# Auditing

Second edition
Michael J. Pratt, B.A.(Econ.), MCom, F.C.A.

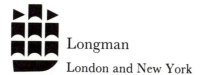
Longman

London and New York

Longman Group Limited
Longman House, Burnt Mill, Harlow
Essex CM20 2JE, England
Associated companies throughout the world

*Published in the United States of America*
*by Longman Inc., New York*

*First published 1982*
*Second edition 1983*

British Library Cataloguing in Publication Data
Pratt, M.J. (Michael John)
   Auditing. – 2nd ed
   1. Auditing
   I. Title
   657'.45       HF5667

   ISBN 0-582-29653-6

Printed in Great Britain
by The Pitman Press, Bath.

# Contents

vi    Contents

x    Contents

# Preface

Auditing has the potential to be one of the most stimulating of all the professional accountant's areas of study. For it combines the most interesting areas of financial accounting (accounts presentation and review) within a framework of inquiry and investigation, and involves a wide range of knowledge and sophisticated techniques. Yet it is often regarded as the most boring subject of all. I certainly found it so when I was studying, although in practice this was far from the case. When I came to teach the subject, both in a professional environment, and subsequently in public and private sector colleges, I quickly discovered that it was perhaps the most difficult of all subjects in which to maintain student interest. For there is such a vast body of knowledge that must be learned and understood. And students cannot practice their knowledge with worked examples in the same way as they can in accounting. But I found after much trial and error in the classroom that interest could be maintained by logical presentation, and by the use of plenty of case studies and anecdotes. I have tried to incorporate all of these into this book. And I have laid emphasis on logical presentation, this being so essential both for the maintenance of interest and for understanding. Without it, the subject degenerates into a huge mass of unrelated facts, with the result that learning becomes a chore, to be performed for the sole purpose of passing an examination.

The old generation of text books has, in my view, been largely responsible for perpetuating (or perhaps even perpetrating!) this unstructured approach, and this, combined with their rigid style and tortuous phraseology, has, I believe, done much to further auditing's poor student image. So I have tried to make this book as readable as possible.

'Auditing' is primarily a book for students, and the structure is such that it is suitable for all levels up to final professional. But it is particularly aimed at the student commencing his study of auditing, to take him through, comfortably I hope, to his finals. First-level professional students can ignore those sections in the final chapters which are marked with an asterisk, and are advised to concentrate on aspects of internal control and testing. Final-year students will profit by a thorough knowledge of the audit of final accounts, and presentation.

The book is not primarily designed for the practitioner, though he may well find the various forms and check lists illustrated to be of some interest. In addition, the practitioner who would appreciate a synopsis of current large-firm procedures may also find value in these pages.

The body of knowledge incorporated here is based on years of research and gradual development in the profession, in both large and small firms alike. In particular I am grateful to the Institute of Chartered Accountants in England and Wales for permission to reproduce extracts from their various publications, to Deloitte, Haskins and Sells for allowing me to include many of their forms and documents and for providing much source material, and to Peat, Marwick Mitchell and Co., for allowing the inclusion of extracts from their audit documentation. But the format herein adopted, together with opinions as to likely and necessary future developments, are entirely my own. These, together with any mistakes, I take responsibility for. Some of what I have to say, even as early as Chapter 1, may well provoke controversy; but only through controversy are problems solved. So if this books helps students to approach their study of auditing with an enquiring mind, then I shall consider this a measure of success.

My grateful thanks go to Ian Marrian and D. Lawrenson of Deloitte, Haskins and Sells and to Professors J. T. Steele and I. Macgregor for kindly reading the manuscript and making helpful comments thereon. Sincere thanks also to the many generations of students with whom I have formulated the teaching approach used in this book. And finally my very best thanks to Helga, my wife, for logic checking the entire manuscript and for suggesting and helping to implement the concept diagrams which I believe to be an important feature of the book.

We are indebted to the following for permission to reproduce copyright material:

*Accountancy* and the author for an extract from the article 'Future of Auditing' by Ian Hay Davison reprinted in *Accountancy* July 1977; American Institute of Certified Public Accountants for an extract from *Statement on Auditing*; Deloitte, Haskins and Sells for accounting check lists in Figs 19.1 (a) and (b) and Appendix 1; Gee & Co. (Publishers) Ltd. for an extract from the 'Address To Small Business Bureau' by John Wakeham, in *The Accountant*, 6 April 1978; Institute of Chartered Accountants in England and Wales for an extract from the 'Accountants' International Steering Group Statement on Materiality', and material from *Accounting Standards, Auditing Standards*, a discussion paper on the *Audit of Small Limited Companies* and Institute Statements on Auditing and Accounting.

For Helga

# I
# What is an audit?

## 1.1 Introduction

If you were to ask the average man in the street about the auditor's work, he would probably tell you that he prevents fraud. Were you to press our layman further, he may paint you a picture of a rather grey individual who buries himself in ledgers, emerging only from time to time to produce sets of figures which are not important anyway.

Such is the image that the auditor has attracted in the past. But it is inaccurate, and unfair. Inaccurate, because the auditor's primary responsibility is neither to prevent fraud, nor to produce figures. Unfair, for his is a highly skilled professional task without which the modern economy could not function.

So what does the auditor do? Well, the word audit itself, derives from Latin, meaning 'to hear'. And in times gone by the accounts of an estate were called over by those who had compiled them, and were 'heard' or audited, by those in authority. Through usage the word has come to denote the *independent* checking and validating of figures which have been produced to account for the usage of funds. The production of such 'accounts' is not part of the audit function, but is the job of the accountant; though sometimes one person will wear both hats, first producing, then checking. This is arguably not desirable in that it could involve a loss of independence – the auditor's *raison d'être*. But more to this later.

I have just stated that it is not the auditor's principal job to prevent fraud, or indeed error. This is so. But clearly where accounts contain substantial undisclosed fraud or error they will not present a reasonable picture of an enterprise's activities. And so, the auditor would be expected not to validate such accounts. Just what constitutes 'substantial' and 'reasonable' is embodied in the concepts of 'materiality' and 'truth and fairness' which will be discussed in more detail later on in the chapter.

## 1.2 Who needs an audit?

The need for audit is as old as business itself. For whenever owners of funds provide capital for an enterprise, there is a need for accounts. If only one person contributes to the project, then he can himself scrutinise the accounts to gain assurance that they are reasonable; he can perform his own audit, assuming that he has sufficient skill and experience. But as soon as a group of people come together to form a joint project, it is no longer feasible for each of them to check and validate the accounts. So it makes sense to appoint one skilled person for the task. And in order that no individual entrepreneur should be accused of having an advantage over the others, it is reasonable to appoint a person independent of both the providers and users of the capital. This concept of independence is extremely important, and is examined in detail in Chapter 2.

Auditing in its modern sense, albeit in primitive form, has been with us since the sixteenth century, when the division first started to grow between those who provided capital, and those who engaged in business activity. As commercial enterprises became more sophisticated, two problems manifested themselves:

1. phony projects sprang up, the only objective of which was to relieve gullible backers of as much finance as possible;
2. the lack of a formal accounting requirement meant that the entrepreneurs of even genuine projects were able to cheat the providers of capital.

The first problem was perhaps the most serious, and was the first to be subject to a long line of legislation, culminating in the latest Prevention of Fraud (Investments) Act in 1958. The information sheets (or 'prospectuses') given to potential backers gradually became subject to stringent controls, and the information in them to independent check. Such checking is not strictly an audit, but may be regarded as an investigation. Investigations will be dealt with in detail in Chapter 22, and you should note that this area is covered in the advanced syllabuses of the professional examinations.

With the advent of 'limited liability' companies in the eighteenth century, the lack of formal accounting requirements gave rise to increasing problems. As is well known, in a limited company, the providers of capital can be called upon for no more than their original investment, to pay off the company's debts. This development enormously facilitated the growth of enterprise, in that large and small investors could safely contribute the amount of money they could afford to lose, and they could exactly quantify the amount at risk. The resulting increase in the number of people providing capital gave rise to the need for legislation to protect investors from the inefficiency and perhaps deceit of their management (who in time became known as 'directors'). Hence the need for formal accounts for the benefit of investors. But it was not until the turn of the twentieth century that a *mandatory requirement* for the audit of limited company accounts, and for the presentation of an audit report to members was finally embodied in the Companies Acts. And it was not until the 1948 Companies Act that anything like realistic accounting and audit safeguards were incorporated into the law. Even now company law lags a long way behind the requirements of the modern business environment. There are many areas of deficiency, as we shall see in Chapters 15 and 23, but the following are perhaps the two most significant:

1. Small companies.
2. The requirements of people, other than shareholders, who are interested in the accounts of business enterprises.

1. Small limited companies have exactly the same rights of limited liability as large listed companies, and in law they have similar reporting requirements in terms of audited accounts. It is arguable that small management-owned companies should only have the rights of limited liability if they have a minimum, substantial paid-up capital (such rules apply already in many European countries). However, here is not the place to discuss such a contentious aspect of company law reform. But what is relevant now is a discussion of audit requirement for such companies. As we have seen, the audit requirement for limited companies grew out of the divorce of the ownership from the usage of funds. But with certain small limited companies where the owners and managers are one and the same (and such 'proprietorship' companies constitute a large proportion of companies on register) there can be no need for an audit in the sense that is envisaged in company law. For there is obviously no need to protect owners from managers, when they are the same people. Not only is the current audit requirement illogical, it is also impractical; but more to this in Chapter 18.

2. Many different classes of people are interested in the accounts of a company, in addition to the shareholders. Creditors will usually have a substantial investment, and bankers too, while the Inland Revenue has (currently) a 52 per cent interest in the company's profits. And yet none of these people receive protection under company law. With one very minor exception (more later), they do not even get a mention. Such people have no rights to receive an audit report, nor are the accounts produced with them in mind. The accounts and audit report are produced for the members. So if things go wrong, they have no rights to sue either directors or auditors, except in very specific circumstances which will be dealt with in Chapter 21.

These two significant contemporary problems will be dealt with in Chapter 18 (The audit of small limited companies), and Chapter 23 (Contemporary developments). But it is important to appreciate these limitations in the current audit requirements, before we proceed to the detail of the book.

## 1.3 Why have an audit?

The answer to this question for a limited company is simple. Company law says you must, and provides for substantial penalties if you do not. But this rather begs the question. So let us look at the advantages that can ensue from having accounts audited. These advantages can be different for various types of organisation, so we will examine each in turn.

### Large limited companies

The main advantage here lies in the protection that is afforded to the shareholders who, in complex organisations, will usually be divorced from management. But in addition other interested parties can gain some confidence from accounts that have been subject to independent audit, even if those accounts have not been

*✗ important.*

produced specifically with third parties in mind. Such confidence is essential to the proper functioning of the economy, for without it trade would decline and companies founder. The audit can be said to inspire the confidence which oils the machinery of business; and, as a further advantage in large companies, the auditor's experience will enable him to make recommendations for improvements in the systems of control which can make the company less susceptible to fraud by its customers, suppliers and employees. Finally the auditor can ensure that the accounts are produced in line with best practice and conform with all relevant standards; such conformity being essential to the proper interpretation of the figures produced.

### Proprietorship companies

We have seen that there is no need for an audit of the accounts of small owner-run limited companies in the sense of protecting the shareholders. But banks, creditors and the Inland Revenue can gain some confidence from the audited accounts, albeit issued to the shareholders, rather than to them; although just how much use such accounts actually are is a matter of debate. This is discussed in Chapter 18. But if the bank and/or the Inland Revenue are satisfied with the shareholders' audited accounts, then clearly the audit has proved useful in minimising explanations and saving time.

Most small companies will not normally require, or practically be able to achieve, the sophisticated control systems that are necessary in larger businesses to safeguard against fraud and error. Nevertheless, the auditor will be able to advise on those checks that may be appropriate to the needs of the firm.

Finally, should the proprietor of a small company ever decide to sell his business, he will be in a much stronger position to ask a good price if he is able to produce authenticated accounts showing how the business has fared over the past few years.

### Partnerships

So far we have concentrated on limited companies, and this reflects practice in professional examinations. But partnerships too can benefit from having an audit, although there is *no statutory requirement* for them so to have. All the advantages quoted above for the proprietorship company apply equally here, and in addition the following benefits may also be derived:

(a) the independent audit could minimise disputes between the partners, and such disputes are a common cause of partnership dissolution;
(b) changes in the partnership will often involve complex changes in capital and goodwill, so that an audited set of accounts will ensure that the new partnership sets out on a sound basis.

### Sole traders

As with partnerships, there is no requirement for sole traders to have their accounts audited, but the advantages quoted above in respect of the proprietor-ship company are equally applicable here.

*Special classes*

Building societies, banks, insurance companies, investment trusts, friendly societies and charities are all special classes of organisation which have their own rules, and which require the production of audited accounts. The audit principles are largely the same, but the approach sometimes different. These are largely specialist audit areas, but a general knowledge about them is required for the professional examinations, and they are, therefore, dealt with in Chapter 22 of this book.

And *in addition to the audit function*, the qualified auditor will be able to offer all his clients a wide range of professional services including accountancy, taxation, company secretarial work, management and financial consultancy, valuations, and even, should it be necessary, advice on bankruptcy proceedings. All this is largely outside the scope of this book, but some of these matters are dealt with in Chapter 22 in so far as they are relevant to the auditing syllabuses of the professional examinations.

## 1.4  Introduction to true and fair

Company law requires that all limited companies appoint an auditor whose task is to express an independent opinion on the reasonableness of accounts produced by the directors for stewardship purposes. But just what constitutes reasonableness is a highly subjective matter. The early Companies Acts required the auditor to certify as to the truth and correctness of accounts, the phrase 'true and correct' implying arithmetic accuracy. And this indeed is largely what early audits concentrated upon. Hence if you look back in old ledgers you will find that many or most of the entries have ticks next to them implying that they have all been individually checked for authenticity and for arithmetical accuracy. But such an approach largely ignores the overall view of the accounts, and would in any event not be feasible with the large multinational corporations of today. Further, it is not possible to certify that any one set of accounts is *the correct* set, because so many accounting areas are susceptible to a wide variety of interpreta-tions and therefore presentations. The treatment of depreciation, stock, goodwill and deferred taxation are all obvious examples of where there are many different possible treatments, each one of which can be justified. Hence there can be no *one* correct set of accounts, and this was recognised in the 1948 Companies Act which required the auditor to express an opinion as to whether the accounts show a true and *fair* view of the state of affairs of the company (balance sheet) and of the profit or loss for the period under review. The concept of fairness is now considered to be far more important than absolute arithmetic accuracy. But just what constitutes true and fair will take us the rest of this book to discover.

However, certain points must be made at this stage. You should note that the auditor now expresses an *opinion* on the accounts; he does not certify them. This must necessarily be so, as where there is the possibility of differing treatments in many different accounting areas, there must inevitably be the possibility of disagreement over what is fair presentation. An auditor will express *his* opinion whether in *his* view the accounts are true and fair. Other people may think differently.

But before you begin to think that this sounds like a recipe for chaos, we can identify a number of important principles which go to make up the concept of Truth and Fairness.

1. *Materiality.* The concept of *materiality* is closely related to that of truth and fairness. In a paper entitled 'Materiality in Accounting', the Accountants International Study Group (see sec. 1.5) concluded that Materiality is essentially a matter of professional judgement. An individual item should be judged to be material if the knowledge of that item could reasonably be deemed to have influence on the users of the financial statement – i.e. if it alters the true and fair view. Just what constitutes materiality is the subject of further discussion in Chapter 11. But a brief word of explanation is appropriate here.

Materiality is a relative concept. What is material in one company may well not be material in another. A £1,000 error in the accounts of a corner shop would probably be material, but in the accounts of ICI Ltd it would not in any way affect the reader's view of the figures presented to him. The Accountants International Study Group states that quantitative guidelines can be identified to help in distinguishing material items, and they suggest figures of 5 to 10 per cent as being the cut-off point, when compared to an appropriate base (much less in certain specific areas).

The concept of materiality is extremely important to the auditor in that it assists him in determining whether the true and fair view has been distorted. In addition, it will indicate to him the amount of work that should be done in any particular audit area. For example, if it transpired that were the entire petty cash of a particular firm to be misappropriated, it would not be material, then little audit work would be necessary in that area for the auditor to be able to express an opinion on the accounts as a whole.

2. *Fraud and error.* Substantial fraud or error may clearly result in accounts which do not show a true and fair view – but only if the fraud or error remains undiscovered. Those that are revealed can be incorporated into the accounts, in order to show a fair picture of the activities of the company in the period under review.

It follows from our discussion of materiality that any *material* fraud or error must be discovered by the auditor, because by definition it will affect the truth and fairness of the accounts. But if a fraud or error would not be deemed to be material, then the auditor is under no obligation to bring it to light; although we will see during subsequent chapters that normal audit procedures can usually be expected to prevent or detect any significant frauds or errors. Furthermore if the auditor discovers, or should discover, any matter of a suspicious nature, then he is under an obligation to probe that matter to the full, regardless of the materiality or time involved. This principle is embodied in the judgement of Lopez LJ in the Kingston Cotton Mill Case of 1898:

'It is the duty of an auditor to bring to bear on the work he has to perform that skill, care and caution, which a reasonably competent, careful and cautious auditor would use. What is reasonable skill, care and caution must depend on the particular circumstances of each case. An auditor is not bound to be a detective or . . . to approach his work with suspicion or with a foregone conclusion that there is something wrong. He is a watchdog and not a bloodhound. . . . If there is anything to excite suspicion he should probe it to the bottom; but in the absence of anything of that kind he is only bound to be reasonably cautious and careful.'

3. *Proper records*. The company must have maintained *proper accounting records*, which adequately explain the transactions that have occurred in the period under review. Otherwise it may be impossible to ascertain whether the accounts show a true and fair view.

4. *Production of accounts*. The accounts must obviously be produced *in accordance with the underlying accounting records* of the company, and must be free from any significant arithmetical inaccuracies.

5. *Verification of assets and liabilities*. The *assets and liabilities of the company must be verified* by the auditor to prove their: Cost; Authorisation for purchase; Valuation; Existence/Obligation; Beneficial ownership; Presentation in the accounts. This is an extremely important audit area, and is fully discussed in Chapter 14.

6. *Accounting concepts*. The accounts should be based on *generally accepted accounting concepts*. As explained in Statement of Standard Accounting Practice (hereafter SSAP) 2, 'Fundamental accounting concepts are the broad basic assumptions which underlie the periodic financial accounts of business enterprises; and the following are generally accepted – Going Concern concept, Accruals concept, Consistency concept, and the Prudence concept'.

7. *Accounting bases*. These are defined in SSAP2 as 'the methods which have been developed for expressing or applying fundamental accounting concepts to financial transactions and items'. As an example, 'Last in first out', 'First in first out', and 'Weighted average' are all acceptable accounting bases for the treatment of stock. The accounting base chosen is known as the company's accounting policy. In order that accounts may show a true and fair view, accounting policies

should be chosen that are:

(a) appropriate to the needs of the business;
(b) in accordance with the Statement of Standard Accounting Practice applicable to the accounting area under review (SSAPs are extremely important for the auditor and are further discussed throughout the book);
(c) consistently applied with previous years (or where a change is deemed to be necessary the effect of such change should be disclosed in the accounts).

8. *Description of figures.* Finally, if the *description of figures* on the accounts is misleading or ambiguous, or the presentation obscure or complicated to a material degree, then the accounts will not show a true and fair view.

The concept of truth and fairness is fundamental to the audit function, and we will frequently be referring to it during the course of the book. But before we move on, it is worth pausing to ask the question . . . 'true and fair to whom?'. For example, the needs of shareholders and creditors are very different; the former are interested mainly in profitability and return, the latter in the likelihood that the company will be able to pay its debts. So it is perhaps unreasonable to expect one set of accounts to be all things to all men. But more to this in Chapter 23.

## 1.5  Professional pronouncements

The accounting and auditing profession is now a highly dynamic one, and so that changes are well documented and brought to the attention of all interested parties, pronouncements are made by a number of bodies on a wide variety of different subjects. The pronouncements with which we are most concerned are those of:

* The Institute of Chartered Accountants in England and Wales (hereafter ICAEW) – Statements on Auditing.
* The Consultative Committee of Accountancy Bodies (hereafter CCAB), whose two important sub-committees are:
  The Accounting Standards Committee (hereafter ASC) – Exposure Drafts and Statements on Standard Accounting Practice.
  The Auditing Practices Committee (hereafter APC) – Auditing Standards.
* The International Accounting Standards Committee (hereafter IASC) – International Accounting Standards.
* The Accountants International Study Group (hereafter AISG) – Studies in Accounting and Auditing.
* The Union Européenne des Experts Comptables Economiques et Financiers (hereafter UEC) – Acceptable Practice statements.
* The International Federation of Accountants (hereafter IFAC).

Reference will be made throughout the book to these various pronouncements, and extracts will be included as appropriate. So it is important at this stage to consider each in turn, and discuss their significance.

*The Institute of Chartered Accountants in England and Wales*

The ICAEW is the professional association that is most concerned in England with public auditing practice, and their members, together with those of the Scottish and Irish Chartered Institutes, and the Association of Certified Accountants, are (with certain exceptions noted in the next chapter) the only people entitled to carry out the audit of limited companies. The ICAEW has for many years now incorporated what is considered to be the best auditing practice into Statements on Auditing, sometimes known as U statements (because they all appear under this heading in the Institute's members' handbook – they are also available for separate purchase). However, many of these statements were withdrawn following the introduction of the Auditing Standards and Guidelines, and it is envisaged that they will all eventually be so superseded. The following is a list of U statements:

U7 Verification of debtor balances: confirmation by direct communication (June 1967)

U9 Attendance at stocktaking (July 1968)

U11 Stock in trade and work in progress (Apr. 1969)

U14 Internal Control in a computer-based accounting system (Dec. 1969)

U15 The audit of computer-based accounting systems (Dec. 1969)

U16 The ascertainment and confirmation of contingent liabilities arising from pending legal matters (Aug. 1970)

U21 Group accounts – reliance on other auditors (Mar. 1976)

U22 Bank reports for audit purposes (Aug. 1976)

U24 Guidance for auditors on the implications of goods sold subject to reservation of title (Dec. 1977)

U26 Auditors' reports – Registered Friendly Societies and Industrial and Provident Societies (Aug. 1978)

U27 Auditors' responsibilities under the Trade Union and Labour Relations Act 1974 (May 1979)

*The Consultative Committee of Accountancy Bodies*

The CCAB includes representatives of the three chartered institutes, as well as the Association of Certified Accountants, and the Chartered Institute of Public Finance and Accountancy (whose members carry out the audit of local governments and public corporations). The Committee speaks with one voice to the government and to the public on all matters hinging on accountancy, including auditing and taxation. We are primarily concerned with the two important sub-committees which issue Statements on Accounting and Auditing, these statements being binding on all members.

*The Accounting Standards Committee*

The ASC is responsible for formulating proposed Accounting Standards (called

Exposure Drafts) and circularising these to members and others for comment. Upon general acceptance, the EDs become Standards, deviations from which must be commented upon in the auditor's report, under pain of disciplinary action for failure so to do. The need for Standards in terms of conformity of accounting practice will be covered in your accounting studies, and there is insufficient room at this stage to go into detail (see Ch. 15). However, all of the Standards have audit implications, and these will be dealt with at the appropriate point in the book, and extracts will be included as necessary. It is desirable that you should have a complete set of the Standards, and they are now available from many sources, including that mine of useful information, *Accountancy* (the journal of the ICAEW). The ICAEW also publishes them in book form. In addition a number of books have included them as an appendix.

To assist your studies, SSAP and IAS checklists are reproduced in Appendix 1, by kind permission of Deloitte, Haskins and Sells. The following SSAPs are currently effective:

1. Accounting for the results of associated companies (issued Jan. 1971, amended Apr. 1982)
2. Disclosure of accounting policies (Nov. 1971)
3. Earnings per share (Feb. 1972, revised Aug. 1974)
4. The accounting treatment of government grants (Apr. 1974)
5. Accounting for Value Added Tax (Apr. 1974)
6. Extraordinary items and prior year adjustments (May 1974, revised Apr. 1975)
8. The treatment of taxation under the imputation system in the accounts of companies (Aug. 1974, revised Dec. 1977)
9. Stock and work in progress (May 1975)
10. Statements of source and application of funds (July 1975)
12. Accounting for depreciation (Dec. 1977)
13. Accounting for research and development (Dec. 1977)
14. Group accounts (Sept. 1978)
15. Accounting for deferred taxation (Oct. 1978)
16. Current cost accounting (Mar. 1980)
17. Post balance sheet events (Sept. 1980)
18. Contingencies (Sept. 1980)
19. Accounting for investment properties (Nov. 1981)

The following Exposure Drafts are still under discussion:

ED27  Foreign currency translations
ED28  Accounting for Petroleum Revenue Tax
ED29  Accounting for leases and hire purchase contracts
ED30  Accounting for goodwill
ED31  Accounting for acquisitions and mergers

Pension Costs is an area which has been cited as in need of standardisation.

*The Auditing Practices Committee*

In June 1978 the APC published discussion drafts of the first three auditing standards and these were finalised in April 1980. These are designed to have the same status as the accounting standards, and hence are the most authoritative source on auditing practice. Their application is mandatory for all members under pain of disciplinary action, and accordingly knowledge of them is vital for professional students.

The three standards introduced so far are 'The Operational Standard', 'The Audit Report' and 'Qualifications in Audit Reports'. The first deals with the general conduct of an audit, and the second and third with the form of the audit report. The standards have been couched in fairly general terms so as to be applicable to all types of company (herein lies a criticism), and each is accompanied by Guidelines designed to assist in the implementation. These Guidelines, the APC has said, are ultimately designed to replace the existing U series of Auditing Statements. If this is so, it would seem to be a retrograde step in that they are less detailed in many respects and less informative. The existing U statements have the same status as Guidelines, and will remain in force until withdrawn.

Each of the Standards, together with the associated Guidelines, will be examined in detail at the appropriate point in the book.

*The International Accounting Standards Committee*

The IASC has a worldwide membership and has similar aims to that of the ASC in England. IASs are currently in force on the following subjects:
1. Disclosure of accounting policies.
2. Valuation and presentation of inventories in the context of the historical cost system.
3. The presentation of consolidated financial statements.
4. Depreciation accounting.
5. Information to be disclosed in financial statements.
6. Statements of changes in financial position.
7. Unusual and prior period items and changes in accounting policies.
8. Accounting for research and development activities.
9. Contingencies and events occurring after the balance sheet date.
10. Accounting for construction contracts.
11. Accounting for taxes on income.
12. Presentation of current assets and current liabilities.
13. Reporting financial information by segment.
14. Information reflecting the effects of changing prices.
15. Accounting for property, plant and equipment.

Professional bodies in member countries have generally agreed that in the absence of a home standard on the subject, then the International standard should be applied. In the (unlikely) event that the two should be in conflict, then the home standard should be applied, but the auditor should specify the respect(s) in which there is non-compliance with the International standard. The requirements of the IASs are included in the Standards checklist in Appendix 1.

### The Accountants International Study Group

The AISG (now disbanded) comprised representatives of the United Kingdom and Canadian Chartered Institutes, and the American Institute of Certified and Public Accountants. Accordingly, although their studies are not official in the way that the Accounting and Auditing standards are, they carry considerable prestige, and therefore authority. We have already come across one in our look at Materiality, but the following is a complete list of studies produced:

1. Accounting and auditing approaches to inventories in three nations 1968.
2. The independent auditors' reporting standards in three nations 1969.
3. Using the work and report of another auditor 1969.
4. Accounting for corporate income taxes 1971.
5. Reporting by diversified companies 1972.
6. Consolidated financial statements 1972.
7. The funds statement 1973.
8. Materiality in accounting 1974.
9. Published profit forecasts 1974.
10. International financial reporting 1975.
11. Comparative glossary of accounting terms 1975.
12. Accounting for goodwill 1975.
13. Interim financial reporting 1975.
14. Going concern problems 1975.
15. Independence of auditors 1976.
16. Audit committees 1977.
17. Revenue recognition 1978.
18. Extraordinary items, prior period adjustments and changes in accounting principles 1974.

### The Union Européenne des Experts Comptables Economiques et Financiers

The UEC was founded in 1951 as an association of European professional accountancy bodies whose aims were to uphold the principles of independence and professional responsibility, and create a sense of unity among European accountants with a view to the overall improvement of professional standards. In pursuance of these aims, in 1974 the UEC began to issue statements of 'acceptable practice', and although these are not mandatory, they do represent authoritative guidelines on best practice, and the three Chartered Institutes together with the Association have agreed to incorporate the principles on which

these statements are based in their own auditing standards in due course. The following statements have been issued so far:
* The disclosure of accounting policies (Apr. 1974).
* Framework of professional ethics for accountants in public practice (Apr. 1975)
* The audit report (July 1975).
* The object and scope of the audit of annual financial statements (July 1978).
* The use of another auditor's work (July 1978).
* The auditor's working papers (July 1978).
* Audit considerations regarding the 'going concern' basis (July 1978).
* Independence (Dec. 1979).

*The International Federation of Accountants*

The IFAC was formed in 1970 with representatives from the accounting bodies of some 50 countries. The International Auditing Practices Committee of IFAC has issued the following Guidelines:
  1. Objective and Scope of the Audit of Financial Statements 1979.
  2. Audit Engagement Letters 1980.
  3. Basic Principles Governing an Audit 1980.
  4. Planning 1981.
  5. Using the Work of Another Auditor 1981.
  6. Study and Evaluation of the Accounting System of Related Internal Controls in Connection with an Audit 1981.
  7. Control of the Quality of Audit Work 1982.
  8. Audit Evidence 1982.
And the International Ethics Committee of IFAC issued a 'Guideline on Professional Ethics for the Accounting Profession' in 1980.

## 1.6 Conclusion

We have now looked in outline at the nature of the auditor's work. And we have seen something of the professional environment within which he operates. Both the nature of work and the professional requirements are in the process of rapid change. And this change is accelerating. Until as late as the early 1970s, auditing was a relatively stagnant profession. This was reflected in the texts available on the subject, so that they remained in print, valid and up to date (almost) for decades. Such cannot be the case now, and auditing texts probably require almost as frequent revision as those on tax. Accordingly a regular review of the accounting press is essential to keep one's knowledge current. It is not realistically possible to absorb all of the knowledge and thoughts that are aired on auditing. For this is rapidly becoming a highly specialised subject. But it is very necessary to keep abreast of all important developments. And for this purpose *Accountancy* magazine is an excellent source of reference (there is even a colour coding of the important bits). *Accountancy* will have copies of all the SSAPs, EDs, IASs, Auditing Standards, etc., as they are introduced, and these can be used to update this text. Any articles commenting on the various statements and standards should prove useful, as well as those discussing likely future developments. An indexing system for copies of the magazine is a good idea to facilitate easy referral, and this can usefully be referenced into this text.

The financial pages of *The Times*, *Guardian*, *Daily Telegraph* or *Financial Times* will give you a more immediate and day-by-day view of what is going on in the financial world and it will reveal what that world has to say about us. It is not currently very impressed, and often downright critical! In particular watch out for comments about qualified audit reports, reports by company inspectors, company failures and frauds, and professional developments.

The approach outlined in subsequent chapters is based on current legal and professional requirements, and builds step by step. In the final chapter, I discuss likely and necessary future changes.

# 2
# Who can be an auditor?

## 2.1 Introduction

We saw in the last chapter that *all* limited companies are required by law to produce audited accounts. There is no such requirement for sole traders and partnerships. For this reason and because the professional examinations concentrate mainly upon limited company audits, the remainder of this book is devoted to company audit practice unless otherwise specified. Although of course, many of the principles are equally applicable to the audit of any type of organisation.

## 2.2 The role of the auditor

The relationship between auditors and shareholders is strange in that although the shareholders appoint the auditors (who are technically their agents), the main discussions all take place between directors and auditors. After the initial appointment, the auditors have nothing to do with the shareholders until the (very brief) report at the AGM. The main relationship develops between directors and auditors, and it is the directors who receive the detailed report on the accounts and accounting system. Such a close working relationship is of course essential for the proper conduct of the audit, but it must always be remembered that the auditors' legal *raison d'être* is as the guardian of the shareholders, in whose interests they should always be working. This theme is further developed later on in the chapter when we discuss the issues of the auditor's independence. But at this stage a study of Fig. 2.1 depicting the relationship between the various parties is important.

## 2.3 Appointment

In law the company (represented by the shareholders in general meeting) appoint the auditors, but in fact it is often the directors that effectively make the appointment. The basic rule in Sec. 14 of the 1976 Companies Act (hereafter CA 1976) is that every company shall at each Annual General Meeting (AGM) appoint an auditor (or auditors) to hold office until the conclusion of the next AGM. There are two exceptions to this rule:

Fig. 2.1  The role of the auditor

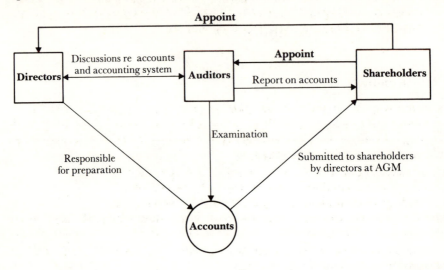

*Note:* There is no provision for communication between
the shareholders and the auditor, other than through
the audit report. Communication is via the directors.

1. The directors may appoint:
   (a) the first auditors until the conclusion of the first AGM;
   (b) auditors to fill a casual vacancy.
2. The Secretary of State for Trade may appoint auditors if the members and
   directors fail so to do.

   In practice the directors will nominate the auditors of their choice, and it is
unusual for this to be questioned by the shareholders. Indeed, it is unusual for
many shareholders to be present at an AGM unless the company is faring badly,
or unless there is a hint of scandal. Only in these circumstances is it likely that the
directors' nomination of auditor will be questioned, and in these circumstances
the directors themselves will often face the possibility of dismissal.

   So normally, if there is a change of auditor, it is instigated by the directors,
sometimes for reason of poor service, or high fee, or perhaps to achieve uniformity
of auditors within a group, but sometimes because of conflict between directors
and auditors. Such conflict can arise through a personality clash or perhaps
through a genuine disagreement on a point of principle. But more seriously it may
happen because the directors put undue pressure on the auditors, perhaps in an
attempt to cover up something in the accounts that should properly be revealed
to the shareholders. And as the power of removal is often effectively, if not in law,
in the hands of the directors, this can represent a serious threat to the shareholders (this is quite apart from the possibility that the auditors may yield to the
pressure in order to safeguard their position – this possibility is examined later in

the chapter when we look at the important issue of the auditor's independence). To help safeguard against this threat, the 1976 Companies Act enacted a number of provisions with regard to the *removal* of auditors.

## 2.4 Removal

An ordinary resolution of the company in general meeting is all that is required to remove the auditor from office, *but* special notice (28 days in writing) to the company is required (note this is *not* a special resolution). Such notice is required in each of the following circumstances:
1. Appointing an auditor other than the retiring auditor.
2. Removing an auditor before the end of his term of office.
3. Filling a casual vacancy where not filled by the directors.
4. Reappointing a retiring auditor who was originally appointed by the directors to fill a casual vacancy.

In the event of the resolution being passed, the company must notify the Registrar of Companies within 14 days.

Sections 14 and 15 of the CA 1976 include certain safeguards:
1. On receipt of a resolution requiring special notice as in 1 or 2 above, the company must send a copy to the auditor.
2. The auditor can then make reasonable representations in writing to the shareholders, and these must be circularised at the company's expense to everyone entitled to receive notice of the meeting; additionally in any notice of resolutions that is given to members, note must be made of the fact that such representations have been received.
3. If the representations are not circularised for any reason, then the auditor has the right to have them read out at the meeting. This is supposed to be a safeguard, but in fact it would seem to be exactly the reverse. For the whole point of sending out such representations must surely be to persuade members of the necessity to attend the meeting in the first place. If no one attends save friends of the directors, then reading out the auditor's reasons why he should not be dismissed would be valueless. One can argue that if the shareholders do not attend their AGM, then they can only have themselves to blame. But such is to ignore the reality of corporate meetings.

There is a provision to safeguard the company from needless expense in circularisation, in the event that the auditor tries to use these provisions as a platform for defamatory matter. Anyone aggrieved by the contents of the representations (and this is most likely to be the directors) can make application to the court to prevent their circularisation (or reading out), and the court then has power to charge the costs of the action to the auditor.

In the event that the auditor is removed, he can still attend the AGM at which his term of office would have expired, or any meeting at which it is proposed to appoint someone to fill the vacancy created by his removal, and he has the right to speak at such meetings on any matter which concerns him as retiring auditor.

## 2.5   Resignation

The CA 1976 allowed for the first time the possibility of the auditor resigning his office, provided in his resignation notice he includes a statement to the effect that there are no circumstances in relation to his resignation that should be brought to the attention of members or creditors. Or in the event that there are such circumstances, he must include a statement as to their nature. He is then empowered to require the directors to convene an Extraordinary General Meeting for consideration of these matters. You should note that this is the very first time in Companies Act legislation that any attempt has been made to safeguard the interests of *creditors*.

## 2.6   Remuneration

The auditor will clearly require remuneration for his work. Indeed, if you look at the accounts of the larger listed companies you will see that audit fees can run into millions of pounds (CA 1981 Sch. 1.53(7) requires that the audit fee must be disclosed). The amount to be paid is fixed by whoever makes the appointment, although normally only the basis of computation will be agreed in advance. The shareholders will later be asked to approve the audit fee at the AGM.

## 2.7   The rights and duties of the auditor

The auditor has specific rights and duties assigned to him by company law, and it is necessary for you to know these thoroughly, as they constitute the basis of audit work. The rights are all-encompassing and include the following:

> *CA 1976:*

1. The right of access at all times ([*sic*] but one should read here all reasonable times!) to the accounting records of the company.
2. The right to require from officers and employees of the company any information and explanations deemed necessary for the purposes of the audit. You should note that it is the auditor who decides what is necessary, and no one can in any way restrict this right, even on grounds of confidentiality. Clearly it would not be appropriate for a first-year audit trainee to demand confidential trade information from the managing director! But if such information were deemed necessary for the purposes of the audit, then it must be made available at a senior level.
3. Rights in relation to general meetings:
   (a) to receive notice;
   (b) to attend;
   (c) to speak on any matter concerning the auditor.

*Sec. 15 CA 1976:*

4. Rights associated with attempts to remove him from office, or not to reappoint him (see sec. 2.4).

*Sec. 18 CA 1976:*

5. Rights to require that subsidiaries and their auditors provide such information and explanations as is deemed necessary for the purposes of the audit of holding companies.

The corresponding duties are onerous. The auditor is obliged to *report to the members* on each set of accounts laid before the company in general meeting, whether *in his opinion*:

1. The Balance Sheet gives a *true and fair view* of the state of affairs of the company as at the balance sheet date.
2. The Profit and Loss account gives a *true and fair view* of the profit (or loss) for the period ended on that date.
3. The accounts *comply with the Companies Acts 1948 to 1981*.

Nothing, and no one can in any way reduce or restrict the auditor's obligations in these respects, and in addition he is obliged under company law to report in the event that he is *not satisfied* on certain specific matters. These are:

1. Whether in the auditor's opinion proper accounting records have been maintained, as prescribed by Sec. 12 CA 1976:
    (a)  complete records of purchases and sales of goods, including, in the case of credit dealings, the names and addresses of buyers and sellers;
    (b)  receipts and payments of cash;
    (c)  assets and liabilities;
    (d)  stocktaking.
    (Requirements (a)–(c) were previously contained in the 1948 Act.)
2. Whether the accounts are in agreement with the underlying records (1948 Act).
3. Whether proper returns, adequate for audit purposes have been received from branches not visited by the auditor (1948 Act).
4. Whether all necessary information and explanations have been received by the auditor (1948 Act).

These matters will be mentioned in the auditor's report, *only if his opinion is adverse*, Keeping the report to a minimum length so as not to confuse.

In addition to these various reporting requirements, the auditor is also obliged to *provide* in the audit report the following Companies Act disclosure information, if the directors fail to so provide in the accounts themselves:

1. CA 1948 Sec. 196 on director's emoluments.
2. CA 1948 Sec. 197 on loans to officers.
3. CA 1967 Sec. 6 on the split of director's emoluments.
4. CA 1967 Sec. 7 on total director's emoluments waived.
5. CA 1967 Sec. 8 on highly paid employees.
    (These sections are fully dealt with in the check list in Appendix 1.)

## 2.8 The qualifications required

The qualifications required to carry out the audit of limited companies are set out in Sec. 161 of the 1948 Companies Act (hereafter CA 1948) and Sec. 13 CA 1976, and the people so entitled are as follows.

1. Members of the following professional bodies:
   Institute of Chartered Accountants in England and Wales;
   Institute of Chartered Accountants in Scotland;
   Institute of Chartered Accountants in Ireland;
   Association of Certified Accountants.
2. People with equivalent qualifications from overseas countries provided that reciprocal arrangements are in force with such countries, and provided that permission is sought and obtained from the Secretary of State.
3. Any person who holds a Department of Trade authority as having had sufficient practical experience prior to August 1947, the date when the CA 1948 was introduced as a Bill.
4. In respect of non-listed companies *only*, any person who holds authority from the Secretary of State as having had sufficient practical experience in the twelve months to November 1966 (the date on which CA 1967 was introduced as a Bill) and was on that date the auditor of at least one exempt private company. A provision in the CA 1976 has prevented any further exemptions under this head.

Certain categories of people are specifically excluded from accepting office as public auditors, and these include:

(a) a body corporate;
(b) an officer or servant of the company;
(c) a partner or employee of an officer or servant of the company.

The body corporate (or company) is excluded on the grounds that the audit is a personal service, so it would be inappropriate for one 'legal person' to oversee the acts of another. Further, a company has the advantage of limited liability, whereas the auditor must be held personally responsible for the quality of his work, and for the opinion that he gives. Officers and servants together with their partners and employees are excluded for the obvious reason of maintaining the auditor's all important independence. Section 455 of CA 1948 defines an officer as a director, secretary or manager, and a servant may be regarded as any full-time employee of the company. And although the auditor's task can be regarded as being a service, he should never place himself in a position 'of service' to the company.

These very limited independence rules will be examined again later on in the chapter when we look at the auditor's independence issue in more detail. But it is worth noting here that there is no legal restriction on blood relations of directors acting as auditor, nor is there any legal restriction on *employers* of directors so acting (for example, where an employee of an audit firm also holds a directorship, there would be no legal objection to that firm accepting the audit appointment of the employee's company).

## 2.9 Current problems in the profession

For those of you who like crunching facts, there has been a lot for you to chew on so far in this chapter. But the issues discussed in the remaining sections are far from cut and dried, with different sections of the profession holding very different opinions. So I shall examine these points upon which there is general agreement, and then look at the points of difference, making it clear where I am expressing my own opinion. But first perhaps a word of warning. The areas to be discussed are controversial in that they involve criticism of certain sections of the profession, and to an extent the CCAB itself. A healthy atmosphere of constructive criticism amongst new entrants to the profession can do nothing but good. And it is probably fair to say that the lack of such an atmosphere in the past has given rise to some of the profession's current problems. But you should perhaps not be too critical in your examination answers!

We must begin with a word of introduction about some of the criticisms currently being levied at the auditing profession. The criticisms largely centre on firstly whether a self-regulating body can ever be truly impartial (or independent), and secondly, if the current standards of auditing are sufficiently high to safeguard the public's interest. The reasons for public concern (frequently expressed in the financial press) stem from the large number of company failures, frauds and mistakes that have hit the headlines during the last few years, in which the auditors have come in for not inconsiderable criticism. The headlines speak for themselves, so here are a few examples:

'Are accounts too serious to be left to the accountants?' – *The Times*.

'Call for sanctions against below standard accountants' – *Financial Times*.

'Auditors should put the community first' – *The Daily Telegraph*.

'Watchdog, bloodhound or lapdog? Auditors are in for an uneasy time' – *Investors Chronicle*.

By no means are these isolated instances, and they are complemented by some heavily critical comments in Company Inspectors' reports:

'(The auditors) were responsible for part of the overstatement by acting without reasonable skill and care in the conduct of the audit.' (Roadships)

'Having regard to the size of the claim and the circumstances surrounding its preparation we believe that both firms of auditors were on notice to exercise particular care in dealing with the matter. It is our view that the auditors did not do so.' (Lonrho)

'We noticed a number of errors where the auditors had failed to follow items through in the course of the audit and see that agreed or necessary provisions were included in the accounts.' (London and County Securities)

In particular, the collapse of London and County Securities caused considerable concern because of the secondary banking collapse and resulting financial crisis that it precipitated. The Company Inspectors' report concluded:

'the auditors should not have signed unqualified audit reports. . . . The main extent of inflation of cash balances was known to the audit partner, . . . and it was so serious as to make the accounts misleading to a material extent.'

Small wonder the concern. Following this, the Secretary of State for Trade instigated a wide-ranging inquiry into the role of auditors, and subsequently the Cross Committee was formed (appointed by the English and Scottish Institutes and the Certified Association) to inquire into professional disciplinary arrangements (its report resulted in a revised statement by the ICAEW on professional independence effective as of 1 January 1980). And in March 1977 a Private Member's Bill was debated which proposed the establishment of a State Audit Board (more later in this chapter), on the grounds that self regulation was not working satisfactorily. The Bill was only narrowly defeated. So clearly there is need for change. And if we do not make improvements ourselves, the matter will probably be taken out of our hands.

Let us now look at the areas in which we are subject to criticism.

## 2.10  The auditor's independence

There can be no doubt that in Professor Edward Stamp's words, 'an auditor is virtually useless as an auditor if he is not independent'. This principle we established in the first chapter when we looked at the auditor's role. And it is logically evident, for you cannot expect one person to check the work of another if he depends on that other in some way. But the problem comes in deciding what can and what cannot make the auditor dependent. Nor is the *fact* of independence alone sufficient, for it is important that the auditor shall be seen to be independent by the people who are relying upon him. Without such evidence confidence fails and the auditor's role is diminished.

We can identify a number of ways in which the auditor's independence may be compromised:

1. Close involvement with the management of the company on a business or personal level. . . . This possibility is largely prevented by the provisions of company law, but you should note the two loopholes already mentioned in sec. 2.8 above.

2. A substantial shareholding in the client company. . . . There could be the risk that auditors may concur with directors' wishes to adjust profits upwards, in order to benefit their own interests. Equally as dangerous, the auditors could be accused of so concurring, even if this was not in fact the case. A side issue often raised in this connection is that auditors, directors and others with substantial shareholdings and inside knowledge may be accused of 'insider dealing' on the Stock Exchange. This is a very real problem, but should not be confused with problems of compromised independence. Such 'insider dealing' has now been treated as a criminal offence, and this would seem the best way of dealing with it.

3. Preparation and audit of the accounts by the same firm. It is hard to see how one person can objectively and independently check the work that he himself has prepared. Indeed, logically it cannot be so. But this problem is more common in small firms and small limited companies. And we have seen that in these companies there is often no need for an independent check on the management on behalf of the shareholders, in that the two are often the same. (The issue of

independent checks on behalf of creditors, etc., must await discussion in a later chapter.)

4. Heavy involvement in other work, such as management consultancy, taxation services, systems design, secretarial work, financial advice, etc., may mean that the fees for 'other services' may be substantially higher than the audit fee itself. To lose the audit would probably be to lose this work too, so substantial financial pressure could be placed upon auditors to concur with directors' wishes. And there is the further danger that the auditors may become, or may appear to become, too involved in the making or formulating of management decisions for them to remain objective.

5. Similar financial pressure could be imposed if one client represented a significant proportion of the audit firms' total fees. This is perhaps not so important with the bigger firms as the loss of one, even large, audit may not be significant – 'you win some, you lose some'. But it could well be very significant to a medium sized firm struggling for survival. And this is an area where considerable concern has been expressed.

6. More subtle is the problem the auditor faces with a client in a difficult financial situation. A qualification may be required to his report. Even a qualification to the effect that the company is no longer a going concern. Such a qualification would of course give the company no further hope of survival. And this almost certainly would not be in the shareholders' interests – interests which the auditor is appointed to serve. The creditors may ultimately benefit from such a qualification if it results in an orderly winding up; but company law at the present time does not require the accounts to show a true and fair view to the creditors. Only the auditor's integrity and level-headed judgement can solve this very tricky problem.

7. Finally, one can point to the whole system itself whereby the auditors are effectively, if not in law (see sec. 2.3), paid and appointed by the directors, and ask if there can ever be real and total independence. He who pays the piper calls the tune. This leads logically to the almost heretical suggestion of a nationalised auditing profession. But as we shall see later in this section this is probably not the answer either.

So now let us look at the solutions that have been put forward to combat some of these problems. In early 1978 the ICAEW published a discussion document on professional independence, and revised Ethical Guidelines were introduced on 1 January 1980. The following is a summary of the major provisions:

1. *Fees.* Recurring fees from one source should not exceed 15 per cent of the gross fees of the practice.

2. *Personal relationships.* These – of partners or staff with client officers or employees, either by blood, marriage or close friendships – could prejudice independence. This applies particularly in the case of any business relationship, and may also apply in the situation where one member of staff works on the audit for many years.

3. *Financial involvement.* This may arise in several ways and can affect objectivity. The following situations should be avoided:

(a) *Shareholdings.* A practice should ensure that it does not have as an audit client a company in which a partner in the practice, the spouse or minor child of such a partner is the beneficial holder of shares, nor should it employ on the audit any member of staff who is a beneficial holder of such shares. Where a practice is asked to report other than in the capacity as auditor, no partner or employee engaged on the assignment should have shareholdings as above. There are certain minor exceptions to allow time for the disposal of such shares acquired involuntarily through inheritance, and in relation to such shares held through unit or investment trusts. Savings in client building societies are only prohibited if they represent a significant amount in relation to the saver.

(b) *Trusts.* A practice should not have as an audit client a public company if a partner in the practice, or the spouse of a partner, is a trustee of a trust holding shares in that company and the holding is in excess of 10 per cent of the issued share capital of the company or of the total assets comprised in the trust. A number of detailed additional provisions also apply.

(c) *Loans.* Neither the practice, nor partners, nor spouses or minor children of partners should make or receive loans to or from a client company.

(d) *Goods and services* from clients should not be accepted on more favourable terms than would normally be granted to employees of the client. Undue hospitality should be guarded against.

(e) *Commission.* Where the practice will earn a commission from a client as a result of his acting upon advice given, care must be taken that the advice is in the best interests of the client, and that the commission is disclosed to him. (Note that the UEC's 1979 Independence statement says that '*in no circumstances*' should a public accountant accept such a commission. A fee should be charged on a proper professional basis, and the accountant should have no financial interest in its acceptance.)

4. *Conflicts of interest.* In cases where conflict of interest may arise there should be full and frank disclosure to those involved, coupled with any action necessary to disengage from one or both positions, the conflicting interests of which have occasioned the difficulty.

5. *Provision of other services to audit clients.* Whilst it is right that members should provide, for audit clients, other services beyond performing the audit, nevertheless care must be taken not to perform executive functions or to make executive decisions. These are the duties of management. In particular members should beware lest, in providing such services, they drift into a situation in which they step across the border-line of what is proper.

6. *Preparation of accounting records:*

(a) A practice should not participate in the preparation of the accounting records of a public company audit client save in exceptional circumstances.

(b) In the case of private company audit clients, it is frequently necessary to provide a much fuller service than would be appropriate in the case of a public company audit client and this may include participation in the preparation of accounting records.

(c) In all cases in which a practice is concerned in the preparation of accounting records of an audit client particular care must be taken to ensure that the client accepts full responsibility for such records and that objectivity in carrying out the audit is not impaired.

7. *Current appointment in a company reported on.* A practice, wherever it may be situated, should not report on a company, even if the law of the country in which the company is registered would so permit, if a partner or employee of the practice is an officer or employee of the company. Nor should a practice report on a company if a company associated with the practice fills the appointment of secretary to the client. It should be particularly noted that this guidance is applicable to members whether they are within or without the United Kingdom and whether they are in practice or not.

8. *Previous appointment in a company reported on.* No one should personally take part in the exercise of the reporting function on a company if he has, during the period upon which the report is to be made, or at any time in the two years prior to the first day thereof, been an officer (other than auditor) or employee of that company.

9. *Liquidation following receiverships.* Where a partner in or an employee of a practice is, or in the previous two years has been, receiver of any of the assets of a company, no partner in or employee of the practice should accept appointment as liquidator of the company.

10. *Liquidation generally.* Where a practice or a partner in or an employee of a practice has, or during the previous two years has had, a continuing professional relationship with a company, no partner or employee of the practice should accept appointment as liquidator of the company if the company is insolvent. Where the company is solvent such appointment should not be accepted without careful consideration being given to the implications of acceptance in that particular case.

11. *Receiverships.* Where a practice or a partner in or an employee of a practice has, or during the previous two years has had, a continuing professional relationship with a company, no partner in or employee of the practice should accept appointment as receiver or as receiver and manager of that company.

12. *Audit following receivership.* Where a partner in or an employee of a practice has been receiver of any of the assets of a company, neither the practice nor any

partner in or employee of the practice should accept appointment as auditor of the company, or of any company which was under the control of the receiver, for any accounting period during which the receiver acted or exercised control.

13. *New clients*. Whenever a practice is asked to accept an appointment, consideration will need to be given to whether acceptance might give rise to a situation in which independence may be compromised whether by a prospective conflict of interest or otherwise. All reasonable steps should be taken to establish that acceptance is unlikely to threaten independence.

These rules would seem to cover most of the potential areas for compromised independence discussed earlier, but two important issues of public concern remain:
1. Involvement in other work.
2. The effect of the audit fee itself.

And these problems the profession seems unwilling to discuss. For example, the ethics paper just cited states '. . . it is right that members should provide for audit clients, other services. . . .'. No attempt is made to justify *why* it is right, and no mention is made of the fact that in America it is considered far from 'right', and is expressly forbidden. Similar comments are made by the CCAB in its reply to the proposed EEC Eighth Directive of Company Law, which covers, among other things, the independence of auditors. It would be unacceptable to 'isolate the activity of auditing from the profession of accountancy as a whole and could only be to the detriment of the public which relies on the profession to carry out audits on the foundation of a wide range of professional experience'. But divorcing auditing from other services does not preclude the auditor from having a wide range of professional experience . . . in other clients. And it may also be questioned whether the public has ever voiced this imputed reliance.

The divorce of auditing from 'Other Services' has been the practice for some time in America, where the SEC (Securities Exchange Commission) does not permit audit firms of listed companies to have any significant accounting functions in those companies. The SEC is a powerful quasi-legal body which has no direct parallel in the UK, so such constraints here would have to come from the government itself. And this is where it may well come from, as the ICAEW ethics document studiously ignores the issue. It is not hard to see why. Such a move would strike at the very structure of the profession which has for so long provided a wide range of other services at the same time as carrying out the audit function. And it is certainly arguable that a change would be of little *practical* benefit to the public. There may even be some disadvantage to the client, in that through the audit function the auditor can gain a knowledge of the firm which can assist him in the provision of other services. Such knowledge would have to be acquired by any other firm that took over the work, and of course at a price to the client. So there is some justification for saying that the benefits would be largely cosmetic.

The profession seems similarly reluctant to tackle the issue of the audit fee itself. The ethics guide gives a maximum of 15 per cent of total practice fee income to come from any one source. On the other hand, the EEC Eighth Directive considers this to be too high, and cites 10 per cent as being the maximum. The CCAB's reply is interesting. It makes the valid point that knowledge of a breach may only become available after the event, such as when the firm's accounts are finalised. But this problem could be easily overcome by a marginal provision allowing the firm to rectify the position (e.g. by resigning the appointment or by the appointment of joint auditors) within a stated time period. However, instead of this suggestion, the CCAB proposes that a figure 'in the region of 15 per cent or 20 per cent will at least make it less likely that the prohibition will be unwittingly breached'. It is hard to see why this should be true. For if the firm is on the margin, the prohibition could be unwittingly breached irrespective of the actual position of that margin. The logical implication of what is being said is that a figure of 100 per cent should be used, as this would ensure that the prohibition could *never* be unwittingly breached!

The ethics guide itself is also somewhat watered down by the inclusion of the following provisions: 'It is recognised that a new practice seeking to establish itself or an old practice running itself down may well not, in the short term, be able to comply with this criterion.' But this is exactly the type of practice that may find itself under pressure. So a very strict definition of 'short term' must be applied.

If the profession as a whole fails to satisfy public opinion, then we invite the government to step in. Self regulation could give way to government control, such a move already having been given impetus by the Eighth EEC Directive (covering audit matters) which stated that 'member states shall ensure that approved persons fulfill their obligations either through appropriate administrative measures or by making such persons subject to professional discipline'. The phrase 'appropriate administrative measures' constitutes an invitation for government interference and legislation.

And as I mentioned earlier, the Private Member's Bill (put forward by Mr Ivor Clemitson) to create a State Audit Board was only narrowly defeated. So it is appropriate to examine what powers such a board would have. The most commonly suggested functions are:
(a) state control of examinations and qualification for membership of professional bodies;
(b) state control over disciplinary matters;
(c) state responsibility for the formulation of auditing and accounting standards;
(d) state control over the appointment of auditors, and/or setting of fees;
and, more extreme . . .
(e) nationalisation of audit firms.
Some advantages could undoubtedly accrue from such moves:
(a) less intransigence resulting from vested interests;
(b) greater real and apparent independence;
(c) greater powers of enforcement as a result of legal as opposed to professional sanctions.

But in my opinion government interference is not the answer for the following reasons:

1. Government interference invites political involvement, and this is arguably not desirable if the profession is to remain objective.
2. Government interference could well induce a rigidity into the profession which would not be in the interests of the development of best practice. Indeed, the formulation of legally enforced rules can take such a time that those rules could well lag even farther behind the requirements of current circumstances than those formulated by self regulation. This is well illustrated by the defects in current company law.
3. It is true that a self-regulating body can probably never be totally impartial. But it is inevitable that the bureaucratic approach of a public regulating authority would result in far greater cost to the shareholder and ultimately to the public. And it is very doubtful whether the benefit derived would justify a further increase in an already heavy burden.
4. There is a very large existing precedent for nationalised auditing in the form of local authority audits. And there is no evidence to suggest that such audits are conspicuously better. Indeed, mistakes there bear a marked similarity to those made in industrial audits.
5. A number of other industrialised countries (e.g. France and South Africa) have considerable state involvement in auditing. But there is little indication that the standards actually achieved are any higher.

However, there is one practical piece of legislation that could and should be introduced – *Audit committees*. Such committees are made up of a majority of non-executive officers of the company, and act as a buffer between the auditors and the directors. This helps to overcome the very real possibility of auditors getting the sack if they disagree with the directors. And this goes to the very root of the independence issue.

This concept was originally introduced in America as long ago as 1940, but became more generally accepted in the 1960s when the American Institute of Certified Public Accountants (AICPA) positively recommended such committees for all quoted companies. They became a mandatory requirement from 1978 when the New York Stock Exchange made them a condition of listing.

The role that an audit committee could undertake is open to discussion, but the following areas would seem to have general application:

(a) be responsible in conjunction with the shareholders for appointing the auditors and fixing their remuneration;
(b) be available for consultation with auditors concerning the accounts and accounting systems, and to assist the auditors in obtaining information;
(c) deal with any material reservations that the auditors may have in connection with the annual accounts or the accounting system, or indeed even the management itself;
(d) ensure that those matters raised in the auditors' management report are speedily and effectively actioned;
(e) review the auditors' procedures to ensure that they are adequate (so the

committee has a two-edged function – not just to oversee the directors).

A further suggestion along similar lines to the audit committee is for a statutory tribunal to be created, to which the auditor could appeal in the event that he considers he is being wrongfully dismissed by the directors. Such a tribunal could be an effective and a comparatively simple expedient, although it would of course cost more of the taxpayers' money.

We must now leave the very delicate issue of independence and move to the related and equally controversial area of audit standards. But you should appreciate that the independence issue is crucial to the whole audit function. Without independence, the auditor is nothing. In fact he is worse than nothing, because he can give credibility to accounts which do not merit it. He becomes like icing on a very stale cake.

## 2.11  Auditing Standards

In addition to questions about his degree of objectivity, the standards with which the auditor carries out his task have also come in for considerable attack. To help counteract such attack, the first draft Auditing Standards, covering operational matters and reporting formats, were issue by the APC in June 1978 (see sec. 1.5) and were finalised in April 1980. The 'Operational Standard' formulates what is currently best practice amongst the bigger firms of auditors. There is clearly merit in telling people how we carry out our audits, but this may not make our performance of the job significantly better. It is the large firms who have come in for most of the criticism. So to formulate their methods into standards does not necessarily solve the problem of poor work. If inadequate skill is the problem (and it may be less so than the lack of objectivity as discussed in sec. 2.10 – to take but one example, the London and County audit partner was aware of . . . 'The main extent of inflation of cash balances'), then the answer must lie in improving the current, inadequate method of training new entrants to the profession.

It is strange that in all the solutions put forward by members of the profession, and outsiders alike, education is seldom mentioned. Yet it must be the answer for the future, albeit not an immediate and demonstrable answer, in the way that written standards could be. Nor is a simple raising of the examination pass mark or fine tuning the existing examination system the way to raise standards. Standards can only be raised by a whole new look at our approach to training, and a recognition that the huge and ever increasing body of knowledge cannot be adequately assimilated in the current minimum of just over three years. Doctors, architects, lawyers all require considerably longer periods of specific training. Is our profession so much easier?

The Standards themselves are very brief, although the Guidelines do give more details. It is possible that the reason why more of the substance of the Guidelines was not included in the Standards is that agreement could not be reached in the District Societies on the matters contained therein. Understandably so, for the practices in small firms are very different. And it is long overdue for the profession to recognise this difference, and to take action accordingly.

It is, however, unlikely that the profession as a whole will ever accept such a move without considerable outside pressure. The reason is simple. A large proportion of the profession is constituted by members in small practice. And they see their position threatened by any move to recognise that small proprietary companies have different requirements to their big brothers quoted on the Stock Exchange. Their fears were clearly expressed by John Wakeham FCA, MP in an address to the Small Business Bureau (text reproduced in *The Accountant*, 6 April 1978). He stated . . . 'It is the job of the leaders of the accountancy profession to devise auditing standards that are readily adaptable to cover these different situations (large and small companies) . . . What will not be acceptable is to end up with some companies having a first-class audit and some companies a second-class audit; or, to put it another way, some auditors being first-class citizens and some second-class.' To state thus is to fail to realise that in listed and proprietary companies we are dealing with two completely different entities with completely different requirements, but the real fear of the small firm is perhaps expressed in the last sentence; the fear of being seen as a second-class citizen. I personally find it hard to understand why anyone should hold this fear, or feel inferior because it is recognised that they are doing a different job. Do we regard the general practitioner as an inferior doctor simply because he does less specialised work than the consultant physician? We do not. And there is similarly no reason to regard the small practitioner as an inferior accountant because his work is less sophisticated.

The Auditor's Operational Standard is reproduced in full below, and together with the associated Guidelines, is referred to throughout the text. The Reporting Standards and Guidelines are reproduced in Chapter 17.

'The Auditors Operational Standard
'1. This Auditing Standard applies whenever an audit is carried out.
'2. Planning, controlling and recording
   The auditor should adequately plan, control and record his work.
'3. Accounting systems
   The auditor should ascertain the enterprise's system of recording and processing transactions and assess its adequacy as a basis for the preparation of financial statements.
'4. Audit evidence
   The auditor should obtain relevant and reliable audit evidence sufficient to enable him to draw reasonable conclusions therefrom.
'5. Internal controls
   If the auditor wishes to place reliance on any internal controls, he should ascertain and evaluate those controls and perform compliance tests on their operation.
'6. Review of financial statements
   The auditor should carry out such a review of the financial statements

as is sufficient, in conjunction with the conclusions drawn from the other audit evidence obtained, to give him a reasonable basis for his opinion on the financial statements.

'7. Effective date

This Auditing Standard is effective for the audit of financial statements relating to accounting periods starting on or after 1 April 1980.'

# 3
## The audit approach – an overview

## 3.1 Introduction

We saw in Chapter 1 that the purpose of an audit is to report upon accounts that have been produced for stewardship purposes. The auditor must examine the accounts, and ascertain whether they are 'true or fair' by reference to the supporting evidence available, which will include:

(a) the accounting books, records and documents;
(b) information and explanations from employees;
(c) confirmations from third parties.

In this chapter we will look at the overall audit approach in order that you may subsequently appreciate how the stages in audit procedures relate to each other. Such an appreciation is essential for a full understanding, and it is my experience that the lack of a logical, structured approach in past teaching has contributed substantially to students' difficulties with this subject.

## 3.2 Alternative approaches

There are many possible approaches to audit work, and no one approach is the only or correct one. And this perhaps adds an element of confusion for newcomers to the subject. However, in the Guidelines to the Operational Standard, the APC lays down certain principles, and it is these which we will examine now. You should note that the audit approach discussed is based upon the requirements of medium and large sized companies. The changes required in, and problems associated with, the audit of small companies will be tackled in Chapter 18.

We can distinguish three possible bases for audit work:

1. *Transactions (or vouching) audit.* This approach involves vouching (proving) all or a large proportion of transactions to documentary evidence.
2. *Balance sheet audit.* This approach involves (amongst other things) the verification of all the assets and liabilities that appear in the balance sheet. By so doing, the profit for the year is automatically proved, assuming that the opening balance sheet was validated in similar fashion (those of you who are familiar with incomplete records will know this principle well; those of you who are not – think about it carefully!).

3. *Systems audit.* In this approach, the auditor examines and tests the client's accounting and other control systems (Internal Control) to see whether or not they constitute a reliable base for the preparation of the accounts.

Clearly it will only be practicable to examine all or a large proportion of the transactions in the smallest of concerns. Such an examination will not in any event guarantee the truth and fairness of the accounts, as evidence of certain transactions may be deliberately concealed from the auditors and no amount of audit work will necessarily bring these to light. Accordingly the *transactions' approach* is not used today, in any other than very small companies. Such companies have their own special audit problems, and these are examined later.

The *balance sheet audit* approach used by itself suffers from similar inherent problems. While it may be possible to adequately verify all the assets and liabilities that appear on the balance sheet, it may well be impossible to prove those that should be there, but are not. Assets or liabilities that are deliberately concealed may be impossible to discover; only a sound system of internal control can prevent such deliberate defalcation (see sec. 3.3 below).

In a company of reasonable size, with shareholders other than the directors and managers, it is necessary to use the *systems approach* to auditing. This approach is based on the premise that the directors are responsible for running the business in an orderly fashion, for safeguarding its assets and for producing accounts which show a true and fair view of the state of affairs of the company and of the profit or loss for the period under review. The auditor will examine the systems developed for these purposes, in order to evaluate to what extent they are likely to form a reliable basis for the preparation of the annual accounts.

These varied approaches may be used in isolation, or in conjunction with each other. Traditionally, an audit was carried out by extensive vouching of transactions, followed at the year end by an examination of the balance sheet. For the reasons looked at above, this is not now considered appropriate, and the current approach is to carry out a systems-based audit during the course of the accounting year, followed by an extensive balance sheet audit at the year end. This combination provides the best assurance that the accounts are true and fairly stated, in that the system which gives rise to the final accounts is proved as reliable, and the accounts themselves are validated by a variety of means which will be examined in detail in Chapters 10 to 14.

## 3.3 Internal control

We saw above that the basis of a *systems audit* is an examination of internal control. Before we can examine the procedures upon which such an audit is based, we must look at the nature of internal control. The Auditing Guideline (hereafter AG) 204 Internal Control defines an internal control system as

'the whole system of controls, financial and otherwise, established by the management in order to carry on the business of the company in an orderly and efficient manner, ensure adherence to management policies,

> safeguard the assets and secure as far as possible the accuracy and reliability of the records'.

AG 202 Accounting Systems states –

> 'The management of an enterprise requires complete and accurate accounting and other records to assist it in:
> '(a)  controlling the business;
> '(b)  safeguarding the assets;
> '(c)  preparing financial statements;
> '(d)  complying with legislation.'

And AG 204 continues:

> 'It is a responsibility of management to decide the extent of the control system which is appropriate to the enterprise. The nature and extent of the controls will vary between enterprises, and also from one part of an enterprise to another. The controls used will depend on the nature, size and volume of the transactions, the degree of control which members of management are able to exercise personally, the geographical distribution of the enterprise and many other factors. The choice of controls may reflect a comparison of the cost of operating individual controls against the benefits expected to be derived from them.'

It is not necessary at this stage for you to understand in detail the nature of internal control; that can wait until Chapter 5. But the concept is crucial to the modern audit approach. And the part it does play may be understood by reference to Fig. 3.1. This depicts the various stages of the audit in brief form so that you can assimilate the sequence of events before proceeding to the detail of the text. You should study this thoroughly, and familiarise yourself with the jargon used at the various stages, noting also the timing which is depicted down the left-hand side of the diagram.

## 3.4  Audit procedure

1. *Record the accounting system*

The first stage in the audit procedure will be to establish and document the system used for recording transactions. To facilitate the subsequent audit work, the documentation will be split into accounting areas such as the Purchases Cycle, the Wages Cycle, the Sales Cycle, Stock and Fixed Assets, and a separate systems record will be made of each. These records can be produced in several ways, but the essence of them is that they allow the auditor to evaluate the system of internal control. Diagrammatic presentation in the form of 'flow charts' is now generally recognised as allowing quicker and more meaningful evaluation of control systems, and it is this method that is usually used by the larger firms in their analysis of substantial client companies. The alternatives are narrative

Fig. 3.1 The audit approach

| Timing | Step no. | Audit stages | Audit documents |
|---|---|---|---|
| Interim audit/s | 1 | Gain an understanding of and record the accounting system. Check system recorded correctly by carrying out 'walk through' tests. Undertake a preliminary review of past financial statements, and the accounting system, with a view to planning the conduct of the audit. | Systems notes, ICQs or flow charts |
| | | | Audit plan |
| | 2 | Evaluate the system of internal control to see if it constitutes a reliable basis for the preparation of the financial statements. | ICQ or ICE |
| Final audit | 3 | Compliance tests – to gain assurance that the client's internal control procedures are being complied with. | Send letter to management re control weaknesses. |
| | 4 | Agree financial statements to underlying records. | Extended trial balance MAP |
| | 5 | Substantive tests – to substantiate the transactions and balances underlying the financial statements. (a) Analytical review (b) Tests of detail (the extent of (b) is determined by 2, 3 and 5a) Verify assets and liabilities. | MAP |
| | 6 | Ensure compliance with Companies Acts. | Companies Act check list |
| | 7 | Ensure compliance with SSAPs, IASs and Stock Exchange requirements. | SSAP check list |
| | 8 | Review for truth and fairness including: Analytical review Going concern audit Post balance sheet events audit Letter of representation. | Audit completion check list |
| | 9 | Partner review. | |
| | 10 | Report: Report to shareholders Report to management. | Audit report Report to management |

Key ICQ – Internal Control Questionnaire
    ICE – Internal Control Evaluation
    MAP – Master Audit Programme

notes or checklists of desirable control features. The relative advantages and disadvantages of each method are discussed in detail in Chapter 7.

AG 202 Accounting Systems suggests:

'As an aid to recording the accounting system, the auditor should consider tracing a small number of transactions (possibly one or two of each type) through the system. This procedure (often known as "walk-through checks") will confirm that there is no reason to suppose that the accounting system does not operate in the manner recorded. The procedure is particularly appropriate where the enterprise has itself prepared the record of the system which the auditor is to use.'

2. *Evaluate the system of internal control*

AG 204 Internal Control states:

'The auditor will need to ascertain and record the internal control system in order to make a preliminary evaluation of the effectiveness of its component controls and to decide the extent of his reliance thereon. 'The evaluation of internal controls will be assisted by the use of documentation designed to help identify the internal controls on which the auditor may wish to place reliance. Such documentation can take a variety of forms but might typically consist of questions asking either:
'(a)  whether controls exist in a system which meet specified overall control objectives [these are often called Internal Control Questionnaires or ICQs]; or
'(b)  whether there are controls which prevent particular specified *frauds, errors or omissions occurring [these, for convenience of differentiation, we can call Internal Control Evaluations or ICEs, although some firms also refer to these as ICQs]*.
'Where the preliminary evaluation indicates that there are controls which meet the objective which the auditor has identified, he should design and Carry out compliance tests, if he wishes to rely on them [see 3 below]. Where, however, the preliminary evaluation discloses weaknesses in, or the absence of, internal controls, such that material error or omission could arise in the accounting records or financial statements, the auditor will move directly to designing and carrying out substantive tests [*see 5 below*] . . .'

3. *Compliance tests*

Compliance tests, as their name implies, are designed to ensure that the internal controls on which the auditor wishes to rely are in fact working properly in practice. The nature of such tests will depend upon the nature of the control, but essentially they involve checking transactions for evidence of compliance. Such evidence might for example be in the form of signatures or stamps on documentation, it might be obtained by physically observing procedures (such as attending a wages payout), or it may be derived by the auditor rechecking figures or computations to ensure no errors have occurred.

Para. 24 of the Guideline states:

'The auditor is not entitled to place any reliance on an accounting system or internal controls based solely on his preliminary evaluation. He should carry out compliance tests to obtain evidence that the controls on which he wishes to rely were functioning both properly *and throughout the period*. It should be noted that it is the control which is being tested by a compliance test, and not the transaction which may be the medium used for the test. For this reason the auditor must record and investigate thoroughly all exceptions revealed by his compliance testing, regardless of the amount involved in the particular transaction. (An "exception" in this context is an occurrence where a control has not been operated correctly whether or not a quantitative error has occurred.)

'If compliance tests disclose no exceptions, the auditor's preliminary evaluation is confirmed and he may reasonably place reliance on the effective functioning of the internal control tested. *He can, therefore limit his substantive tests* on the relevant information in the accounting records.'

### 4. *Agree financial statements to underlying records*

At the year end, it is necessary to check that the accounts produced are in accordance with the underlying records. This is a specific requirement of the CA 1976, and it is clearly of the utmost importance, as undiscovered errors or irregularities here could nullify all previous work. However, it is normally a routine test, which will be carried out by checking the accounting records to the trial balance, and then the trial balance to the profit and loss account and balance sheet.

### 5. *Substantive tests*

Substantive testing is designed to substantiate the transactions and balances underlying the financial statements, and it is carried out in two ways:
(a) Analytical review (over-all analysis);
(b) Tests of detail.

The *analytical review* can usefully be carried out before performing tests of detail and it has the following purposes:
(a) to ascertain whether there is an acceptable business explanation for any unusual trends, fluctuations or interrelationships revealed by the review;
(b) to obtain (without examining detail) reasonable assurance that particular items are substantially correct.

By highlighting significant fluctuations or unusual items, the review identifies material problem areas that can then be investigated by procedures which are appropriate to the particular circumstances. The review is discussed in detail in Chapter 10, so suffice to say here that it will consist of a variety of techniques including comparisons to budget, comparison with previous years' results and ratio analysis.

If the client's system of accounting records is both soundly conceived and carefully maintained, the review will reveal a clear logical pattern in the results –

a pattern that is consistent with a knowledge of the client's business. This pattern will be based on relationships within the system: relationships such as those between sales and the cost of sales, between the cost of sales and stocks and between stocks and purchases. The existence of such a consistent pattern in the results constitutes persuasive evidence that the final accounts will present a true and fair view.

The *testing of detail* will be achieved by retracing the procedural steps followed in the accounting process, by recalculating computations, by checking casts and summaries, allocations and postings and by direct confirmation of balances through external confirmation. *Such tests can be kept to a minimum provided*:

(a)  the internal control evaluation reveals no significant weaknesses;

(b)  the compliance tests disclose no exceptions;

(c)  the analytical review reveals no unexplained peculiar trends or relationships.

However, in the words of para. 16 of AG 204:

> 'If the compliance tests have disclosed exceptions which indicate that the control being tested was not operating properly in practice, the auditor should determine the reasons for this. He needs to assess whether each exception is only an isolated departure or is representative of others, and whether it indicates the possible existence of errors in the accounting records. If the explanations he receives suggests that the exception is only an isolated departure, then he must confirm the validity of the explanation, for example by carrying out further tests. If the explanation, or the further tests confirm that the control being tested was not operating properly throughout the period, then he cannot rely on that control. In these circumstances the auditor is unable to restrict his substantive testing unless he can identify an alternative control on which to rely. Before relying on that alternative control he must carry out suitable compliance tests on it.'

Where there are no controls on which to place reliance, or the auditor has decided it will be more efficient to disregard the existence of internal controls, he will need to design and carry out substantive tests in such a way as to obtain reasonable assurance that material error or omission has not occurred. In these circumstances, it may be impossible to be satisfied that the accounts show a true and fair view, because in the absence of internal controls it may not be possible to discover assets or transactions that have been deliberately concealed.

In practice it is often possible to combine Compliance testing and Substantive tests of transactions, in that they both concentrate on the same accounting records. Many of the tests will be the same or similar, but the reasons for performing them are very different. So provided this is remembered, it is possible to design an audit programme which can considerably reduce the overall amount of detailed work required, by combining aspects of these two types of tests.

Some firms combine these tests in preprinted Audit Programmes (often called Master Audit Programmes or MAPs) which have a general application to all clients. These forms can assist in ensuring a systematic approach to the work and that no areas are missed, but care needs to be taken that the job does not become stereotyped with a resulting lack of the initiative and perception so necessary for satisfactory audit work.

At the conclusion of the procedures indicated in the stages above, the auditor will be in a position to decide whether the accounting records will constitute a reliable basis for the preparation of the final accounts.

### Verification of assets and liabilities

Verification is a technical term implying the confirmation of the existence, ownership and value of assets, and the existence and amount of liabilities. The extent of such substantive testing of balances will be dictated by the quality of the internal control, and the confidence (or otherwise) given by the analytical review. Verification procedures are extensively covered in Chapter 14.

### 6. Ensure compliance with the Companies Acts

This step is again a specific requirement of the Companies Acts, and with the considerable number of disclosure requirements, it is very necessary that there should be an independent check on the people that have produced the accounts. Many audit firms are kind to their employees and do not expect them to re-member all these requirements! Instead a Companies Act checklist will be used, incorporating all the requirements in note form and in the order normally met with in a set of accounts. Such a pre-printed form will be applicable to all clients, and can considerably reduce the time taken at this stage, and lessen the possibility of overlooking any of the disclosure provisions. A copy of the Companies Act checklist, kindly supplied by Deloitte, Haskins and Sells, is included in Appendix 1 to this book.

### 7. Ensure compliance with SSAPs, IASs and Stock Exchange requirements

Compliance with SSAPs, IASs and Stock Exchange requirements is not a specific requirement of the law (except in so far as non-compliance distorts the true and fair view). However, the professional bodies have sanctions (the ultimate being disqualification from membership) against members who sign accounts that do not so comply. And the Stock Exchange likewise has sanctions in that it can restrict a company's quotation.

Compliance is important in order to facilitate comparison between different companies, and to enable the proper interpretation of the figures produced. In order to check for compliance in client company accounts, many firms have pre-printed checklists which incorporate all the disclosure requirements in note form, and are of general application to all clients. Copies of such checklists, again kindly supplied by Deloitte, Haskins and Sells, are included in Appendices 2 and 3B to this book.

8. *Review for truth and fairness*

(a) *Analytical review.*   During the course of the year the auditor will examine ratios and relationships between figures to help determine the amount of detailed testing required. The emphasis will be on profitability and performance, whereas at the year end the emphasis will change towards those ratios and figures which show credit ratings and liquidity. Normally, accounts are drawn up on the assumption that the company is a '*going concern*', and the auditor must satisfy himself that the assumption is justified. Also sufficient knowledge of the client's future trading prospects is necessary to enable a critical examination of the director's report, the chairman's statement, and any other information that is given in the accounts brochure.

(b) *Post balance sheet events audit.* A substantial period can elapse between the accounting year end, and the presentation of the accounts at general meeting. Material events occurring after the year end, but before the AGM, could have a substantial effect on those accounts, and in extreme cases could render them totally meaningless. So it is necessary for the auditor to ensure that all such events have been incorporated into the financial statements in the way that will be examined in Chapter 16.

(c) *Review of directors' minutes.* The directors' minutes and other books such as the register of charges and the seal register should be scrutinised for matters affecting the accounts; for example, capital commitments or contingent liabilities.

(d) *Letter of representation.* As a final stage, a letter of representation should be obtained from the directors to the effect that the financial statements are true and fairly stated. Such a letter in no way relieves the auditor of any liability, but it does point out to the directors that the accounts are primarily their responsibility.

9. *Partner review*

Before signing the accounts the partner will review all the work that has been done to assure himself that he is in a position to express an opinion on the accounts. He will pay particular attention to the presentation of the accounts, to the analytical review and to the appropriateness of the various accounting policies used.

## 3.5  Timing of audit work

Audit work may be carried out in total at the end of the accounting year. However, this can give rise to a number of problems:

(a) there may be a heavy demand on audit staff at certain times in the year, because most accounting periods end on one of the quarter days and in particular on 31 December. This can mean that audit staff are not available and that the final accounts can be delayed;

(b) detailed checking may be reduced unreasonably in order to speed up the production of the final accounts;
(c) there may be a long delay between the recording of an entry by the client and the examination of that entry by the auditor. This may result in problems in checking because of poor recollection by the client and because of difficulties in locating documentation.

The solution to these problems is to have one or more 'interim' audits during the year, and the majority of the systems work will be undertaken at the interim/s. However, it will be necessary to carry out further compliance tests at the year end to ensure that the internal controls upon which the auditor is relying have been working satisfactorily *throughout* the year. In addition, substantive tests must be conducted during the final audit to substantiate the transactions that have occurred since the interim visit.

## 3.6 Audit reports

In Chapter 1 we saw that the auditor was required to express his opinion as to whether accounts presented to him represented a true and fair view of the state of affairs of the company and of the profit or loss for the period under review. If all the stages of the audit hitherto discussed have proved to be satisfactory, then the auditor will be in a position to express such an opinion. However, in the event that the auditor is not satisfied with the reliability of the accounting system, or if the accounts contain figures or information which may mislead shareholders to a material extent, then the auditor must consider qualifying his report. In Chapter 17 we look in more detail at the form such qualifications may take.

## 3.7 Reporting to management

We have seen that the primary function of the auditor is to report to the shareholders in general meeting. However, it is now normal practice also to issue a 'Report to Management'. The 'Report to Management' will contain (inter alia) notes as to the following:
(a) weaknesses in internal control and recommendations as to how they may be rectified;
(b) breakdowns in the accounting systems and any material errors arising;
(c) additional audit time necessitated as a result of weaknesses in the internal control system, or occasioned by the client's failure to adhere to timetables;
(d) unsatisfactory accounting procedures or policies, and recommendations as to how they may be improved;
(e) suggestions as to how financial and accounting efficiency may be improved;
(f) constructive suggestions not necessarily related to accounting procedures but noted by the auditor during the course of his investigations, with the benefit of an outsider's viewpoint.

These reports should normally be sent at least once a year, but it is necessary to point out control weaknesses as soon as possible. These control weaknesses may then be rectified at an early stage, so as to reduce the possibility of error or fraud, and to prevent the need for extensive transaction testing. An important purpose of the reports is to put on record the existence of weaknesses, in order to clarify responsibility for any event stemming from failure by the directors to follow the auditor's recommendations. Clearly the matters should be discussed at an appropriate level before the report is written, in order to avoid antagonising clients through misunderstandings. The final report should contain only significant items, listed in order of importance, and should be phrased in a constructive manner. It should be sent to the directors with a copy to the chief accountant, and an answer should be requested and followed up.

While the 'Report to Management' is not strictly part of the auditor's reporting function, it is increasingly becoming a more significant feature of his work, and can be seen as extending the audit role beyond that of purely checking the historic accounts and then reporting to shareholders.

## 3.8   Conclusion

In this chapter we have looked in outline at the ways in which the external auditor may approach the task of expressing an opinion on the annual accounts of his client companies. In subsequent chapters we will examine in more detail the concepts so far introduced.

# 4
# Commencing an audit

## 4.1 Before engagement

Before an auditor accepts a new appointment, he should communicate by letter with the retiring auditor to see if there is any professional reason why the appointment should be refused. Such communication is an ethical as opposed to a legal requirement, and it can also be seen as a matter of professional courtesy to the previous holder of the post. The duty to communicate should be explained to the potential client, from whom authority must be obtained before writing. If such authority is not forthcoming, or if the existing auditor is prevented from revealing anything of the client's affairs, then the appointment should not be accepted; for such would be a strong indication that something is amiss. Normally the communication will be a routine matter, but occasionally circumstances may be revealed which could affect an acceptance decision. Such circumstances may range from failure to pay fees, to dubious trading practices, and even to undue pressure being placed upon auditors to comply with directors' wishes concerning the accounts. The requirement to communicate may be seen as one of the ways in which the profession seeks to protect itself against this latter, ever-present risk, which was discussed in sec. 2.10 on audit independence.

If the audit is that of a limited company, the scope of the work is defined by statute. But if the client is a partnership or sole trader, then it will be very necessary to discuss the precise scope of the work that is required, carefully distinguishing between audit and accountancy work and any other services. The extent of any audit work must be precisely defined to ensure that there are no misunderstandings as to the amount of work that is to be (and can feasibly be) done. And whatever the type of audit, at this stage it will also be appropriate to discuss the basis for charging the fee. These and other matters must be put in writing to safeguard the auditor in the case of future legal disputes, and this is best achieved by an engagement letter as discussed below.

## 4.2 The engagement letter

The engagement letter has the following functions:
1. To define the scope of the audit in the event that it is not defined by statute.
2. To confirm any verbal agreements, including the basis on which fees will be charged.

3. To confirm any other services which are to be provided, or to point out other services which may possibly be of interest and value to the client.
4. To distinguish between accountancy and audit work.
5. To emphasise that the directors are primarily responsible for producing 'true and fair' accounts.
6. To explain in outline how the auditor will approach his task; this can assist considerably in preventing future misunderstandings.
7. To stress that the audit should not be relied upon necessarily to prevent or detect fraud and error as this is not its main purpose; although it should also be stressed that normal audit procedures can be expected to considerably reduce the likelihood of such occurrences (see sec. 1.4).

Many audit firms have standard engagement letters to cover different circumstances. Two copies of the letter should be sent, one to be signed and returned by the client as acknowledgement of, and agreement to, the terms contained therein. By way of example, copies of the standard form of letters used by Deloitte, Haskins and Sells for both statutory and non-statutory audits are reproduced in Fig. 4.1 by kind permission.

Fig. 4.1  Specimen engagement letters

### Specimen engagement letter for company audits with ancillary services

This illustrates the form that an engagement letter for a company should normally take, except where it is necessary to vary it to suit individual requirements and circumstances.

Following our appointment as auditors of the company, and in confirmation of our recent discussion with . . . . . . . . . . . . . . . . . . . . . . . . ., we set out below our responsibilities as auditors and our understanding of the further services which it was agreed between us we should perform.

1. Audit
    (a) We have been appointed auditors of . . . . . . . . . . . . . . . . . . . . . . . . . . . . . . . . .
        Limited and of the undermentioned subsidiaries;
        . . . . . . . . . . . . . . . . . . . . . . . Limited
        . . . . . . . . . . . . . . . . . . . . . . . Limited
        . . . . . . . . . . . . . . . . . . . . . . . Limited
        and of certain (all) dormant or moribund subsidiaries.
    (b) Our function as auditors under the Companies Acts is to examine financial statements prepared by the directors for presentation to the shareholders, and to express our opinion on them as required by the Companies Acts.
    (c) To enable us to express our opinion, we shall make such tests and enquiries as we consider necessary. The nature and extent of our tests will vary according to both our assessment of what is material in the context of the company's financial statements, and also our assessment of the company's system of internal control. We shall report to the company's management any material weaknesses in the company's system of internal control which come to our notice and which we think should be brought to their attention.
    (d) Our audit is designed to enable us to express our opinion on the company's financial statements. It should not be relied upon to disclose defalcations or other irregularities, but if they exist, the audit tests that we undertake may discover them.
    (e) The foregoing does not cover the work of maintaining the accounting records or the preparation of financial statements, since this is the responsibility of the company's officials.

     (f)  As auditors of the holding company we shall make such enquiries regarding financial statements of the subsidiaries and associated companies as we consider are necessary. It should not be assumed that such enquiries impose responsibilities on us for any matters relating to subsidiaries or associated companies of which we are not auditors, where those matters could be known only to the auditors of the companies concerned in their capacity as such.

2. Accounting and other services (as appropriate)

It was agreed that we should carry out certain accounting services, namely:

     (a)  To prepare final accounts for approval by the Board from draft accounts prepared by the company's staff.

     (b)  To prepare group accounts for approval by the Board.

     (c)  To type and print the financial statements and the directors' report.

It was agreed that we will report on the profits and the wages for the purposes of the company's consequential loss insurance policy.

It was agreed that we will act as financial advisers on any matters which you refer to us.

3. Taxation services (as appropriate)

It was also agreed that we would assist with the following taxation services, namely:

     (a)  To prepare the provisions for taxation for inclusion in the financial statements.

     (b)  To prepare the company's tax computations and to submit them to, and agree them with, the Inland Revenue Authorities.

     (c)  To act as taxation advisers on any matters which you refer to us.

4. Fees

Our fees are computed on the basis of the time necessarily occupied on the company's affairs by partners and staff of different seniority, depending on the degree of responsibility and skill involved. Unless otherwise agreed, our fees will be charged separately for each of the main classes of work mentioned above.

We shall be grateful if you will kindly acknowledge receipt of this letter, the terms of which will continue to apply until they are varied by a subsequent letter. If the contents are not in accordance with your understanding of our discussion, we shall be pleased to consider the matter further with you.

### Specimen engagement letter for pension fund and other non-statutory audits

This illustrates the form an engagement letter for a pension fund or other non-statutory audit should normally take, except where it is necessary to vary it to suit individual requirements and circumstances.

In confirmation of our meeting with . . . . . . . . . . . . . . . . . . . . . . . we set out below our understanding of the services which it was agreed we should perform.

1. Audit

     (a)  You have appointed us auditors of the AB Pension Fund (the EY Social Club) (C & D Partnership) under the terms of paragraph . . . . . . of the Trust Deed (Rules, Partnership Deed, etc.).

     (b)  Our function as auditors is to examine the financial statements prepared by . . . . . . . . . . . . . . . . . . . . for presentation to . . . . . . . . . . . . . . . . . . . . and to express our opinion on them.

     (c)  To enable us to express our opinion, we shall make such tests and enquiries as we consider necessary. The nature and extent of our tests will vary according to both our assessment of what is material in the context of the financial statements, and also our assessment of the system of internal control. We shall report to . . . . . . . . . . . . . . . . . . . . any material weaknesses in the system of internal control which come to our notice and which we think should be brought to their attention.

     (d)  Our audit is designed to enable us to express our opinion on the financial statements. It should not be relied upon to disclose defalcations or other irregularities but if they exist, the audit tests that we undertake may discover them.

(e) The foregoing does not cover the work of maintaining the accounting records or the preparation of financial statements, since the work is the responsibility of . . . . . . . . . . . . . . . . . . . . . . .

(Note: if the client also requires us to prepare financial statements this should be set out under the heading 'Accounting and other services'.)

2. Accounting and other services
3. Taxation
4. Fees

Our fees are computed on the basis of the time necessarily occupied on the Pension Fund's (Social Club's) (Partnership's) affairs by partners and staff of different seniority, depending on the degree of responsibility and skill involved. Unless otherwise agreed, our fees will be charged separately for each of the main classes of work mentioned above.

We shall be grateful if you will kindly acknowledge receipt of this latter, the terms of which will continue to apply until they are varied by a subsequent letter. If the contents are not in accordance with your understanding of our discussion we shall be pleased to consider the matter further with you.

## Specimen engagement letter for a sole trader, a trust or any other organisation where no audit is requested

This illustrates the form that an engagement letter for a sole trader, a trust, or any other organisation, where no audit is requested, should normally take, except where it is necessary to vary it to suit individual requirements and circumstances.

In confirmation of our meeting, we set out our understanding of the services it was agreed we should perform.

1. Accountancy
   (a) It was agreed that we would prepare annual financial statements for your consideration. We understand that you (the trust) (the organisation) will supply the information required for us to complete the preparation of the financial statements. We shall not audit or otherwise review the financial statements unless specifically instructed by you.
   (b) We shall report to you (the trustees, etc.), with such variation as we consider necessary, that we have prepared without undertaking an audit, the financial statements from the accounting records presented to us and from the information and explanations given to us, and that they are in accordance therewith.
   (c) We wish to emphasise that the control over, and the responsibility for, the prevention and detection of defalcations or other irregularities, errors, or omissions must rest with you. You should instruct us specifically if you require us to undertake an investigation to discover any defalcations or irregularities that may exist.
2. Taxation
3. Fees

Our fees are computed on the basis of the time necessarily occupied on your (the trust's) (the organisation's) affairs by partners and staff of different seniority, depending on the degree of responsibility and skill involved. Unless otherwise agreed, our fees will be charged separately for each of the main classes of work mentioned above.

We shall be grateful if you will kindly acknowledge receipt of this letter, the terms of which will continue to apply until they are varied by a subsequent letter. If the contents are not in accordance with your understanding of our discussion we shall be pleased to consider the matter further with you.

## 4.3 Commencement procedures

Once a satisfactory reply has been received from the retiring auditor, and the engagement has been documented in the form of an engagement letter, the auditor can begin collecting the information necessary to commence his detailed work. This will include:

1. A copy of the regulations (if any) of the client, e.g. Memorandum and Articles of Association, or partnership agreement, or club rules.
2. Details as to the nature of the business.
3. Details of physical locations of factories, offices, shops, etc.
4. An organisation chart of the client's staff, with special emphasis on those employees with whom the auditor is likely to have regular contact.
5. An accounts manual, or other details as to the accounting system and the accounting records of which it is composed.
6. Copies of previous annual accounts (see sec. 4.4).
7. Details of the financial history of the company, noting whether it is listed or unlisted, and whether it is director controlled (see sec. 4.4).
8. Names and addresses of the client's advisers, including solicitors, stockbrokers, bankers and management consultants.
9. Copies of important documents, such as leases, debenture deeds and major contracts.

During the course of acquiring this information it can be extremely valuable to visit the client's various locations, and to meet the employees with whom the auditor is likely to have frequent dealings. In this way a very valuable initial impression can be gained of the efficiency of the company and of the sort of problems that may be encountered during the course of the audit.

The above information and the initial impressions will be recorded in a Permanent File which will be used for any information of permanent value to the audit. This file will be further discussed in sec. 4.5.

## 4.4 Planning and controlling an audit

The information so far acquired will be used in planning the audit. When planning a new audit, the auditor should first consider the nature of the company itself, especially whether it is director controlled (the audit role changes, effectively, if not in law, if the company is proprietor managed).

As every student of management accounting knows, planning and control are essential to the financial success of every business, and this applies nonetheless to the business of auditing. But for the auditor, planning and control are not only essential to profitable operation, they are also vital to ensure that professional standards are both maintained and improved.

Paragraph 2 of the Auditor's Operational Standard lays down the standards of audit planning required. It states (somewhat vaguely): 'The auditor should adequately plan, control and record his work. Auditing Guideline 201 on planning, reproduced below, gives a little more detail on how this standard should be applied:

> 'Background:
> 'The form and nature of the planning required for an audit will be affected by the size and complexity of the enterprise, the commercial environment within which it operates and the reporting requirements to which it is subject. In this context the auditor should aim to provide an effective and economic service within an appropriate timescale.
> 'Adequate audit planning:
> '(a) establishes the intended means of achieving the objectives of the audit;
> '(b) assists in the direction and control of the work;
> '(c) helps to ensure that attention is drawn to critical aspects of the audit; and
> '(d) helps to ensure that the work is completed expeditiously.
> 'In order to plan his work adequately the auditor needs an understanding of the nature of the business of the enterprise, its organisation, its methods of operating and the industry in which it is involved, so that he is able to appreciate which events and transactions are likely to have a significant effect on the financial statements.
>
> 'Procedures:
> 'The auditor should consider the outline audit approach he proposes to adopt [see Ch. 3], including the extent to which he may wish to rely on internal control, and any aspects of the audit which need particular attention. He should also take into account in his planning any additional work, which he has agreed to undertake.'

Preparatory procedures which the auditor should consider include the following:

> '(a) reviewing matters raised in the audit of the previous year which may have continuing relevance in the current year. [In the event that the audit is a new one, ratios and trends should be computed from the previous accounts to determine the existence of any likely problem areas, and particular attention should be paid to any previous qualifications made.]
> '(b) assessing the effects of any changes in legislation or accounting practice affecting the financial statements of the enterprise.
> '(c) reviewing interim or management accounts where these are available and consulting with the management and staff of the enterprise. Matters which should be considered include current trading circumstances, and significant changes in (i) the business carried on, (ii) the enterprise's management.
> '(d) identifying any significant changes in the enterprise's accounting procedures, such as a new computer based system.
> '(a) The auditor should also consider:

  (i)   the timing of significant phases of the preparation of the
        financial statements;
  (ii)  the extent to which analyses and summaries can be prepared by
        the enterprise's employees;
  (iii) the relevance of any work to be carried out by the enterprise's
        internal auditors.
'(b)  The auditor will need to determine the number of audit staff
      required, the experience and special skills they need to possess and
      the timing of their audit visits. He will need to ensure that all audit
      staff are briefed regarding the enterprise's affairs and the nature and
      scope of the work they are required to carry out. The preparation of a
      memorandum setting out the outline audit approach may be helpful.
'(c)  On joint audits there should be consultation between the joint
      auditors to determine the allocation of the work to be undertaken and
      the procedures for its control and review.'

The Guideline goes on to discuss control procedures, and begins by pointing
out that:

'Management structures vary between firms of auditors and this Auditing
Guideline should be interpreted in the context of the particular structure
within each firm. The Guideline has, however, been written on the basis
that the audit is carried out by a reporting partner and his staff.
'The reporting partner needs to be satisfied that on each audit the work is
being performed to an acceptable standard. The most important elements
of control of an audit are the direction and supervision of the audit staff
and the review of the work they have done. The degree of supervision
required depends on the complexity of the assignment and the experience
and proficiency of the audit staff.

'Procedures:
'The nature of the procedures needed to control an audit and the extent
to which they need to be formalised cannot be precisely specified as they
depend on the organisation of the audit firm and the degree of delegation
of the audit work. The procedures established should be designed and
applied to ensure the following:
'(a)  Work is allocated to audit staff who have appropriate training,
      experience and proficiency.
'(b)  Audit staff of all levels clearly understand their responsibilities and the
      objectives of the procedures which they are expected to perform.
      Audit staff should be informed of any matters identified during the
      planning stage that may affect the nature, extent or timing of the
      procedures they are to perform. They should be instructed to bring to
      the attention of those to whom they are responsible any significant
      accounting or auditing problems that they encounter.
'(c)  The working papers provide an adequate record of the work that has
      been carried out and the conclusions that have been reached.

'(d) The work performed by each member of the audit staff is reviewed by more senior persons in the audit firm. This is necessary to ensure that the work was adequately performed and to confirm that the results obtained support the audit conclusions which have been reached.

'The final stages of an audit require special attention. At this time, when pressures are greatest, control of the audit work is particularly required to ensure that mistakes and omissions do not occur. The use of an audit completion checklist, with sections to be filled in by the reporting partner and his staff, will help to provide such control.

'Where matters of principle or contentious matters arise which may affect the audit opinion the auditor should consider consulting another experienced accountant. This accountant may be a partner, a senior colleague, or another practitioner. If another practitioner is consulted, confidentiality of the client's affairs must be maintained.

'The auditor should also consider how the overall quality of the work carried out within the firm can best be monitored and maintained.'

These procedures outlined in the Guideline offer little *practical* advice on audit planning and control. Indeed, you may even think that they are but little more than common sense. The probable reason for this almost deliberate vagueness is that procedures necessarily vary from firm to firm, and it would be wrong to imply that any one approach is more desirable than another. Especially so, as the Guidelines will almost certainly come to be used as the basis of best practice in future law suits. However, a further reason for the lack of detail lies in the fact that the Guidelines are designed to cover the audit of all situations from multi-nationals down to the £100 proprietorship company. And as the audit approach is very different in these various types of company, the Guidelines must inevitably keep to basic principles only. Although the Guidelines find it necessary to keep to basic principles, a more structured presentation can be helpful to an understanding of the issues raised. For this reason a suggested possible approach to the planning and control of *larger* audits is included here. This is not to imply that small audits do not require controlling. But just as internal control procedures in small companies can be much less formalised because of close management involvement, so too, in smaller firms of auditors, there is less need for formalised planning and control.

You should note that the approach suggested here is by no means the only possible one, and that the sequence and documents used are for illustration only.

The essential ingredients of planning and control in any business environment are a soundly conceived organisation structure, and appropriate budgetary procedures, and this is nonetheless true in an audit firm. The *organisation* adopted in most of the larger firms involves a pyramidic structure as illustrated opposite.

The *Partner* will be responsible for the overall audit, and he will sign the final accounts (although he may well wish to consult with other partners over any difficult audit or accounting matter). In addition, he will often approve the detailed plan of audit work, and will carry out a final review of that work once it

Partners
|
Managers
|
Accountant in Charge
|
Audit Assistants

has been completed, prior to signing the accounts. It will be the partner's responsibility to ensure the provision of up-to-date advice on all professional matters (such as current accounting practice, taxation, EDP, etc.), and to provide a continuity of relationship which may well not be present lower down the pyramid. To him will also fall the task of negotiating the fee.

A *Manager* will be appointed for each job, and he will be responsible to a partner for the satisfactory completion of that job. The manager's initial responsibility will be to prepare provisional timings and costings for the audit, and to agree the timings with the client. These commitments must be coordinated to ensure that there are sufficient staff available at the right grade to cover the requirements of the clients. This will normally be achieved by producing a staff forecast in matrix form, showing available staff on one axis, and clients' requirements by date on the other. Shortages and surpluses will be immediately apparent, and may be coped with by either borrowing or lending from or to other audit managers (or as an extreme measure, hiring temporary staff). From the available staff, it will be the manager's job to select an appropriate accountant in charge, and to brief him as to the work required. The manager will review the audit plan and related budget that will be prepared by the accountant in charge, and monitor the work as it progresses to ensure targets are kept. At the conclusion of the audit work the manager will review the working papers in detail before they are submitted to the partner for final review.

The *Accountant in Charge* (or audit senior) will control the day-to-day operation of the audit, but the degree of autonomy that he has will very much depend on a particular firm's policy, and the personalities of the managers, as well as of course upon the accountant's own expertise. Typical responsibilities would be:
(a) collect detailed information for the preparation of the audit plan;
(b) delegate specific areas to audit assistants;
(c) plan and supervise the day-to-day running of the audit;
(d) review progress by comparison of the actual time spent to the budget;
(e) ensure the thorough preparation of working papers and the orderly presentation of these to the manager and partner for review.

*Audit Assistants* will be responsible to the Accountant in Charge for the detailed work of the audit. They will be expected to produce ordered working papers in accordance with the principles set out in sec. 4.5 below.

A proper organisation structure provides the basis for planning and control, but sound *budgetary procedures* are essential for their successful operation. Three documents can usefully be produced, which, for convenience here, I will call: A. Manpower Plan; B. Audit Plan; and C. Audit Budget.

### *A. Manpower plan*

We have already seen that the manager will usually produce a manpower plan to coordinate the work within his group of jobs. But in addition, a manpower plan will also need to be produced, which makes provisional allocations of staff to managers. Alternatively manpower planning may be done centrally throughout the firm.

### *B. Audit plan*

The audit plan will be a formulation of the way in which the audit is to be carried out. As we saw in Chapter 3, the audit approach will be dependent upon the reliance that can be placed upon internal control, and analytical review, because this will dictate the amount of substantive testing that will be required. Accordingly it will not be possible to finalise the audit plan until the Internal Control has been evaluated, and the initial analytical review completed. This matter is further considered in Chapters 8 and 10. But, in order that you may gain a better appreciation of the typical stages in the preparation of the audit plan, a checklist for planning is reproduced below:

#### Checklist for planning, supervision and review

The purpose of the auditing procedures set out in this programme is to assist the planning, and control of the audit. The procedures should normally be completed by the Accountant in Charge of the Audit.

Preparing for the first interim audit visit

1. Examine the correspondence, report, billing and permanent audit files to ascertain:
   (A) The terms of the engagement including reporting responsibilities and deadlines.
   (B) Any other matters of audit significance.
2. Review prior year working papers and systems file. Look for problem areas, excessive or inefficient procedures.
3. If the firm does tax work for the client, consult the tax specialist and review and record the current tax position in the working papers.

Handling the initial discussion with the client

4. Discuss with the chief accountant (or his equivalent):
   (A) Whether there have been or will be any significant changes in the client's business, accounting procedures or staff.
   (B) If there are any likely problem areas.
   (C) The effect on the accounts of new legislation, SSAPs, EDs and pronouncements of regulatory bodies.
   (D) The production of a detailed timetable for the preparation of the accounts, and the provision of supplementary schedules analysing the main figures in a form suitable for inclusion in the current audit file. Also discuss the outline arrangements for the stock count.
   (E) The retention of all data that will be required during the audit, e.g. computer files, suppliers' statements, account reconciliations, etc.

5. Establish, by discussion and observation, the extent to which recommendations made in any previous report to management have been implemented.
6. (A) Arrange for members of the audit team to visit specific client locations as necessary.
   (B) Where necessary arrange for the manager or the partner to visit the client to follow up any matters arising from the initial discussion with the chief accountant.

Making a preliminary review of the records

7. Perform an analytical review to establish the credibility of the results to date.
8. Read the minutes of all meetings of shareholders, of directors and of any committee whose decisions may affect the accounts. (Ensure in each case that the meeting is valid and that the minutes are properly approved.) Prepare extracts or obtain copies of all minutes that are relevant to the accounts.
9. Review any changes made to the Memorandum and Articles of Association or to loan agreements. Consider whether such changes will require disclosure in the accounts.
10. If the client has an internal audit department, read any reports this department has submitted to management, noting the action taken.
11. Update the permanent file. Remove working papers no longer needed. The permanent file should contain only items of continuing relevance.

Delegating specific audit areas to the audit team

12. Obtain a detailed trial balance. Divide the accounts in the trial balance into appropriate audit areas. Define these areas in an audit testing plan and cross reference the trial balance to this plan.
13. Allocate the audit areas to the audit team and ensure that they are briefed as to the method of working, budget, deadlines, working papers, etc.

Reviewing and evaluating internal control

14. Supervise the updating of the systems file. Check that:
    (A) The client's principal officials and their areas of responsibility have been recorded.
    (B) The client's books of account and the methods of recording (e.g. computer, mechanical, slip system, manual) have been set out. (If a computer is used, check that the details of equipment, applications and programs summarised in the systems notes are up to date.)
    (C) The control features of the client's significant accounting systems have been properly documented by means of flow-charts or other systems notes, and have been confirmed by walk-through tests, which have been recorded in the working papers.
15. Supervise the reviews of the client's accounting systems and controls. ICQs/ICEs should be used where possible. Any alternative procedures adopted should be recorded in the working papers.
16. Evaluate the results of the above reviews to identify significant weaknesses in internal control, taking into account the effects of any general factors such as:
    (A) Budgetary controls,
    (B) Internal Audit.
    Where reliance has been placed on any of the more general control factors, a record must be made in the working papers of such reliance, together with the reasons therefore.
17. Determine and record on which accounts and to what extent reliance can be placed on the system of internal control and thereby restrict the level of tests of detail.

Extending and developing the analytical review

18. Decide if it is possible to extend analytical review procedures to reduce the level of tests of detail.

Planning the nature and extent of tests of detail

19. Determine the nature and extent of the tests of detail required on each account or group of accounts in the trial balance. Coordinate the work on related audit areas (e.g. income and related assets) to ensure maximum efficiency.
20. If there is any reason for special concern as to management's attitude, competence, or credibility with respect to matters affecting the accounts, discuss the implications of these matters with the audit manager as soon as possible.
21. If present business conditions indicate potential future difficulties for the company, discuss the implications of this with the audit manager as soon as possible.

Planning the timing of audit work

22. Review the client's year-end procedures and timetable and ensure that they appear adequate for the client to prepare the accounts, and for the firm to audit them, within the deadline. Advise the client where it is apparent that he may save time and effort by making estimated rather than unnecessarily precise closing entries.
23. Prepare a detailed timetable for audit work, analysing it into audit areas, and indicating dates and members of staff involved. Investigate and inform the manager immediately of any significant deviation from the provisional timings or costings.

Attending to possible problem areas

24. Ensure that the balances appearing on the prior year's audited accounts have been correctly brought forward in the general ledger. This will normally be achieved by reference to last year's working papers.
25. As early as possible during the first audit visit:
    (A) Review any instructions issued by the client for the preparation of branch returns.
    (B) Ensure that the client will provide an adequate ageing analysis of debtor balances.
    (C) Arrange for the preparation and typing of confirmation letters, bank letters and other routine correspondence.

### C. Audit budget

The audit budget will be used for controlling the day-to-day work of the audit. The budget will be based on the previous year's audit, but with timings modified for known inefficiencies, or changes in circumstances. (In the case of new work, the partner and manager will make a provisional estimate of time based upon their experience and knowledge of the company.) Actual time taken will be compared to budget on an ongoing basis, and the accountant in charge will be responsible for explaining the reasons for any variations. An example of such a budget form as used by Deloitte, Haskins and Sells is reproduced in Fig. 4.2.

## 4.5 Recording the work done

The Operational Standard Guidelines cite the following reasons for preparing audit working papers:

'(a) The reporting partner needs to be able to satisfy himself that work delegated by him has been properly performed. The reporting partner can generally only do this by having available to him detailed working papers prepared by the audit staff who performed the work.

'(b) Working papers provide, for future reference, details of problems encountered, and adequate evidence of work performed and conclusions drawn therefrom in arriving at the audit opinion. [The guideline does not state as much, but such evidence is necessary to safeguard the auditor in the event of a future law suit.]

'(c) The preparation of working papers encourages the auditor to adopt a methodical approach.'

And in addition, we can cite the following further advantage:

(d) Working papers provide a basis for planning the following year's audit.

The Guidelines go on to provide certain basic principles in regard to the contents of working papers:

'Audit working papers should always be sufficiently complete and detailed for an experienced auditor with no previous connection with the audit subsequently to ascertain from them what work was performed and to support the conclusions reached.

'Working papers should be prepared as the audit proceeds so that details and problems are not omitted.

'Audit working papers should include a summary of all significant matters identified which may require the exercise of judgement, together with the auditor's conclusions thereon. If difficult questions of principle or judgement arise, the auditor should record the relevant information received and summarise both the management's and his conclusions. It is in such areas as this that the auditor's judgement may subsequently be questioned, particularly by a third party who has the benefit of hindsight. It is important to be able to tell what facts were known at the time the auditor's conclusion was reached, and to be able to demonstrate clearly that, based on these facts, the conclusion was reasonable.'

Working papers can conveniently be split into three: Permanent file; Systems file; Current file.

*Permanent file*

The permanent file will contain information of permanent value to the audit. As such it will be used by new members of the audit team in familiarising themselves with the company, and by the accountant in charge in his planning function. The file will be a constant source of reference, and can prevent the possibility of irritating the client by asking the same questions year in, year out. Typical contents of the file were reviewed earlier in the chapter when we were dealing with commencement procedures, so I will not repeat them here. But it is worth making the point that no two firms will record precisely the same information in their permanent file. Some firms, for example, will include systems information here, while others will relegate this to a separate systems file.

Fig. 4.2  Time record

**TIME RECORD (in hours)**
**(excluding supervisory time)**

CLIENT ........................................................   PREPARED BY ........................... DATE...........................

PERIOD ........................................................   REVIEWED BY ........................... DATE...........................

| Staff Name (Block Capitals) | Initials Used | Category | | | | | | | | | |
|---|---|---|---|---|---|---|---|---|---|---|---|
| | | | | | | | | | | | |
| | | | | | | | | | | | |
| | | | | | | | | | | | |
| | | | | | | | | | | | |
| | | | | | | | | | | | |
| | | | | | | | | | | | |
| | | | | | | | | | | | |
| Total (a) to equal total (b) below | | | | | | | | | | | |
| Planning Supervision and Review | : Review and evaluation of internal control | | | | | | | | | | |
| | : Analytical review | | | | | | | | | | |
| | : Audit testing plan, supervision and daily reviews | | | | | | | | | | |
| | : Final audit review | | | | | | | | | | |
| | : Presentation of final acs. & dir. report | | | | | | | | | | |
| General Matters—(A.I.C.) | : Minutes | | | | | | | | | | |
| | : Trial balance and adjustments | | | | | | | | | | |
| Letters to Management and Constructive Services | | | | | | | | | | | |
| Sample Selection (all areas) | | | | | | | | | | | |
| Transaction Testing | : Sales and other credit entries | | | | | | | | | | |
| | : Purchases and other debit entries | | | | | | | | | | |
| | : Payrolls | | | | | | | | | | |
| | : Journal and general ledger | | | | | | | | | | |
| Balance Testing | : Share capital, reserves & long term liabilities | | | | | | | | | | |
| | : Taxation — review of provision | | | | | | | | | | |
| | : Creditors and accruals | | | | | | | | | | |
| | : Other current liabilities | | | | | | | | | | |
| | : Fixed assets | | | | | | | | | | |
| | : Investments | | | | | | | | | | |
| | : Stocks & work in progress — stock count | | | | | | | | | | |
| | — other procedures | | | | | | | | | | |
| | : Debtors & prepayments — confirmations | | | | | | | | | | |
| | — other procedures | | | | | | | | | | |
| | : Bank and cash balances | | | | | | | | | | |
| | : Other current assets | | | | | | | | | | |
| Audit of Consolidation | : Prior planning | | | | | | | | | | |
| | : General work | | | | | | | | | | |
| Accountancy Work | : Preparation of accounts | | | | | | | | | | |
| | : Preparation of tax computation | | | | | | | | | | |
| | : Preparation of consolidation | | | | | | | | | | |
| Updating of permanent and systems audit files | | | | | | | | | | | |
| | | | | | | | | | | | |
| | | | | | | | | | | | |
| Travelling | | | | | | | | | | | |
| Total (b) | | | | | | | | | | | |

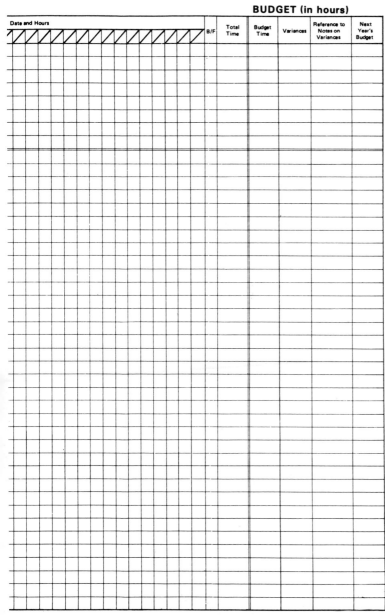

BUDGET (in hours)

0113

Whatever the precise contents, and whatever the order, it is essential that the permanent file is kept up to date by the removal of irrelevant or outdated information, and the insertion of current material.

*Systems file*

The systems file, or files, can conveniently be used to record the way in which the client's internal control and accounting systems operate. Typically this will be in the form of flow charts recording each of the accounting areas, supplemented where necessary by narrative notes.

*Current file*

The current file will contain all the working papers in relation to the current year's audit, and these can be quite extensive. Again no two firms will order their current file in precisely the same way, but a typical format would be as follows:
A.  Index.
B.  Control papers:
    Copy of Accounts as signed
    Report to Management
    Letter of representation
    Comments by partner, detailed reviewer and accountant in charge
    Schedule of significant ratios
    Companies Act checklist
    Stock Exchange and SSAP checklist
    Audit completion checklist
    Time record and budget
    Extended trial balance
    Extracts from minutes, statutory books and contracts.
C.  Supporting schedules for each of the figures in the accounts.
D.  Internal control evaluations.
E.  Analytical Review.
F.  Audit Programme including notes of errors found and action taken.

Most large firms of auditors now use working papers which are standardised in terms of their contents and sequence. The Operational Standard Guidelines point out that:

> 'The use of standardised working papers may improve the efficiency with which they are prepared and reviewed. Used properly they help to instruct staff and provide opportunities to delegate work while giving a means to control its quality.
> 'However, despite the advantages of standardising the routine documentation of the audit (e.g. checklists, specimen letters, standard organisation for the working papers), it is never appropriate to follow mechanically a "standard" approach to the conduct and documentation

Fig. 4.3 Example of working paper

| | | | | | Prepared by | Initials | Date | | Schedule No. | |
|---|---|---|---|---|---|---|---|---|---|---|
| Abraxis Yachts Ltd. | | | | | | M.I.P. | 23.7.81 | | B/S | |
| Year ended 30 June 1981 | | | | | Reviewed by | A.M. | 2.8.81 | | 25 | |
| TRADE and OTHER CREDITORS - Accrued Expenses | | | | | | | | | | |
| | | | | | | | | | | |
| | | | | | | | | | | |
| 1980 | | | | | | | | | 1981 | |
| | | | | | | | | AUDIT WORK | | |
| 14761 | | Works wages - overtime | | | | | | 1 | 17273 | ℓ |
| | | earned w/e 26/6 pd 3/7 | 14373 | | | | | | | |
| | | - estimated 29 & 30th. | 2900 | | | | | | | |
| 25000 | | Holiday Pay | | | | | | 2 | 26000 | ℓ |
| 2000 | | Provision for salesmens' bonus | | | | | | 3 | 2000 | ℓ |
| 3493 | | Rent of factory qtr. to 30/6 - paid 3/7 | | | | | | L | 3493 | ℓ |
| 1700 | | Electricity - estimated 2 months | | | | | | L | 1200 | ℓ |
| 350 | | Telephone - estimated 2½ months | | | | | | L | 350 | ℓ |
| 723 | | Interest payable to 30/6 - paid 1/7 | | | | | | 5 | 2990 | ℓ |
| 3600 | | MJP and Co. audit fee | | | | | | 4 | 4250 | ℓ |
| 3000 | | Provision for unascertained liabilities | | | | | | 6 | 3000 | ℓ |
| £ 54027 | | | | | | | | £ | 60556 | ℓ |
| | | | | | | | | | B/S | |
| | | ℓ Per trial balance | | | | | | | | |
| | | Audit Work | | | | | | | | |
| | | 1. Checked with supporting evidence, compared to previous period | | | | | | | | |
| | | and accepted. | | | | | | | | |
| | | 2. Holiday pay year runs from 1/8 to 31/7 Annual paid | | | | | | | | |
| | | holiday = two weeks, average weekly payroll = £14,000 | | | | | | | | |
| | | ∴ 2 × 14,000 / 12 × 11 = £25,667 - say £26,000 | | | | | | | | |
| | | 3. Calculation checked to sales records, and contracts of employment. | | | | | | | | |
| | | 4. As confirmed by letter June '80. | | | | | | | | |
| | | 5. Payment vouched - amount due confirmed by bank letter. | | | | | | | | |
| | | 6. Provision has remained at £3000 for many years. | | | | | | | | |
| | | Apparently not required as system for accruing | | | | | | | | |
| | | liabilities is adequate. But can stay as not material. | | | | | | | | |
| | | 7. All July invoices to date over £500 scrutinized for | | | | | | | | |
| | | other accruals — None found. | | | | | | | | |
| | | | | | | | | | | |
| | | Conclusion | | | | | | | | |
| | | | | | | | | | | |
| | | Accrued expenses fairly stated. | | | | | | | | |

of the audit without regard to the need to exercise professional judgement.'

This last point cannot be emphasised too strongly. For without doubt the most common reason for inadequate audit practice is the slavish adherence to ancient audit programmes. Programmes which often dictate the vouching of vast quantities of documentation with little rhyme or reason therefore; or if there was reason once, it has long since been forgotten. Such rigid programmes lead to a mindless approach to the work, which is thus rendered several stages worse than useless. And this is well illustrated by an internal audit review I once undertook. The internal audit department in question was of the old school, with audit programmes that originated with Pacioli and had changed little since! Part of the sales programme involved the vouching of at least 50 per cent of the sales invoices for the year. Now vouching sales invoices is of limited value anyway, as we will see later, but 50 per cent of those in a comparatively large company was bordering on insanity. And this is seemingly what the internal audit assistants thought too. For I inquired just how long this job took, and was given a figure which when divided by the number of invoices in question, produced a time per invoice of just two seconds. Long enough to put a tick on the invoice. But no more. Futile, and soul destroying, so that I could almost guarantee that any other procedures that they had undertaken would also be of but limited value. So at the risk of being repetitive, I repeat – an inquiring and imaginative approach to an audit is essential, for without it enthusiasm dies and the whole purpose of the work is lost.

### Example of working paper

Figure 4.3 presents an example of a schedule supporting the figure for accrued expenses in the balance sheet of a company. You should note:
(a) schedules should always be signed and dated by the preparer and by the reviewer;
(b) schedules should always be referenced either to the financial statements, or to an index;
(c) comparative figures should always be given where appropriate;
(d) the extent of audit work should be indicated, or reference made to supporting audit programmes;
(e) a conclusion should always be given.

We must now begin to look in more detail at the current approach to auditing procedures. And we must commence with an examination of the principle upon which this approach is largely based – Internal Control.

# 5
## Principles of internal control

## 5.1 Introduction

Paragraph 5 of the Auditor's Operational Standard states:

'If the auditor wishes to place reliance on any internal controls, he should ascertain and evaluate those controls and perform compliance tests on their operation.'

Auditing Guideline 204 defines an internal control system as:

'The whole system of controls, financial and otherwise, established by the management in order to carry on the business of the enterprise in an orderly and efficient manner, safeguard its assets, and secure as far as possible the completeness and accuracy of the records.'

An internal control system should include both internal check and internal audit (see secs. 5.6 and 5.7).

We saw in Chapter 3 that one of the first audit stages is to review and evaluate the client's system of internal control. One of the main objectives of so doing is to establish the extent to which the system can be relied upon in determining the nature, extent and timing of substantive testing (substantive tests are performed in order to obtain reasonable assurance that the accounts are not materially mis-stated). In addition, the evaluation will constitute the basis upon which we will decide whether proper accounting records have been maintained in accordance with the 1976 Companies Act.

## 5.2 The significance of internal control

If the system of internal control is good, it will act like a filter and so prevent or detect mis-statements. It follows that a good system will justify a reduction in the normal level of substantive testing. However, substantive testing procedures cannot be eliminated altogether, because it must always be remembered that the auditor reports on the *substance* of the reported figures, and not on the system which produces those figures. Furthermore, even the best system of internal control is subject to certain limitations in practice. For clients' staff often mis-understand instructions, or exercise poor judgement, act carelessly, or just become plain bored! All of this means that internal check procedures can collapse, and in any event, procedures that depend for their effectiveness on the fact that duties are segregated can obviously be circumvented by collusion between the staff. Finally, procedures that are designed to ensure that transactions are executed and recorded in accordance with management's authorisation may be ineffective if managers themselves perpetrate errors or irregularities – either in dealing with transactions, or in making estimates when preparing the accounts.

The process of reviewing and evaluating the system of internal control should never be omitted, even if it is suspected in advance that the system is poor. For although the auditor may decide to place no reliance at all on internal control (and therefore not to restrict the extent of substantive testing), it is still necessary for him to understand the system in order to determine the *nature* and *timing* of the substantive testing. Especially so, as a weak system may allow items to be omitted entirely from the client's records. Accordingly the client's controls must be examined to discover if there is any scope for such omissions, and to obtain satisfaction that adequate accounting records have been maintained. In some situations, the system of internal control may be so inadequate that it will be impossible to express an opinion on any accounts based thereon.

## 5.3  Errors and irregularities

Where a company's financial statements are materially mis-stated, it is usually because the records which underlie those statements contain material errors, or material irregularities, or both. Before we look in detail at how internal control can prevent these, it may be useful to classify just how they can occur.

By definition, errors are unintentional. Most audit problems involve situations which have resulted from errors made by the client's management or staff either in recording transactions, or in making judgement valuations (especially at period ends when time pressure is greatest). In book-keeping terms, errors can be classified as:

(a)  failing to make a book entry;
(b)  making an incorrect book entry;
(c)  making an incorrect calculation;
(d)  losing a supporting document;
(e)  making a posting to an incorrect ledger account.

Common examples of errors include the failure to accrue for goods and services which have been received but have not yet been billed, failure to evaluate the doubtful element in the debtor's figure and failure to invoice all despatches to customers. Clearly, anything that can happen by accident can also be made to happen. And this gives us a means of classifying irregularities. Irregularities, although they bear a superficial resemblance to errors, are perpetrated deliberately. In book-keeping terms, they can be classified as:

(a)  suppressing a book entry;
(b)  making an improper book entry;
(c)  making an improper calculation;

(d)  manipulating or suppressing a supporting document;

(e)  making an improper posting to a ledger account.

Irregularities can also be classified as either *distortions*, or as the *concealment of defalcations*. Distortion involves deliberately misrepresenting the operating results or the financial position. A simple example of distortion is where profit is artificially inflated (for example, by inflating the valuation of stock, or by including as sales goods that were despatched after the end of the accounting period). Distortion does not necessarily involve the company in loss of assets (though it could result in an irrecoverable tax charge), but it can potentially be the more serious irregularity. For the deliberate intention of the perpetrators (usually senior officials) is to mislead the shareholders by producing accounts which show other than a true and fair view. For example, the distortion may be designed to manipulate the Stock Exchange quotation, or perhaps just to keep the directors in office. But whatever the reason, the auditor will be under an obligation to find the matter and report it to the shareholders.

Whereas distortion does not usually involve the company in any loss of assets, defalcation does. The concealment of a defalcation will usually involve manipulating the appropriate records, and it will either be temporary, or (if the internal control is sufficiently weak) permanent. However, often the matter will not be sufficiently material to alter the true and fair view, and as such the auditor will not necessarily be under an obligation to find and report upon it. Although if he discovers anything to excite suspicion, he is obliged to probe it to the full, even if the matter is apparently of little consequence. Even if the auditor discovers a material fraud, he may not necessarily be obliged to comment upon it in his report, for it may be sufficient if the matter is incorporated into the accounts; although any frauds that take place at a senior level will normally be of considerable concern to the shareholders as they will affect the credibility of the management.

## 5.4  Administrative and accounting controls distinguished

Internal controls are sometimes divided into:

1. Administrative controls
2. Accounting controls

*Administrative controls* are those controls which are designed primarily to enable the company to carry on its business in an orderly manner: they include the overall organisational structure and those procedures and records which management use when authorising transactions. The authorising of transactions is a management function which is directly associated with the responsibility for achieving the objectives of the organisation. It is, therefore, the starting point in the process of establishing the accounting control of transactions.

*Accounting controls* are those controls which are primarily designed both to safeguard the assets of a company and to maintain accurate and reliable records. They therefore include certain aspects of the company's organisational structure and the detailed controls over the access to, and the condition of, the company's assets. They also include controls over the prompt and correct recording of all valid transactions.

These definitions are not mutually exclusive, for some of the procedures and records comprised in the accounting controls may also be involved in the administrative controls. For example, a company may classify sales records and cost records by products for two reasons: first to provide accounting controls, and second, to assist in making management decisions such as those concerned with pricing. In practice, therefore, the distinction between these pieces of terminology is not very significant. It is mentioned here, so that you are familiar with the distinction if you meet it elsewhere.

## 5.5 Accounting controls

Accounting controls are many and complex, so before we look in detail at how they apply to different aspects of the company's business, we must examine the underlying concepts. But in advance of this, a glance at Fig. 5.1 may assist your understanding of this area, which is often a problem to students, and which is treated, for some reason, very cursorily in most texts on auditing.

To understand the way in which accounting controls operate, we must first discuss the meaning of *accountability*. We can define accountability as the condition which exists when an employee who handles assets or records, or who performs duties, can be held to account for the performance of the responsibilities that have been delegated to him. Although the dictionary definitions of the words accountability and responsibility are almost identical, within the context of accounting controls we must distinguish between them. For example, an employee must be made responsible for the company's cash balances, but without effective accounting controls it may be impossible to hold him to account for the way in which he discharges his responsibility. Accordingly the system of accounting controls must be designed in such a way that either there is automatic check on the work of each employee, or it is a straightforward matter for a senior official to check that each employee is discharging his responsibility correctly. With such a system of accounting controls, top management can delegate responsibility to employees without losing control of the activities which those employees perform.

Accounting controls operate by:

1. Establishing accountability for each transaction by recording the existence of, and the responsibility for, that transaction; this recording must be done clearly, and as early as possible after the transaction takes place.
2. Maintaining an effective record of this accountability, from the time it is established to the time it is effectively discharged.
3. Providing evidence of the discharge of accountability.
4. Using the existence of accountability in order to carry out routine checks both on the reliability of the records and on the existence and value of the assets.

Fig. 5.1 Internal control concepts

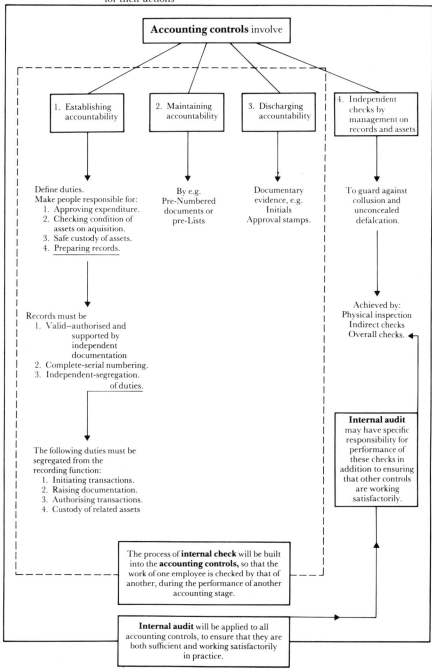

Sound Internal Control involves making employees
**Responsible** for various tasks
Accounting controls make the employees **Accountable**
for their actions

**Accounting controls** involve

1. Establishing
accountability

2. Maintaining
accountability

3. Discharging
accountability

4. Independent
checks by
management on
records and assets

Define duties.
Make people responsible for:
1. Approving expenditure.
2. Checking condition of
assets on aquisition.
3. Safe custody of assets.
4. Preparing records.

By e.g.
Pre-Numbered
documents or
pre-Lists

Documentary
evidence, e.g.
Initials
Approval stamps.

To guard against
collusion and
unconcealed
defalcation.

Records must be
1. Valid–authorised and
supported by
independent
documentation
2. Complete-serial numbering.
3. Independent-segregation.
of duties.

Achieved by:
Physical inspection
Indirect checks
Overall checks.

The following duties must be
segregated from the
recording function:
1. Initiating transactions.
2. Raising documentation.
3. Authorising transactions.
4. Custody of related assets

**Internal audit**
may have specific
responsibility for
performance of
these checks in
addition to ensuring
that other controls
are working
satisfactorily.

The process of **internal check** will be built
into the **accounting controls,** so that the
work of one employee is checked by that of
another, during the performance of another
accounting stage.

**Internal audit** will be applied to all
accounting controls, to ensure that they are
both sufficient and working satisfactorily
in practice.

*Establishing accountability*

The first step in establishing accountability in any area must be to define the duties which need to be performed, and then to allocate to specific staff the responsibility for performing those duties. Accordingly, a clearly defined organisational structure is a prerequisite for accountability. For unless duties have been defined and allocated, unauthorised actions become difficult to detect. To take an example, normally remittances from debtors have to be made available to a number of employees, in that they must be counted, prepared for banking and banked. Unless management stipulates which employees should perform each aspect of this work, it may not be possible to establish who is accountable for any subsequent shortages.

Accountability for particular duties is greatly improved where those duties are defined in a manner which all other members of staff can easily recognise. Such definition may be achieved by organisational charts, procedural manuals, job specifications or special instructions. But the objective is that each employee concerned should know to whom he is responsible, what he is responsible for and who is responsible to him. And he should preferably be given a written copy of these duties, which he should then be asked to confirm. Employees will of course be considerably assisted in carrying out their duties if facilities are provided which physically reduce the opportunities for unauthorised people to interfere with the records. Such facilities include segregated areas, lockable storerooms and ledger cabinets and safes.

Once the responsibility for performing specific duties has been clearly defined by an organisational structure, it becomes feasible to safeguard assets by making specified people accountable for them. This involves making someone responsible for:
(a) examining and approving the expenditure involved in acquiring the asset;
(b) checking the condition of the asset when it is acquired;
(c) preparing a reliable record of each asset as soon as possible after it has been acquired;
(d) keeping the assets in safe custody.
Note also that controls must extend to cover liabilities. For the authority to set up a liability implies the authority to release assets to settle that liability.

It should be emphasised here that accountability cannot safeguard assets against defalcation by custodians who are not concerned about concealing their theft. Accountability is, therefore, normally supplemented by management spot checks, and controls to mitigate the effect of isolated defalcations. Examples of the latter include limits on the amount that can be withdrawn on one cheque, and limits on the amount of cash held on the premises.

We have seen that accountability is primarily established by means of records. Accordingly it is important that these records should be VALID, COMPLETE, ACCURATE and INDEPENDENT. Validity as to account code, period and propriety can be established by having all initiating documents approved by management, and supported by documents from independent sources (e.g.

suppliers' invoices or debtors' remittance advices). Completeness can be secured by having all internal documentation pre-serially numbered, and subsequently checked for serial number order. Accuracy can be achieved by internal check of costs, cross costs, extensions and postings. But independence is the most important requirement, for the record will only be reliable if the person who has prepared it is independent. And he will not be independent if he has any form of access to the asset, including any authority to dispose of it. Indeed, we can distinguish five specific functions in the actioning of any transaction, that should be kept strictly separate if independence is to be assured:

1. Initiating the transaction.
2. Raising the relevant documentation.
3. Authorising the transaction.
4. Having custody of the related assets.
5. Recording in the accounting records.

We will refer again to these five separate stages in Chapter 6 when we look at the accounting controls necessary in the different accounting areas (wages, sales, purchases, etc.). But you should commit these to memory now as you should find them useful in putting a structure on what can otherwise appear to be a series of isolated requirements.

*Maintaining accountability*

Accounting transactions go through many recording stages after initiation (see Fig. 5.2) and each of these stages gives an employee an opportunity to manipulate

Fig. 5.2 Recording stages

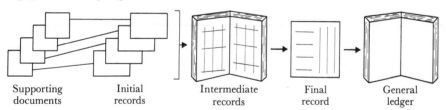

| Supporting documents | Initial records | Intermediate records | Final record | General ledger |

the record which holds him accountable, should he be able to gain access to it. It follows that a COMPLETE, ACCURATE and VALID record must be maintained *at each stage* in the processing of a transaction, from inception to completion. This can be achieved in a variety of ways, such as by prenumbering the intermediate documents, preparing pre-lists of documents (with a subsequent independent check back to the pre-list), or by the maintenance of independent control accounts.

*Discharging accountability*

Once an employee has properly discharged his assigned duties he must indicate the fact by initiating a document, writing a brief report, signing a register or similar action. This evidence not only holds the employee concerned accountable, but it also provides control over other employees who might attempt to perpetrate irregularities. A specific example should prove useful here. When a purchase order is placed upon a supplier, the buying officer can be made accountable through the use of a prenumbered purchase order, supported by an independently authorised goods requisition. When the goods are received, a prenumbered goods received note can be created. And this provides evidence that the purchase order has been fulfilled and that accountability for the goods has been transferred to the storekeeper. As items from the stock are issued, approved requisitions can be used, and these provide evidence that accountability for these items has now been transferred to the employee who withdrew them from the stores. Later, as goods are manufactured or assembled from these items, a stock transfer form can be created, and the finished products placed in the stores. The stock transfer form provides evidence that the storekeeper is now accountable for the finished goods. As finished goods are sold and despatched, a despatch note can be created, and this discharges the storekeeper's accountability. Finally, an invoice will be prepared, and this provides evidence that the accounts department is accountable for collection of the debt.

### Checks on records and assets

But none of these accounting controls will be effective in discouraging errors and irregularities unless management ensures that the controls are actually working in practice. Such assurance can be achieved either by *internal check* or by *internal audit*, and often a combination can be used to advantage.

## 5.6　Internal check

Management normally build checking procedures into the accounting process itself. This *internal check* is provided by segregating duties in such a way that no one person can initiate, authorise, conduct and record a transaction from start to finish *without his work coming under the surveillance of at least one other person*. And internal checks should be made, not only at each point where details are entered from documents on to subsequent records, but also at any stage where *significant action* is based on the documents. For example, before cheques are signed, supporting documents should be checked to confirm that they are both valid and appropriate.

Clearly it is not only the documents that must be safeguarded, for it is the assets themselves that need the protection. And this is best achieved by *checking from the record to the asset itself*. Such routine checks of assets include physically inspecting stocks, investments and cash balances, together with the reconciling of bank balances to bank statements. In addition to direct checks on the custody of assets, *indirect checks* can also prove useful. For example, employees' duties can be allocated in such a way that statements to customers are prepared and mailed by, and any replies routed to, employees who do not normally handle remittances. In this way, those employees indirectly check the work of the employees who normally receive remittances.

In addition to the specific checks so far discussed, *overall checks* can be made on the books of account. Such checks include balancing the general ledger at frequent intervals, and reconciling the control accounts with subsidiary ledgers (such as those kept for stores, trade debtors and trade creditors). But you should note that these checks will be invalidated if they are performed by employees who have direct or indirect access to realisable assets since the authority to check the records also carries with it the authority to alter them. Nor will the checks be satisfactory if they are performed by an employee who is in any way dependent upon the person whose work is being checked. For example, it would clearly be unsatisfactory for a subordinate to check the work of a head of department.

## 5.7 Internal audit

Large companies will often supplement their internal check procedures with internal audit. Such internal audit will be carried out by specially assigned staff, and will consist of a review of the operations, procedures and records of the business. The scope will vary from business to business, but in every case the main objective should be to assure management that the accounting controls are both adequate, and working effectively in practice.

It is useful here to comment upon the relationship that exists between the external and the internal auditor:

1. They both have a *common interest* in ascertaining whether there is an effective system of internal check, and in ensuring that the system is working satisfactorily in practice.
2. But there is a *fundamental difference* in that the scope and responsibility for the work are prescribed respectively by statute and by management. And as the internal auditor's work is controlled by management, the external auditor must be very cautious before placing reliance upon it.
3. Nevertheless there is a *similarity of work* in that both sets of auditors will examine internal control and accounting records, verify assets and liabilities and pursue similar lines of observation and enquiry.
4. It follows, therefore, that there are possible *areas for coordination*:
   (a) the external auditor may assist in determining whether internal check procedures are being properly complied with;
   (b) the internal auditors' programme may include spot cash counts and visits to branches which the external may rely on;
   (c) the internal auditors can assist the externals in familiarising themselves with the accounting system, and can act as a liaison between the externals and other members of the client's staff;
   (d) at the year end the internals can assist in detailed scheduling procedures.

At the very least, the internal auditor may provide assistance in that he can strengthen the system of internal control upon which the external auditor relies. In determining the extent to which the internal auditor contributes towards the control system, the following factors should be considered:

(a) the qualifications of the appointed staff (in themselves qualifications mean little, but their *absence* can be significant);

(b) the length of service of the appointed staff (newly appointed staff may have insufficient knowledge of the system to be of much assistance; on the other hand, staff who have been with the company for most of their careers may think the systems are wonderful simply because they do not know anything else!);

(c) the internal audit programme can give an indication of the ability of the internal auditors (have the programmes changed in the last twenty years?!) and the extent to which they have been completed will give an idea of the audit effectiveness;

(d) along similar lines, the internal audit reports will give a good idea about the quality of the audit staff, and in this context it may be appropriate to note what action (if any) has been taken on the reports by management (for if management take but little notice of the internals, this would not strengthen an externals' opinion of their effectiveness);

(e) the level of internal audit reporting is also significant; the reports should be made to the highest level of management (i.e. the Board of Directors), for only at this level can the necessary independent action be taken; it will clearly be inappropriate for the reports to be made to the Chief Accountant, for he has a vested interest in making sure that inadequacies in his systems of control are not made public.

But even if all these points prove satisfactory, you should remember that the external auditor can only rely on the internal as one feature in the whole system of internal control. Internal audit is not a substitute for a proper evaluation of the overall controls present. Nor does it justify omitting substantive testing (though it might justify a reduction therein, in that the system of control as a whole can be strengthened). And the most important limitation lies in the fact that in the last resort the internal auditors are dependent upon senior management. Accordingly they offer little check on the actions of management themselves.

## 5.8 Summary of types of internal control

The appendix to the Audit Guideline on Internal Controls provides a summary of the various types of internal control. So a study of this now may help you to assimilate the contents of this chapter.

'1. Organisation. Enterprises should have a plan of their organisation, defining and allocating responsibilities and identifying lines of reporting for all aspects of the enterprise's operations, including the controls. The delegation of authority and responsibility should be clearly specified.

'2. Segregation of duties. One of the prime means of control is the separation of those responsibilities or duties which would, if combined, enable one individual to record and process a complete transaction. Segregation reduces the risk of intentional manipulation and error and increases the element of checking. Functions which should be separated include those of authorisation, execution, custody, recording and in the case of a computer based accounting system, systems development and daily operations.

'3. Physical. These are concerned mainly with the custody of assets and involve procedures and security measures designed to ensure that access to assets is limited to authorised personnel. This includes both direct access and indirect access via documentation. These controls assume importance in the case of valuable, portable, exchangeable or desirable assets.

'4. Authorisation and approval. All transactions should require authorisation or approval by an appropriate responsible person. The limits for these authorisations should be specified.

'5. Arithmetical and accounting. These are the controls within the recording function which check that the transactions to be recorded and processed have been authorised, that they are all included and that they are correctly recorded and accurately processed. Such controls include checking the arithmetical accuracy of the records, the maintenance and checking of totals, reconciliations, control accounts and trial balances, and accounting for documents.

'6. Personnel. There should be procedures to ensure that personnel have capabilities commensurate with their responsibilities. Inevitably, the proper functioning of any system depends on the competence and integrity of those operating it. The qualifications, selection and training as well as the innate personal characteristics of the personnel involved are important features to be considered in setting up any control system.

'7. Supervision. Any system of internal control should include the supervision by responsible officials of day-to-day transactions and the recording thereof.

'8. Management controls. These are the controls exercised by management outside the day-to-day routine of the system. They include the overall supervisory controls exercised by management, the review of management accounts and comparison thereof with budgets, the internal audit function and any other special review procedures.'

You should remember the key internal control objectives in relation to recording and processing:

VALIDITY
COMPLETENESS
ACCURACY
INDEPENDENCE

# 6
## Practical aspects of internal control

## 6.1 Organisation structures

Before we look in detail at the practical aspects of internal control, a glance at typical large company organisation structure is necessary, as the type of organisation dictates the type of controls that will be appropriate. We are primarily concerned with the structure dealing with accounting information flows, but the production organisation will also be important to us from the point of view of accounting for stocks and work in progress. So illustrative organisation charts are included (Figs. 6.1 and 6.2) covering both these areas. But you should note that although these are typical structures, they are by no means the only arrangements possible.

The auditor's field of interest covers most of the business's activities. For although primarily he will be concerned with the actions of central accounts, accounting information will be generated by many departments. And it is the auditor's task to see that all this information is reliable.

## 6.2 Practical aspects of internal control – introduction

The detailed application of internal control concepts can be a very dry area of study. Of this there is no doubt. But traditional teaching methods have not helped. The important thing is to understand the significance of the controls. For in practice you will have check lists to assist you in remembering them. And for examination purposes, questions are no longer phrased in the traditional (very unimaginative and valueless) way of '*list* ten internal check requirements covering . . .'. Much more now, you will be required to interpret and evaluate controls or perhaps to suggest appropriate controls to cover given situations. Accordingly the emphasis here is on understanding.

I have adopted the approach of putting the considerations in the context of typical, simple systems, such as may be used in a medium sized manufacturing company. Note that service or retail businesses could have similar systems, except that the conversion cycle and manufacturing wages would be excluded. The considerations are ordered as to the sequence of events, and set within the framework of the segregation of duties principle discussed in the previous chapter. The danger of this approach is that it may be assumed that the sequence of

Fig. 6.1 Accounting information flow – organisation chart

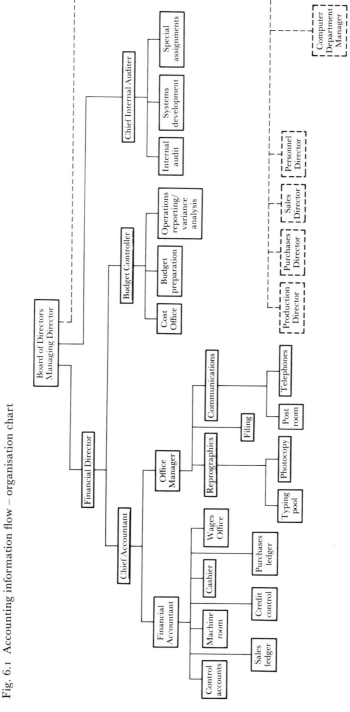

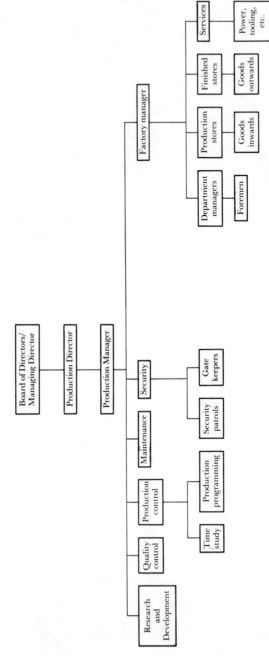

Fig. 6.2  Production – organisation chart

events and the format of controls illustrated is the only one possible. It must be stressed now that this is not so, for there are as many possible systems as there are companies needing them. But with this warning in mind, it should be a simple matter to extract the main principles from the approach suggested. And these principles will be further illustrated in the following ways:

(a)  examining the most common types of fraud that can arise in the absence of proper controls (this chapter);
(b)  discussing evaluation methods (Ch. 8);
(c)  evaluating internal control systems using case studies (Ch.9).

A whole book could (and perhaps should!) be written on control systems alone. So the considerations discussed here can only cover straightforward situations, although the principles will have general application.

## 6.3  Transaction 'cycles'

The traditional classification of operations for internal control purposes was as follows:

(a)  cash and cheques received (including cash and bank balances);
(b)  cheque and cash payments;
(c)  wages and salaries;
(d)  purchases and trade creditors;
(e)  sales and trade debtors;
(f)  stock (including work in progress);
(g)  fixed assets and investments.

But it is now perhaps more usual to classify transactions in accordance with 'Cycles': Sales Cycle; Purchases Cycle; Wages Cycle; Conversion Cycle (stock and work in progress). And this is the principle that has been adopted here. Reference to the model in Fig. 6.3(a) should illustrate the relationship between these 'cycles' which are then broken down into their component stages in Fig. 6.3(b). You should note the necessary segregation of duties in each of these 'cycles', as discussed in Chapter 5:

1.  Initiating the transaction.
2.  Raising the relevant documentation.
3.  Authorising the transaction.
4.  Recording the transaction in the accounting records.
5.  Custody of the related assets.

## 6.4  Quantity control of sales and purchases

Before we begin to look in detail at the transaction 'cycles' it is worth noting that the best control of sales and cash is by means of quantity reconciliation, if the type of business makes it possible. Particularly appropriate for the retail trade, the technique can be used to advantage in many businesses. Let us take the

Fig. 6.3 Transaction cycles

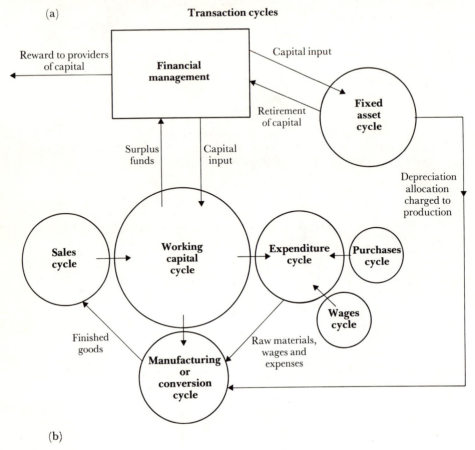

(a)                        **Transaction cycles**

(b)

*The sales cycle*

The whole sales cycle can be broken down into the following operations –

| | |
|---|---|
| Ordering and despatch of goods | (a) Approval of sales order |
| | (b) Checking of credit limit |
| | (c) Preparation of despatch documentation |
| | (d) Despatch of goods |
| Invoicing | (e) Preparation of invoice |
| | (f) Processing of invoice – sales journal/invoice listing |
| | (g) Processing of invoice – debtors ledger |
| | (h) Preparation of statement |
| Credit note and adjustments | (i) Preparation of credit note for valid claims for short deliveries of defective goods |
| Receiving and recording of cash/cheques | (j) Initial recording of cash received |
| | (k) Entry of cash received in cash book |
| | (l) Preparation of deposit slip and payment into bank |
| | (m) Posting of receipt to debtors ledger |

| | (n) | Checking of cash book with bank statement |
| General recording | (o) | Posting to general ledger |
| | (p) | Agreement of control account |
| Overdues | (q) | Following up overdue debt |

### The purchases cycle

The whole purchases cycle can be broken down into the following operations –

| Ordering | (a) | Requisition of goods |
| | (b) | Ordering goods |
| Receipt of goods | (c) | Receipt of goods |
| | (d) | Checking of goods |
| | (e) | Claims for short deliveries or defective goods |
| | (f) | Putting goods into store |
| Processing invoice and | (g) | Receipt of invoice |
| setting up liability | (h) | Checking of invoice |
| | (i) | Coding of invoice |
| | (j) | Overall approval of invoice |
| | (k) | Processing of invoice – purchase journal/invoice listing |
| | (l) | Processing of invoice – creditors ledger |
| Payment | (m) | Reconciliation of creditors ledger account with suppliers statement |
| | (n) | Selection of items for payment |
| | (o) | Preparation of cheque |
| | (p) | Approval of cheque |
| | (q) | Signature on cheque |
| | (r) | Entry of cheque in cash book |
| | (s) | Posting of payment to creditors ledger |
| General | (t) | Checking of bank statement with cash book |
| | (u) | Posting to general ledger |
| | (v) | Agreement of control account |

### The payroll cycle

The payroll can be broken down into the following operations –

| Employment | (a) | Employment of individual |
| | (b) | Preparation of personnel record |
| Record of work done | (c) | Production of the clockcard/piece work record |
| | (d) | Authorisation of hours worked/piece work totals |
| Calculation of pay | (e) | Calculation of gross pay (including overtime) |
| | (f) | Calculation of deductions |
| Preparation of payroll | (g) | Preparation of payroll |
| | (h) | Preparation of payroll summary |
| | (i) | Preparation of note/coin analysis |
| | (j) | Authorisation of payroll for payment |
| Payment | (k) | Preparation of cheque for cashing at bank |
| | (l) | Signature on cheque |
| | (m) | Collection of cash from bank |
| | (n) | Preparation of cheque/credit transfer |
| | (o) | Make-up of wage packet |
| | (p) | Pay out/distribution of cash or cheques |
| | (q) | Unclaimed wages/cheques |
| Recording | (r) | Posting of payroll summary to the general |

ledger and production records
(s)   Settlement of liabilities for deductions
(Based on Peat, Marwick, Mitchell and Co. audit documentation)

*The conversion cycle*

The process of accounting for the conversion of raw materials into finished goods will vary considerably from company to company depending on the nature of operations, and in particular on whether the company is operating on unit, job or process costing. But the principal procedures will include accounting for:

1. Material requisitions       – charging raw materials to the appropriate work in progress (WIP) account or cost centre.

2. Labour                      – analysing labour expense to the appropriate WIP account or cost centre.

3. Manufacturing overhead      – allocation and apportionment of overheads into the appropriate cost centres, and absorption into units of WIP.

4. Transfer to finished goods  – calculation of cost of finished goods transferred out from WIP.

Critical to the control over the conversion cycle will be the use of control accounts for material, labour, overheads, work in progress and finished goods.

example of a publican who wishes to control the activities of his bar manager. This can simply be achieved by the following weekly (or other appropriate interval) reconciliation:

|        | Opening stock |
|--------|---------------|
| Add    | Purchases for the period |
| Less   | Closing stock |
| Less   | Allowance for wastage |
| Add    | Percentage for known mark up on cost |
| =      | Cash takings |

If the amount banked does not come to the amount per the above reconciliation, the bar manager is either a drunkard or a thief!

Now this is not meant to be a book about fraud, for fraud is only one aspect of auditing. So I do not intend here to discuss all the tricks that bar managers can (and do!) get up to – nor the techniques for preventing them. But you should note the important principle illustrated by this example, for it is a useful technique that can be employed in small and large businesses alike.

## 6.5 The sales 'cycle'

*Sales – Internal Check*

### Sales department

The sales department should acknowledge orders received in detail on sequence controlled acknowledgements. The object of this is to initiate the 'accounting trail' and to reduce the possibility of misunderstandings with customers. The sales department should also be responsible for fixing selling prices and delivery dates, and any special discounts should be approved by a senior official.

### Credit control

But before an order is processed, the customer's credit worthiness must be reviewed by the credit control department. If the order is from an existing credit customer, checks must be made to ensure that the new order will not put the account over the predetermined credit limit. If the customer has not had previous dealings with the company, bank and trade references should be obtained, and possibly credit agencies consulted.

### Despatch department

The despatch department will be responsible for packing the ordered goods, on the basis of despatch documentation approved by sales department and credit control. A goods outwards note should be raised for each consignment and this must be done either by the despatch department or by the gatekeeper. These goods outwards notes (GONs) should be serially controlled to assist in ensuring that no goods leave the premises without being invoiced. Copies of the despatch documentation should be sent with the goods, one copy as advice to the customer, and a second copy to be signed by the customer and returned to the company as proof of delivery.

### Accounts

To ensure all goods leaving the premises are invoiced, the GON sequence should be checked prior to raising invoices, and each GON should be checked to ensure that an invoice is raised upon it.

### Sales ledger

The sales ledger department will be responsible for recording invoices against the appropriate debtor. To ensure that all the invoices are included, the documentation should be serially numbered and the sequence should be checked prior to recording.

### Assistant accountant

The ledgers should be balanced monthly, and agreed with an independently held debtors' control account. Although the detail of this work will be performed by the sales ledger department, it should be checked at a senior level. Once the accounts are reconciled, statements should be sent to customers, because they can provide an independent check on the overstatement of debts or the under-statement of remittances received. For this reason the statements should be sent out by a senior official, after (test) checking the balances on the statement to the ledger. Queries from customers should be referred to staff other than those who maintain the ledgers.

A senior official should be responsible for authorising the write off of bad debts and the approval of credit notes. And since such authority is equivalent to the power to write cheques, stringent safeguards are required. These will include the requirement for appropriate supporting vouchers (e.g. solicitor correspond-ence/goods returned notes) and properly raised and approved documentation.

### Credit control

Finally credit control should be responsible for reviewing accounts regularly to ensure that none have exceeded their credit limits, and to discover any balances which are overdue. Such overdue balances should be pursued immediately using properly formulated procedures (such as warning letters, and then reference to solicitors or credit collection agencies).

### Sales – fraud

In the absence of the above controls, the following are examples of types of fraud that become possible:

### 'Teeming and lading'

This can occur when sales ledger clerks also have access to cash receipts (or are in collusion with the cashier). But the fraud is only likely to remain undiscovered for long if the accounts are very chaotic and there is no regular independent check. If a system is very bad, cash or cheque receipts could simply be mis-appropriated, and the amount not credited to the debtor's account (or so credited, and the books allowed to remain out of balance). But it is likely that sooner or later someone will check the account, possibly in response to a customer query. So to cover up the defalcation a credit could be made to the account in respect of money received from another customer. The second customer's account will then be overstated but this may not matter if accounts are not checked until they are long overdue. Even if only small amounts are removed on each such manipu-lation, over a period of time this fraud (of teeming and lading) can reach a substantial size. Normally the perpetrator will become more greedy, and his system of interlocking frauds will become so complicated that the edifice will collapse. But perhaps not before the company has lost a substantial sum of money. Money which is unlikely ever to be recovered, even if the employee is caught. The sending of statements, and the independent resolving of customer queries thereon, can do much to prevent this fraud.

*Collusion between customer and sales invoicing*

If such collusion occurs invoices may not be raised, or may be raised only for a reduced amount. Such fraud can involve substantial sums of money, but can be prevented by proper sequential control over despatch documentation, and subsequent independent check of despatch documentation to invoices.

*Failure to raise despatch documentation*

If goods are allowed out of the premises without proper despatch documentation the matter may never be discovered (except possibly by stock check and re-conciliation of sales to purchases, when it will be far too late). So every precaution must be taken to prevent this possibility. And this is best achieved by having the minimum number of entrances to the premises, with a guard at each entrance checking documentation in respect of all goods leaving.

*Improperly raised credit notes*

False credit notes can be used either to cover up the misappropriation of cash, or to reduce a customer's debt if the perpetrator is in collusion with the customer. The false writing off of bad debts can be used in the same way.

*Receipts in respect of debtor accounts – internal check*

The cashier function must be kept strictly separate from any of the sales procedures in order to forestall 'teeming and lading' as already discussed.

*Post room*

Most moneys will be received through the post, so there must be adequate controls over opening the mail. These will include the involvement of at least two people, the one opening, the other recording the amounts received in an 'initial cash listing'. This latter forms the initial record of money received and as such is an important control to prevent subsequent defalcation. Cheques should immediately be stamped 'not negotiable – account payee only', and all moneys should then be passed as soon as possible to the cashier. He should sign for the amounts received, and the post room should retain a copy of their initial record, together with the cashier's signature. A useful check could be made on the cashier if the post room were to send customer remittance advices together with a copy of the 'initial cash listing' direct to sales ledger for recording amounts received. In this way the cash book could subsequently be reconciled to the debtors control account to ensure that all amounts have been correctly included. This latter check could usefully be performed by the internal audit department.

*Cashier*

The cashier should record the moneys received, and should bank them daily, to avoid having large amounts on the premises. At least two copies of the bank pay-in slip must be completed; one for the bank, and the other to be stamped by the bank and returned as proof of deposit. Provided the drawers' names are completed in full on the slip, this can provide some basis on which to subsequently check if the correct accounts have been credited. But it is not a very satisfactory basis, for banks will seldom check in detail the names on the copy pay-in slip, so it is better to rely on the independent posting of the sales ledger as discussed above. The person who makes out the pay-in slip should not take the money to the bank, for if there are any irregularities these may be discovered by the person banking the money. Of course he could himself perpetrate a fraud by altering the pay-in slip, but this may well be suspicious to bank officials. If teeming and lading is suspected (and for it to occur, accounts *must* be incorrectly credited), then it may be necessary to obtain the bank copy of the pay-in slip in order to carry out a reliable investigation.

### Ledger accounts

The sales ledger department will record the amounts received on the basis of remittance-received advices. If no such advice is included with the payment, then the post room could usefully make out such a form based on as much information as is available. Indeed there could be some advantage in having all remittances entered on serially numbered internal remittance-received advices, and copies of these could then be used to post the various books of account. The sales ledger control account should be independently maintained, preferably by a more senior official. And this account should be regularly and independently reconciled to the cash book and sales ledger.

### Receipts in respect of debtor accounts – fraud

It should not be thought that moneys received are immune from fraud, simply because they are in the form of cheques. Nothing could be further from the truth, for cheque frauds are easily and commonly perpetrated. And they will normally be carried out by slightly altering the company's name on the cheque to a similar but fictitious name, in which a bank account can then be opened and the amounts paid in. This possibility can only be forestalled if there is proper segregation of duties in accordance with the principles discussed above.

### Receipts in respect of over the counter sales

Cash sales are always highly susceptible to fraud, and it is almost impossible to entirely eliminate the risk. There is not sufficient room in this book for a detailed discussion of the controls necessary, but the following principles are important:
1. Wherever possible the best control over cash sales is quantity reconciliation as discussed earlier in the context of sales.
2. Close supervision is in any event essential in order to reduce the temptation for employees to 'pocket' takings.
3. Employees should not be allowed to work on their own if it can possibly be avoided. For temptation will be reduced if collusion is necessary before fraud can occur.

4. Wherever possible there should be an independent record of moneys received. A cash register with a till roll can provide such a record, though there is always the danger that the employee will simply not 'ring up' the receipt. Or he may ring it up, but for a reduced amount. Though the customer himself can provide some check here, provided the register is clearly on display.

5. The best method is to segregate the point of sale from the point of cash receipt, and to have some record of the sale created which can subsequently be checked to the cash register. Such record may be constituted by a simple cash invoice, or it may be a very sophisticated system such as employed in some large chain stores (for example, John Lewis Partnership). Electro-magnetic/Bar code stickers are here stuck on all products. A computerised till reads the bar code, and automatically records the price, while at the same time up-dating stock records. So cash takings can be reconciled with completely accurate sales figures.

None of this can of course prevent out and out theft by either customers or employees, although close supervision can go a long way to forestall it. Shop-lifting is now a multi-million pound business, and an allowance is commonly built into retail prices for what is politely known as 'stock shrinkage'. And there is evidence to suggest that fraud/theft by employees is becoming just as much of a problem. As auditors, we have a part to play in instigating control procedures that can forestall such crime.

*Cashier on holiday*

Arrangements must be made for a senior official to take over the cashier's function when he is on holiday. A cashier who consistently refuses to take a holiday automatically creates suspicion, for the implication is that he has something to hide.


## 6.6 The purchases 'cycle'

*Purchases – internal check*

### *Requisitioner*

Only specified employees should have the power to requisition goods, and then only up to an authorised limit, such limits increasing with the level of seniority. The requisition should be made on serial numbered documentation and should be sent to the buying department.

### *Buying department*

The buying department will be charged with the responsibility for negotiating the best prices and delivery dates from suppliers and ensuring that appropriate quality goods are obtained. The advantages of a central buying function include:
(a) ability to buy in bulk and reduction in volume of small (expensive) orders;

(b)  knowledge of most reliable suppliers;

(c)  planning of optimum reorder times and quantities.

But the most important advantage from the auditor's point of view is the fact that the existence of a separate buying department considerably strengthens internal control; for user departments are prevented from ordering goods without the order first being independently checked. And at the same time the user department can act as a check on the buying department itself, provided requisition notes are used and independently checked.

The order should contain information about price and delivery date requirements, and a delivery address should be quoted. And for subsequent internal purposes the account code should be entered showing to which account in the ledger the purchase should be charged. Several copies of the order will be required:

(a)  supplier,

(b)  buying department,

(c)  accounts department,

(d)  requisitioner (to advise him that the matter is in hand),

(e)  goods inwards (to know what to expect).

The documents should also be serially numbered. Colour coding of the different copies can also be useful.

### Goods inwards

Goods should be received in specially designated areas, and control is best established at the gate by having goods received notes raised there. The GRNs should be serially numbered to facilitate cut-off procedures at the year end (provided the last number issued in the year is known those that remain uninvoiced at the year-end can be accrued in the accounts). Numbering will also strengthen internal check, in that it reduces the possibility of introducing fake documents. And this is important because the GRN is the prime supporting document for subsequent invoice approval. A copy of the GRN should go direct to accounts for this purpose, and a copy should also be sent to the buying department for matching off in their uncompleted order file. Another copy should go to the inspection department for checking that the goods delivered correspond to the order and are of the correct quality and quantity. Shortages should immediately be notified to accounts in order that the appropriate credit may be claimed.

### Accounts department

The accounts department will receive the invoices and should date stamp them on receipt. Accounts will also collect the relevant supporting documents (copy orders, GRNs and inspection reports) and on this basis will approve the invoice for payment, completing the various steps indicated on the approval stamp illustrated in Fig. 6.4. Such a stamp can provide very useful control in that any missing stage can be seen at a glance, and those people actioning each stage must take responsibility by initialling the appropriate box. This provides a moral check and also enables management to pin point any employees whose work is

Fig. 6.4 Invoice approval stamp

| Check | Date | Initials |
|---|---|---|
| Cast, cross-casts and extensions | | |
| Prices | | |
| GRN | | |
| Order | | |
| Inspection note | | |
| Accounts code | | |
| Approved | | |
| Authorised for payment | | |
| Paid | | |

particularly slack.

Invoices should be numbered on arrival, and can be controlled in one of two ways:

(a)  slip system (voucher system);

(b)  ledger system.

In the *slip system* of accounting for purchases, the invoices themselves constitute the record. They will be numbered, and brief details of them will be recorded in a memorandum register. The slip system is often encountered with EDP methods of accounting, and in such circumstances the memorandum register may also be computerised. As invoices are paid they will be eliminated from the register, and the accounting entries will be credit cash, and debit stock or the appropriate expense account. Accordingly payment is only made on validly approved invoices, and for each payment appropriate supporting documentation must be presented to the official responsible for signing the cheque. In this way good control is maintained. However, the disadvantages of this system can lie in the difficulties sometimes associated with establishing the year-end creditors' figure. No problems will be experienced if the memorandum register is kept up to date. But often it will not be. And invoices can be lost, so that on some audits with this kind of system one can end up estimating the creditors and qualifying the accounts accordingly.

On the other hand the *ledger system* of accounting for purchases maintains a continuous record of creditors by building them into the double entry process. A personal account will be opened for each supplier and invoices will be credited there immediately on receipt. Payment will be made on ledger balances; and herein lies the problem. For a balance will be made up of several invoices, and so you move away from the principle of one supporting document, one payment. So it becomes easier for an employee intent on fraud to confuse the authorising signatory, especially as the latter will be a senior official with much pressure on his time. Often too much pressure for the routine (but vital) task of checking supporting documentation.

### Authorising for payment

The process of authorising invoices for payment is of vital importance, because all previous checks are worthless if this stage is omitted or performed slackly. And yet it often is performed slackly, because unreasonable demands are made on those officials responsible. The system will often demand that all invoices are reviewed; but with large firms this could amount to many hours work a day if it is done properly. It is therefore much more realistic to require the presentation of all supporting documentation, but only the actual examination of a percentage on a random basis; although a 100 per cent check could occasionally be made. However, if this method is used the sample actually selected should be scrutinised thoroughly and it would be usual to include those suppliers whose names were unfamiliar. The purchases not examined in detail should be checked to ensure that the documentation is, prime facie, in order.

### Purchases – fraud

In the absence of the above controls, the following are examples of the types of fraud that become possible:

### False charges from suppliers

If suppliers are in collusion with company employees, fictitious charges can be approved for payment, with a share subsequently going to the employee. This can most easily occur at the goods inwards stage, and is particularly possible if the inspection procedures are inadequate.

### Submission of false invoices

False invoices can be inserted at any stage in the processing, and provided false supporting documentation can be produced, then there is little to prevent this type of fraud. Typically the perpetrator will set up a phony company with impressive looking stationery and invoice the client for goods not supplied. It may not even be necessary for him to acquire phony supporting documentation, provided his responsibilities are late in the processing sequence, and provided there is no detailed management check at the approval stage.

### Re-presentation of supporting documents

Unless documentation is cancelled at the time the cheque is signed, it is possible for a genuine invoice to be re-presented for a second payment. If the perpetrator is in league with the supplier, he can obtain a percentage of the payment as his share in the crime, and the company can lose substantial sums of money in this way.

*Cheque payments – internal check and fraud*

### Authorisation

Cheque payments will be authorised on the basis of validly approved supporting documentation (see above).

### Cashier and cheque signing

The cashier will normally draw the cheques, which should be crossed 'Account payee only – not negotiable', and should then go to the first cheque signatory for signing. It is normal practice to have two signatories on all cheques above a stated minimum amount, the second signatory acting as an internal check on the work of the first. Limits as to the amount that can be signed for should be imposed on signatories; and it is imperative that supporting vouchers are cancelled at the time of signing, for a very common fraud is the re-presentation of used but uncancelled supporting documentation.

### Despatch of cheques

Once the cheques are signed they should immediately be despatched to the recipient. On no account should they be returned to anyone who has had anything to do with their preparation or authorisation – especially not to the cashier, for in the right hands signed cheques are as good as cash; it takes only a little skill to be able to alter the name or amount on the cheque. And this will be especially easy for the cashier because the cheque will be in his writing, and it could have been drawn originally with alteration in mind. So if the payee's name can be altered, the cashier only has to open a bank account in the fraudulent name and money can be withdrawn easily and painlessly. Such a fraud will probably be discovered in that the genuine supplier will ultimately demand payment; but a large quantity of money could be extracted in the meantime, and this fraud can be especially dangerous if combined with other types of falsification.

### Recording cheque payments

The cashier will record the cash book, and the other side to the double entry (either a debit to the supplier or straight to expense) will normally be made on the basis of the cashier's record. But it would be dangerous to give the original copy of the cash book to general ledger for posting, as entries could then be altered. It is better to send only a duplicate copy, and this will normally be the case except in very unsophisticated systems; although there would be considerable advantage in posting from totally independent records, including those derived from the accounts department.

### Suppliers' statements

If purchase ledger accounts are maintained, there can be some advantage in an independent reconciliation of these to suppliers' statements. But too much reliance should not be placed on this, as many suppliers now do not send statements; and an incomplete check is largely invalid.

It is also unwise to use suppliers' statements as the sole documentation in support of cheque payments. Staff could be in collusion with suppliers to approve excessive statements, or totally fictitious statements could be introduced. So all payments should be supported by invoices, GRNs and inspection notes, with the statement possibly being used as an additional supporting voucher.

*Cash payments – internal check*

Cash payments will normally be via petty cash, and this is best controlled by employing the 'imprest system'. In this system a fixed sum or 'imprest' is assigned to the petty cashier, and more cash can only be obtained on the production of the vouchers that have been redeemed in respect of payments made. The advantages of such a system are as follows:

(a) the fixed balance prevents escalation of the amount held – so the amount at risk can be kept small;

(b) the system is inherently self checking, for each time a reimbursement is required, the petty cashier must present his records to the official responsible (normally the cashier) for examination;

(c) reconciliation of cash book to petty cash book is facilitated.

The system works as follows:

1. Each payment should be supported by a voucher signed by the recipient's immediate superior, and where appropriate, vouchers should be supported by independent invoices or receipts.

2. Vouchers should be cancelled on payment, in order to preclude their further use. This can be achieved by numbering them and dating them as they are entered in the petty cash book. And the chief cashier should also cancel them when they are presented in support of a reimbursement request.

3. The amount of the imprest should be as low as possible, and the number of floats in use should also be kept to a minimum.

4. IOUs should not be allowed, nor should cheques be cashed out of petty cash.

5. No other receipts should go into petty cash or the system will be invalidated.

6. The chief cashier should check the reconciliation of the petty cash book at the time of reimbursement, and he should sign the book accordingly.

7. Spot cash counts can usefully be made, possibly by the company's internal auditors, and at the same time reconciliations and reimbursements from the main cash book can also be checked.

*Cash payments – fraud*

The most common fraud in this area is the re-presentation of supporting vouchers, but this can be prevented by the safeguards indicated above. Falsified vouchers can also be used to extract money from the company, but the amounts involved here are normally trivial. With these exceptions, a properly run imprest petty cash is reasonably well protected from material fraud. But if an imprest system is not used, then the opportunities are much greater, for it becomes much harder to check the reimbursement requests.

*Bank and cash balances*

Money in all forms is highly susceptible to misappropriation. For this reason reconciliations must be carried out regularly by senior independent officials. The financial accountant or an assistant is an appropriate person to reconcile the bank statement to the cash book, and this should be done preferably every week. Outstanding items should be thoroughly cleared, especially if they remain outstanding for a period of time. Spot checks on the petty cash are also necessary. These can usefully be performed by the financial accountant or internal audit staff, and the cash should be both counted and reconciled to the petty cash book. This latter should be cast and cross cast, and should itself be cross checked with reimbursements from the main cash book.

## 6.7 The wages 'cycle'

*Wages – internal check*

The internal control principles involved in wages and salaries are largely the same, with the exception that for the former there is the additional problem of handling large volumes of cash. For practical purposes the two are treated as the same here, but you should note that controls must apply to all forms of remuneration, from the directors' to the shop floors'. Stringent controls must be maintained over the wages cycle because extreme accuracy, and, in the case of hourly paid wages, at the same time speed are called for from clerks. The wages must be ready by payday, but overpayments resulting from mistakes are unlikely to be returned! And as well as the possibility of expensive mistakes, the large quantities of cash also give rise to the temptation to commit fraud. It is interesting to note that approximately 58 per cent of UK employees are still paid in cash, as opposed to only 2–3 per cent in the USA.

### Personnel department

The personnel department will be responsible for hiring and firing employees. They will also be responsible for authorising alterations in rates of pay in respect of promotions or general pay increases. The existence of a separate department negotiating these matters is extremely important from the auditor's point of view, because an independent record can be maintained of all personnel in employment. And this can provide a very useful check on the work of the wages department. Serially numbered change documents should be used to notify wages department of all changes and a copy should be retained by the personnel department for subsequent checking.

### Timekeeping

Clock cards or time sheets will normally be used to record the hours worked. In either case the amounts stated need to be independently verified.

*Clock cards.* Clock cards are the traditional means of recording hours, but 'clocking in' is subject to many abuses unless carefully monitored. It will be necessary to have the clocking-in process observed, and this has traditionally been achieved by the use of a timekeeper. But this is seldom a satisfactory solution, for the timekeeping function will inevitably not be a highly paid one. And so the employee assigned the job may well be susceptible to bribes from his workmates to overlook certain irregularities. An alternative is to have the 'clock' in such a position that it can be observed by management. But management may well not be there 'bright and early' in the morning. Nor are they likely to be there when the night shift comes and goes. So perhaps it is better to combine the time-keeping function with that of security. Although whatever method of control is used, it would be dangerous to rely on the clock alone. Cards should be approved by the employee's immediate superior, and the internal auditors can play a useful function here by carrying out spot checks, and reconciling personnel records to those in the wages department. If cards are used, blanks must be carefully controlled to prevent fraudulent ones being entered into the system. The exact number of cards for the week should be made out by the personnel department on the basis of their independent records, and they should be clearly identified by date.

*Time sheets.* Time sheets are often used, as these can be incorporated into the costing function. The sheets should be approved by the employee's immediate superior, and where the nature of the company allows, there should be regular reconciliation to the production records.

### Wages office

The approved clock cards or time sheets will be sent to the wages department whose job it is to produce the payroll. But within the wages department there will be several functions that should ideally be kept separate. The sequence of events will probably be as follows and the work distributed as indicated.

### Employee
    A. Check the hours worked as calculated by the foreman.
       Calculate the gross pay by reference to the employee's personal card showing his wage rate.
    B. Check the calculation of gross pay.
       Calculate net pay by reference to tax tables, and employee's personal record.
    C. Check net pay calculation.
       Check the casts and cross-casts of the payroll.

Several copies of the payroll will be needed as follows:
    Approval.
    Wages office.
    Cost office.
    General ledger (showing analysis of labour expense).
    Payslips.

We are primarily concerned with the copy that goes for approval. This should always be the original, as carbon copies are comparatively easily altered.

*Approval*

The payroll should be approved by a senior member of the management team, and this will often be the chief accountant. The person approving the payroll must to a large extent rely on the internal checks built into the system for preparing the payroll. But he can carry out a useful overview as follows:

1. Cast and cross-cast the payroll.
2. Check the payroll for duplicated names and/or unusually high payments.
3. Check the number of employees on the payroll to personnel department records.
4. Carry out a week-over-week reconciliation of total pay as follows:

|  | Last week's net pay. |
| --- | --- |
| Add | Starters, and increases in pay rates per personnel department records. |
| Less | Leavers. |
| Add/less | Increase/reduction in hours worked from production records. |
| Add/less | Changes in tax or other deductions. |
| = | This week's net pay. |

(this technique can provide strong evidence that the payroll is materially correct; although clearly it will be difficult to reconcile down to the last £).

*Signing the cheque*

Once the payroll is approved, the cheque can be drawn. Often the person approving the payroll will be one signatory to the cheque. But there should be at least one other signature by an independent senior official who should also examine the payroll, although in less detail.

*Distribution*

The money can now be collected from the bank and distributed. But it is important to build internal checks into these stages, for any attempted frauds up until this point will be less serious if the perpetrator has difficulty in actually getting his hands on the money. So the sequence of the remaining stages is shown below with an indication on the right hand column how the work may be split.

| Drawing the cheque | – | Cashier |
| --- | --- | --- |
| Collecting the money from the bank | – | Security firm |
| Filling the pay envelopes | – | Independent employees |
| Distributing the cash to the employees | – | Other independent employees and foremen. |

The employees who fill the envelopes should have had no previous dealings with the compilation of the payroll. They should count the money before beginning their work, and only the exact amount of cash should be withdrawn from the bank. In this way it becomes immediately apparent if an error has been made in filling the envelopes. The envelopes themselves should be designed so that it is possible for the employee to check that the amount is correct before opening. And queries should clearly not be accepted afterwards.

Once the envelopes are filled, they should be counted and given to a second batch of independent employees who should check the number of packets handed over, before distributing them to the employees. The foremen should accompany the payout in order to identify the correct employees. It is normal practice to obtain a receipt from the employee, although this is of limited value, for no one can be expected to know the signatures of all the employees. Pay-packets should not be given to other employees in the event that the recipient is absent; rather they should be returned to the safe, and rebanked as soon as possible, with a Postal Order or registered letter being subsequently sent to the employee. A register of unclaimed wages should be maintained, and strictly controlled.

### Wages – fraud

In the absence of the above controls the following are examples of the types of fraud that become possible.

#### Dummy names

If a proper independent record of employees is not maintained, the insertion of dummy names on the payroll becomes possible. Fictitious names may be invented, or employees who have retired or left employment may be retained on the payroll. Often this fraud is perpetrated by the wages office, but the foreman may also be in a position to obtain money in this way; though he will only be able to do so if there is additionally no independent check on the payout. The wages department too will be prevented from benefiting by this fraud, provided they are prevented access to the money by the techniques discussed above.

#### Overstatement of gross pay

If the wages clerk is in collusion with an employee on the shop floor, it will be possible for the gross pay to be overstated, and for the employee to be overpaid. The wages clerk could receive a refund of part of the overpayment, and provided the amounts involved are not excessive such a fraud would be very difficult to trace; but the likelihood of it occurring can be reduced if the calculation is checked by an independent clerk (although the power to check is the power to alter, so the second clerk could now be in a position to carry out the fraud). The only redeeming feature here is that the fraud will probably eventually be revealed by someone (who does not receive the bonus!) telling tales. If the wages clerk wished to be especially greedy he could overstate the gross pay on the payroll, but enter the correct amount on the payslip. And in this way he could retain the entire overpayment for himself; although, again, for this to be success-ful it is necessary for the clerk to have access to the cash.

*Overstating the payroll*

A very simple fraud that can be prevented very simply by casting the payroll at the time of approval (though in practice on large payrolls this is seldom done, as senior management, or even their assistants, will not usually have the time).

*Clock card frauds*

These are many and varied, but the amounts involved are usually comparatively small. Though this does not mean that they can be ignored, for fraud often has a snowballing effect. Very simply, one employee may 'clock out' for a number of his friends, so that if turns are taken, each employee can obtain useful extra weekly income! And in time this fraud can amount to a considerable sum of money lost to the company. However, it can be prevented by adequate supervision of clocking procedures and by ensuring that clock cards are properly authorised. As an alternative fraud, clock cards may be re-used if they are not strictly controlled by a numbering and date system. And it may also be possible to 'create' false employees if blank clock cards can be obtained. These latter should be controlled by the personnel department and only the correct number issued each week.

*Deductions*

These are also susceptible to fraudulent activity, but the perpetrator here has to be a little more subtle. It is difficult to manipulate payments to the Inland Revenue or for National Insurance, unless the controls over cheque payments (see before) are particularly weak. However, more typically, deductions in respect of sports clubs, canteen funds, trade union subscriptions, etc., can be misappropriated, especially if the perpetrator also has dealings with those funds. Overpayments can then simply be requested and the excess removed before payment into the fund. For this reason, no one in accounts or wages department should have control of such funds, and cheque requests in respect of deductions should be carefully scrutinised.

## 6.8 Stock and fixed assets

The control requirements here are primarily concerned with custody procedures, whereas so far we have been dealing with accountability for transactions. Custody procedures are of prime importance because of course all fraud involves misappropriating assets. So these procedures will be examined in detail in Chapter 14 on the verification of assets and liabilities. But some principles must be noted at this stage for these will be very significant when it comes to the overall evaluation of accounting systems, which we will tackle in Chapter 8 by means of 'key control questions'. It is not appropriate to introduce here generalised systems for controlling these assets, for the requirements of different companies vary tremendously with the nature of their operations. So we will examine only the all important 'segregation of duties' that will be required in these areas. And then we will look at the types of fraud that can typically occur in the absence of strong controls.

*Stock*

### Segregation of duties

*Receiving, checking and recording goods inwards.* These are as discussed in the context of purchases.

*Custody procedures.* These are normally achieved using segregated, lockable areas under the control of a storeman who is held accountable by means of stock records.

*Maintenance of stock records.* This should be performed by someone who has no access to the physical stock, and has no responsibility for sales or purchase records.

*Reconciliation of physical quantities to stock records.* Such reconciliations are vital for the prevention/detection of fraud, and to ensure that the stock figure in the accounts shows a 'true and fair view'. The internal auditors are appropriate officials to control the stock count and subsequent reconciliation; and discrepancies should be referred to the highest level of authority, and should be investigated immediately.

*Write off of damaged, slow moving and obsolete stocks.* Such stocks may be revealed by the periodic stock checks, or they may come to light during the ordinary course of business. But in either event it is essential that the authority for writing off should come from a senior independent official, and then only on the basis of appropriate documentary evidence.

*Control of scrap and waste products.* Scrap and waste products can be of considerable value in certain types of industry. But they can be very difficult to control. So it is essential that calculations of estimated scrap and waste should be compared regularly with the actual amounts. Any significant differences should be investigated immediately.

### Stock fraud

Stock frauds are many and varied, and here the distinction between 'distortion' and 'concealment of defalcation' is very clearly in evidence. Many senior level frauds involve the manipulation of stock values to show other than a true and fair view. But this is outside the scope of this chapter, and will be dealt with in Chapter 14 on verification of assets and liabilities. For here we are primarily concerned with the controls necessary to prevent defalcation.

*Theft.* If custody procedures are sufficiently weak, it will be possible for employees to simply remove stock from the premises. Some such 'stock shrinkage' is almost inevitable, but it can be kept to a minimum by properly controlled storerooms, and strict security measures at the points of access to the factory.

*Concealment of theft by write-offs.* If those who have access to stocks also have the authority to make write-offs in the records for damage, etc., then theft can be very easily concealed.

*Manipulation of records to conceal theft.* If people who have access to stock are also permitted to record either the stock records, or records of sales or purchases, book quantities can be manipulated so that they correspond with the actual quantities of stock on hand.

### Fixed assets

As with stock, the value placed on fixed assets is susceptible to distortion. This will be discussed in Chapter 14. So here we will concentrate on those controls necessary to prevent defalcation. For although fixed assets are often very large and very immovable (no one is going to steal the main factory!) some can be small, highly portable and very stealable. Motor cars, bulldozers and power tools all spring to mind. And such items as these can often be very valuable indeed. So it is essential that they are adequately controlled.

#### Segregation of duties

*Authorisation of capital expenditure.* This should be performed by senior levels of management, and it is normal to place limits on the competence of each manager, with major items of expenditure being sanctioned by the board itself.

*Accounting records.* The maintenance of accounting records should be performed by someone who has no access to the fixed assets, and has no responsibility for authorising purchases or sales thereof. Care must be taken to ensure that a proper distinction is drawn between capital and revenue items.

*Plant and property registers.* Detailed registers of fixed assets as to location, value, etc., are vital for proper control. But many companies do not maintain them. As auditors we should always encourage their use, and there will be a more detailed discussion of their importance in Chapter 14. If fixed asset registers are maintained, the clerk responsible should have no involvement with the assets themselves or with the general ledger, or with sales or purchases of fixed assets. In this way his records can provide totally independent evidence but this will only be of value if checked regularly to the assets themselves and reconciled to the general ledger. This work should be performed by independent employees, and again the internal auditors would be appropriate.

*Sale, scrapping or transfer of fixed assets.* The responsibility for taking assets out of the company's service should be reserved for the highest levels of management, and then only on the basis of properly approved documentation.

*Fixed assets – fraud*

*Theft.* Small portable items may simply be stolen from the premises. This can be prevented by ensuring that someone is accountable for all items of equipment, and by having appropriate security measures at all points of access to the factory. Additionally there should be regular reconciliations of the plant register to the physical assets and explanations of discrepancies should be sought from the persons accountable.

*Manipulation of records to conceal theft.* If people who have responsibility for assets are also in a position to write up the accounting records or the plant register, then they will be able to conceal a misappropriation by altering the books accordingly.

*Premature scrapping.* An employee who has physical control of assets as well as the responsibility for sanctioning their scrapping, may scrap items prematurely, in return for a 'kickback' from a scrap dealer with whom he is in league.

*Sale at below market value of assets which are no longer required, but which have not yet reached retirement age.* This type of fraud is particularly common in construction and heavy plant industry, where very expensive items of equipment have but a very limited useful life. It is comparatively difficult for an outsider to determine the value of such assets. So the specialist plant manager may be able to arrange the sale at below real value to a dealer with whom he is in collusion (or even to a company he sets up for the purpose).

*Use of company assets for private purposes.* This practice will inevitably happen to some degree on a minor scale, but major frauds can also occur in this way. For example, one computer manager succeeded in convincing his inexpert board of directors that far greater computer capacity was necessary than was actually in fact the case. With the spare capacity the manager made a considerable profit for himself by selling computer time to other local businesses. One plant manager I encountered (and I am sure there are many more like him), also made himself large amounts of money by sub-contracting major items of construction equipment to other construction companies; the fees going straight into his pocket! This type of fraud can be difficult to prevent if the senior management have insufficient technical expertise to know the capacity of fixed assets actually required; although the internal audit department can play a useful role here by making spot checks on the location and condition of assets, and by comparison to the plant register.

## 6.9   Investments

Investments are by very definition valuable, so every precaution should be taken over their safekeeping. The necessary *segregation of duties* is as follows:

*Authorisation of purchases and sales.* These should be performed by a very senior level of management, possibly even the board of directors. And those responsible should have no concern with cash or the custody of documents of title.

*Maintenance of investment register.* This should be performed by a clerk who has no access to the documents of title, and no responsibility for authorising purchases or sales. The register should periodically be reconciled with the investment account in the general ledger, and the documents of title should periodically be vouched. The internal auditors would be appropriate officials to carry out this work.

*Maintenance of records.* An independent clerk should be responsible for comparing contract notes with purchase and sale authorisations, and for ensuring that charges have been correctly calculated. Additionally arrangements should be made for dealing with share transfers, for ensuring that share certificates are received/delivered and that bonuses, rights issues, capital repayments and dividends or interest are received and properly accounted for. The internal auditors can play an important part in ensuring that this work is performed satisfactorily.

*Documents of title.* Adequate custody procedures must be maintained for documents of title, and two senior officials should have responsibility for them. Access to the documents should be by the two officials acting jointly.

*Investments – fraud*

*Purchase/sale on own account*

If investment managers are in league with stock brokers they may be able to manipulate transactions so that purchased shares which go down in value are bought in the name of the company, whereas some of those that go up are bought in the name of the manager. A no-lose situation! And very difficult to detect except in the long run if the manager's investment record appears to be particularly unsatisfactory. Investment managers can be particularly vulnerable to 'persuasion' by stock brokers, because the latter are dependent on the manager for their business. And very big business it can be too, with large values of shares changing hands, each with a percentage to the broker. So that a good lunch is not necessarily all that could come the way of the investment manager in return for his favours!

*Misappropriation of assets*

This may be possible, if officials having access to cash also have the responsibility for authorising the sale of investments, or have custody of the documents of title. This fraud should be discovered by regular reconciliations, but the amounts at risk can be so large that the possibility of ultimate detection may not be a sufficient deterrent – provided the perpetrator has sufficient time to leave the country!

# 7
# Recording the accounting system

## 7.1 Methods of recording systems

Paragraph 3 of the Auditor's Operational Standard states that:

> 'The auditor should ascertain the enterprise's system of recording and processing transactions and assess its adequacy for the preparation of financial statements.'

The first stage in the review of a client's system of internal control is to record the system in a way which allows for easy analysis. There are a number of alternative methods of recording:

1. *Narrative notes.* These are perhaps the most adaptable means of recording, but they can be cumbersome to use, difficult to interpret and review, and awkward to change. It is also difficult to identify if any part of the system has been omitted. And there is the additional difficulty associated with reading other people's handwriting! This method is most likely to be appropriate in small businesses, and to specific overall aspects of the systems in larger enterprises (see 3 below).

2. *Check lists (ICQs).* These are pre-printed documents asking specific questions to which a negative answer normally implies a weakness in control. ICQs help to ensure that all basic control points are considered, and in the context of control evaluation they can be extremely useful. But they are not efficient as the sole means of recording the details of an accounting system, for they can then become very cluttered, with a consequent difficulty in interpretation.

3. *Flow charts.* These are a graphic representation of the flow of documents through an accounting system, with each check or control recorded on the lines of flow and with segregation of duties highlighted. This method ensures as far as possible the completeness of recording, because a missed stage results in the flow line simply stopping in mid page. The method also eliminates the need for lengthy narrative and it is easy to understand and extract the salient points of control and any related weaknesses. In addition the standardisation of format makes for ease of assimilation. However, the method does not facilitate the recording of physical, personnel, supervision or management controls, which are usually best contained in narrative notes.

Flow charts are widely and correctly regarded as a very important tool in the evaluation of systems. However, you should remember that a flow chart is not an end in itself. It is primarily designed to reveal the absence of essential accounting controls, so a disproportionate amount of time should not be spent on recording details which are irrelevant to this purpose. Flow charts are time consuming, and therefore expensive to prepare, and thought must always be given to their cost effectiveness. In many cases it will not be appropriate to prepare flow charts at all.

You should not assume that the above three techniques are mutually exclusive. Indeed, we shall see in the next section that systems files for other than small businesses will often contain all of these methods of recording.

## 7.2  The information required

The necessary information will be obtained by interviewing the client's officials and staff, and by referring to relevant documents such as manuals of procedures and job descriptions. The detail required will vary from client to client, but we can identify four important elements that will be necessary whatever the audit:

1. *An overall organisation chart.* The organisation chart should show the principal departments of the company, together with a description of their functions and the number of people employed therein (important later for assessing internal control). In addition, the titles and names of all responsible officials should be recorded along with their lines of responsibility within the organisation.

2. *A list of the principal books of account, with a brief description of how each is kept.* Records can of course be kept in many ways, ranging from hand-written ledgers, through accounting machines to the most sophisticated real time computerised data processing systems. It is essential for a satisfactory review of internal control to have precise details of the methods used.

3. *Information as to accounting information flows and controls.* This will normally be in the form of flow charts, unless the size or type of organisation makes a different method of recording more appropriate. Whatever method is used, it is important to record the person who is responsible at each stage for the authorising, the recording and the custody of the relevant assets and records.

4. *Narrative notes on appropriate accounting controls, particularly with reference to the accountability of employees in each audit area.* For example, authority limits for cheque signing, together with specimen signatures would be noted. And in addition a brief description would also be included of any relevant administrative controls.

## 7.3  Preparing flow charts

The flow chart will be designed to highlight the ways in which duties are segregated together with any internal checks that the system contains. The charts can be prepared in different ways and many of the large firms have their own versions. No one form is necessarily to be preferred over another, as long as they all fulfil this prime objective. So if you are already familiar with a method different from that portrayed here, you are not required to unlearn all that you know! But the flow charting method explained in this chapter, and used throughout the remainder of the book, is convenient and simple to use and it has been widely adopted throughout the profession both in this country and overseas. Even if you already know an alternative system, in order that you may obtain the most value out of Chapter 9 containing evaluation case studies, I recommend that you familiarise yourself with the very simple symbols explained in the following sections. The symbols, together with the accompanying explanation and sample charts, are drawn from the training manuals of Deloitte, Haskins and Sells.

Flow charts will usually be prepared for any part of an accounting system which processes large volumes of transactions, such as:

the sales 'cycle',
the purchases 'cycle',
the wages 'cycle'.

For convenience of preparation and review, it is necessary to prepare one section of a system independent of the others, but it will usually be necessary to link them by cross referencing, especially in such obvious areas of overlap as purchases/ stock.

The information for the preparation of the charts will inevitably usually come from management, so it is necessary to confirm that the details are correct. For you may be given wrong information, not necessarily because management wish to deceive you, but simply because they themselves have an incorrect understanding of how the systems are actually working in practice. Often systems are gradually changed by junior employees who see an easier (but perhaps less satisfactory) way of accomplishing a particular task. And these changes can go unnoticed by senior officials, especially in the absence of internal audit. Accordingly, we must carry out 'walk-through' tests as discussed in Chapter 3 to confirm the information given to us. You should not confuse these tests with compliance tests, which are designed to see whether the system has been complied with throughout the period in question. Having ascertained that the system has been recorded as it is supposed to operate, the charts should be reviewed with senior officials to ensure that they also comply with their understanding of procedures.

Before we proceed to the detail of preparation, a brief word as to examinations is appropriate here. It is comparatively rare that examinations test the ability to draw flow charts (though subsequent examinations may prove me wrong!). This is necessarily so, for flow charts take a long time to produce and are also difficult to allot marks upon. But if you are faced with one in an exam, you should ensure that you concentrate on that which the examiner is likely to want to see:

(a) the understanding of the discipline of a flow charting system (you should of course provide a key);
(b) the ability to highlight the appropriate segregation of duties and internal checks.

You should not spend a long time going into immense detail, and nor should you attempt to make your chart into a work of art in the limited time available.

A more effective test is for the examiner to provide a flow chart depicting an accounting system and to ask for an evaluation thereof. I have been using this system for many years in internal examinations, but it is more difficult in external examinations where the examiners cannot rely on all candidates knowing the same flow charting scheme.

## 7.4 Flow charting symbols and techniques

*Showing the separation of functions*

If you take a glance at the sample flow chart reproduced on pages 106–09 (Fig. 7.1), you will see that there are separate columns for each function, identified across the top of the page. These emphasise the division of responsibilities, the segregation of duties and the system of internal check, and as such are extremely important in the subsequent review procedures. So care should be taken in ensuring that the appropriate split is made. It may be sufficient to record the work of a whole department in one column, or it may be necessary to record the work of each individual within the department. Which of these approaches applies depends on the nature of the system, and the separation of functions involved.

*Showing the flow and the processing of documents*

Document flow is shown by continuous lines. Vertical lines indicate the passing of time, whereas horizontal lines show the movement of documents from one control area to another. It follows that the general flow must always be down the page, thus showing the processing of documents according to time sequence. Diagonal lines should never be used, as they have no meaning in this system, and will accordingly confuse another reader. You should try to avoid crossing document flow lines, and this can usually be achieved by careful design of the chart before you begin the detailed drawing. Such crossing lines serve to confuse, but if they cannot be avoided the fact that the flows have no relationship with each other can be denoted by using the following 'hump-bridge' symbol.

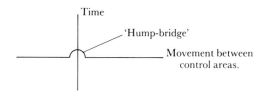

Information flow is shown by a broken line, which will always be horizontal and never vertical. Some common examples of the flow of information are: the preparation of one document from the information contained in another, the posting of a ledger account, and the checking of one document with another.

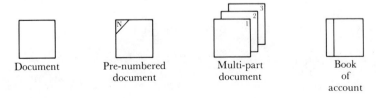

– – – – – Information flow lines

*Showing the documents and books of account*

| Document | Pre-numbered document | Multi-part document | Book of account |
|----------|------------------------|----------------------|------------------|

Documents or books should only be shown when they are first 'set-up', and the title should be entered within the square, or close alongside. Where documents are brought forward from previous charts, or where the charts have become very complicated, it may be appropriate to restate the document by 'ghosting' in the following manner:

'Ghost' document

It would not be correct to show an unbroken square again, for this would imply that a new document was being introduced. Where documents are transferred from one chart to another, the following connector symbol should be used:

Connector

If documents are attached to each other this should be shown on the chart by joining the two flow lines in the following way:

*Showing operations and checks*

Operation            Check

A check is distinguished from an operation, because it has a special audit significance. So the right-hand symbol should always be used where an operation constitutes an accounting control. Where the comparison of one document with another checks both documents, this will be depicted as follows:

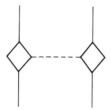

But if the comparison checks only one document, then a combination of the operation and check symbols must be used.

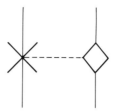

The operation of filing will be depicted by an inverted triangle, against which letters can be placed to symbolise different types of filing as follows:

| Order | Permanent filing | Temporary filing |
|---|---|---|
| Alphabetic | ▽ A | ▽ TA |
| Numeric | ▽ N | ▽ TN |
| Date | ▽ D | ▽ TD |

Each operation must be numbered to facilitate subsequent reference to control evaluation documents.

*Showing alternative procedures*

Alternative procedures may be shown either by way of narrative description, or by way of flow charts. If the alternatives are relatively simple, they may both be shown on the main chart, but more complicated alternatives may have to be relegated to a subsidiary chart.

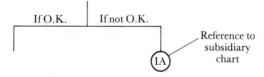

Where documents are sent outside the company, an arrow can be used with a narrative description of the destination. Where documents are destroyed, the word destroyed is normally written at the end of the flow line.

Document sent out          Document destroyed

*Showing narrative*

You will note from the flow chart example (Fig. 7.1, pp. 106–09) that sufficient space has been left for a minimal amount of narrative down the left-hand side of the page. In the main, the symbols are sufficient explanation of the actions taking place, but a brief note will be necessary to explain the precise nature of some operations, and details of the person performing the tasks should also be included. The narrative must be made immediately opposite the step on the chart, and should be numbered accordingly. For this reason, you should write the narrative as you draw the chart, as otherwise insufficient space may be left.

*Showing EDP systems*

Additional symbols are necessary where the client uses computerised data processing.

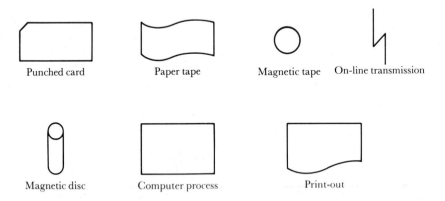

Punched card          Paper tape          Magnetic tape          On-line transmission

Magnetic disc          Computer process          Print-out

## 7.5 Flow chart example

You should carefully study the flow chart shown in Fig. 7.1, which depicts a typical purchasing operation for a larger company from the initial ordering stage through to the final payment. A narrative explanation of the various steps is included at the bottom of each chart as an aid to understanding. As well as noting the flow chart techniques involved, you can usefully also look for the internal control present in this system, paying special attention to the segregation of duties, and the checks denoted by the diamond symbol.

## 7.6 Narrative notes

At the beginning of the chapter I stated that narrative notes would normally be necessary in addition to the flow charts of accounting controls. We can identify four important areas where such notes can often be useful:

1. *Recording the information that management receive.* Management supervision is an essential ingredient for effective overall internal control. So it is important that we know the basis upon which management exercise their supervision. Is sufficient detail provided for effective control? For example, are monthly or quarterly accounts produced? Or perhaps is too much information produced so that it cannot be assimilated or used for immediate decision making?

2. *Recording the budgetary control system.* Budgetary control also plays an important part in overall control. So brief notes can usefully be made about the budgetary control system, to facilitate an evaluation of its effectiveness. Particular reference should be made to procedures for dealing with variances, for we will see later that these can have a special audit significance.

3. *Client's accounting manuals and instructions.* Extracts or complete copies of manuals and other accounting instructions should be obtained for the audit file. And at the first audit they should be reviewed to assess the likelihood of the effective communication of the various (usually complex) accounting procedures, for the breakdown in such communication is a common cause of audit problems.

4. *Recording details of the internal audit function.* As we saw in Chapter 5, internal audit can form a very useful part of overall internal control. So in order to be able to assess the internal audit effectiveness we must record sufficient details along the lines discussed in sec. 5.7 above.

## 7.7 Conclusion

In order to satisfy ourselves that we have a correct understanding of the internal control system, we must carry out a brief 'walk through' test on each of the areas under review, as discussed in Chapter 3. This test consists of tracing a few transactions in each accounting area from inception, through to final recording. In this way we can both gain familiarity with the system, and ensure that we have recorded it correctly in our flow charts or systems notes. For example, Fig. 6.3(b) showed the transaction cycles broken down into procedural stages. The 'Walk through' test would follow these procedures through, at each stage check-

# Fig. 7.1 Example of flow charts

Purchases: Chart No 1 – Ordering, delivery and invoice approval

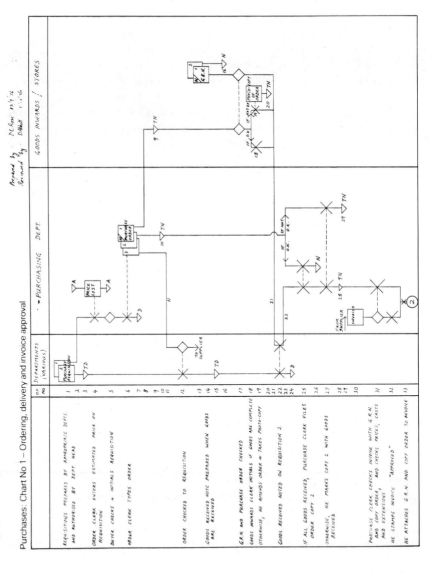

Flow chart
operation
No.

1 Purchase requisitions are prepared (in duplicate) by various departments requiring goods. The requisitions are authorised by the departmental heads. The top copy is passed to purchasing department, whilst the

2 second copy is temporarily filed in date order in the requisitioning department.

3

4 Order Clerk enters estimated prices from suppliers' price lists.

5 The Buyer checks and initials the requisition. Then a

6 three part pre-numbered purchase order set is typed by the Order Clerk from the requisition. The

7 requisition is filed in date order in the purchasing department.

The purchase order is then distributed as follows:

Copy

8 1. Passed to the goods inwards department/stores

9 where it is filed temporarily in numerical order.

10 2. Retained in the purchasing department, in a temporary file (in numerical order).

11 3. Passed to the requisitioning department where it

12 is checked against the second copy of the purchase

13 requisition. It is then sent out to the supplier. The

15 requisition is then filed temporarily in date order.

14 When the goods are received, a pre-numbered goods received note is made out in duplicate by the goods

16 inward department. The second copy is filed in

17 numerical order. The top copy is checked with the copy purchase order.

18 If the goods are in accordance with the order, the

19 Goods Inwards Clerk initials it; otherwise he notes

20 any differences on it and takes a photocopy of the amended order which he retains in a temporary file (in numerical order).

21 The copy order and GRN are attached and sent to the requisitioning department.

22 Details of goods received noted on the purchase requisition.

23 The GRN and copy order are passed back to the Purchase Clerk in the purchasing department.

24 The purchase requisition is filed permanently (in date order).

25 If all the goods have been received the Purchase

26 Clerk transfers the copy order to a permanent file (in

27 numerical order). Otherwise he notes the goods

29 received on the copy order and returns it to a temporary file.

28 The GRN and attached copy order are filed temporarily.

30 When the supplier's invoice is received, it is checked with the goods received note and copy order by the

31 Purchase Clerk. He also checks the invoice for prices, casts and extensions. He then stamps the

32 invoice 'Approved' and attaches the goods received

33 note and copy order to the invoice.

Purchases: Chart No 2 – Bought ledger and payments procedure

Prepared by : D.L.Ross 14/9/76
Reviewed by : D. Abbott 5/4/76

| OP. NO. | PURCHASING DEPT. | BOUGHT LEDGER CLERK | CHIEF ACCOUNTANT | CASHIER | COMPANY SECRETARY | NOMINAL LEDGER CLERK |
|---|---|---|---|---|---|---|

INVOICES NUMBERED SEQUENTIALLY — 35
ACCOUNTS CODING ENTERED — 36
LEDGER & DAYBOOK IN BURROUGHS MACHINE — 37, 38
DAYBOOK TOTAL AGREED WITH PRE-LIST — 39, 40, 41
REQUISITION & ADVICE PREPARED SIMULTANEOUSLY — 42, 43
REQUISITIONS TESTED WITH INVOICES — 44, 45
INVOICES CANCELLED — 46
REQUISITIONS SIGNED — 47, 48, 49, 50
CHEQUE & PAYMENTS SHEET PREPARED FROM REQUISITION — 51, 52
SECRETARY COMPARES CHEQUE WITH REQUISITION — 53
HE SIGNS CHEQUE & OBTAINS A DIRECTOR'S SIGNATURE — 54, 55, 56
PAYMENTS POSTED TO BOUGHT LEDGER — 57, 58, 59
— 60, 61, 62
PAYMENTS POSTED TO NOMINAL LEDGER — 63
— 64
DAYBOOK POSTED TO NOMINAL LEDGER — 65, 66

| Flow chart operation No. | |
|---|---|
| 34 | The invoices are pre-listed in the Purchasing Department. The batches of invoices, goods received notes and copy orders are then passed to the Bought Ledger Clerk, together with the pre-list. The Bought |
| 35 | Ledger Clerk numbers the invoices sequentially and |
| 36 | enters the accounts coding on the invoice. He then |
| 37 | posts the invoice to the bought ledger, on a Burroughs accounting machine. The proof sheet |
| 38 | forms the bought daybook. |
| 39 | He agrees the daybook total with the pre-list and |
| 40 | files the latter (in date order). The bought ledger is in |
| 41 | alphabetical order. |
| 42 | The Bought Ledger Clerk prepares simultaneously (from the bought ledger sheet) cheque |
| 43/44 | requisitions and remittance advices. The last two |
| 43/44 | documents and the supporting invoices are passed |
| 45 | to the Chief Accountant, who tests the requisitions |
| 46/47 | with the invoices. He cancels the invoices and signs |
| 48 | the requisitions. The invoices are then returned to the |
| 49 | Bought Ledger Clerk, who files them in numerical order. |
| 50 | The cheque requisitions and remittance advices are passed to the Cashier. He prepares the cheques from the requisitions; the cash payments sheet is also |
| 51 | prepared, being a copy of the cheques. |
| 52 | The cheque is attached to the remittance advice and passed with the cheque requisition to the Company Secretary. |
| 53 | He compares the requisition and cheque. |
| 54 | He signs the cheque and obtains a director's signature. |
| 55 | The cheque and remittance advice are dispatched to the supplier. |
| 56 | The cash payments sheet is passed back to the |
| 57 | Bought Ledger Clerk who posts it to the bought ledger, and then files the ledger sheets in alphabetical order. |
| 60 | The cheque requisitions are passed back to the |
| 58 | Cashier who then files them in date order. |
| 59 | The cash payments sheet and bought daybook sheet are passed to the Nominal Ledger Clerk. He posts |
| 61/62 | them to the nominal ledger and files both sets of |
| 63/64 | sheets in date order. |
| 65/66 | |

ing relevant documentation for authority, approvals and calculations, and ensuring that the transaction followed the predetermined internal control route.

These tests can be performed at any convenient stage in the audit, but they will usually be completed before the evaluation procedures. It will not usually be necessary to repeat such tests on subsequent audits, unless the accounting system changes.

We have now collected sufficient information to enable us to begin our review of a client's system of internal control. Remember that this information-gathering process is not an end in itself, but is merely a stage in the process of reaching an opinion as to the truth and fairness of the company's periodic financial statements.

# 8
# Evaluating the accounting system

## 8.1 Introduction

We have seen in previous chapters that we evaluate a client's accounting system in order to decide if it constitutes a reliable basis for the preparation of the annual accounts, and to determine the required amount of substantive testing. If the internal control is very weak, it may not be possible to express any opinion at all on the accounts presented. If on the other hand the internal control is strong, we can minimise the amount of substantive testing used in arriving at an opinion.

It is necessary to examine a system from three points of view:
1. Is there a possibility of defalcation/fraud, either permanent, or temporary?
2. Is there a possibility of undiscovered errors occurring?
3. Is there a possibility of the accounts being deliberately distorted?

Just how this evaluation will be tackled varies from firm to firm, and it would be wrong to suggest that any one method is necessarily superior to another, for each may have advantages in specific circumstances. We have already looked at the general principles involved, during the course of Chapter 3. And we saw that there were two basic approachs, both involving the use of questionnaires:
1. Designed to determine if desirable internal controls are present.
2. Using *key control questions* to determine if specific frauds/errors are possible.
The former questionnaires we called ICQs, and for convenience of differentiation the latter we labelled ICEs.

During the course of this chapter we will look at both these approaches and determine their relative merits.

## 8.2 Internal Control Questionnaires (ICQs)

ICQs were first used on a major scale in Britain towards the end of the 1960s. They represented the first attempt at a formalised, more systematic approach to the audit of the ever more complex, large corporations. ICQs were originally (and still are) used in two ways – either as a means of recording and evaluating information on internal control; or simply as a means of evaluation. Used in the former fashion, the ICQs will typically ask whether certain controls are performed, and if so, when, how and by whom. It is now generally considered that such questionnaires become too complex and cluttered for meaningful evaluation, and that systems information is best recorded in the form of flow charts, or systems notes as appropriate. If the controls are recorded in this latter way, the questionnaire will normally be answered simply by Yes or No, indicating whether or not a desirable control exists. The questions will all be so designed that a 'No' answer indicates a weak control situation.

The ICQs will usually be formulated so that there is one covering each of the accounting areas discussed in Chapter 6. And in addition, there will probably be one dealing with general financial matters. The example ICQ (Fig. 8.1) is a traditional one covering cheque payments, and is based on the approach in Auditing Statement U4. You will see that the questions approximately follow the sequence of the accounting system, and cover the various desirable checks and controls that we discussed in Chapter 6. Look at the questions themselves, as well as at the format, and try to think why each question is being asked. If necessary refer back to Chapter 6 for inspiration! You will see that there are 'Yes' and 'No' columns, to be ticked as appropriate, and a 'not applicable' column could also be added. A column is included for reference to systems notes, and this is important for the manager/partner review after completion. Then a column is included for referencing to the audit test programme (see Ch. 13). And finally there is plenty of space for comments. Here the accountant completing the ICQ will record the extent to which he considers any weakness material. He may be able to point to other controls which mitigate a particular weakness. Or he may consider that the weakness is very serious indeed. Whichever, his judgement will constitute the basis of determining the subsequent amount of substantive testing.

ICQs facilitate the orderly evaluation of the internal control present in a system. They eliminate the possibility of matters being overlooked, as may be the case were the auditor to rely on his memory of desirable controls. And they provide the basis for the manager/partner review of the opinions reached by the staff in the field. They also provide documentary evidence of the basis of audit conclusions, in the event that the auditor's judgement is subsequently challenged in a court of law.

However, there is the danger that ICQs can provoke a rather styilised approach to the job, for they concentrate on the controls themselves, rather than upon the fraud or error that the controls are designed to forestall. It is essential that the audit is conducted in a searching and enquiring manner, always bearing in mind the types of problem that may arise. With ICQs it is very easy to forget the significance behind each question. And if this happens, much of their value is lost. For this reason most of the major firms have adopted the Internal Control Evaluation approach (though not necessarily under this name).

Before we leave the ICQs, we must briefly consider their means of completion. ICQs of the 'who, when and how' kind are often given to the client for him to complete. I do not consider this appropriate, for the client may well not comprehend the full significance of a given question, and may accordingly not fill in the answer correctly. At the very least the auditor should fill in the questionnaire together with the appropriate client official, after the latter has had time to study

Fig. 8.1 Internal control questionnaire – cheque payments

Internal control questionnaire – cheque payments
*Client* – Fundamentals Ltd

*Prepared by*: MJP
*Date*:

| Steps | Yes | No | Ref. to Systems Notes | Ref. to Map | Comments |
|---|---|---|---|---|---|
| 1. Are cheques crossed and marked 'A/C Payee' and 'Not Negotiable'? | | | | | |
| 2. Are unused cheque books kept in safe custody? | | | | | |
| 3. Is the function of drawing cheques independent from those of ordering goods, payroll preparation, approving invoices and signing cheques? | | | | | |
| 4. Are cheques drawn only against authorised vouchers, remittance advices, etc.? | | | | | |
| 5. Are supporting documents produced to each cheque signatory before payment is made? | | | | | |
| 6. Are at least two signatories required on cheques and are they controlled as to limits of authority? | | | | | |
| 7. Are authorised vouchers immediately stamped paid, or otherwise cancelled to prevent duplicate payment? | | | | | |
| 8. Are the cheques mailed without being returned to the drawers of the cheques? | | | | | |
| 9. Is there independent check to ensure proper discounts are being obtained where possible? | | | | | |
| 10. If cheques carry pre-printed signatures is there adequate control? | | | | | |
| 11. Is the use of blank cheques prohibited? | | | | | |
| 12. Where mechanical signing devices are used, are they under strong control? | | | | | |
| 13. Is there strict control over payments on account and cheques drawn for cash? | | | | | |
| 14. Are all cash payment sheets and cash books checked for casts and cross casts? | | | | | |
| 15. Are all direct debits and standing orders checked for accuracy and authority? | | | | | |
| 16. Is there adequate control over the posting of cash payments to the appropriate general ledger accounts? | | | | | |

the document. In this way, useful clues can be derived as to the official's knowledge of the system, his confidence in it and his thoughts as to problem areas. This can be derived as much by what he does not say, as by what he reveals.

ICQs of the 'yes/no' kind should always be completed on the basis of the systems information derived from client interviews or documentation. Considerable judgement is often necessary to complete them properly, and if not actually completed by the accountant in charge, they should certainly be reviewed by him before the manager/partner review.

## 8.3 Internal Control Evaluations (ICEs)

The format of ICEs varies from firm to firm, even more than that of ICQs. But the principle remains the same – for each aspect of a system, a key control question will concentrate on the frauds or errors that could occur.

There follows a series of 'key control questions', covering the accounting cycles discussed in Chapter 6, extracted from audit documentations provided by Peat, Marwick, Mitchell and Co., and used with their kind permission:

*The Sales Cycle*

1. Can any goods be despatched or leave the premises without being invoiced? Services be rendered without being invoiced? (Including goods on consignment, goods to other branches, samples, etc.)

2. Can goods be sent to a bad credit risk? Overdue accounts escape follow up?

3. Can invoicing errors occur (sales invoiced but not recorded, sales invoiced incorrectly)?

4. Can cash/cheques be received but not banked (including teeming and lading)?

5. Can monies from cash sales be improperly dealt with by
   – persons initially receiving cash?
   – persons handling cash from initial receipt to final banking?

6. Can debtors accounts be improperly credited?

*The Purchases Cycle*

1. Can liabilities be set up for goods or services which are either not authorised or not received?

2. Can liabilities be incurred but not recorded
   (a) for goods
   (b) for services and sundries?

3. Can payments be made if not properly documented or authorised, e.g. incomplete documentation, forged/fraudulent documentation, inadvertent duplicate payments, etc.?

4. Can charges be allocated to the wrong general ledger account?

5. (a) Can goods be returned to suppliers without being recorded in stores and financial records?
   (b) Can claims/credit notes for short deliveries not be raised or recorded?

*The Wages Cycle*

1. Can persons other than genuine employees be paid through the payroll (including fraudulent double payments for leavers, holiday pay, etc.)?

2. Can employees be paid for work not done or unclaimed wages misappropriated?

3. Can payroll errors occur (starters, leavers, rate changes, etc.)?

4. Can deductions from gross pay be improperly made or misappropriated?

5. Can the payroll be inflated in other ways?

*General Cash*

1. Can miscellaneous receipts be omitted?

2. Can non-trading or petty cash payments be made if not authorised?

3. Can cash balances be misappropriated or improperly used?

*General Ledger*

1. Can unauthorised journal entries be processed?

2. Can errors be made in subsidiary ledgers?

*Stocks*

1. Can stocks be lost or pilfered?

2. Can stocks be consumed or wasted without proper recording?

3. Can work in progress be over or understated?

*Fixed Assets*

Can fixed assets be acquired or disposed of without proper authority or recording?
(Based on Peat, Marwick, Mitchell and Co. audit documentation)

In practice, each key control question would be supported by detailed control points to be considered in the context of the system being evaluated. But these detailed points are not necessary for our purposes here, for such matters were extensively dealt with in Chapter 6 on Practical aspects of internal control. So, in the light of Chapter 6, you should now consider the sort of controls that would be necessary to satisfy each control question. But first an example – Key control question 1 of the purchases cycle asked 'Can liabilities be set up for goods or services which are not authorised or not received?'. Controls necessary to prevent such fraud/error may include:

(a) orders based on requisitions originating from outside buying department;
(b) defined authority limits for buyers;
(c) authorisation of purchase orders by someone other than originator and recorded on copies retained;
(d) pre-numbered purchase orders;
(e) approval of expenditure in excess of that on original order;
(f) procedure for reviewing currency of standing orders;
(g) properly designated goods receiving area properly staffed;
(h) independent checking procedure for goods received, including part deliveries;
(i) adequate inspection of goods received;
(j) pre-numbered goods received notes;
(k) invoices received in a department which is separate from buying;
(l) invoices checked against order (including prices and discounts) and goods received notes;
(m) invoices checked for casts and extensions;
(n) overall invoice approval when all steps completed;
(o) authority obtained for opening new accounts in creditors' ledger;
(p) independent creditors' ledger department;
(q) maintenance of independent creditors' ledger control account, and independent reconciliation thereof.

Key control questions can be formulated in many ways, and the only absolute criteria is that all aspects of a system must be covered. An alternative approach to that illustrated above is to concentrate on the controls necessary to prevent specific error or fraud. The basis of this approach (as adopted by Deloitte, Haskins and Sells) is as follows:

*The likelihood of defalcation can be evaluated by determining whether segregation of duties is satisfactory. And the possibility of error can be considered by looking at the checks present in the system in the light of the various types of error possible. The possibility of distortion (normally by senior officials) cannot be readily determined by questionnaires, but may be revealed during the course of evaluation procedures by looking out for signs that the management are under pressure.*

We will now deal in detail with the defalcation and error reviews before looking at distortion. The reviews for defalcation and error may be performed simultaneously or separately, with the latter having some advantage in terms of focusing the attention of the reviewer on the types of problem possible. So for instructional purposes this is the approach I have used here. But you should note that, in practice, it may be appropriate to completely review one accounting area before moving to the next. Before proceeding to the detail of the following

Fig. 8.2 The process of internal control evaluation

ICQs ask whether desirable controls are present in the
accounting system under evaluation.
*whereas*
ICEs concentrate upon the types of possible mis-statement
in the financial statements under review.

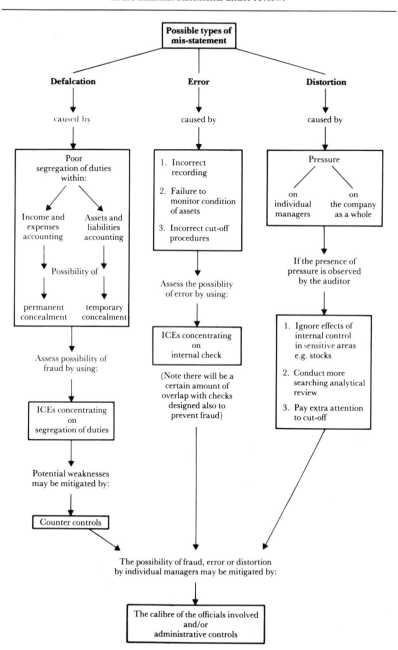

sections, a study of Fig. 8.2 may assist your understanding of the approach now adopted.

## 8.4 ICEs – review for defalcation

This review will be designed to determine what potential exists for deliberately concealing a defalcation of company assets by manipulating records. The assets which need to be considered are those which are both material and readily realisable, and these will clearly include cash and bank balances, stock and often fixed assets, together with any other asset considered vulnerable in the circumstances of a particular audit.

### *Types of defalcation*

A company may suffer the defalcation of a readily realisable asset in the following three ways:

1. An asset may be intercepted before it is recorded. For example, a cashier may take and cash a debtor's remittance cheque and not record its receipt.
2. An asset may be removed after it has been recorded, either by preventing its further use (for example, by not banking a cheque received), or by improperly disposing of it (for example, by issuing an unrecorded cheque).
3. An asset may be diverted after it has been recorded, by improperly converting a proper payment (for example, by increasing the amount of a signed cheque, cashing it, paying the payee the amount due and pocketing the difference). Alternatively, an asset may be diverted by miscrediting the contra for a recorded asset (for example, an employee who has an account with his employer may credit a debtor's payment to his own account).

### *The effect of concealed defalcations*

If a readily realisable asset is misappropriated, then the relevant ledger account must be wrong, since it will overstate the true position. Or alternatively (as in the case where a cheque payable to a creditor is diverted), a liability account could be understated.

To *temporarily* conceal a defalcation, the records must be manipulated each time the relevant assets are checked (if they are never checked, no problems!). This might be achieved for example by incorrect bank reconciliations, by false entries in stock sheets or by 'teeming and lading' on debtors' accounts. This effectively carries the fraud forward in the balance sheet.

To conceal the defalcation *permanently* on the other hand, the shortage will have to be charged to the profit and loss account. This can be achieved either by overstating expense records (e.g. purchases on credit, sales returns, etc.), or by understating income records (e.g. credit sales or miscellaneous income). If a permanent concealment is not discovered during the period in which it occurs, it is unlikely ever to be discovered. Examples of such concealment include the paying of fraudulent invoices, and the insertion of fictitious names on a payroll.

It follows therefore that we will review the possibility of permanent conceal-ment by assessing the segregation of duties in the income and expenses area, and we will examine the likelihood of temporary concealment by assessing the segregation of duties in the balance sheet area.

*Permanent concealment*

The chart shown in Fig. 8.3 (based on that used by Deloitte, Haskins and Sells) covers the segregation of income and expense duties and facilitates the evaluation of the likelihood of permanent defalcation. Along the top of the chart in Blocks A to E there are the five different situations in which persons have access to assets. And down the side of the chart the nine different types of income/expense record are listed. The review process is based on inserting the names of client officials in the boxes provided on the chart, in accordance with the instructions. Note that the names of persons who handle the records are entered all the way across the appropriate row (e.g. Mr Fiddle appears all the way across Row 1). Where the same name appears in one of the blocks, and in one of the rows below, then there is the possibility for fraud. Those areas which are blanked out in the chart have no potential scope for concealing a defalcation. You should thoroughly study the chart and consider the potential dangers that lie in each of the unblanked boxes.

But first an example may help. You will see on the chart that the name of Mr Fiddle, who handles receipts after initial recording, has been recorded in Block B. And the name of Mr Honest, who handles signed cheques, has been recorded in Block C. Mr Honest does not have access to any of the records, so his name does not appear again. But Mr Fiddle appears in Row 1 because he posts the total of the sales journal to the general ledger. So he could misappropriate a cheque received and conceal the defalcation by understating the record of sales made subsequently to that debtor. You will note that this weakness is denoted by a ring around Mr Fiddle's name on the chart. And in the absence of counter controls to mitigate the weakness, we would not be able to reduce substantive testing in this area.

A system of internal control is not necessarily weak merely because a particular person has access to both assets and to the relevant records, because the system may include other controls that counter the potential weakness. For convenience, we will call these *counter controls*, and their operation can be illustrated by con-tinuing the example above. If Mr Fiddle posts incorrectly from the sales summary to the control account in the general ledger, this may be discovered if an in-dependent person posts the sales ledger before the summary is prepared. Of course it will be necessary for an independent person to also frequently reconcile the control account, for this check to be effective. Another illustration of a counter control would be where an employee independently examines all paid cheques for alterations. In this way diverted cheques should be discovered.

You will see on the chart that the key control questions are recorded down the right-hand side. Once the boxes and rows are filled in, the auditor is then in a

Fig. 8.3 Review chart for permanent concealment of defalcation

| | RECORDS | BLOCK A<br>Names of the persons who handle receipts before initial recording. | | BLOCK B<br>Names of the persons who handle receipts after initial recording. | | BLOCK C<br>Names of the persons who issue cheques singly or handle signed cheques. | |
|---|---|---|---|---|---|---|---|
| CLIENT ............................................ | | | | | | | |
| PERIOD............................................ | | | | *FIDDLE* | | *HONEST* | |
| | | Names of the persons who: | | Names of the persons who: | | Names of the persons who: | |
| | | Prepare or test the records | Cast or handle the records | Prepare or test the records | Cast or handle the records | Prepare or test the records | Cast or handle the records |
| ROW 1<br>Credit sales records | Initial records or supporting documents | | | | | | |
| | Intermediate or final records | | *FIDDLE* | | *(FIDDLE)* | | *FIDDLE* |
| | | | | | Cross out the names that do not also appear in row 4 | | |
| ROW 2<br>Cost of sales records | Initial records or supporting documents | | | | | | |
| | Intermediate or final records | | | | | | |
| ROW 3<br>Sales returns and allowances records | Initial records or supporting documents | | | | | | |
| | Intermediate or final records | | | | | | |
| | | | | | Cross out the names that do not also appear in row 4 | | |
| ROW 4<br>Receipt records | Initial records or supporting documents — Collections of trade debts | | | | | | |
| | Initial records or supporting documents — Cash sales and miscellaneous receipts | | | | | | |
| | Intermediate or final records<br>(ICQ page 6 — question 15) | | | | | | |

| BLOCK D | BLOCK E |
|---|---|
| Names of the persons who disburse pay-rolls singly or who handle pay packets or signed pay cheques. | Names of the persons who have sole cust-ody of other readily realisable assets. |
| | |

PREPARED BY.................................................
(Accountant-in-charge)

DATE................................

REVIEWED BY.................................................
(Manager)

DATE................................

| Names of the persons who: | | Names of the persons who: | | Key Questions | Tick | |
|---|---|---|---|---|---|---|
| Prepare or test the records | Cast or handle the records | Prepare or test the records | Cast or handle the records | | Yes | No |
| | | | | Is the segregation of duties adequate to prevent or detect the concealment of defalcation by the under-statement of sales? | | |
| | | | | Is the segregation of duties adequate to prevent or detect the concealment of defalcations by the over-statement of cost of sales? | | |
| | | | | Is the segregation of duties adequate to prevent or detect the concealment of defalcations by the over-statement of sales returns and allowances? | | |
| | | | | Is the segregation of duties adequate to prevent or detect the concealment of defalcations by the over-statement of discount? | | |
| | | | | Is the segregation of duties adequate to prevent or detect the concealment of defalcations by the under-statement of receipts not credited to debtor accounts? | | |

CLIENT ..........................................

PERIOD ..........................................

| | BLOCK A<br>Names of the persons who handle receipts before initial recording. | BLOCK B<br>Names of the persons who handle receipts after initial recording. | BLOCK C<br>Names of the persons who issue cheques singly or handle signed cheques. |
|---|---|---|---|
| | | *FIDDLE* | *HONEST* |

| RECORDS | | Names of the persons who: | | Names of the persons who: | | Names of the persons who: | |
|---|---|---|---|---|---|---|---|
| | | Prepare or test the records | Cast or handle the records | Prepare or test the records | Cast or handle the records | Prepare or test the records | Cast or handle the records |
| ROW 5<br>Purchase records | Initial records or supporting documents | | | | | | |
| | Intermediate or final records | | | *FIDDLE* | | *FIDDLE* | |

Cross out the names that do not also appear in row 6

| | | | | | | | |
|---|---|---|---|---|---|---|---|
| ROW 6<br>Payment records | Initial records or supporting documents | | | | | | |
| | Intermediate or final records | | | | | | |
| ROW 7<br>Wage records | Initial records or supporting documents | | | | | | |
| | Intermediate or final records | | | | | | |
| ROW 8<br>Salary records | Initial records or supporting documents | | | | | | |
| | Intermediate or final records | | | | | | |
| ROW 9<br>Journal and general ledger | Initial records or supporting documents | | | | | | |
| | Intermediate or final records | | | | | | |

| BLOCK D | BLOCK E |
|---|---|
| Names of the persons who disburse pay-rolls singly or who handle pay packets or signed pay cheques. | Names of the persons who have sole custody of other readily realisable assets. |
|  |  |

PREPARED BY.................................................
(Accountant-in-charge)

DATE...............................

REVIEWED BY.................................................
(Manager)

DATE...............................

| Names of the persons who: | | Names of the persons who: | | Key Questions | Tick | |
|---|---|---|---|---|---|---|
| Prepare or test the records | Cast or handle the records | Prepare or test the records | Cast or handle the records | | Yes | No |
|  |  |  |  | Is the segregation of duties adequate to prevent or detect the concealment of defalcations by the over-statement of purchases? |  |  |
|  |  |  |  | Is the segregation of duties adequate to prevent or detect the concealment of defalcations by the over-statement of payments not debited to creditor accounts? |  |  |
|  |  |  |  | Is the segregation of duties adequate to prevent or detect the concealment of defalcations by the over-statement of wages? |  |  |
|  |  |  |  | Is the segregation of duties adequate to prevent or detect the concealment of defalcations by the over-statement of salaries? |  |  |
|  |  |  |  | Is the segregation of duties adequate to prevent or detect the concealment of defalcations by writing them off via the journal or in preparing the general ledger? |  |  |

position to answer the key question by either Yes or No. A 'Yes' answer indicates that control is satisfactory, and that substantive testing can accordingly be minimised. A 'No' answer indicates unsatisfactory segregation of duties, and it is then up to the auditor to determine the extent to which there is real danger. This judgement will be made in the light of counter controls, but you should note that such controls are more prone to failure than a direct control; for the counter control may simply not be performed, or performed inadequately.

*Temporary concealment*

Temporary concealment of a defalcation is possible by overstating assets, or understating liabilities. The review chart shown in Fig. 8.4 assesses the likelihood by reference to segregation of duties, along the lines of the chart for income and expenses.

Fig. 8.4  Review chart for temporary concealment of defalcation

## ICE for Temporary Concealment of Defalcation

### Key control question

Is the segregation of duties adequate to prevent or detect the concealment of defalcation by the overstatement of assets or the understatement of liabilities, in that none of the persons listed below carry out any of the following functions:
1. Handle receipts before initial recording?
2. Handle receipts after initial recording?
3. Issue cheques singly or handle signed cheques?
4. Disburse payrolls singly or handle signed payroll cheques?
5. Have sole custody of other readily realisable assets and their related records?

### Fixed assets

Persons who post the subsidiary records of fixed assets unless independently checked by physical inspection . . . . . . . .
Persons who check subsidiary records of fixed assets by physical inspection and investigate differences . . . . . . . .
Persons who reconcile subsidiary records with control accounts . . . . . . . .

### Investments

Persons who post the subsidiary records of investments unless independently checked by physical inspection . . . . . . . .
Persons who check subsidiary records of investments by physical inspection and investigate differences . . . . . . . .
Persons who reconcile the subsidiary records of investments with the control accounts in the general ledger . . . . . . . .

### Intangibles and deferred charges

Persons who post the subsidiary records of intangibles and deferred charges . . . . . . .
Persons who reconcile the subsidiary records of intangibles and deferred charges with the control account in the general ledger . . . . . . . .
Persons who authorise transfers to and from the intangibles and deferred charges records . . . . . . . .

### Creditors, accruals and provisions

Persons who post the subsidiary records of creditors unless independently checked by reconciliation with suppliers' statements ........
Persons who reconcile the subsidiary records of creditors with suppliers' statements ........
Persons who reconcile the subsidiary records of creditors with the control account in the general ledger ........

### Debtors and prepayments

Persons who post the subsidiary records of debtors unless checked by the independent preparation and despatch of statements to all customers ........
Persons who prepare or despatch statements to customers, or receive or investigate queries, or who authorise transfers between individual debtors accounts ........
Persons who reconcile the subsidiary records of debtors with the control account in the general ledger ........
Persons who approve the write-off of debtors ........

## Stock (periodic system)

## Key control questions

### Existence

Do the stocktaking instructions and procedures ensure that persons who have sole custody of stocks do not:
(a) have sole responsibility for counting items, or
(b) have access to stocktaking sheets or tags, at any time, or
(c) act as experts where stocks are difficult to identify?

### Valuation

Do the valuation procedures ensure that persons who have sole custody of stocks do not have sole responsibility for:
(a) valuing any item of stock, or
(b) extending, casting or otherwise summarising the stock sheets, or
(c) reconciling physical stocks with the stock control account in the general ledger and investigating any significant differences?

You should note that exhaustive though such reviews can be, they should not be expected to reveal all the possibilities for fraud. For example, no controls can forestall the danger of defalcation if two or more employees act in collusion (though the auditor should always be on the look out for suspicious circumstances, such as married couples or blood relatives checking each other's work, or more subtly where personalities are such that one person is dominated by another).

Apparent weaknesses in control may be mitigated by strong administrative controls. And the danger associated with uncontrolled officials may be offset by the calibre and seniority of such persons. But these are all areas where the auditor's mature and experienced judgement is required. So you will see that it is not all just auditing 'by numbers'!

## 8.5 ICEs – review for error

Although adequate segregation of duties can prevent the possibility of fraud, it may not necessarily prevent errors being made. Both can render the accounts materially misleading. So we need to ensure that:

(a) the final records of transactions contain *only* valid transactions, and also contain *all* transactions;
(b) all assets are maintained in good condition;
(c) the recording of the movement of assets is synchronised with the physical movements of those assets, so that a clean 'cut-off' is achieved at the end of the accounting period.

### Controls over recording

If the accounting system is to process only valid transactions, it is essential that the documents used for recording should be properly authorised and executed. For example, purchase invoices need to be supported by purchase orders that have been approved at the appropriate level, and by documentary evidence that the goods concerned have been received. Checks to ensure proper processing will include the checking of approvals, calculations, account allocations and postings, as well as the regular reconciliation of general ledger control accounts with subsidiary ledgers, and of bank accounts with bank statements.

### Controls over the condition of assets

The condition of assets must be regularly and properly reviewed in order to ensure that asset values are not over-recorded. A company's assets may deteriorate or be lost if, for example, those persons who have responsibility for establishing control over the granting of credit to customers, or for storing stocks in suitable locations, or for insuring company property, fail so to do.

### Controls over cut-off

The essence of a cut-off procedure is that initially a cut-off point is established on prenumbered despatch notes and goods received notes, and then later all the items up to that cut-off point are accounted for in the records. Unless this is done, purchases, sales or stock could be wrongly stated in the accounts. For example, where there is a time lag between the despatching of goods and the recording of those despatches as sales, items of stock which have been despatched before the year-end stocktaking may not be recorded as sales until the new year; and sales, therefore, could be understated.

To illustrate these points, key control questions are shown in Figs. 8.5 and 8.6 for sales. These questions are all designed to test whether a system is susceptible to error. Subsidiary questions follow each key question, and these should be used in answering the key question correctly.

Fig. 8.5 Example of internal control evaluation for error – sales

## ICE Review for Error Sales

|  | Yes | No |
|---|---|---|
| Are controls designed to ensure that all goods despatched or services rendered are subsequently invoiced? | ___ | ___ |

Consider:
Are despatch records or services rendered records prepared for all sales of:
(a) Goods?
(b) Services?
Are all appropriate independent records (such as despatch records, customer purchase orders, service records or contracts) accounted for (by sequence checks or other methods) and are they compared with initial credit sales records to ensure that all goods and services are charged to customers?
Are invoices prepared and mailed promptly after the despatch of goods or the rendering of services?

| Are controls designed to ensure that all amounts invoiced are recorded in the accounts? | ___ | ___ |
|---|---|---|

Consider:
Are sales invoices checked in respect of:
(a) Prices and terms?
(b) Quantities?
(c) Extensions and casts?
Are sales records controlled by being prenumbered and checked to ensure that all sales are included in:
(a) Initial records?
(b) Intermediate records?
(c) Final records?
(d) Postings to the general ledger accounts?
Are sales records checked to ensure that all casts and cross-casts are correct in:
(a) Initial records?
(b) Intermediate records?
(c) Final records?
Are sales recorded in the correct accounting period (i.e. the period in which goods are despatched or services are rendered):
(a) At interim accounting dates during the financial year?
(b) At the balance sheet date?

| Are controls designed to prevent the raising of invalid sales credit notes? | ___ | ___ |
|---|---|---|

Consider:
Is the issue of sales credit notes supported by adequate evidence?
Are sales credit notes approved by an appropriate official?
Are sales credit notes checked in respect of:
(a) Prices?
(b) Quantities?
(c) Extensions and casts?

| Are controls designed to prevent invalid sales returns and allowances being recorded in the accounts? | ___ | ___ |
|---|---|---|

Consider:
Are sales returns and allowances records controlled by being prenumbered or checked to ensure that only valid sales returns and allowances are included in:
(a) Initial records?
(b) Intermediate records?
(c) Final records?
(d) Postings to the general ledger accounts?

Are sales returns and allowances checked to ensure that all casts and
cross-casts are correct in:
(a) Initial records?
(b) Intermediate records?
(c) Final records?
Are final records checked to ensure that postings to the general ledger
accounts are correct?

Fig. 8.6 Example of internal control evaluation for error – debtors and prepayments

## Debtors and Prepayments

|  | Yes | No |
|---|---|---|

### Existence and ownership

Are controls designed to prevent invalid debtors being recorded in the
accounts?
Consider:
Are sales records prepared or checked to ensure that only valid sales are
included in:
(a) Initial records?
(b) Intermediate records?
(c) Final records?
(d) Postings to the general ledger accounts?
Are sales returns and allowances records prepared or checked to ensure
that all sales returns and allowances are included in:
(a) Initial records?
(b) Intermediate records?
(c) Final records?
(d) Postings to the general ledger accounts?
Are sales returns and allowances recorded in the correct accounting period
(i.e. the accounting period in which the corresponding sales are made):
(a) At interim accounting dates during the financial year?
(b) At the balance sheet date?
Are customer statements prepared and despatched to all customers
promptly and with reasonable frequency?
Are the subsidiary records of debtors reconciled with the general ledger
accounts promptly, thoroughly and with reasonable frequency (state period
. . . . . . . . weekly/monthly/quarterly)?

### Valuation

Are controls designed to prevent the despatch of goods or the rendering of
services to customers who are a bad credit risk?
Consider:
Are customers' purchase orders (or their equivalent) approved before
despatch of goods or the rendering of services:
(a) As to prices?
(b) As to credit and other terms?

Are controls designed to prevent doubtful debtors being included in the
accounts at full value?
Consider:
Does a responsible official review an aged analysis of debtors reasonably
frequently and investigate debtors outstanding for longer than the normal
credit period?

## 8.6 ICEs – considering the results

Where weaknesses are revealed by the ICEs, we must see whether they are mitigated by the calibre of the officials involved, or by administrative controls. An auditor is entitled to rely upon the honesty of senior officials, unless there is any matter which arouses suspicion, such as:

(a) the granting of excessive powers either to new employees or to employees of comparatively low calibre;

(b) a policy of paying wages that are below the average for the locality or the industry;

(c) the unexplained extravagance of any employee;

(d) the refusal of an employee to take his due holiday (which may be because he wishes to avoid having his duties subjected to the independent scrutiny of a relief employee);

(e) employees who either adopt an uncooperative or antagonistic attitude to auditors, or who appear to be excessively cooperative;

(f) the unexplained domination of any department, branch, or activity by one particular person;

(g) books of accounts which are consistently written up a long time after the transactions which they record have taken place;

(h) filing systems where, for no apparently good reason, documents are difficult to retrieve.

Where specific problems manifest themselves, it is usually appropriate to carry out tests on the specific weakness in order to obtain satisfaction that no material frauds have been perpetrated. So long as the system is generally satisfactory, it may still be appropriate to reduce the level of substantive testing.

Where the ICEs reveal the possibility of error, it will be necessary to decide whether the danger is mitigated by other controls, such as:

(a) the management's practice of studying variances from cash forecasts, standard costs, budgets or the results of prior periods;

(b) a system of either assignment or responsibility reporting (where each employee is continuously assessed and reported upon by his superiors);

(c) quality control procedures (particularly if these are substantiated by independent production control procedures);

(d) the use of either production and stock statistics, or perpetual records to trace shortages in stocks;

(e) engineering or supervisory reviews of a kind that hold employees to given standards of performance (e.g. in respect of material usage and the number of hours worked);

(f) the intimate personal knowledge that some members of management may have of operating and financial activities, which enable them to detect irregularities. This is likely to apply more to small companies, but it may also be applicable in some departments or branches of larger companies;

(g) overall tests by supervisory personnel (such as reconciling production figures and stock quantities with sales, applying tests of gross profits, carefully scrutinising turnover statistics or reviewing comparative costs);

(h) the operation of an effective and well-organised internal audit department, which reports directly to top management.

## 8.7 Review for distortion

We saw earlier that distortion is likely to occur where there is pressure on management; either as a result of the current or future unsatisfactory performance of the company as a whole, or of individual managers.

*Unsatisfactory performance of the client's business as a whole*

The auditor should first look for *signs of deterioration.*
1. In the recent past –
    (a) a declining trend in the company's normal trading income or profits;
    (b) a declining trend in the performance of the company, as compared with the performance of other companies in the same industry;
2. In the near future –
    (a) a significant dependence on new products or new services where these involve uncertainties as regards either technical development or market potential;
    (b) signs that the demand for the client's products or services may decline (e.g. increasing competition, a saturated market or the obsolescence of the client's products);
    (c) a significant dependence on one or two suppliers for essential raw materials, or a few customers for the majority of the sales turnover;
    (d) the possible adverse effects on the business of government action.
    The likelihood of *difficulty in meeting financial obligations* should then be examined. For example, the following situations would cause concern:
(a) the proceeds of short-term borrowings invested in assets which can only be realised in the long term;
(b) the expected cash flow for the year is inadequate to meet both the anticipated requirements for working capital and payments to investors;
(c) restrictions on future availability of credit;
(d) repayment of a loan due in the near future, but insufficient funds.
    Finally the auditor should have regard to circumstances which may indicate that *more significance will be placed upon the accounts than usual.* For example, where:
(a) the client's past performance has been significantly better than the industry average;
(b) the client's management plans to shortly issue loans or equity stock;
(c) a contest for control of the company appears likely;
(d) the accounts may be used in connection with litigation;
(e) a profit forecast has been previously made (and appears unlikely to be met).

*Unsatisfactory performance of individual members of management*

If the performance of individual members of management is unsatisfactory, or if their attitude or competence is likely to be questioned, they may be tempted to improve their personal positions by distorting the true results. Indications of this possibility include:

1. Significant differences in operating or accounting philosophies between new members of management and their predecessors.
2. Unrealistic budgets, which may cause middle management to distort the accounts to produce the results that the budgets demand.
3. Remuneration which is derived to a large extent from bonuses or commissions.
4. Earlier profit forecasts, which seem to have been unduly optimistic.

*Distortion is most likely to be achieved by:*
(a) altering judgement valuations of assets or provisions;
(b) capitalising items which should be charged against profit;
(c) manipulating the cut-off procedures at the balance sheet date. Management are less likely to distort the accounts by inventing large volumes of transactions (although the gigantic 'Equity Funding' fraud in America was a significant exception to this).

*If the possibility of distortion is suspected,* then one or a combination of the following techniques will be necessary:
(a) ignoring the effect of internal control in such sensitive areas as stocks, debtors, creditors, and fixed assets;
(b) conducting a particularly searching analytical review (especially of the figures towards the end of the year);
(c) increasing the extent of cut-off tests.

In extreme cases, it may be necessary to increase the overall amount of substantive testing. But you should note that simply because circumstances indicate the possibility of distortion, it does not necessarily mean that distortion has occurred. The client's officials may even be honest!

## 8.8 Compliance testing

Before we can be confident in our evaluations, we must carry out compliance tests to ensure that the accounting system (upon which the internal control evaluation has been based) has been working satisfactorily throughout the year. Only after such tests have been completed can we determine whether we can safely rely upon internal control as a means of reducing substantive testing.

We must ensure that all controls upon which we place reliance have been working properly *throughout the year.* So it is essential that transaction tests are chosen from the entire period. Compliance tests will be performed on any procedure upon which reliance is placed. For example, if we have based our reliance on the validity of overtime claimed, on the fact that a foreman approves all overtime worked, we must check that this procedure has been complied with. So it will be helpful in designing compliance tests to note during our evaluation procedures those procedures that we are in fact relying upon.

The way in which a procedure will be tested for compliance depends upon whether or not written evidence is available. *Written evidence* will be examined as a normal part of detailed testing (two examples of this kind of evidence are the completion of a checking stamp on a purchase invoice, and the signature of an authorised official on an invoice as evidence of approval). So it makes sense to carry out compliance testing based on written evidence at the same time as substantive testing, and on the same transaction sample (for this reason, a detailed discussion of the principles involved in sample selection has been left until we examine substantive testing in Chapters 10, 11 and 12). But it must be said that simultaneous testing is not always appropriate, and some firms may prefer to have positive evidence that they can rely on internal control before proceeding to their substantive tests. In this case separate samples will be chosen for the tests at each stage. Note that the principles of depth testing (see sec. 12.4) are particularly applicable in these circumstances.

Simultaneous completion only applies in any event to situations where there is (or should be) written evidence of compliance. Where the internal control procedure provides *no written evidence* that it has in fact been carried out, then discreet enquiry and observation will have to be used. And to do this effectively involves using a mixture of common sense and ingenuity. It will always be preferable to observe a procedure casually, rather than making formal arrangements, and it follows, therefore, that we stand a better chance of obtaining the necessary evidence if we carry out our audit work in the department which is being audited (rather than hiding away in the audit room!).

If the compliance testing shows that the system of internal control is not operating in practice, it will of course be necessary to revise our evaluation in accordance with the way in which it is actually working. This may mean that the volume of substantive testing will have to be increased. You should note that in compliance testing it is not the amount of an error that is important – materiality is not relevant in this context. For any error, no matter what the size, indicates that the client's own checking system is not working properly. And this is what is of immediate concern to us.

## 8.9 Reporting to management

Once we have evaluated the client's internal control system, we should discuss any weaknesses with the appropriate officials involved. This will eliminate the possibility that we may have misunderstood the operation of the system, and, more important, will enable the company to take corrective action. And the quicker such corrective action is taken, the less substantive testing that will be necessary in the *remainder* of the year (note that substantive testing in the area of weakness cannot be reduced until the time that effective corrective action is taken).

All significant weaknesses should be discussed with the chief accountant (or equivalent) after discussion with the official responsible (if fraud is suspected, it will be necessary to go directly to senior management). And it will then be necessary to document these matters in a report to management. This report should be addressed to the board of directors, with a copy to the chief accountant (or if the company has an audit committee – unlikely! – it should be addressed to them; see Ch. 2).

The timing of the report will vary. It will often be useful to complete the compliance testing before submission, in order that breakdowns in the accounting system may be included in addition to the weaknesses discovered through evaluation. On the other hand, serious weaknesses should be reported upon immediately. So it will often be appropriate to submit more than one report. In any event, a report will usually be sent after each audit attendance, and certainly should be made at the completion of the final audit. In this latter report, comments will be made in addition to those on weaknesses and breakdowns in internal control. These will include issues concerning the final accounts, such as accounting policies and presentation. But more to this later.

A well drafted report can serve to extend the role of the audit beyond that of simply reporting upon the periodic accounts, as it can assist the management in running their company more efficiently. And this in turn can help to promote a constructive relationship between auditor and client management, which will assist in the conduct of future audits. On the other hand, if things should go wrong, the report may possibly protect the audit firm against subsequent recriminations. For if weaknesses are merely discussed without confirmation in writing, there is always the danger that the client could blame the auditors for any subsequent problems resulting from failure to rectify these weaknesses. And the auditors would have no documentary defence.

It is essential that the report is both realistic and constructive (for this reason, I prefer not to use the common term 'Letter of Weakness' when describing the report; such a description has a negative and critical implication, which could antagonise management). So the '*Report to Management*' should contain appropriate recommendations concerning all weaknesses in internal control, which should be commented on in their order of significance. And the recommendations should be both practical, and as economic as is feasible. In no circumstances should measures be recommended which are likely to result in costs disproportionately heavy in relation to the assets or liabilities involved. A reply should be both requested and followed up.

Both breakdowns and weaknesses in internal control may well necessitate audit work in excess of what would otherwise be required. Accordingly it will be necessary to advise the client in the report as to the likely extra time required, and of course to warn him of the higher fee!

The final report to management will be dealt with in Chapter 17.

## 8.10 Conclusion

Armed with our evaluation of the likelihood of defalcation, error or distortion, we can now determine:

1. Whether the accounting system is sufficiently reliable to enable us to express an opinion on the figures produced, and to report to the effect that proper

accounting records have been maintained, and if so,

2. The amount of substantive testing necessary for us to express such an opinion.

Remember that we can derive our confidence in the accounts in three ways: internal control, tests of detail and analytical review. It is never appropriate to eliminate any of these techniques, but the proportion of confidence that will be derived from each will vary from audit to audit. Some firms use mathematical formula to determine the proportions, and this can have advantages in terms of conformity of approach, and a disciplined application of a firm's procedures. But in the last resort it becomes a matter of judgement. And here there is no substitute for experience. In Chapters 10 and 11 we discuss just how the volume of substantive testing may be determined, based on the assessment of internal control. But now for some case studies to test your understanding of internal control procedures.

# 9
## Case studies in systems evaluation

## 9.1 Introduction

We have seen that the current audit approach relies on an evaluation of the accounting system. Now a problem that some students of auditing face is that they have little familiarity with the accounting systems of larger corporations, which are usually the basis of examination questions.

It is clearly not possible to evaluate something that you do not understand. So the following case studies have been included to give an illustration of the overall accounting information flow within a business, to demonstrate the principles of internal control that were introduced in Chapters 5 and 6, and to give practice in evaluation techniques. There are case studies covering the major aspects of business transactions. Each case study is based upon a simplified accounting information flow system depicted in the form of a flow chart. To help demonstrate the meaning and significance of internal controls, fundamental weaknesses have been introduced into the systems, and the dangers of these weaknesses, together with possible corrective action, are explained in the form of a report to management (see sec. 8.9).

You should initially approach a case study by reading the flow chart several times to familiarise yourself with the system. Then try to identify the main weaknesses in internal control; both those which could give rise to error, and those that could allow fraud to occur. Remember the segregation of duties principle:

Initiation – Authorisation – Raising Documentation – Custody of Related Assets – Recording in the Accounting Records.

And you may find it helpful to refer to the ICEs in the previous chapter, and to the general principles discussed in Chapter 6. You could usefully fill in the fraud/error review charts to give practice in their completion. No specific names of employees have been given, for this would make the case studies unnecessarily voluminous. But the required result will be achieved by entering the department title into the segregation of duties boxes. This would indeed be entirely realistic assuming we had made the audit judgement that persons in a given department were dependant upon each other. For each weakness that you identify, you should try to draft an appropriate recommendation, in accordance with the principles discussed in sec. 8.9. If you then formulate these into a report to management, it will be a good day's work! But don't cheat and look at my example reports first!

## 9.2 Case study number one – the sales cycle

*Introduction*

Fundamentals Ltd is a wholesale company supplying the electrical trade. It carries approximately 3,000 stock lines featured in its catalogue, and no other items are sold. The company's capitalisation is £1 million, the average annual turnover £2 million, and the average annual net profit after corporation tax is £150,000.

Customers receive a trade order form which contains a list of all the company's products together with their part numbers, cost and a space to enter the quantity required. A new form is sent out with each completed order.

The organisation of the company is illustrated by Fig. 9.1. Figure 9.2 shows the accounting system–sales function. Figure 9.3 shows the report to management.

Fig. 9.1 Organisation chart of Fundamentals Ltd

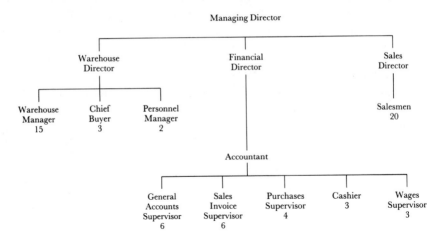

Figures indicate number of employees per department

Fig. 9.2 Fundamentals Ltd – sales cycle

| Notes | Step | Warehouse | Sales invoicing |
|---|---|---|---|
| Order received from customers by post or phone order received by telephonist and order form made out by her | 1 | | |
| Order serially numbered by clerk | 2 | | |
| Delete lines not available | 3 | | |
| Goods per order selected and packed | 4 | | |
| Extensions calculated | 5 | | |
| Each order is pre-listed | 6 | | |
| Four-part invoice set made out and serially numbered with order numbers | 7 | | |
| Invoice checked to pre-list | 8 | | |
| Pre-list destroyed | 9 | | |
| Top copy of invoice stapled to order | 10 | | |
| Invoice and order attached to goods | 11 | | |
| Blank order form enclosed | 12 | | |
| Invoice order and blank order sent to customer | 13 | | |

| Sales | | | | Sales invoicing | General accounts |
|---|---|---|---|---|---|
| Notes | Step | Warehouse | | | |
| Serial numbering checked | 14 | | | | |
| Invoice 2 filed numerically | 15 | | | | |
| Invoice 3 filed in alphabetical order | 16 | | | | |
| Invoice 4 filed in awaiting posting file | 17 | | | | |
| All invoices for posting are pre-listed | 18 | | | | |
| Invoices are posted to sales ledger twice a week. A statement and a proof sheet are produced at the same time as the individual and control sales ledger cards are posted. (If no sales A/C card the operator prepares one from information on invoice) | 19 | | | | |
| Proof sheet agreed with pre-list | 20 | | | | |
| Pre-list filed in date order | 21 | | | | |
| Proof sheet posted to sales A/C in general ledger | 22 | | | | |
| Proof sheet filed in date order | 23 | | | | |
| Invoices filed alphabetically | 24 | | | | |
| Sales A/C returned to NCR ledger tray | 25 | | | | |

Note: NCR = National Cash Register CO. accounting machine

Pre-list
Proof sheet
Control card
Sales Ledger account card
Statement
Sales Account/General Ledger
Invoice 2
Invoice 3
Invoice 4

Sales

| Notes | Step | General accounts | | | Cashier |
|---|---|---|---|---|---|

| Notes | Step |
|---|---|
| Cash book sent to general accounts twice a week | 26 |
| Receipts posted to sales A/C, statement, control card and proof sheet simultaneously | 27 |
| Total of proof sheet agreed to cash book | 28 |
| Statements sent out once a month by machine supervisor | 29 |
| Total of sales A/Cs. listed monthly by machine operator | 30 |
| List of A/Cs. agreed to control card monthly by machine operator | 31 |
| List filed in date order | 32 |
| Sales A/C and control card returned to NCR tray. Proof sheet filed in date order | 33 |
| Cash book returned to cashier | 34 |

*Note*

1. The sales ledger goes to assistant accountant for credit control purposes

2. The warehouse manager has sole responsibility for issuing credit notes to customers

Fig. 9.3 Fundamentals Ltd – report to management

Fundamentals Ltd

The Managing Director

cc The Chief Accountant

Dear Sir,

We write to formally draw your attention to certain areas of weakness in your company's internal control, which we discovered during our recent audit attendance. We consider it essential that these weaknesses be remedied in order to reduce the likelihood of fraud and error, so as to ensure that the accounting system may prove a reliable basis for the preparation of the annual financial statements. We would point out that these matters have already been discussed with appropriate company officials.

1.0 *Warehouse*

1.1 We are concerned over the fact that the warehouse has complete control over accepting orders, despatching goods and raising sales invoices. Goods could be despatched on fraudulent orders, and sales invoices never raised. Alternatively sales invoices may be understated if collusion between employees and customers occurs.

1.2 In order to prevent any irregularities, we strongly recommend that the sales function be divorced from the warehouse, with invoices being sent by sales invoicing department directly to customers. We further suggest that all goods despatched should have a serially numbered goods outwards note raised on them, and that no goods should be allowed out of the gates without such a note. These notes can subsequently be used to ensure that all goods despatched have sales invoices raised in respect of them.

2.0 *Credit control*

2.1 We noted that the debtors accounts are checked by the Accountant once a month only for long overdue accounts.

2.2 We feel that the system would be considerably strengthened if the creditworthiness of new customers was checked before granting credit, and if credit limits were checked before the despatch of goods.

3.0 *Credit notes*

3.1 The present arrangements for granting credit notes are not satisfactory in that the warehouse staff could conceal the misappropriation of goods by raising false credit notes.

3.2 Employees from other than the warehouse or sales sections, should approve credit notes, and then only on the basis of Goods Returned Notes or other appropriate documentation.

4.0 *Sales ledger*

4.1 There is no assurance that all invoices are posted to the sales ledger because the invoice sequence test is carried out on the invoice copy which is immediately filed. The posting copies of the invoice should be checked for sequence by the sales ledger department, prior to posting. In addition it may be useful to have a pre-list of invoices raised in Sales Invoicing and independently checked to the Sales Ledger proof sheet.

4.2 Furthermore the practice of sending the cash book to General Accounts for posting should be discontinued. The cash book could be manipulated to conceal fraud.

4.3 The monthly reconciliation of control accounts to the subsidiary sales ledger is not a strong check as it is not independently verified. An independent senior official should check this reconciliation, at the same time checking totals of cash received from the cash book and totals of invoices raised, from the pre-list mentioned in 4.1 above.

4.4 Before despatch, statements should be checked to the reconciled subsidiary ledger by an independent person, as a precaution against 'teeming and lading'.

5.0 *Telephone orders*

5.1 The present practice of accepting telephone orders could lead to errors or irregularities, as mistakes are easily made over the phone and there is no documentary proof that an order has been validly placed by a genuine customer.

5.2 Accordingly we would recommend that only written orders be accepted. We appreciate that this may not always be possible, but would recommend that any urgent orders placed by phone should be approved by a senior official and confirmed immediately in writing.

6.0 *Orders*

6.1 In addition to our comments in 5.0 above we feel that the orders themselves need a greater degree of control. The company does not at present retain a copy of the order so that there is nothing to refer back to for checking customer queries. More seriously, as the order is at present the despatch document, there is nothing against which to check that all goods outwards have been invoiced and recorded.

6.2 We suggest that the orders be serially numbered and a duplicate retained. The serial numbering can be related to the invoice numbering, and a sequence check can be carried out to ensure all goods outwards are invoiced and recorded in the sales ledger.

7.0 *Efficiency*

7.1 We note that out of stock items are simply deleted from orders.
We feel that customer relations and profitability could be considerably improved if provisions were made:

(i) to advise customers of non-availability,

(ii) to obtain out of stock items,

(iii) to process uncompleted orders.

We point out that the above observations do not arise from any special survey, but came to our attention during the course of usual audit procedures. Hence they are not necessarily exhaustive.

We consider it imperative that these weaknesses be remedied as soon as possible, and would point out that their presence has necessitated a greater degree of audit work than would otherwise have been the case. We would be pleased to discuss any of these matters further, and would be grateful if in due course you would advise us in writing of the action you propose to take or have taken in relation to each of the points raised.

Yours faithfully,
M. J. Pratt, BA, FCA

## 9.3  Case study number two – the purchases cycle

*Introduction*

Better Buying Ltd is an engineering company with 1,000 employees, a turnover of £20 million, and a capitalisation of £5 million. The organisation of the company is illustrated by Fig. 9.4. Figure 9.5 shows the accounting system–purchases function. Figure 9.6 shows the report to management.

## 9.4  Case study number three – the wages cycle

*Introduction*

Wasteful Wages Ltd is a manufacturing company with approximately 250 employees paid on time work. There is a personnel department consisting of a manager and secretary, and a wages department with four clerks and a supervisor. The accounting system for wages is handwritten. Figure 9.7 shows the accounting system – wages function. Figure 9.8 shows the report to management.

Fig. 9.4 Better Buying Ltd – organisation chart

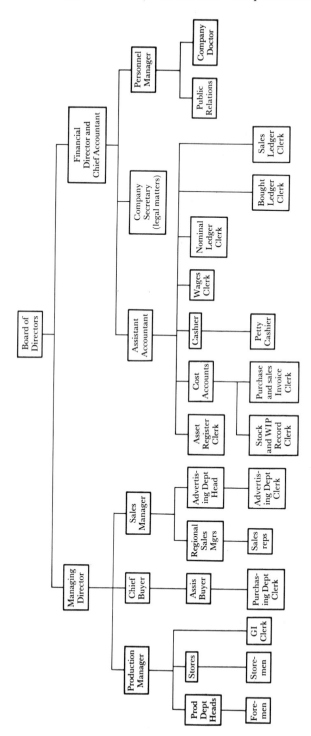

Fig. 9.5 **Better Buying Ltd – purchases cycle**

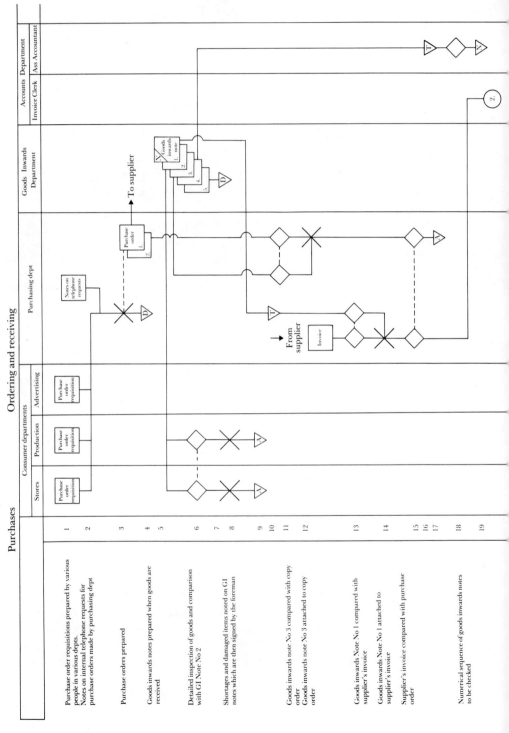

Purchases

Ordering and receiving

| | |
|---|---|
| 1 | Purchase order requisitions prepared by various people in various depts. |
| 2 | Notes on internal telephone requests for purchase orders made by purchasing dept |
| 3 | Purchase orders prepared |
| 4 | Goods inwards notes prepared when goods are |
| 5 | received |
| 6 | Detailed inspection of goods and comparison with GI Note No 2 |
| 7 | Shortages and damaged items noted on GI |
| 8 | notes which are then signed by the foreman |
| 9 | |
| 10 | |
| 11 | Goods inwards Note No 3 compared with copy order |
| 12 | Goods inwards note No 3 attached to copy order |
| 13 | Goods inwards Note No 1 compared with supplier's invoice |
| 14 | Goods inwards Note No 1 attached to supplier's invoice |
| 15 | Supplier's invoice compared with purchase |
| 16 | order |
| 17 | |
| 18 | Numerical sequence of goods inwards notes to be checked |
| 19 | |

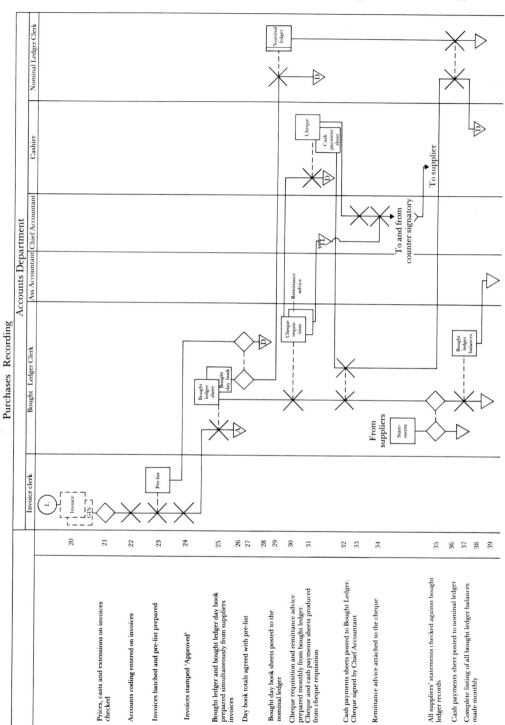

Fig. 9.6 Better Buying Ltd – report to management

Better Buying Ltd

The Managing Director

cc The Chief Accountant

Dear Sir,

We write to formally draw your attention to certain areas of weakness in your company's internal control, which we discovered during our recent audit attendance. We consider it essential that these weaknesses be remedied in order to reduce the likelihood of fraud and error, so as to ensure that the accounting system may prove a reliable basis for the preparation of the annual financial statements. We would point out that these matters have already been discussed with appropriate company officials.

1.0 *Requisitioning*

1.1 At present purchase order requisitions are prepared by various people in various departments. In order to reduce the likelihood of fraudulent requisitions, only duly authorised people in each department should be allowed to requisition goods. And the number of people so authorised should be kept to a minimum.

1.2 Telephone requisitions are currently part of the system. Formal written requisitions can act as a check on the purchasing department, if they are examined at the authorisation stage. But telephone requests nullify this check, because any order placed without a requisition could be explained away in this manner. We accordingly recommend that telephone requests should always be subsequently supported by a duly authorised requisition.

2.0 *Purchasing department*

2.1 There would seem to be no authorisation procedure in relation to requisitions, and no approval procedure in relation to orders placed. Senior officials should be designated for both these tasks.

2.2 Only two copies of the purchase order are produced. There would be advantage in preparing additional copies to notify the requisitioner that the order has been placed (and thus to prevent the possibility of duplicate requisitions), and to advise goods inwards of what to expect. More important, a copy of the order should go to the accounts department for purposes of approving the invoice when it subsequently arrives.

2.3 Goods are inspected by the user departments for shortages and damaged items, but only on the basis of the goods inwards notes, not by reference to the order. Furthermore, deficiencies are merely noted on the Goods Inwards Note, which is then filed. An inspection note should be raised at this stage, and sent to the accounts department, to be used as part of the approval procedure. This will also enable accounts to raise debit notes for the shortages to the supplier concerned.

3.0 *Purchasing department*

3.1 Controls over the purchasing department are currently very weak, for there is little to prevent junior officials in the department from raising orders for purchases of items for their own benefit. Alternatively they could introduce fraudulent invoices into the system in order to misappropriate company funds.

3.2 We accordingly recommend that invoice approval should not be carried out in the purchasing department. Instead, copies of approved orders, approved requisitions, goods inwards notes and inspection notes should all be routed to accounts department. Invoice approval can then be carried out by an independent official on the basis of approved documentation.

4.0 *Invoice approval*

4.1 The present invoice approval procedure is weak because of the inadequate segregation of duties as discussed in 3.0 above.

4.2 The accounts coding should be entered on the invoice on the basis of coding noted on the order. The accounts clerk cannot necessarily be expected to know what each order is for, on the basis of invoice and GIN alone. Accordingly there is a danger of mis-allocation.

4.3 Although the assistant accountant checks the numerical sequence of GINs, there is little value in the procedure because no attempt is made to ensure that all goods are recorded in purchases by matching GINs to invoices.

5.0 *Payment authorisation*

5.1 At no stage are supporting documents to a payment examined by a senior official. Either the invoice clerk, or the bought ledger clerk are in a position to enter false invoices into the system for payment. And as genuine invoices are not cancelled (other than by the invoice clerk's own approval stamp) they could be represented in support of a second (fraudulent) payment. So it is essential that a senior official, such as the assistant accountant, authorises all, or possibly a selected sample, of the invoices before a cheque is drawn. And at the same time he should cancel them to prevent subsequent re-presentation.

5.2 Indeed, the bought ledger clerk would not even have to produce fraudulent documentation to perpetrate fraud, for the cheque is drawn and signed on the basis of the remittance advice that he produces. So remittance advices should perhaps be prepared by an independent person.

5.3 A pre-list is currently used to check that all invoices are included in the bought day book. While this may be a useful check against error, it would be a stronger control if it was carried out independently by the assistant accountant. In this way, the activities of the bought ledger clerk could be subject to internal check.

5.4 Remittance advices are routed independently to the chief accountant. So he has a basis upon which to ensure the cheque has been completed correctly by the cashier. However, this control is weakened by the fact that the signed cheque is returned to the cashier, who is thus in a position to fraudulently alter it to commit a defalcation. Alteration could be straightforward, as the cheque will be in the cashier's writing, and could have been drawn originally with alteration in mind. Either the payee or the amount could be altered. The former perhaps to a name in which the cashier has an account, the latter to misappropriate funds through collusion with a supplier, or perhaps by cashing the cheque, paying the supplier the correct amount, and pocketing the difference.

6.0 *Reconciliations*

6.1 Statements are currently checked against bought ledger records, but there is no evidence that accounts are reconciled and differences thoroughly investigated. Furthermore, the checking is now performed by the bought ledger clerk, and as we pointed out above, he is in a very strong position to perpetrate fraud. A check on the reconciliations by an independent person would accordingly strengthen control.

6.2 A list of bought ledger balances is currently prepared and retained by the chief accountant, but no attempt is made to reconcile this list with the nominal ledger control account. This reconciliation could usefully be performed by the assistant accountant on a regular basis.

We point out that the above observations do not arise from any special survey, but came to our attention during the course of usual audit procedures. Hence they are not necessarily exhaustive.

We consider it imperative that these weaknesses be remedied as soon as possible, and would point out that their presence has necessitated a greater degree of audit work than would otherwise have been the case.

We would be pleased to discuss any of these matters further, and would be grateful if in due course you would advise us in writing of the action you propose to take or have taken in relation to each of the points raised.

Yours faithfully,
M. J. Pratt, BA, FCA

Approx 250 employees on time work

Hourly paid wages

| Op. no. | Personnel dept (Personnel manager and secretary) | Factory | Wages dept | Cashiers dept |
|---|---|---|---|---|

Employee records (1 to 7)
Change documents raised for starters and leavers, changes in wage rates and in deduction amounts — 1

Entered on employees' personal records — 2

3

Entered on personal wage record — 4

5

Filed in clock number order — 6

7

Payroll preparation (8 to 21)

Clock card received from factory — 8, 9

No of hours to be paid calculated — 10

Hourly pay rate entered on clock card — 11

Gross pay calculated (hrs and rate)
Gross pay entered (simultaneously by carbon) on personal wage record, payroll and payslip — 12

13

PAYE calculated by reference to Tax Code No (on records card) and tax tables — 14

15

Other deductions entered from details on personal wage record — 16

Deductions totalled and net pay calculated — 17

18

Employers NHI, pension contributions per dept added to payroll — 19

Payroll columns totalled by depts and overall and totals cross cast — 20

21

Document labels in diagram: Change document; Personal record; Clock card; Personal wage record; Payroll; Payslip; Tax tables

Fig. 9.7  Wasteful Wages Ltd – wages cycle

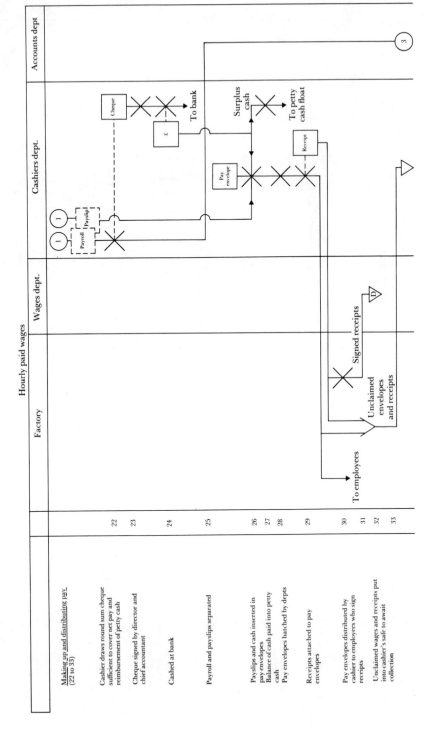

Hourly paid wages

| | Factory | Wages dept. | Cashiers dept. | Accounts dept |
|---|---|---|---|---|

Making up and distributing pay
(22 to 33)

22  Cashier draws round sum cheque sufficient to cover net pay and reimbursement of petty cash

23  Cheque signed by director and chief accountant

24  Cashed at bank

25  Payroll and payslips separated

26  Payslips and cash inserted in pay envelopes
27  Balance of cash paid into petty cash
28  Pay envelopes batched by depts

29  Receipts attached to pay envelopes

30  Pay envelopes distributed by cashier to employees who sign receipts
31
32  Unclaimed wages and receipts put into cashier's safe to await collection
33

Hourly paid wages

| | Wages dept | Cashiers dept | Accounts dept |

Accounting entries and payment of deductions (34 to 49)

| | |
|---|---|
| 34 | Journal entry prepared |
| 35 | Journal entry posted to |
| 36 | nominal ledger |
| 37 | Monthly payroll summary produced |
| 38 | |
| 39 | |
| 40 | |
| 41 | Cheque requisitions for deductions prepared |
| 42 | Cheques prepared |
| 43 | Passed to Director and Chief Accountant for signature |
| 44 | |
| 45 | |
| 46 | Requisitions entered in cash book |
| 47 | Cash book posted to nominal |
| 48 | ledger |
| 49 | |

Fig. 9.8 Wasteful Wages Ltd – report to management

The Managing Director

Wasteful Wages Ltd

cc The Chief Accountant

Dear Sir,

We write to formally draw your attention to certain areas of weakness in your company's internal control, which we discovered during our recent audit attendance. We consider it essential that these weaknesses be remedied in order to reduce the likelihood of fraud and error, so as to ensure that the accounting system may prove a reliable basis for the preparation of the annual financial statements. We would point out that these matters have already been discussed with the appropriate company officials.

1.0 *Clock cards*
1.1 Clock cards are currently issued within the factory. Control could be strengthened if the cards were prepared by the personnel department on the basis of their independent records. This would prevent additional fraudulent cards being introduced into the system, especially if a list of employees on roll was sent weekly by the personnel department direct to the wages approval authority.
1.2 At present clock cards are not approved before submission to the wages department. Hours worked should be checked and authorised by foremen, or departmental managers.

2.0 *Wages department*
2.1 There is no evidence that any checks are made on the calculations of hours worked, gross pay or net pay. Checks should be built into the system to reduce the possibility of error, and to necessitate collusion before fraud can be perpetrated. Hours worked could be first calculated in the factory, and checked in the wages department. And gross and net pay calculations could be checked by suitable division of duties between the five members of the wages department. Casts and cross-casts should also be checked before approval.
2.2 A copy of the payroll could usefully be retained in the wages department for use in answering queries from employees, and for subsequent audit check.

3.0 *Payroll approval*
3.1 At present there is no system for approving the payroll, which goes straight from the wages department to the cashier, who then prepares a cheque. This makes the system very vulnerable to fraud, either

within the wages department (where there is anyway no internal check), or by the cashier. In particular, the cashier is in a strong position to perpetrate undetected fraud, for he deals with all stages in the payment procedure subsequent to and including the cashing of the wage cheque. So he could simply overstate the amount required, and pocket the difference. Furthermore, he has access to the only copy of the payroll (see 2.2), which he could alter to conceal the fraud. Accordingly even subsequent audit work may not necessarily bring a fraud to light.

3.2 Accordingly we recommend that the top copy of the payroll should go directly to the chief accountant or his assistant for approval purposes. Approval procedures should include casting and cross-casting the payroll, checking employees on roll to the personnel department report (see 1.1), checking for large or other unusual payments and reconciling to the previous week's payroll. And of course the amount on the payroll should be checked to the drawn cheque.

3.3 Furthermore, the cashier and all persons who have been involved in payroll preparation should be excluded from any duties in connection with the payout. In this way, even if manipulation is attempted, it will be difficult for the perpetrators to gain access to the money.

4.0 *Drawing payroll cash*

4.1 At present a round sum of money is drawn to cover the net pay and a reimbursement of petty cash. This is not a sound practice as manipulations can be readily concealed with this system. Instead, the exact amount of money for the net pay should be drawn, so that the payroll can always be related to the cash book. Then the exact amount of money can be given to those responsible for filling the pay envelopes, and this can act as a check against error.

4.2 The cash should be drawn from the bank, and the pay envelopes filled by someone other than the cashier, for reasons discussed in 3.0 above.

4.3 The pay envelopes are currently issued by the cashier alone. As already mentioned, the cashier is not an appropriate person for this function, but in any event, the foremen should also be present at the payout, so as to identify employees.

5.0 *Unclaimed wages*

5.1 Unclaimed wages are currently returned to the cashier's safe to await collection. This is not a good practice, as it could facilitate manipulation of cash balances at subsequent petty cash counts. And its presence provides temptation for misappropriation. Instead, the moneys should be banked and drawn again as required. Alternatively, they may be sent to the employee's address by registered mail, or by cheque or postal order, subject to approval being obtained from the employee. An unclaimed wages register should be maintained.

6.0 *Payroll deductions*

6.1 The system for payroll deductions is also susceptible to fraud, for no documentary proof of the deductions is presented to the cheque signatories at the time of signature. Currently the wages department makes out cheque requisitions which are passed to the cashier for the preparation of the cheques, and to the chief accountant for signature. We recommend that control accounts for deductions be opened in the nominal ledger, and that payments be made on the reconciled balances therein. Payroll summaries could be inspected by the chief accountant at the time of signature.

We point out that the above observations do not arise from any special survey, but came to our attention during the course of usual audit procedures. Hence they are not necessarily exhaustive.

We consider it imperative that these matters be remedied as soon as possible, and would point out that their presence has necessitated a greater degree of audit work than would otherwise have been the case. We would be pleased to discuss any of these matters further, and would be grateful if in due course you would advise us in writing of the action you propose to take or have taken in relation to each of the points raised.

Yours faithfully,
M. J. Pratt, BA, FCA

# 10
# The nature of audit testing

## 10.1 Audit evidence

Our evaluation of accounting systems, and the associated compliance tests, have been carried out with a view to determining the reliance we can place on internal control for the prevention of fraud and error. This in turn enables us to determine the nature and amount of audit evidence that we need to acquire through substantive testing. The Auditing Guideline *Audit Evidence* discusses these matters, and emphasises the importance of substantive tests. The Guideline points out the main considerations that the auditor will need to bear in mind, and introduces the most important procedures that he will use.

### 'Introduction

1. Paragraph 4 of the Auditing Standard *The auditor's operational standard* states that:
   "The auditor should obtain relevant and reliable audit evidence sufficient to enable him to draw reasonable conclusions therefrom."

### 'Background

#### 'The nature of audit evidence

2. Audit evidence is information obtained by the auditor in arriving at the conclusions on which he bases his opinion on the financial statements. Sources of audit evidence include the accounting systems and underlying documentation of the enterprise, its tangible assets, management and employees, its customers, suppliers and other third parties who have dealings with, or knowledge of, the enterprise or its business.

3. The sources and amount of evidence needed to achieve the required level of assurances are questions for the auditor to determine by exercising his judgement in the light of the opinion called for under the terms of his engagement. He will be influenced by the materiality of the matter being examined, the relevance and reliability of evidence available from each source and the cost and time involved in obtaining

it. Often the auditor will obtain evidence from several sources which, together, will provide him with the necessary assurance.

## 'Sufficiency

4. The auditor can rarely be certain of the validity of the financial statements. However, he needs to obtain sufficient relevant and reliable evidence to form a reasonable basis for his opinion thereon. The auditor's judgement as to what constitutes sufficient relevant and reliable audit evidence is influenced by such factors as:
   (a) his knowledge of the business of the enterprise and the industry in which it operates;
   (b) the degree of risk of misstatement through errors or irregularities; this risk may be affected by such factors as:
      (i) the nature and materiality of the items in the financial statements;
      (ii) the auditor's experience as to the reliability of the management and staff of the enterprise and of its records;
      (iii) the financial position of the enterprise;
      (iv) possible management bias;
   (c) the persuasiveness of the evidence.

## 'Relevance

5. The relevance of the audit evidence should be considered in relation to the overall audit objective of forming an opinion and reporting on the financial statements. To achieve this objective the auditor needs to obtain evidence to enable him to draw reasonable conclusions in answer to the following questions. (Audit objectives are stated in brackets.)

*Balance sheet items*

(a) Have all of the assets and liabilities been recorded? (completeness)
(b) Do the recorded assets and liabilities exist? (existence)
(c) Are the assets owned by the enterprise and are the liabilities properly those of the enterprise? (ownership/obligation)
(d) Have the amounts attributed to the assets and liabilities been arrived at in accordance with the stated accounting policies, on an acceptable and consistent basis? (accuracy/valuation)
(e) Have the assets, liabilities and capital and reserves been properly disclosed? (presentation/disclosure)

*Profit and loss account items*

(f) Have all income and expenses been recorded?
(g) Did the recorded income and expense transactions in fact occur?
(h) Have the income and expenses been measured in accordance with

the stated accounting policies, on an acceptable and consistent basis?

(i) Have income and expenses been properly disclosed where appropriate?

### 'Reliability

6. Although the reliability of audit evidence is dependent upon the particular circumstances, the following general presumptions may be found helpful:

   (a) documentary evidence is more reliable than oral evidence;

   (b) evidence obtained from independent sources outside the enterprise is more reliable than that secured solely from within the enterprise;

   (c) evidence originated by the auditor by such means as analysis and physical inspection is more reliable than evidence obtained from others.

7. The auditor should consider whether the conclusions drawn from differing types of evidence are consistent with one another. When audit evidence obtained from one source appears inconsistent with that obtained from another, the reliability of each remains in doubt until further work has been done to resolve the inconsistency. However, when the individual items of evidence relating to a particular matter are all consistent, then the auditor may obtain a cumulative degree of assurance higher than that which he obtains from the individual items.

## 'Procedures

### 'Obtaining audit evidence

8. Audit evidence is obtained by carrying out audit tests which may be classified as "substantive" or "compliance" according to their primary purpose. Both such purposes are sometimes achieved concurrently. Substantive tests are defined as those tests of transactions and balances, and other procedures such as analytical review, which seek to provide audit evidence as to the completeness, accuracy and validity of the information contained in the accounting records or in the financial statements. Compliance tests are defined as those tests which seek to provide audit evidence that internal control procedures are being applied as prescribed.

9. The auditor may rely on appropriate evidence obtained by substantive testing to form his opinion, provided that sufficient of such evidence is obtained. Alternatively, he may be able to obtain assurance from the presence of a reliable system of internal control, and thereby reduce the extent of substantive testing. The audit procedures which are

appropriate when the auditor wishes to place reliance on the enterprise's internal controls are set out in the Auditing Guideline *Internal Controls.*

**'Techniques of audit testing**

10. Techniques of audit testing fall into the following broad categories:
    (a) *Inspection* – reviewing or examining records, documents or tangible assets. Inspection of records and documents provides evidence of varying degrees of reliability depending upon their nature and source (see paragraph 6b above). Inspection of tangible assets provides the auditor with reliable evidence as to their existence, but not necessarily as to their ownership, cost or value.
    (b) *Observation* – looking at an operation or procedure being performed by others with a view to determining the manner of its performance. Observation provides reliable evidence as to the manner of the performance at the time of observation, but not at any other time.
    (c) *Enquiry* – seeking relevant information from knowledgeable persons inside or outside the enterprise, whether formally or informally, orally or in writing. The degree of reliability that the auditor attaches to evidence obtained in this manner is dependent on his opinion of the competence, experience, independence and integrity of the respondent.
    (d) *Computation* – checking the arithmetical accuracy of accounting records or performing independent calculations.

*Analytical review procedures*

11. In addition to the above techniques, there are analytical review procedures, referred to in paragraph 8 above. These procedures include studying significant ratios, trends and other statistics and investigating any unusual or unexpected variations. The precise nature of these procedures and the manner in which they are documented will depend on the circumstances of each audit.

12. The comparisons which can be made will depend on the nature, accessibility and relevance of the data available. Once the auditor has decided on the comparisons which he intends to make in performing his analytical review, he should determine what variations he expects to be disclosed by them.

13. Unusual or unexpected variations, and expected variations which fail to occur, should be investigated. Explanations obtained should be verified and evaluated by the auditor to determine whether they are consistent with his understanding of the business and his general knowledge. Explanations may indicate a change in the business of

which the auditor was previously unaware in which case he should reconsider the adequacy of his audit approach. Alternatively they may indicate the possibility of misstatements in the financial statements; in these circumstances the auditor will need to extend his testing to determine whether the financial statements do include material misstatements.'

It is very easy to become lost in all the detailed considerations governing testing. To help you to keep the overall picture in mind, Figs. 10.1 and 10.2 show the main points contained in Chapters 10, 11 and 12.

## 10.2 Testing terminology

Of itself, terminology is of no great importance in terms of performing the job. However, in terms of passing examinations and convincing people you know what you are talking about, it is very important! For if you use terminology

Fig. 10.1 Audit tests – testing procedures and methods

| Tests | | Purpose | Audit testing procedures and techniques | Methods of sample selection |
|---|---|---|---|---|
| **'Walk through'** | | Ensure correct recording of accounting system. Preliminary evaluation | Depth testing Inspection Observation Enquiry Computation | Judgemental |
| **Compliance** | | Confirm internal control procedures operating satisfactorily | Depth testing Inspection Observation Enquiry Computation | Judgemental Stratified Random Systematic/ Interval Monetary unit Statistical |
| **S u b s t a n t i v e** | **Tests of detail** | Substantiate transactions and balances underlying financial statements | Depth testing or directional testing Inspection Observation Enquiry Computation | |
| | **Analytical review** | | Corroborate relationships among accounts using: ratio analysis regression analysis correlation | |

Fig. 10.2  Audit testing

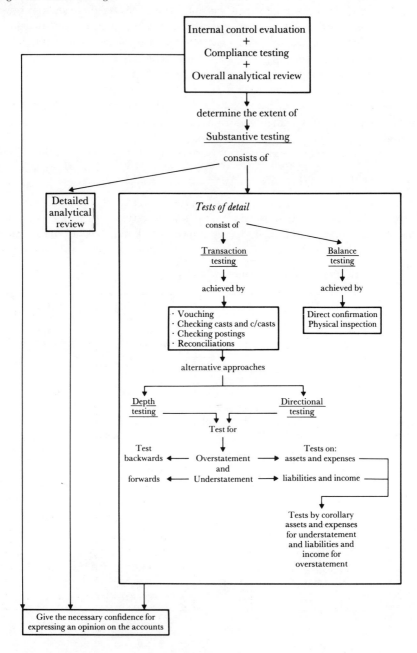

incorrectly, an examiner may naturally assume that you have misunderstood not only the term, but the technique it describes. Auditing terms are no more than a shorthand, used to save describing a technique each time it is mentioned. However, a problem comes in the fact that different firms use this shorthand in different ways. And herein is a very real source of confusion to students. So here I have kept to terms which are generally accepted within the profession, as evidenced by the Auditing Standards.

We have already encountered most of the terms in previous chapters, but a reminder here will do no harm:

*Walk through test.* This is designed to ensure that the auditor has a proper understanding of how the internal control systems work, carried out by following one transaction through from its initiation to final recording in the accounting records.

*Compliance tests.* These are designed to test the extent to which internal control systems have been operating throughout the year in accordance with laid down procedures.

*Substantive tests.* These are designed to substantiate the completeness, accuracy and validity of the transactions and balances contained in the accounting records and financial statements. Substantive tests consist of:
1. Analytical review – designed to help locate material mis-statements in the accounts by comparing transactions and balances with related items both for the same period, and for previous periods.
2. Tests of detail – designed to substantiate individual items in the accounts, and so to gain assurance either about the validity of similar transactions, or about the details that underlie account balances.

The American 'Statement on Auditing No. 1' in para. 320.70 particularly well explains the role of substantive testing, and an extract is accordingly reproduced below:

'The evidential matter required . . . is obtained through two general classes of auditing procedures: (a) tests of details of transactions and balances and (b) analytical review of significant ratios and trends and resulting investigation of unusual fluctuations and questionable items. These procedures are referred to . . . as "substantive tests". The purpose of these procedures is to obtain evidence as to the validity and propriety of accounting treatment of transactions and balances or, conversely, of errors or irregularities therein. Although this purpose differs from that of compliance tests, both purposes are often accomplished concurrently through tests of detail.'

## 10.3 Analytical review procedures

The draft Auditing Guideline *Review of Financial Statements* issued in summer 1978 provided a useful summary of the nature of analytical review. These comments were not included in the final standards, perhaps because it was felt they applied mainly to large companies. But they are nonetheless extremely useful and extracts are accordingly reproduced below:

'The precise nature of the analytical review and the manner in which it is documented will depend on the circumstances of each audit, but will include a study of significant ratios, trends and other statistics and an investigation of any unusual or unexpected variations disclosed, together with their monetary effect.

'The auditor should ensure that his audit working papers contain the completed results of the analytical review. These might comprise:

(a) the outline programme of the review work;
(b) the summary of significant figures and relationships for the period;
(c) a summary of comparisons made with budgets and with previous years;
(d) details of all significant variations considered;
(e) details of the results of investigations into such variations;
(f) the audit conclusions reached;
(g) information considered necessary for assisting in the planning of subsequent audits.

'Some examples of analytical review procedures now follow:

'1. The auditor should undertake a review of the financial statements to gain an overall appreciation of the figures involved and to assess the materiality of each in relation to the financial statements as a whole. The assessment should be designed to enable the auditor to answer the following questions:
   (a) what financial data, ratios or other statistics exist which might be significant to the business?
   (b) with what other data should they be compared?
   (c) are there any variations which would be expected to occur in the data identified?

'2. The data available for use in an analytical review is of three types:
   (a) financial data such as figures in the financial statements, management accounts or budgets, account balances and entries in the accounting records;
   (b) non-financial data such as production and employment statistics;
   (c) ratios and percentages developed directly from the financial and non-financial data.

'3. The comparisons which can be made will depend on the nature, availability and relevance of the data available. The following comparisons should usually be made:
   (a) amounts appearing in financial statements should be compared with corresponding amounts of preceding periods, other related amounts and, when available, with budgets and forecasts; these figures should also be broken down into subcomponents to

determine monthly trends and to isolate particular amounts which have been combined;

(b) non-financial data should be compared with entries in the accounting records and with other financial data;

(c) ratios and percentages appropriate to the business developed from individual financial amounts and non-financial data, should be compared with those of preceding periods and, when available, with budgets, forecasts and published industry statistics.

'4. In smaller enterprises comparisons of individual financial amounts might be made by examining the monthly trends from the nominal ledger figures and by a review of the books of original entry.

'5. The auditor needs to exercise imagination, skill and judgement in deciding which ratios, percentages and statistics will, with the aid of appropriate comparisons, provide useful insight into the enterprise's operations. For this purpose he should possess a good understanding of the business and the economic and commercial environment in which it operates.

'6. Once the auditor has decided on the comparisons which he intends to make in performing his analytical review, he should determine what variations he expects to be disclosed by them. The auditor is concerned not only with large or unexpected variations, but also with expected variations which fail to occur. Some of the factors that should be considered in determining the variations that can be expected to occur are:

(a) general inflation;

(b) change in prices of the specific goods and services used by the enterprise;

(c) seasonal factors affecting the enterprise or the industry;

(d) specific factors such as industrial disputes within the enterprise itself or within any of its major suppliers or customers;

(e) changes in the general level of business activity in the economy as a whole;

(f) changes in the level of business activity in the industry;

(g) technological advances rendering products or services obsolete;

(h) planned expansion or contraction of the operations of the enterprise;

(i) governmental action affecting such matters as labour, taxes, energy usage, regulation or inspection of manufacturing processes, price or wage constraints and foreign exchange.

'7. In an analytical review, unusual or unexpected variations, and expected variations which fail to occur, should be investigated. Explanations obtained should be verified and evaluated by the auditor to determine whether they make sense in relation to his understanding of the business, his general knowledge and judgement. Explanations may indicate a change in the business of which the auditor was previously unaware in which case he should reconsider the adequacy of his audit approach. Alternatively they may indicate the possibility of errors or mis-statements in the financial statements; in these circumstances the auditor will need to extend his testing to determine whether the financial statements do include material errors or mis-statements.'

Much of the analytical review will be based on accounting ratios. To illustrate how these ratios can be used by auditors, the ones most commonly employed are discussed below. The schedule (Standard accounting ratios) set out below shows how the ratios could be incorporated into a working paper.

*Standard accounting ratios*

*Gross profit as a percentage of sales*

1. The ratio of gross profit as a percentage of sales provides an important guide to the accuracy of the accounts. Any changes in this ratio over a period of time might indicate that there has been a genuine shift in trading conditions. However, they might also indicate the existence of material errors, distortions, or frauds.
2. When the change in the gross profit percentage is caused by genuine trading factors, we may expect to find one or more of the following features:
   (a) an improvement or, alternatively, a decline in cost efficiency;
   (b) an increase or, alternatively, a decrease in selling price;
   (c) a change in the mix of sales.
3. Where the features in the previous paragraph are not present, the shift in the gross profit percentage may well be caused by factors which will give us cause for concern, such as:
   (a) the under-statement or the over-statement of stocks;
   (b) stock losses;
   (c) the under-statement or the over-statement of sales;
   (d) the under-statement or the over-statement of costs.
4. The factors in (c) and (d) above usually result from the client not having adequate procedures for synchronising the book entries that record purchases or sales with the delivery or despatch of goods.

*Net profit as a percentage of sales*

5. The ratio of net profit as a percentage of sales discloses variations in expenses once the factors listed as affecting the ratio of gross profit as a percentage of sales have been taken into account. The breakdown of expenses into groups of related items (e.g. selling, administration and finance), and the calculation of the percentage to sales of each group, is a valuable elaboration which may cause us to examine the percentage to sales of individual items.
6. Naturally, if it is possible for us to make a further analysis of sales and related

costs – particularly by products – it simplifies our work of isolating the reasons for, and the areas of, any variations. If we use a physical quantity of sales (e.g. weight or units) in place of a monetary value, it helps us in assessing the effect of changes in price and volume.

*Net profit to capital employed*

7. The ratio of net profit to capital employed (expressed as a percentage) is the basic ratio that investment analysts use in assessing a company's performance from year to year and, more particularly, in comparing one company with another. It is a yardstick of how well management has utilised the funds invested in the business. In this context 'net profit' is taken before tax, interest and extraordinary items. Capital employed is taken as total assets less current liabilities at the beginning of the period.

8. In making internal comparisons within a particular business, this ratio serves only as a starting point: it is useful as a general indicator of progress over a period of years, but it needs to be amplified. In using this ratio, therefore, we need to examine the underlying factors to explain movements in the ratio; and even if there is no fluctuation, our investigation may reveal that there have been significant compensating changes in the constituents.

9. There are many different ways that can be used to show how profitably funds are employed. Depending on the purpose of the exercise, or on the particular circumstances of a business or industry, the composition of the profit figure and of the assets employed may be varied. For instance, it might be desirable to exclude from capital employed all or part of bank overdrafts and other short-term loans (if these were of a semi-permanent renewable nature). Indeed, it might be appropriate to go even further and relate profits to total operating assets.

*Sales to capital employed*

10. The ratio of sales to capital employed indicates how intensively capital is utilised. Thus, if the ratio of net profit to capital employed is rising, and there is no comparable rise in the ratio of net profit to sales percentage, the ratio of sales to capital employed must be rising. The more intensive the use of capital the better – provided that improvements in this ratio are not achieved by serious inroads into profit margins, and provided also that the business is not running the risk of over-trading.

*Sales to net current assets*

11. The ratio of sales to net current assets at the beginning of the period (and the ratio of sales to the constituents of current assets) indicates how effectively management is utilising the company's working capital. Viewed from the standpoint of performance, a high ratio is desirable. However, viewed from the standpoint of credit rating, too high a rate of turnover can indicate a shortage of working capital; and it may give early warning of a strained credit position.

*Cost of sales to stocks and work in progress*

12. The ratio of the cost of sales to stock and work in progress at the beginning of the period indicates the rate at which stocks and work in progress are being converted into sales. It also indicates whether the level of stocks held is justified in relation to sales. An unduly slow rate of stock turnover means that working capital is being tied up and that liquidity is being reduced. There is a risk of losses due to obsolescence and deterioration, and also a risk that unnecessary costs are being incurred for storage space. An unduly slow rate of stock turnover may also indicate that the buying, stock control, and production planning functions are inadequate. An adverse trend in this ratio can raise doubts about the value placed on stocks in the balance sheet and, in particular, can raise the question of whether adequate provision has been made for those stocks which it may not be possible to dispose of in the course of normal trading.

13. There may be good justification for a high level of stocks being held at a particular point in time: for example, a company may have taken advantage of bulk purchasing, or may have stocked up in preparation for a major contract. However, considerations of matters such as these must be balanced against the need for liquid working capital to continue the business during the time that it takes for stocks to be converted into sales.

14. It might be thought that a high level of turnover of stocks is an ideal to strive for. Certainly it may indicate that stocks and production are well managed, that available working capital is fully utilised, and that there is high liquidity. However, a high level of turnover of stocks may, in some cases, give cause for concern. It may mean, for example, that stocks have been reduced to such dangerously low levels that it is not possible to meet delivery dates or to increase turnover. By contrast, if stocks are conservatively valued, the turnover is high.

15. We must take seasonal fluctuations in stock levels into account, particularly since companies tend to draw up annual accounts at the time when their stocks are at their lowest level. Using average stock levels in relation to sales will discount seasonal distortions.

16. To obtain true stock turnover, we should use the cost of sales rather than the selling value, although in certain circumstances we may need to use the selling value. It may be that the only source available to us is the published accounts (e.g. when we are examining trade investments or making inter-firm comparisons). Alternatively, it may be that the cost of sales is not readily available, or that we know that it is affected by variations in the allocations of costs between the periods we are comparing. We may be able to draw valid conclusions from stock turnover based on selling value, but marked variations in profit margins could distort the true physical turnover position.

*Current assets to current liabilities*

17. The ratio of current assets to current liabilities where both are taken at the close of the period (which is known as the working capital ratio) was the

first ratio that was used in analysing balance sheets. It is still of prime importance – particularly to creditors. An often-quoted standard for this ratio is not less than 2 : 1, but it is unwise to place reliance on predetermined standards. It is preferable instead, when looking at a particular company, to devote attention to trends. A declining trend in this ratio indicates, prima facie, that the company is becoming short of working capital and may have difficulty in meeting its current obligations (perhaps because it has expanded its trading too rapidly or else because it has invested too heavily in fixed assets without having adequate resources).

18. An increasing trend may indicate that there is excessive liquidity because assets are being utilised badly. However, we should not draw firm conclusions about this without first referring to trends in supporting and associated ratios.

### Liquid assets to current liabilities

19. In the context of the ratio of liquid assets to current liabilities, liquid assets are current assets less stocks and work in progress. This ratio is known as the liquidity ratio, and it supplements the working capital ratio. It is a more severe test of financial safety in that it deals only with those assets that are quickly available for paying short-term creditors.

### Collections period

20. The collections period in days is usually calculated by deducting progressively from the trade debtors the sales for the previous months, noting the number of days in each month. For example, the debtors at the end of June are likely to include sales for June and May (61 days) and part of the sales for April (say 4/5th or 24 days). The collection period is, therefore, 85 days. Ideally, the collection period which is obtained by this calculation should be the same as the period embraced in the standard credit terms which a company offers.

21. From an audit point of view, any marked adverse difference there is between the actual collection period and the period in the standard credit terms, and any declining trend there is in the actual collection period, would cause us to have doubts about the effectiveness of the system of credit control and the adequacy of the provision for bad and doubtful debts. If we found, in a particular case, that the collection period had been extended because credit terms had been relaxed as a matter of policy, we should need to exercise even greater caution about credit control and the creation of provisions, since this situation would indicate that there had been a general decline in trading conditions. Because we had insufficient information, it might be necessary for us to modify this ratio and to compare total debtors (including prepayments) with total disclosed sales. Doing this would provide valid trends but, clearly, distortions could arise if either prepayments and other debtors or cash sales were material. Conversely, it might be desirable to compute separate collection periods for those classes of sales (e.g. hire

purchase sales and other credit sales) which are subject to considerable fluctuations in volume and terms because of government restrictions.

*Shareholders' funds to total assets*

22. One way in which to test the fundamental financial stability of a company is to consider how the operating assets have been financed. There are only two basic sources of funds – the proprietors (be they shareholders, partners, or sole traders), and the outside lenders (who may range from long-term debenture holders through to unsecured trade creditors). Maintaining a proper balance between those two sources is of prime importance, and so the ratio of shareholders' funds to total assets is of great significance. A company that works with a high proportion of borrowed money produces the potential of a high rate of return on the proprietors' funds. However, it also incurs the burden of high interest charges and a high risk of insolvency should the business falter. A situation such as this is even more dangerous if the outside funds are represented to a high degree by current liabilities: therefore, the ratio of current liabilities to shareholders' funds is a further ratio that we need to consider.

*Standard Accounting Ratios – example of working paper*

Client . . . . . . . . . . . . . . . . . . . . . . . . . . . . . . . . . . . . . . . . . . . . . . . . . . . . . . . . . . . . . .

|  | 1979 | 1980 | 1981 | 1982 | 1983 |
|---|---|---|---|---|---|
|  | £000 | £000 | £000 | £000 | £000 |
| Accounts figures |  |  |  |  |  |
|   Credit sales |  |  |  |  |  |
|   Total sales |  |  |  |  |  |
|   Cost of sales |  |  |  |  |  |
|   Gross profit |  |  |  |  |  |
|   Net profit |  |  |  |  |  |
|   Stock and work in progress |  |  |  |  |  |
|   Debtors |  |  |  |  |  |
|   Liquid assets |  |  |  |  |  |
|   Total current assets |  |  |  |  |  |
|   Total current liabilities |  |  |  |  |  |
|   Net current assets |  |  |  |  |  |
|   Fixed assets |  |  |  |  |  |
|   Total assets |  |  |  |  |  |
|   Total liabilities |  |  |  |  |  |
|   Capital employed |  |  |  |  |  |
|   Shareholders' funds |  |  |  |  |  |
| Profit ratios |  |  |  |  |  |
|   Gross profit to sales |  |  |  |  |  |
|   Net profit to sales |  |  |  |  |  |
|   Net profit to capital employed |  |  |  |  |  |
| Trading ratios |  |  |  |  |  |
|   Sales to capital employed |  |  |  |  |  |

Sales to net current assets
Cost of sales to stocks

Solvency ratios
Current assets to current liabilities
Liquid assets to current liabilities
Collections period

Capital ratios
Shareholders' funds to total assets
Current liabilities to shareholders' funds

## 10.4 Tests of detail – introduction

Substantive tests of detail can be designed to substantiate *both transactions and balances*. And here we must introduce two more pieces of jargon – vouching and verification. These two terms are often used indiscriminately, and hence are often a source of confusion to students. The generally accepted usage is very simple:

*Vouch* – to prove the authenticity of a recorded *transaction*;

*Verify* – to prove the authenticity of the recorded amount of assets and liabilities (*balances*).

*Vouching* will be achieved by comparing entries in the accounting records with appropriate vouchers. For example, we may wish to authenticate entries that have been made on account of trade purchases. We could do this by vouching the debit side of purchase records to invoices, orders and goods received notes. Our major concern during such a vouch will be to prove that the purchase was authorised. We will also want to make sure that the items acquired were compatible with the needs of the business (for example, a television set delivered to the chief buyer's address might arouse our suspicion!). These tests will be designed to detect fraud, but in addition we will need to be on the look out for error:

(a) did the transaction occur in the accounting period under review?

(b) are all calculations, extensions, discounts and casts arithmetically correct? (miscalculations may of course also be used to perpetrate fraud).

(c) is the allocation to the general ledger account appropriate, and has proper distinction been drawn between capital and revenue?

The procedures so far listed will constitute substantive testing. But at the same time as carrying out these tests, the auditor will also be on the look-out for evidence that the client's own checking procedures have been operating correctly (such evidence may consist of initials, signatures, stamps, etc., on the relevant document). And in this way compliance testing can be combined with substantive testing in the same vouch.

*Verification* will be achieved by confirming the following factors about an asset or liability balance:

**C**ost – the original amount at which the asset or liability was acquired.

**A**uthorisation – that there was proper authority to acquire the asset or incur the liability.

**V**aluation – the valuation of liabilities will normally be at cost; but not necessarily so with assets.

**E**xistence – in the case of assets, do they exist, or have they been lost, stolen, caught fire, or otherwise deteriorated?

**B**eneficial.

**O**wnership – the assets may exist, they may have value, and the company may even have paid for them, but does it own them? . . . Or for example, is the title faulty, or has the company acquired them on mortgage or hire purchase?

**P**resentation – is the presentation in the accounts:
  (a) clear and unambiguous
  (b) appropriate to the nature of the business
  (c) in accordance with relevant accounting standards
  (d) consistent with previous years (or if not, so stated)?

Remember these principles (CAVEBOP!), for they are crucial when it comes to the detailed verification of assets and liabilities, which we will be dealing with in Chapter 14.

But now I must complicate matters slightly. I stated that vouching relates to transactions, and verification to balances. But it is not quite as simple as this for two reasons:

1. Vouching is only one of the techniques that will be used in proving transactions.
2. The technique of vouching will also be used in verification procedures.

We will deal with (1) in Chapter 12 on designing transaction tests of detail. But (2) requires a word of explanation. Clearly balances are derived from earlier transactions. So it follows that when verifying a balance we may have cause to vouch the transaction that gave rise to it. For example, when proving the cost of an asset, we will vouch to the related purchase invoice. So you can see that vouching can be part of verification procedures, but never vice versa.

You should note that verification objectives are similar to, but not the same as, the audit objectives explained in 10.1. To verify an account balance, it is necessary to carry out the above procedures. However, in addition, evidence will be necessary in support of the COMPLETENESS of the balance. This will not normally be possible by testing the amount itself, for reasons which are explained in 12.1. Completeness of balances will normally be proved by:

1. Proving the completeness of recording and processing of related transactions, and/or
2. Reliance on analytical review, and/or
3. Balance testing as explained in 10.5 below.

## 10.5 Tests of detail – transaction and balance testing

We can test an account in two ways:
1. By checking individual transactions in, and the casts of, the account in the financial year concerned – *transaction testing*;
2. By checking the balance of the account – *balance testing*.

Both methods are valid, and either or both can be used, depending on which is administratively more convenient in the circumstances.

### Transaction testing

Transaction testing involves retracing the procedural steps followed in the accounting process, vouching, recalculating computations and checking summaries, allocations and postings. This method requires larger sample sizes than does balance testing, and so it will normally only be used when the alternative is either not possible, or inadequate.

### Balance testing

Balance testing involves agreeing or reconciling similar information that has been generated from different sources. For example, balance testing would include the confirmation of bank or debtor balances by applying direct to the independent parties concerned. Another example would be the physical inspection of the plant, machinery and stock that underlie the relevant general ledger accounts.

The two methods can be combined in testing one account. For example, debtors can be verified at an interim date by direct confirmation from the debtors, and transactions from then until the year end can be vouched in order to confirm the year end balances.

As a generalisation, balance testing will usually be more appropriate for testing balance sheet figures, whereas transaction testing will normally be used in respect of income and expenses. But this will not always be the case as we will discover when we deal in detail with transaction and balance testing in Chapters 12, 13 and 14. However, first we must look at the ways in which samples may be selected for testing purposes.

# I I

# Sampling and statistical sampling

## 11.1 Selecting the sample

Samples can be selected in two principal ways:
1. Subjectively, or
2. Using statistical method.

Subjective sampling is based on the auditor's judgement as to the quantity and incidence of items to be selected, and hence it is often known by the somewhat euphemistic title of *judgement sampling*. Such samples can be perfectly satisfactory, provided they are properly designed. But regretfully this is often not the case. For it is all too easy for a particular month's vouchers to be selected, simply because they happen to be on top of the pile. Or worse, perhaps just because the audit programme says so.

Such slack work is never justified, and is usually valueless. So if we are to use judgement sampling, we must obey certain principles:
1. The sample must be chosen so as to be *representative* of the entire population – in transaction testing, transactions should be selected from the entire year, and in balance testing, all balances should be given a chance of selection.
2. Where items are selected on the basis of the fact that they 'look peculiar', we must be conscious that we are exercising personal *bias* and that the results of testing could well represent a distorted view of the errors in the population. Such bias is more appropriate in compliance testing, in that any error may be significant if it reveals that the internal control has failed to work properly. But for substantive testing, we gain little advantage if we select peculiar items which are representative only of themselves, for we reveal nothing about the population as a whole. Hence the technique of random sampling may be used to advantage, in that it can eliminate the intentional or unintentional application of personal bias. And this is the first step towards statistical sampling.

*Random sampling* involves the selection of the sample on a purely random basis. The principle can be applied in a more or less sophisticated fashion. Days or weeks can be selected on a random basis from the year. Or the selection may be made on the basis of batches, though it is best to select on the basis of a population which is entirely prenumbered. If this is the case, you merely need the starting and concluding numbers for the period under review, and the specific items to be tested can be chosen randomly on the basis of their unique numbers. This will normally be achieved by the use of random number tables. However, where the population is not prenumbered, these tables are not appropriate and the usual alternative is *Interval Sampling*. This method involves selecting items at regular numeric intervals, starting from a point chosen at random. A more sophisticated version of the same technique is called *Cumulative Monetary Sampling*, and this weights the sample in favour of the more material items. This is achieved by adding cumulatively the monetary amount of each entry or balance in the population, and making the selection on the basis of monetary as opposed to numeric intervals. Although of course this will not be possible in the case of non-monetary populations such as, for example, goods outwards notes when testing for understatement of sales ledger balances.

Whichever method of selection is chosen, it is important that all items in the population have a chance of being picked, and it must be ensured that the population is itself free from bias. For example, if we used interval sampling to select from sales ledger balances, starting at random at 83 and selecting at 100 balance intervals, our sample would be biased if all large accounts had been placed for convenience in the first 50 numbers.

Both random number and interval sampling can necessitate considerable work to extract the sample, so there is much advantage in having them selected by computer program, if the accounting system so permits. If this is not the case, the extent of work is normally only worthwhile if the actual volume of items to be tested is reduced by the use of statistical sampling.

*Stratified sampling* may be used in conjunction with either judgement or statistical sampling, but again it is more appropriate to the latter in terms of the work involved. This technique involves re-ordering the items in the population so that they are listed in stratas, all items in a given strata being of approximately the same materiality. So for example, if we were selecting debtor balances for confirmation, we could stratify the balances – £0 to £100, £100 to £1,000, £1,000 to £5,000, £5,000 to £10,000 and £10,000 and over. We could then select progressively more from each of these strata, so that we weight our test in favour of the more material accounts, thereby testing a high proportion of the monetary value of the population, while perhaps only selecting a small number of the total balances. Although there is a danger in this, in that it will often be the small, less often checked accounts which will be used for the purposes of fraud.

The two techniques above are often, but not always, used in conjunction with *Statistical sampling*. Statistical sampling involves selecting the *quantity* of items to be tested, in accordance with a mathematical formula. And the formula enables the auditor to reach a statistically valid *conclusion* about the entire population from which the test is drawn. Such testing is best suited to large volume transactions, such as tests of detail on purchases, sales, wages, inventory and debtors; but then only in the larger company. For a statistical sample takes a long time to set up, and the time involved is not justified if the population is only small. Furthermore, the laws of probability (on which statistical sampling is based) are not applicable in the case of small populations.

The ability to reach a valid and statistically proveable conclusion is clearly advantageous when it comes to discussing with management weaknesses in their internal control (compliance testing), or errors in the accounts that need correcting (substantive testing). For the management will be unable to refute the auditor's statements on the grounds of unrepresentative testing. However, while statistical sampling certainly has its place in modern auditing, opinions vary in the profession as to the extent to which it should be used. Some firms use it for all volume tests of detail, whereas others require the express permission of the partner to devote time to the technique. The reason for the disparity lies in mistrust of applying mathematical techniques to what is essentially a highly intuitive and subjective art. Auditing is not a science, and many people consider that the application of formulae only serves to reduce the application of the very necessary audit initiative. And in any event, many subjective decisions have to be made before a statistical sample can be selected, so it can be argued that adding a formula at the end is little more than cosmetic. There is some validity in this argument, but provided the auditor is conscious of the dangers, I consider the technique to be advantageous for larger client companies because:

1. A statistically valid conclusion can be placed on the result of the sample, and the audit risk can be quantified. Although the validity of the conclusion will be dependent on the underlying assumptions, at least the auditor is forced to specify the assumptions that he is making.

2. The extent of the items to be tested can be limited, thus saving time. Testing beyond a certain amount adds very little to audit evidence about an account, as we will see later in the chapter. So the extra time involved is largely wasted. And although a statistical sample does take a long time to set up, the same sample can be used for more than one type of test. For example, a stock sample could be used for checking stores records, physical existence, prices and scrutinising for slow-moving items.

3. The technique of statistical sampling brings with it a useful discipline, for the exact nature of the test, the size and nature of the population, the nature of an error and the confidence level that is required from the sample all have to be specified.

This concept of confidence level is crucial, and must be examined before we can proceed to the detailed aspects of statistical sampling.

## 11.2 Confidence levels

Obviously, when using any form of sampling technique, we can never be 100 per cent certain that we are right in our conclusions. For even if we select 99 out of every 100 items for testing, it may just be that number 100 contains a material error. So we have to decide what level of confidence is required, to enable us to express an opinion on the accounts.

The confidence required from detailed tests will depend on the confidence obtained through internal control and analytical review. An example of the relationship between these three factors is illustrated by Fig. 11.1. The level of confidence to be derived from each factor is a subjective decision, which can only

Fig. 11.1 Sources of audit confidence

Audit confidence is derived from:
    Internal control
    Analytical review
    Tests of detail
Tests of detail can never be eliminated, but the confidence to be derived from them will be dictated by the confidence obtained from internal control and analytical review.

    Examples of the relationship between these three sources of confidence are given in the following 'pie' diagrams, taking the full circle to be the total amount of confidence required:

A. A situation where the internal control is good, and an effective analytical review can be performed.

B. A situation where the internal control is only moderate, but an effective analytical review can be performed.

C. A situation where the internal control is poor, but a reasonable analytical review can be performed.

D. A situation where the system of internal control is poor, and no reliance can be placed on analytical review.

In situation D, it may well be impossible to express an opinion on the accounts, because although tests of detail can give us confidence that there is no overstatement, they cannot prove whether or not understatement has occurred due to the deliberate concealment of transactions.

be made on the basis of mature audit judgement. But many firms have laid down quantitative guidelines to assist in making this decision. Among such firms, it is generally accepted that a minimum confidence level of 95 per cent must be obtained from a combination of all the factors. And some firms have gone even further by ascribing *reliability factors* to various confidence levels. But you should note that such a technique is normally only used with statistical sampling. By way of example, the reliability factors used by Deloitte, Haskins and Sells are reproduced in Fig. 11.2. These factors are derived from the Poisson distribution which forms the basis for the firm's Sampling Plan.

It follows that we must achieve a total confidence adding up to whatever number we choose to represent 95 per cent – in this case 3.0. So if we are confident that the internal control system will detect, for example, 80 per cent of material mis-statement occurring in the accounting process, we can ascribe to it an R factor of 1.6 (it would be unrealistic to place much more than 90 per cent confidence in an internal control system, because of the inherent drawbacks of internal control, as discussed in Ch. 5). So from the chart you can see that we need a further 1.4 R to reach our required confidence level. This we will obtain from analytical review and tests of detail. Though you would in any event not normally go much below 0.5 R on tests of detail, because of their importance, as previously discussed.

But of the two substantive testing procedures, analytical review and tests of detail, only the confidence ascribable to the latter is statistically quantifiable, for only an individual transaction is either capable of being substantiated, or not. The analytical review is totally subjective, and a firm must accordingly come up with its own policy decisions as to how much reliance can be placed upon various levels of review. More than 63 per cent or an R of 1.0 would seem to be excessive. So, continuing our example:

| | | |
|---|---|---|
| Internal control gives 80% confidence | R = | 1.6 |
| Assume for example that the analytical review gives 33% confidence | R = | 0.4 |
| | | 2.0 |
| Balance required from Tests of Detail | R = | 1.0 |
| | | 3.0 |

The actual risk can be restated thus:

| | | |
|---|---|---|
| Total risk that there is mis-statement in the accounts | | – 100% |
| Risk that the client's internal control system has not detected the mis-statement. Confidence level 80% | risk | – 20% |
| Risk that undetected mis-statement will not be revealed by analytical review. Confidence level of 33% | risk | – 67% |

Fig. 11.2 Reliability factors

The table set out below shows the relationship of reliability (R) factors to confidence levels and consequent risks. For example, if we were to consider subjectively that the client's system of internal control would detect 75 per cent of the material mis-statement occurring in the accounting process, we could quantify this confidence by ascribing to it an R factor of 1.4. This would leave a further R factor of 1.6 to be found from our substantive testing to leave us with an acceptable overall risk of 5 per cent.

| Reliability factor R | Confidence level % | Consequent risk % | Further reliability factors required to reach total R = 3.0 | Confidence level % | Consequent risk % | Approximate overall risk (product of all risks) |
|---|---|---|---|---|---|---|
| 3.0 | 95 | 5 | — | — | — | 5 |
| 2.9 | 94 | 6 | 0.1 | 10 | 90 | 5 |
| 2.8 | 94 | 6 | 0.2 | 18 | 82 | 5 |
| 2.7 | 93 | 7 | 0.3 | 26 | 74 | 5 |
| 2.6 | 93 | 7 | 0.4 | 33 | 67 | 5 |
| 2.5 | 92 | 8 | 0.5 | 39 | 61 | 5 |
| 2.4 | 91 | 9 | 0.6 | 45 | 55 | 5 |
| 2.3 | 90 | 10 | 0.7 | 50 | 50 | 5 |
| 2.2 | 89 | 11 | 0.8 | 55 | 45 | 5 |
| 2.1 | 88 | 12 | 0.9 | 59 | 41 | 5 |
| 2.0 | 86 | 14 | 1.0 | 63 | 37 | 5 |
| 1.9 | 85 | 15 | 1.1 | 67 | 33 | 5 |
| 1.8 | 83 | 17 | 1.2 | 70 | 30 | 5 |
| 1.7 | 82 | 18 | 1.3 | 73 | 27 | 5 |
| 1.6 | 80 | 20 | 1.4 | 75 | 25 | 5 |
| 1.5 | 78 | 22 | 1.5 | 78 | 22 | 5 |
| 1.4 | 75 | 25 | 1.6 | 80 | 20 | 5 |
| 1.3 | 73 | 27 | 1.7 | 82 | 18 | 5 |
| 1.2 | 70 | 30 | 1.8 | 83 | 17 | 5 |
| 1.1 | 67 | 33 | 1.9 | 85 | 15 | 5 |
| 1.0 | 63 | 37 | 2.0 | 86 | 14 | 5 |
| 0.9 | 59 | 41 | 2.1 | 88 | 12 | 5 |
| 0.8 | 55 | 45 | 2.2 | 89 | 11 | 5 |
| 0.7 | 50 | 50 | 2.3 | 90 | 10 | 5 |
| 0.6 | 45 | 55 | 2.4 | 91 | 9 | 5 |
| 0.5 | 39 | 61 | 2.5 | 92 | 8 | 5 |
| 0.4 | 33 | 67 | 2.6 | 93 | 7 | 5 |
| 0.3 | 26 | 74 | 2.7 | 93 | 7 | 5 |
| 0.2 | 18 | 82 | 2.8 | 94 | 6 | 5 |
| 0.1 | 10 | 90 | 2.9 | 94 | 6 | 5 |

Risk that mis-statement undetected by both internal control, and analytical review, will not be revealed by tests of detail.

Confidence level 63%                                    risk  –  37%

Overall Risk – $100 \times 20 \times 67 \times 37\% = 4.96\%$

or, Confidence Level approximately   95%

Now this does not mean that we are automatically going to be wrong 4.96 per cent of the time. For we have started off with the 100 per cent assumption that there is a material mis-statement in the first place. And this may well not be the case, as all the client's staff could well be both honest and diligent! Furthermore, the internal control system may well work more effectively than is indicated by the minimum confidence that we ascribe to it. And of course there is always the chance that audit staff may apply initiative and skill outside the minimum rules that a firm may lay down!

## 11.3 Materiality

The extent of tests of detail will be based upon:
(a) the degree of reliance that can be placed on internal control;
(b) the extent of inconsistencies discovered through the use of analytical review techniques;
(c) the materiality of the figures in question.
We have discussed the first two factors in detail during this and previous chapters, but the issue of materiality has only been briefly raised in Chapter 1. So before we can proceed to the detail of statistical sampling, a further discussion is necessary here.

We saw in sec. 1.4 that materiality is essentially a matter of professional judgement, and that an individual item should be judged material if the knowledge of that item could reasonably be deemed to have influence on the users of a financial statement. The issue of materiality arises in two situations:
1. Determining the extent to which detailed audit work should be performed in specific areas.
2. Determining whether errors, or other mis-statements have affected the true and fair view.

The principles for determining materiality apply equally to both (although we are concerned only with the former situation at the moment) and are concisely stated in the report entitled *Materiality in Accounting* by the Accountants' International Study Group. The following is an extract from the report:

> 'An amount is not material solely by reason of its size; other factors including those set out below must be considered in making decisions as to materiality:
> 'A. The nature of the item – i.e. whether it is:
> 1. a factor entering into the determination of net income
> 2. unusual or extraordinary
> 3. contingent upon an event or condition
> 4. determinable based upon existing facts and circumstances
> 5. required by statute or regulation;
> 'B. The amount itself, in relation to:
> 1. the financial statements taken as a whole

2. the total of the amount of which it forms, or should form a part

3. related items (e.g. if the figure under review is the doubtful debt provision, then debtors would be a related item)

4. the corresponding amount in previous years or the expected amount in future years.'

The study group reached the conclusion that quantitative guidelines as to materiality could and should be developed, and that these could be in the range of 5 to 10 per cent when compared to an appropriate base. Below 5 per cent would not normally be deemed material (except for certain transactions such as those which must be disclosed by statute, e.g. directors' fees). Above 10 per cent would ordinarily be material, and between 5 and 10 per cent, the matter would have to be determined in relation to the circumstances.

Let us take a specific example. Assume all of a company's stock was held at the main factory store, with the exception of a small quantity held in a distribution depot at another location. The question will arise as to how much audit work should be performed on the stock at the depot. Does it, for example, require the auditor to personally attend there? And, how much detailed testing should he perform? To answer these questions, we need to consider internal control, analytical review and materiality, as stated at the beginning of this section.

1. How strong is the internal control at the depot? For example, are independent continuous records maintained at head office of all despatches to, and deliveries authorised from, the depot? Does the internal audit department visit the depot and make spot checks?

2. Does the analytical review indicate any inconsistencies? For example, is the stock at the depot *materially* greater or smaller than for previous years? How does the percentage of stock to cost of sales at the depot compare with that at the main factory?

3. Is the amount in question material? For example, what is the percentage of stock at the depot to total stock? And what is the percentage of stock at depot to total assets?

If internal control is good, and the analytical review reveals no inconsistencies, then tests of detail can be kept to a minimum, even if the stock in question is considered material. And if the stock is not material, then minimum work need be performed in the area even if the internal control or analytical reviews are less than satisfactory (though clearly it will be appropriate to point out these matters to the directors, and if suspicious circumstances are discovered, then the auditor is under an obligation to probe the matter to the full, regardless of the materiality). If, on the other hand, the stock is considered material, and the internal control is weak, then the auditor will not be able to restrict tests of detail, especially if the analytical review reveals possible inconsistencies. In this situation, up to 100 per cent of transactions/balances would have to be tested, depending on the degree of weakness and the nature of tests and sampling techniques used.

If statistical sampling is used, materiality will automatically be taken into account in determining the extent of tests of detail, in that it will be used in deciding the relevant precision limits.

## 11.4 The requirements for statistical sampling

The required confidence is the starting point for producing a statistical sample, but other matters will also need consideration. So let us have a complete list:

1. *Confidence level* (see sec. 11.2).

2. *Precision limits.* The precision with which we can describe the attributes of a given population. For example, our sample may be chosen such that the errors in the population can be proved to be within ±5 per cent of the monetary value. But how precise do we require this percentage to be? The bigger our sample, clearly the more precise we can be, but we can never be completely precise for the same reasons as we can never be 100 per cent confident. The degree of precision required will depend on the materiality of the items in question. And this should be considered in the light of the comments in sec. 11.3. For example, if £3,000 of errors in a sales ledger population of £100,000 would be considered to be just not material, then ±3 per cent would be our precision limits. From this you will deduce that confidence level and precision limits are essentially inter-related, and the two combine together to determine the quantity of testing.

3. *Population.* It is necessary to determine the unit of the population; for example, voucher, ledger entry or line on a stock sheet. And it is necessary to discover the size of the population. Pre-numbered populations can be advantageous in that selection can be by random number tables. However, most audit sampling plans now use *interval selection*, which does not require pre-numbering, but simply necessitates a population that is readily accessible for counting the intervals. (For example, lines in a ledger or on a computer print-out would be sufficient.)

4. *Errors.* We must determine the significance of potential errors, for this will in turn determine the way in which we conduct our tests. For example, in compliance testing any error will be significant irrespective of its monetary value, because any failure in internal control procedures reduces the reliance that we can place on those procedures. And hence tests of detail will have to be extended. It is not the size of the error that is significant in these circumstances, but its nature (indeed there may be no monetarily quantifiable mis-statement at all – e.g. a payroll may not have been check cast, but it may still be correct). With substantive testing, on the other hand, we are interested in discovering whether there is material mis-statement, so in this situation it is purely the amount of the error that is relevant.

## 11.5 Statistical sampling procedures

There are many different types of statistical sampling plan, but whatever type is used, the procedures for conducting a test will be as follows:
(a) decide on the relevant confidence level, and precision limits;
(b) calculate the sample size using an appropriate formula, or tables designed for the purpose;
(c) select the sample using random methods;
(d) carry out the necessary tests;
(e) appraise the results.
The most common types of plan adopted by auditors are:
Acceptance sampling (with discovery sampling a variation) or
Estimation sampling, which may be used to determine:
(a) population variables, or
(b) population attributes.

*Acceptance sampling*

Acceptance sampling is designed to enable the auditor to accept or reject a population on the basis of the errors discovered in the sample. The auditor has to specify an acceptable error rate, and his sample will then reveal whether this has been exceeded. But the answer will be numeric rather than financial, so materiality cannot be used to determine the acceptable rate. Accordingly, the technique is of limited value, except possibly in the case of compliance testing, where it is the fact that a particular error has occurred, which is significant, rather than the actual size of the error. For example, assume that we have a population of 5,000 items, and that our required confidence level and precision limits necessitate the selection of 300 items for testing (the sampling plan will dictate the numbers of items to be selected for a given confidence level and precision limits). We may have specified that for internal control to be deemed satisfactory there must be errors in no more than 2 per cent of the population. This condition will be satisfied if we discover no more than six errors in the sample that we test. If this quantity is exceeded, the population would be rejected, and the internal control would be deemed unsatisfactory.

The principle of *discovery sampling* is similar to that of acceptance sampling and it differs largely only in format. Again it is only of real value in compliance testing. It is used in connection with the discovery of very significant compliance failures, or frauds, and enables the auditor to select a sample size which will assure him of discovering at least one error of the type being tested, if the error rate in the population as a whole exceeds the predetermined limit. If no errors are found, this indicates that the errors in the population as a whole are within the limit.

*Estimation sampling*

Estimation sampling is the most usual sort of plan adopted by auditors. The technique may be used either to estimate *variables* from a population or to estimate *attributes*. A variable sample is normally used to estimate the total monetary value of the population, and this should then be compared with the actual value in the client's records. Or alternatively it may be used to discover the value of certain characteristics of the population; for example, obsolete or slow moving stock in an inventory valuation. An attribute sample, on the other hand, will normally be used to determine the error rate of the population, and this rate will then be compared with the maximum rate that the auditor is prepared to accept.

### Estimation sampling for variables

Let us take an inventory test as an example, and assume that we require a confidence level of 90 per cent and a precision limit of $\pm 2$ per cent. The number of items to be tested will be calculated by reference to the formula used in the sampling plan, or by reference to appropriate tables. We will then carry out the necessary tests on the stock balances that we extract and list any errors discovered. These errors will then be applied to the total of the sample balances to obtain an adjusted figure. So assume further that the monetary value of the sample as selected was £10,000, and that after adjustment for errors discovered it became £9,850. Now $\pm 2$ per cent of £10,000 allows a range of £9,800 to £10,200, and £9,850 is within that range. So we can conclude with 90 per cent confidence that the value of the whole population is correct $\pm 2$ per cent. But if the adjusted sample had fallen outside the required limits, then extra work would have had to be performed, in the form of additional sample(s). This/these would be pooled with the original sample, and the population could be accepted were the pooled sample to fall within the required limits. But if after one or two repeats of the test the population were still to lay outside the acceptable range, it would be reasonable to conclude that the account is not fairly stated. There are then three choices:

1. Verify 100 per cent of the stock balances.
2. Require the client to check the entire account, and start back at the beginning of the testing.
3. Conclude that no amount of testing will reveal the true figures in that the errors indicate an extremely weak control situation. In this case there will often be no alternative but to qualify the accounts.

You may come across a fourth choice in some texts and that is to lower the confidence level or precision limits used in calculating the sample. But I do not consider that appropriate, unless these figures were incorrectly calculated in the first place.

### Estimation sampling for attributes

Estimation sampling for attributes is normally used to determine the extent of any errors in a population, and hence it will usually be applied to compliance testing. For example, let us assume that we wish to test the internal control in relation to purchase invoice approval. First we must determine the confidence that we require (or think we will be able to achieve) from the results of our testing. This has already been discussed in sec. 11.2, so let us assume a 90 per cent level here. We must then decide what constitutes an acceptable error rate. With variable sampling, errors were expressed in terms of their monetary value, but with attribute sampling they are expressed in terms of yes or no. So, for example, did an appropriate official authorise the invoice for payment, and sign it accordingly? If not, this would constitute an error.

The extent of errors allowable will be based on our knowledge of the client's system, and accordingly on the confidence that we ascribe to it, combined with our judgement as to what is acceptable in the circumstances. The acceptable rate will be less, as the controls or checks become more critical. So testing for failure to cast and cross-cast an invoice may well require less precision than testing for failure to authorise for payment; though it may well be more convenient to select a composite error limit for all compliance tests on the same population, as these can then all be performed at the same time.

Let us assume that a 2 per cent error rate is the maximum acceptable. As with variable sampling, precision limits must also be specified, but here understatement is not relevant, for we are only interested in the maximum error. So if we further assume that $\pm 1$ per cent are our precision limits, as 2 per cent is the maximum amount we set for the error rate, we must use 1 per cent as our estimated error rate for the purposes of calculating the sample size. This is explained by:

$1\%$ = estimated rate $+ 1\%$ maximum overstatement = $2\%$ maximum error rate allowed.

The actual rate may of course be as low as $1\% - 1\% = 0\%$. But it is the maximum error which is significant, whereas with variable sampling, either over or under-statement may be relevant. The sample will be evaluated by determining whether or not the error rate in the sample is equal to or less than the estimated rate of 1 per cent. If this is the case, we can conclude that the error rate in the population as a whole is not greater than the maximum acceptable rate of 2 per cent. If on the other hand, the sample reveals an error rate in excess of the estimated rate, then we would conclude that internal control procedures had not been complied with. We would accordingly revise our estimate of the reliance that could be placed on internal control; and this would of course in turn result in an increase in substantive testing.

Of the two types of estimation sampling, variable sampling is the most useful, for it can be applied for the purposes of both substantive and compliance testing. Attribute sampling will normally only be used in circumstances where variable sampling is not possible; in that, the population has no identifiable monetary values. In this latter case it will only be possible to reach a conclusion from the sample, in respect of compliance with internal control procedures.

## 11.6 Conclusion

Tables are available to calculate the sample size, given the confidence level and precision limits required, and the size of the population; or formulae may be used for the calculation. Alternatively we may give the job to a computer already programmed with the formula.

I do not consider it appropriate here to illustrate the use of these tables and formulae, for each firm will have its own variant; so to show one to the exclusion of others would serve only to confuse. In any event, it is an extremely complicated area upon which whole books have been written, so to deal with the detail in just a few pages would be spurious. For examination purposes, you are advised to concentrate on the principles as illustrated here. If you are employed by an audit firm you could usefully study your firm's statistical sampling plan, if one is in use. Alternatively you may find the following references useful for further study:

T. W. McRae. *Statistical Sampling for Audit and Control*. John Wiley and Sons (1974).
D. M. Roberts. *Statistical Auditing*. American Institute of Certified Public Accountants (1978).
T. M. F. Smith. *Statistical Sampling for Accountants*. Accountancy Age and Prentice Hall International (1976).
Herbert Arkin. *Handbook of Sampling for Auditing and Accounting* (this contains many useful tables). McGraw-Hill (1974).

There is much literature on this subject, but I have found these references to be the most useful. And they should certainly keep you busy!

# 12
# Tests of detail – transaction testing

## 12.1 Over- and understatement

When we test any account, we are looking for any *over-* or *understatement* which will materially affect the truth and fairness of the financial statements. But only through balance testing can we determine *both* in the same test. And even balance testing may not always reveal understatement. For example, whereas a confirmation from the bank of the bank balance can be relied on to reveal both over- and understatement, a debtors' confirmation will be highly unlikely to reveal understatement, as a debtor will hardly reply to the effect that he owes *more* than the amount to be confirmed!

With transaction testing, however, we can only *ever* reach a conclusion about the *overstatement* of items in the given population from which we select our test. Understatements through omission will never be revealed by examining a sample, because there is clearly no chance of selecting items that have been omitted from the population. Consequently to test an account for understatement, we must select the sample from a reciprocal population, i.e. we would check from the initiation through to the conclusion of a transaction; for example, if we want to check whether sales have been understated, it is clearly useless to select from the sales account. A selection from despatch records could be appropriate, and this could be tested through to sales account to ensure that all have been included. Note that detection of over/understatement through causes other than omission statistically stands the same chance whichever the test direction.

We must always make sure that our tests operate in the correct direction to achieve the desired audit objective. A brief story may better illustrate this point. I once observed (from the sidelines) an internal auditor discussing with a yacht marina manager the tests he wished to perform on yacht berth rental. Now such a business is susceptible to fraud, for yacht owners would be very pleased to obtain a cheap berth by paying cash direct to the manager. So commonsense would indicate a spot test to ensure that yachts in the marina were also in the records. But our auditor was of the old school, more used to 'ticking' than thinking. And he designed his test the wrong way round. He took a sample of yachts from the records and went to locate these in the marina. And obviously this proved nothing, as he had no chance of discovering yachts which were there, but for which no record had been made. His error was compounded by the fact that the manager had suggested this approach as being easier!

## 12.2 Approaches to testing

Each firm will adopt its own approach to designing transaction tests, and each approach will have its merits and its problems. It is not feasible to illustrate all these approaches, for much depends on the nature of the audit problem. So here I shall concentrate on principles. And the main principle is that tests should be designed with the audit objective in mind. Does the direction of test achieve the desired objective?

What is never acceptable, however, is mindless adherence to dated, tattered audit programmes, the origin of which lies in the mists of time, and the reasoning for which is often non-existent. But these programmes, regretfully, still characterise the approach of some firms. . . . It is up to us to rid the profession of these soul-destroying documents, and to *think* what our tests are designed to achieve.

## 12.3 Procedures in transaction testing

The testing of transactions will be achieved in the following ways:
1. Vouching (see Ch. 10).
2. Checking casts and cross-casts (technical terms for adding up and adding across in a ledger or other accounting record).
3. Checking postings (the transfer of a balance or total from one accounting record to another, e.g. the total of the credit sales day book could be check posted to the debtors' control account).
4. Reconciliations (e.g. reconciliation of the bank account with the cash book to assist in proving the records of receipt and payment transactions).

But the arrangement of the tests will depend on the approaches adopted. One such approach is that of depth testing.

## 12.4 Depth testing

Depth testing is a term used to denote the tracing of transactions through from their inception to final recording. An obvious concept, but nevertheless one which has been adopted only comparatively recently. The term applies not just to transaction testing, but to walk through and compliance testing as well. You will no doubt recall that the definition of walk through testing was similar to that given for depth testing above, but you should not regard the two as synonymous. For walk through testing specifically refers to the preliminary check that the auditor performs to satisfy himself as to his understanding of the system; depth testing refers to the overall concept. Similarly, compliance testing could also be carried out in depth test format, there being some advantage in terms of having a logical test sequence. However, you should remember that reliance will not necessarily be placed on all aspects of a control system, and accordingly compliance tests will not be needed for all of it.

But now let us apply the principle of depth testing to transaction tests of detail in the sales 'cycle':

| A typical sales cycle of a manufacturing enterprise would include the following procedures: | INTERNAL CONTROL DIVISIONS | POSSIBLE DOCUMENTATION |
|---|---|---|
| (a) determination of pricing and discount policies; | initiation | customer order |
| (b) approval of sales order; | of the | despatch |
| (c) checking of credit limit; | transaction | authority |
| (d) preparation of despatch documentation | | goods outwards note (GON) |
| (e) despatch of goods; | custody of the related assets | |
| (f) preparation of invoice; | | invoice |
| (g) processing of invoice – sales day book/ invoice listing/posting to sales ledger; | raising the | sales day book sales ledger |
| (h) preparation of credit note for valid claims for short deliveries, defective goods or pricing errors; | relevant documentation | credit note |
| (i) preparation of customers' statements; | | statements |
| (j) listing of cash/cheques received; | post room | cash/cheque diary |
| (k) entry of cash/cheques receipts in cash book; | cashier | cash book |
| (l) preparation of paying-in slip and payment into bank; | | pay-in slip |
| (m) posting of cash/cheques to sales ledger; | recording in | |
| (n) posting totals to nominal ledger; | the accounting | nominal ledger |
| (o) agreement of sales ledger control account; | records | |
| (p) following up overdue debts; | | |
| (q) writing-off bad debts and assessing necessary provisions. | senior official | journal entries |

Remember that in *one* test we can only check for either *understatement or overstatement*. As an example let us test the sales and debtor accounts for *understatement*, which could of course result from either defalcation or error or possibly from distortion if management wish to understate profit perhaps for tax reasons. Now we know that to test for understatement we check from initiation to conclusion, so we therefore must ensure:

1. Only valid orders are despatched.
2. All despatches are correctly invoiced.
3. All invoices are recorded in the ledger.
4. And, in the case of debtors, all credit note, bad debt write-offs, or cash credits are genuine.

Try to follow the logic of these stages, for then you will be able to design a programme for any situation. Note that the term vouching implies checking for all the points discussed earlier in Ch. 10.

### 1. *Only valid orders are despatched*

Clearly we must select from despatch documentation for this test. For if we select from orders, we stand no chance of picking despatches that were made on invalid documentation. So we must examine GONs and vouch these to orders, checking for evidence of 1, 2 and 3 above.

### 2. *All despatches are invoiced*

It will no doubt be clear that you should also select from GONs for this test; for obviously by selecting from invoices there would be no chance of choosing despatches upon which no invoice was raised. But at the same time we must vouch the invoice itself to orders and price lists to check for understatement through fraud or error. This test will of course also reveal overstatement through error.

### 3. *All invoices are recorded*

To ensure all invoices are recorded, we must post from invoices to sales day book, and sales day book to sales and debtors control accounts, or straight to the control accounts if it is feasible. The reverse test, although possibly easier, would only check for overstatement.

### 4. *All credit note or bad debt write-offs are genuine*

This will involve selecting a sample of such write-offs from the debtors ledger, and vouching these to supporting documentation, and for evidence of authority. Note that simply vouching credit notes or journal entries to supporting documents will not be sufficient, for fraudulent entries may be made in the ledger with no supporting documents at all.

### *Cash credits*

In respect of cash credited to debtor accounts, it may be necessary to check to the cash book and/or initial cash listings to prove that cash credits have not been overstated by an employee in collusion with a customer. Such a fraud, however, is not likely except in the instance of very weak controls, so extensive testing would be unusual in this regard.

### *Overstatement*

Overstatement of sales or debtors may be revealed by simply reversing the depth test, and checking from the ledger accounts back to source documentation. Sales returns will have to be checked for understatement by checking from goods returned notes through to the ledger accounts. And cash credits will have to be checked for understatement by checking from initial cash listings to cash book, and bank statement, and cash book to debtors' ledger. In the event that 'teeming and lading' is suspected it may be necessary to obtain the original deposit slips from the bank and check these to the debtors' subsidiary ledger accounts, to ensure that the correct account has been credited.

As an alternative to transaction testing of debtors' ledger accounts, balance testing may be employed to check for overstatement. And as this will normally be quicker and more effective, this method will normally be employed. But more to this in Chapter 14.

*Casting and reconciliations*

So far we have carried out both vouching and posting. But our four principles in sec. 12.3 included casting and reconciliations as well. So think what we can cast and reconcile! Clearly all the books of account that we have examined should be test cast and cross-cast (the vouchers will be cast as part of the vouching procedure), as under- or overstatement may have occurred through error in this way. And then finally reconciliation should be performed between the sales ledger control account, and the total of the sales subsidiary ledger.

*Designing substantive depth tests*

The design of a test should always take into account the most likely form that a mis-statement might take. The principles illustrated by the foregoing test design in respect of sales and debtors should enable you to design transaction tests for the other accounting cycles. And you should now attempt to draft suitable programmes. But to assist you, the chart shown in Fig. 12.1 depicts the most probable forms of mis-statement for each accounting cycle, in respect of error, defalcation and distortion. The lower half of the chart then depicts the direction and nature of tests (in outline) in respect of both over- and understatement. Note that balance testing has been substituted for transaction tests whenever this is likely to be more effective or expedient. The chart is only intended to be indicative; other tests will be necessary in the circumstances of a particular audit. The direction of test only is indicated, and no attempt has been made to list all the documents and records that would be examined during the course of a test. The tests indicated assume that basic control documents exist. In their absence, alternative tests will have to be designed, and the auditor may wish to consider whether proper accounting records have been maintained sufficient for audit purposes.

Example audit programmes are included in Chapter 13, covering sales, purchases and wages, and based on directional testing principles as discussed in the next section.

## 12.5 Directional testing

You will have seen from the last section that depth testing can result in some duplication of effort, in that the same account has to be tested forwards and backwards. Now clearly, in a double entry system of accounting, a mis-statement in

Fig. 12.1 Substantive testing procedures in over- and understatement

| Potential mis-statement | Error | Sales | Debtors | Purchases | Creditors | Wages |
|---|---|---|---|---|---|---|
| | | | | Over or understatement | | |
| | Defalcation | Under | Under/over | Over | Over/under | Over |
| | Manipulation or distortion | Over/under | Over/under | Under/over | Under/over | Unlikely |

**Substantive tests for:**

| | Sales | Debtors | Purchases | Creditors | Wages |
|---|---|---|---|---|---|
| Over statement | Ledger accounts to GONs — GINS (for returns inwards) to ledger accounts | Balance testing (by direct confirmation) | Ledger accounts to GINs — GONs (for returns outwards) to ledger accounts | Ledger accounts to GINs — GONs (for returns outwards) to ledger accounts — Cash book (and perhaps returned cheques) to creditors ledger | Ledger accounts to source documents (payroll, clock cards, personnel dept records, etc) |
| Under statement | GONs to ledger accounts (sales account and debtors' ledger) — Credits in ledger accounts for returns inwards to GINs | Credits for remittances and bad debts to source documents (e.g. initial cash listing, correspondance and bad debts) | GINs to purchases account (particularly near year end re. cut off) | Balance testing (by direct confirmation) | See Note 2 |

Notes

1. GON = Goods outward note
   GIN = Goods inward note

2. No test necessary as unlikely that complete omission of a transaction will have occurred. Understatement through error statistically stands the same chance of detection whichever the test direction

3. Only the principal type/direction of test has been shown. Other tests may be necessary in the circumstances of a particular audit

one account inevitably means that there is a mis-statement in another, provided of course that the books balance. For example, if we discover that an asset account is overstated, it must mean either:

(a) another asset account balance is understated, or
(b) a liability account balance is overstated, or
(c) an income account balance is overstated, or
(d) an expense account balance is understated.

Suppose a debtor confirmation revealed a transposition in a debtor's account, so that he had been debited with £2,100 instead of £1,200. The effect of this will be to overstate both debtors and income by £900. By discovering the overstatement of debtors, we also reveal the overstatement of income. We can use this principle of *directional testing* to help minimise the amount of audit work required.

As we saw in sec. 12.1, all accounts are subject to both overstatement and understatement. But different types of account are often more susceptible to material mis-statements in one direction rather than in the other. For example, if senior management want to distort the accounts, they are most likely to do so by overstating assets, or understating liabilities. If, on the other hand, defalcation has occurred, it is most likely to result in the understatement of income, or the overstatement of expenses. So it follows that we should design our primary tests to check the four types of account for the appropriate mis-statement.

If we check all assets and expenses for overstatement, and all liabilities and income for understatement, it follows from the logic above that we must by corollary check all assets and expenses for understatement and all liabilities and income for overstatement at the same time. And in so doing we can considerably reduce the audit work required.

The following matrix shows tests on the most likely form of mis-statement for each type of account, and demonstrates the secondary effect that the tests will have. You will see that in this way all accounts can be checked for both over- and understatement, without necessarily performing tests on each account.

| Type of account | Purpose of primary test | Resulting corollary test |  |  |  |  |  |  |
| --- | --- | --- | --- | --- | --- | --- | --- | --- |
| | | Assets | | Liabilities | | Income | | Expenses |
| Assets | O | U | or | O | or | O | or | U |
| Liabilities | U | U | or | O | or | O | or | U |
| Income | U | U | or | O | or | O | or | U |
| Expenses | O | U | or | O | or | O | or | U |

But, some words of caution:

1. If we use the double entry principle to minimise our work in this way, we are very dependent on the trial balance. So the usual tests on the trial balance (which were mentioned in Ch. 3) become even more important.
2. Extreme care must be taken to test *all* debit balances for overstatement, and *all* credits for understatement, for an omission of one effects more than just that account.

I should say that this directional testing approach is a comparative innovation, and you should in no way think that this system is universally adopted. Many firms will adopt the straightforward depth test approach to auditing transactions, using balance testing as appropriate. If designed properly, such tests will be perfectly satisfactory in that the account will be tested for both over- and under-statement. But it may not be the most economical way of conducting an audit. Examples of master audit programmes using the directional approach are reproduced on pages 195–99.

# 13
# Audit programmes

## 13.1 The function of audit programmes

Records must be made of all compliance and substantive tests that are performed, and these records will serve the following purposes:
(a) to record work done for purposes of the partner review;
(b) to record who performed the work (and therefore provide a possible indicator of its likely quality);
(c) to provide evidence of work done in the event of subsequent legal proceedings;
(d) to help ensure a methodical approach to the work;
(e) to facilitate transfer of work in the event of new staff being engaged on the audit;
(f) to assist in planning the subsequent year's audit.

The records may either be completed as the work progresses, or they may be in the form of pre-printed programmes. These latter will itemise objectives to be achieved, and/or procedures to be adopted, and staff will be required to sign for the quantity of work performed, identifying at the same time the items selected for testing. Sometimes the programmes will go one step further, by specifying the quantity of testing to be performed. But I would strongly criticise such documents, on the grounds that they are likely to produce an unthinking 'tick and go home' approach to the work, for the quantity of testing must be based on the quality of the internal control, and on the reliance that can be placed on the analytical review; and these will not be known until the relevant audit work has been performed, each year.

But audit programmes can have considerable advantages provided they can be used flexibly. It may sometimes be necessary to draft a programme specifically for a particular client, but this will normally only be the case with very specialist companies. And once written such a programme can provide the basis for audit test procedures (but not quantities) in subsequent years.

Most of the larger firms, however, will use Master Audit Programmes that can be readily adapted to any client company. These Master Audit Programmes (or MAPs) will describe particular objectives to be achieved and/or procedures to be adopted, rather than list specific documents and records to be checked, for the programmes obviously have to be couched in fairly general terms in order to have widespread application. A properly drafted, pre-printed programme can have the following advantages in addition to those mentioned earlier in respect of test records:

(a) facilitates a logical and methodical approach to the work, and reduces the likelihood of significant tests being omitted;

(b) assists inexperienced auditors in conducting test programmes, and accordingly assists in staff training;

(c) communicates the wishes of the partners regarding the testing policy of the firm;

(d) provides a consistent approach throughout the firm and with all clients, making for improved efficiency and reduced audit time, while also facilitating staff movement between jobs.

The disadvantage of MAPs lies mainly in the fact that they can generate an unthinking approach to the work by stifling initiative. But this is only likely to be the case if the programmes and the firm's audit and training policies are themselves unimaginative.

MAPs are undoubtedly invaluable on the job, but for theoretical training purposes they are of limited value. For in my experience, students attempt to memorise the MAPs to the exclusion of understanding why tests are required. This is totally unsatisfactory, for two reasons:

1. Examination questions are becoming increasingly conceptual and a far cry from the traditional 'List 12 tests for . . .', which was prevalent not so long ago. Such memory questions are educationally bankrupt, but nonetheless easier for the student who has not been taught to think about what audit procedures are designed to achieve.

2. There are a lot of tests to remember. If you understand why they are necessary, you do not have to remember them.

## 13.2 Types of audit programme

It follows from what I have just said, that you will not find a complete set of Master Audit Programmes included here! What follows is a selection to illustrate the points that were made in earlier chapters, and to demonstrate the form that such documents might take.

Whichever type of programme is used, certain key features should be present, and these you should note:

1. MAPs will normally be available for each of the key transaction cycles and balance sheet areas, and each will be associated with an ICQ or ICE. Indeed, sometimes the ICE and the MAP are combined in a single document.

2. Space will be included on the MAP for the extent of the tests, reference to the associated ICQ/ICE, and conclusions reached. The document should also always be dated and signed.

3. Space will be available for any additional procedures thought necessary.

Obviously any split of testing procedures will be somewhat artificial because accounting systems are closely interrelated. Nevertheless, a split is necessary to make the work manageable, and to facilitate delegation. So the question arises as to how the split should be made.

Compliance and substantive testing procedures can be shown either separately or together. However, it is now generally considered best not to specify compliance tests in detail in that the auditor will not necessarily wish to rely on all controls, and in any event the nature of controls, and hence the nature of testing, varies considerably from client to client.

Tests on income and expenditure cycles and assets and liabilities can be combined in one programme (e.g. sales and debtors) or dealt with in separate programmes. In that income and expenditure will normally be proved by transaction testing, and assets and liabilities will normally be verified by balance testing, there can be some advantage in having separate programmes. But you should note that in practice there must be close co-ordination between those members of the audit team engaged on related areas.

For demonstration purposes master audit programmes are shown in Fig. 13.1 covering Credit Sales, Credit Purchases and Wages. These MAPs are based on those used by Deloitte, Haskins and Sells and utilise the principles of directional testing discussed in sec. 12.5. If traditional depth testing is used, additional tests may have to be designed in accordance with the principles illustrated in Fig. 12.1 (for example, sales may be tested for overstatement by checking from ledger accounts to goods outwards notes, but this particular test would only normally be necessary if distortion was suspected).

Further examples of directional test MAPs covering debtors and creditors are included at the end of the appropriate sections in Chapter 14, after discussion of the relevant principles of verification.

Fig. 13.1 Master audit programmes – directional tests

## Audit area – Credit sales

Audit objective – the objective of the procedures set out in this programme is to obtain reasonable assurance that credit sales are not materially understated.

### Investigating compliance with internal control procedures

Where reliance has been placed on the client's internal control procedures, test that the controls on which we are relying have been complied with, and record the details of such tests in the working papers.

### Tests of detail

Test for omission and other under-statement in the accounting records of sales charged to debtors, by selecting from appropriate records of potential sales transactions and tracing the selected items through to the relevant income account in the general ledger, as follows:

1. Select from the most appropriate records the items to be examined (see note below). Test for completeness of these records by examining the system for preparing and controlling such records, by testing the numerical sequence (if any) of the records, and/or by any other procedures which are appropriate.
   *Note: The records from which the sample is selected should as far as possible satisfy the following requirements.*

    (a) *the records should if practicable be independent of the sales recording system;*

    (b) *the records should be complete in the sense that for each sale that has been made, there is a related item in the independent records;*

    (c) *the records should if practicable be such that the probability of selecting a particular item is proportionate to the value of the potential sale;*

    (d) *the records should enable the potential sales to be identified at the earliest possible stage in the recording process.*

2. Compare the records selected in procedure (1) above with the initial sales records, for correct quantities.
3. Check the selling price of these initial sales records with the relevant independent records (such as official catalogues, price lists, etc.), and check the extensions and casts.
4. Check the VAT on sales selected for testing, and test the proper recording of these items in the VAT account in the general ledger.
5. Compare these initial sales records with the intermediate and final records, testing these records for under-statement of the casts, and for under-summarisation of the sales income.
6. Compare the credits in the final records examined in procedure (5) above with the relevant income account(s) in the general ledger.
7. Test the casts of these income accounts and prove the final balances arithmetically.

Test the transactions in the last few days of the year to ensure that sales have not been under-stated as follows:

    Compare major despatches as shown in the despatch records in the last few days of the year with the copy sales invoices. Trace these copy invoices, via the sales accounting records, to the credit of the sales account. In doing this, ensure that these despatches have been included as sales in the year under review.

*Note: This test should be carried out in conjunction with the cut-off procedures relating to the over-statement of debtors.*

Select from the general ledger accounts, sales returns and allowances to be tested for over-statement.

Examine the relevant supporting documents for:

(a) Approval, and

(b) Other independent evidence of validity (such as goods returned records, correspondence, sales invoices, and remittance advices from customers).

Test the transactions in the last few days of the year to ensure that sales returns and allowances have not been over-stated, as follows:

    Examine major sales returns and allowances debited, in the last few days of the year, to the sales returns account or to the sales account (as appropriate). Compare these sales returns with the supporting evidence (such as goods returned records, correspondence with customers, and the relevant sales invoices). In doing this, ensure that the sales returns have been recorded in the correct financial year.

*Note: This test should be carried out in conjunction with the cut-off procedures relating to the over-statement of debtors.*

## Audit area — Purchases on credit

Audit objective — the objective of the procedures set out in this programme is to obtain reasonable assurance that purchases on credit are not materially overstated.

### Investigating compliance with internal control procedures

Where reliance has been placed on the client's internal control procedures, test that the controls on which we are relying have been complied with, and record the details of such tests in the working papers.

Tests of detail

Select from the general ledger accounts items to be tested for over-statement.
1. Examine the initial purchase records and supporting documents (such as purchase orders and goods received records) for:
   (a) approval;
   (b) other independent evidence of validity; and
   (c) correctness of the allocations to the general ledger accounts.
2. Cast the initial purchase record (usually the purchase invoice).
3. Examine the terms of sale of suppliers selected for the above tests, and identify those suppliers that have included reservation of title in their terms of trade. The year end liability to these suppliers should be tested for under-statement (see paragraph 15(A) of the MAP for creditors, accruals and provisions, Fig. 14.9).
   *Note: Where credit entries (e.g. purchase credits and cash discounts) have been identified in taking out our debit sample, ensure that these credit entries are being tested for under-statement using the relevant MAP.*
4. Examine also the relevant paid cheques for the correctness of the relevant details (such as the date, the payee, the amount and the signatures), and investigate any alterations or unusual endorsements.
5. Where any selected debit entries have not been paid by the year-end, ensure that these are included in creditors at that date.
6. List on a working paper the names of the suppliers whose transactions have been tested. These suppliers will form part of the creditors confirmation sample (see paragraph 3(A) of the MAP for creditors and accruals, Fig. 14.9).

Test the transactions in the last few days of the year to ensure that purchases have not been over-stated, as follows:
Compare major purchases as shown in the purchases account in the last few days of the year with the receiving records, to ensure that the goods or services were received or performed before the year end.
*Note: This test should be carried out in conjunction with the cut-off procedures relating to the under-statement of liabilities.*

Test for the omission and other under-statement in the accounting records of purchase returns and allowances, as follows:
1. Select from the most appropriate independent records of purchase returns and allowances (such as goods returned records, inspection reports and correspondence with suppliers) and compare with the initial purchase returns and allowances records.
2. Check the VAT on purchase returns selected for testing, and test the proper recording of these items in the VAT account in the general ledger.
3. Test the initial purchase returns and allowances records and the relevant intermediate and final records for under-statement of casts and for under-summarisation of purchase credits.
4. Compare the credits in the final records with the relevant general ledger accounts.
5. Test the casts of these general ledger accounts and prove the final balances arithmetically.

Test the transactions in the last few days of the year to ensure that purchase returns and allowances have not been under-stated, as follows:
1. Examine the evidence of purchase returns and allowances (such as goods returned records, inspection reports, correspondence with suppliers, and the relevant purchase invoices) for the last few days of the year and the first few weeks after the year-end. Trace major items in these records, via the credit notes and the accounting records, to the credit of the purchases returns account or the purchases account as appropriate. In doing this, ensure that these purchase returns have been recorded in the correct financial year.
2. Examine major purchase returns credited, in the first few weeks after the year-end, to the purchase returns account or to the purchases account as appropriate. Compare these returns with the relevant supporting evidence (such as goods returned records, inspection reports, correspondence with suppliers, and the

relevant purchase invoices). In doing this, ensure that these purchase returns have been recorded in the correct financial year.

*Note: This test should be carried out in conjunction with the cut-off procedures relating to the under-statement of liabilities.*

## Audit area – Wages

Audit objective – the objective of the procedures set out in this programme is to obtain reasonable assurance that wages are not materially overstated.

### Investigating compliance with internal control procedures

Where reliance has been placed on the client's internal control procedures, test that the controls on which we are relying have been complied with, and record the details of such tests in the working papers.

### Tests of detail

1. Select individual items for examination using either procedure (A) or procedure (B) below:
   *(Note: Procedure (B), the payroll selection reconciliation method, can be used in the following circumstances:*
   *(i) Where we have evaluated the internal control over wages and salaries as good.*
   *(ii) Where we have obtained satisfactory results from our analytical review for credibility.*
   *(iii) Where we have reviewed the week by week/month by month payroll data, which is reconciled by management or is closely controlled by management budgets, and have received satisfactory explanations for all significant discrepancies revealed by our review.)*
   (A) (i) From the general ledger payroll accounts select (on the basis of the total debit entries in these accounts) the accounts to be sampled.
       *(Note: If a costing system is used it may be necessary to select directly from payroll records and prove the postings to the general ledger in total.)*
       (ii) From each payroll account selected under procedure (i) above select individual payrolls to be examined, testing the casts of the debit entries in these accounts for over-statement.
       (iii) From each payroll selected under procedure (ii) above select individual employees' pay to be examined, testing the casts of the payroll for over-statement.
   (B) Where we can use the payroll reconciliation method, select three payrolls for testing as follows:
       (i) At the interim audit visit select two payrolls for testing – one a current payroll and the other selected at random.
       (ii) At the final audit visit select a further payroll at random.
       (iii) Where only one audit visit is carried select three payrolls from the year at random.
       For each payroll selected under (i) to (iii) above select individual employees' pay to be examined.
   (C) In addition, select all individuals who prepare, handle or approve employee status change documents, payroll master files or payrolls.

2. Carry out the following procedures in respect of each employee selected for examination:
   (a) Obtain evidence of employment by examining independent employee records, by personal contact, or by enquiry of other independent employees.
   (b) Examine the relevant supporting documents (such as employee status change documents, payroll master files, and employees' time, piece and bonus records) for:

    (1) Approval.
    (2) Other independent evidence of validity and,
    (3) Correctness of the gross pay calculations.
(c) Obtain the payroll for the pay period from which the employee was selected, and scrutinise it for possible duplicate payments to that employee.
(d) Test that deductions from pay have been properly accounted for, as follows:
    (i) Test for under-statement of credit entries in the deduction accounts in the general ledger. Use the sample of the employees checked under procedures (a) to (c) above. For each employee selected check that the various deductions from gross pay have been correctly recorded in the initial, intermediate and final records and in the general ledger deduction accounts. Test for under-casting of deductions in each of these records.
    (ii) In respect of all the payrolls dealt with above, check that the total deductions plus the total net pay equals the total gross pay.
(e) For employees paid in cash, observe the making up of pay packets and the distribution of pay to employees, paying special attention to unclaimed pay (compliance test).
(f) For employees paid by cheque, examine the paid cheque for the correctness of the relevant details (such as the date, the payee, the amount and the signatures), and investigate any alterations or unusual endorsements.

3. Check the total net pay recorded on all the payrolls selected above, to the paid cheque or other payment details.

4. Where the payroll selection reconciliation method of selecting individuals for testing has been used, carry out the following additional procedures:
    (a) For each employee selected review the cumulative pay for the year for amounts over basic pay.
    (b) Cast the selected payrolls and compare the totals of gross pay and deductions of the selected weeks or months with the equivalent totals of all other payrolls in the year.
    (c) Cast all the weekly or monthly payroll summaries and agree the postings to the general ledger.
    (d) Scan the general ledger payroll accounts to ensure that there are no payroll postings which have not been checked under (c) above.

# 14
# Verification of assets and liabilities

## 14.1 Introduction

In sec. 10.4, I introduced the term verification. Now that we have concluded our discussion of transaction testing, the next stage is to examine the asset and liability verification procedures that will take place at, or towards, the year end. Remember the principles introduced in sec. 10.4; *cost, authorisation, valuation, existence, beneficial ownership, presentation.* Not all of these will be applicable to all assets and liabilities. But they serve as a reminder of the sorts of questions to be asked. And if you are given an examination question on this topic (very likely), they can serve as a framework for your answer.

The initial stages of verification can be achieved in one of two ways – transaction or balance testing. Or a combination can be used. For example, we may verify sales ledger balances by proving the transactions that gave rise to the balances (transaction testing), by proving the balances to independent evidence such as external confirmations (balance testing), or by a combination of the two. Whatever method is used, an extremely important part of the verification process is that of ensuring that the balance is properly presented in the accounts.

Proper presentation includes:

1. Presentation in accordance with the appropriate statement on Standard Accounting Practice, International Accounting Standard, and UEC requirement.
2. Adoption of accounting policies which are appropriate to the circumstances of the company.
3. Consistent application of accounting policies – or where a change in policy is deemed necessary, disclosure of such change in accordance with SSAP6.
4. Presentation in accordance with the Companies Acts, Stock Exchange, and Fourth Directive requirements.

The facts of such presentation are discussed in this chapter. The conceptual background to the varying requirements, together with the action to be taken over contentious matters, can await Chapter 15, although certain points must be made briefly here.

*Accounting and auditing*

Much of the audit work during verification will involve checking for proper presentation; and this involves a thorough knowledge of accounting, accounting standards and company law. Such knowledge I must assume at this stage, for there is insufficient space here to deal in detail with all relevant accounting issues. So I shall concentrate on contentious *audit* matters, and pay particular attention to those areas which traditionally present the auditor with problems (for example, stock, debtors, fixed assets and research and development). Synopsis of the main points contained in the SSAPs have been included where appropriate, but you should certainly have complete copies of all of these for reference. However, to further assist your studies, SSAP and Companies Act check lists are reproduced in Appendix 1.

*Appropriateness of accounting policies*

The SSAPs often allow several accounting policies in a given set of circumstances. For example, FIFO, weighted average and unit cost are all allowable methods of establishing the cost of stock. So the question can often arise as to whether the particular accounting policy chosen is appropriate. It will often fall to the auditor to decide on this appropriateness, and in so doing, he will consider the general practice in the trade, the previous practice in the company and the requirements of the true and fair view.

It may sometimes occur that the requirements of appropriateness will override those of the SSAP itself. For example, Tate and Lyle Ltd (the well known sugar manufacturers) had for many years used the policy of base stock in accounting for cost of stock. This policy was expressly ruled out by SSAP9 when it was introduced, but the Tate and Lyle directors still believed it the most appropriate method for their company. So they continued to use it. And the auditors concurred with their presentation, giving the accounts a 'True and Fair' report, although in these circumstances they were then obliged to state the non-compliance in their report, while at the same time making specific reference to their agreement with the treatment.

*Changes in accounting policy*

Changes in accounting policy may sometimes be necessary either to comply with new legislation or Accounting Standards, or for purposes of more appropriate disclosure. Should such a change be necessary, it must be disclosed by way of a note to the accounts, and the financial effect of the change must be disclosed as a Prior Year Adjustment, in accordance with SSAP6. That is, the opening balance of the relevant account must be adjusted to the closing basis of valuation, and the contra entry must be made on the after tax profit in the income statement. For example, assume that the basis of stock valuation in a company was changed from LIFO to FIFO in a period of inflation, as a result of the introduction of SSAP9. The relevant accounting entries would be: debit opening stock, credit after tax profit.

With these points on presentation in mind, let us proceed to the detail of verification procedures. For the sake of logical treatment, I have dealt with the various assets and liabilities in accordance with the order in which they are likely to occur in a vertical balance sheet. Under some headings, more detail is introduced on control and systems procedures, where this is relevant to the way in which the auditor will carry out his verification. This chapter is accordingly a very long one. So you can take a rest between each sub-heading!

## 14.2 Pre-audit work by the client

The auditor is very dependent on the client for the satisfactory and prompt conclusion of year-end work, for much information will be necessary before verification work can begin. So it is appropriate to advise the client well in advance of the sort of things that we expect; and to receive his agreement thereto. Figure 14.1 shows a suggested list of pre-audit work that should be performed by the client.

Fig. 14.1  Pre-audit work

### Suggested timetable for pre-audit work to be performed by the client

(To be amended as appropriate to fit the circumstances of each individual client.)

The company . . .

General

1. is to prepare the trial balance at the year-end, before taxation and other adjustments.
2. will make any necessary adjustments to the trial balance to include the agreed adjustments and tax provisions.
3. will complete the accounts by . . . . . . . . . . . . . . . . . . . . .

Bank and cash balances

1. will close its cash book promptly at the close of business on . . . . . . . . . . . . . . .
   will prepare bank reconciliations.
2. will arrange for independent persons to count small cash funds and undeposited receipts, etc. as at . . . . . . . . . . . . . . . . . . . .
   and will provide schedules of these counts, and
   will also arrange with the audit staff for all large cash funds and unbanked receipts, etc. to be counted by the custodians in the presence of the audit staff as at the above date.
3. will obtain certificates of funds and/or stocks in the hands of, and loans to, employees at the year-end, and will deliver these certificates to the auditors. (*Note*: Any expenses included by employees in the relevant certificates will be excluded from cash in hand in the company's accounts.)

Debtors and prepayments

1. will agree the total of the sales ledger balances at the end of . . . . . . . . . . . . . . . (together with the monthly statements) with the control account in the general ledger.
2. will agree the total of the sales ledger balances at the year-end with the control account in the general ledger, and produce an aged list of the balances.
3. will prepare a schedule of notes and bills receivable at the year-end.

4. will prepare a schedule of miscellaneous accounts receivable at the year-end.
5. will prepare a schedule of debit balances appearing in the purchase ledger at the year-end together with an explanation of each item.
6. will review the provision for doubtful debts at . . . . . . . . . . . . . . . . . . . with a brief reconsideration at the year-end in the light of the latest available information, and will prepare a schedule showing how the provision has been calculated.
7. will agree or reconcile the balances due from the holding and other group companies at . . . . . . . . . . . . . . . . . . and will prepare a schedule of such balances and reconciliations.
8. will prepare a schedule of the balances due from the holding company and other group companies at the year-end.
   (*Note*: The auditors will make their own arrangements for confirming the balances directly with the  companies concerned.)
9. The company will prepare a schedule of prepayments and deferred charges at the year-end.

## Stocks

1. will inform the auditors when physical counts are to be made and will supply the auditors with copies of the detailed instructions for such counts.
2. will reconcile the physical stocks with the book records as at . . . . . . . . . . . . . . . and will prepare schedules which set out the balances and explain any differences.
3. where the physical count(s) is (are) made prior to the year-end, will prepare a schedule summarising the movements for intervening purchases, production, and sales.
4. will review the obsolete and slow-moving stocks before the year-end, and will supply the auditors with a copy of the subsequent report to management and of the authorisation for any write-down.
5. will make a brief reconsideration of the obsolete and slow-moving stocks at the year-end, and will notify the auditors of any changes made to the earlier report.
6. will prepare a schedule showing details of unrealised profits on goods not yet sold outside the group.

## Fixed assets

1. will prepare schedules of fixed asset additions, disposals and scrappings, and of major items charged to revenue.
2. will prepare a summary of fixed assets and depreciation, including movements during the year, and schedules showing the depreciation computations for the year.

## Creditors and accruals

1. will agree the total of the purchase ledger balances with the control account in the general ledger, and will prepare a suitable listing of the balances.
2. will prepare a detailed schedule of accrued expenses.
3. will make available a list of the credit balances appearing on the sales ledger as and when the purchase ledger balances are listed.
4. if it is necessary to verify the purchase ledger balances at a date previous to the year-end, will prepare a schedule setting out the balances at . . . . . . . . . . . . . . .
5. will agree or reconcile balances due to the holding company and other group companies at . . . . . . . . . . . . . . . and will prepare a schedule of such balances and reconciliations.
6. will prepare a schedule of the balances due to the holding company and other group companies at the year-end.
   (*Note*: The auditors will make their own arrangements for confirming the balances directly with the companies concerned.)

## Taxation

will compute the tax charge and prepare a schedule showing how this charge is calculated.

## Directors' remuneration

will prepare a schedule setting out the directors' remuneration in detail for the period . . . . . . . . . . . . . . . . . . .

## Employees' remuneration

will prepare a schedule which details those employees whose remuneration is in excess of £10,000 per annum.

## Capital commitments

will prepare a schedule of its outstanding capital commitments at the end of the year.

## Profit and loss account schedules

The auditors will let the company know by . . . . . . . . . . . . . . . . . . . what profit and loss account schedules they need, and the company will provide what they are able to, and the auditors will prepare the remainder; agreement on the responsibility for the preparation of these schedules is to be reached before the year-end.

## Management representations

1. The auditors will provide drafts as appropriate.
2. The final letters/representations will be completed and will be signed by the managing director and the chief accountant on the day the accounts are ready for signature.

## Appropriations to reserve and proposed dividends

The company will notify the auditors in writing of any appropriations to reserve or proposed dividends for their inclusion in the accounts.

## Directors' report

The company will prepare the directors' report.

## Chairman's statement

A copy of the draft chairman's statement will be supplied to the auditors.

## Accounts

1. The accounts are to be printed by . . . . . . . . . . . . . . . . . . .
2. The accounts are to be signed by Mr . . . . . . . . . . . . . . . . . . . and Mr . . . . . . . . . . . . . . . . . . as directors.
3. The accounts are to be signed by the auditors.
4. The accounts are to be sent to shareholders on . . . . . . . . . . . . . . . . . . .

Copies of all the above schedules and documents should be sent to the auditors by a specified person, by a specified date.

## 14.3 Fixed assets

We can distinguish four main types of fixed asset that will be encountered in the average company: Land and Buildings; Fixtures and Fittings; Plant and Machinery; and Motor Vehicles. The verification approach will be essentially similar in all of these. However, land, because of its special nature, requires separate treatment. In all cases, a thorough knowledge of SSAP12 is essential. Note that for all assets and liabilities brought forward balances should be checked to the previous years' working papers, as a matter of course.

*Land and buildings*

*Cost and authorisation.* The cost of land and buildings acquired during the year should be vouched to appropriate documentation, such as contracts of sale, surveyors' certificates and solicitors' correspondence and the authorisation for purchase should be proved by reference to the directors' minutes. In particular, the distinction between capital and revenue must be noted, and a check made to ensure that all appropriate items have been capitalised; for example, company labour and materials expended on building extensions are often overlooked. Wherever possible it is necessary to distinguish between the cost of land, and the cost of the buildings that sit on it. This split is necessary in order to comply with the depreciation provisions of SSAP12.

*Valuation.* All fixed assets purchased for use by the business will normally be valued on the basis of depreciated historic cost – with one exception. SSAP12 states that freehold land should not be depreciated, except in the event that the reduction in value is due to depletion through, for example, mining (in which case the proper term for the diminution in value of such a wasting asset would be amortisation), or if the loss is due to changed economic circumstances, such as for example a by-pass construction affecting the value of a fuel station. The reason for not depreciating freehold land is obvious when one looks at the definition of depreciation – depreciation is the allocation of historic cost over the useful life of the asset. As land has no finite useful life, it can have no depreciation, for there is no basis for the calculation. Freehold buildings, should however, be depreciated, and the auditor must check that the estimated useful life is reasonable, and that the calculations have been correctly made.

SSAP19, Accounting for Investment Properties requires that investment properties should be included in the balance sheet at their open market value.

Because of the effects of inflation, freehold land and buildings are often re-valued to approximate market value on a periodic basis. In my view, there is little logic in singling out land and buildings for treatment in this way, when the effects of inflation on other assets are not noted. On the other hand, maintained at original value, the figure for land in the balance sheet will be totally meaning-less after a few years (or less). This is one of the anomalies of historic cost account-ing. In practice some companies revalue, others do not. And we therefore lose the comparability which SSAPs are designed to achieve. Our function as auditors is to ensure that any revaluation is reasonably made by competent personnel, and that the names or qualifications of those personnel are disclosed in the accounts together with the date of the revaluation. Where buildings are revalued, they must still be depreciated, but now on the basis of their revaluation value, spread over their remaining useful life. The profit arising on revaluation of either land or buildings must be debited to the appropriate asset account, and the credit will be added to reserves. Profit arising on the realisation of a fixed asset will, if material, be an extraordinary item in the income statement in accordance with SSAP6 (if you have forgotten about Extraordinary items, you should quickly revise your knowledge by reference to the SSAP6 check list in the Appendix).

Leasehold land and buildings are not depreciated, for the proper term is amortisation. Such an asset will be amortised over the life of the lease, and it is the auditor's task to check that the appropriate calculation is made correctly. You will, I am sure, remember that leasehold property must be disclosed in the accounts, split as between short and long leases, a long lease being defined as one of more than fifty years' duration.

*Existence.* The existence of land and buildings should not normally be difficult to prove. You may even be sitting in the building, if it is the office block! But if the assets are situated abroad, then there may be a problem. In these circumstances it will be appropriate to ask an associate firm (or other reliable professional body) in the overseas country to view the premises for you, to ascertain that the value ascribed is reasonable and to report formally to that effect. No auditor is expected to be a professional valuer when it comes to checking valuations, but he is expected to judge what is, and what is not, reasonable. Failure so to do, in respect of overseas property developments, has resulted in many mis-stated accounts and indeed subsequent legal action against the auditors.

*Beneficial ownership.* All forms of land and buildings are often subject to mortgage, so the auditor has to be particularly careful to ensure that such charges are correctly disclosed in the accounts. The charges should be recorded in the company's register of charges, but if the directors deliberately wish to conceal their existence you will of course not find reference there. However, they are not normally difficult to discover, in that reference will be made in the title deeds; indeed, the mortgagor will probably retain the deeds as security. But second and third mortgages can sometimes be overlooked, so all loans to the company should be investigated to see if they are secured.

The title to the property must also be examined to ensure that it is validly in the name of the company. This will be straightforward in the case of registered land, because a certificate of ownership can be obtained from the Land Registry (Government body). However, not all land is registered, so in the case of non-registered land, the title deeds and conveyances must be carefully examined to ensure that the title is prima facie vested in the client's name. I say prima facie, for the auditor is not expected to be an expert in conveyancing, and if there is an obscure defect in the title dating back to some early faulty conveyance, the auditor would not normally be expected to discover it where solicitors had failed so to do. But if there were suspicious circumstances, such for example as the directors performing their own conveyancing, then the auditors would be put on their guard and should consider obtaining expert professional opinion. Deeds should automatically be checked on every audit. It is not sufficient to merely examine them superficially, and check for example that a seal remains unbroken, such as was done by the auditors of the now well known Grays Building Society. They failed to properly check deeds held as security for loans on mortgage; and this was one of the (many) reasons why they failed to discover the chairman's multi-million pound fraud.

*Presentation.* Proper presentation involves the split of all the fixed assets into appropriate classes, and the following matters must be disclosed:
(a) the depreciation methods used;
(b) the useful lives, or the depreciation rates used;
(c) the total depreciation for the period;
(d) the gross amount of the depreciable assets, and the related accumulated depreciation.
In particular, the split between freehold and leasehold land must be shown, together with the split between long and short term leases.

### Plant and machinery/fixtures and fittings

*Cost and authorisation.* The cost of material, plant, etc. acquired during the year must be vouched to supporting vouchers. Carriage inwards, installation charges and other related expenditure should be capitalised, and the auditor should ensure that these have been included as appropriate.

*Valuation.* As with property, plant, etc., will be valued at depreciated historic cost. The auditor's responsibility here is to:
1. Ensure that the accounting policy for depreciation is appropriate. For example, if the diminution in value of the asset is related largely to time, it would not normally be appropriate to use a reducing balance method – straight line should be used.
2. Ensure that the accounting policy is in accordance with SSAP12.
3. Consider whether the useful lives of the assets are appropriate. This can often be difficult, in that the auditor will not be an expert in all the types of asset that his client companies may acquire. But there are several ways in which the reasonableness of the figures can be checked. The auditor may well have experience of similar assets in other client companies, or information may be available from the manufacturers of the plant. Though perhaps it is better to look to the company's disposal account. If this shows considerable gain or loss on assets disposed during the year, it would be reasonable to suppose that the company is not good at estimating the useful lives of its assets. And accordingly this year's estimates should be thoroughly investigated. It may

even transpire that the company simply uses percentage estimates with no real attempt at accurate prediction of useful lives. Particular attention should be paid to this area, for it is one specific way in which senior management sometimes attempt to distort accounts; for altering the useful lives of assets can considerably affect the depreciation charge, and hence the profit.

4. Check that the calculations are correctly made.

*Existence.* The existence of plant, etc., should normally be checked by physical inspection, wherever it is material. And here I must digress a little, for the only way in which the auditor can reasonably check the existence of plant is through the medium of a plant or fixed asset register.

*The Fixed Asset Register* is an important independent accounting record which we as auditors should encourage clients to maintain. In order for this record to be sufficiently independent to have value, the person maintaining it must have no responsibilities for:

(a) ordering or authorising the purchase of fixed assets;
(b) custody of fixed assets;
(c) authorising the disposal of fixed assets;
(d) maintaining general ledger accounts;
(e) custody of readily realisable assets.

Any of these functions performed by the register clerk could render the register unreliable, in that there would be inadequate segregation of duties, and fraud could occur without necessarily being detected. But assuming that the register is properly maintained, it can provide the following advantages for the client, and for the auditor:

(a) internal control can be strengthened in that there will be an independent record of all fixed assets, as to location, responsibility, etc., and this record can be independently checked to the assets themselves on a periodic basis, perhaps by the internal auditors;
(b) accurate depreciation records can be maintained in respect of each asset. The alternative to a register is normally a bulk account with a percentage depreciation rate applied to the whole account. This leads to inaccurate depreciation charges, inaccurate disposal calculations, and specifically, non-compliance with the provisions of SSAP12, in respect of appraisal of useful lives;
(c) the auditors can only reasonably check the completeness and existence of assets if they have a detailed record of their nature and location. To work from the general ledger is almost impossible;
(d) records for tax purposes (capital allowances claimed) and accounting treatment of government grants can be maintained in the register;
(e) SSAP16 covering Current Cost Accounting is based on the concept of deprival value. It is now accordingly necessary to have information about the net realisable value of the asset, about its replacement cost, and about its economic value. This information will be best maintained in some sort of fixed asset register.

SSAP12, and point (e) above, have added weight to the auditors' consistent requests for clients to adopt plant registers. And there are now signs that these requests are gradually being heeded. If a register is maintained, then it can usefully contain the following information:
(a) plant number;
(b) location and responsibility for custody;
(c) nature and description of asset;
(d) cost and date of purchase;
(e) estimated useful life, and residual value;
(f) accounting policy for depreciation (straight line, reducing balance, etc.);
(g) accumulated depreciation and net book value;
(h) gain or loss on disposal;
(i) capital allowance and government grant details;
(j) deprival value details.

Once the plant register has been reconciled to the general ledger, the auditor can check the assets for physical existence, by reference to the numbers and locations recorded. A 100 per cent check will seldom be necessary unless internal control is very weak, or unless fraud is suspected. Indeed, this may well be one of the areas in which the auditor can place considerable reliance on the internal auditors.

The existence of motor vehicles can sometimes present problems in checking – for they may not stay still long enough to be ticked! In particular, transport fleets or contractors' plants can provide special difficulties. It may not be sufficient in these circumstances to check registration numbers only – for unscrupulous people have been known to swop these around! So manufacturer's engine and chassis numbers may need to be used in the event that suspicions are aroused. You will recall my comments in Chapter 6 on the vulnerability and value of contracting plant, so this should always be borne in mind when conducting existence checks.

*Beneficial ownership.* While plant, etc., is not usually subject to mortgage, it is often acquired under hire purchase, and sometimes a floating charge may be granted over such assets. In the event that plant is acquired under hire purchase, the auditor must check that the accounting treatment is appropriate. The asset should be shown at cost, excluding hire purchase interest, and the hire purchase creditor should be shown inclusive of interest, with the interest shown as a deduction therefrom, in so far as it has not been written off to the income statement. It is also acceptable to show the hire purchase creditor as a figure net of interest, but in my opinion this is not good practice. This in any event is an instance where the commercial substance of a transaction takes precedence over its legal form; for in law the asset is not the property of the hirer until such time as he makes the final payment. But provided the company is a going concern, it is reasonable to treat it as an asset from the date of acquisition. In addition to checking the accounting treatment of the hire purchase, the auditor should check that the calculation of interest has been correctly made. He must further ensure that no assets are on hire purchase, other than the ones stated. This will not ordinarily be a problem as the purchase documentation should reveal any hire purchase agreement. But if there is a possibility of distortion, due perhaps to a severe cash shortage, then this matter may need more careful attention. For motor vehicles, there is a service known as Hire Purchase Information (or HPI) which can provide details as to whether a vehicle is on hire purchase with any of the major companies. Primarily for the benefit of the motor trade, this information could also be of value to the auditor in certain circumstances.

Floating charges should be revealed by the company's register of charges, but again this will not be the case if there has been deliberate distortion. So the terms of any loan to the company should be carefully scrutinised to check for any evidence of security.

*Presentation.* Presentation was discussed in the context of land and you should refer again to the points made there.

## 14.4 Investments

*Cost.* The cost of investments acquired during the year should be vouched to contract notes and brokers statements or, in the event of unlisted companies, possibly to solicitors' correspondence.

*Authorisation.* The purchase should be checked for authorisation, at the appropriate level; either that of the board of directors in the case of major purchases (directors' minutes will be relevant here), or that of the investments manager in the event of routine dealing.

*Valuation.* The valuation of the investments should be at the lower of cost or market value, in the case of investments held as current assets. In the case of assets held as fixed assets, diminution in value would normally only be recognised if it was both permanent and material. Market value of listed investments should be checked to the ruling mid market price (half way between buying and selling price) on the last day of trading before the company's year end. This information can be obtained from the Exchange Telegraph Company (EXTEL), or from a newspaper of the appropriate day. The market value must be quoted as a note to the accounts, if cost is used as the valuation base. If the securities are unlisted, then the directors are required to provide a valuation, and the auditors should check this by reference to the accounts of the company concerned, together with any other available evidence.

*Existence and beneficial ownership.* The share certificates should be inspected, in so far as they are available, but broker's notes are normally considered sufficient independent evidence. If distortion is suspected, there is the possibility that investments could have been sold in advance of the year end, but the sale not declared in the accounts, thereby boosting cash, and overstating investments. So brokers' statements around the year end should be thoroughly examined and reconciled for unrecorded sales. But if there has been deliberate distortion, then another broker may well have been used. So it will be necessary to check the cash records for any large unexplained influx of cash around the year end.

In some cases securities may be held by third parties, banks being an obvious example. It is always preferable that the auditor should himself examine securities, but in some cases it may be appropriate to accept the written certificate of a third party, provided that third party is truly independent, and provided that custodianship of securities is a normal part of the certifying businesses activities. Such a certificate from a bank would normally be acceptable, and indeed the normal bank letter (see sec. 14.9) will usually contain a request for information in respect of any securities held. But a certificate from stockbrokers of securities held would not be acceptable, as the holding of securities is not a normal part of their business. This was well proved in the 1924 case of The City Equitable Fire Insurance Company, where the auditors were held to be negligent for relying on a stockbroker's certificate in respect of a substantial portfolio of investments. The stockbrokers (the senior partner of which was also the chairman of City Equitable) had fraudulently pledged the investments to cover losses on unauthorised dealings in other clients' investments. The principles to be derived from this case are:

1. Certificates should not be accepted from third parties unless the matter being certified is in the ordinary course of that third party's business.
2. Certificates should not be accepted from third parties unless they are truly independent (in this case of course the independence was lost by virtue of the involvement of the chairman in both businesses).

*Note* that these principles have general application to *all* certificates from third parties.

## 14.5 Intangibles

The intangible assets with which the auditor is most concerned are Research and Development and Goodwill. These will often be material, whereas other types of intangible such as patents, trademarks, royalties, and copyrights seldom are. In these latter, the audit work will mainly involve vouching the cost, and ensuring that this is written off over a suitable period of time.

Here I shall concentrate on Research and Development and Goodwill because these are special problem areas for the auditor. For this reason, they warrant slightly different treatment from our 'CAVEBOP' approach adopted so far.

### Research and development

There have been a number of examples of company collapse that can partly be attributed to over indulgence in research and development on unprofitable products. Furthermore, these collapses have in no way been indicated by the preceding financial statements. For research has commonly been capitalised in the past, and auditors have made little attempt to discover whether the value ascribed to it is in any sense realistic. The most obvious example of this is the collapse of the 'Blue Chip' company Rolls-Royce. Huge amounts of R & D were capitalised in the Rolls-Royce accounts, and there was, in actual fact, very little chance of much of this being recovered.

So following this, and other events, SSAP13 on Research and Development was introduced in December 1977. The SSAP drew a distinction between pure research on the one hand, and development work on the other; the former to be written off against income, and the latter to be capitalised. The distinction is based on whether there is the likelihood of a marketable, profitable product being derived from the specific work being undertaken. Until such time as this can be reasonably assured, then the expenditure should be written off, on the grounds of prudence. Let us take a specific example to illustrate the point. Assume that a drug company has been undertaking research for many years in attempts to discover a cure for a particular disease. Until such time as the cure is discovered, and appears feasible for commercial production, expenditure must be written off. But once a suitable drug has been produced, the costs of development work in testing and refining the product can be capitalised. They should then subsequently be written off against income, from such time as the product comes on to the market, and over the anticipated market life.

In making this distinction, the SSAP takes into account the accounting concepts of *matching* costs with revenue, and *prudence*. Clearly research is a necessary expense in earning revenue, and can reasonably be matched against it. However, there is no telling when, and if, the associated revenue will materialise, so prudence suggests that the expenditure should be written off.

The auditor's role in respect of Research and Development is to ensure that this distinction is correctly drawn, and in particular to ensure that no amount is capitalised without a reasonable expectation of its recovery. Easy in theory, extremely difficult in practice. For the issues involved will usually be extremely complex and technical. Indeed, it could well be that they are only understood by a very few individuals in the particular company. So to a certain extent the auditor is inevitably in the hands of the directors. Distortion of the accounts is the possibility, and overstatement the only real worry. Accordingly, if the auditors are in doubt they should insist that the items in question be written off on the grounds of prudence. In reaching a decision, they should bear in mind the company's past experience in predicting its successful products, the likely future economic climate and the thoroughness with which the matters relevant to SSAP13 have been investigated by the client.

## Goodwill

Goodwill is perhaps the most peculiar of all assets, for it cannot be distinguished from the company. Even other intangibles, although they can neither be seen nor touched, can be so distinguished, and a value can accordingly be ascribed to them. But there is no reliable basis for determining the value of goodwill. It normally only arises on the face of a balance sheet in the event that a business is purchased for an amount in excess of the book value of the assets. This excess, or 'purchased goodwill', has to be shown somewhere to make the books balance, so it is shown as an asset. Which indeed it is, for clearly the skill of the labour force, the situation of the company, good relations with customers, etc., all contribute to the company's profitability. But the problem comes in quantifying this asset, when it is acquired through trading development, as opposed to through purchase. In these circumstances it is difficult, if not impossible, to reach an accurate evaluation, so an entry for goodwill seldom appears in the accounts of such companies. This means of course that there is a lack of comparability, so essential for meaningful interpretation of accounts. But in practice I do not consider the matter to be a serious one, for investment analysts will almost always ignore any value placed on goodwill, in effect deducting it from the value of the shareholders' equity. Thus putting it back on the same footing as the company that has no goodwill recorded.

At the time of writing, there is no accepted standard on goodwill, and various accounting practices are adopted. Some companies keep goodwill in their accounts at original cost, showing it as an intangible asset. Others will write it off against income, over such a period as is consistent with not materially affecting the recorded profit in any one year (the write off will constitute an extraordinary item – see SSAP6). Yet another method is to write goodwill straight to reserves. But perhaps the method which most appropriately reflects the true situation as viewed by analysts is to net off the amount against shareholders' equity on the face of the balance sheet. This then puts all companies on the same footing, whether they have purchased their goodwill or developed it, while at the same time recording the amount that has been paid for net assets, in excess of their cost. (See also sec. 15.7 for a discussion of Fourth Directive requirements in respect of goodwill.)

## 14.6 Stock and work in progress

Stock perhaps presents the greatest verification problems of any asset, largely because the amounts involved are invariably material, directly affect profit and are subject to both misappropriation and distortion.

However, the audit approach still fits into our CAVEBOP formula; but first a reminder about analytical review procedures, because they can be particularly useful in an examination of stock. The ratio of stock to cost of sales should be calculated for each significant type of stock, and for each significant location. If this information is also available for previous months and years, then a useful overall picture of likely problems, can be derived. If plotted on a graph, the following types of pattern may emerge (see Fig. 14.2):

1. A steady pattern, suggesting no obvious problems. Or at least, if there are any, they have been there for a long time!
2. A steady build up of stock, suggesting possible overstocking, and at the very

Fig. 14.2 Stock ratios

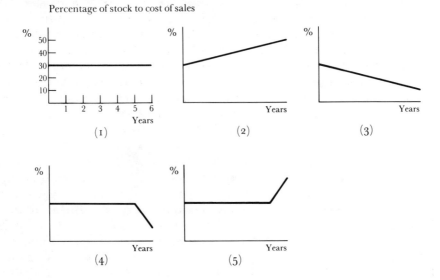

Percentage of stock to cost of sales

least inefficient use of assets. More seriously, such a trend could suggest the presence of slow moving or obsolete stock which may need to be written down in value.

3. A steady reduction in stock, suggesting possible liquidity problems. This may result in reduced sales later, and could possibly be a first indicator that the company is in a dangerous financial position. Consequently this could have implications for the accounts produced on a going concern basis (see sec. 16.2).

4. Where has the stock gone?! Suggests a possible fraud, or serious error in the accounts, or possibly a reduction in stock in anticipation of a future decline in sales. This latter is not a problem if only in one class of stock, but has serious implication if across the whole range.

5. Dramatic build up of stock this year. Look to possible distortion of the accounts by senior management, probably as a result of a valuation manipulation.

Armed with this advance impression of likely problem areas, we can proceed to the detail of verification.

*Cost and authorisation*

The cost of the stock will be vouched to supporting documentation, such as invoices for raw materials and cost records for work in progress and finished goods. Remember that the items to be included as cost of finished stock are strictly specified by SSAP9. The direct costs of raw materials and labour are to be included, together with an appropriate proportion of production overheads. But selling and administrative expenses are specifically excluded. The auditor must ensure that these distinctions are correctly drawn. You should also remember that there are many possible accounting bases in respect of the ascertainment of cost. So it is up to the auditor to decide whether the accounting base chosen is appropriate, consistently applied and in accordance with SSAP9. The accounting bases allowable are: FIFO, Weighted Average or Unit Cost, with LIFO and Base Stock being specifically excluded in normal circumstances. Clearly the various calculations in respect of cost must also be checked by the auditor. If a standard costing system is used, the auditor must ensure that the appropriate proportions of any variances on direct costs and production overheads are applied to the standard value of year end stock.

*Valuation*

SSAP9 prescribes that stock should be valued at the lower of cost or net realisable value. Net realisable value (NRV) can be defined as the amount that would be realised on the open market in the ordinary course of business, less the costs of putting the item into a saleable condition and less the costs of sale. It is up to the auditor to ensure that the NRV of all of the assets is correctly assessed, and that the comparison between cost and NRV is calculated properly and in accordance with SSAP9. The SSAP states that comparisons shall be by individual units of stock, or categories, but it is not permitted to make the comparison simply on a basis of the total cost of all stock, and the total NRV.

*Existence*

Before we look in detail at the practical steps that the auditor will undertake to verify the existence of stock, it is appropriate to look at the case law which defines his legal position in this regard.

*Legal position*

The ancient but oft-quoted Kingston Cotton Mill case of 1896 ruled that it was no part of an auditor's duty to take stock, and that a stock certificate was sufficient audit evidence from the management, in the absence of suspicious circumstances. It is still the case that the auditor is not required to take stock, for this is the duty of the directors; but an auditor is certainly not now entitled to rely solely on a stock certificate. Let us examine further, subsequent case law in order to ascertain the current position.

In 1932, the case of Westminster Road Construction and Engineering Company extended auditors' responsibilities. The auditors were successfully sued on several counts, in particular for their failure to discover substantial overstatements in the work in progress sheets, as a result of which a dividend was incorrectly paid. In this case, the distortion could have been discovered had the auditors called for the underlying stock work sheets; but they did not, and were accordingly held to be negligent. Note at this stage, there is still no suggestion that the auditors should actually be present to witness the count. But this position was dramatically changed in 1939 by the extremely important American case of

McKesson and Robbins. The auditors, Price Waterhouse and Co., failed to discover a fraud of gargantuan proportions, in which stocks and debtors were overstated by some 23 million dollars. The subsequent investigation revealed that the overstatement was in no sense subtly performed and could have been revealed had the auditors made any attempt to 'gain physical contact with the inventory either by test counts, by observation of the inventory taking, or by a combination of these methods' (extract from US Securities Exchange Commission report). But such was not the usual practice by auditors of the day, as obvious a test as it may seem, though it quickly became the practice in the United States. Not so in the UK. Even the successful criminal prosecution of an auditor in the 1954 case of *R. v. Wake & Stone* failed to stir the UK profession out of its apathy in connection with audit attendance at stocktaking. The managing director of Wake & Dean Ltd wilfully overvalued the company's stock of timber in a prospectus report by overstating the actual quantities present. And Mr Stone, the auditor, happily accepted all that Mr Wake told him without checking the basis of arriving at the quantities stated (in fact they were derived on the basis of the total cubic capacity of the warehouse – so air and timber were valued alike!). Mr Wake went to prison. Mr Stone was fined £200 and told that he had been so 'excessively careless as to be reckless'. An understatement to say the least.

But following all this, the Institute's 1962 Auditing Statement U2 on stock and work in progress was less than positive in regard to audit attendance at stocktakes. U2 stated: 'where the auditors consider that such a step would be of assistance to them in the performance of their duties, and would be reasonable and practicable in the circumstances, they may attend occasionally at one or more of the locations to observe the actual stocktaking. This may be particularly helpful in the first year in which the audit is undertaken, and thereafter from time to time, particularly when there have been changes in the procedure or where there are no stock records other than the annual inventory'. But this half-hearted approach was changed by two very important cases in the 1960s. The fraud at Allied Crude Vegetable Oil Refining Corporation of New Jersey was one of the biggest that the world has ever known. It became known as 'the great salad oil swindle', and total losses ran to hundreds of millions of dollars. The fraud involved the manipulation of future commodity prices of crude vegetable oil, through artificially created stocks. The methods used to create these stocks were many and varied, but all involved deceiving the stocktakers and auditors as to the quantities of oil held in above-ground petroleum-type storage tanks. Figure 14.3 tells some of the story. But it still took the UK a few more years and a very expensive court case before the Institute made a positive move on stocktake attendance.

In 1967 the liquidator of Thomas Gerrard and Sons Ltd succeeded in an action against the company's auditors. The managing director of the cotton spinning company (who was also a major shareholder) manipulated cut-off procedures and included non-existent stocks in the accounts in order to pay huge dividends, which were of course effectively then being paid out of capital. The auditors relied on the Kingston Cotton Mill case . . . unsuccessfully; for the judge

Fig. 14.3 Stock fraud

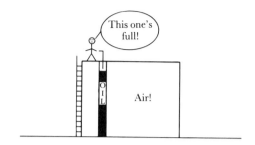

✓ = audit checked

pointed out that this decision also made reference to the 'absence of suspicious circumstances'. And here there were those in plenty, for many sales and purchase invoices at the year end had been deliberately and obviously altered. The judge further observed that in these circumstances the auditors should reasonably have attended the stocktaking.

Shortly following this, in 1968, the Institute issued Auditing Statement U9, advising positively that auditors should attend at stocktakes for the purpose of *observing* the client's procedures and ensuring that they were likely to result in a reliable count.

It is appropriate now to examine U9 to see the requirements that go to make up satisfactory count procedures, and the checks that the auditor will carry out during his attendance. But first another slight digression to look at the difference between perpetual and periodic inventory, for this difference determines to an extent the type of audit work that will be performed.

### Perpetual and periodic inventory

*Perpetual inventory.* This describes the system whereby the quantities of stocks are continually maintained through detailed stock records which note the purchase and the movement of individual stocks. This may be achieved through the use of 'bin cards' at the stock location, or by centrally maintained records based on goods inwards notes and stores requisitions. Or a combination may be used. Whatever the system, for these records to have any value, they must be independently checked to the physical stocks; this process being known as

*Continuous stocktaking.* The internal auditors are appropriate persons to carry out this task, which must be performed on a regular and systematic basis, such that all stocks are counted in rotation, at least two or three times a year. Provided that these stockchecks reveal no significant errors or discrepancies, the auditors may rely on the figures thereby produced, subject to carrying out audit procedures, to ensure that control is satisfactory. These procedures will include test checks on the underlying documentation, and observation of the continuous stocktake procedures.

*Periodic inventory.* This will have to be employed in the event that the perpetual system is deemed unsatisfactory, or if no such system exists. A periodic inventory system is based on total counts of the stocks at the period end, and perhaps at one or more other occasions during the year. This may then be compared to any total stock records that are maintained, or reconciled to the known cost of sales figures.

U9 largely relates to the periodic system, and is shown in Fig. 14.4.

Fig. 14.4 U9. Attendance at stocktaking (issued July 1968)

## U9. Attendance at stocktaking

*General considerations*

1. Although it is not the auditors' duty to take stock, they must satisfy themselves as to the validity of the amount attributed to this asset in the accounts which are the subject of the audit. In determining the nature and extent of the audit steps necessary for this purpose the auditors must examine the system of internal control in order to assess its effectiveness relative to the ascertainment and evaluation of stock and work in progress. (The auditors' examination of a client's system of internal control is described in Statement on Auditing No. 4, paragraph 19.) An important element in this system is the client's procedures for ascertainment of the quantities of stocks on hand and their condition. In most circumstances the best method by which the auditors can satisfy themselves as to the effectiveness of the application of the client's stocktaking procedures is by observation of those procedures. Normally this will be done on a test basis and it will not be necessary for the auditors to observe the application of the stocktaking procedures to the whole of the stock or to the stock at all locations. The extent of the auditors' test observation will depend on their assessment of the soundness of the system prescribed by the client.

2. *Therefore wherever it is practicable and stock-in-trade and work in progress is a material factor in the business, the auditors should satisfy themselves as to the effectiveness of the application of the client's stock-taking procedures by observation on a test basis of these procedures whilst the stocktaking is in progress.*

3. The presence of auditors at stocktaking does not relieve the management in any way of their responsibilities; in order to avoid misunderstanding the auditors should make it clear to the management that the reason for their

attendance is not to take stock but to satisfy themselves as to the effectiveness of the application of the client's procedures. The auditors are neither stocktakers nor valuers, nor have they any responsibility for supervising the stocktaking. Their presence is to enable them as auditors to consider the adequacy and effectiveness of the client's procedures. They will, however, be ready to advise or make recommendations, just as they would on other matters when they consider that the system of internal control is weak or is not being properly carried out.

4. While it will not normally be necessary for the auditors to observe the application of the client's procedures in their entirety or at all locations, the auditors' tests should cover a representative selection of the stock and of the procedures. Where stock is held at a number of locations, the selection of the location or locations to be visited by the auditors may be planned so as to cover all significant locations over a period of years. The extent of their tests will be for them to decide. There may be instances where it is not practicable to test the client's procedures by attendance and observation of the stocktakings taken earlier in the year, or upon continuous or periodical the auditors cannot readily attend. Where the auditors cannot observe the stocktaking, for any reason, they should adopt some or all of the additional procedures suggested in paragraphs 18–20 below.

*Client's stocktaking procedure*

5. The amount at which stock is stated in the accounts may be based upon a physical stocktaking at the year-end or upon information taken from stock records. Stock records may in turn be substantiated by complete physical stocktakings taken earlier in the year, or upon continuous or perioidcal physical stocktakings, or upon combinations of these in relation to various sections of stock. Under some accounting systems it is common practice for work in progress to be based solely upon cost records (see Statement on Auditing No. 11, paragraph 11). Where stock at the year-end is based on a physical stocktaking earlier in the year, the client's procedures should include a review of entries in the intervening periods. Unusual variations from the normal pattern should be explained. These procedures will involve comparison of the amount at the year-end with previous years and with current production and sales to check that these also appear to follow a normal pattern.

6. Where stock is based on records substantiated by continuous or periodical physical stocktakings, the procedures should ensure that:
   (a) adequate stock records are kept up to date;
   (b) each category of stock is checked at least once a year and a record of checks maintained;
   (c) if the checking is continuous, it is done systematically over the year, or if periodic, at suitable times such as when stocks are low or have reached a specific re-order point;
   (d) all differences are properly investigated and the records amended accordingly.
   A schedule of differences with action taken should be maintained.

7. The procedures for carrying out a physical stocktaking vary in detail according to the size and circumstances of the business and the nature of its stock records. Definite instructions, preferably in writing, should be issued in all cases, however, for the guidance of those who will be engaged in the actual stocktaking. The procedures will consist essentially of:

(a) identification of the articles and their ownership;
(b) counting, weighing or measuring;
(c) reporting of stocks which are damaged or otherwise defective;
(d) recording the information.

8. Although considerations will differ in each case, there are certain general procedures which can be applied in most stocktakings but which may need some adaptation to meet particular circumstances, such as where the stocktaking is on a continuous basis:

(a) the stocktaking should be planned well in advance and carried out carefully and systematically by persons fully informed of the duties involved. Those taking part should include persons familiar with the various sections of stock, and where practicable supervisors and checkers drawn from departments which have no control over the usual custody or movement of stock. Where specialist knowledge is necessary to identify the nature or quality of items of stock, the client should ensure that personnel properly qualified for this purpose other than those responsible for custody of the stock are available at the stocktaking. In exceptional circumstances it may be desirable for the services of an independent expert to be utilised, e.g. for the chemical analysis of samples taken at the time of the stocktaking from bulk stocks of high value;

(b) the whole of the stocktaking area should be divided into section for control purposes, and the movement of stock during the stocktaking should preferably be suspended or, if this is not practicable, it should be strictly controlled;

(c) arrangements should be made to ensure a proper 'cut-off'. This means that despatch documentation should have been originated for all goods despatched before stocktaking and, if still on hand, for all goods in which the property has passed to the customer. The latter must not be included as stock when the count is made. The procedures should ensure that the appropriate sales invoices are recorded in the correct financial period. Also liabilities should be set up for all goods received and included in stock, and for all goods purchased the property in which has been passed to the client. These should be included in stock even though they are not then on the company's premises. Where only certain sections of stock, such as raw materials, work in progress, finished goods, etc., are being taken physically, the arrangements should ensure a proper 'cut-off' between the various sections;

(d) arrangements should be made to identify slow-moving, obsolete or damaged stock;

(e) arrangements should be made to ensure that goods held in safe custody for others are not recorded as part of the client's stock;

(f) arrangements should be made to confirm and record in the stock sheets details of goods held for the company by outside parties (see paragraph 16 below).

9. The client's stocktaking procedures should also call for records of the following information, which should be available to the auditors during and at the conclusion of the stocktaking:
(a) details of stock movement during the count;
(b) last numbers of goods inward and outward records;
(c) details of the numbering of stock sheets issued, of those completed and of those cancelled and unused.

*Suggested audit procedures*

10. The audit steps relating to observation of the stocktaking by the auditors will cover three stages: *before, during* and *after* the stocktaking. The procedures described below are intended to be a broad outline which will need adaptation to meet the circumstances of the client, for example where a client's stocktaking is based on records substantiated by continuous physical stocktakings.

*Before stocktaking*

11. Before the stocktaking the auditors will need to study the client's stocktaking instructions (preferably before they are issued), to become familiar with the location of the stocks and to plan the work they are to undertake during the stocktaking. The work to be undertaken will depend on the auditors' evaluation of the client's procedures, as contained in the instructions and explanations given by the client. The auditors will be concerned to see that the client's procedures are adequate in the light of the circumstances. These circumstances will include the locations at which stock is held, the quantities on hand and the values of the stocks, the factors affecting the condition of stocks and the possibilities of the existence of obsolete or slow-moving stocks. Where these procedures are considered to be weak or defective they should be discussed with the client before the stocktaking instructions are issued with a view to changes being made to remove the defects.

*During stocktaking*

12. The main task during stocktaking will be to ascertain whether the client's employees are carrying out their instructions properly. It may be sufficient to watch the counting and recording as it is done by the client's employees, but it would usually be advisable for the auditors to test the efficiency of the counting by arranging for a count or a recount of selected items in their presence. In arranging for items to be counted or recounted in their presence it will be advisable for the auditors to select items from both the count records and the factory or warehouse floor for tracing from one to the other. The test selection should include a reasonable proportion of high value items.

13. Auditors should make such notes as they consider necessary during the course of their observation, for follow-up. These notes will normally include the following:
    (a) details of items of stock selected by the auditors so that the particulars may be checked to the final stocksheets;
    (b) lists of items actually counted in the auditors' presence;
    (c) details of any stock noted by the auditors as being obviously defective, damaged or slow-moving;
    (d) details of instances where the client's stocktaking procedures were not carried out.

14. Where serious inaccuracies or irregularities are revealed during the course of the auditors' observations it may be necessary to arrange for certain sections of, or the whole of, the stock to be recounted.

*After stocktaking*

15. The information obtained by the auditors at the stocktaking should be

followed up when finally reviewing the amount at which the stock is stated in the accounts. The steps taken to do this will include the following:

(a) a check of the 'cut-off', using the details of stock movements and of the last numbers of goods inwards and outwards notes (see paragraph 9 (a) and (b));

(b) a test that the final stocksheets have been properly prepared from the count records and include all stocks belonging to the company. The test will be made by reference to the details of the stock-sheet numbering noted by the client (see paragraph 9 (c)) and also the notes made by the auditors (see paragraph 13);

(c) a follow-up of all outstanding queries.

16. Stocks belonging to the company but held by others should be shown as such in the stocktaking records. The auditors should examine the confirmations obtained by the company from the custodians and, where the amounts of such stocks are material, the auditors should independently obtain confirmations from the custodians in selected cases. They should also examine reports on any periodic inspections of the stock made by the company's own employees and should make enquiries as to the standing of the custodians where the circumstances warrant it.

### If attendance during stocktaking is not practicable

17. As stated in paragraph 4 above, there may be occasions when it will not be practicable for the auditors to observe the client's stocktaking. In such cases they should carry out such additional procedures (distinct from and extra to those usually followed when forming an opinion on stocks) as in their judgement, as skilled professional men, are necessary in the circumstances to satisfy themselves that:

(a) the records of the stocktaking produced to them represent a substantially correct inventory of the stocks and work in progress owned by the company on the stocktaking date; and

(b) the condition of the stocks and work in progress has been properly assessed.

18. The additional procedures to be followed for this purpose will depend on the circumstances which make it impracticable for the auditors to attend for the purpose of observing the stocktaking. In some instances, such as where stock is held overseas, it may be possible for the auditors to arrange for a suitably qualified agent to attend the stocktaking on their behalf and for him to report to them.

19. In other instances auditors who have numerous client companies, which may have a common accounting date and which take stock on the date, may find that their resources in manpower are insufficient for them to attend on every client for the purpose of observing at least some part of the stocktaking. If auditors find that they cannot attend every year, this does not relieve them of their responsibilities. They will have to consider carefully whether the alternative procedures available to them will be sufficient to discharge those responsibilities in the circumstances of each of the clients concerned. Where the client has a well-developed system of internal control and of stock recording it will usually be possible for the auditors to substantiate to their satisfaction the validity of the stocktaking records. This can be done by arranging for the test counts of selected items to be made at an earlier or later date when a representative can attend and observe.

20. In the case of smaller businesses, however, the systems of internal control are necessarily more elementary and in many instances the records of the annual stocktaking are not supported by any continuous stock records. Sometimes it may be possible to arrange for the stocktaking to take place on a date close to the accounting date at a time when the auditors can attend and for records of movements of stocks in the intervening period to be maintained. These records must be in such a form that the auditors can satisfy themselves as to their reasonable accuracy.

21. If, however, the auditors are unable reasonably to satisfy themselves as to the reliability of the stocktaking, and stock is a material factor in the business, they will have no alternative but to make an appropriate qualification in their report on the accounts.

Let me remind you that these various thoughts on attendance at stocktaking all stem from the auditor's need to prove the *existence* of the stock. The next stage in our formula is proving beneficial ownership.

*Beneficial ownership*

Debentures or other loans to the company may well be secured by a 'floating charge' on the stocks of the company, and if this is the case then this secured charge should be revealed as a note to the accounts. But a more problematical issue for the auditor arises under this heading. In January 1976 the Court of Appeal dramatically altered the law in regard to normal trading transactions in the now famous case of *Aluminium Industrie Vaassen B.V. v. Romalpa Aluminium Ltd.*

Normal commercial law states that title to goods passes to the buyer once they are delivered on a valid contract. If the buying company goes into liquidation, then the seller will probably lose his stock and his money. Such has been the case for centuries. But the Romalpa case ruled that transactions could be made *subject to reservation of title* until such time as the buying company makes payment, provided that such reservation is clearly stated in the appropriate sales documentation. The rights of the selling company over unpaid-for stock may even extend to goods produced from the stock, and to the sale proceeds therefore.

So in a strictly legal sense stock subject to such reservation should not be included in a buying company's accounts until paid for. But in fact the accounting treatment acknowledges that *the commercial substance of the transaction takes precedence over its legal form,* and the amounts are shown as sales by the selling company, and as stock by the buying company. But this assumes a situation where a company is a going concern. In the event that the buying company would seem to be in a doubtful financial position, then the amounts in question should be removed from both stock and creditors, although in this situation many more adjustments will be necessary, and these are discussed in sec. 16.2.

Assuming that the commercial basis of presentation is adopted, it will be necessary to reveal in a note to the accounts of the buying company that creditors of the appropriate amount are secured by specific stock. This information could of course be extremely material to the proper interpretation of the asset position, and may be very important, for example, to bankers considering the granting of a loan, perhaps based on a floating charge.

The auditor of both buying and selling companies must ensure that the accounting policy adopted in regard to reservation of title (i.e. legal basis or commercial basis) is disclosed in the notes to the accounts, and the buying company auditor must ensure that the extent of any secured stock is disclosed. Guidance on the necessary audit work is given by the Institute Auditing Statement U24 which is accordingly reproduced in Fig. 14.5.

Fig. 14.5 U24. Guidance for auditors on the implications of goods sold subject to reservation of title (issued December 1977)

## U24. Guidance for auditors on the implications of goods sold subject to reservation of title

*Introduction*

1. The case of *Aluminium Industries Vaassen B.V. v. Romalpa Aluminium Limited* (*the Romalpa Case*) by which a seller reserved his title to goods sold and to the proceeds from the re-sale of such goods until they had been paid for by the buyer, has caused widespread concern to auditors. The accounting implications are dealt with in Statement V24 to which reference should be made and accordingly this statement is limited to providing some guidance on the additional work which this case imposes on auditors.

*Audit approach*

2. *Purchaser.* The following audit approach is suggested:
   (a) ascertain what steps the client takes to identify suppliers selling on terms which reserve title by enquiry of those responsible for purchasing and of the board;
   (b) ascertain what steps are taken to quantify the liability to such suppliers for balance sheet purposes, including liabilities not yet reflected in the creditors' ledger;
   (c) where there are material liabilities to such suppliers:
      (i)   if the liabilities are quantified in the accounts, review and test the procedures by which the amounts disclosed have been computed;
      (ii)  if the directors consider that quantification is impracticable, but have either estimated the liabilities or indicated their existence, review and test the information upon which their disclosure is based;
      (iii) consider the adequacy of the information disclosed in the accounts;
      (iv)  ensure that the basis on which the charge for taxation is computed takes account of the accounting treatment adopted and, where necessary, is adequately disclosed.
   (d) where liabilities to such suppliers are said not to exist or to be immaterial, review the terms of sale of major suppliers to confirm that this is so;
   (e) obtain formal written representation from the directors either that there

are no material liabilities of this nature to be disclosed or that the information disclosed is, in their view, as accurate as it is reasonably possible to achieve.

3. *Supplier.* So far as the audit of a supplier is concerned, reservation of title will normally only be relevant to the valuation of accounts receivable. When a provision for bad or doubtful debts is contemplated, the ability to adopt assets in settlement will have a bearing on the value of the debt.

*Legal and practical considerations*

4. Reservation of title depends on the terms of each contract between purchaser and supplier and difficulty may be experienced in interpreting the contractual relationship between the parties. There is at present no clear legal view as to the effect of contracts containing Romalpa-type reservation of title, for example, as applied to goods which may have been mixed with other materials or used in the manufacture of new products and to the sale proceeds of such new products. However, the following matters, *inter alia*, would appear to be relevant:

   (a) The contractual relationship. The form of contractual relationship between the parties may not be clear. Where the wording of the documents indicates that the purchaser is acting as agent or bailee or custodian, the purchaser may be accountable to the supplier for the goods or proceeds of sale; if, on the other hand, the purchaser is acting as principal, which may well be the majority of cases, it would appear that in England and Ireland a security may arise which may need to be registered under Section 95, Companies Act 1948, or Section 93 Companies Act (Northern Ireland) 1960, or Section 99 Companies Act 1963 (Republic of Ireland) before it is effective. Under the law of Scotland it is not, however, possible in the case of corporeal moveables for any valid right of security to be created in favour of the supplier under a reservation of title condition.

   (b) Have the supplier's terms of trade been adequately brought to the purchaser's notice?

   (c) Has the purchaser explicitly or impliedly – for example, by not refuting them – agreed to the supplier's terms?

   (d) Has the purchaser specifically excluded reservation of title, for example, by a clause in his purchase order?

   (e) Has the supplier reinstated his terms by means of a new offer expressed in an 'order-acknowledgement'?

5. If there is doubt about the legal effectiveness of terms of trade which purport to reserve title, consider whether any legal opinion obtained by the directors supports the manner in which the assets and liabilities have been treated. Where material amounts are subject to doubt in this respect, the directors should be encouraged to obtain a legal opinion. Exceptionally, if they decline to do so, the auditor may need to consider obtaining legal advice himself.

6. Where the contractual relationship or the amounts involved cannot be determined so as to enable the directors to disclose the position in the accounts, the auditor should ensure that a note adequately explains the situation.

7. In considering the practical effects of reservation of title it will be necessary to establish the extent to which the supplier can trace or identify his interest in the goods. The following points, *inter alia*, appear to be relevant:

(a) Are the goods separately identifiable in the form in which they were delivered from other identical goods already supplied and paid for by the purchaser?

(b) Where the goods have been subject to processing, are they still identifiable, for example, as partly completed or finished stocks?

(c) Can the goods be traced to, or identified with, particular debts?

(d) Can the cash proceeds of debts be traced or distinguished so as to enable them to be adopted by the supplier; for example, paid into a bank account opened for the purpose of the transaction or paid into a general bank account in credit at the time the proceeds were deposited?

(e) Where cash identifiable as in (d) above has been applied in the acquisition of other assets, can those assets be traced or identified?

*Other circumstances*

8. Where an opinion other than an audit opinion is requested, for example, an opinion for debentures deed or loan purposes, the implications of goods sold subject to reservation of title will need to be assessed having regard to the purpose of the opinion required.

In July 1979 the Appeal Court decision in *Borden (UK) Ltd v. Scottish Timber Products Ltd*, amplified the *Romalpa* decision.

The effect of the retention clause in *Romalpa* had been to create the fiduciary relationship of bailor and bailee in place of that of seller and buyer. Accordingly Aluminium Industrie Vaassen BV (hereafter AIV) had the equitable right to trace their goods (aluminium foil) into the hands of the bailee (Romalpa) in a situation of insolvency. They had the further right to trace the proceeds of sale of products made from the foil up to the amount of the debt for foil, because the retention clause provided that such goods would be sold on an agency basis. But according to the ruling in *Borden*, if the foil had been mixed with other goods, then the tracing remedy would no longer have been available. Borden confirmed that a contractual charge could be created over mixed goods by a retention clause, but for a remedy to be available under this head, the charge would have to be registered under Sec. 95 of the CA 1948.

AIV succeeded because they only claimed the return of foil still in Romalpa's possession, and the proceeds of the sale of foil which had not been mixed with other goods.

*Borden* failed because they were aware that Scottish Timber could only store their goods (resin) for a day or two, and that it would then be mixed with other goods in making chipboard. So there could be no bailor and bailee relationship. For a retention clause to succeed on a bailor/bailee basis, then all or a part of the goods must be capable of being redelivered. If mixed with other goods almost immediately, then such return is not possible, and the clause must be void. The *Borden* retention clause did not create a principal and agent relationship, so the potential remedy of tracing proceeds was not available. Nor did the clause create a contractual charge over mixed goods. And even had it done so, the Appeal Court gave the opinion that the clause would have been void unless registered under Sec. 95.

The question of reservation of title was also considered by the High Court in the 1979 *Monsanto* case (*Re Bond Worth*). Again the supplier, *Monsanto* Ltd, could not prove its reservation clause to be effective. The clause attempted to set up a trust over supplies of Acrilan, and over the proceeds of resale therefrom and the products made therewith. But the effect of the clause was to create floating equitable charges to secure payment. And Monsanto was not allowed to 'trace' the proceeds of sale and was unable to rely on the charges, because they had not been registered in accordance with Sec. 95 CA 1948.

*Presentation*

Stocks and work in progress should be sub-classified on the face of the balance sheet, or in notes, in a manner which is appropriate to the business and so as to indicate the amounts held in each of the main categories. The accounting policies in respect of stock must be disclosed, as of course must the effect of any changes therein.

## 14.7 Long-term contracts

Long-term contracts are those for which the estimated life is longer than one accounting period. Because of the artificial nature of periodic accounts, and the matching concept, it is necessary to ascribe some proportion of the profit on a contract to each of the accounting periods that it covers. Although against the matching concept, one could argue that to comply with the realisation concept profit should not be taken until the completion of the contract. Where two accounting concepts oppose each other in this way, it is normal to take into account the prudence concept which rules that the alternative adopted should be the one that minimises the reported profit. Nevertheless, despite this, SSAP9 rules that an appropriate amount of profit should be taken each year. The decision as to what is appropriate presents special problems for the auditor.

*Cost and authorisation*

The cost incurred to date on a contract (i.e. the work in progress) can be checked by routine vouching to supporting documentation.

*Valuation*

The basis of valuation in the balance sheet will be: cost plus attributable profit, less foreseeable losses and progress payments (both received and receivable). Accordingly it is necessary to determine the appropriate amount of profit that can be taken on the contract.

The method of deriving the *attributable* profit is shown by the formula:

$$\frac{\text{Total Costs to Date}}{\substack{\text{Total anticipated}\\ \text{costs on the contract}}} \times \substack{\text{Anticipated}\\ \text{total profit}} \times \substack{\text{Allowance}\\ \text{for prudence}} \times \substack{\text{Attributable}\\ \text{profit}}$$

This derives the total profit that can be taken on the contract to date. From this of course must be deduced any profit that has been taken in previous years, to determine the attributable profit for the year.

You should note the following points:
1. Total costs will be derived from the budgeted total costs for the contract.
2. Total profit will be derived from the contract price less total budgeted costs.
3. It is necessary to take into account prudence when determining the amount of attributable profit. This does *not* mean that you necessarily take two-thirds

of the anticipated profit as some older texts would have us believe. You must take into account the likelihood of the profit figure being achieved. This will be a function of:

(a) time (the longer the contract has to run, the less easy the profit is to determine);
(b) the company's proven ability to estimate its costs;
(c) the nature of the contract, e.g. a fixed price contract would be considered far more risky than one which allowed for cost escalation; a 'cost-plus' contract would carry very little risk at all.

You will see that the whole basis of this calculation is the company's estimate of its future costs. So this is where the auditor must lay considerable emphasis, for it is here that the directors may seek to distort the accounts by the use of unrealistic estimates. Now clearly this is in effect an audit of future trading, more in the nature of a profit forecast. Accordingly conventional historic cost techniques will not be appropriate and alternative methods must be adopted, appropriate to the circumstances. These may include:

1. Examine the company's budgets and budgetary system. Do they seem a reliable basis for determining future costs? Or do the figures appear to be little more than guesswork?
2. Compare the costs to date on the contract with the original budget. If these relate reasonably, then it will give some confidence that the future costs are also reasonably stated.
3. Compare the results of previous contracts completed, with the original budgets, to determine the company's ability at forecasting.

Fig. 14.6 Debtor ratios

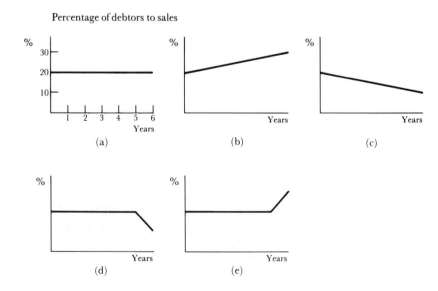

Percentage of debtors to sales

(a)

(b)

(c)

(d)

(e)

4. Perform detailed tests to substantiate the future costs by reference to technical data, and reports from any independent personnel.
5. Check on contract progress in relation to any penalty clauses for late delivery.
   Once the auditor has satisfied himself that the future costs are fairly stated, he should check the calculation of attributable profit, taking into account the concept of prudence, on the basis of points raised earlier.
   If it becomes apparent that a loss will be made on the completed contract, then such a loss must be charged against income in the year in which it is first foreseen; and if profit has already been taken on the contract in previous years then such profit must also be written back along with the total loss. So the rule is, include all anticipated losses, but only a prudent proportion of attributable profit.

*Presentation*

SSAP9 requires the disclosure of long term contracts as follows:

| | |
|---|---|
| Work in progress at cost, plus attributable profit, less foreseeable losses | £ – |
| *Less* cash received and receivable as progress payments as at the balance sheet date | – |
| Value of long-term contracts | £ – |

## 14.8 Debtors and prepayments

*Debtors*

*Analytical review techniques.* These have particular application to debtors as well as to stock. If the percentage of debtors to credit sales is plotted over a number of years, indicative patterns may emerge, as shown below (see also Fig. 14.6).
(a) a steady pattern revealing no specific problems;
(b) a steady increase, indicating weakening credit control, and the consequent granting of excess credit (unless the increase is the result of a deliberate policy to increase sales). Possibility of 'teeming and lading';
(c) steady decline, indicating tightening of credit control. Normally a good sign, unless accompanied by a fall-off in sales in which case it may indicate a working capital problem which the directors are trying to solve by calling in debtors more quickly;
(d) dramatic fall this year. One possibility could be deliberate distortion, perhaps by manipulating cut-off so that end of year sales and debtors have been omitted;
(e) dramatic rise this year. May again be the result of deliberate distortion,

perhaps by manipulating cut-off so that some of next year's sales and debtors have been included. There is also the possibility of a substantial defalcation. (Note that cut-off is an extremely important audit matter, and the tests necessary to ensure its correctness are fully cited in the MAPs on pp. 237 and 250.)

The quality of the internal control, combined with the results of the analytical review, will as usual determine the extent to which the debtor balances need to be substantiated by tests of detail. The tests of detail may be accomplished either by means of transaction or balance testing. It will normally be appropriate to test for understatement by means of transaction tests from the despatch records through to the sales ledger (as previously discussed), and for overstatement by balance testing using direct communication.

*Direct communication.* This involves communicating directly with the debtor himself for independent confirmation of the existence and amount of the debt due. Such confirmation may reveal understatement as well as overstatement, but it cannot be relied upon so to do, as the debtor may reply dishonestly in the event that the balance is understated, and he will definitely do so if he is acting in collusion with a company employee to perpetrate fraud. Direct communication provides more reliable evidence in respect of overstatement than proof by reference to supporting documents (delivery notes, orders and invoices), though this may have to be resorted to in the event that direct communication proves impossible (such as with some overseas customers). Subsequent payment plus supporting documentation would constitute reliable evidence in such circumstances.

Direct communication has been common practice since the 1960s, and Institute Statement U7 issued in 1967 positively recommended such an approach. This method is now adopted as a matter of course by almost all of the larger audit firms, and it has positive advantages even with smaller client companies.

Two methods are possible: *positive* or *negative*.

In the *positive* method the debtor is asked to reply, confirming the amount he believes due, regardless of whether or not he agrees with the amount stated in the request. Whereas in the negative method he is only asked to reply if he disagrees. The logic of this latter method is that it is only in the debtor's interest to reply if the amount is overstated. And if this is the case, he will reply under either the negative or the positive approach.

Under the positive method, if the balance is understated then he will either not reply, or confirm the amount as stated; unless he is exceptionally honest! So it may be thought that just as much reliable information is revealed by the negative method as by the positive one.

However, the *negative* method gives no proof as to whether the request has ever been received, and considered. It is, therefore, unreliable, and should only ever be used where there is strong internal control. It may then be appropriate, if a large number of small accounts are to be tested. But it can never be used in conjunction with statistical sampling, as a positive reply is then necessary from each debtor that is sampled.

*Carrying out the circularisation*

The auditor himself has no right to circularise the client's debtors. This must be an act of the client himself, though it follows that for the test to have any value strict control must be maintained by the auditor. If the client is reluctant to allow a circularisation, this would immediately cast doubt as to the validity of the debtor figure. And if the auditor is unable to obtain reliable alternative evidence, he would have to qualify his report to the extent that he had been unable to obtain all the information he deemed necessary for the purposes of the audit.

*Selecting the sample*

Debtor circularisation is a particularly suitable application for statistical sampling, the use of which in a large ledger can reduce the number of debts to be circularised to a manageable quantity. Only by selecting randomly will the results of the sample be representative for substantive testing purposes. So whether or not statistical sampling is used, the majority of the sample should be selected on a random basis. Stratified sampling techniques can usefully be employed so that a higher proportion of high value accounts is selected. Debit balances on purchases ledger should be included in the population.

In addition to the random sample, it may also be appropriate to subjectively select certain categories of account for compliance testing purposes. For example:

1.  Old unpaid accounts. These may be fictitious balances to conceal defalcation, or there may be a genuine dispute, both of which could cause overstatement.
2.  Accounts with round sum payments. This may indicate 'teeming and lading', or that the debtor cannot pay the full amount. Note that in this latter case conclusive evidence in support of the validity of the debt may not be obtained from direct confirmation, as the debtor may confirm the amount due but be unable to pay.
3.  Accounts with nil balances would be left out of a cumulative monetary sample, but it may be appropriate to select some in the event of weak control. In such circumstances there could be the possibility of a duplicate (concealed) set of books with genuine balances being maintained by company employees or management to perpetrate fraud. Such understatement may be revealed by the circularisation.
4.  Credit balances on the sales ledger should be circularised (they should be included in the creditors' circularisation if one is to be undertaken). Such balances could have been fraudulently set up with a view to subsequent fraudulent payment. It should be said, however, that transaction testing may additionally have to be employed in these circumstances as the customer may be in collusion with a company official, and would accordingly reply dishonestly. The client may be reluctant to allow you to advise his customers of credit balances, in case they have been overlooked. Such objections may be resolved by omitting the balance figure from the confirmation request.
5.  Accounts where credit or discount seem excessive or where credit periods are habitually exceeded without follow up would require investigation as collusion between a company employee and the customer may be indicated, or it may

be that credits are being used to conceal the defalcation of receipts. Both possibilities would necessitate investigation for understatement by transaction testing, but the latter possibility could also give rise to a potential overstatement of a balance as a result of an as yet unconcealed defalcation of receipts.

When selecting subjectively in the above manner, the auditor should be conscious that he is exercising bias and that the results of his sample will not be representative for substantive testing purposes, although of course under/overstatement revealed in this way should be adjusted. If the random or subjective samples reveal significant compliance failures, indicating that the client's control systems are not working satisfactorily, then the auditor would have to extend his sample in order to be sufficiently confident that the debtors are not materially mis-stated (note that practical problems may be encountered in this regard, as the publication of the accounts may be materially delayed by a further circularisation). The auditor should also consider whether the compliance failures are so significant as to cast doubt on the reliability of the accounting records as a whole.

### Sending the request

The requests can usefully be sent at the same time as the statements, so that they stand a chance of being looked at and so that the customer has something against which to reconcile the amount due. It is particularly important that the date of the confirmation is clearly in evidence as well as the amount to be confirmed. The auditor should ensure that the sales ledger control account reconciles to the sales subsidiary ledger at the time of selecting the sample, and that he maintains strict control of the sample from that time. This even necessitates him posting the confirmation requests himself, for if a member of the client's staff has access to the requests, he is then in a position to withhold them and to send false replies himself, in the event that he wishes to conceal a manipulation.

### Follow-up procedures

The replies should all be sent directly to the auditors and there should be a procedure for prompt follow-up. If replies are not received within a set time period (approximately three weeks), then second and then third requests should be sent in an attempt to receive a reply. In some cases, however, customers may refuse to reply or may be unable to do so because of their accounting system. If after three requests there is still no reply forthcoming, it will be necessary to enlist the client's help, and perhaps to telephone the debtor concerned. Clearly only senior officials, independent of the sales department, should be involved here, for it may be that the customer does not even exist. If it transpires that the customer cannot reply for technical reasons, his system may still allow the confirmation of specific invoices, in which case such a confirmation should be arranged.

Attempts should be made to follow-up all accounts selected for testing, and this is particularly important in the case of statistical sampling, where the plan will probably only allow for a very small number of non replies. The most usual recalcitrants are government departments and overseas customers.

The procedures so far are largely designed to prove the *cost* and *existence* of debtors, but they do not necessarily prove their *valuation*. It will be necessary to review the sales ledger for the existence of bad and doubtful debts. Bad debts should be written-off, and doubtful debts should be provided against, and the auditor must clearly ensure that this is correctly done. So the following tests should be performed:

(a) obtain an ageing analysis of debts from the client, and investigate old balances. This may be done in conjunction with the circularisation, particularly if the possibility of disputed invoices is suspected;

(b) analyse solicitor's correspondence for evidence of bad debts;

(c) compare percentage of bad debts written off over previous years to debtors, with this year's provisions for doubtful debts. Compare provision for doubtful debts with that of previous years;

(d) investigate basis of calculation of provision for doubtful debts.

### Prepayments

Prepayments are susceptible to error because they are not checked by the double entry system. The auditor must ensure that last year's prepayments are written back, and this is a good place to begin the examination of those of the current year. Prepayments do not change much from year to year, so a comparison of this year's schedule with that of last year should prove informative. Any items missing, or items substantially greater or less than last year, should be thoroughly investigated. But in the first year of trading such a comparison will not be available. So the auditor must rely on his knowledge of the accounts which frequently contain prepayments, such as rent, rates, insurance and advertising. Such accounts should be examined in detail to determine whether prepayments have been understated. But overstatement is perhaps our primary concern in so far as prepayments are concerned. So the schedule of prepayments should be vouched to supporting documentation to determine the authenticity of the amounts included (see also para. 14 of the MAP for Debtors and Prepayments on page 239).

The matters discussed in this section are now incorporated into a directional test MAP (see Fig. 14.7).

## 14.9 Bank and cash

The substantive tests required in relation to bank and cash will be designed mainly to prove the *existence* of the balances stated in the records.

### Bank

The client's year-end reconciliation of the cash book and bank statements should be checked as a matter of course by the auditor, and particular attention

Fig. 14.7 MAP for debtors and prepayments

*The purpose of the auditing procedures set out in this section of the programme is to obtain reasonable assurance that DEBTORS AND PREPAYMENTS are not materially over-stated.*

| | Work performed by | Reference to supporting working paper |
|---|---|---|

### Investigating compliance with internal control procedures

1. Where reliance has been placed on the client's internal control procedures, test that the controls on which we are relying have been complied with, and record the details of such tests in the working papers.

### Tests of detail

### Confirming the existence of trade debtors

*(Note: Debtors may be confirmed at the balance sheet date or at an interim date. If an interim date is chosen the follow-up procedures set out in paragraph 9 of this MAP must also be applied.)*

2. Obtain a list of trade debtors at the confirmation date and test these debtors for over-statement by carrying out the audit procedures set out in paragraphs 3, 4 and 5 below. Wherever possible, use as the list the client's analysis of debtor accounts.

3. Test the list as follows:
   (A) Agree or reconcile the total of the list with the debtors control account in the general ledger.
   (B) Test the casts of the list for over-statement.
   (C) Test the individual items on the list for over-statement, by applying the procedures set out below:
       (1) Select debit balances from the list of debtors or invoices outstanding.
       *(Note: Test for under-statement of credit balances, using the tests required to verify creditors — see MAP for creditors, accruals and provisions.)*
       (2) In respect of the selected balances, send out positive confirmation requests.
       *Note:*
       *(a) Where the client prepares the confirmation requests, check that they have all been properly prepared. Retain a copy of the working paper that lists all accounts selected.*
       *(b) Obtain the signature of the client's official on each request.*
       *(c) Mail the request direct, and do not use the client's staff or facilities for this purpose.*
       *(d) After a reasonable period of time, send out second request to those debtors who have not*

| | Work performed by | Reference to supporting working paper |
|---|---|---|

*responded.*

(3) Where the debtor will not confirm the balance in writing, try (with the client's permission) to obtain confirmation by telex or telephone.

(4) Review each reply that we receive. In cases where the debtor disputes the balance, request the client to investigate the reasons for all differences. Establish the validity of the differences and prepare a schedule of the differences and their subsequent disposal. *Note: It is important to investigate thoroughly any instances where the debtor disputes the amount paid by him or the date on which the client's records indicate payment was received. Factors such as these may indicate 'teeming and lading'.*

4. Where we are unable to obtain confirmation of a debtor's balance obtain evidence (by applying appropriate procedures) that the balance was a bona fide debtor of the client at the conformation date. The appropriate alternative procedures consist of:

(A) Checking the opening balance of the account with the list of balances at the previous year-end, testing the casts of the account during the year and agreeing the balance, and

(B) Testing the outstanding items with independent evidence of validity – including customers' orders, despatch records and subsequent payments (where these can be substantiated by remittance advices or other independent means), and

(C) Testing for the under-statement of payments etc. by discussing the outstanding items with a responsible official who is independent of the cash receiving function.

5. Where confirmation procedures are not applied, select individual balances from the list of debtors and carry out procedures listed in paragraph 4 above.

6. Prepare a summary of the confirmation procedures applied under paragraphs 2 to 5 above and of our conclusions.

## Testing the valuation of trade debtors

7. Test trade debtors for collectability and for under-statement of the doubtful debts provision as follows:

(A) Obtain reasonable assurance that the client's listing of overdue accounts has been correctly prepared by checking it with the sample selected in procedure 3(C)(1). Check the casts of each column and agree the total with the debtor's control account.

(B) Select overdue items from the client's listing of overdue accounts and check and investigate the extent to which they are collectable by reviewing credit reports, correspondence and other independent evidence.

Work
performed
by

Reference
to
supporting
working
paper

(C) Establish the reasonableness of formulae used to calculate general provisions. Review generally the client's bad debt experience for the current and recent financial years and establish the reasons for significant differences. Check the calculations on which the provision is based.

8. Test the bad debts written off against the provision during the year for overstatement by selecting debts written off and checking them with such independent evidence of validity as correspondence with solicitors, debt collection agencies etc.

## Following up an interim confirmation of trade debtors

9. Where the procedures in paragraphs 2 to 8 above were applied to a date other than the balance sheet date, apply the following additional procedures:
    (A) Test for over-statement of trade debtors at the balance sheet date by examining the transactions in the intervening period from the confirmation date to the balance sheet date, as set out below:
        (1) Test the credit sales in the intervening period for over-statement, as follows. Select debit entries from the debtors control account and compare these with the final sales records. Select individual transactions by sampling these final records and the related intermediate and initial sales records. Check these transactions with independent evidence of validity, such as customer orders, delivery notes signed by the debtors, despatch records, etc.
        (2) Test the sales returns and allowances in the intervening period for under-statement, as follows. Examine the evidence of sales returns and allowances (such as goods returned records, correspondence with customers, and the relevant sales invoices). Trace major items in these records to the credit notes and (via the accounting records) to the credit of the debtors control account. In doing this ensure that these sales returns were recorded in the correct financial year.
        (3) Test the receipts from debtors in the intervening period for under-statement, as follows. Examine customers' remittance advices, and any other available independent evidence. Trace major items in these records (via the accounting records) to the credit of the debtors control account. In doing this, ensure that these receipts were recorded in the correct financial year.
    (B) Review and summarise the movements on the debtors control account from the confirmation date to the balance sheet date and establish the reasons

for all unusual fluctuations. Compare the individual
balances which were selected for confirmation at the
——interim date with the corresponding balances at the
balance sheet date, and investigate major
differences.

## Testing the cut-off of debtors

10. Test for any over-statement of debtors as at the balance
sheet date that has arisen from recording transactions in
the wrong financial year. Do this by testing for over-
statement of sales and for under-statement of sales
returns and receipts, in the following manner:

(A) Test for over-statement of credit sales in the period
immediately preceding the year-end, as follows.
Compare major billings as recorded in the debtors'
control account (or other appropriate accounting
record of billings) in the last few days of the year,
with evidence of the date on which goods were
despatched or services were rendered. In doing this,
ensure that the billings are for sales made during the
financial year under review. (The evidence of
despatch should preferably comprise the
customer's acknowledgement of delivery or service
(such as signed delivery notes) or, failing that, the
client's despatch records.)

(B) Test for under-statement of sales returns and
allowances in the period immediately preceding the
year-end, as follows:

(1) Examine the evidence of sales returns and
allowances (such as goods returned records,
correspondence with customers, and the
relevant sales invoices) for the last few days of
the year and the first few weeks after the year-
end. Trace major items in these records to the
relevant credit notes and (via the accounting
records) to the credit of the debtors' control
account. In doing this, ensure that the sales
returns and allowances have been recorded in
the correct financial year or, alternatively, that
adequate provision for sales returns and
allowances has been made as at the year-end.

(2) Compare major sales credit notes in the first
few weeks after the year-end with the relevant
supporting evidence (such as goods returned
records, correspondence with customers, and
the relevant sales invoices). In doing this,
ensure that these credit notes have been
recorded in the correct financial year or,
alternatively, that adequate provision for sales
returns and allowances has been made as at the
year-end.

(C) Test for under-statement of receipts from debtors in
the last few weeks of the year, as follows. Examine

customers' remittance advices, listings of
remittances, and any other independent evidence.
Trace major items in these records (via the
accounting records) to the credit of the debtors'
control account. In doing this, ensure that these
receipts were recorded in the correct financial year.
*Note: The cut-off tests set out above should be carried
out in conjunction with the cut-off procedures relating to
the under-statement of sales and the over-statement of
sales returns and allowances – see the MAP for income
and expenses – credit sales, and sales returns and
allowances.*

## Reviewing the trade debtors

11. Review generally the list of balances as at the balance
sheet date. Compute trade debtors as a percentage of
sales and as the number of days' sales outstanding.
Compare these ratios with those of preceding years and
obtain satisfactory explanations for any significant
differences. Determine that the balances have been
correctly classified for balance sheet purposes and in
particular that:
    (A) Material credit balances have not been deducted from
    debtors (except where there is a right to set-off).
    (B) Inter-group balances have been classified correctly.
    (C) Balances due from any person or company which is
    in any way 'connected' with the client arise from
    bona fide transactions on an 'arm's length' basis.

## Testing of loans

12. Obtain a list of loans at the balance sheet date or, where
appropriate, as at an interim date. Test this for over-
statement, as follows:
    (A) Agree the total with the balance of the control
    account in the general ledger.
    (B) Test the casts of the list for over-statement.
    (C) Select loans from the list, or where the loans bear
    interest, from the sources specified in the note
    below. Test the selected items for over-statement as
    follows:
        (1) Obtain written confirmation direct from the
        individual borrowers.
        (2) Compare the selected loans with adequate
        evidence of ultimate collectability. Do this by
        checking that the interest and principal are
        being paid on time and that the loan is not in
        default of the loan agreement. Also, determine
        that the loan is adequately secured, by confirming
        that the client has a charge on the security and
        by examining evidence of the existence and
        value of the security (such as correspondence,
        the borrower's accounts, etc.). Where necessary,

   review the loans with responsible client
   officials.
   (3) In the case of those selected loans which were
       made during the financial year, compare with
       the relevant supporting documents for:
       (i)  Approval by the board of directors or by
            other designated officials or committees, and
       (ii) Other independent evidence of validity
            (such as loan agreements and evidence of
            receipt).
   *Note: Where the loans bear interest, the selection should
   be made instead from the list of loans at the beginning
   of the year and from the loans made during the year.
   The items selected should then be used for:*
   *(A) Testing the loans for over-statement – as in
        procedure (C) above, and*
   *(B) Testing for under-statement of loan interest, by
        checking that the interest relating to the selected
        loans has been included in the relevant income
        account in the general ledger.*

## Testing of other debtors and prepayments

13. Obtain a list of other debtors as at the balance sheet date
    or, where appropriate, as at an interim date. Test this for
    over-statement, as follows:
    (A) Agree the list with the balances on the relevant
        accounts in the general ledger.
    (B) Test the casts of the list for over-statement.
    (C) Select debtors from the list and test them for over-
        statement by applying procedures similar to those
        set out in paragraph 12(C) above.
    (D) Determine the nature and bona fides of all
        significant debtors, paying particular attention to
        amounts due from any person or company which is
        in any way connected with the client.

14. Obtain a list of prepayments as at the balance sheet date
    or, where appropriate, as at an interim date. Test this for
    over-statement, as follows:
    (A) Agree the list with the balances on the relevant
        accounts in the general ledger.
    (B) Test the casts of the list of over-statement.
    (C) Select prepayments from the list and test them for
        over-statement by comparing them with supporting
        independent documentation and with the
        corresponding amounts in prior years.

## Loans to directors or employees

15. Identify loans made to, or debts due by either directors,
    or employees, and consider the disclosure of such loans
    in the accounts.

should be paid to proving the reconciling items. This will normally be easily achieved by checking that unpresented cheques and uncleared lodgements appear on the bank statements early in the new year. If they do not appear thorough investigation will be necessary, as manipulation of the cash balance or fraud would be indicated. Substantial unpresented cheques may indicate that the bank balance is being deliberately reduced for balance sheet purposes, possibly because a high balance is often considered indicative of poor utilisation of funds and reflects badly upon the directors. Lodgements uncleared by the bank after a few days are more serious in that fraud or distortion would appear almost certain. Banks normally take only a short time to clear effects, so those uncleared after about a week will probably be fictitious. They may have been inserted by management to conceal a shaky liquidity position, or by an employee to conceal a misappropriation elsewhere. The auditor must discover which has occurred, and if the latter, substantial investigation could be required to determine the extent of the fraud.

Normally, however, the bank reconciliation will prove a routine matter, and the only step remaining will be to obtain directly from the bank a certificate confirming the balances as at the year end. The main purpose of this *bank certificate* is to authenticate the bank statements which could be fraudulent. This is not so far fetched as it may seem, as I discovered on the audit of a small printing works in London. The accountant had for several years been siphoning funds from the company and had concealed his defalcation by entering the correct, overstated amounts in the cash book, and then having bank statements printed to match! It was a printing company after all! The previous auditors had failed to call for a bank certificate. The accountant disappeared shortly after being asked to write to the bank requesting that they confirm directly to the auditors the balances outstanding. The request must be made by the client, for the auditor has no right to require such action from the client's bank – but the reply must go directly to the auditors. In addition to confirming the balances on all accounts as at the close of business on the last day of trading in the company's accounting year, the bank will be requested to confirm certain other matters. These are all included in a 'standard letter of request for bank report for audit purposes' included in audit guidance statement U22, which is reproduced in Fig. 14.8.

## Cash

Petty cash balances will often be counted by the auditor, though they will seldom be material. They are counted because of their susceptibility to fraud, and because management often hold the view that this is a traditional audit area. However, we can often delegate this work to the internal audit staff, provided they are regarded as reliable, in accordance with the considerations discussed in sec. 5.7.

So far as possible all cash balances should be counted at the same time, to prevent the possibility of substitution. And the counts should be performed at the

Fig. 14.8 U22. Bank reports for audit purposes (issued August 1977)

# U22. Bank reports for audit purposes

*Introduction*

1. The practice of obtaining independent certificates or reports from banks is essential to the proper discharge of auditors' responsibilities. Bank reports assist auditors to verify the existence of liabilities and the existence, ownership and proper custody of assets; they also provide other information relevant to the audit of accounts.

2. For many years, letters of request to banks were relatively simple and uniform, but they have recently tended to become complex and varied as a result of increased complexity in business and banking practices. Changes in the methods used by banks for keeping customers' records, especially with the development of computers, have also contributed to the problems of extracting the information at the time and in the form requested.

*Standard letter of request*

3. The information which auditors regularly need from banks is substantially the same for most audits, and can be contained in a standard letter of request. The use of such a letter, designed to cover all normal banking activity and to facilitate the extraction of information from banking records, should smooth the processing of these audit requests. Areas for particular audit attention should also be clearly exposed if answers are received which call for further enquiry.

4. As the clearing banks operating in the United Kingdom keep their customer records in a more or less similar manner, the use of a standard letter should facilitate the efficient preparation of their replies, particularly as much of the work falls at a period of peak activity for the banks. The banks accept the need for their assistance in these matters, and a standard letter should give them a clearer understanding of auditors' requirements.

5. Auditors should therefore adopt the practice of requesting information from banks in the form of the standard letter set out in Appendix 1 and in accordance with the procedures in paragraphs 7 to 10 below. Appendix 2 to this statement sets out explanations of items which are incorporated in, or specifically excluded from, the standard letter. *It is stressed that this standard letter is for audit purposes only. It should not be used when members are only concerned with the preparation of accounts of, for instance, sole traders, partnerships or other non-statutory organisations.*

*Authority to disclose*

6. Banks will require the explicit authority of their customers to disclose the requested information. They will always require such authority in writing, and this may be obtained either on each occasion a bank report is requested or as an authority which continues until further notice. In the former case it is recommended that the authority should be evidenced by the customer's countersignature to the letter of request; in the latter case the clearing banks state that the letter of request must refer to the customer's written authority given on a specified earlier date. The clearing banks state that, in the case of a joint account, the authority must be given by all parties to

the account. In the case of security lodged by a third party, his authority for disclosure will have to be obtained and produced to the bank.

*Procedure*

7. Auditors should adopt the following procedure in connection with requests to banks for audit purposes:
   (a) The standard letter set out in Appendix 1 to this statement should be sent on each occasion by the auditor on his own note-paper to the manager of each bank branch with which it is known that the client holds an account or has dealt since the end of the previous accounting reference period.
   (b) Auditors should ensure that the bank receives the client's authority to permit disclosure. The clearing banks state that this authority must be evidenced by either:
      (i) his countersignature to the standard letter; or
      (ii) a specific authority contained in an accompanying letter; or
      (iii) a reference in the standard letter to his specific written authority, given on a specified earlier date, which remains in force.
   (c) Wherever possible, the letter should reach the branch manager *at least one week in advance* of the date of the client's financial year-end.
   (d) The dates to be entered on the standard letter are normally the closing dates of:
      (i) the client's accounting reference period for which the report is requested; and
      (ii) the client's previous accounting reference period for which a full bank report was compiled. If, exceptionally, audited accounts are produced other than for an accounting reference period, alternative dates should be substituted.
   (e) In reviewing the bank's reply, it is important for auditors to check that the bank has answered all questions in full.
   (f) Auditors will need to check the authenticity of any letters not received *directly* from the bank branch concerned. If an auditor receives a bank report without having made a previous request, he should check with the branch concerned that the report has been prepared in compliance with the terms of the standard letter.

8. The standard letter should be used in its complete form for all audit requests in respect of year-end accounts and should not be altered or extended. In certain circumstances supplementary requests for additional information may be required for audit purposes. For administrative reasons the letter containing these supplementary requests should be submitted as far as possible at the same time as the standard letter.

9. If a non-standard letter of request is used for standard information, or if requests are made after the date of the appropriate year-end, banks may have difficulty in complying with the requests, and some of the information required may not be readily available.

10. For certain purposes other than verification for year-end accounts (for example for work of an accounting nature, interim audits and accountants' reports on solicitors' accounts), it may only be necessary to seek confirmation of selected items from the standard request. In such cases the letter should not be headed 'standard request for bank report'.

11. By agreement with the clearing banks, the standard letter should be used as from 1 December 1976.

*Bank reports for audit purposes*

## Appendix 1

STANDARD LETTER OF REQUEST FOR BANK REPORT
FOR AUDIT PURPOSES

The Manager

_____ (Bank)

_____ (Branch)

Dear Sir,

_____ (Name of customer)

STANDARD REQUEST FOR BANK REPORT
FOR AUDIT PURPOSES

In accordance with your above-named customer's instructions given

1. hereon
2. in the attached authority
3. in the authority dated _____ already
   held by you

} Delete as appropriate

please send to us, as auditors of your customer, the following information relating to their affairs at your branch as at the close of business on _____ and, in the case of items 2, 4 and 9, during the period since _____.

Please state against each item any factors which may limit the completeness of your reply; if there is nothing to report, state 'NONE'.

It is understood that any replies given are in strict confidence, for the purposes of our audit.

*Bank accounts*

1. Full titles of all accounts, together with the account numbers and balances thereon, including NIL balances:
   (a) where your customer's name is the sole name in the title;
   (b) where your customer's name is joined with that of other parties;
   (c) where the account is in a trade name.

*Notes*
(i) Where the account is subject to any restriction (e.g. a garnishee order or arrestment) or exchange control considerations (e.g. 'blocked sterling', 'external account'), this information should be stated.
(ii) Where the authority upon which you are providing this information does not cover any accounts held jointly with other parties, please refer to your customer in order to obtain the requisite authority of the other parties.

2. Full titles and dates of closure of all accounts closed during the period.

3. The separate amounts accrued but not charged or credited as at the above date, of:
   (a) provisional charges (including commitment fees) and
   (b) interest.

4. The amount of interest charged during the period if not specified separately in the bank statement.

5. Particulars (i.e. date, type of document and accounts covered) of any written acknowledgement of set-off, either by specific letter of set-off, or incorporated in some other document or security.

6. Details of loans, overdrafts and facilities, specifying agreed limits and in the case of term loans, date for repayment or review.

*Customer's assets*

7. (a) *Security*: Please give
   (i) details of any security formally charged to the bank, including the date and type of charge;
   (ii) particulars of any undertaking to assign to the bank any assets.

   If a security is limited to a specific borrowing, or if there is a prior, equal or subordinate charge, please indicate.

   (b) *Assets held but not charged*: Please give details.

*Contingent liabilities*

8. All contingent liabilities, viz.:
   (a) Total of bills discounted for your customer, with recourse;
   (b) Details of any guarantees, bonds or indemnities given to you by the customer in favour of third parties;
   (c) Details of any guarantees, bonds or indemnities given by you, on your customer's behalf, stating where there is recourse to your customer and/or to its parent or any other company within the group;
   (d) Total of acceptances;
   (e) Total of forward foreign exchange contracts;
   (f) Total of outstanding liabilities under documentary credits;
   (g) Others – please give details.

*Other information*

9. A list of other banks, or branches of your bank, or associated companies where you are aware that a relationship has been established during the period.

Yours faithfully,

*Bank reports for audit purposes*

DISCLOSURE AUTHORISED
For and on behalf of

_____ (Name of customer)

_____ ⎫ Signed in accordance with the
⎬ mandate for the conduct of the
_____ ⎭ customer's bank account.

year end, so that the petty cash fund cannot be paid into the bank account to boost that account, either for purposes of distortion, or to conceal a fraud. The count must be performed in the presence of the petty cashier, who should be asked to sign the count sheet, which should also be signed, dated and have the time of the count inserted by the auditor. The petty cashier's presence is necessary for he could otherwise say that the auditor is responsible for any shortages!

All funds under the control of the cashier must be counted at the same time, again to prevent the possibility of substitution. And this applies even if the funds are not directly part of the company's assets. For example, trade union funds held by the cashier in the company's safe should be counted at the same time as the petty cash, and the balance checked to appropriate records. Though this may present you with problems in actual practice! For this reason the petty cashier ideally should have no control over any other fund.

Vouchers making up the balance of the imprest should be checked for authenticity, and any items such as IOUs or advance slips should be carefully investigated. These should be prohibited in a good system of control. The petty cash book could usefully be cast and cross-cast at the same time, and reconciled to the main cash book. And reimbursements could then be checked for evidence of proper authorisation.

## 14.10 Creditors and accruals

### Creditors

Creditors may be substantiated either by transaction tests, or by balance tests. Traditionally, transaction tests have been used to check for both over- and understatement, though it is often difficult to obtain complete confidence about understatement in this way, unless the internal control is very strong and there is little opportunity for interference by senior management. For this reason it is now common practice amongst the larger firms to circularise creditors in a similar way to debtors. This has been traditionally resisted by clients, on the grounds that the circularisation could reveal to suppliers any overstatement in the client's records, to which the supplier would happily agree! But this objection can be obviated, by omitting the balance from the request and asking the creditor to insert the amount due.

### Accruals

Considerable attention must be paid to accruals at the year end, for these are not checked by the double entry system, and are accordingly susceptible to error. And this is also an area in which the senior management may seek to distort the accounts. It is obviously essential to ensure that last year's accruals are written back, and this is a good basis on which to begin the examination of those of the current year. Accruals do not ordinarily alter much from year to year, so any that are missing in the current year, or that are substantially greater or smaller, would call for thorough investigation. Accruals in relation to trade creditors should be checked by reference to those end of year goods received notes which are unmatched with supplier invoices. (See also paras 11–14 of the MAP for creditors, accruals and provisions in Fig. 14.9 and Fig. 4.3.)

## 14.11 Deferred taxation

Deferred taxation results from the fact that the Inland Revenue use different rules for calculating profit from those of financial accounting (e.g. capital allowances – depreciation). These different rules normally result in a reduced profit for tax purposes in the short term, as a means of encouraging investment. But in the long term there may be a potential payment of this deferred taxation. In the past no reference to this has been made in financial accounts, so that it was almost impossible to compare the net of tax profits of different companies; for some companies would have considerable potential for deferred taxation, and others would have very little at all. After-tax profit nowadays is considered to be the best indicator of a company's performance, so comparability of the net of tax position has become important.

### SSAP11

The first attempt at regularising this area came in 1975 with PSSAP11 on deferred taxation. In simple terms, this standard required that all timing differences be provided for in the accounts. This standard had the definite advantage that it was absolute, with little room for subjective judgement, and consequently few audit problems beyond checking the calculations. Comparability was in a sense assured, but provisions were being made for taxation charges which may never actually have been paid to the Inland Revenue (for example, as long as a company continues to reinvest the proceeds of the sale of capital items, then no capital gains tax will arise because of 'roll-over' relief; but PSSAP11 required that deferred tax be provided in all circumstances). For this reason PSSAP11 met with much opposition, and many companies, including ICI Ltd, bluntly refused to comply. As a result the standard (which was only provisional) was withdrawn in 1976, and was replaced by ED19, which subsequently became SSAP15 in October 1978.

### SSAP15

By contrast, SSAP15 is highly subjective and gives rise to considerable audit problems, because the directors are allowed to omit a provision for deferred taxation if they can demonstrate with *reasonable probability* that the provision will not be required in the future. The onus of proof is on the directors, but the auditors have to satisfy themselves as to the 'reasonable probability'. This can be a highly subjective matter involving an assessment of future profitability and capital expenditure over a period of several years. But before we look at the audit work

Fig. 14.9  MAP for creditors, accruals and provisions

*The purpose of the auditing procedures set out in this
section of the programme is to obtain reasonable assurance
that CREDITORS, ACCRUALS and PROVISIONS are not
materially under-stated.*

| | Work performed by | Reference to supporting working paper |
|---|---|---|

## Investigating compliance with internal control procedures

1. Where we have placed reliance on the client's internal
   control procedures, test that the controls on which we are
   relying have been complied with, and record the details
   of such tests in the working papers.

## Tests of detail

*(Note: Where the client keeps book records of stocks,
trade creditors should be confirmed at the date of the
physical stockcount. Where this date is not the balance
sheet date it will be necessary to apply the additional
procedures set out in paragraph 10 of this MAP.)*

## Testing the inclusion of creditors

2. Obtain a list of creditors at the confirmation date and
   apply the following procedures:
   (A) Agree or reconcile the total of the list with the
       general ledger account(s).
   (B) Cast the list.
   (C) Establish whether or not the list appears reasonable,
       by reviewing it for creditors which are obviously
       mis-stated, or which have clearly been omitted.

3. Select creditors' balances at the confirmation date on the
   following bases:
   (A) Select from those creditors whose provision of goods
       or service we have tested under the MAP for
       income and expenses, and
   (B) Select from the list of creditors at the beginning of
       the year in order to cover those accounts which had
       significant balances at the beginning of the year.

4. Confirm each selected balance as follows:
   (A) Where a statement from the creditor is available,
       compare this with the balance and ask the client to
       investigate any difference.
   (B) Where a statement from the creditor is not available,
       request the creditor to confirm his balance in
       writing.
       *Notes:*
       *(For creditor accounts such as rentals, public
       utilities, payroll deductions etc., direct confirmation
       is not required if the maximum unrecorded liability
       can be reasonably estimated.)*
       *(1) Where the client prepares the confirmation
       requests, check that they have all been properly*

*prepared. Retain a copy of the working paper that lists all accounts selected.*

*(2) Obtain the signature of the client's official on each request.*

*(3) Mail the requests direct, and do not use the client's staff or facilities for this purpose.*

*(4) After a reasonable period of time, send out second requests to those creditors who have not responded.*

(C) Where the creditor will not confirm his balance in writing try (with the client's permission) to obtain confirmation by telex or telephone.

(D) Review each reply that we receive. If the balance confirmed differs from the balance in the client's records, request the client to investigate the reasons. Establish the validity of the differences and prepare a schedule of the differences and their subsequent clearance to our satisfaction.

5. Where we are unable to confirm a creditor's balance:
   (A) Consider alternative ways in which we may satisfy ourselves that all liabilities to the creditor have been accrued (e.g. by selecting payments debited to the creditor's account after the confirmation date and ensuring that, where necessary, correct accruals have been made in the correct accounting period). Record in the audit working papers the work done and the conclusions reached.
   (B) Sample the debit entries to the creditor's account and establish their validity by examining paid cheques, credit notes or other relevant evidence. Agree the opening balance on the account with the list of creditors at the previous year-end, and test the casts of the account.

6. Test for the over-statement of any debit balances included in the liabilities at the confirmation date, using the tests required to verify debtors and prepayments (see MAP for debtors and prepayments).

7. Prepare a summary of the results of our confirmation of the creditors selected under paragraph 3 above and of our conclusions.

## Applying complementary procedures

*(Note: The confirmation procedures set out above are designed to ensure that there is not a significant amount of unrecorded liability to:*

*(A) Those suppliers with whom the client has done a significant amount of recorded business, and*

*(B) Those creditors who had significant balances at the beginning of the year.*

*In addition, the procedures set out in steps 8 and 9 below must be applied in order to ensure that there is not a*

| Work performed by | Reference to supporting working paper |
|---|---|
| | |

*material amount of unrecorded liability either to unrecorded creditors or to those recorded creditors whose transactions have been so greatly under-stated in the records that their chance of selection was significantly reduced).*

8. Consider which sources (independent of the general ledger) it is appropriate in the circumstances to investigate and test for the purpose just stated.

9. Carry out such procedures as may be necessary, and in particular:
   (A) Investigate the client's procedure which ensures that all receiving records are accounted for and result in the accrual of a liability. Test this procedure by such methods as may be appropriate in the circumstances.
   *Note: These methods will normally include:*
   *(1) Testing the sequence of records.*
   *(2) Selecting receiving records from each location and tracing those selected through the system to the accrual of the liability.*
   (B) Investigate and test the client's procedure which ensures that goods and services ordered from suppliers are delivered to the client, and which ensures that the related liabilities are duly recorded (i.e. paid or accrued).

## Following up an interim confirmation of creditors

10. Where the procedures in paragraphs 2 and 3 above are applied at any date other than the balance sheet date, apply the following additional procedures:
    (A) Test for under-statement of the credits to creditors' accounts as at the balance sheet date, by examining the transactions in the intervening period from the confirmation date to the balance sheet date, as follows:
       (1) Test for under-statement of the credit purchases in the intervening period, by applying to these purchases the procedure set out in paragraph 9 above.
       (2) Check that purchases and expenses in the intervening period which have been selected under the MAP for income and expenses have been either accrued at, or paid by, the balance sheet date.
    (B) Select debit entries to the creditors control account in the intervening period and:
       (1) Test the selected purchases returns and allowances in the intervening period for over-statement, by comparing the debit entries with the supporting evidence (such as goods returned records, inspection reports, correspondence with suppliers, and the relevant purchase invoices). In doing this, ensure that these

Work
performed
by

Reference
to
supporting
working
paper

purchase returns have been recorded in the correct financial year.

(2) Test the selected payments to suppliers by comparing them with the relevant debits in the bank statement and with the paid cheque. In doing this, ensure that each payment was debited by the bank within a reasonable time after the date of payment.

(C) Review and summarise the movements on the creditors' control account from the confirmation date to the balance sheet date, and establish the reasons for all unusual movements.

(D) Compare the individual balances which were selected for confirmation at the interim date with the corresponding balances at the balance sheet date, and investigate major differences.

## Testing the cut-off of creditors

11. Test for under-statement of creditors as at the balance sheet date (and at the stock taking date if appropriate) arising from the recording of transactions in the wrong financial year. Do this by testing for under-statement of purchases and for over-statement of purchase returns and payments, as follows:

(A) Test for under-statement of the credit purchases in the period immediately preceding the year-end, by the following procedures:

(1) Compare major entries in the receiving records in the last few days of the year with the accounting records. In doing this, ensure that the goods and the services concerned have been either paid for, or included in, creditors or accrued liabilities at the year-end.

(2) Select from purchase and expense records for the first few week after the year-end. Ensure (by referring to receiving records or by other appropriate means) that those purchases and expenses which relate to the period before the year-end were accrued as liabilities at the year-end.

(B) Test for over-statement of the purchase returns and allowances in the period immediately preceding the year-end, by comparing major returns debited to the creditors' control account in the last few days of the year with the supporting evidence (such as goods returns records, inspection reports, correspondence with suppliers, and the relevant purchase invoices). In doing this, ensure that these purchase returns have been recorded in the correct financial year.

(C) Test for over-statement of the payments to suppliers in the period immediately preceding the year-end, by comparing major payments debited to the creditors' control account in the last few days of the year with

Work
performed
by

Reference
to
supporting
working
paper

the relevant debit entries in the bank statement. In
doing this, ensure that each payment was debited by
the bank within a reasonable time after the date of
payment.

*Note: The cut-off tests set out in paragraph 11 above
should be carried out in conjunction with the cut-off
procedures relating to the over-statement of purchases
and the under-statement of purchase returns and
allowances — see the MAP for income and expenses —
purchases and purchase returns and allowances.*

12. Examine unprocessed invoices and check that all
significant amounts relating to the year under review have
been accrued at the balance sheet date.

## Testing accruals and provisions

13. Test for omission and other under-statement of accrued
liabilities and provisions, by examining supporting
documentation and by checking calculations to ensure
that adequate (but not excessive) provision has been
made for the items listed below. Where there is no
independent evidence available concerning the amount of
any accrual, test the debits to accrual accounts by
comparing with internal evidence of validity and with
paid cheques etc.
(A) Periodic payments (e.g. rent, utilities, insurance, etc.).
(B) Accrued salaries, wages and employer's social
security contributions.
(C) Accumulated holiday pay.
(D) Accrued commissions and bonuses.
(E) Accrued pension and retirement costs.
(F) Payroll deductions (e.g. P.A.Y.E., social security, and
pension scheme contributions).
(G) Professional charges.
(H) Directors' remuneration.
(I) Royalties and similar charges.
(J) Further expenditure for 'completed work' and for
after-sales service (warranty and similar matters).
(K) Pending or unbilled inter-company expense
allocations.
(L) Value Added Tax.

14. In addition, test for omission of other accruals and
provisions, by comparing with accruals and provisions in
previous years, by comparing with expenses incurred
during the year, by enquiry, and by other appropriate
methods.

## Reservation of title

15. (A) By using the information obtained in the MAP for
income and expenses — purchases, ensure for the
selected suppliers that the year-end liability for
goods purchased subject to reservation of title is not
under-stated.

| | Work performed by | Reference to supporting working paper |
|---|---|---|

(B) Test the items comprising the disclosed secured liability for over-statement.

(C) Review the tax correspondence to ensure that it is appropriate for the tax computation to be prepared on the 'commercial' basis.
*Note: The 'commercial' basis of the contract is that the goods are treated as purchases in the accounts of the purchasing company and sales in the accounts of the selling company. The 'legal' basis means that the relevant goods are not treated as a sale or purchase until the buyer has paid for them.*

(D) Record in the working papers the work done and the enquiries made.

## Pension funds

16. Establish that there is appropriate provision or disclosure in the accounts by carrying out the following procedures:

(A) Review the latest available information on the company's funds. This review should include an examination of:
    (1) the most recent actuarial valuation.
    (2) any correspondence with the actuary since the date of the valuation.
    (3) the latest accounts of the funds.

(B) Ascertain that there are not known events since the last actuarial valuation (such as the granting of substantial additional benefits to members or increases in the number of members of the scheme due to mergers) which might invalidate the actuary's most recent conclusions and recommendations.

(C) Determine what arrangements have been or will be made for funding the scheme and whether or not these are in accordance with the recommendations of the actuary.

(D) Record in the working papers the work done and the conclusions drawn.

## Reviewing and testing contingent liabilities

17. Obtain or prepare a working paper of contingent liabilities (including liabilities for bills discounted, letters of credit issued on behalf of third parties, purchase commitments, guarantees to third parties, damage claims by third parties, lawsuits, etc.).

18. Test that these are correctly stated and that no significant items have been omitted:

(A) In respect of lawsuits, claims and other actions against the client, by:
    (1) Enquiring of, and discussing with management, the policies and procedures adopted for identifying, evaluation and accounting for legal actions against the company.

(2) Obtaining from management an up-to-date description and evaluation of all lawsuits, claims and other legal actions that existed at the date of the balance sheet (matters which have been referred to the company's solicitors should be so indicated).

(3) Obtaining assurances from management as of the date that the accounts are approved in writing, that they have disclosed all matters requiring to be disclosed.

(4) Examining documents in the client's possession concerning lawsuits, claims and other legal actions including correspondence and bills from solicitors.

(5) Arranging for letters of audit enquiry to be sent to the client's solicitors. These letters should always be sent by the client but the replies should be addressed to us.

(B) In respect of other possible contingent liabilities by:

(1) Examining minutes and bank certificates.

(2) Discussing the contingencies with responsible client officials.

19. Record in the working papers the work done, the names and status of the client officials with whom these matters were discussed, and the conclusions drawn.

## Reviewing the classification of balances

20. Examine the listing of liabilities as at the balance sheet date, and reclassify debit balances, non-current balances, and inter-group balances where appropriate.

## Setting-off of balances

21. Ensure that:

(A) A legal right of set-off exists where debtor and creditor balances have been set-off.

(B) The client has made all known material set-offs in the accounts.

## Reviewing the level of creditors

22. Review the level of creditors and its relationship to purchases. Compare with the previous year and investigate any significant differences.

that may be involved, let us note *the ways in which a potential charge for deferred taxation can arise*:

1. Short-term timing differences; for example, as a result of the disallowance of a provision until actually paid. Such differences must *always* be provided against.
2. Capital allowances/depreciation. Capital allowances can be at the rate of 100 per cent in the first year, whereas 'depreciation will normally be much lower.
3. Stock relief, on the increase in cost of stock, year over year.
4. Debit balances may arise as a result of trading losses or advanced corporation tax.
5. Revaluation surpluses, and roll-over relief in respect of sales of capital items. Note that ACT and deferred tax in respect of trading losses cannot be set off against such capital items.

*Items 2 to 5 above may not need a provision if the conditions contained in Paragraph 28 of SSAP15 are complied with:*

> It will be reasonable to assume that timing differences will not reverse and tax liabilities will not crystallise if, but only if, the company is a going concern and:
> a. the directors are able to foresee on reasonable evidence that no liability is likely to arise as a result of reversal of timing differences for some considerable period (at least three years) ahead; and
> b. there is no indication that after this period the situation is likely to change so as to crystallise the liabilities.

*So we can distinguish the audit functions as follows:*
1. Check the calculation of timing differences in respect of 1–5 above.
2. Check the directors' view of the extent of the provision required by:
   (a) ensuring the company is a going concern;
   (b) examining the evidence upon which the directors base their assumption of no timing difference reversals.
3. Ensure that the presentation in the accounts is in accordance with SSAP15 and is comprehensive and unambiguous.

Stage one should prove a routine matter, and the auditors will always examine whether the company is a going concern, for many valuation bases will change if it is not. This latter area is fully discussed in Chapter 16, so now we can go straight to examining the difficulties associated with determining the reliability of evidence in support of a reduction in the provision.

Evidence will be necessary in respect of each category of deferred tax, and it may be reasonable to reduce one, but not another. The main category likely to cause difficulty is: *capital allowances.*

Evidence in support of a reduction of this provision must be based on proof of at least the maintenance of existing levels of investment in real terms. For once investment begins to decline, then deferred tax liabilities could crystallise.

The maintenance of existing capital investment levels is dependent upon the sales and profitability of the company. So in a sense the auditor is required to perform a profit forecast for at least three years ahead (three years being the minimum time period quoted in the SSAP). This is directly opposed to Institute Statement S23 which advises members not to comment on profit forecasts of more than one year ahead. The ASC in a statement accompanying SSAP15 counter this point by saying that 'whereas in a profit forecast many factors are outside the control of the directors, capital expenditure and inventory levels are, to a certain extent, within the control of the directors'. This is a weak argument, for profitability clearly affects investments, and if there is no likelihood of profit then the directors will not prudently invest, although it may well be within their control so to do. But it can be said that the auditor is only required to assess whether profitability is likely to fall or not rise sufficiently to warrant or support planned capital expenditure; he does not have to assess precisely what the profitability is going to be. And this does make his job much easier.

Audit evidence will inevitably have to be based largely on the company's budgets and longer term forecasts. *The procedures an auditor might adopt are*:

(a) assess the trend of past investment in capital items to see whether it is falling or rising, or perhaps whether there is no consistent pattern;

(b) assess the company's past profit performance to see whether falling or rising, and compare this performance with the company's previous budgets and estimates to determine its ability in forecasting – good forecasting in the past would give more confidence for the present;

(c) assess the company's investment, cash and profit forecasts for reliability. Determine whether they have been conscientiously made on the basis of reasonable data, or whether they are something more approaching guesswork;

(d) examine the directors' minutes for evidence of policy changes which might affect future investment;

(e) take note of the economic situation, with particular reference to the client's own industry, and assess the vulnerability of the company to economic or legislative changes, and to labour disruption or material or component shortages.

Quite a task. But if the auditor cannot satisfy himself as to the quality of evidence in support of a reduction in the provision, he should insist on the full amount being provided. The extent to which he needs to investigate the above matters can, to a degree, be mitigated if the company already has a large backlog of unused capital allowances.

Provision will not normally be necessary on the revaluation surpluses of land and buildings (as would have been the case under SSAP11), because of the availability of 'roll-over' relief, provided sale proceeds are reinvested. Accordingly the auditor should only insist on a provision in the event that the directors both sell the revalued property, and decide not to reinvest.

In November 1980 the Inland Revenue introduced a new scheme for stock relief. Under this scheme there will be no clawback of stock relief unless the business is discontinued or substantially curtailed. So deferred taxation would only need to be provided if such circumstances were envisaged.

The amounts provided in respect of each category of deferred taxation should be shown separately, and any debits in respect of ACT or trading losses should be shown as a deduction from the total. These amounts should be shown in the balance sheet as a liability and not as part of the shareholders' funds. In the Profit and Loss account they should be shown as a charge for taxation in addition to the mainstream corporation tax. SSAP15 also provides that the full potential amount of deferred taxation split between the categories must be shown by way of a note to the accounts. Note that the complete disclosure requirements are included in the SSAP check list in Appendix 2.

## 14.12 Capitalisation

### Share capital

Any issue of shares during the year should be checked to board minutes for authority, and to the company's Memorandum of Association to ensure that the authorised share capital has not been exceeded. The correct recording of moneys received should be vouched, and the correct treatment of any share premium ascertained. Remember that the only allowable purposes for which a share premium account may be used are:
(a) to issue fully paid bonus shares;
(b) to write off preliminary expenses, or expenses of share or debenture issue;
(c) to write off discounts on shares or debentures;
(d) to provide for a premium payable on the redemption of redeemable preference shares.
Share transfer procedure should be examined in principle, but a share transfer audit is a special assignment which will be dealt with in Chapter 22.

### Reserves

Movements on reserves must be shown either in the balance sheet, the profit and loss account, the director's report or in notes, so the proper authorisation and recording of such movements must be vouched by the auditor. The relevant disclosure requirements are dealt with in the Companies Act check list in Appendix 3, but in brief, material amounts of reserves must be classified under appropriate headings, with the Capital Redemption Reserve Fund and the Share Premium Account shown separately, and the aggregate amount clearly identified.

### Debentures

An issue of debentures must be checked for authority by reference to the director's minutes, and the Articles of Association to ensure that the borrowing is not *ultra vires*. Any discounts and premiums should be shown in a separate account in the balance sheet, with the debentures themselves shown at nominal value. Discounts should be written off against profit over such a period of years as is consistent with not distorting the profits of any one year, that period to be not longer than the life of the debenture; although there is no legal or professional requirement to force the directors to take such action if they do not so wish. Any premium would be shown as a capital reserve, or may be used to write off preliminary expenses of issue. It will be necessary to examine the trust deed or debenture to ensure that all the terms of issue have been complied with, and to determine if there is any security for the loan. Such security would of course have to be shown by way of a note to the accounts, and should also appear in the company's register of charges. The trust deed will also reveal the nature of the interest payable, and the auditor must check that the appropriate amount of any interest outstanding has been accrued in the accounts.

## 14.13 Capital commitments

Capital commitments must be disclosed by way of a note to the accounts in accordance with the 1967 Companies Act. Accordingly the auditor must perform sufficient work to ensure that such amounts are fairly and completely stated. This information will normally be acquired from the directors in the Letter of Representation (see Chapter 16), but work must be performed to confirm the amounts stated. The place to begin will be the directors' minutes, which should be reviewed for evidence of authority to place capital contracts. The capital expenditure budget should also be examined and informal discussions with appropriate middle management staff may prove useful. Finally, correspondence with solicitors should be examined to discover whether any instructions have been placed for drawing up or vetting contracts. Remember that a distinction must be made in the note, between expenditure authorised by the directors, and contracts that have actually been placed.

## 14.14 Contingencies

SSAP18 Accounting for Contingencies defines a contingency as 'a condition which exists at the balance sheet date, where the outcome will be confirmed only on the occurrence or non-occurrence of one or more uncertain future events. A contingent gain or loss is a gain or loss dependent on a contingency'. For example, potential damages as a result of the unfavourable outcome of a pending court case, would be a contingent liability. The 1967 Companies Act provides that 'the general nature of any other contingent liabilities not provided for and where practicable, the aggregate amount or estimated amount of those liabilities, if it is material', should be shown by way of a note to the accounts.

SSAP18 on contingencies, and International Accounting Standard 10 on Contingencies and Events Occurring After the Balance Sheet Date make further disclosure requirements. The requirements of IAS10 are fully met by compliance with SSAP18, so only the latter is reproduced here:

*Standard accounting practice*

15. In addition to amounts accrued under the fundamental concept of prudence in SSAP2 'Disclosure of accounting policies', a material contingent loss should be accrued in financial statements where it is probable that a future event will confirm a loss which can be estimated with reasonable accuracy at the date on which the financial statements are approved by the board of directors.

16. A material contingent loss not accrued under para. 15 above should be disclosed except where the possibility of loss is remote.

17. Contingent gains should not be accrued in financial statements. A material contingent gain should be disclosed in financial statements only if it is probable that the gain will be realised.

18. In respect of each contingence which is required to be disclosed under paras. 16 and 17 above, the following information should be stated by way of notes in financial statements:
    (a) the nature of the contingency; and
    (b) the uncertainties which are expected to affect the ultimate outcome; and
    (c) a prudent estimate of the financial effect, made at the date on which the financial statements are approved by the board of directors; or a statement that it is not practicable to make such an estimate.

19. Where there is disclosure of an estimate of the financial effect of a contingency, the amount disclosed should be the potential financial effect. In the case of a contingent loss, this should be reduced by:
    (a) any amounts accrued; and
    (b) the amounts of any components where the possibility of loss is remote.
    The net amount only need be disclosed.

20. The estimate of the financial effect should be disclosed before taking account of taxation, and the taxation implications of a contingency crystallising should be explained where necessary for a proper understanding of the financial position.

21. Where both the nature of, and the uncertainties which affect, a contingency in respect of an individual transaction are common to a large number of similar transactions, the financial effect of the contingency need not be individually estimated but may be based on the group of similar transactions. In these circumstances the separate contingencies need not be individually disclosed.

Provisions should always be made in the financial statements themselves for any losses that can be estimated with reasonable accuracy, and the occurrence of which is reasonably probable. Gains on the other hand should only be included if they are reasonably certain to occur. Accordingly the auditor must determine:

1. Whether all potential gains and losses have been ascertained.
2. Whether all necessary provisions have been made in respect of losses that can be determined with reasonable accuracy.
3. Whether adequate disclosure has been made of all contingent gains or losses including sufficient detail of the circumstances surrounding each item.

Most contingencies should be revealed during the course of normal audit work, but in particular the following should be kept in mind:

(a) guarantees made on behalf of other companies or individuals;
(b) bills discounted not matured;
(c) pending legal cases.

(a) and (b) will normally be revealed by the bank letter, and (c) may be revealed by reference to solicitor's correspondence and the directors' minutes. And these may also provide evidence of other possible contingencies.

The assessment of contingent liabilities in respect of pending legal matters is often a difficult audit area. Accordingly the ICAEW issued auditing statement U16 covering this matter, after consultation with the Law Society, and this is reproduced in Fig. 14.10.

Fig. 14.10 U16. The ascertainment and confirmation of contingent liabilities arising from pending legal matters (issued August 1970)

## U16. The ascertainment and confirmation of contingent liabilities arising from pending legal matters.

1. It is the duty of directors to ensure that proper account is taken of all liabilities, including contingent liabilities, in the preparation of company financial statements. From the audit viewpoint, pending lawsuits and other actions against the company may present problems both of ascertainment and appraisal.

2. The following audit procedures are suggested for the verification of the existence of such claims though they will not necessarily provide the auditor with adequate information of the likely amounts for which the company may ultimately be responsible:

   (a) Reviewing the client's system of recording claims and the procedure for bringing these to the attention of the management or board.

   (b) Discussing the arrangements for instructing solicitors with the official(s) responsible for legal matters (for example the head of the legal department (if any) or the company secretary).

   (c) Examining the minutes of the board of directors and/or executive or other relevant committee for references to, or indications of, possible claims.

   (d) Examining bills rendered by solicitors and correspondence with them, in which connection the solicitors should be requested to furnish bills or estimates of charges to date, or to confirm that they have no unbilled charges.

   (e) Obtaining a list of matters referred to solicitors from the appropriate director or official with estimates of the possible ultimate liabilities.

   (f) Obtaining a written assurance from the appropriate director or official that he is not aware of any matters referred to solicitors other than those disclosed.

3. In appropriate circumstances, auditors may decide to obtain written confirmation from third parties of certain representations made by directors; for example, the identification and appraisal of contingent liabilities. In the field of legal actions the normal and proper source of such confirmations is the company's legal advisers.

4. Requests for such confirmations should be kept within the solicitor-client relationship and should thus be issued by the client with a request that a copy of the reply should be sent direct to the auditors.

5. In order to ascertain whether the information provided by the directors is complete, auditors (especially in certain overseas countries) may decide to

arrange for solicitors to be requested to advise whether they have matters in hand which are not listed in the letter of request, and to provide information as to the likely amounts involved. When considering such a non-specific enquiry, auditors should note that the Council of the Law Society has advised solicitors that it is unable to recommend them to comply with requests for information which are more widely drawn than the specimen form of wording set out in paragraph 6 below.

6. In these circumstances, the enquiry should normally list matters identified as having been referred to the company's legal advisers in accordance with paragraph 2(e) above. The following form of wording, appropriate to specific enquiries, has been agreed between the Councils of the Law Society and the Institute of Chartered Accountants in England and Wales as one which may be properly addressed to, and answered by, solicitors:

'In connection with the preparation and audit of our accounts for the year ended . . . the directors have made estimates of the amounts of the ultimate liabilities (including costs) which might be incurred, and are regarded as material, in relation to the following matters on which you have been consulted. We should be obliged if you would confirm that in your opinion these estimates are reasonable.

| Matter | Estimated liability including costs.' |
|--------|--------------------------------------|

7. The Council of the Institute of Chartered Accountants in England and Wales understands the reasons for the view of the Council of the Law Society regarding non-specific enquiries, but nevertheless believes that there may be circumstances in which it is necessary as an audit procedure for an enquiry of a general nature to be addressed to the solicitors in order to confirm that the information provided by the directors is complete in all material particulars.

8. If the outcome of the enquiries set out in paragraphs 2 and 5 above appears satisfactory, auditors would not normally regard the absence of a corroboration of the completeness of a list of legal matters as a reason in itself for qualifying their report. If the enquiries lead to the discovery of significant matters not previously identified, the auditors will wish to extend their enquiries and to request their clients to address further enquiries to, or arrange a meeting with, the solicitors, at which the auditors will wish to be present. If, however, having regard to all the circumstances, the auditors are unable to satisfy themselves that they have received all the information they require for the purpose of their audit, they must qualify their report.

## 14.15 Conclusion

We have now examined the procedures necessary for substantiating the year-end balances of all the most usual types of asset and liability. During the course of this examination we noted the most important disclosure requirements, and these are completely recorded in the SSAP and Companies Acts check lists in the Appendices. But before we proceed to the concluding stages of the audit, it is appropriate to look in more detail at the need for disclosure, the likely and necessary future developments in this direction and the steps that the auditor must take in the event of non-compliance. The next chapter is devoted to this end.

# 15
# Disclosure requirements

## 15.1 The need for disclosure

Successive Companies Acts have required progressively more and more disclosure of financial information to shareholders, and this trend is certain to continue. For, it is argued, the more information an accounts user has the better he is able to reach appropriate decisions (for example, to continue to hold his shares, or to sell them). And the less able are the directors to deceive, through ambiguous or confusing presentation. All this is undoubtedly true, but disclosure, held out by many as a sacred cow, is not of itself a total answer for curing accounting ills, for several reasons:

1. There is clearly a limit to the amount of disclosure that can be made in a competitive economy, without the information being prejudicial to the company's trading interests.
2. Disclosure of disparaging remarks by auditors concerning a company's control systems or other operations could lead to a loss of confidence in the company, which could be prejudicial to shareholders in terms of their stock quotation, and ultimately to creditors also, if the company is forced into an unnecessary liquidation. Behind-the-scenes rectification of minor weaknesses may in the long run be better for all.
3. Excessive disclosure of unnecessary detail can serve only to confuse.
4. Disclosure is of comparatively little value without conformity of accounting treatment – conformity, both with previous period practice within the company, and with the practice in other similar businesses. For conformity brings with it comparability. And very few accounts have much meaning in isolation.

Companies Acts have enacted a considerable body of legislation specifying various matters that must be disclosed. You will of course have come across most of these during the course of your accountancy studies, so reference has only been made during the course of this book to those matters which are of particular significance or problem to the auditor.

However, the Companies Acts are nowadays considered nowhere near sufficient in terms of their disclosure requirements. Accordingly they have been supplemented by various professional pronouncements, which, while they do not have the force of law behind them, do have the sanctions of the professional bodies concerned. The pronouncements with which we are most concerned were discussed in sec. 1.5, but here is a list to remind you:

> Statements of Standard Accounting Practice
> International Accounting Standards
> Stock Exchange Pronouncements
> UEC pronouncements
> All of these requirements are included in the check lists in Appendices 2 and 3).

In addition, the Fourth Directive on Company Law of the EEC lays down specific compliance provisions for public accounts, although in the main they do not much alter the UK position (see sec. 15.7 for a more detailed discussion). These provisions will in due course be incorporated into the UK law. Again you will be familiar with many of the above requirements from your financial accounting studies. But the SSAPs in particular, are of special concern for the auditor, because it will often fall to him to decide whether the requirements have been interpreted correctly in a given set of circumstances, whether accounting policies are appropriate and whether there has been consistent compliance with relevant standards.


## 15.2  The need for conformity

It is sometimes argued that total disclosure of accounting policies allows the accounts of different companies to be compared, even if differing policies are used by those companies, for the effects of the differences can be assessed. But the practical difficulties of making such an assessment, in my view, render comparison almost impossible. So there is every need for standardisation of accounting treatment in the way that the SSAPs and IASs are designed to achieve, though I believe that these standards often do not go far enough, in that many allow considerable discretion on the part of the directors.

Argument against standardisation largely centres on the fact that the exercise of judgement is at the heart of professional work, and that standardisation eliminates judgement. It would seem to me that the exercise of judgement comes in formulating suitable standards in the first place, and then in ensuring that financial statements comply. But this point aside, it would seem that there is no necessary merit in judgement *per se*, unless it produces more meaningful figures. And surely figures can only be really meaningful if there is a generally accepted basis for computation.

It is true that companies do differ, so in some specific cases it may be that one accounting policy will be more appropriate than another. For example, certain types of asset may more appropriately be depreciated by a reducing balance method than by straight line depreciation. But in general those formulating the standards should consider whether one basis of treatment is likely to be significantly more appropriate than another. If both would equally do, then what purpose is there in allowing a choice?

There is a considerable need for the consolidation of the various Companies Acts now on the statute book. At present there are the 1948, the 1967, the 1976, the 1980 and the 1981 Acts each with overlapping and cross-referenced requirements. And in addition a substantial company law reform is also necessary. But this can await discussion in Chapter 23.

## 15.3 The 1980 Companies Act

The 1980 Companies Act introduced a number of important reforms, of which the following is a summary of those significant for our purposes:

1. Distinction is drawn between 'public' and 'private' limited companies, with only the former being able to offer shares and debentures to the public. A 'public' company must state the fact in its name, and must have an issued share capital of at least £50,000 with at least one-quarter paid. *There is no minimum requirement for a 'private' company, and this is in my view extremely unfortunate.*

2. A company may not make a distribution which would reduce its net assets below the aggregate of its called up share capital and undistributed reserves (undistributed reserves consist of the excess of accumulated unrealised profit over accumulated unrealised losses).

3. Auditors are given added power, by a provision that no distribution may be made on qualified accounts, unless the auditors have stated in writing that their qualification is not material for the purposes of determining the permissibility of the distribution.

4. The long-standing audit problem of deciding whether a loan to a director was 'in the ordinary course of business' and therefore exempt from disclosure is removed by the requirement for all loans to directors or people 'connected' with directors to be disclosed. Loans to directors are in general prohibited unless they are either for the purposes of business expenditure (and either approved by general meeting or not more than £10,000 and repayable within six months) or made in the ordinary course of business on normal terms (favourable terms are allowable if the loan is for expenditure of not more than £50,000 on a dwelling-house and similar loans are made to other employees).

5. Moves are made in the Act towards restricting 'related party transactions'. A director or 'connected' person may not enter into a contract with the company for the purchase or sale of any non-cash asset, the value of which exceeds £50,000 or 10 per cent of the company's net assets, unless there is an approving resolution by general meeting of the company. Contracts entered into in contradiction of this provision are voidable at the instance of the company (with certain specific exceptions).

Where a director has a material interest in a contract (in the opinion of the other directors) and value of property, etc., provided by the company exceeds £5,000 or 1 per cent of the company's net assets, the accounts must disclose the name of the director and the nature of the contract and the director's interest.

6. At last 'insider dealing' is outlawed by company law. Insiders are defined

as an officer or employee of the company or a related company, or an individual who occupies a position which gives him access to not readily available information which could, if disclosed, materially affect the price of securities and which it would be reasonable to expect a person in his position not to disclose except for the proper performance of his duties. Such insiders are prohibited from dealing on a Stock Exchange with any securities of the company with which they are connected (or have been connected within the previous six months) if they have information which is not readily available and which could materially affect the price of securities if disclosed. Nor can they procure another person to deal in those securities, or give their information to another in the knowledge that the other person will make use of it for the purpose of dealing. A 'connected' person dealing outside a Stock Exchange must declare his status before making a deal. The Secretary of State has authority to appoint inspectors with wide powers to investigate any suspected contravention of these provisions.

## 15.4 The 1981 Companies Act

The 1981 Companies Act incorporates many of the provisions of the EEC Fourth Directive. A distinction is made between large, medium and small companies, with medium and small companies being entitled to take advantage of provisions enabling them to submit abridged accounts to the Registrar of Companies. Medium sized companies can submit a modified income statement and reduced disclosure of additional information. Small companies may submit an abbreviated balance sheet only with no income statement or directors' report. Medium companies are defined as those which fulfil two or more of the following criteria for the current and preceding financial year:

Turnover not more than £5,750,000
Balance sheet total not more than £2,800,000
Number of employees not more than 250

Small companies are defined as those which satisfy two of the following criteria for the current and preceding financial year:

Turnover not more than £1,400,000
Balance sheet total not more than £700,000
Number of employees not more than 50

In circumstances where a company takes advantage of the exemption provisions S152 p. 7 requires from the auditor's report that in their opinion the conditions for exemption are met. In addition to this special report the full audit report as required by Section 14 of the 1967 Act must be submitted to the Registrar of Companies.

The audit requirement for dormant companies is removed by the 1981 Act provided specific conditions are met.

As well as changing the content of annual financial statements for different sizes of company, the 1981 Act in Schedule 8 sets out a number of prescribed reporting formats for different types of company for the presentation of income statements, balance sheets and additional information. These prescribed formats must be complied with under penalty of law.

The 1981 Act gives statutory authority to many of the principles underlying SSAPs. The requirements of the 1981 Act are included in the disclosure checklist in Appendix 1.

## 15.5 Statements of Standard Accounting Practice

Companies should comply with the SSAPs unless a specific SSAP makes an exception. Normally companies will comply with these provisions, but occasionally the auditor may discover a non-compliance. This will usually be a mistake by the client and the auditor should in this case advise the client of the correct treatment, and ensure that the financial statements are changed accordingly.

But it may sometimes arise that the directors refuse to comply with SSAP provisions, either because they disagree with those provisions (for example ICI Ltd and SSAP11) or because they believe that the provisions are inappropriate for their company. In any event, if there is a non-compliance, the auditor must make reference to this in the first part of his audit report, unless the non-compliance is fully documented in the notes to the accounts on accounting policies, or elsewhere. In the event that the auditor considers the departure unjustified, he should quantify the effect of the departure in his report, or state that such a quantification cannot be made, in either event giving details of the nature of the departure. And he should then qualify his report by either:

(a) stating that the accounts do not show a true and fair view . . . or

(b) stating that subject to the non-compliance, the accounts show a true and fair view.

The former qualification would only be made in extreme cases, when the non-compliance was such as to render the accounts as a whole misleading. An example of this would be a non-compliance with SSAP2, in respect of the 'Going Concern' concept. In normal circumstances however, only one item, or at most a group of items, in the accounts will be affected making only those specific items misleading. Accordingly, the accounts as a whole may still show a true and fair view subject to this exception.

The most common departure from standard accounting practice is in respect of SSAP9 on stock and work in progress. I have already mentioned the oft quoted case of the Tate and Lyle Co. Ltd, which, with the auditor's concurrence, continued to use base stock accounting despite the prohibition in the SSAP. A similar example is provided by the Steetley Co. Ltd of Manchester. Their accounts for 1977 did not comply with SSAP9 in that all fixed overheads were written off immediately instead of a proportion being carried forward in stocks as required. They considered this treatment more prudent and appropriate to their manufacturing processes, overhead structure and control systems. And the auditors agreed, though, as was then required, they made note of the non-compliance in their report, adding 'We are in agreement with the treatment adopted'.

An example of an audit report covering non-compliance with an SSAP is given in sec. 17.4.

## 15.6 The Stock Exchange

All companies listed by the Stock Exchange are required to comply with the Listing Agreement as contained in 'Admission of Securities to Listing' published by The Stock Exchange. The requirements include certain information which must be circulated with the annual report of the directors. These requirements are all contained in the Stock Exchange requirements check list reproduced in Appendix 1. The requirements themselves should present few audit problems, other than straightforward checking for compliance.

## 15.7 The Fourth Directive

The Fourth Directive on Company Law of the European Economic Community was adopted on 25 July 1978, and laid down quite specific requirements for the preparation and presentation of company accounts. Member states were required to enact legislation to implement the directive by 10 August 1980, and implementation could be delayed by a further eighteen mouths. So the first accounts to be published under the provisions are likely to be those for financial years ending in 1982, with disclosure of the corresponding amounts for the previous year.

By European standards, the United Kingdom is comparatively advanced in terms of presentation and disclosure requirements in accounts. And the format required under the new provisions necessitates little change in existing practice. However, the new accounting practice and disclosure requirements do make some changes necessary. At the time of writing this is a recent development, so I believe it useful to depart from my practice so far, and to document in the main body of the text those changes in existing practice which are necessitated by these provisions: The changes are listed below in article number order:

30. Separate disclosure must be made of the tax on ordinary trading activities and extraordinary items. At the moment, SSAP6 requires that extraordinary items be shown net of tax, but there is no requirement for the separate disclosure of the amount of tax.

34. The formation expenses of the company must be written off over not more than five years, and dividends must not be paid until reserves cover the expenses not yet written off. There is no such requirement at present.

37.1. Goodwill is to be written off over not more than five years, or over its useful life if a member state specifically permits. At the time of writing goodwill is the subject of a proposed Exposure Draft, and presumably the CCAB will take account of this requirement in the draft. But currently, there is no requirement to write off goodwill, and there is a variety of treatment, as discussed in sec. 14.5. I myself do not favour the EEC provision. Why write off over five years; why not six or ten, etc.? Indeed why write off at all? And the concept of writing off over the useful life is interesting. For how do you determine the useful life of goodwill, which is in effect the company? You are really asking how long will the company remain a going concern. The directors will clearly hope indefinitely; so they could quite reasonably take infinity as the amortisation base!

40.2. Disclosure is required, if material, of the difference between the value of stock as stated in the balance sheet, and the market value. This of course is not required at present. The concept of market value has not been used in UK accounting since ED11 proposed the lower of cost or market value as the basis of stock valuation. This latter was rejected in favour of net realisable value, which is a much more useful concept. But possibly the EEC provision will be interpreted in this way. Because how do you assess the market value of work in progress, for example? This point aside, the provision is a useful one, in that it can enable a reader of the financial statements to determine the actual amount of equity that there is in stock. And for example, this could be relevant to the granting of credit, or loans.

43.1. In respect of other companies in which the company holds an interest of
(2) 20 per cent or more (this percentage may be reduced at the member state's discretion), the following must be disclosed:
(a) Proportion of capital held;
(b) Capital and reserves;
(c) Profit or loss for the latest financial year for which accounts adopted.
At present such companies would be consolidated. In the holding company's own accounts only the name, country of incorporation and description and proportion of shares held would at present be disclosed, where more than a 10 per cent interest is held.

43.1. The security for any loans must be identified. At present it is sufficient to
(6) state that a loan is secured. This is clearly a useful provision.

43.1. This article requires net turnover to be disclosed split as to activity and area.
(8) Activity split is currently required by law, but geographical split is only required for listed companies by the Stock Exchange, and then only in the unaudited directors' report.

43.1. Average numbers employed must be disclosed by category, and employee
(9) costs split as to (a) wages and salaries, (b) social security costs and (c) pension. At present there is no requirement for the split by category of the numbers employed, and only the aggregate staff costs need be shown. And this again only in the unaudited directors' report.

46. The directors' report must disclose:
(a) a review of the company's development;
(b) significant events occurring after the financial year end;
(c) comment on future development;
(d) comment on research and development.
There is no current requirement for such comment, and normally only the briefest indication is given. And then only in listed companies.
From the point of view of the auditor, the only other particularly significant

268 Disclosure requirements

provision of the Fourth Directive is that which allows member states to relieve small companies from the requirement to have their accounts audited. A small company is here defined as one which does not exceed any two of the following criteria:

> balance sheet total = 1 million European Units of Account
> net turnover     = 2 million European Units of Account
> average number of staff during the financial year = 50

(A European Unit of Account is based on an average of European currencies.) A government Green Paper has asked for views on the relaxation of small company audit requirements along these lines. I personally believe that the EEC size limit is too large. In my opinion, the relaxation should not be based on size, but on the nature of the company – as to whether it is manager or proprietor operated. And in either event, I believe that there should be an audit review of the accounts as a protection for creditors and others who may seek to rely on them, and as a precaution to ensure that the advantages of limited liability are not abused. But more about this in Chapter 18.

## 15.8 Conclusion

It is the auditor's task to ensure that all professional and legal requirements are complied with, or to report to the members in the event of non-compliance. This will usually be a routine matter which can best be achieved by the use of check lists, such as those in the Appendices. These allow the systematic appraisal of the accounts, and ensure that no provisions are overlooked. For your examinations, however, you will need to know these provisions.

We can now proceed to the concluding stage of the audit, and then to the audit report.

# 16
## Concluding an audit

## 16.1 Letters of representation

A letter of representation will normally be sought by the auditor from the directors at the concluding stage of the audit. The purpose of this letter is to confirm various matters stated in the accounts, particularly those which concern questions of fact or judgement which are difficult for the auditor to prove objectively. For example, there is no need to obtain a representation about the amount of the bank account balance, because that can be objectively proved. But there is need to obtain a representation to the effect that there are no contingent liabilities other than those stated, for it is difficult in practice to prove this. This does not mean, however, that the auditor can rely on these representations from the directors to the exclusion of other audit work, as perhaps was once the case with, for example, stock certificates. The representations will simply be one more piece of evidence to add to evidence obtained through testing and enquiry. And in the absence of such other evidence, it would be a very rash auditor indeed who relied on representations to save him from a potential negligence claim. Though it must be said, that the usefulness of representations was increased by the 1976 Companies Act which made it a criminal offence to recklessly supply auditors with false or misleading information. Negligence or fraud is no longer a necessary prerequisite before the directors can be held criminally liable.

This latter change in the law has, of course, made directors more reluctant to sign such a letter; though it should be pointed out to them that the accounts are primarily their responsibility anyway, and that the representations are merely designed to confirm matters already contained therein. And this is perhaps the main use of the letter – to ensure that the directors both fully appreciate the matters that have been stated in the accounts, and are taking full responsibility for them. In the event that the directors refuse to sign, the auditors should endeavour to determine the reason why. The directors may have reservations about one specific aspect of the accounts, or about the accounts as a whole. Or they may simply not understand what they are being asked to sign, or appreciate their responsibility in relation to the accounts. Whichever, it is a serious matter. If the latter, every effort should be made to explain the position. But if the directors have material reservations, they presumably relate to some matters which have not been revealed to the auditors. In which case the auditors will either have to carry out extra work to discover the nature of the reservations, or to qualify the accounts, probably stating that they are unable to express an opinion, because they have not received all necessary information and explanations.

The letter of representation will often be a standard part of audit stationery. It will be filled in by the auditors, and then given to the directors to sign. An example of such a document is reproduced in Fig. 16.1 by kind permission of Deloitte, Haskins and Sells:

Fig. 16.1 Standard letter of representation

### An example of a representation letter

Date . . . . . . . . . . . . . . . . . . .

Dear Sirs,
In connection with your examination of the accounts for the year ended . . . . . . . . . .
we confirm, to the best of our knowledge and belief, that at that date

### Deferred taxation

1. Deferred taxation has been provided by the liability/deferral method in respect of all timing differences of a material amount, except where there is a reasonable probability that the timing differences will not reverse within a period covering at least the next three years.
   (a) When assessing the probability that timing differences in respect of accelerated capital allowances and stock appreciation relief will not reverse within the next three years, the directors considered and reviewed the latest management estimates of capital expenditure and stock levels. The estimates of capital allowances, depreciation and stock levels for each of the next three years are as follows:

   |                   | 1980 £000 | 1981 £000 | 1982 £000 |
   |-------------------|-----------|-----------|-----------|
   | Capital allowances |           |           |           |
   | Depreciation       |           |           |           |
   | Stock levels       |           |           |           |

   The directors have had no indication that, after this period the timing differences in respect of accelerated capital allowances and stock appreciation relief will reverse.
   (b) EITHER – On the basis of these estimates, the directors consider that timing differences in respect of accelerated capital allowances and stock appreciation relief will not reverse in the foreseeable future. Therefore, no provision for deferred taxation is required in respect of these timing differences.
   OR – On the basis of these estimates, the directors consider that timing differences in respect of accelerated capital allowances and stock appreciation relief amounting to £ . . . . . . will reverse in the foreseeable future. Accordingly, a partial provision for deferred taxation amounting to £ . . . . . . is required.
   (c) When assessing the probability that timing differences will not reverse in respect of unrealised surpluses on the revaluation of fixed assets and also of surpluses on the disposal of those fixed assets that are subject to rollover relief, the directors considered the future plans of the company. On the basis of those plans, the directors consider that none of these fixed assets will be sold. However, if any of these fixed assets are sold, the directors consider that there will be sufficient rollover relief available to ensure that the originating timing differences will not reverse. Therefore, no provision for deferred taxation is required in respect of either unrealised surpluses on

the revaluation of fixed assets or on surpluses on the disposal of those fixed assets that are subject to rollover relief.

## Liabilities, provisions and commitments

2. Provision has been made in the accounts for:
   (a) All liabilities which existed at the balance sheet date (other than contingent liabilities in respect of which no actual liability is expected to arise).
   (b) All losses expected to arise from events (including the placing of forward contracts) which had occurred by the balance sheet date.
3. Except as indicated in the accounts, none of the liabilities, including those secured by reservation of title, was, at the balance sheet date, secured on any assets of the company, and the assets in the balance sheet on that date were then owned by the company free of any charge or lien in favour of third parties.

   *Following the discussion in the 'ROMALPA' case, the Institutes' guidance statement (English Institute Statement V24) recommends, in relation to liabilities secured by reservation of title:*
   *(a) Where material, disclosure of the fact that liabilities are so secured, and*
   *(b) When practicable, quantifying the amount of these liabilities.*
4. All commitments to buy or sell securities or businesses, bonus or profit-sharing arrangements, share capital or other options, or other undertakings which were not in the ordinary course of business, or which might have an adverse effect upon this company, have been provided for or noted in the accounts.
5. At the balance sheet date there were no material contingent or potential liabilities under claims, or pending or threatened litigation, and there were no other material contingent liabilities other than those provided for or noted in the accounts.

   *The terms contingent liabilities and claims apply to, but are not limited to, such items as discounted or assigned debts; accommodation endorsements; guarantees; warranties; sureties; open balances on letters of credit; unsatisfied judgements; additional taxes of which there is present knowledge based upon either formal or informal advice; and pending or prospective claims or other proceedings, whether or not in litigations, such as those involving injuries, damages, defective goods, patent infringements, additional payments, other breaches of contracts, and refunds and penalties arising from alleged violation of laws or government regulations.*
6. The correct amounts of contracts for capital expenditure not provided in the accounts, and capital expenditure authorised by the directors but not contracted for at the balance sheet date, are as stated in the accounts.
7. The amounts set aside as provisions for liabilities, losses and the diminution in the value of assets, are not greater than the sums reasonably required for those purposes.

## Assets

8. The net book amounts at which the premises, plant and equipment are stated in the balance sheet were arrived at:
   (a) After taking into account all expenditure which represented capital outlay on these assets, but no expenditure of a revenue nature.
   (b) After writing off all amounts relating to items which had been sold or scrapped by the balance sheet date.
   (c) After providing for depreciation at a rate sufficient to cover obsolescence, as well as wear and tear, and thus to reduce the net book amounts of the assets to their residual value by the time they become no longer economically useful to the company.
9. In arriving at the amount at which raw materials, work in progress and finished stocks are stated in the balance sheet:
   (a) Account has been taken only of items which are the property of the company at the balance sheet date, and, except as indicated in the accounts, are free from all material liens and encumbrances.

  (b) Account has been taken of the whole of the raw materials, stores, and finished products in the company's ownership at the balance sheet date.

  (c) The costs of all goods have been properly recorded in the books of the company, and the basis on which stocks have been valued are consistent with those used for the preceding period.

  (d) Adequate allowance has been made for all prospective losses on realisation, including those expected because stocks are redundant, obsolete, excessive, or defective.

  (e) Stocks purchased for which amounts have not been entered as liabilities, stocks returned by customers without credit to their accounts, and stocks billed to customers in advance of despatch and which are properly recorded as sales, are excluded.

10. The debtors (after provisions) shown in the balance sheet are expected to produce on realisation in the ordinary course of business at least the net amounts at which they are stated.

11. Deferred expenditure and prepayments included in the balance sheet are deferred to be matched against income which can properly be expected to accrue after the balance sheet date.

12. The valuation of the company's investments in unlisted shares and debentures has been considered and accepted at a board meeting on . . . . . . . . . . . . . . . . . . for the purpose of showing a directors' valuation of these investments in the accounts.

13. The balance sheet includes all cash and bank accounts, and all other assets of the company in accordance with accounting principles generally accepted in the United Kingdom.

14. All income which arose up to the date of the balance sheet has been brought into account in accordance with the company's accounting policies.

## Other matters

15. All material agreements and transactions are described fairly in the accounting records that have been made available for your audit and that were used for the preparation of the accounts.

16. All full minutes of general shareholders' meetings, directors' meetings, and other committees of executives have been disclosed to you.

17. Disclosure has been made in the accounts of all matters necessary in order to show a true and fair view of the company's financial position, including transactions with related parties on other than 'arm's length' or normal commercial terms.

  *The term 'related parties' includes organisations under the same control as the company, when control is defined as the power to direct or cause the direction of management or policies, whether through ownership, by contract, or otherwise; shareholders who own more than 10% of the voting shares; directors and senior management and their immediate families; associated companies; and any other party who can prevent the company from pursuing its separate interests.*

18. Except as provided for or noted in the accounts there have been no events which have occurred since the balance sheet date and which have had or may have a material effect on the financial position of the company at that date, or the results of operations for the period then ended.

           Yours faithfully,

Signature:        Signature:

Title:           Title:

(Usually this letter should be signed by the managing director and by the finance director.)

## 16.2 Going concern?

The valuation bases adopted in the accounts will assume that the company is a going concern, in accordance with SSAP2. So it follows that auditors must carry out sufficient work to ensure that this assumption is justified. This means seeking evidence that the company is likely to continue trading for at least a further twelve months. Or more practically, to ensure that there is no evidence to the contrary.

The following are the sort of danger signals that should be watched for:

1. Falling trend of sales and/or profitability.
2. Liquidity problems and/or a weak, or falling ratio of current assets to current liabilities.
3. Vulnerability to economic or legislative changes, or operation in a highly competitive market. If the latter, is the company keeping abreast of current developments, or is it slipping behind?
4. Supply problems or labour disruption.
5. Over dependence on a few suppliers, customers or products.
6. Finance problems such as: high gearing ratio; dependence on short-term costly finance, such as hire purchase; purchase of long-term assets with short-term finance; loan repayment due shortly with insufficient funds to cover.
7. Working capital problems, such as a heavy reliance on creditor financing, or a dangerous reduction in stock, which could prejudice sales.
8. Over trading.
9. Substantial research and development not yet justified by products (Rolls-Royce).
10. Reductions or cancellations of capital projects.
11. Large capital investment with unrealistic returns.
12. Dependence on overseas holding company for finance or trade.

(The APC, in its bulletin *True and Fair*, points out (some) of these considerations and suggests that the going concern basis should be reconsidered if the auditor cannot satisfy himself that his client will stay in business 'in the foreseeable future'.)

If these or similar problems are identified, then the auditor should be on his guard, and should make a thorough investigation of cash flow forecasts, profit forecasts and budgets for the ensuing period. The assumptions contained therein should be carefully scrutinised and corroborated by independent evidence in so far as possible, and there should be discussion with appropriate officials. In particular the cash budget should be analysed to ensure that there is sufficient credit available to cover short-term requirements. If necessary, confirmation should be gained from the bank as to the availability of overdraft or similar facilities. In the absence of such forecasts, or in the event that they reveal a dangerous situation, then the auditor will have to reconsider whether it is appropriate to adopt the going concern basis of preparation. Indeed, the very absence of a basic budgetary process would be strong evidence to suggest that, by virtue of inadequate management, the company would be unable to survive a crisis.

In the event that the auditor considers the company not to be a going concern, then he should advise the directors accordingly and ensure that the accounts are prepared on a market value, or 'break-up' basis. If the directors refuse to comply, then the auditors will have to qualify the accounts as a whole, to the effect that they are not true and fair. Whether or not the directors comply, it is a very serious move indeed, for it will give the company little further hope of survival, as existing credit will be drawn in, and no further credit is likely to be obtainable.

Over the last few years liquidations have averaged some 10,000 a year, and scarcely any of these companies have had their immediately preceding reports qualified to the extent that the company is not a going concern. And yet the signs are almost invariably there. One wonders how much this has to do with auditors being involved in last-minute rescue operations, which may be hopelessly prejudiced by a qualification. Note that such a situation is not expressly forbidden by the ICAEW's new independence rules, as one could reasonably have expected.

The auditor cannot rely on an assessment of the going concern situation simply at the date of the balance sheet, for the accounts will not become public knowledge until much later, just before the Annual General Meeting. So it will be necessary to take into account any events which take place after the year end and before the AGM, which may affect the company as a going concern. This matter is further discussed in the next section.

## 16.3 Events after the balance sheet date

Financial accounting inevitably has to artificially split a company's trading into periods. But the auditor cannot ignore events that occur subsequent to a period end, simply because the accounts are closed. Indeed, the period after the year end is extremely valuable for the auditor, in that it can be used to confirm many features about the accounts (outstanding cheques and uncleared lodgements in the bank account are obvious examples). But the question arises, what subsequent events should be taken into account, and how should they be treated in the accounts? SSAP17 deals with Accounting for Post Balance Sheet Events, and defines such an event as one which occurs between the balance sheet date and the date on which the financial statements are approved by the directors.

The following extracts are taken from SSAP17:

> Events occurring after the balance sheet date may be classified into two categories: 'adjusting events' and 'non-adjusting events'.
> *Adjusting events* are post balance sheet events which provide additional evidence of conditions existing at the balance sheet date. They include events which because of statutory or conventional requirements are reflected in financial statements.
> *Non-adjusting events* are post balance sheet events which concern conditions which did not exist at the balance sheet date.
>
> *Standard accounting practice*
>
> 21. Financial statements should be prepared on the basis of conditions existing at

the balance sheet date.

22. A material post balance sheet event requires changes in the amounts to be included in financial statements where:
    (a) it is an adjusting event; or
    (b) it indicates that application of the going concern concept to the whole or a material part of the company is not appropriate.

23. A material post balance sheet event should be disclosed where:
    (a) it is a non-adjusting event of such materiality that its non-disclosure would affect the ability of the users of financial statements to reach a proper understanding of the financial position; or
    (b) it is the reversal or maturity after the year end of a transaction entered into before the year end, the substance of which was primarily to alter the appearance of the company's balance sheet.

24. In respect of each post balance sheet event which is required to be disclosed under para. 23 above, the following information should be stated by way of notes in financial statements:
    (a) the nature of the event; and
    (b) an estimate of the financial effect, or a statement that it is not practicable to make such an estimate.

25. The estimate of the financial effect should be disclosed before taking account of taxation, and the taxation implications should be explained where necessary for a proper understanding of the financial position.

26. The date on which the financial statements are approved by the board of directors should be disclosed in the financial statements.

Some events will not be easily defined in terms of their category, and hence it will be difficult to determine the period affected. For example, assume that subsequent to the year end it transpires that the net realisable value of a material quantity of year end stocks has fallen below cost. The question arises, when did the fall in value occur? This will have to be discovered in order to determine which period to charge. But practically this may prove a problem.

Because of the importance of post balance sheet events, it is now standard practice in the larger firms to conduct a subsequent events programme. Such a programme would include:

1. A comparison of significant accounting ratios before and after the year end. Explanations should be sought for any material differences, as such differences may indicate the presence of adjusting or non adjusting events. Consideration must also be given to any indications in these ratios that the company may no longer be a going concern.

2. An examination of all material provisions and contingent liabilities at the latest date feasible prior to the signing of the accounts, to determine whether there is any additional evidence which may effect the original estimates used.

3. A review of directors' minutes subsequent to the year end in particular looking for:
    (a) those matters referred to in 16.2;
    (b) major new contracts, or losses of major customers/contracts;
    (c) capital expenditure commitments;
    (d) changes in accounting policy;
    (e) new borrowings or share issues;

    (f)  extraordinary or abnormal transactions;

    (g)  changes in market conditions, or products.

4. Discussions with senior officials concerning the findings in 1 to 3 above, and any related matters. These discussions should be thoroughly documented, and any necessary adjustments should be made in accordance with SSAP17.

## 16.4 Current cost accounting

A common misconception is that Current Cost Accounting (CCA) purely adjusts for inflation. This is not so; it adjusts for all price level changes, regardless of whether they are induced by inflation or by other market forces. Inflation is only adjusted for in-so-far as it is reflected in *specific* price movements. Granted it was the increasing levels of inflation in the 1970s that stimulated the development which, after various false starts, culminated in the adoption of SSAP16 on Current Cost Accounting in March 1980. But this should not disguise the fact that SSAP16 is much more than just an inflation accounting standard. It represents a fundamental change in the basis upon which accounts are produced. It is a move away from accounting for historic costs, which can to some degree be objective, towards accounting for value (value to the business/deprival value), which can be highly subjective. And herein lie the potential problems for the auditor.

This is not to say that valuation plays no part in historic cost accounting. Of course many companies have for years been carrying land and buildings at valuation; some companies also revalue certain items of plant and machinery; stock is sometimes reduced to net realisable value (NRV), and investments are sometimes shown at market value. But with CCA, valuation is the rule not the exception; the basis of accounting rather than a periodic adjustment. So the auditor will have to rely much more on his judgement of value. And the exercise of judgement brings with it the opportunity for other people to question that judgement, particularly with the benefit of hindsight.

Now of course judgement has always been at the heart of the professional accountant's and auditor's work. For the production of historic cost accounts is by no means an objective science, as (*inter alia*) the appropriateness of accounting policies has to be determined, and compliance with accounting standards has to be ensured. But CCA introduces a further level where subjective judgement must be applied. For the auditor must additionally determine whether the valuation bases chosen are reasonable, in particular for stock and fixed assets. Such reasonableness has to be determined not by objective (in part) principles of historic cost, but by subjective economic concepts of deprival value.

### The effect of CCA upon the auditor's work

In considering the detailed effect of CCA upon the auditor's work, I must assume a thorough knowledge of SSAP16 and associated Guidelines, just as I have had to assume a thorough knowledge of other aspects of accounts preparation.

The development of CCA is still in its infancy, and the audit thereof has barely yet been conceived! And yet it must now be both born and mature very rapidly, for (contrary to many auditors' hopes) SSAP16 prescribed that current cost accounts form part of listed and large unlisted companies' financial statements. Hence they are subject to audit. Moreover, companies are given the option either to produce their accounts in historic format, with supplementary CCA statements, or to produce their primary accounts in CCA format. This means that auditors may have to comment specifically on whether CCA statements are true and fair. They may not be able to escape with comment along the lines that the statements have been 'properly prepared', as was the case with statements produced in accordance with the Hyde Guidelines which preceded SSAP16. Auditing guideline on 'Auditors' reports and SSAP No. 16, "Current Cost Accounting"' states that it is appropriate for an auditor to consider giving a 'true and fair' report on unabridged current cost accounts unless they are of an experimental nature.

At this stage of the development of CCA, I personally believe that the SSAP16 provisions are unfortunate in two respects:

1. *The mandatory requirement for examination by auditors of the current cost accounts, and reference thereto in the audit report.* It may have been preferable in the first instance to have required supplementary CCA statements, which could have been made subject to audit examination and report at such time as generally accepted bases of preparation had been agreed. Such a period could then have been seen as a time of transition, and the status of the CCA statements would have been in no doubt. Whereas at the moment, the value of 'flexibly prepared' information could, in many people's eyes, be somewhat dubious.

The ASC, on their own admission, hold the view that flexibility in the first few years of mandatory CCA is necessary to assist further development. Accordingly the standard is very brief, associated guidance notes are not mandatory and there is very little prescription about methods to be used when preparing CCA statements. With this I wholly agree at this stage. But it does mean that there will be a large diversity of methods used in practice, which could serve to reduce the very comparability which the standard is designed to enhance. Furthermore, there could be considerable difficulty in the audit of such statements because of the lack of criteria by which to assess reasonableness.

2. *The option to produce the primary accounts in either CCA or historic cost format.* This option could further serve to reduce comparability, as many companies (particularly those making embarrassing super profits) will opt to produce CCA only accounts, while others (whose profits are perhaps not so good) will want to emphasise the historic cost accounts, with only supplementary CCA accounts. It would have been better to specify one method of compliance for all.

But all this aside, the necessity for price level/value accounting is in no sense denied. So let us now look at those specific ways in which the auditor will be affected by CCA.

SSAP16 is mandatory for all listed companies, and for large unlisted companies (see page 456). The standard is only advisory in-so-far as other business entities are concerned, but it is anticipated that it will ultimately be universally adopted.

## Additional areas of audit involvement

### The objective of CCA

The objective of CCA is to reflect the impact of specific price changes on a business entity (note it does not reflect the change in the general purchasing power of money) when determining profits, and preparing a balance sheet. In determining profits the objective is achieved in two stages:

1. The current cost operating profit is determined as the surplus after allowing for the impact of price changes on the funds needed to continue the existing business and maintain its operating capability, whether financed by share capital or borrowing;
2. The current cost profit attributable to shareholders is then determined after allowing for the effect of financial gearing.

In the balance sheet the objective is met by including assets at their value to the business (which in the case of stock and fixed assets will normally be current replacement cost).

It follows that the auditor must have a thorough knowledge of the adjustments necessary to historical data to produce current cost profit figures:

the depreciation adjustment,
the cost of sales adjustment,
the monetary working capital adjustment
    and
the gearing adjustment.

And in addition, he will have to thoroughly understand the economic principles of deprival value, which constitutes the value to the business of a company's assets. Deprival value normally equates to replacement cost, but in certain specific circumstances the value to be derived from further use or the net realisable value on disposal may constitute the value to the business. The auditor will have to recognise the economic situations which could give rise to each of these bases of valuation, and will have to have the expertise to determine if they have been correctly calculated.

### Indices

Specific indices of price movements of various categories of asset are probably the most usual way of establishing replacement cost. These can be either internally or externally prepared. Of the external indices the most authoritative, and therefore most usually used are those published by the Central Statistical Office. Its booklet *Price Index Numbers for Current Cost Accounting* gives indices for fixed assets and stock for both specific industries and specific types of asset. There is also a booklet covering indices for overseas countries. But even if such authoritative indices are used, the auditor will still have to ensure that the specific index chosen is the relevant one.

In the event that the company uses an in-house index, the auditor will have to examine it to ensure that the weighting is reasonable, and that the index reflects the actual price movements of those assets on which it is to be employed. Comparison to externally generated data will be preferable but may not always be possible. Computerised accounting systems may include a program which allows for the ongoing preparation and updating of indices for each category of asset. In the absence of an external means of validation, the auditor may have to examine the program to ensure that it is correctly written and based on sound statistical principles. Here it may be necessary to obtain expert advice, so no doubt the larger audit firms will develop specialists in this field.

### Stock accounting systems

In-so-far as the balance sheet valuation of stock is concerned, replacement cost is not so very different from a LIFO or NIFO basis of calculation. So few practical difficulties should be experienced here. Although it should be said that the comparison of replacement cost to net realisable value assumes a much greater importance, in that there is a much greater chance of replacement cost being in excess of NRV than there is in the case of FIFO.

But the basis of calculating cost of sales under CCA can involve a considerable change. In a company which chooses to use the averaging method of calculating the cost of sales adjustment (normally only used in a company with little fluctuation in stock levels), there need be little change in the stock accounting system in that index adjustments can be made to the historical cost figures; so the main audit problem is likely to be evaluating the choice of index. But the averaging method may not suit more sophisticated companies, or companies with lengthy stock holding periods and/or large stock fluctuations, which will have to develop accounting systems (probably computerised) for establishing replacement cost at the point of sale. Accordingly, the auditor now has to have a greater understanding of those factors likely to affect index movements, such as the nature of stock holdings, fluctuations in purchasing patterns and in sources of supply, and changes in raw material mix.

### Fixed assets – land and buildings

Land and buildings have to be revalued regularly. This means that the auditor will now be more frequently involved in the area of property valuation than has hitherto been the case. Although it is anticipated that qualified valuers will be employed for this work, the auditor cannot entirely subrogate his responsibilities to the valuer. He will have to ensure that the basis of valuation is suitable for CCA in that it complies with the Royal Institution of Chartered Surveyors' *Guidance Note on the valuation of fixed assets for Current Cost Accounting*. And in particular, he will have to have regard to:

1. *Valuation intervals*. The decision when to value is at the directors' discretion, but it will be up to the auditor to determine whether the directors are exercising

their discretion reasonably. So the auditor will require a knowledge of the movement in general and specific property values to determine the materiality of likely changes in his client's assets since the date of the last valuation. In the event that directors place their own valuation on properties in the interval between professional valuations, then the auditor will have to ensure that such adjustments are appropriate in relation to market trends. He may of course seek advice from a valuer to this end.

2. *Valuations performed internally.* Larger companies may well have their own property departments with personnel who are well qualified to perform valuations, and in this case the company will most certainly wish to use them. The auditor will have to decide when, and the extent to which he will wish to confirm such valuations by reference to external valuers.

3. *No open market value.* Some properties, such as highly specific factory premises, may have no readily determinable market value, because they have no alternative use. In these circumstances, the valuation will be based on replacement cost, depreciated to the extent of the proportion of the useful life that has already expired. The auditor will need to understand when depreciated replacement cost is an appropriate valuation base, and have a knowledge of the movement in building costs in the intervening period between valuations so as to be able to audit directors' interim valuations. Again, he may seek expert advice independent of the company.

4. *Completeness of valuation.* With a large portfolio of properties, perhaps spread as to location, and therefore valued by different valuers, there could be some difficulty in ensuring that all properties have been included, and that there are no overlapping valuations. This could especially be the case if the company has itself provided the details of the properties, such as title, mortgages, restrictive covenants, rents and tenancies. In this case, the auditor will have to substantiate the information provided for valuation purposes, and again in this he may need to seek expert opinion.

5. *General purpose and specific land and buildings.* In the case of general purpose (non specific) land and buildings, market value will usually be taken as the replacement cost, for replacement would normally be achieved by purchase on the open market. But as mentioned earlier, it may not be possible to obtain a market valuation for some specific properties. In these circumstances, the cost of buying the land and building anew would have to be calculated, and the resulting replacement cost of the building then adjusted for depreciation.

In the event that the 'recoverable amount' which can be obtained from either using or selling the property is lower than replacement cost, then that recoverable amount will constitute the deprival value. The recoverable amount is calculated by taking the greater of the amounts which can be recovered, either through further use of the premises or through sale. In the case of properties which can be valued on a market basis, then no problems are likely to arise in this connection, because the buy in values (replacement cost) are unlikely to be materially different from the selling values (net realisable value).

However, in the case of highly specific properties valued on depreciated replacement cost, the net realisable value will not be relevant as no market exists. Accordingly the recoverable amount will be the future benefits to be derived from further use of the property. SSAP16 (unlike ED18) does not mention discounted cash flow calculations as a means of quantifying such future benefits, but it is hard to imagine how else they could be derived. This issue awaits clarification.

One can think of many situations where the recoverable amount is most likely to be lower than net replacement cost – certain British Leyland factories for example, or British Steel foundries. In circumstances of poor anticipated profits or losses, the economic value would be almost nil. Deprival value in these circumstances would simply be the realisable value of the land alone, less the costs of demolishing the buildings sitting on it! Potential large-scale write-offs of property values could have interesting political connotations in some industries. But that is of no concern here. What is of concern is the incredible difficulties that the auditor could face in this regard. Apart from the possibility of pressure on auditors not to reduce values, the evaluation of the reasonableness of present value calculations (if used) will in most circumstances be extremely difficult. For it implies looking many years in the future and assessing the useful life and likely profitability, and then determining what proportion is reasonably applicable to the building. Many people consider meaningful calculations to be impossible.

And yet such calculations must be done in companies with poor profitability and highly specific property (which in view of the collapse of the heavy engineering sector often go hand in hand), in order to comply with the principles of CCA. So probably in practice the most pragmatic and the most accurate, will be to take net land values only in instances where no market value can be applied to buildings and the company's profit outlook is poor. Or perhaps reverting to historic cost may be an alternative solution, at the risk of defiling the purity of CCA!

*Fixed assets – plant and machinery*

The deprival value of plant and machinery will, as with property, be the lower of depreciated replacement cost, or recoverable amount; recoverable amount to be taken as the higher of estimated realisable value or economic value. In a profitable concern the recoverable amount will usually be the higher, so the replacement cost can then be calculated either by reference to suppliers' price lists or by the use of indices, and it can then be depreciated in accordance with the life expended. But in the event that the recoverable amount is lower than replacement cost, either because use is to be discontinued, or because of poor profitability, the recoverable amount must be calculated in order to determine the appropriate deprival value.

The need to assess the reasonableness of such deprival value calculations presents the auditor with special problems:

1. *Fixed asset registers.* Greater detail is required than in the past of individual asset identities, cost details, depreciation bases and age. These are best contained in a fixed asset register as discussed in sec. 14.3. But very many companies do not have such systems. So the auditor will need to determine whether an appropriate fixed asset accounting system has been introduced and maintained, in order that a satisfactory audit of CCA may be possible.

2. *Aggregation of assets for value calculations.* As when comparing cost to NRV under SSAP9, a company may wish to aggregate certain of its assets when comparing replacement cost to recoverable amount. In some cases, aggregation of assets into an appropriate 'economic unit' will be essential, as the assets may have no value individually. The auditor will have to check that the basis of such aggregation is reasonable. Ideally all assets/'economic units' should be compared on an individual basis, but this may not always be feasible in the first instance because of inadequate fixed asset accounting. Aggregation of similar assets/units would be reasonable, but the aggregation of the assets of an entire plant would not normally be so, unless they are so interrelated in terms of physical relationship and in terms of the industrial process that they serve that there is no practical means of distinguishing them. In between these extremes lies a grey area in which the auditor can only rely on his judgement of what seems fair in the circumstances. In this regard, the auditor will have to obtain a much greater understanding of industrial processes and machinery. And even then, in many circumstances he may have to call upon expert advice.

3. *Data bases for valuation calculations.* We have seen that net replacement cost will normally constitute deprival value. But there are several acceptable methods of calculating net replacement cost. This gives a further area of management judgement which must be examined by the auditor. Index adjusted historic cost, suppliers' price lists, or expert opinion are all possible valuation bases, but each may be inappropriate in certain circumstances. In particular, index adjusted historic cost will be inappropriate when there has been substantial technological change, when the historic purchase price was affected by special circumstances or when there is no suitable index for a specific asset. The auditor will have to have or be able to obtain sufficient technical information to enable him to determine whether a chosen valuation base is appropriate. If suppliers' price lists are used, he will have to have sufficient technical understanding of the relevant plant to ensure that the suppliers' prices relate to plant which is equivalent in nature to that belonging to the company.

Calculation of the depreciation charge is a straightforward accounting matter which should not present the auditor with any special difficulties. He will have to bear in mind the manipulatory possibilities occasioned by the requirement to regularly assess the useful lives of assets for depreciation purposes.

*Closing entries*

The calculation of the closing adjustments to profit present few conceptual difficulties for the auditor, and his work here will be largely concerned with ensuring that the client has performed such calculations correctly. But to the extent that the monetary working capital adjustment allows for subjectivity with regard to those items to be included, the auditor could be called upon to decide what is and what is not appropriate.

Monetary working capital (MWC) ordinarily consists of trade debtors, prepayments, bills receivable, and stocks not subject to a cost of sales adjustment, less trade creditors, accruals and trade bills payable, in-so-far as they all relate to day-to-day operating activities as opposed to capital transactions. But MWC can also include bank and cash balances or overdrafts, in-so-far as they relate to the financing of fluctuations in stock, debtors or creditors, if their inclusion is necessary to avoid a misleading calculation of current cost profit. Just what proportion of a bank balance can be said to relate to such fluctuations can be a highly subjective decision, more related to economic theories of the reasons for holding money, than to accounting. But directors may have to make such a decision, and auditors will have to evaluate the propriety thereof. It is not unreasonable to anticipate that directors will be particularly keen to suggest that overdrafts are exclusively the result of working capital fluctuations and therefore subject to adjustment and that bank balances exist entirely for speculative reasons, and accordingly no MWC adjustment should be made. For overdrafts would result in a MWC credit to profit, and bank balances would result in a MWC debit. So the auditor will have to consider whether the balance or overdraft really is used to finance working capital fluctuations. In practice and in theory, this is difficult to determine, for investment theory holds that management has available a 'central pool of finance' from which *all* investment is taken. A particular form of finance is not normally allocated to a specific form of investment.

*Overseas companies*

Not many auditors will be faced with having to examine the CCA accounts of overseas subsidiaries. But for those that do, the problems could be considerable:
1. Deprival value information may be difficult to obtain because of inadequate accounting systems, and because of insufficient locally generated information (such as indices). Sufficiently competent valuers may also be difficult to find in less sophisticated countries. And there is an increased likelihood of there being no market for certain types of asset.
2. The people producing the CCA information may have little experience or training in so doing, with the result that the figures they produce could be highly dubious.
3. 2 above is essentially a short-term problem in that training can be provided, but it may not be so easy to persuade the overseas company of the necessity for such training in the event that the company is only partially owned.

4. Even if the overseas company can produce the figures, there may be no local firm with sufficient training or expertise to audit them. This could result in considerably extra audit cost and time, if UK personnel have to be sent out to audit the CCA accounts of material overseas holdings.

### Existing SSAPs

'Existing standards issued for use with historical cost accounts apply to CCA except where a conflict arises from the conceptual differences between the systems.' So says SSAP16. Such conflict inevitably arises in almost every standard, and the auditor will have to bear a heavy burden in resolving that conflict. It would be useful if a detailed analysis could be provided of just which aspects of each standard are, and are not applicable to CCA.

### The auditor's responsibility

The various areas of increased managerial judgement considered in the preceding pages all serve to increase the extent to which the auditor must apply his own judgement. And this can serve to increase the audit risk. An auditor can obviously be criticised, and indeed considered negligent, if he fails to take sufficient steps to establish reasonableness. But what is sufficient and what is reasonable can be open to wide interpretations. It is to be hoped that in the early days courts will be reluctant to litigate in cases of divergent but honestly held opinions as to reasonableness. And in the meantime, the auditing profession should perhaps press for SSAP16 to be made much more specific, as soon as practical experience of the operation of CCA makes this possible.

### Necessary audit procedures

Below is an outline list of the principal audit procedures that should be followed in a CCA audit, above and beyond those procedures already considered in the context of historic cost.

1. Assess whether the indices in use by the company are reasonable in relation to the nature of the company's stocks and fixed assets. If the company uses internally generated indices, examine the basis of computation.

2. Assess whether the basis of calculation of deprival value of stock and fixed assets is satisfactory, and test check the calculations. Evaluate for reasonableness the basis of any aggregation made for purposes of comparison of replacement cost to recoverable amount.

3. Consider the necessity for employment of an external valuer for the valuation of the company's land and buildings. Where internal valuation is considered satisfactory, ensure that such valuation is reasonable in regards to known market price movements.

4. Ensure that the bases of the calculations of:
   (a) the depreciation adjustment;
   (b) the cost of sales adjustment;

(c) the monetary working capital adjustment;

(d) and the gearing adjustment

are appropriate, and that the calculations are correctly made. Ensure that the basis of those items included in the monetary working capital is satisfactory.

5. Check the basis for, and the calculation of, all other adjustments to historical cost figures.

6. Ensure that complete information on CCA accounting policies is disclosed, so that readers should not be misled by the adjusted figures.

7. Ensure that there is consistency between information in historic accounts, and that in CCA statements, when both are provided. Where there is a conflict between the requirements of historic accounting standards and SSAP16, ensure that such conflict is satisfactorily resolved.

Towards the end of 1980 the APC issued an auditing Guideline to assist in the formulation of audit reports on Current Cost Accounts. This is now reproduced below.

*Auditors' reports and SSAP No. 16, 'Current cost accounting'*

### Introduction

1. This auditing Guideline is intended to assist auditors when reporting on statements produced by enterprises in accordance with Statement of Standard Accounting Practice No. 16 'Current cost accounting' (SSAP 16). It should be read in con conjunction with the Explanatory Foreword to auditing Standards and Guidelines (including the glossary of terms) and the auditing Standards 'The audit report' and 'Qualifications in audit reports'.

### Background

2. An enterprise will, when complying with SSAP 16, provide current cost accounting (CCA) information in one of the following forms:
   (a) the presentation of historical cost accounts as the main accounts with supplementary current cost accounts which are prominently displayed;
   (b) the presentation of current cost accounts as the main accounts with supplementary historical cost accounts; or
   (c) the presentation of current cost accounts as the only accounts accompanied by adequate historical cost information.

3. Annual financial statements of enterprises coming within the scope of SSAP 16 are required to include current cost accounts. Therefore, when reporting on such financial statements the auditor should report on the current cost accounts included therein.

4. The objective of the management of an enterprise preparing current cost accounts should be that they give a true and fair view under the current cost principles described in SSAP 16. Equally, the objective of the auditor should be to give his opinion in true and fair terms. However, in the early years of CCA it is expected that many enterprises will continue to present historical cost accounts as the main accounts. In such cases the current cost accounts will be supplementary to the historical cost accounts on which the auditor reports in accordance with any statutory obligation.

*Supplementary current cost accounts*

5. The supplementary current cost accounts may in practice take the form of either unabridged or abridged accounts. An unabridged set of supplementary current cost accounts is for the purpose of this guideline deemed to be a set of accounts, which together with notes, give all the information required for accounts intended give a true and fair view under current cost principles of the state of affairs and results for the year. Such a set of accounts go beyond the minimum requirements of SSAP 16. Other forms of accounts, including those drawn up in a form similar to that shown in the Appendix to SSAP 16, are for the purpose of this guideline, abridged accounts.

6. Enterprises which consider that they have developed an appreciation for CCA as a whole and its application in their particular circumstances, will be in a position to go beyond presenting the minimum information required by SSAP 16 and prepare an unabridged set of current cost accounts and notes which together are intended to show a true and fair view. Where such unabridged accounts are supplementary to the main accounts, the auditor should report in true and fair terms, referring to the accounting policies and methods used, in an additional paragraph to the report on the historical cost accounts. A suitable form of wording is as follows:
'In our opinion the supplementary current cost accounts set out on pages x to x have been prepared in accordance with the accounting policies and methods described in notes x to x and give, under the current cost principles described in SSAP 16, atrue and fair view of the state of the company's affairs at 31 December 19. . and of its results for the year then ended.'

7. However, in the case of many enterprises the objectives of the management, set out in para 4 above, will not be achivable because they have not yet developed the necessary appreciation and experience. The preparers of the current cost accounts of these enterprises will not therefore be in a position to claim that their supplementary current cost accounts, do give a true and fair view. Where the supplementary accounts are abridged, or where the supplementary accounts are unabridged but their experimental nature is made clear in the accounts, it will not be appropriate for the auditor to report on such supplementary current cost accounts in true and fair terms. Nevertheless, in these cases, it will be helpful to the user of the current cost accounts to know whether in the opinion of the auditor, the accounting policies and procedures adopted comply with the provisions of the SSAP 16. Therefore, it is recommended that in these cases the auditor's report be expressed in terms which confirm 'compliance' and be set out in an additional paragraph to his report on the historical cost statements.

8. A form of wording which will be suitable for 'compliance' reports on abridged accounts is:
'In our opinion the abridged supplementary current cost accounts set out on pages x to x have been properly prepared, in accordance with the policies and methods described in notes x to x, to give the information required by Statement of Standard Accounting Practice No. 16.'

9. If the auditor concludes that it is necessary to qualify his opinion on the supplementary current cost accounts, the qualification should be framed in accordance with the auditing Standard 'Qualifications in audit reports'.

*Main current cost accounts*

10. Where an enterprise chooses to present current cost accounts as the main or only accounts, the auditor will usually have a statutory obligation to report in 'true and fair' terms.

11. In these cases the provisions of the auditing Standards 'The audit report' and

'Qualifications in audit reports' apply directly. All such reports should refer specifically to the current cost principles as described in the relevant notes setting out the particular accounting policies and methods adopted to comply with SSAP 16.

12. When reporting on current cost accounts which are the main or only accounts, it will not normally be necessary to make separate reference to the historical cost information presented either in the form of supplementary statements or in the form of additional notes. Nevertheless, the scope paragraph of the audit report should make clear that such information has been subjected to examination by the auditor.

### Failure to present current cost accounts

13. Where an enterprise to which SSAP 16 applies does not present current cost accounts, it is not appropriate merely because of this omission, for the auditor to qualify his opinion on the historical cost accounts. However, he should refer to the omission using wording on the following lines for an additional final paragraph to his report – 'The financial statements do not contain the current cost accounts required by statement of Standard Accounting Practice No. 16'.

I have not attempted to cover all the accounting problems that the auditor will encounter in his examination of CCA accounts. For this is largely an accounting matter which will no doubt be dealt with extensively in your accounting courses. And there is insufficient space here for such an examination. But those matters which I have discussed are those which go to the root of the *audit* problems raised by the introduction of SSAP 16 . . . only time will resolve many of these problems.

## 16.5 Related party transactions

The auditor is obliged by the 1980 Companies Act to ensure disclosure of any significant contracts in which directors or others 'connected' with directors have a material interest, together with any loans or guarantees given to or on behalf of directors, or others 'connected' with directors.

In this context 'connected' persons include:

(a) the director's spouse, child or step-child;

(b) a body corporate with which the director is associated – association includes: ownership of one-fifth of the share capital, or control over one-fifth of the voting rights in general meeting by director and persons 'connected' with him;

(c) trustees of trusts, the beneficiaries of which include the director or 'connected' persons.

It is also considered by many that holders of a substantial quantity of the company's shares, and providers of substantial finance also constitute 'related parties'. Indeed, it is now generally considered that shareholders have a right to be informed of any material transactions, where the full amount of the proper benefit did not accrue to the company, as a result of the company's trading at other than 'arm's length'.

The following *types of transaction* could be involved:
(a) sales/purchases at other than normal prices;
(b) granting of loans at other than normal terms of interest or repayment (loans to directors or 'connected' persons are in any event prohibited by the 1980 Companies Act except in so far as concerns loans of less than £5,000 made either in the ordinary course of a banking company's business (and on normal terms), or for the purposes of expenditure on a dwelling house providing similar loans are generally made to company employees);
(c) exchange of assets at other than market value.

The following *audit procedures* could be adopted to ensure the identification and proper treatment of related party transactions:
1. Identify potential related parties by examining:
    (a) the register of shareholders for substantial holdings;
    (b) the annual return for evidence of other directorships held by the directors;
    (c) the financial records for evidence of associated companies or pension funds;
    (d) a list of 'connected' persons (as defined by the 1980 Companies Act), supplied by the directors.
   Information about any suspected related parties must be given to all members of the audit team, so that they may be aware of their existence during the course of normal audit work.
2. Examine directors' minutes and solicitor's correspondence for any evidence of other than arm's-length transactions.
3. Examine the terms of any significant loans, to ensure that they are on a normal commercial basis.
4. Confirm the nature of any guarantees given.
5. Collect evidence of any significant transactions with related parties during the course of normal audit procedures. Confirm that such transactions are on a commercial basis, by comparison with similar transactions involving normal trade customers.
6. Investigate the sales and general ledgers for material debts from related parties, and ensure that they are collectable. This could involve obtaining information from credit agencies or audited accounts, or in the case of a private individual, a bank reference. At the same time the transactions that gave rise to the debt could be investigated to determine whether they were on a normal commercial basis.

In particular, the auditor should consider the collectability of debts with related parties, for there have been a number of company failures in the past, which have highlighted inadequate investigation of such debts. If the auditor is not satisfied with the results of any of his investigations above, he will be forced to qualify his report in the event that the item in question is material.

## 16.6 The final review

The Auditor's Operational Standard states that:

> 'The auditor shall carry out such a review of the financial statements as is sufficient, in conjunction with the conclusions drawn from the other audit evidence obtained, to give him a reasonable basis for his opinion on the financial statements.'

Before an audit firm will be prepared to express an opinion on accounts, senior members of the firm will review the adequacy of audit work performed, together with the presentation and content of the accounts themselves. In smaller firms this review will be performed by the partner in charge of the job, with reference to partner colleagues on any difficult points. In larger firms a manager will probably review the work, prior to its examination by the partner. Whatever the review procedure, the accountant in charge of the day-to-day audit work should ensure that his work is ready for review by:

1. Inspecting the statutory books to ensure they are up to date, and the Articles and Memorandum to ensure no provisions have been contravened.
2. Ensuring that all the necessary stages in the audit procedure have been completed and documented, and that the permanent and systems files have been brought up to date.
3. Completing the overall analytical review schedules.
4. Ordering the working papers in standard format, and referencing them to the index.
5. Reviewing the accounts for presentation.
6. Preparing final comments sheets on outstanding or contentious points which require a decision at manager or partner level.
7. Drafting a letter to management (see next chapter).
8. Completing the audit time schedule, comparing to budget and providing an explanation of variances, and preparing a provisional budget for the subsequent year.

These various matters can usefully be the subject of an audit completion check list to ensure that the accountant in charge does not overlook any points when under pressure at the concluding stages of the audit. The sort of points to be included in such a check list are amplified below.

### Audit Completion Checklist

#### Completing the Analytical Review

i    Review the transactions for the year with major customers, suppliers, borrowers and lenders to ensure:
   (a) that the accounting treatment of these transactions is in accordance with the relevant contract or agreement;
   (b) that there are no matters which require disclosure in the final accounts.

ii    Examine large, unusual or non-recurring transactions and any guarantees given or received — especially those arising near the year-end.

iii    Check that all items in the balance sheet and detailed profit and loss account have been compared with the previous year and ensure that explanations are recorded in the working papers, explaining all significant variations.

iv Ensure that all figures used in analytical reviews have been agreed with the figures in the final accounts.
v Ensure that final accounting ratios have been worked out and compared with the previous year, and that all significant variations have been adequately investigated.
vi Ensure that conclusions have been reached and recorded of the results of the analytical review to support (where applicable) the reliance placed on it in individual audit areas.

**Inspecting the Statutory Books**
Inspect the following statutory registers and ascertain whether prima facie the information they contain is up to date:
(A) Register of directors and secretary.
(B) Register of directors' share and debenture interests.
(C) Register of interests in shares (to be kept if the company is listed).
(D) Register of charges.
(E) Share Register.
Ensure the minutes of all meetings of shareholders, of directors and of any committee whose decisions affect the accounts are complete, and follow through any relevant financial matters to the accounts.

**Borrowing limits**
Ensure that any restrictions on the client's borrowing or on its operations, which are contained in the Memorandum or Articles or in trust deeds and loan agreements, have not been infringed. Summarise in the working papers any restrictions and relevant conclusions that we have reached on these matters.

**Questionable Payments by Clients**
(A) Review material contracts for terms and conditions and identify any significant expenses or deductions from income disclosed by either analytical review or detailed testing, which are not prima facie within the scope of the contract.
(B) Bring such payments to the attention of the manager or partner responsible for the audit.
(C) In cases not involving payments in the United Kingdom we may not require disclosure of these payments in the accounts provided the following procedures are adopted:
    (i) Ensure that the payments were actually received by the person specified.
    (ii) Ensure that the payments were made wholly in connection with the furtherance of the client's business operations.
    (iii) Obtain a form of representation approving the payments signed by all the directors of the company and, if applicable, by the holding company.

**Working papers**
Ensure that the working papers are complete and that they adequately support the audit report. They must:
(A) Be indexed, cross referenced to both the accounts and the trial balance, dated, initialled and cast.
(B) Show corresponding figures and audit work done, and state whether the accounting policies adopted are reasonable and consistent with those used in the previous year.
(C) Describe how errors and irregularities were dealt with.
(D) Show conclusions as to the accuracy of the figures and the fairness of their representation in the accounts.
Prepare the 'final points on accounts' schedule containing:
(A) A concise summary of the client's operations and financial position.
(B) A summary of the conclusions reached as to whether or not:
    (i) all tests are complete;
    (ii) all items are fairly presented in the accounts.
(C) A list of any matters on which the Accountant in Charge is not satisfied.
(D) A list of the work which has not been completed.

## Memorandum and Articles

Ensure that:

(A) The company has not entered into any transactions likely to infringe its objects clause.
(B) Reserves are maintained in accordance with requirements.
(C) Where appropriate the directors have held their qualification shares during the requisite period.
(D) The directors' emoluments are in accordance with the Articles of Association, minutes, agreements or other authorisations.

## Presentation of figures in the accounts

Ensure that all classifications and descriptions in the accounts are appropriate both for the current year and for the corresponding period, and that descriptions cannot be misinterpreted and are not ambiguous.

Ensure that there is consistency of description for the same items in the balance sheet and consolidated balance sheet. Ensure that the accounts cast and that corresponding figures agree with the previous year's accounts. Check that the note references in the accounts are correct.

Ensure that disclosure has been made in the accounts of any exchange restrictions affecting any of the company's assets.

Ensure that the company has complied with any other legislation (i.e. other than the Companies Acts) to which it is subject which includes accounts requirements.

Ensure that the accounts disclose related party transactions where this disclosure is necessary for a true and fair view to be disclosed in the accounts.

## Auditor's report

Ensure that the auditors' report is correctly titled and addressed and that it clearly identifies all the pages or documents that we are reporting on.

Ensure that the auditors' report correctly refers to:

(A) The company's name.
(B) The basis of accounting, i.e. historical or current cost.
(C) The profit or loss.
(D) The year or period.
(E) The accounting date.

Check that proper accounting records have been kept and that the accounts agree with the accounting records.

Ensure that any matters for which adequate information or explanation have not been received are recorded in the working papers.

## Directors' report

Ensure that the directors' report satisfies the following conditions:

(A) That there is no information contained in the report which either conflicts with the accounts or is misleading.
(B) That all necessary statutory disclosures have been made.

## Chairman's report

Ensure that the chairman's report satisfies the following condition:

That there is no information contained in the statement which either conflicts with the accounts or is misleading.

## Drafting the report to management

Using the information collected during the audit to prepare a draft report to management and determine the level of management to which it should be addressed.

Check that the report to management is factually correct and deals helpfully with all the client's main accounting and control problems which came to light during the course of the audit and on which we are competent to comment.

Check that the working papers support all comments and opinions in the report to management.

Ensure that the working papers record the names and reactions of client officials with whom the report to management was discussed.

### Audit completion

Obtain a letter of representation from the directors of the company. Ensure that it is dated immediately prior to the date of the auditors' report.

Ensure that arrangements have been made for the directors' report, auditors' report and accounts to be signed.

Ensure that arrangements have been made for the appropriate printing and distribution of office and client sets of accounts.

Where necessary ensure that arrangements have been made for the attendance by the partner or his representative at the client's AGM.

Draft the bill for the audit fee and arrange with the manager for billing. Ensure that the working papers explain any significant deviation of actual time from budgeted time.

### Forward planning

At the conclusion of the audit, consider and record ways in which the efficiency of the audit might be improved the following year. In particular, consider how time might be saved and whether certain procedures could be performed at an interim rather than the final visit.

Ensure that the client will retain all the data that will be required for the following year's audit, e.g. computer files, suppliers' statements, account reconciliations, etc.

Prepare a provisional budget for the following year's audit.

Open a new file for the following year's audit and place in it all forward planning working papers.

The manager will review the work from a detached viewpoint, and assess whether the accountant in charge has performed his work satisfactorily. In particular he should ask himself the following questions:

1. Is there anything to indicate that the audit team was unable to obtain audit evidence for forming a firm conclusion about any matter?
2. Is any evidence in the working papers incomplete?
3. If reliance has been placed on oral representations, do the working papers record the name of the person giving them and the date, and would written representations be more satisfactory?
4. Is there any reason to believe that the client's management have followed unacceptable accounting policies, or have made under or over estimates, or have been inconsistent in their method of accounting?
5. Is there adequate documentation to support the audit team's conclusions as to the acceptability of unusual accounting policies, or as to the accounting estimates the client's management have used?
6. Is there any evidence to suggest that the audit team have failed to relate all the parts of the audit evidence to the accounts as a whole?
7. Is the presentation of the accounts true and fair in relation to the audit evidence collected?

The accountant in charge will carry out any necessary extra work to answer questions raised by the manager's review, and then the work will be ready for final review by the partner.

At this final review, the partner will:

(a) determine whether sufficient work has been performed to enable him to express an opinion on the accounts. He will be particularly concerned that the manager has signed to the effect that all test programmes and check lists

are complete, and that all necessary audit evidence has been collected;
(b) determine whether, in overall terms, the accounts 'make sense';
(c) assess the presentation of the accounts for truth and fairness;
(d) determine whether there are sensitive or contentious areas in the audit, and if so, whether the working papers would enable the firm to successfully defend itself in the event of its report being challenged;
(e) finalise the report on the accounts (see next chapter);
(f) agree the final draft of the letter to management (this may be done at a slightly later stage).

Extra audit work may be necessary as a result of the partner's review. As this work will probably relate to problem or sensitive areas, it is particularly important that it is thoroughly documented.

## 16.7 Conclusion

Once the reviewer's comments have been cleared with the manager, and then with the reviewer himself, the financial statements are ready to be signed. But they should not be signed until:
(a) a letter of representation has been signed by management;
(b) the directors have themselves signed the financial statements.
In the next chapter we deal in detail with the audit report itself, and the report which will be sent to management on the conclusion of the audit.

# 17
# Audit reports

## 17.1 The nature of the report to members

As we saw in sec. 2.7, the Companies Act 1948 requires the auditors of a limited company to report to the members, whether or not the financial statements laid before their annual general meeting, *show a true and fair view* of the state of the affairs of the company and *comply with Companies Act legislation.* In addition they must report in the event that they are *not satisfied* in respect of certain matters contained in the 1948 to 1981 Acts (see sec. 2.7 for details). And they must *provide* certain information, in the event that it is not supplied by the directors in accordance with the provisions of the 1948 and 1967 Acts (again see sec. 2.7).

The minimum reporting standards required by law are amplified by professional standards, extracts from which are reproduced in secs. 17.2, 17.3 and 17.4.

If the accounts satisfy the auditor in all respects, he will issue what is known as an *unqualified* report. But if he considers that the accounts do not show a true and fair view, or that certain prescribed information is missing, he will *qualify* his report accordingly. But he will only take such a step if it proves impossible to persuade the directors to change the accounts so that they are satisfactory, or if the accounting system is such that no amount of audit work will enable the expression of an opinion.

## 17.2 Auditing standard – the audit report

'Statement of Auditing Standard

'1. This Auditing Standard applies to all reports in which the auditor expresses an opinion on financial statements intended to give a true and fair view of the state of affairs, profit or loss and, where applicable, source and application of funds. The Standard is not intended to override the statutory exemptions granted in respect of certain types of enterprise but is intended to apply to the audit reports relating to such enterprises in other respects.

'2. The audit report should identify those to whom it is addressed and the financial statements to which it relates.

'3. The auditor should refer expressly in his report to the following:
   (a) whether the financial statements have been audited in accordance

with approved Auditing Standards;

(b)  whether in the auditor's opinion the financial statements give a true and fair view of the state of affairs, profit or loss and, where applicable, source and application of funds; and

(c)  any matters prescribed by relevant legislation or other requirements.

### '6.  True and fair

'6.  The majority of audit reports are issued under the Companies Acts which normally require the use of the words "true and fair view". For the purpose of this Standard, therefore, the phrase "true and fair view" has been retained. When expressing an opinion that financial statements give a true and fair view the auditor should be satisfied, *inter alia*, that:

(a)  all relevant Statements of Standard Accounting Practice have been complied with, except in situations in which for justifiable reasons they are not strictly applicable because they are impracticable or, exceptionally, having regard to the circumstances, would be inappropriate or give a misleading view; and

(b)  any significant accounting policies which are not the subject of Statements of Standard Accounting Practice are appropriate to the circumstances of the business.

### '7.  Reference to accounting convention

'7.  The auditor should refer in his report to the particular convention used in preparing the financial statements if he considers it necessary in order to avoid misunderstanding.

### '8.  Emphasis of matter

'8.  As a general principle the auditor issuing an unqualified opinion should not make reference to specific aspects of the financial statements in the body of his report as such reference may be misconstrued as being a qualification. In rare circumstances, however, the reader will obtain a better understanding of the financial statements if his attention is drawn to important matters. Examples might include an unusual event, accounting policy or condition, awareness of which is fundamental to an understanding of the financial statements.

'9.  In order to avoid giving the impression that a qualification is intended, references which are intended as emphasis of matter should be contained in a separate paragraph and introduced with a phrase such as "We draw attention to . . ." and should not be referred to in the opinion paragraph. Emphasis of matter should not be used to rectify a lack of appropriate disclosure in the financial statements, nor should it be regarded as a substitute for a qualification.'

Note that the auditor is only required to include reference to the accounting convention, if he considers it necessary to avoid a misunderstanding. It may have been better to specify whether or not reference to the accounting convention used need be made. For its inclusion in some reports and not others may of itself lead to confusion. However, in most of the Guideline example reports this reference is included. So its inclusion will presumably become standard practice.

An example of an *unqualified* audit report is given in the notes to the 'Audit Report' standard:

'Auditors report to the members of ...............................

We have audited the financial statements on pages ...... to ...... in accordance with approved Auditing Standards.

In our opinion the financial statements (which have been prepared under the historical cost convention as modified by the revaluation of land and buildings) give a true and fair view of the state of the company's financial affairs at 31 December 19 ....... and of its profit and source and application of funds for the year then ended and comply with the Companies Acts 1948 to 1981.'

## 17.3 Auditing standard – qualifications in audit reports

'Statement of Auditing Standard.
'1. When the auditor is unable to report affirmatively on the matters contained in paragraph 3 of the Auditing Standard "The Audit Report" he should qualify his report by referring to all material matters about which he has reservations. All reasons for the qualification should be given, together with a quantification of its effect on the financial statements if this is both relevant and practicable. Additionally, reference may need to be made to non-compliance with legislation and other requirements.
'2. A qualified audit report should leave the reader in no doubt as to its meaning and implications for an understanding of the financial statements. To promote a more consistent understanding of qualified reports the forms of qualification described in this standard should be used unless, in the auditor's opinion, to do so would fail to convey clearly the intended meaning.
'3. The nature of the circumstances giving rise to a qualification of opinion will generally fall into one of two main categories:
   (a) where there is an uncertainty which prevents the auditor from forming an opinion on a matter (*uncertainty*); or
   (b) where the auditor is able to form an opinion on the matter giving rise to the qualification but this conflicts with the view given by the financial statements (*disagreement*).
Each of these categories gives rise to alternative forms of qualification

depending upon whether the subject matter of the uncertainty or disagreement is considered to be fundamental so as to undermine the view given by the financial statements taken as a whole.

'4. The forms of qualification which should be used in different circumstances are shown below:

| Nature of circumstances | Material but not fundamental | Fundamental |
|---|---|---|
| Uncertainty | 'SUBJECT TO' OPINION | DISCLAIMER OF OPINION |
| Disagreement | 'EXCEPT' OPINION | ADVERSE OPINION |

' – In a disclaimer of opinion the auditor states that he is unable to form an opinion as to whether the financial statements give a true and fair view.

' – In an adverse opinion the auditor states that in his opinion the financial statements do not give a true and fair view.

' – In a "subject to" opinion the auditor effectively disclaims an opinion on a particular matter which is not considered fundamental.

' – In an "except" opinion the auditor expresses an adverse opinion on a particular matter which is not considered fundamental."

Explanatory notes further amplify the standard, and, because of the extreme importance of qualified reports these are reproduced in full below. (I have italicised those points which are especially important):

'Introduction

'There are occasions when, in order to convey clearly the results of his audit, the auditor needs to depart from the form of wording normally used for unqualified audit reports. Such departures are generally referred to as qualifications. The principles set out in this Standard are intended to make qualified audit reports more understandable by developing *a consistent use of language* to distinguish the types of qualification appropriate to different circumstances.

'Reasons for qualification

'As indicated previously, circumstances which give rise to a qualification of opinion in an audit report may be in the nature of *uncertainty or disagreement*.

'Circumstances giving rise to *uncertainties* include the following:

(a) *Limitations in the scope of the audit*. Scope limitations arise if the auditor is *unable for any reason to obtain all the information and explanations which he considers necessary* for the purpose of his audit; for example, inability to carry out an audit procedure considered necessary, or the absence of proper accounting records.

(b) *Inherent uncertainties*. Inherent uncertainties result from circumstances in which it is *not possible to reach an objective conclusion* as to the outcome of a situation due to the circumstances themselves rather than to any limitation of the scope of audit procedures. This type of uncertainty may relate to major litigation, the outcome of long-term contracts or doubts about the ability of the enterprise to continue as a going concern. Inherent uncertainties will not normally include instances where the auditor is able to obtain adequate evidence to support estimates and use his experience to reach an opinion as to their reasonableness; for example as regards collectability of debts or realisability of stock.

'The wording in expressing the audit opinion describes the effect of uncertainties on that opinion and does not distinguish those arising from a limitation of scope from those which are inherent. The cause of the uncertainty will be described elsewhere in the audit report.

'Circumstances giving rise to *disagreement* include the following:

(a) *departures from acceptable accounting practices* where:
   (i)   there has been failure to comply with a relevant Statement of Standard Accounting Practice (SSAP) and the auditor does not concur;
   (ii)  an accounting policy not the subject of an SSAP is adopted which in the opinion of the auditor is not appropriate to the circumstances of the business; or
   (iii) exceptionally, an SSAP has been followed with the result that the financial statements do not present a true and fair view.

(b) *disagreement as to the facts or amounts* included in the financial statements.

(c) *disagreement as to the manner or extent of disclosure* of facts or amounts in the financial statements.

(d) *failure to comply with relevant legislation or other requirements.*

### 'Small enterprises

'The auditor needs to obtain the same degree of assurance in order to give an unqualified opinion on the financial statements of both small and large enterprises. However, the operating procedures and methods of recording and processing transactions used by small enterprises often differ significantly from those of large enterprises. Indeed, many of the controls which would be relevant to the large enterprise are not practical, appropriate or necessary in the small enterprise. *The most effective form of internal control for small enterprises is generally the close involvement of the directors or proprietors. This involvement will, however, enable them to override controls and purposely to exclude transactions from the records.* This possibility can give rise to difficulties for the auditor not because there is a lack of controls but because of insufficient evidence as to their operation and the completeness of the records.

'In many situations it may be possible to reach a conclusion that will support an unqualified opinion on the financial statements by combining the evidence obtained from extensive substantive testing of transactions with a careful review of costs and margins. However, in some businesses such as those where most transactions are for cash and there is no regular pattern of costs and margins, the available evidence may be inadequate to support an opinion on the financial statements.

'There will be other situations where the evidence available to the auditor is insufficient to give him the confidence necessary for him to express an unqualified opinion but this uncertainty is not so great as to justify a total disclaimer of opinion. In such situations the most helpful form of report may be one which indicates the need to accept the assurances of management as to the completeness or accuracy of the accounting records. Such a report should contain a "subject to . . ." opinion. It would only be appropriate to use this form of report if the auditor has taken steps to obtain all the evidence which can reasonably be obtained and is satisfied that:

(a) the system of accounting and control is reasonable having regard to the size and type of the enterprise's operations; and is sufficient to enable management to give the auditor the assurances which he requires;

(b) there is no evidence to suggest that the assurances may be inaccurate.

### 'Disclosure of reasons for qualifications

'The audit report should include a brief recital of the reasons for a qualification and should quantify the effects on the financial statements if this is relevant and practicable. Whilst reference may be made to relevant notes in the financial statements such reference should not be used as a substitute for a description of the basic circumstances in the audit report.

'The auditor should refer in his report to all material matters about which he has reservations. Thus, a qualification on one matter should not be regarded as a reason for omitting other unrelated qualifications which otherwise would have been reported.

'The manner in which the reasons for qualifying are disclosed is for the auditor to decide in the particular circumstances of each case, but the overall objective should be clarity. The inclusion of a separate "explanatory" paragraph before the paragraph in which the auditor gives his opinion is likely to be the clearest method of outlining the facts giving rise to the qualification.

### 'Statutory requirements

'The auditor will also need to consider whether the circumstances which give rise to his qualification impinge on his statutory duties to report. For instance, shortcomings in the sales records which give rise to a qualified opinion on the financial statements will generally mean that proper accounting records have not been maintained. Similarly, limitations in scope may mean that the auditor has not obtained all the information and explanations he considers necessary.

### 'Omission of statements of source and application of funds

'SSAP10 requires, with certain specified exceptions,* that financial statements should include a statement of source and application of funds. Omission of such a statement from financial statements to which SSAP10 applies presents a particular problem to the auditor in that the omission of a funds statement does not justify, on this ground alone, a qualified report on the profit and loss account and balance sheet.

'It is considered that the standards set out in this statement will be met if the auditor reports the omission of a funds statement by adding a separate paragraph which follows his opinion. An example of the manner in which this matter could be reported is set out below:

"The financial statements do not specify the manner in which the operations of the company (group) have been financed or in which its financial resources have been used during the year as required by Statement of Standard Accounting Practice No. 10." '

*Note:*

(a)  the auditor is not required to produce a funds statement himself;
(b)  SSAP10 and reporting is further discussed in Auditing Statement U23, which is not reproduced as the main points are contained here.

### 'Materiality

'In deciding whether to qualify his audit opinion, the auditor should have regard to the materiality of the matter in the context of the financial statements on which he is proposing to report. In general terms a matter should be judged to be material if knowledge of the matter would be likely to influence the user of the financial statements. Materiality may be considered in the context of the financial statements as a whole, the balance sheet, the profit and loss account, or individual items within the financial statements. In addition, depending upon the nature of the matter, materiality may be considered in relative or absolute terms.

'If the auditor concludes that, judged against the criteria he believes to be most appropriate in the circumstances, the matter does not materially affect the view given by the financial statements, he should not qualify his opinion.

---

* The main one being if the company has less than £25,000 turnover.

'Where the auditor has decided that a matter is sufficiently material to warrant a qualification in his audit report, a further decision is required as to whether or not the matter is fundamental, so as to require either an adverse opinion or a disclaimer of opinion on the financial statements as a whole. An uncertainty becomes fundamental when its impact on the financial statements is so great as to render the financial statements as a whole meaningless. A disagreement becomes fundamental when its impact on the financial statements is so great as to render them totally misleading. The combined effect of all uncertainties and disagreements must be considered.

*'It is emphasised that the adverse opinion and the disclaimer of opinion are the extreme forms of the two main categories of qualification of opinion arising from disagreement and uncertainty. In most situations the "except" or "subject to" form of opinion will be the appropriate form to use; the adverse opinion and the disclaimer should be regarded as measures of last resort.'*

## 17.4  Auditing Guideline – Audit Report Examples

The Auditing Guideline 'Audit Report Examples' illustrates the types of qualification most likely to be required. The Guideline is reproduced in full below:

'List of Examples.
'Forms of Unqualified Audit Report.
1. Companies without subsidiaries and complying with Companies Acts (Great Britain).
2. Companies submitting group accounts and complying with Companies Acts (Great Britain).
3. Companies without subsidiaries and complying with Companies Acts (Ireland).
4. Emphasis of matter – transactions with a group company.
'Forms of qualified audit report.
'Note: Examples are based on legislation applicable to Great Britain. Minor modifications may be necessary if the audit report is required to comply with legislation applicable to Ireland.

| Form | Circumstances |
| --- | --- |
| *Uncertainty – material but not fundamental:* | |
| 5. Subject to – scope | No stock count at a branch |
| 6. Subject to – scope | Acceptance of management assurances (small business) |
| 7. Subject to – inherent uncertainty | Going concern |
| 8. Subject to – inherent uncertainty | Major litigation |

| Form | Circumstances |
|---|---|
| *Uncertainty — fundamental:* | |
| 9. Disclaimer — scope | Accounting breakdown |
| 10. Disclaimer — scope | Inability to substantiate cash transactions |
| 11. Disclaimer — inherent uncertainty | Valuation of long-term construction contracts |
| *Disagreement — material but not fundamental:* | |
| 12. Except — departure from Statement of Standard Accounting Practice | Failure to apply SSAP 4 |
| 13. Except — disagreement as to facts | No provision for doubtful debt |
| 14. Except — non-compliance with legislation | Company omitted information on overseas associated companies and at date of issue of financial statements has not obtained Department of Trade agreement |
| *Disagreement — fundamental:* | |
| 15. Adverse — departure from Statement of Standard Accounting Practice | Long-term contracts carried at cost with no provision made for losses in accordance with SSAP 9 |
| 16. Adverse — disagreement as to facts | Goodwill no longer justified at balance sheet amount |
| *Multiple qualification:* | |
| 17. Subject to and except | Based on Examples 5 and 13 |

## 'EXAMPLE 1: UNQUALIFIED AUDIT REPORT

**'Companies without subsidiaries — Great Britain**

'AUDITORS' REPORT TO THE MEMBERS OF . . . . . . . . . . . . . . . . . . . . . . .

'We have audited the financial statements on pages . . . . . . to . . . . . . in accordance with approved Auditing Standards.

'In our opinion the financial statements, which have been prepared under the historical cost convention as modified by the revaluation of land and buildings, give a true and fair view of the state of the company's affairs at 31 December 19 . . . . and of its profit and source and application of funds for the year then ended and comply with the Companies Acts 1948 to 1981.

## 'EXAMPLE 2: UNQUALIFIED AUDIT REPORT

**'Companies submitting group accounts – Great Britain**

'AUDITORS' REPORT TO THE MEMBERS OF . . . . . . . . . . . . . . . . . . . . .

'We have audited the financial statements on pages . . . . . . to . . . . . . in accordance with approved Auditing Standards.

'In our opinion the financial statements, which have been prepared under the historical cost convention as modified by the revaluation of land and buildings, give a true and fair view of the state of affairs of the company and the group at 31 December 19. . . . and of the profit and source and application of funds of the group for the year then ended and comply with the Companies Acts 1948 to 1981.

## 'EXAMPLE 3: UNQUALIFIED AUDIT REPORT

**'Companies without subsidiaries – Ireland**

'AUDITORS' REPORT TO THE MEMBERS OF . . . . . . . . . . . . . . . . . . . . .

'We have audited the financial statements on pages . . . . . . to . . . . . . in accordance with approved Auditing Standards and have obtained all the information and explanations we considered necessary.

'In our opinion proper books of account have been kept by the Company and the financial statements, which are in agreement therewith and have been prepared under the historical cost convention as modified by the revaluation of land and buildings, give a true and fair view of the state of the company's affairs at 31 December 19 . . . . and of its profit and source and application of funds for the year then ended and comply with the Companies Act . . . . . . . . . . . .

## 'EXAMPLE 4: UNQUALIFIED AUDIT REPORT

**'Emphasis of matter: transactions with a group company**

'AUDITORS' REPORT TO THE MEMBERS OF . . . . . . . . . . . . . . . . . . . . .

'We have audited the financial statements on pages . . . . . . to . . . . . . in accordance with approved Auditing Standards.

'We draw attention to note . . . . which outlines a number of transactions with the parent company during the year without which the company would have incurred a loss.

'In our opinion the financial statements, which have been prepared under the historical cost convention, give a true and fair view of the state of the company's affairs at 31 December 19 . . . . and of its profit and source and application of funds for the year then ended and comply with the Companies Acts 1948 to 1981.

'Notes

'1. The explanatory paragraph may appear before or after the opinion paragraph.

'2. It should be noted that the opinion paragraph does not refer to the explanatory paragraph. The use of words such as "with this explanation" or similar phrases would in effect "qualify" the opinion.

### 'EXAMPLE 5: QUALIFIED AUDIT REPORT

#### 'Uncertainty — subject to: no stock count at a branch

'AUDITORS' REPORT TO THE MEMBERS OF . . . . . . . . . . . . . . . . . . . . . .

'We have audited the financial statements on pages . . . . . . to . . . . . .
Our audit was conducted in accordance with approved Auditing Standards except that the scope of our work was limited by the matter referred to below.

'One branch of the company did not carry out a physical count of stock at 31 December 19 . . . . and there were no practicable alternative auditing procedures that we could apply to confirm quantities. Accordingly, we have been unable to obtain all the information and explanations considered necessary to satisfy ourselves as to the existence of stock valued at £ . . . . at 31 December 19 . . . . which is included as part of the total stock of £ . . . . in the balance sheet. In our opinion, in the case of the stocks referred to above, proper accounting records have not been kept as required by Section 12, Companies Act 1976.

'Subject to the effects of any adjustments which might have been shown to be necessary had a physical count of the branch stock been carried out, in our opinion the financial statements, which have been prepared under the historical cost convention, give a true and fair view of the state of the company's affairs at 31 December 19 . . . . and of its profit and source and application of funds for the year then ended and comply with the Companies Acts 1948 to 1981.

### 'EXAMPLE 6: QUALIFIED AUDIT REPORT

#### 'Uncertainty — subject to: acceptance of management assurances (small business)

'AUDITORS' REPORT TO THE MEMBERS OF . . . . . . . . . . . . . . . . . . . . .

'We have audited the financial statements on pages . . . . . . to . . . . . .
Our audit was conducted in accordance with approved Auditing Standards
having regard to the matters referred to in the following paragraph.

'In common with many businesses of similar size and organisation the
company's system of control is dependent upon the close involvement of
the directors/managing director, [who are major shareholders]. Where
independent confirmation of the completeness of the accounting records
was therefore not available we have accepted assurances from the
directors/managing director that all the company's transactions have been
reflected in the records.

'Subject to the foregoing, in our opinion the financial statements, which
have been prepared under the historical cost convention give a true and
fair view of the state of the company's affairs at 31 December 19. . . . . .
and of its profit and source and application of funds for the year then
ended and comply with the Companies Acts 1948 to 1981.

'Notes

'1. Paragraphs 11 to 13 of the Auditing Standard *Qualifications in Audit
    Reports* outline the circumstances where this form of report might be
    appropriate.
'2. The auditor should consider referring to the specific areas of the
    financial statements in which he has had to rely on assurances.
'3. Where the lack of evidence of the operation of internal controls coupled
    with the inability to adopt alternative auditing procedures to
    compensate is regarded as so fundamental as to prevent an effective
    audit being carried out, a disclaimer such as that set out in Example 10
    will be appropriate.

## 'EXAMPLE 7: QUALIFIED AUDIT REPORT

**'Uncertainty – subject to: going concern**

'AUDITORS' REPORT TO THE MEMBERS OF . . . . . . . . . . . . . . . . . . . . .

'We have audited the financial statements on pages . . . . . . to . . . . . . in
accordance with approved Auditing Standards.

'As stated in note . . . . . . the company is currently negotiating for long-
term facilities to replace the loan of £ . . . . . . which becomes repayable on
[a date early in the next financial year]; continuation of the company's
activities is dependent upon a successful outcome to these negotiations.
The financial statements have been drawn up on a going concern basis
which assumes that adequate facilities will be obtained.

'Subject to a satisfactory outcome of the negotiations referred to above, in our opinion the financial statements, which have been prepared under historical cost convention, give a true and fair view of the state of affairs of the company and the group at 31 December 19 . . . . and of the profit and source and application of funds of the group for the year then ended and comply with the Companies Acts 1948 to 1981.

*'Note*

'Where there is uncertainty as to an enterprise's ability to continue as a going concern a "subject to" opinion will generally be the more appropriate form of qualification, provided that the going concern assumption upon which the financial statements have been based is made clear together with the nature of the related uncertainty.

## 'EXAMPLE 8: QUALIFIED AUDIT REPORT

### 'Uncertainty – subject to: major litigation

'AUDITORS' REPORT TO MEMBERS OF . . . . . . . . . . . . . . . . . . . . . . . . . . . .

'We have audited the financial statements on pages . . . . . . to . . . . . . in accordance with approved Auditing Standards.

'As more fully explained in note . . . . . . to the financial statements a claim has been lodged against a subsidiary company in respect of one of its major contracts. The claim calls for rectification and for substantial compensation for alleged damage to the customer's business. The directors have made provision for the estimated cost of rectification but no provision for compensation as that part of the claim is being strongly resisted. At this time it is not possible to determine with reasonable accuracy the ultimate cost of rectification and compensation, if any, which may become payable.

'Subject to the adjustment, if any, that may be required when the claim referred to above is determined, in our opinion the financial statements, which have been prepared under the historical cost convention, give a true and fair view of the state of affairs of the company and the group at 31 December 19 . . . . and of the profit and source and application of funds of the group for the year then ended and comply with the Companies Acts 1948 to 1981.

## 'EXAMPLE 9: QUALIFIED AUDIT REPORT

### 'Uncertainty – disclaimer: accounting breakdown

'AUDITORS' REPORT TO THE MEMBERS OF . . . . . . . . . . . . . . . . . . . . . . .

'We have audited the financial statements on pages . . . . . . to . . . . . .
Our audit was conducted in accordance with approved Auditing Standards
except that the scope of our work was limited by the matter referred to
below.

'As stated in note . . . . . . , a fire at the company's computer centre
destroyed many of the accounting records. The financial statements
consequently include significant amounts based on estimates. In these
circumstances we were unable to carry out all the auditing procedures, or
to obtain all the information and explanations we considered necessary.

'Because of the significance of the matter referred to in the preceding
paragraph, we are unable to form an opinion as to (i) whether the financial
statements give a true and fair view of the state of the company's affairs
as at 31 December 19 . . . . and of its profit and source and application of
funds for the year then ended, (ii) whether proper accounting records have
been kept, or (iii) whether the financial statements comply in all respects
with the Companies Acts 1948 to 1981.

'Notes

'1. This disclaimer of opinion would apply irrespective of the accounting
convention adopted. Reference to an accounting convention should
therefore be omitted from the opinion paragraph because such a
reference might imply that a different form of opinion could be given
under a different accounting convention. In order to distinguish the
financial statements from statements prepared under an alternative
convention, it may be appropriate to include a reference to the
accounting convention in the first paragraph of the report viz ". . . the
financial statements on pages . . . . . . to . . . . . . , which have been
prepared under the historical cost convention. Our audit was
conducted in accordance with approved Auditing Standards except
that . . ."
'2. The notes to the financial statements would clearly identify which
amounts are estimates.

## 'EXAMPLE 10: QUALIFIED AUDIT REPORT

'Uncertainty – disclaimer: inability to substantiate cash transactions

'AUDITORS' REPORT TO THE MEMBERS OF . . . . . . . . . . . . . . . . . . . . . . .

'We have audited the financial statements on pages . . . . . . to . . . . . .
Our audit was conducted in accordance with approved Auditing Standards
except that the scope of our work was limited by the matter referred to
below.

'A major part of the company's income comprises cash sales. There was no system of control over such sales upon which we could rely for the purpose of our audit and there were no satisfactory procedures which we could adopt to verify the completeness of the income. We were therefore unable to obtain all the information and explanations we considered necessary. Consequently, we were unable to satisfy ourselves as to the completeness and accuracy of the accounting records.

'Because of the significance of the matter referred to in the preceding paragraph, we are unable to form an opinion as to (i) whether the financial statements give a true and fair view of the state of the company's affairs at 31 December 19 . . . . and of its profit and source and application of funds for the year then ended, (ii) whether proper accounting records have been kept, or (iii) whether the financial statements comply in all respects with the Companies Acts 1948 to 1981.

'Notes

'1. In this particular case the lack of evidence of the operation of internal controls coupled with the inability to adopt alternative auditing procedures to compensate has been regarded as so fundamental as to prevent an effective audit being carried out.

'2. If the system of internal control over the major areas of the company's affairs is considered to be adequate and the limitations are confined to non-fundamental areas, it might be appropriate to describe the areas in which there are limitations and to give a "subject to" opinion. See Example 5 for a method of reporting when a scope limitation is confined to a specific area.

'3. This disclaimer of opinion would apply irrespective of the accounting convention adopted. Reference to an accounting convention should therefore be omitted from the opinion paragraph because such a reference might imply that a different form of opinion could be given under a different accounting convention. In order to distinguish the financial statements from statements prepared under an alternative convention it may be appropriate to include a reference to the accounting convention in the first paragraph of the report viz ". . . the financial statement on pages . . . . . . to . . . . . . ., which have been prepared under the historical cost convention. Our audit was conducted in accordance with approved Auditing Standards except that . . ."

### 'EXAMPLE 11: QUALIFIED AUDIT REPORT

'Uncertainty – disclaimer: valuation of long-term construction contracts

'AUDITORS' REPORT TO THE MEMBERS OF . . . . . . . . . . . . . . . . . . . . . .

'We have audited the financial statements on pages . . . . . . to . . . . . . in accordance with approved Auditing Standards.

'As indicated in note . . . . . . the estimates of losses to completion of long-term construction contracts depend on a number of assumptions including those relating to substantially increased production and productivity which have yet to be achieved. In view of these uncertainties we are unable to confirm that the provision of £ . . . . . . is adequate.

'Because of the significance of this matter, we are unable to form an opinion as to whether the financial statements give a true and fair view of the state of the company's affairs at 31 December 19 . . . . and of its profit and source and application of funds for the year then ended.

'In other respects the financial statements in our opinion comply with the Companies Acts 1948 to 1981.

'Notes

'1. It is assumed for the purpose of this example that the amount of the provision for losses on long-term construction contracts is of overwhelming significance in relation to the net assets of the company.
'2. In this case the area of uncertainty is well defined so that the auditor is able to reach an opinion as to whether the financial statements in other respects comply with the Companies Acts. Such a conclusion would not normally be possible where wide ranging scope limitations are involved as instanced in Examples 9 and 10.
'3. This disclaimer of opinion would apply irrespective of the accounting convention adopted. Reference to an accounting convention should therefore be omitted from the opinion paragraph because such a reference might imply that a different form of opinion could be given under a different accounting convention. In order to distinguish the financial statements from statements prepared under an alternative convention, it may be appropriate to include a reference to the accounting convention in the first paragraph of the report, viz. "We have audited the financial statements on pages . . . . . . to . . . . . . , which have been prepared under the historical cost convention. Our audit was conducted in accordance with approved Auditing Standards".

## 'EXAMPLE 12: QUALIFIED AUDIT REPORT

### 'Disagreement – except: failure to apply SSAP 4

'AUDITORS' REPORT TO THE MEMBERS OF . . . . . . . . . . . . . . . . . . . . . . .

'We have audited the financial statements on pages . . . . . . to . . . . . . in accordance with approved Auditing Standards.

'As explained in note . . . . . . regional development grants have been credited in full to profits instead of being spread over the lives of the relevant assets as required by Statement of Standard Accounting Practice No. 4; the effect of so doing has been to increase group profits before and after tax for the year by £ . . . . . . (19 . . . . £ . . . . . .).

'Except for the effects of accounting for regional development grants in the manner described in the preceding paragraph, in our opinion the financial statements, which have been prepared under the historical cost convention, give a true and fair view of the state of affairs of the company and the group at 31 December 19 . . . . and of the profit and source and application of funds of the group for the year then ended and comply with the Companies Acts 1948 to 1981.

*'Note*

'It might also be appropriate to indicate the cumulative effect on retained profits where the amount is significant.

## 'EXAMPLE 13: QUALIFIED AUDIT REPORT

**'Disagreement – except: no provision for doubtful debt**

'AUDITORS' REPORT TO THE MEMBERS OF . . . . . . . . . . . . . . . . . . . . . . .

'We have audited the financial statements on pages . . . . . . to . . . . . . in accordance with approved Auditing Standards.

'No provision has been made against an amount of £ . . . . . . owing by a company which has been placed in liquidation since the year end. The liquidator has indicated that unsecured creditors are unlikely to receive any payment and in our opinion full provision should be made.

'Except for the failure to provide for the amount described above, in our opinion the financial statements, which have been prepared under the historical cost convention, give a true and fair view of the state of the company's affairs at 31 December 19 . . . . and of its profit and source and application of funds for the year then ended and comply with the Companies Acts 1948 to 1981.

*'Note*

'This is an example of a simple qualification. More explanation might be required in the middle paragraph if there were additional complications such as a consequential material overstatement of the tax provision.

## 'EXAMPLE 14: QUALIFIED AUDIT REPORT

### 'Disagreement – except: information not disclosed

'AUDITORS' REPORT TO THE MEMBERS OF . . . . . . . . . . . . . . . . . . . . . .

'We have audited the financial statements on pages . . . . . . to . . . . . . in accordance with approved Auditing Standards.

'As explained in note . . . . . . the information concerning overseas investments acquired during the year has not been disclosed in accordance with Section 4(1) of the Companies Act 1967.

'In our opinion the financial statements, which have been prepared under the historical cost convention, give a true and fair view of the state of the affairs of the company and the group at 31 December 19 . . . . and of the profit and source and application of funds of the group for the year then ended and except for the omission of the disclosure concerning overseas investments referred to above comply with the Companies Acts 1948 to 1981.

*'Notes*

'1. The note to the financial statements might explain that to give the information as to the identity and shareholdings of the new investments would harm the company's business and that application would be made to the Department of Trade for exemption in accordance with Section 4(3) of the Companies Act 1967.
'2. The lack of disclosure in this case does not impair the true and fair view shown by the financial statements.

## 'EXAMPLE 15: QUALIFIED AUDIT REPORT

### 'Disagreement – adverse opinion: contract losses not provided for in accordance with SSAP9

'AUDITORS' REPORT TO THE MEMBERS OF . . . . . . . . . . . . . . . . . . . . . .

'We have audited the financial statements on pages . . . . . . to . . . . . . in accordance with approved Auditing Standards.

'As more fully explained in note . . . . . . no provision has been made for losses expected to arise on certain long-term contracts currently in progress because the directors consider that such losses should be offset against expected but unearned future profits on other long-term contracts. In our opinion provision should be made for foreseeable losses on individual contracts as required by Statement of Standard Accounting Practice No. 9. If losses had been so recognised the effect would have been to reduce the profit before and after tax for the year and the contract work in progress at 31 December 19 . . . . by £ . . . . . .

'In view of the significant effect of the failure to provide for the losses referred to above, in our opinion the financial statements do not give a true and fair view of the state of the company's affairs at 31 December 19 . . . . and of its profit and source and application of funds for the year then ended.

'In other respects the financial statements in our opinion comply with the Companies Acts 1948 to 1981.

'Notes

'1. If the effect of the departure is considered to be fundamental to the profit and loss account and balance sheet but not to the funds statement, the final two paragraphs should be modified along the lines used in Example 16.
'2. It has been assumed in this example that the need to provide for losses arose during the year and comparative figures are not affected.
'3. This adverse opinion would apply irrespective of the accounting convention adopted. Reference to an accounting convention should therefore be omitted from the opinion paragraph because such a reference might imply that a different form of opinion could be given under a different convention.

'In order to distinguish the financial statements from statements prepared under an alternative convention, it may be appropriate to include a reference to the accounting convention in the first paragraph of the report, viz. "We have audited the financial statements on pages . . . . . . to . . . . . . which have been prepared under the historical cost convention. Our audit was conducted in accordance with approved Auditing Standards."

## 'EXAMPLE 16: QUALIFIED AUDIT REPORT

### 'Disagreement — adverse opinion: goodwill

'AUDITORS' REPORT TO THE MEMBERS . . . . . . . . . . . . . . . . . . . . . . . . .

'We have audited the financial statements on pages . . . . . . to . . . . . . in accordance with approved Auditing Standards.

'Goodwill included in the consolidated balance sheet at £ . . . . . . relates to a subsidiary which has incurred material losses during the year. In our opinion there are insufficient grounds to support the directors' contention that the subsidiary can be expected to become profitable in the foreseeable future. Accordingly we consider that goodwill should be written off in the consolidated financial statements and the investment in the subsidiary should be written down by a similar amount in the holding company's financial statements.

'Because of the significance of the foregoing matter, in our opinion the financial statements do not give a true and fair view of the state of affairs of the company and the group at 31 December 19 . . . . and of the profit of the group for the year then ended.

'In our opinion, the financial statements give a true and fair view of the source and application of funds of the group for the year ended 31 December 19 . . . ., and, except for the matter set out above, comply with the Companies Acts 1948 to 1981.

*'Notes*

'1. In this case it has been assumed that, as the writing off of goodwill does not affect the total funds generated from operations, the statement of source and application of funds has not been affected. The validity of this assumption will need to be considered in the light of individual circumstances.

'2. This adverse opinion would apply irrespective of the accounting convention adopted. Reference to an accounting convention should therefore be omitted from the opinion paragraph because such a reference might imply that a different form of opinion could be given under a different convention. In order to distinguish the financial statements from statements prepared under an alternative convention, it may be appropriate to include a reference to the accounting convention in the first paragraph of the report, viz. "We have audited the financial statements on pages . . . . . . to . . . . . . which have been prepared under the historical cost convention. Our audit was conducted in accordance with approved Auditing Standards."

### 'EXAMPLE 17: QUALIFIED AUDIT REPORT

**'Multiple qualification – based on Examples 5 and 13**

'AUDITORS' REPORT TO THE MEMBERS OF . . . . . . . . . . . . . . . . . . . . . .

'We have audited the financial statements on pages . . . . . . to . . . . . . Our audit was conducted in accordance with approved Auditing Standards except that the scope of our work was limited by the matter referred to below.

'One branch of the company did not carry out a physical count of stock at 31 December 19 . . . . and there were no practicable alternative auditing procedures that we could apply to confirm quantities. Accordingly, we have been unable to obtain all the information and explanations considered necessary to satisfy ourselves as to the existence of the stock quantities valued at £ . . . . . . at 31 December 19 . . . . and included as part of the total stock of £ . . . . . . in the balance sheet. In our opinion in the case of the stocks referred to above proper accounting records have not been kept as required by Section 12, Companies Act 1976.

'No provision has been made against an amount of £ . . . . . . owing by a company which has been placed in liquidation since the year end. The liquidator has indicated that unsecured creditors are unlikely to receive any payment and in our opinion full provision should be made.

'Subject to the effects of any adjustments which might have been shown to be necessary had a physical count of the branch stock occurred and except for the failure to make provision against an amount receivable, in our opinion the financial statements, which have been prepared under the historical cost convention, give a true and fair view of the state of the company's affairs at 31 December 19 . . . . and of its profits and source and application of funds for the year then ended and comply with the Companies Acts 1948 to 1981.'

## 17.5 The report to members – conclusion

The number of qualified audit reports per annum has increased considerably in recent years. The reasons for this are many, but the following are particularly important:
(a) proliferation of accounting standards, the non-compliance with any of which could lead to a qualified report;
(b) significant advances in standards of auditing in the last decade;
(c) increase in the disclosure requirements, of company law and of various other bodies such as the Stock Exchange;
(d) number of legal decisions against auditors, heavily critical Department of Trade inspectors' reports, and heavily critical press comment in the wake of massive unpredicted company failures and frauds.

All of this has made the auditor much more conscious of the need to qualify. Unfortunately many of the qualifications have been designed more to protect the auditor against subsequent recriminations than to be of real value to the reader. Qualifications must be specific and unambiguous. And, if the auditor is not prepared to express an opinion, he must clearly state why not. If he has reservations about the accounts, he should clearly state the specific circumstances of those reservations. He should always ask himself whether the qualification gives information useful to the reader in evaluating the accounts.

The standardisation of wording in the Guideline examples is an extremely welcome move in terms of bringing more meaning to the somewhat 'tarnished' audit report. However, I personally do not believe that the same standards and reports are applicable to both large and small companies. And I believe that this must ultimately be recognised by the profession.

A number of matters which affect the auditor's report, remain to be discussed in detail:

1. Audit reporting in small companies – Chapter 18.
2. Reporting to interested parties, other than the members – Chapters 18 and 23.
3. Group accounts – reliance on other auditors – Chapter 19.

This chapter has concentrated on the form of the audit report itself. So these detailed considerations are left until subsequent chapters.

## 17.6 The report to management

*(Note: this topic was introduced in sec. 8.9, in advance of the case studies incorporating reports to management. The topic is further discussed here, in the context of the final report which will be given at the year end.)*

The main purpose of the 'report to management' (otherwise known as 'letter of weakness', 'letter to management' or 'internal control letter') is to point out any material weaknesses in the system of internal control which were revealed by the audit work. These matters may then be corrected by the management, and this will enable a reduction in audit work in future years. It may also obviate the possible need for a qualified report, and, in the event of subsequent problems resulting from failure to correct a weakness, can protect the audit firm against recriminations.

The report to management can be useful in promoting the essential constructive relationship with the client management, and can be seen as extending the role of the auditor beyond that of merely reporting to the members on the annual accounts. Although a comparatively recent development, it has nowadays become an essential ingredient in the conduct of both large and small audits alike.

The contents of the year-end report would include the following topic headings. The order cited would be appropriate.

1. Weakness in internal control together with recommendations for correction.
2. Breakdowns in internal control, together with comment on any material error/fraud arising. (Note the distinction between a weakness and a breakdown. The former occurs when the systems themselves are fundamentally unsatisfactory, the latter where the systems are satisfactory, but there has been a failure to operate them correctly. A weakness necessitates an improvement in the system, a breakdown necessitates the enforcement of the laid down procedures.)
3. Details as to additional audit time spent because of:
   (a) weaknesses or breakdowns in the control systems;
   (b) failure of client to adhere to timetables.
   (This information will be given to justify the higher fee that will be charged as a result!)
4. Inadequate or inappropriate accounting practices. (Here the auditor may wish to document any disagreement with the directors' accounting practice/s, which may have led to a qualified report. Or he may wish to point out to the

directors changes which must be made as a result of new standards or legislation.)

5. Suggestions concerning financial and accounting efficiency. (By virtue of his detached examination, the auditor may be able to suggest ways in which accounting efficiency may be improved. This is above and beyond comments concerning adequacy of controls. For a control system may be extremely sound, but hopelessly inefficient and unnecessarily costly.)

6. Other constructive services. (Again, with the advantage of an outsider's viewpoint, the auditor may be able to point out other ways in which the company may be able to operate more efficiently and profitably. For example, time-consuming procedures may have been carried out for so long, that no one questions whether there is a quicker way of performing them.)

7. Conclusion. The following points should be made-
   (a) the comments in the report do not result from any special survey, but came to the auditor's attention during the course of normal audit procedures. They therefore cannot be relied upon to deal exhaustively with *all* weaknesses and errors in accounting procedures and records;
   (b) reference to previous reports should be made if there has been no improvement in the matters mentioned therein;
   (c) a reply should be requested;
   (d) offer should be made of additional clarification as may be appropriate.

A report will usually be drafted at the conclusion of both the interim and final audits. The interim report will contain mainly reference to internal control, and should be sent as soon as possible after the conclusion of the audit attendance, in order that the management may rectify the weaknesses/breakdowns as soon as practicable. Illustration of such reports is contained in the case study in Chapter 9. The final report would contain the matters referred to above, and would reiterate those matters from the interim report which have not yet been rectified. A reply to the matters raised should be both requested and followed up.

# 18
# The audit of small limited companies

## 18.1 To audit or not?

The relevance of independent audit for small limited companies has been the subject of much discussion in recent years. And a strong lobby has developed for the complete abolition of the audit requirement in such companies. This lobby was given added impetus by the EEC Fourth Directive which allowed member states to exempt certain small companies from audit, and by a government Green Paper on 'Company Accounting and Disclosure' which asked for views as to whether the UK should take advantage of these provisions.

Following the publication of this paper, the CCAB published a discussion document on 'Small Companies: the need for audit?'. This document presents impartially the arguments for and against audit exemption and asked for the views of all interested parties. It provides an excellent background to the debate, and is, therefore, reproduced in Fig. 18.1.

Fig. 18.1 Small companies: the need for audit?

### Small companies: the need for audit?

### Background

1. All enterprises incorporated under the Companies Acts are required to have their financial statements audited. An audit may be described as an independent examination of the financial statements of an enterprise conducted with a view to the expression of an opinion on whether or not those statements show a true and fair view. In order to form such an opinion the auditor accumulates evidence relating to both the completeness and accuracy of the entries in the records which underlie the financial statements. Having formed his opinion on the truth and fairness of the financial statements (and on compliance with certain other statutory regulations) an auditor is required to express his opinion in the form of a report. These reporting requirements have remained substantially unchanged since they were introduced in the Companies Act 1947.

2. When the EEC Fourth Directive is incorporated into the UK company law the form and content of financial statements will, to a much greater extent than hitherto, be prescribed by law, but the requirement that those statements should show a true and fair view will remain. The same Directive requires member countries to legislate for companies to have their financial statements

audited but permits member countries to exempt certain small companies from that requirement.

3. The laws of nearly all our European partners do not require small companies to have their financial statements audited; a similar situation applies in the United States. In Australia, New Zealand and parts of Canada the former statutory requirements for such enterprises to appoint auditors have been repealed.

4. The publication of the Government's Green Paper on Company Accounting and Disclosure which discusses company legislation designed to implement the Fourth Directive accepts that now is an appropriate time to review the suitability of the present state of the law on this subject within the United Kingdom and, if appropriate, to introduce changes.

5. The present law does not differentiate in any way between the audit requirements of large and small companies, of public and private companies, nor of limited and unlimited companies.

6. Although the legal framework within which auditors operate has been generally static for many years the business environment has changed significantly. A wider range of users has become increasingly aware of the level of assurance which they should be able to obtain from audited financial statements. Criticisms and comments made in court cases and in Department of Trade Inspectors' reports have increasingly related not only to accounting shortcomings but also to the role of the auditor. These factors have been a significant influence in the changes which have taken place in audit practice and in particular in the change towards higher standards of independent evidence in place of management representations.

7. These developments have taken place initially in the large company sector. However, because the Companies Acts prescribe the same audit report for all companies irrespective of size, the same audit requirements apply to both large and small companies. Some of these may not be appropriate to small companies.

8. Furthermore, it is important that from time to time a reappraisal should be made of the value to users of the services which auditors provide. The cost of an audit to a small company should represent value to the business or to other users of its financial statements. Otherwise there is a risk that the statutory requirement to have an audit may be absorbing funds which could instead be spent on the provision of other services that the accountant can and should give and which would help management in the commercial development of the enterprise.

9. The companies referred to in this paper as 'small companies' are those forming the bottom tier of the classification set out in the Green Paper. A copy of that classification forms Appendix 1 to this paper.

## To audit or not

10. The case for retaining the present system of requiring accounts of all small companies to be subject to a statutory audit rests on the value of the audit to those who have an interest in their affairs. Principal among such interested parties are:
* shareholders
* banks and other institutional creditors
* trade creditors
* taxing authorities
* employees
* management

11. The proposals for change envisage that small companies should be

permitted to opt out of the requirement for audit. They do not call into question either the need for the directors to produce financial statements which show a 'true and fair' view or the value of such statements: indeed, the suggestion* that directors should be required to acknowledge their responsibility for the financial statements by attaching thereto a suitable declaration applies equally to such proposals. Furthermore, the proposals recognise the need to protect the rights of minorities. The subject which is considered to be open for debate is whether the benefit of the compulsory audit of the financial statements of small companies justifies the attendant cost.

12. The arguments for and against change which tend to be put forward when the interests of each of the parties referred to in para. 10 above are considered are set out in para. 13 to 31 below, together with a consideration of some of the other factors involved. This paper does not attempt an evaluation of the validity of these views on which readers' comments are requested.

*Shareholders*

### The case for the status quo

13. Shareholders who are not connected with the management of a company need reassurance that their interests are being properly protected. An audit provides an independent opinion of the fairness of management's annual financial report on the progress of the business. Furthermore, in the case of a small company having minority shareholders who are not involved in the management the discipline of an annual audit discourages the major shareholders from treating the company's assets as their own personal property and ʳrotects the interests of the minority.

14. Financial statements are often of particular importance to shareholders in small companies because they provide virtually the only information available to determine the value of their shares. Valuations for taxation purposes are generally substantially based on financial statements and frequently the provisions in the articles of private companies include a requirement for the transfer price of shares to be determined by a valuation based on the financial statements. It is accordingly particularly important that these statements should be fair and an audit provides valuable assurance of this fact.

### The case for change

15. The value of independent audit to shareholders in some, perhaps many, cases is not disputed. But it is argued that there are also many cases where the independent audit is of little value to the shareholders or where the cost is disproportionate to its value. This position often arises:
(a) where all the shareholders are also directors and actively involved in the management of the company;
(b) where those shareholders who are not involved in the management of the company have complete confidence in the probity of the directors, e.g. by reason of close kinship or long association; or
(c) where the size and nature of the enterprise is such that it is not reasonably practicable to provide the auditor with all the necessary evidence, with the result that any audit report would be so heavily qualified as to be of little value.

16. Accordingly it is argued that it is unreasonable and oppressive to impose the audit requirement in all cases: the law should be amended to provide

*'Improvements to company law', a memorandum submitted in June 1977 to the Secretary of State for Trade on behalf of the accounting bodies (para. 121).

shareholders with the option to resolve that audit may be dispensed with, under appropriate conditions. For example, it might be provided that the agreement of the holders of at least 90 per cent of all shares would be necessary for a resolution dispensing with audit.

### Banks and other institutional creditors

#### The case for the status quo

17. Financial statements are of value to banks and institutional lenders both as a basis for taking lending decisions and as a means of monitoring the continuing security of advances made. Clearly, they must also value the additional assurance as to the accuracy of the financial statements that is provided by the independent examination and attestation of the auditor. Indeed they would probably be reluctant to rely at all on financial statements which constituted the wholly unsupported representations of management. Qualification of an audit report reduces but does not eliminate its value.

#### The case for change

18. Although financial statements form a part of the information which banks or other institutions will use when deciding whether or not to make an advance, greater reliance is generally placed on the manner in which the bank account has been conducted and on management accounts and cash flow projections. Comparisons of the projections with out-turn are also important.

19. If a bank or other institution considers that it needs audited financial statements as a means of monitoring the progress of the borrowing enterprise, it would be able to make an audit a condition of granting the loan. It is open to question whether banks and other institutions do, in fact, place more reliance on the audited financial statements of small limited companies than on the financial statements of unincorporated businesses of similar size which although unaudited, have nearly always been prepared by a qualified accountant.

20. It is difficult to justify the retention of the requirement for all small companies to undergo an audit of their financial statements merely for the benefit of those of their number that may want to borrow money from lenders who wish to have financial statements audited.

### Trade creditors

#### The case for the status quo

21. Trade creditors are concerned that the goods they supply to their customers will be paid for in due course, and accordingly they will seek assurance that the companies with which they do business are financially sound. Valuable evidence on this matter is provided by the companies' financial statements which are available for inspection at Companies House. Often creditors will not inspect customers' financial statements themselves, but they will rely on reports from credit agencies for whom the Companies House files are a valuable source of information. The value of this information is reduced if not independently verified.

#### The case for change

22. In most cases credit worthiness is only investigated when an account is first opened, when the level of credit is significantly increased or when a debtor is seen to be in trouble; it is rarely reviewed on a continuous basis.

23. Financial statements of small companies are generally filed with the

Registrar of Companies too late to be of relevance for the short terms under which trade credit is commonly allowed. Consequently, financial statements, whether audited or not, can at best only be of limited value to trade creditors. Suppliers wishing to investigate the credit worthiness of the small firm are more likely to rely on trade references and personal contacts.

## Taxing authorities

### The case for the status quo

24. The tax authorities are among the largest users of financial statements. The Inland Revenue uses them as a basis for the computation of profit for the purposes of corporation tax. The Customs and Excise uses the financial statements of an enterprise as a means of cross-checking the figures of turnover and expenses contained in VAT returns. The value of the financial statements is clearly enhanced by the addition of an independent audit opinion.

### The case for change

25. It is questionable whether the Inland Revenue places greater reliance on audited financial statements of small companies than on the unaudited statements received from sole traders and partnerships. Inspectors of Taxes tend to be more influenced by the reputation of the accountant or firm of accountants associated with the information than with the expression of a particular form of opinion, or even of no opinion at all. Certainly, the recently instituted 'in depth' enquiries have not been confined to unincorporated businesses.

26. The Customs and Excise authorities use financial statements as a means of verifying the accuracy of figures contained in VAT returns. The detailed information which they require is, therefore, generally contained in the trading account of a company and is not explicitly the subject of the auditor's report.

## Employees

### The case for the status quo

27. Although the statutory rights to information given to trade unions under the 1975 Employment Protection Act do not specifically include audited financial statements, the public availability of those statements makes them a natural part of the overall evidence used by a union in conducting collective bargaining. Furthermore, individual employees can, if they wish, examine audited accounts placed on public record with a view to assessing the prospective viability of their employer's business.

### The case for change

28. It is unlikely that in a small business the employees will be interested in the audited financial statements either as a tool for wage negotiations or as a means of assessing the prospective viability of the business. Profit in such enterprises is in any event heavily influenced by the amount of directors' remuneration and by the extent of low interest loans from the directors.

## Management

### The case for the status quo

29. Because small companies generally have neither the resources nor the need to maintain complex accounting systems, an audit provides an independent

check on whether the business is performing as management believes to be the case. It also provides an independent check on the accuracy and adequacy of the basic book-keeping procedures performed by the company's own staff. An audit will often provide valuable incidental benefits such as recommendations for improvements to the systems of accounting and control and the detection of fraud and error.

### The case for change

30. Financial statements provide a check on whether the business is performing as management believes to be the case only to the extent to which the information supplied to the accountant has been given honestly and accurately by the management. In such cases an audit opinion on those financial statements is unlikely to add anything to management's knowledge of the results.

31. Furthermore, management frequently benefits from the advice and assistance of practising accountants in preparing and in organising and evaluating the information on which management takes the commercial decisions appropriate to the business. Such advice might more readily be sought if the regulatory function of audit no longer masked the accountant's potentially more useful roles as financial adviser and management consultant. He could, moreover, act as trustee for substantial family shareholdings without the constraints of requirements to remain independent.

### The price of limited liability

#### The case for the status quo

32. Limited liability is a substantial benefit conferred on the shareholders of a limited company. They can seek the return appropriate to a risk investment while restricting their risk to a predetermined sum. In return for this benefit it is reasonable that collectively they should be publicly accountable by placing the company's accounts on public record and by obtaining an independent attestation of their truth and fairness. If the privilege of limited liability is worth having, the cost of an audit, including the cost of maintaining adequate auditable systems of accounting, should be paid willingly. If the value of limited liability is not worth this price, the related benefits can reasonably be withheld.

#### The case for change

33. Although public accountability (i.e. the filing of accounts) is a valid price to ask for the benefits of limited liability, in no other area of business activity is compliance with the law monitored in the comprehensive manner provided by an audit. Furthermore, in many small businesses the benefits of limited liability have been eroded by the giving of personal guarantees to lending institutions. In any event the law currently requires the accounts of unlimited companies to be audited in just the same way as those of limited companies.

### The cost and availability of audit evidence

#### The case for the status quo

34. As already indicated changes have taken place in audit practice which have resulted in the auditor requiring higher standards of independent evidence in place of management representations. If the auditor attempts to carry out an audit and is unable to obtain sufficient relevant and reliable audit evidence the

draft APC auditing Standards* require him to qualify his report. The type of qualification likely to be appropriate to the circumstances of many small companies was published as Example 17 in a supplement to the draft auditing Standards and Guidelines. The text is given in Appendix 2. This approach is considered to be acceptable.

### The case for change

35. In some small companies because of the personal involvement of the proprietor, the level of independent audit evidence which the auditor of a larger organisation would reasonably expect cannot be provided. In other small companies this level of audit evidence may be available, but the cost of collecting and evaluating it may well be disproportionate to the benefit arising either to the company or to users of its financial statements.

36. The auditor is not entitled to treat wholly unsupported assurances from management as reliable audit evidence. Where he is unable to obtain sufficient independent evidence, the draft auditing Standards require him to qualify his report along the lines of Example 17 (Appendix 2). Although it is impracticable to be precise about the extent, it is expected that the adoption of the draft APC auditing Standards and Guidelines will result in a significant number of such qualified reports on smaller companies. A widespread increase in qualifications in this context could well do harm to the standing of the audited financial statements of such companies. Removal of the statutory audit requirement would be a way to avoid this unwelcome risk.

## The development of auditing Standards

### The case for change

37. It was the need to ensure that audited financial statements meet the reasonable expectations of users that led to the publication by APC of the draft auditing Standards and Guidelines mentioned above and in the context of identical audit objectives these Standards and Guidelines must apply to all companies. The wording of the audit report is prescribed by the statute and the accountancy profession cannot lay down standards of performance which lead to the same words carrying different meaning according to the size of company.

38. It would not be acceptable to improve the standards of auditing in those larger companies which are clearly publicly accountable without increasing the standards of auditing for companies of all sizes. The retention of the compulsory audit requirement for small companies will inevitably lead to compromises and delays in the important task of further developing standards of auditing for larger companies.

39. As mentioned earlier, users expectation of the value of the auditor's attestation of annual accounts is increasing. Furthermore, the auditor who fails to meet those expectations has become progressively more likely to be pursued by means of legal action. For this and other reasons standards of auditing have developed significantly during recent years, a trend which can be expected to continue.

## The alternative to an audit

40. If the case for changing the present statutory requirement for the audit of

* Published by Auditing Practices Committee, May 1978.

small companies were to be accepted there would appear to be two basic alternatives available, either:
(a) a statutory requirement for an examination differing from an audit in its purpose and therefore in its methods; or
(b) no legal requirement for an external examination of the financial statements.

In either case standards to be observed by accountants associating their names with the unaudited financial statements of limited companies would need to be laid down by the profession. If there were no statutory requirement for an external examination of the financial statements, such standards would not necessarily be observed if the financial statements were prepared by an unqualified accountant.

### The nature of a review

41. Those who have argued in favour of the abolition of the audit requirement for small companies have generally proposed that the alternative should be an accountant's 'review' but there has been no unanimity as to what a review would be. Those favouring retention of the audit requirement have not unreasonably criticised the concept of review on the grounds that it was vague and ill-defined. It would seem worthwhile, therefore, to set out the main principles and objectives of a review and in so doing to draw on the experience of countries where this form of external examination of financial statements is already used.

42. In order to describe a review, to analyse the appropriate scope of the work and how it would differ from an audit and to discuss the reporting problems that would arise, it is helpful to refer again to certain of the relevant arguments:
(a) in the circumstances of small companies, the collection of the independent evidence necessary to support an audit opinion involves in many cases a cost which is out of proportion to the value of that opinion; and
(b) in a significant number of small companies the independent evidence necessary to support an audit opinion may not be available at any cost.

43. The point at issue is not the truth and fairness of the financial statements but rather, whether it is either worthwhile or possible to obtain adequate independent audit evidence as a basis for an audit opinion on such statements. A review could be described as a procedure whereby an accountant, relying upon the assumption that his client has made a full and fair disclosure of all the relevant information, satisfies himself (after completing work in accordance with an approved review standard) that on the basis of the information and explanations so provided the financial statements give a true and fair view.

44. It should be noted that the accountant would not be entitled to assume that the client has the necessary competence in accountancy to produce financial statements.

45. Under these circumstances there would thus be no requirement for independent corroborative evidence to support the information provided. The reviewer, therefore, would not require to collect independent evidence nor to carry out an examination of internal control. He would, however, usually require to make at least a limited examination of the accounting system, in case the information provided by management was not as accurate or as complete as management believed.

46. There would be four main parts to a review (which are largely based on the precautions that a competent accountant would take if he were preparing the statements himself), namely:
(a) establishing that the client has employed reasonable procedures to ensure

the accuracy of his financial statements, including:

(i) having books and records which are reasonably adequate for the purpose of recording transactions and providing the necessary information;

(ii) employing satisfactory procedures for such matters as ascertaining stock;

(iii) taking reasonable precautions to verify the accuracy of the statements by such means as reconciling bank statements, reviewing suppliers' statements received after the balance sheet date etc.

(b) reviewing the accounting policies adopted by the client for consistency and appropriateness and reviewing with him the significant judgemental areas in the statements, such as the recoverability of debts, stock obsolescence, depreciation, etc.;

(c) carrying out analytical review procedures on the statements with a view to identifying anomalies or unexpected items or relationships and obtaining satisfactory explanations for them;

(d) reviewing the financial statements as a whole for fairness of presentation, compliance with statutory disclosure requirements and compliance with accounting Standards.

47. A check list of procedures which might be carried out in conducting a review forms Appendix 3 to this paper.

48. As a result of his work, the reviewer might come to an adverse conclusion on one or more of the above aspects. In this case he would need to consult with the client as to what further steps could be taken to ensure that the directors discharge their statutory duty to prepare accounts which do show a true and fair view.

49. The sort of review procedures outlined in this paper are similar to those already adopted by many practising accountants in connection with their work on unaudited financial statements. However, the procedures would need to be further developed and refined in the light both of any specific statutory requirements and of comments from interested parties.

*Reporting on a review*

50. In formulating a report appropriate to a review, it should be borne in mind that the accountant has not collected any *evidence* on which to base an *audit opinion* on the financial statements; therefore he cannot express such an opinion. To avoid the possibility of any misunderstanding by the reader it is desirable that his report includes a clear statement to that effect.

51. There are three basic options:

(a) the simple disclaimer of opinion, e.g. because the scope of our engagement is limited to the review of the financial statements we have not carried out an audit and accordingly we express no audit opinion on the financial statements';

(b) positive assurance to the extent that the scope of the work justifies such assurance; this could take a form such as 'the financial statements are in accordance with the underlying records and with the explanations and information given to us. We have not carried out an audit and accordingly express no audit opinion on the financial statements';

(c) some form of negative assurance, e.g. 'we are not aware of any circumstances which suggest that the financial statements do not show a "true and fair view" '.

52. The first has the merit of making clear that the accountant does not express an audit opinion: it is therefore safe but has little other merit and it can

reasonably be argued that whoever pays the reviewer has not got any assurance for his money. The second adds little to the information conveyed by the first. Negative assurance, as in the third option, may be considered to be unsatisfactory on the grounds that it only has meaning in the context of a clearly defined work scope: unless the reader knows precisely the work done before giving the report he cannot determine what value can be placed on it. It is suggested, however, that this would be the most useful option available in the circumstances and is similar to the type of report used in the United States where the review of small company financial statements is established.

53. On this basis and provided that an acceptable operational standard relating to review work is first published by the recognised accountancy bodies, the following form of accountants' report is suggested:

*Accountants report to the members of XYZ Limited*

'We have reviewed the accompanying financial statements set out on pages . . to . . in accordance with approved review standards and have obtained the information and explanations which we required for this purpose.

Our review which consisted primarily of enquiries, comparisons and discussions was substantially less in scope than an audit, and in particular did not include the independent verification of information supplied to us. It is, therefore, inappropriate for us to express an audit opinion on the financial statements.

Having carried out our review, we report that the financial statements are in accordance with the underlying records. We are not aware of any material respects in which the financial statements do not show a true and fair view of the state of the company's affairs at 31 December 1979 and of its profit for the year ended on that date or fail to comply with the Companies Acts.'

54. The following points should be noted:

(a) The first paragraph is necessary to define the scope of the work with precision: it is based on the assumption that there will be a standard developed by the Auditing Practices Committee and published by the recognised accountancy bodies which will be the yardstick for performance. If the scope of review is defined in some other way (e.g. by legislation) this paragraph will require appropriate amendment.

(b) The words 'have obtained all the information and explanations which we required' are considered necessary to meet the circumstances where a modification is necessary because the reviewer is either not satisfied as to the procedures taken to ensure accuracy (para. 46(a)) or is dissatisfied with the results of his analytical review (para. 46(c)). If these words were omitted it seems that the reviewer could give a standard 'unmodified' report even when he had these serious misgivings.

(c) The second paragraph is designed to explain in broad terms what a review is and to contain the essential disclaimer of opinion. It is helpful to specify the main area in which a review differs from an audit, namely the absence of independent verification.

(d) The final paragraph is an appropriate 'negative assurance' founded on a definition of the work done. The reviewer cannot give this assurance unless he is satisfied with the results of his review of accounting policies and principal judgemental decisions (para. 46(b)) and his overall review of the financial statements (para. 46(d)).

55. Users of financial statements which had been reviewed by a qualified accountant in the way described above would therefore have some assurance regarding those statements. In many cases the level of assurance resulting from a review should be sufficient for such users. Furthermore, the time and thus the cost of carrying out such a review, while not insignificant could be expected to

be materially less than that needed to carry out an audit of the same financial statements.

*Legislating for a review*

56. Certain restrictions and safeguards would need to be provided if the law is amended to allow companies to opt out of the present statutory audit, e.g.:
(a) they had less than a defined number of shareholders;
(b) they were below a specified size (within the criteria provided by the Fourth Directive);
(c) a large majority of shareholders (perhaps as large as 90%) approved the change.

57. If the principles of a review were to be introduced by statute the legislation would need to recognise the fact that the reviewing accountant would not necessarily obtain independent evidence of the representations of directors regarding the financial statements of the company concerned.

58. The legislation would need to provide that companies that elected not to have an audit would appoint a reviewing accountant. The present provisions relating to the qualifications, appointment and dismissal of auditors would be extended to apply to reviewing accountants.

59. Legislation might lay down requirements for the reviewing accountants on the following lines:
(a) The reviewing accountant should make a report to the members on the financial statements examined by him.
(b) The review report should state whether the financial statements are in accordance with the accounting records and whether the accountant is aware of any material respects in which the financial statements:
    (i) do not show a true and fair view of the state of the company's affairs and of its profit; or
    (ii) fail to comply with the Companies Acts;
(c) The reviewing accountant in preparing his report on the above should make such enquiries as will enable him to form an opinion to the following matters:
    (i) whether the company has employed reasonable procedures to ensure the accuracy of its financial statements, including:
        * having books and records which are adequate for the purpose of recording transactions and providing the necessary information;
        * taking reasonable precautions to verify the accuracy of the statements;
    (ii) whether the accounting policies adopted by the client are consistent and appropriate.
    If the reviewer comes to an adverse conclusion on one or more of these aspects he must state that fact.
(d) The reviewing accountant is not required to obtain independent evidence in support of the entries in the accounting records or of the other information and explanations supplied to him.

60. Details of the work which should be carried out by an accountant before signing a review report would be promulgated by the accountancy bodies.

61. If the option of a review were to be introduced by statute, it is questionable whether it should be applied to the whole of the category of companies described in the Green Paper as 'bottom tier' (see Appendix 1). The problems of obtaining adequate audit evidence discussed in paras. 34–36 would generally not apply to the larger companies in this tier and it is accordingly for discussion whether those size criteria are appropriate for these purposes.

*The voluntary approach*

62. An alternative approach would be for the law to remain silent on the consequences for companies which elected not to have an audit. In these circumstances the accountancy bodies would lay down both the manner in which members would allow their names to be associated with such unaudited financial statements and, as in para. 58 above, the work which should be carried out before allowing their names to be so associated.

63. Thus a company which elected not to have an audit and whose financial statements were prepared by an accountant who was a member of one of the s161 bodies would automatically have its financial statements reviewed. If, however, a company elected not to have an audit and its directors decided to have its financial statements prepared by an unqualified accountant there would be no legislative or professional supervision over any assurances given on those financial statements.

*The issues*

64. Readers are invited to consider and comment on the paper and in particular to consider the following which seem to be the fundamental issues:

(a) Is it appropriate that audit in its present form should continue to be mandatory for all small companies?

(b) If the answer to (a) is 'yes', is it acceptable that a significant number of companies are likely to receive audit reports qualified along the lines of Example 17 (Appendix 2)?

(c) If the answer to (a) or (b) is 'no', should a small company which chooses not to have an audit be required by law to have its financial statements reviewed?

(d) Should the right to choose a review apply to all companies coming within the description 'bottom tier' set out in the Green Paper, or should the right be more restricted (see para. 61 above)?

# Appendix 1: Extract from the Green Paper 'Company Accounting and Disclosure'

*Part A: the broad approach*

### *Chapter 1: classification of companies*

1. In order to provide a more appropriate framework within which the law relating to company accounts can be developed, it is intended to introduce a three tier classification of companies so that different accounting and disclosure requirements can be applied to each category of company. The three categories will be as follows:

*Top tier*: all companies listed on the Stock Exchange and all other companies which exceed two of the following three criteria:

* turnover £5 million
* balance sheet total £2.5 million
* average number of employees 250

*Middle tier.* All public companies not included in the top tier and all private companies which do not fall within either the top tier or the bottom tier.

*Bottom tier.* Small private companies which do not exceed two of the following three criteria:

* turnover £1,300,000
* balance sheet total £650,000

\* average number of employees 50.

Additionally, for the purpose of the accounting requirements a subsidiary of a public company may not be treated as a small private company. Furthermore any company in a group which, taken as a whole, does not fall within the criteria for the bottom tier may not be treated as a small private company.

2. It is proposed that small private companies, defined above, should be called *proprietary companies* but there would be no requirement for such companies to indicate their status in their names.

3. The criteria used to define the three tiers are close to the maximum figures included in the Fourth Directive.

## Appendix 2: Example 17 – Qualified audit report in Draft Auditing Guidelines. Now replaced by example 6 in the final Guidelines. (See 17.4.)

## Appendix 3: Example of a review check list

These initial questions are designed so that the replies may be evaluated to determine whether or not further enquiries or procedures are required. This illustrative check list is not intended to be exhaustive or to be followed slavishly. The circumstances of each engagement should be considered carefully.

*Preliminary considerations*

1. Are the services to be provided mutually agreed and has an engagement letter been issued?
2. Nature of business
(a) What kind of business is carried on?
(b) Has the company, complied with the statutory requirements for exemption from audit?
(c) Where is business carried on?
3. What are the significant
(a) assets and liabilities?
(b) sources of revenue?
(c) costs and expenses?
4. Has consideration been given to matters arising from:
(a) prior period financial statements?
(b) prior period working papers and related files?
(c) prior period accounting problems?
5. What books and records are kept
(a) general ledger?
(b) cash book?
(c) petty cash book?
(d) purchase day book?
(e) sales day book?
(f) wages/salary book?
(g) nominal ledger?
(h) sales ledger?
(i) purchase ledger?
(j) costing records?

*Items in the financial statements*

6. Cash and bank
(a) Has a bank reconciliation been prepared?
(b) Have old or unusual outstanding items in the bank reconciliation been reviewed and adjusted where necessary?
(c) Has cash been counted and agreed with records?

7. Debtors
(a) Is the sales ledger control account in agreement with the listing of debtor accounts?
(b) Has provision been made for doubtful debts?
(c) What method was used to determine the provision?
(d) How has the cut-off with sales been effected?
(e) Have subsequent receipts been reviewed?
(f) Has aged analysis of debts been provided?
(g) Have material credit balances been reviewed and appropriately classified?
(h) Has VAT been reconciled with returns?

8. Stock and work in progress
(a) When was stock counted?
(b) Are procedures designed to arrive at a proper and consistent count?
(c) Have stock sheets been reviewed as to quantities, prices, calculations, etc?
(d) Have consignment stock, stock held for others or stock held by others been considered?
(e) What is the basis of valuation? Is such basis consistent?
(f) Have provisions for obsolescence been considered?
(g) How has the cut-off of purchase/stock/sales, goods in transit, returned goods, etc., been effected?

9. Prepaid expenses: have all significant prepayments been set up?

10. Investments (loans, mortgages, investments, etc.)
(a) Have opening balances been reconciled to closing balances?
(b) Have gains and losses on disposal been recorded?
(c) Has investment income been accounted for?
(d) Has current/non-current classification been made?
(e) Has value been considered?

11. Fixed assets
(a) Have opening balances of fixed assets and accumulated depreciation been reconciled to closing balances?
(b) What significant changes have occurred in owned or leased fixed assets?
(c) Have gains or losses on disposal been recorded?
(d) Have fixed assets been capitalised on a consistent basis?
(e) Has the repairs and maintenance account been reviewed?
(f) Are fixed assets stated at cost?
(g) What are the depreciation methods and rates? Are they consistent?
(h) Is property mortgaged or otherwise encumbered?

12. Other assets
(a) What is the nature and amount of other assets?
(b) What is the amortisation policy? Is it consistent?
(c) Has current/non-current classification been made?
(d) Are the assets realisable at their stated value?

13. Creditors and accruals
(a) Is the purchase ledger control account in agreement with the listing of creditors?
(b) What procedures have been followed which are designed to result in all major creditors being recorded?

(c)  Are suppliers' statements reconciled with ledger accounts?
(d)  Are there any undisclosed short-term liabilities?
(e)  Have all significant accruals been set up?
(f)  Are secured liabilities appropriately described?
(g)  Have subsequent payments been reviewed?
(h)  Have VAT, PAYE and NHI been reconciled with returns?
    14.  Long-term liabilities
(a)  Has current/non-current classification been considered?
(b)  Is interest payable recorded?
    15.  Tax
(a)  Has the relationship between the tax provision and pre-tax result been considered?
(b)  To what extent are past tax liabilities agreed?
(c)  Have assessments and computations been reviewed?
(d)  Has deferred taxation been considered?
    16.  Other liabilities
(a)  What is the nature and amount of other liabilities?
(b)  Has current/non-current classification been made?
(c)  Have contingent liabilities and capital commitments been considered?
    17.  Statutory requirements
(a)  Maintenance of statutory books?
(b)  Annual return filed?
    18.  Overall review: has appropriate consideration been given to:
(a)  the inter-relationship of items in the financial statements?
(b)  a comparison of significant components of the profit and loss account (in light of current operating and economic conditions) with budgets and/or figures for preceding periods?
(c)  significant operating ratios?
    (i)  gross profit;
    (ii)  debtors to sales.

    19.  Are there any events which occurred after the end of the financial period which would have a significant effect on the financial statements or would be significant to readers of the financial statements?

    20.  Has trial balance been agreed?

    21.  Have opening balances been agreed with last year's financial statements?

    22.  To what extent are there differences? Quantify and indicate treatment.

    23.  To what extent have significant estimates been included?

*Final consideration for the accountant*

    24.  Have the financial statements and 'Accountants Report' been discussed with the client?

    25.  Is the client satisfied that the financial statements are complete and accurate?

    26.  Are there any representations by the client regarding full disclosure which should be documented?

    27.  Do the financial statements comply with the appropriate disclosure requirements of the Companies Acts and the accounting Standards?

    28.  Are the financial statements in accordance with the accounting records?

    29.  Have the accounting policies adopted been disclosed and are they in accordance with accounting Standards?

    30.  Based on the information provided and the review performed and so far as you know, are the accounting concepts and policies adopted in respect of

material items in the financial statements appropriate to the organisation?

31. Is the form and content of the 'Accountants Report' appropriate to this assignment and in particular are you aware of any respects in which the financial statements do not give a true and fair view, or in which there has been a failure to comply with law?

32. Additional questions.

The CCAB well explain the issues as usually discussed, but they miss the principal illogicality of the current requirements: an audit can be defined as an 'official examination of accounts'; but to have any meaning, that examination must be performed for some specific purpose. According to current company law, a statutory audit must be made on *all* limited company statutory accounts, for the purpose of *reporting to the members*, whether or not the directors' accounts show a true and fair view, and comply with the Companies Acts. But if the members are also the directors, there can be no purpose in reporting to members whether they are misleading themselves with their own accounts! So it is clear that current company law must be inappropriate in respect of proprietorship companies. Of this there can be no doubt. The only argument comes in determining how the current law should be changed. Should it be changed:

(a) to change the audit requirement for small companies;
    or
(b) to alter the reporting requirements so that the real interested parties are protected – e.g. creditors, the bank, the Inland Revenue together with any minority shareholders?

This opens up the entire debate, for if we adopt the latter course such an extension of audit responsibility cannot just apply to small companies. For creditors, banks, the Inland Revenue, etc., are every bit as interested in the accounts of large companies as well as small. So the change in the law would have to apply to all companies.

Would the profession as a whole welcome such an extension in its responsibility? If the answer is *yes*, then clearly we as a profession should recommend an early change in the law making us responsible to creditors and other interested parties, as well as to members. But if, as I suspect, the answer is *no*, then the logical course of action is to change the existing small company audit requirement. (I am for the moment ignoring the possibility of a 'backdoor' extension of liability through the law of tort – see Chapter 21.)

## 18.2  Practical problems

Were we to retain the audit requirement for all companies, and extend reporting responsibility, practical problems would arise in applying the *same rules* to *all* companies, because proprietorship and stewardship companies are very different creatures indeed:

1. In small companies there is often a *lack of evidence of the operation of internal control*, such that heavy reliance has to be placed on management representations as a basis of audit evidence. Sufficient work can often be performed to determine whether assets are overstated, but it is commonly not possible to obtain objective evidence to prove the extent (if any) of understatement of assets, liabilities and income. For this we have to rely on management representations which cannot be objectively proved. So the accounts will only be true, if the directors are telling the truth.

2. Small companies often require *qualified reports* in that there are inadequate accounting controls or inadequate accounting records. In either situation, the auditor should state that he is unable to express an opinion, or at best give a 'subject to' report. So the reader of the report gains little assurance about the accounts themselves. He is told that the accounting system is weak, but he could probably have guessed that anyway from his knowledge of the company. The trend appears to be towards much more frequent disclaimers of opinion (where once the accounts may have been signed as true and fair). Audit reports in these circumstances may be of limited value.

3. *Ethical standards.* As we saw in Chapter 2, there is a strong case for suggesting that auditors should have no part in the preparation of financial statements, or in the giving of financial advice. The logic of this suggestion is that the auditor cannot independently express an opinion on work that he has himself performed, or on advice that he has himself given. The need for this increase in real and apparent independence is strong in the case of the large company auditors who have come in for heavy criticism in the wake of recent company failures and frauds (for example, company inspectors enquiring into the affairs of Bernard Russell Ltd were critical of the fact that one of the joint auditors had substantial involvement in accounts preparation). But in smaller companies it is impractical and unnecessary to have the audit function separated from the function of accounts preparation and financial advice. Costs would increase considerably and service may conceivably decline.

4. *Procedural standards.* I quote from a paper given by Ian Hay Davison (managing partner of Arthur Andersen), in *Accountancy* magazine, to a conference on auditing standards:
'As we raise the standards of auditing in order to match public pressures, it is becoming clear that we can no longer expect auditing standards appropriate to a publicly quoted company to apply to a corner grocery shop. Yet both, assuming that the shop is incorporated, are governed by the Companies Acts and have to be audited under the same provisions. Our dilemma is that the complicated needs of ICI cannot be met by rules which make sense for the one-man business, and standards that fit the proprietary company are much too loose for the stewardship company. It is clear that a legal separation is needed between the audit requirements of proprietorship and stewardship companies. To the stewardship company, the public quoted company, where management and ownership are separated, the full rigour of auditing standards must be applied. On the accounts of such companies, it is appropriate to express a "true and fair" view.'

The same principles can apply to all companies, but the same procedures cannot. And standards consisting purely of principles are too vague to be of any practical value.

## 18.3 Dual standards?

It follows from the practical considerations outlined above that if we continue to have the same audit requirements for all companies, there may well be the need for the application of *dual standards*; dual standards or reporting, of ethics and of procedures. But in my opinion, dual standards are not desirable for the following reasons:

1. If the adherence to an audit standard is necessary for the giving of an un-qualified report, it is illogical to suggest that because a company is small the standard is no longer appropriate. If we need standards, then we need con-sistent standards.

2. If a small company has been examined at a lower level, then it cannot expect the same degree of audit assurance as its larger brothers. It follows that the audit report would have to specify which standards had been applied. And this could quickly lead to misunderstanding on the part of readers, and could possibly be detrimental to the credibility of the audit function as a whole.

Dual standards are not acceptable, but *different* audit requirements for proprietary companies are necessary to recognise the different level of accountability that exists therein. While it is usually possible in proprietor managed companies to determine the likelihood of error and employee fraud, it is commonly not possible to formulate an opinion on the extent (if any) of management manipulation. I believe that the legal reporting requirements and the Auditing Standards should recognise this fact.

## 18.4 The way ahead

I do not believe that it is appropriate to completely abandon the audit require-ment in proprietorship companies because there would then be nothing to safe-guard against total abuse of the limited liability status by directors, and no protection would be afforded to minority shareholders, or to creditors, banks and other third parties. Granting such readers the special right to request an audit (subject to provisions to safeguard against frivolous or malicious requests) is a possibility. But in my view, it would not be appropriate to include all third par-ties. For such a right would then be inconsistent with the rights of third parties in larger companies, who would continue to have only the members' report as assurance. Totally abandoning the audit requirement in small companies, subject to shareholder approval, is also not the answer, for third parties would not then even receive the minimal assurance afforded by the members' report.

So my suggestions are as follows:

1. A requirement for a minimum paid up share capital before the granting of

limited liability status, and that loans by directors should not be preferential to creditors. Such rules already apply in some European countries, and they could do much here to prevent abuse of limited liability privileges by a small number of unscrupulous companies.

2. A review requirement to determine:
   (a) whether financial statements are arithmetically accurate, agree to underlying records and are produced on the basis of accepted accounting standards, and in accordance with company law;
   (b) whether the accounts are plausible in relation to the known circumstances of the company;
   (c) whether the company appears to be solvent, and likely to remain so for the ensuing period.

3. Minority shareholders to have the right to require a full audit, subject again to safeguards to prevent vexatious requests.

My definition of a review just stated goes beyond what is envisaged by the CCAB in that it includes a review of the company's solvency. The logic of this additional requirement is as follows:

In a conventional audit, a solvency review will be made as part of the 'Going Concern' audit. But it is of prime concern also to all readers of small company accounts. It may be achieved with a great deal less testing than would be necessary in a conventional audit, because it will be sufficient to test only for the overstatement of assets, and for the understatement of liabilities. This can be achieved largely through balance testing – circularisation of debtors and creditors, attendance at stocktaking, direct communication with banks, subsequent payment checks, etc. It is normally the understatement of income and net assets that is difficult to test for in the absence of internal controls, and this would not be required under these proposals. In certain instances, it may still be necessary to rely on management representations (e.g. the absence of contingent liabilities), but readers could be given a large measure of assurance.

These suggestions are both personal and comparatively radical, but I believe they could do much to meet objections on all sides. The small practitioner would continue to have a role to play, and that role would be of much more practical value. The business community and the company's customers would gain greater assurance from these requirements. For these account users are only really concerned with whether the company is likely to stay solvent long enough to pay its debts, and to fulfil its contractual obligations. The minority shareholder also receives the best protection available, because he can demand a complete audit if circumstances allow.

## 18.5 The main issues

In para. 64 of their discussion paper, the CCAB pose questions fundamental to the small company audit issue. And it is appropriate now to provide some answers to these questions.

(a) and (b) *Appropriateness of existing arrangements*
It cannot be appropriate to retain the audit in its current form for all small companies. The existing arrangements are illogical, impractical, inequitable and probably misleading.

(c) *The need for a review*
Some form of review of financial statements is essential to safeguard against the possibility of the total abuse of limited liability status (control against which is, under existing arrangements, in need of strengthening).

(d) *Who can choose a review?*
I do not believe this is the correct question. More appropriately we can ask, 'should a review be mandatory instead of an audit?' I have conducted research which shows that the vast majority of companies would choose to retain the audit requirement were they given the option. So in the vast majority of cases all the problems associated with auditing small companies would remain. These problems only disappear if *no* audit is required (though minority shareholders should have the right to request an audit should one prove to be possible).

## 18.6 The practice overseas

A comparison of the overseas practice in relation to small company audits is not necessarily indicative in that company structure and business and legal encoronments in different countries. But were we to discover that the majority of other countries saw either no, or a limited, requirement for audit in small companies, then it should at least make us wonder whether we might be wrong, rather than everybody else! And the following analysis does in fact show that we are distinctly out of step. It is particularly instructive to note that Australia and New Zealand have dropped the small company audit requirement. Their company law and business systems are, of course, substantially based on those in the UK.

## 18.7 Conclusion

The formulation of Auditing Standards and the development of an associated conceptual base to auditing has crystalised the different levels of accountability applicable in proprietary and public companies. Almost all auditing research has centred around the reporting requirements of listed companies, and it is on this basis that Standards have primarily been devised. I believe that research is necessary into the specific requirements of proprietory companies, and that specific Standards should be devised accordingly. The American 'compilation', 'review' and audit options may provide a starting point in this regard.

Any proposal for reform in this area will give rise to many detailed problems of implementation. But it is important that the discussion should primarily centre

Fig. 18.2 Small companies: audit practice overseas

# Overseas Audit Requirements

*Germany*

Audit mandatory for Public Companies (AG), but no audit requirement for Private Companies (GmbH) unless they deal in banking or insurance, or exceed two of the following three criteria:
1. Balance Sheet total in excess of DM 125 million.
2. Turnover in excess of DM 250 million.
3. Number of employees in excess of 5,000.

*France*

Audit mandatory for Public Companies (SA), but not for Private Companies (SARL) unless their capital exceeds FF 300,000.

*Holland*

Audit mandatory for Public Companies (NV), but not for Private Companies (BV), unless they are banking or insurance companies, or have an issued capital exceeding 500,000 guilders.

*Switzerland, Sweden, Denmark and Belgium*

Audit mandatory for all limited companies.

*Australia*

Exempt 'Proprietary' companies do not require an audit, if all members agree.

*Canada*

Private or 'Closely Held' companies do not require an audit.

*New Zealand*

Private Companies do not require an audit if shareholders so agree.

*USA*

A statutory audit or examination of accounts is not generally required for non-public entities (i.e. anything other than a listed company). The AICPA has, however, laid down very specific standards for the 'Compilation and Review of Financial Statements' of non-public entities (statement issued December 1978). No report on the unaudited financial statements of such an entity may be issued unless the provisions of this statement have been complied with. Here the distinction between an audit, a 'compilation' and a 'review' is very clearly defined, and every effort has been made to ensure that no confusion arises in the minds of users. The statement could be very useful in formulating similar provisions for the UK.

It should be noted that while there is no statutory requirement for a review in the USA, most companies voluntarily choose to have an audit or a 'review', primarily for the benefit of providers of finance.

around the requirements rather than around the detail. That the current audit requirements are long overdue for change, it would seem to me there can be no doubt.

In Spring 1980 the ICAEW responded to the Government's Green Paper concerning the abandonment of the audit requirement, with a qualified 'no'. Their decision was based on the lack of pressure for change by small companies themselves and by a vote of roughly half the members (who bothered to register an opinion) against change. The report to government noted that the decision may have to be reviewed within the next few years in the light of continuing professional developments.

The 1981 Companies Act retains the audit requirement for small companies (though it reduces the disclosure requirements). So it would seem that the status quo is to be preserved for the time being.

In March 1981 the UK Government published a consultative document entitled 'A New Form of Incorporation for Small Firms'. This work was based on a memorandum by Professor Laurence Gower, a recognised authority on company law. The motivation behind this document was the wish to eliminate unnecessary legal formalities for small family businesses, where many requirements of company law are superfluous because 'of the close relationship between the members, or because the limited liability for which disclosure is required is circumscribed in practice as creditors obtain personal guarantees from the directors' (extract from the report).

A memorandum from Professor Gower included in the document, questions the appropriateness of the 'present type of audit' for small companies. As an alternative Professor Gower suggests the filing of an accountant's certificate which would declare no more than that 'the company had remained solvent throughout the accounting period'. Companies taking advantage of this (and other simplifying provisions) would need to be incorporated under different rules which would in turn incorporate additional safeguards for creditors such as the director's liability to include his initial capital contribution plus loans. It would appear that the Government is behind this move to produce a simpler regime for small businesses.

Professor Gower's proposals accord very strongly with my own feeling that solvency is the extent to which the public interest in proprietary companies needs to be protected by company law. But Gower has approached the problem as an academic and as a lawyer. Accountants need to consider two additional points:

1. To be able to comment on a company's solvency, accountants will still have to conduct a limited examination of the accounts to determine whether assets do indeed exceed liabilities. And that examination will have to go further than that commonly proposed under the title of 'review' in that assets and liabilities may have to be substantiated. My proposals above cover this issue.
2. Although the public interest requires only the guarantee of solvency, users of small company accounts, such as banks and the Inland Revenue, will almost

certainly continue to demand some assurance from accountants that company accounts are properly prepared. So standards of accountants' involvement with unaudited financial statements must be designed and implemented.

# 19
# The audit of group accounts

## *19.1 Introduction to legislation and professional pronouncements

The Companies Acts require the directors of a holding company to produce consolidated accounts which show a true and fair view of the state of affairs and the results of the company and its subsidiaries so far as they concern the members of the holding company. There are a few exceptions, which I shall remind you of in the Group Accounts check list reproduced in the next section.

SSAP14, entitled Group Accounts, was introduced by the ASC in September 1978, and became mandatory from 1 January 1979. The SSAP does not significantly extend the legal requirements, but deals largely with matters of detail. In this chapter I have departed from my normal practice of covering the detailed accounting requirements by way of the appendices, for with Group Accounts the major part of the audit work will be to ensure that the legal and accounting requirements are complied with. So in sec. 19.2 following, a Standard Accounting Practices check list is reproduced covering Group Accounts (SSAP14) and Associated Companies (SSAP1 as amended). This checklist also contains reference to the legal requirements, so you could usefully check your knowledge of the SSAP and the law, before proceeding to sec. 19.3, which deals with the audit of Group Accounts.

Section 14 CA 1967 requires the auditor of a holding company to report on consolidated accounts. And Sec. 18 CA 1976 provides that subsidiary (or secondary) auditors must supply such information and explanations as the holding company's auditors deem necessary. Section 18 further requires directors to obtain necessary audit information from subsidiaries incorporated overseas. Consideration of the extent to which the holding company's auditors (sometimes known as primary auditors) can rely on the work of secondary auditors will normally be an important part of Group Accounts audit work. This matter is fully dealt with in Auditing Statement 21, which is accordingly reproduced in sec. 19.4 (Fig. 19.3).

# *19.2 Accounting requirements – SSAP 14 and SSAP 1 Check list

## Fig. 19.1(a) Group accounts check list

| | Reference | Yes/No N/A |
|---|---|---|
| If the company has subsidiaries, the financial statements must include group accounts. Group accounts are not required, however, where the company is itself the wholly-owned subsidiary of another company incorporated in Great Britain (but see Section E below for information to be disclosed in the notes to the holding company's financial statements). | 1948 S 150(1), (2)(a) SSAP 14 para 19 | |
| Group accounts should be in the form of a single set of consolidated financial statements that cover the holding company and all its subsidiaries at home and overseas unless one, or more, of the circumstances in steps 1 or 3 apply. | SSAP 14 para 15 1948 S 151 | |

Part 6 is divided into five sections that cover standard and non-standard situations. The sections are as follows:

Section A:  Consolidated financial statements

Section B:  Subsidiaries excluded from consolidation

Section C:  Group accounts other than consolidated financial statements

Section D:  Subsidiaries excluded from group accounts

Section E:  Group accounts not prepared

Only the relevant section(s) of Part 6 should be completed. In any one situation, Section A, or Section C, or Section E will be relevant. Where Section A is relevant, Sections B and/or D may also be relevant. Where Section C is relevant, Section D may also be relevant.

**Section A**

Group accounts in the form of consolidated financial statements must comply with the accounting and the disclosure requirements set out in this section of Part 6.

| | Reference | Yes/No N/A |
|---|---|---|
| 1.  Has a subsidiary been excluded from consolidation only where one of the following applies: | SSAP 14 para 21 | |
| (a)  Its activities are so dissimilar from those of other companies in the group that consolidated financial statements would be misleading? | | ... |
| (b)  The holding company, although owning itself or through other subsidiaries, more than half the equity share capital of the subsidiary, either: | | |
| (i)  Does not own share capital that carries more than half the votes? or | | ... |
| (ii)  Has contractual or other restrictions imposed on its ability to appoint the majority of the board of directors? | | ... |
| (c)  It operates under severe restrictions that significantly impair control by the holding company over the subsidiary's assets and operations for the foreseeable future? | | ... |
| (d)  Control of the subsidiary is intended to be temporary? | | ... |
| 2.  Where consolidated financial statements are prepared that deal with a subsidiary that comes within the scope of the circumstances in step 1, have the directors justified and stated the reasons for reaching the conclusion that the resulting group accounts give a fairer view of the financial position of the group as a whole? | SSAP 14 para 22 | ... |
| 3.  Has a subsidiary been excluded from group accounts only where one of the reasons permitted by 1948 S 150(2)(b) applies? | SSAP 14 para 20 | ... |

*Notes:*

*(a)  The reasons permitted by 1948 S 150(2)(b) are:*

  *(i)  It is impracticable, or would be of no real value to members of the company because of the insignificant amounts involved or would involve expense or delay out of all proportion to the value to the members of the company.*

  *(ii)  The result would be misleading, or harmful to the business of the company or any of its subsidiaries.*

  *(iii)  The business of the holding company and that of the subsidiary are so different that they cannot reasonably be treated as a single undertaking.*

*(b)  Department of Trade approval is necessary for exclusion on the ground that the result would be harmful or on the ground that the businesses differ.*

| | | Reference | Yes/No N/A |
|---|---|---|---|
| 4. | Except where provisions specifically do not apply to consolidated financial statements, do the consolidated financial statements combine the information contained in the separate financial statements of the holding company and the subsidiaries consolidated with such adjustments, if any, that the directors think necessary? | 8 Sch 61 | ... |
| 5. | Do the consolidated financial statements in giving the information required by step 4 comply so far as practicable with the requirements of Schedule 8 and with the other requirements of the Companies Acts 1948 to 1981 as if they were the financial statements of an actual company? | 8 Sch 62 | ... |
| | *Note:* | | |
| | *This requirement does not override any requirements of the Companies Acts 1948 to 1981 that apply specifically to group accounts.* | 8 Sch 64 | |
| 6. | Is there a description of the bases on which subsidiaries have been dealt with in the consolidated financial statements? | SSAP 14 para 15 | ... |
| 7. | When preparing the consolidated financial statements has the holding company used uniform accounting policies? | SSAP 14 para 16 | ... |
| | Where group accounting policies have not been adopted in the financial statements of a subsidiary, have appropriate adjustments been made in the consolidated financial statements? | | ... |
| | Where it is impracticable to make appropriate adjustments and different accounting policies are used: | | |
| | (a)    Are they generally acceptable policies? | | ... |
| | (b)    Is there disclosure of: | | |
| |     (i)    The different policies used? | | ... |
| |     (ii)    An indication of the amounts of the assets and liabilities involved? | | ... |
| |     (iii)    Where practicable, an indication of the effect on results and net assets of the adoption of different policies? | | ... |
| |     (iv)    The reasons for using different policies? | | ... |
| 8. | Wherever practicable for the purposes of consolidated financial statements, have the financial statements of all subsidiaries been prepared: | SSAP 14 para 17 1948 S 153 | |
| | (a)    To the same accounting date as the holding company? | | ... |
| | (b)    For identical accounting periods as the holding company? | | ... |
| 9. | If a subsidiary does not prepare its formal financial statements to the same date as the holding company and if it is not practicable to use for consolidation purposes special financial statements drawn up to the same date as those of the holding company, have appropriate adjustments been made to the consolidated financial statements for any abnormal transactions in the intervening period? | SSAP 14 para 18 | ... |
| | In addition, where the financial year of any subsidiary does not coincide with that of the company, are the following disclosed: | 8 Sch 70 | |
| | (a)    The date on which the year of each such subsidiary ending last before that of the company ended or the earliest and latest of those dates? | | ... |
| | (b)    The reasons why the company's directors consider that the financial year of any such subsidiary should not end with that of the company? | | ... |
| | (c)    The names of the principal subsidiaries that have different year ends? | SSAP 14 para 18 | ... |
| 10. | If special financial statements drawn up to the same date as those of the holding company have been used for consolidation purposes, has the Secretary of State's consent been obtained? | SSAP 14 para 18 1948 S 152(4) (1981 S 2) | ... |
| 11. | Where the accounting period of a principal subsidiary is of a different length from that of the holding company, is the accounting period involved stated? | SSAP 14 para 18 | ... |
| 12. | Where a subsidiary has been purchased, has the purchase consideration been allocated between the underlying net tangible and intangible assets (other than goodwill) on the basis of fair value to the acquiring company? | SSAP 14 para 29 | ... |
| | If this is not done by means of adjusting the values in the books of the acquired company, has it been done on consolidation? | | ... |
| | *Note:* | | |
| | *Any difference between the purchase consideration and the value ascribed to net tangible assets and identifiable intangible assets (e.g. trade marks, patents or development expenditure) will represent premium or discount on acquisition.* | | |

| | | Reference | Yes/No N/A |
|---|---|---|---|

13. In the case of material additions to, or disposals from, the group, do the consolidated financial statements contain sufficient information about the results of the subsidiaries acquired or sold to enable shareholders to appreciate the effect on the consolidated results? — **SSAP 14 para 30** — ...

14. Where there is a material disposal, does the consolidated profit and loss account include: — **SSAP 14 para 31**

   (a) The subsidiary's results up to the date of disposal? — ...

   (b) The gain or loss on the sale of the investment (i.e. the difference at the time of the sale between the proceeds of the sale and the holding company's share of its net assets together with any premium (less any amounts written off) or discount on acquisition)? — ...

15. Has the effective date for both the acquisition and the disposal of a subsidiary been taken as the earlier of either the date on which consideration passes or the date on which an offer becomes or is declared unconditional? — **SSAP 14 para 32** — ...

16. Have outside or minority interests in the share capital and reserves of subsidiaries consolidated been disclosed as a separate amount in the consolidated balance sheet and not shown as part of shareholders' funds? — **SSAP 14 para 34** — ...

   Are debit balances recognised only if there is a binding obligation on minority shareholders to make good losses incurred and they are able to meet this obligation? — ...

17. Have the profits or losses attributable to outside or minority interests been shown separately in the consolidated profit and loss account after arriving at group profit or loss after tax but before extraordinary items? — **SSAP 14 para 35·** — ...

   Have minority interests in extraordinary items been deducted from the related amounts in the consolidated profit and loss account? — ...

18. Is the extent of any significant restrictions on the ability of the holding company to distribute the retained profits of the group (other than those shown as non-distributable) disclosed? — **SSAP 14 para 36** — ...

## Section B

**Where a subsidiary is excluded from consolidation,** the consolidated financial statements must comply with the additional accounting and disclosure requirements set out in this section of Part 6.

19. Where a subsidiary is excluded from consolidation because of dissimilar activities (step 1(a)), do the group accounts include separate financial statements for that subsidiary? — **SSAP 14 para 23** — ...

   Do these separate financial statements include the following:

   (a) A note of the holding company's interest? — ...

   (b) Particulars of intra-group balances? — ...

   (c) The nature of transactions with the rest of the group? — ...

   (d) A reconciliation with the amount included in the consolidated financial statements for the group's investment in the subsidiary (which should be stated under the equity method of accounting)? — ...

   *Note:*

   *Separate financial statements of subsidiaries with similar operations may be combined if appropriate.*

20. Where a subsidiary is excluded from consolidation because of lack of effective control (step 1(b)), is it dealt with in the consolidated financial statements on one of the following bases: — **SSAP 14 para 24**

   (a) Under the equity method of accounting if in all other respects it satisfies the criteria for treatment as an associated company under SSAP 1? — ...

   (b) If the criteria are not met, as an investment at cost or valuation less any provision required? — ...

21. Where a subsidiary is excluded from consolidation because of severe restrictions (step 1(c)), is the amount of the group's investment in the subsidiary stated in the consolidated balance sheet at the amount at which it would have been included under the equity method of accounting at the date the restrictions came into force? — **SSAP 14 para 25** — ...

   Have no further accruals been made for its profits or losses? — ...

   If the amount at which the investment is stated has been impaired by a permanent decline in value of the investment, has provision for the loss been made through the consolidated profit and loss account? — ...

| | Reference | Yes/No N/A |
|---|---|---|
| When determining any necessary provision, were investments considered individually and not in aggregate? | | ... |
| 22. Where a subsidiary is excluded from consolidation because of severe restrictions (step 1(c)), are the following disclosed in the group accounts: | SSAP 14 para 26 | |
|   (a)  Its net assets? | | ... |
|   (b)  Its profits or losses for the period? | | ... |
|   (c)  Any amounts included in the consolidated profit and loss account in respect of: | | |
|     (i)  Dividends received? | | ... |
|     (ii)  Writing down of the investment? | | ... |
| 23. Where a subsidiary is excluded from consolidation because control is intended to be temporary (step 1(d)), is the temporary investment in the subsidiary stated in the consolidated balance sheet as a current asset at the lower of cost and net realisable value? | SSAP 14 para 27 | ... |
| 24. In respect of subsidiaries excluded from consolidation, are the following disclosed in the group accounts: | SSAP 14 para 28 8 Sch 69 | |
|   (a)  The reasons for excluding the subsidiary? | | ... |
|   (b)  The names of the principal subsidiaries excluded? | | ... |
|   (c)  Any premium or discount on acquisition (see step 12) to the extent that it is not written off? | | ... |
|   (d)  A statement of any qualifications in the auditors' report or in any notes to the subsidiary's financial statements for the year ending with or during the year of the company that are material from the point of view of members of the company? | | ... |
|   (e)  The aggregate amount of the total investment in the subsidiaries under the equity method of valuation? | | ... |
|   (f)  If the information required by any one of (a), (d) or (e) above is not obtainable, a statement to that effect? | 8 Sch 69(5) | ... |
| *Note:* | | |
| *The information in (e) is not required where the company is the wholly-owned subsidiary of another company incorporated in Great Britain and a note to the financial statements includes a statement that, in the opinion of the directors, the value of the company's interests in the subsidiaries is not less than the amount at which the interests are stated in the balance sheet.* | 8 Sch 69(4) | |

**Section C**

**Group accounts in a form other than consolidated financial statements** must comply with the disclosure requirements set out in this section of Part 6.

| | Reference | Yes/No N/A |
|---|---|---|
| 25. Where group accounts are not prepared as consolidated financial statements, do they give the same or equivalent information as that required to be given in consolidated financial statements? | 8 Sch 68 | ... |
| 26. Is there a description of the bases on which subsidiaries have been dealt with in the group accounts? | SSAP 14 para 15 | ... |
| 27. Where a group prepares group accounts in a form other than consolidated financial statements in circumstances different from those set out in step 1, have the directors justified and stated the reasons for reaching the conclusion that the resulting group accounts give a fairer view of the financial position of the group as a whole? | SSAP 14 para 22 | ... |

**Section D**

**Where a subsidiary is excluded from group accounts** (as opposed to consolidated financial statements), the group accounts must comply with the additional disclosure requirements set out in this section of Part 6.

| | Reference | Yes/No N/A |
|---|---|---|
| 28. Where a subsidiary has been excluded from group accounts for one of the reasons permitted by 1948 S 150(2)(b) (step 3): | SSAP 14 para 20 | |
|   (a)  Is the reason for the exclusion stated? | | ... |
|   (b)  Do the resulting financial statements give a true and fair view of the position of the group as a whole? | | ... |
| 29. In respect of subsidiaries excluded from group accounts, is the information required by step 24(a), (d), (e) and (f) disclosed? | 8 Sch 69 | ... |

| | Reference | Yes/No N/A |
|---|---|---|

**Section E**

**Where a holding company does not prepare group accounts,** the holding company's financial statements must comply with the disclosure requirements set out in this section of Part 6.

| | | Reference | Yes/No N/A |
|---|---|---|---|
| 30. | Where a holding company does not prepare group accounts, is the information required by step 24(a), (d), (e) and (f) disclosed? | 8 Sch 69 | ... |

## Fig. 19.1(b) Associated companies check list

| | SSAP 1 Para | Yes/No N/A |
|---|---|---|

If a company or group has investments in associated companies (as defined in paragraphs 13-16 of SSAP 1), the financial statements must comply with the accounting and the disclosure requirements set out below.

*(Note: Paragraph 65 of Schedule 8 to the Companies Act 1948 permits the equity method of accounting in consolidated financial statements where the directors consider that a body corporate is so closely associated with the holding company or any subsidiary consolidated as to justify the use of the method in respect of that investment.)*

| | | SSAP 1 Para | Yes/No N/A |
|---|---|---|---|
| 1. | Where the interest of the investing group or company is not effectively that of a partner in a joint venture or consortium and it amounts to 20% or more of the equity voting rights but it is not treated as an associated company, are the accounting treatment adopted and the reasons for adopting this treatment stated? | 38 | ... |

*Note:*

*The standard specifies that "in those cases where disclosure of the reason would be harmful to the business, the directors may omit the information, after consultation with their auditors".*

| | | SSAP 1 Para | Yes/No N/A |
|---|---|---|---|
| 2. | Where the interest of the investing group or company amounts to less than 20% of the equity voting rights but the interest is treated as an associated company, is the basis on which significant influence is exercised stated? | 38 | ... |
| 3. | In respect of each of the principal associated companies, are the following disclosed: | 49 | |
| | (a) Its name? | | ... |
| | (b) The proportion of its issued shares of each class held by the investing group? | | ... |
| | (c) An indication of the nature of its business? | | ... |

**Profit and Loss Account Items**

| | | SSAP 1 Para | Yes/No N/A |
|---|---|---|---|
| 4. | Is income from investments in associated companies brought into account on the following bases: | 18 | |
| | (a) In the investing company's own financial statements — dividends received and receivable? | | ... |
| | (b) In the investing group's consolidated financial statements — its share of profits less losses of associated companies? | | ... |

*Note:*

*These bases need not be applied to those interests in partnerships and non-corporate joint ventures where it is appropriate to account for a proportionate share of individual assets and liabilities as well as profits or losses.*

| | | SSAP 1 Para | Yes/No N/A |
|---|---|---|---|
| 5. | Do the investing group's consolidated financial statements disclose the following: | | |
| | (a) In profit before tax — its share of profits less losses of associated companies? | 19 | ... |
| | (b) In taxation — the tax attributed to its share of profits of associated companies? | 20 | ... |
| | (c) Its share of the aggregate net profits less losses retained by associated companies? | 22 | ... |
| 6. | Do extraordinary items in the consolidated profit and loss account include the investing group's share of the aggregate extraordinary items of associated companies (unless this amount would not be classified as extraordinary in the context of the investing group)? | 21 | ... |

| | SSAP 1 Para | Yes/No N/A |
|---|---|---|
| Where material, is the amount included separately disclosed? | | ... |
| 7. Do items such as turnover and depreciation exclude the investing group's share of the associated companies' turnover and depreciation? | 23 | ... |
| 8. If the results of one or more associated companies are very material in the context of the investing group, is there separate disclosure of items such as total turnover, total depreciation charges and total profits less losses before taxation of the associated companies concerned? | 23 | ... |

*Note:*

*When judging materiality, regard should also be had to the scale of the associated companies' operations in relation to those of the investing group.*

| | SSAP 1 Para | Yes/No N/A |
|---|---|---|
| 9. Except where it is a wholly-owned subsidiary, has an investing company that does not prepare consolidated financial statements shown the information required either by preparing a separate profit and loss account, or by adding the information in supplementary form to its own profit and loss account in such a way that its share of the profits of the associated companies is not treated as realised for the purposes of the Companies Acts 1948 to 1981? | 24 | ... |

**Balance Sheet Items**

| | SSAP 1 Para | Yes/No N/A |
|---|---|---|
| 10. Is the interest in associated companies shown on the following bases: | | |
| (a) In the investing company's own financial statements — either at a valuation or at cost less amounts written off? | 25 | ... |
| (b) In the investing group's consolidated financial statements — at the total of: | 26 | |
| (i) Its share of the net assets other than goodwill of the associated companies stated, where possible, after attributing fair values to the net assets at the time each interest was acquired? | | ... |
| (ii) Its share of any goodwill in the associated companies' own financial statements? | | ... |
| (iii) The premium paid, or discount, on the acquisition of the interest (to the extent that it has not been written off)? | | ... |

*Note:*

*Item (i) must be disclosed separately, but items (ii) and (iii) may be combined.*

| | SSAP 1 Para | Yes/No N/A |
|---|---|---|
| 11. Do the consolidated financial statements disclose the following: | | |
| (a) The total of loans to associated companies from the group? | 27 | ... |
| (b) The total of loans from associated companies to the group? | 28 | ... |
| (c) The investing group's share of the post-acquisition accumulated reserves of the associated companies and any movements on those reserves (including amounts that have not passed through the profit and loss account)? | 31 | ... |
| (d) Where applicable, the fact that the accumulated reserves of overseas associated companies would be subject to further tax on distribution? | 31 | ... |
| (e) The extent of any significant restrictions on the ability of an associated company to distribute its retained profits (other than those shown as non-distributable)? | 40 | ... |
| 12. Are trading balances between the investing group and the associated companies included under either current assets or current liabilities (and separately disclosed if material)? | 29 | ... |
| 13. If the interests in associated companies are very material in the context of the group, is more detailed information given about the associated companies' tangible assets, intangible assets and liabilities? | 30 | ... |

*Note:*

*See Note to step 8.*

| | SSAP 1 Para | Yes/No N/A |
|---|---|---|
| 14. Where there has been a permanent impairment in the value of items (ii) and (iii) in step 10(b), have they been written down and is the amount written off in the period separately disclosed? | 32 | ... |
| **15. Where an associated company has a deficiency of net assets but is still regarded as a long-term investment and is supported in some way by its shareholders, is the investing group's share of the deficiency of net assets reflected in the consolidated financial statements?** | 33 | ... |

| | SSAP 1 Para | Yes/No N/A |
|---|---|---|
| 16. Where an investment is made in an unincorporated entity and a liability could arise in excess of that resulting from taking account only of the investing group's share of net assets (for example, as a result of joint and several liability in a partnership), has the investing group considered whether it would be prudent either to include an additional provision or to recognise a contingent liability for this excess? | 34 | ... |
| 17. Except where it is a wholly-owned subsidiary, has an investing company that does not prepare consolidated financial statements shown the information required either by preparing a separate balance sheet or by adding the information in supplementary form to its own balance sheet? | 35 | ... |

**Other Matters**

| | | |
|---|---|---|
| 18. Do the associated companies prepare their financial statements either to the same date as, or to a date that is not more than six months before, or shortly after, the date of the investing group's financial statements? | 36 | ... |
| 19. If financial statements not coterminous with those of the investing group are used and the effect is material, are the facts and the dates of the year ends disclosed? | 37 | ... |
| 20. If the investing group has used financial statements already issued by the associated company, has it ensured that later information has not materially affected the view shown by those financial statements? | 37 | ... |
| *Note:* | | |
| *If the associated company is listed on a recognised stock exchange, only published financial information should be disclosed.* | 36 | |
| 21. Where the effect is material, has the investing group made 'consolidation adjustments' to exclude such items as unrealised profits on stocks transferred to or from associated companies and to achieve reasonable consistency with group accounting policies? | 39 | ... |
| 22. Where an associated company has subsidiary or associated companies, is the investing group's share of the results and net assets based on the group financial statements of the associated company? | 42 | ... |
| 23. Where the investment in an associated company is held by a subsidiary in which there are minority interests, do the minority interests in the investing group's consolidated financial statements include the minority share of the subsidiary's interest in the results and net assets of its associated companies? | 41 | ... |
| 24. Has the effective date for both the acquisition and the disposal of an interest, or part interest, in an associated company been taken as the earlier of either the date on which consideration passes or the date on which an offer becomes unconditional? | 44 | ... |
| 25. When an investment in a company ceases to fall within the definition of an associated company, is it stated in the consolidated balance sheet at the carrying amount under the equity method at that date? | 43 | ... |
| *Note:* | | |
| *The carrying amount should be adjusted if dividends are subsequently received out of profits earned prior to the change of status or if there is any impairment in value.* | | |

**Treatment of Associated Companies in Current Cost Accounts**

| | | |
|---|---|---|
| 26. Where the associated companies do not prepare current cost accounts and the investing group includes current cost information based on directors' best estimates, is this fact disclosed? | 48 | ... |
| 27. Does the investing group's current cost consolidated profit and loss account include its share of profits less losses of associated companies (after interest and the associated companies' gearing adjustments but before tax) on a current cost basis? | 46 | ... |
| 28. Has the investing group's gearing adjustment been calculated by applying its gearing ratio to its current cost adjustments which should include its share of the associated companies' current cost adjustments (including gearing)? | 47 | ... |
| 29. Are investments in associated companies shown in the current cost consolidated balance sheet on the basis set out in step 10(b), but with net assets (except goodwill) on a current cost basis? | 45 | ... |
| *Note:* | | |
| *The figures for goodwill and premium or discount on acquisition should be the same as in the historical-cost balance sheet provided that fair values were attributed to the other assets at the date of acquisition of each interest.* | | |

## *19.3  Audit of group accounts

The audit of group accounts can be split into three sections:
1. Obtaining and confirming information about subsidiaries.
2. Checking consolidation working papers.
3. Reviewing the work of secondary auditors.

### 1. *Information about subsidiaries*

The audit procedures set out in the following programme should be completed before commencing work on the consolidation itself.

Fig. 19.2  Information about subsidiaries

*The purpose of the auditing procedures set out in this programme is to obtain reasonable assurance that INVESTMENTS IN SUBSIDIARIES AND BALANCES DUE BY/TO GROUP COMPANIES are not materially mis-stated.*

#### Investments in subsidiaries

1. Obtain or prepare schedules of investments in subsidiaries showing for each company:
   (A) Number of shares or debentures held at the beginning of the year and their book value.
   (B) Additions and disposals during the year, noting the dates.
   (C) Number of shares or debentures held at the end of the year and their book value.
   (D) Percentage of share capital in issue held at beginning and end of year.
   (E) Country of incorporation and registration.
   (F) For companies carried at valuation show original cost and date and basis of valuation.
2. Verify additions and disposals during the year with agreements, board minutes, etc.
3. Check the accounting treatment of profits or losses on disposals during the year.
4. Confirm at the year-end, the existence and ownership of all investments. Do this either:
   (A) By inspecting the documents of title, or
   (B) By obtaining confirmation from independent third parties.
5. Review the value at which each subsidiary is carried in the accounts by reference to their net assets, and ensure that provision is made for any diminution in value.
6. Check that all income which relates to the investments has been included in the investment income account in the general ledger. Do this by referring to the accounts of the relevant companies.

#### Balances due to/due by subsidiaries, fellow subsidiaries and the holding company

7. Obtain or prepare a working paper of the balances with other group companies at the year-end.
8. If balances with group companies have not been agreed by the companies themselves in writing, obtain independent confirmation of the balances from the auditors of the companies. Investigate all material differences revealed and ensure correct treatment in the accounts.
9. Where any of the above companies do not have the same balance sheet date as this company, agree the balance at both dates. Review with the auditors of the other company any transactions between the two balance sheet dates (paying

particular attention to cash movements and administration charges) to ensure that these transactions are fairly presented after the accounts of the companies have been consolidated into the group's accounts.
10. Review transactions with other group companies for a period before and after the year-end to ensure that there is consistency of cut-off and accounting treatment.
11. Ensure that adequate provision has been made against group indebtedness where necessary.

2. *Checking consolidation working papers*

Particular attention must be paid to the calculation of:
(a) goodwill or reserves arising on acquisitions during the year;
(b) pre-acquisition and post-acquisition profits;
(c) minority interests;
(d) adjustments for inter-company profit in stock;
(e) agreements of inter-company indebtedness;
(f) cancellations in respect of inter-company cash in transit;
(g) adjustments for inter-company cash in transit;
(h) turnover, excluding inter-group trading;
(i) adjustments in respect of group companies with different accounting period ends;
(j) taxation, including any claims for group relief.
    The consolidated accounts must of course comply with all relevant accounting and legal requirements, so the normal checklists can be used.

3. *Reviewing the work of secondary auditors*

The primary auditor is solely responsible for the holding company accounts. Regretfully, reports still appear which state that the accounts of certain subsidiaries were examined by other auditors. This may be so, but the fact certainly should not be stated in the auditor's report, for it could give the impression that the primary auditors do not take responsibility for the effect of these subsidiaries on the group. Whereas in fact they cannot escape such responsibility.
    The procedures for reviewing the work of secondary auditors are in many ways akin to those used in assessing the work of internal auditors. This matter is discussed in Auditing Statement U21, which is reproduced in full in Fig. 19.3.

# *19.4  Reliance on other auditors – U21

Fig. 19.3  U21. Group accounts – reliance on other auditors

## U21.  Group accounts – reliance on other auditors

### Part 1 – introduction

*Subsidiary companies*

    2. Sections 150 to 152 of the Companies Act 1948 provide that where at the

end of its financial year a company has subsidiaries, group or consolidated accounts shall be laid before the company in general meeting, and that such group accounts shall give a true and fair view of the state of affairs and profit or loss of the company and its subsidiaries dealt with thereby as a whole, so far as concerns members of the company.

*Associated companies*

3. Statement of Standard Accounting Practice No. 1 ACCOUNTING FOR THE RESULTS OF ASSOCIATED COMPANIES M1 requires the investing group or company, except in certain circumstances, to incorporate in its accounts its share of the profits less losses of its associated companies.

*Company partnerships and joint ventures*

4. Where a company acts as a member of a partnership or joint venture the relevant figures of its interests in such consortium activities will normally be included in the accounts of the company itself.

*Duties of directors*

5. The directors of a primary company have a duty to produce group accounts which show a true and fair view, and consequently they need to satisfy themselves that amounts taken from the accounts of other group companies and interests are sufficiently reliable to be properly incorporated into the group accounts.

*Duties of auditors*

6. Section 14 of the Companies Act 1967 provides that in the case of a holding company submitting group accounts its auditors ('the primary auditors') shall expressly state whether, in their opinion, the group accounts have been properly prepared in accordance with the provisions of the Companies Acts 1948 and 1967 and whether they give a true and fair view of the state of affairs and profit or loss of the company and its subsidiaries dealt with thereby, so far as concerns members of the company. This opinion is wholly their responsibility. They are not relieved of this responsibility where group accounts contain amounts, which may be material, relating to other companies of which they are not the auditors, nor is the responsibility discharged by an uninformed acceptance of the accounts of those other companies, even if they have been independently audited. Whilst they are entitled to take account of the extent of the work and the report of other auditors, nevertheless they should conduct such further enquiries as they consider necessary in order to satisfy themselves that, with the inclusion of figures which they themselves have not audited, the group accounts disclose a true and fair view.

7. The principles set out in paragraphs 5 and 6 above apply whether the results to be incorporated are those of subsidiary, associated or consortium companies. The principal matters on which the primary auditors need to be satisfied before relying on accounts not audited by them are set out in Part 2 hereof, and the need to consult with other auditors is considered in Part 3.

# Part 2 – the primary auditors' responsibilities

8. As the primary auditors have the sole responsibility for the opinion expressed in the auditors' report on the group accounts, amongst the principal matters which they need to examine before relying on accounts not audited by them are:
   (a) accounting policies
   (b) availability of information
   (c) scope of work of the secondary auditors
   (d) the materiality of the amounts involved.
   These matters are discussed in the following paragraphs.

*Accounting policies*

9. The primary auditors should discuss with the primary company's directors, or other responsible officials, the accounting policies and arrangements in force throughout the group in order to ensure that these are in their opinion appropriate to and consistent with the proper preparation of the group accounts. In many cases the directors will have adopted accounting policies on a uniform basis throughout the group. This will help the primary auditors in assessing whether the accounts present a true and fair view of the group as a whole.

10. In certain exceptional cases it may not be possible or desirable for the directors of a primary company to require their accounting policies to be adopted in the accounts of other group companies as these are normally the responsibility of their directors, who in many cases will have to consider the interests of minority shareholders. Moreover local legislation may require the adoption of accounting policies different from those of the primary company. In such circumstances the primary auditors should check that the directors of the primary company have obtained from the other group companies such information as is necessary to enable them to make the appropriate adjustments. Where it is necessary to incorporate in the group accounts figures based on different accounting policies for a material section of the group, the primary auditors should ensure that those policies are fully explained in the group accounts.

*Availability of information*

11. The directors of a holding company should be able to exercise sufficient control over, and to secure sufficient information from its subsidiaries to satisfy themselves that the group accounts give a true and fair view and disclose all the information required by statute and other appropriate regulations.

12. In the case of associated companies, the control by the directors of the investing company may be less complete than in the case of subsidiaries; nevertheless it follows from the definition of 'associated company' that the directors of the investing company will normally be in a position to ensure that the necessary financial and accounting information is made available to the primary auditors. In the case of associated companies which are listed on a recognised stock exchange, only published financial information should be used for incorporation in the accounts of the investing company.

13. The primary auditors have the responsibility for verifying that the directors

of the primary company have taken the necessary steps to provide the information discussed in paragraphs 11 and 12 above. If the primary auditors find that the directors of the primary company lack information about the accounting policies, items for disclosure, or consolidation adjustments relating to the accounts of other group companies they must ask for the omission to be made good. It may also be necessary to seek permission to obtain the additional information direct from the other companies or from their auditors. It is important for the primary auditors to discuss these requirements at an early date with the directors of the primary company.

*Scope of the work of the secondary auditors*

14. Before the primary auditors form their opinion on the group accounts, they need to determine whether in their opinion the underlying accounts are acceptance for the purpose of incorporation in the group accounts. In arriving at this opinion, the primary auditors will need to consider at least the following matters:
    (a) have all the material aspects of the underlying accounts been subject to an audit examination? If so,
    (b) are they, as primary auditors, aware of any reasons why they should not rely on the work and reports of the secondary auditors?

15. The answer to paragraph 14(b) will depend on:
    (a) what is the primary auditors' knowledge of the standard of work of the secondary auditors?
    (b) what auditing 'standards' govern the work of the secondary auditors?
    (c) what are the auditing requirements in the country in which the secondary auditors work?
    (d) who appointed the secondary auditors and to whom do they report?
    (e) has any limitation been placed on the work of the secondary auditors, or are they free to decide the scope and levels of their audit tests?
    (f) are the secondary auditors independent in all respects?
    (g) is the nature and extent of the secondary auditors' examination adequate and reasonable *in the judgement of the primary auditors* to provide a sound basis on which the primary auditors can form their opinion?

16. Before drafting their report, the primary auditors will also need to consider:
    (a) whether the 'secondary auditors' reports contain any qualifications which should be incorporated in the primary auditors' report; and
    (b) whether any answers to the above questions require the primary auditors to qualify their report.

17. It follows from the considerations set out in paragraphs 14 to 16 above, that in all cases the secondary auditors should appreciate that the accounts of the company which they are auditing will ultimately be an ingredient of the group accounts and that they should therefore be prepared to co-operate with the primary auditors and make available to them such information as they may require in order properly to discharge their duties as auditors of the group accounts.

*Materiality*

18. In deciding how extensive their enquiries ought to be, and therefore in selecting the type of audit procedures required, the primary auditors will need to consider the materiality of the amounts involved in so far as

concerns the members of the primary company. (See Council Statement
V10 THE INTERPRETATION OF 'MATERIAL' IN RELATION TO ACCOUNTS.) The
primary auditors may only need to review in detail each year those
secondary companies which are judged to be material.

## Part 3 – consultations with other auditors

19. In all material cases the primary auditors will need to consult the auditors of
other group companies so that they may be familiar with the auditing
procedures and standards applied by the auditors of the other subsidiary
and associated companies (the secondary auditors). However, they should not
contact the secondary auditors until they have received proper authority by
means of arrangements made through the respective boards. In conducting
these consultations the primary auditors would normally use one or more of
the following procedures:
   (a) requests for written explanations of the secondary auditors' procedures
   and findings, and of the secondary company's accounting policies,
   supplemented as necessary by:
   (b) oral explanations;
   (c) examination of audit files, working papers and any relevant management
   letters.

20. In practice it is often found convenient to use audit questionnaires for
completion by the secondary auditors. Care should be exercised in using such
questionnaires, which may not be particularly helpful unless they are:
   (a) suitably compiled with the specific circumstances of the group in mind
   (including the degree of control exercised over the subsidiary and
   associated companies);
   (b) discussed in advance with the secondary auditors;
   (c) properly completed.

21. If the primary auditors are not satisfied as a result of the above review, or if
they need to obtain independent confirmation of additional accounting
information required specifically for the group accounts, they should arrange
for additional audit tests to be conducted, either directly by the secondary
auditors on their behalf, or conjointly with them. Only in exceptional
circumstances are primary auditors likely to need to conduct their own tests
independently of the secondary auditors. It should be borne in mind that the
secondary auditors are fully responsible for the standard of their own work
and reports on the subsidiary or associated companies' accounts, and that
the additional tests discussed above are those required solely for the audit of
the group accounts.

22. It follows from the above considerations that it is important, in order that
the secondary auditors may be aware in advance of the primary auditors'
requirements, to arrange for consultations to take place when the secondary
auditors are planning their audits and not to defer such consultations until
the audits have been completed. Such a procedure is especially necessary
where overseas firms of auditors are involved. Among the benefits which may
arise from such advance consultations are:
   (a) that the secondary auditors may be advised as to the standard of audit
   required to enable their work to be relied on in the preparation and
   audit of the group accounts; and
   (b) that the secondary auditors will be encouraged to discuss any proposed
   qualifications in their own reports with the primary auditors.

## Part 4 – other considerations

*Reference to other auditors*

23. The primary auditors are fully responsible for their opinion on the group accounts and need not for this reason refer in their report to the fact that the accounts of some subsidiary or associated companies have been audited by other firms. Such a reference may be misleading as it may be taken to imply a limitation of the scope of the primary auditors' opinion. This in no way takes away from the secondary auditors their responsibility for the audit of their client companies' accounts.

24. It is considered, however, that the shareholders of the primary company are entitled to know that the accounts of some of the companies in the group have been audited by other auditors and the materiality of those companies to the group, and accordingly that appropriate information should be disclosed. A suitable way in which this information may be included is to state in the schedule of principal subsidiary and associated companies (or in the directors' report or in the notes to the accounts), which of those companies have been audited by the other auditors. It is desirable to indicate the significance to the group of the companies that have been so audited by reference to the amount of their assets, sales or profits or losses before tax.

*The absence of an audit*

25. The fact that the accounts of a subsidiary or associated company are not subject to regular audit, for example, because it is situated in a country in which there are no requirements for audit, does not alter the duty of the directors of the primary company to prepare accounts which disclose a true and fair view. If the amounts involved may be material (see paragraph 18 above) the primary auditors should request the directors of the primary company to arrange for an audit to be carried out, otherwise it may be impossible for them to report that the group accounts disclose a true and fair view.

*Branches*

26. In the case of branches, it may be necessary for the primary auditors to arrange for audit work to be carried out by local auditors. Such auditors act on behalf of the primary auditors, who must take full responsibility for the work of the local auditors. The primary auditors should ensure that the specified procedures have been properly carried out by the local auditors.

## *19.5 Audit reports on group accounts

The information that some subsidiaries were audited by other firms should not be mentioned in the auditor's report, but should be contained in the list of principal subsidiaries contained in the financial statements themselves.

Provided that in the auditor's opinion the group's financial statements show a true and fair view and comply with the Companies Acts, the auditor will be able to issue an unqualified audit report along the lines of Example 2 in the Audit Report Guidelines of the APC (see p. 303). However, qualifications will be necessary in the following circumstances:

1. Qualifications in any of the subsidiary companies, if that subsidiary is material to the group. If the subsidiary's qualification is only in respect of specific items, then no reference need be made in the holding company report, unless those specific items are material to the group.
2. Primary auditors are unable to obtain satisfactory information with regard to material subsidiaries, or material amounts are consolidated from unaudited accounts. This will necessitate a 'subject to' report.
3. Material disagreement by the auditors with any of the consolidation calculations could result in a 'disclaimer' or 'except' report.
4. Non-compliance with legal or professional requirements for disclosure (CA 1967 or SSAP14).
5. Any matter which could lead to qualification in the accounts of companies without subsidiaries would normally also require a qualification in the accounts of a group.

## 20

# The audit of computerised accounting systems

## 20.1 Introduction

Auditing has become a very specialised area of the professional accountant's work. And computer auditing is a further specialisation in itself. Indeed, many of the large firms now have computer auditing specialists for different types of computer. And these specialists will be called in to assist the normal audit team, whenever the latter feels that the complexity of the systems has exceeded their level of competence.

But computers of the 'mini' variety, with most of the attributes of their larger 'main frame' relations, have now become so cheap (less than an accountant's annual salary – though it is often not realised that the software packages and organisational backup can often cost several times this amount) that they are within the range of almost any business. And they will become, in real terms, even cheaper. So no audit firm, no matter how small, can afford to ignore the existence of computers any longer. It is true that the purpose of the audit is in no way altered – to report to the members whether, in the auditor's opinion, the accounts show a true and fair view. . . . But the ways in which the auditor will arrive at his opinion, *can* (though not necessarily *will*) be considerably different.

It behoves all qualified accountants to have sufficient a working knowledge of computers, and computer auditing, to determine the effect of the computer on their work; and to determine when their level of competence has been exceeded. We cannot all be computer audit experts; just as we are not all taxation experts. But we should all know the principles that are involved, be able to give advice in the more simple situations, and know when and where to call for help. To provide this knowledge is the purpose of this chapter . . . as well as to enable you to pass examinations.

Most of you will have studied the workings of computers either at Foundation Level, or as a subject in its own right (which indeed it is). For this reason and through sheer pressure on space, I have assumed a basic knowledge of procedures and controls, and have concentrated on the application of these to auditing. Sufficient detail is included for the purposes indicated in the previous paragraphs. But for those of you who would like to study the subject in greater depth, I have included at the end of the chapter a bibliography of those relevant books which I have found to be the most useful.

## 20.2 The effect of computers on audit work

I emphasise again, that the computer does not affect the auditor's primary responsibility of reporting on the accounts. But it may affect the ways in which he carries out his tests. If the computer is used as little more than a glorified accounting machine, it may still be possible to carry out conventional substantive testing by reference to suitable 'hard copy' – to audit 'around the computer'. But without reference to the internal control over computer operations it will not be possible to limit the volume of substantive testing. And without this limitation the audit of large volume transactions will be very costly and time consuming indeed.

Even disregarding considerations of speed and economy, the auditor will often be obliged to involve himself in the evaluation of computer systems because many of these will occasion, to some degree, a 'loss of audit trail', i.e. it will not be possible to trace a transaction through from its initiation to conclusion by reference to visual records. Such a loss can occur through a wide variety of reasons (discussed later), but the most usual is a heavy reliance on 'management by exception'. For example, management may no longer require a complete print-out of sales ledger balances; simply an exception report showing those balances which are overdue, or in excess of their credit limit. But whatever the reason for the 'loss of audit trail', it will then usually no longer be possible to treat the computer as a 'black box', and to 'audit around' it. Instead, 'through the computer' audit techniques (test packs and computer audit programs) will have to be used, and this will necessarily involve a degree of expertise in computers, and computer systems.

*The auditor's work on a computerised system will be affected by the following factors:*

### 1. Complexity

Normal manual accounting systems evolve on an ad hoc basis over a considerable period of time and, in the majority of cases, can be changed relatively easily and quickly. On the other hand, computerised accounting systems are:
(a) planned and implemented over a considerable period;
(b) often costly and difficult to change after they are operational (although with the new generation of equipment this is becoming less the case);
(c) often operated by people who do not have an accounting background, and are not, therefore, familiar with accounting controls.

This means that the auditor should specify those controls that he considers necessary, well before a system is implemented. Amendments later may be neither economical, nor even feasible. This implies a close involvement at the systems planning stage, in a way which has not hitherto been necessary (though it must be stated that this often does not occur). And it also implies that the auditor must have, or be able to obtain, the necessary expertise for meaningful participation.

### 2. Concentration of records in the computer department

For a computer to be an economical proposition, it is normal to find that a major proportion, if not all, of a client's volume processing will be computerised. This means that records of sales, purchases, cash, wages, etc., will all be handled at some stage by the same personnel. Thus, the all important segregation of responsibilities can break down, unless there is adequate organisational control within the computer department itself. This the auditor will have to have sufficient expertise to determine.

### 3. *Timing of tests – visibility of records*

In computerised accounting systems much of the data is produced and stored on magnetic media (tapes and discs). Once hard copy of the data has been produced (and even sometimes when it is not) it is normal to retain data on magnetic media for only a limited time. The auditor will require access to data in magnetic form for testing 'through the computer'. Therefore, it will be necessary to alert the client to this requirement some months before the audit attendance, to ensure that data is retained in suitable form. For some tests, hard copy may be required. In this case, it will be necessary to advise the client of those print-outs which are needed in addition to those normally produced (though the auditor cannot reasonably request a large volume of extra print-outs, unless internal control is weak – see p. 392), and those that should be retained rather than destroyed. The lack of complete visible records means that *the auditor must pay much more attention to planning his tests in advance.* The necessary planning can of course be a useful discipline, but it does bring the disadvantage of directing the attention of the client's employees to those areas to be tested. Suitable means of overcoming this problem must be devised to suit the circumstances of each audit.

### 4. *Effect on internal control*

(a) The client's management will perform less checks on the documents which support a transaction. For example, calculations and casts are performed once only – by the computer program. Accordingly, to compensate for this, alternative controls must be available. The most important alternative controls are those over initial testing of the program, controls over subsequent amendment and the use of validation checks within the program to ensure that calculated and processed results fall within acceptable limits.

(b) The authorisation function (such as the decision whether or not to accept a particular sales order) may appear to be built into the computer program. In fact, of course, it is given to those persons who wrote the program, as well as to those who set up the data in the master files which the computer uses to accept or reject the data (for example, a credit limit on a customer account could be used as a basis of accepting a customer order). Hence the control over program development and master file set-up assumes a vital importance.

(c) The use of a computer introduces into the accounting system those personnel who are required to design, program and maintain the systems, and also those personnel who are needed to run the computer and handle the data. And this all adds extra potential for fraud, and consequently requires the design of suitable extra controls.

### The effect of real time data processing

As computerised systems become more complex, so does the work of the computer auditor become more sophisticated. On line, real time data processing with multiprogramming capabilities, (i.e. the input of transaction data at the time the transaction takes place, into a computer, capable of dealing with many programs simultaneously) once rare, are now commonplace. For example, many airlines have remote computer terminals with visual display units (VDUs) at passenger 'check points' with direct access into the central computer for purposes of booking, registration and fare payment. Many banks and building societies also make extensive use of real time processing. And many industrial and commercial accounting systems employ remote terminals for the input of cost details and sales. The use of real time applications in small businesses is also growing.

The main body of this chapter will concentrate on the conventional 'batch processing', but the additional control requirements of 'real time' data processing will be dealt with in sec. 20.11.

### The effect of mini- and micro-computers

Perhaps the biggest danger of all lies in the small computers. The new generation of 'mini-computers' are computers in every sense of the word. But they are as small as a desk, do not require strict environmental control and are cheap. They can sit in the corner of an office, and can perform all those functions of a small business hitherto carried out by several clerks. They are designed with simple programs which are flexible in use, and easy to operate. Access for input is usually simple in the extreme, via a key-board terminal, and the output is immediately seen on a VDU. All of this means that the mini-computer is often seen by management just as a better type of accounting machine, such as they might previously have used. And they accordingly do not realise the need for computer type controls. As a result the machine is often accessible to everyone in the office, with each person using it as required. The potential for fraud in these circumstances is vast, the danger from computer failure immense and the risk of data loss (such as a lost sales ledger file with no back-up, or a lost master file), potentially disastrous. I emphasise that administration, systems development and procedural controls are every bit as important in a mini-computer installation as with its main frame brother. And if such controls are not introduced and maintained, the auditor would be forced to conclude that proper accounting records, as defined by the 1976 Companies Act, are not being kept, and would be obliged to report to this effect.

## 20.3 Advantages of a computer for audit purposes

However, the computer can *assist* the auditor as well as providing him with problems.

1. Computers allow the keeping of much *more detailed records*; for example, on

stock movements and values, and the information can be much more up to date and readily retrievable. Such records make for more accurate accounting, improve the management's overall control and assist the auditor in his testing, particularly with analytical review. For example, an analysis of detailed stock movements by location can be of considerable assistance in establishing the fairness of the stock valuation. In the past detailed information such as this has often not been available, or if available, not readily accessible.

2. Computers have a *repetitive ability* in a way that a person does not. So if a computer makes a calculation correctly the first time it will continue to do so, except in the event of an uncontrolled fault (which with new generation equipment is less likely – gone are the days when you had to listen for valves going pop!). This means that the auditor can place reliance on a small volume of compliance testing.

3. Computers have a much greater *mathematical ability* than human beings (even, or perhaps especially, human beings with calculators!), so less testing needs to be performed on arithmetic and casts.

4. The computer can make *regular reconciliations* (e.g. of sales control to sales subsidiary ledger), which may otherwise only be performed intermittently.

5. A normal part of a computer's reporting procedures will be the use of *rejection and exception reports*. Rejection reports will indicate the reasons why the computer program (via its program controls) has rejected certain input data. Exception reports will indicate any items which are outside pre-determined limits (e.g. a debt which is overdue, or a wage payment beyond £120 a week).

The volume of *rejections* will give the auditor a very good idea of the standard of input documentation, and the fact that incorrect documents are rejected can reduce errors to a minimum, provided of course that the program controls are properly designed.

*Exception reports* are the basis of management by exception. For example, the credit control manager will not have to review the entire sales ledger for overdue amounts. Instead the computer will provide him with a list. Indeed it can go one better than that, by sending out reminder letters, and then suitable threats at the appropriate time. So the credit control manager can concentrate on those accounts which require subjective judgement, as opposed to pre-determined action.

Exception reporting improves control, which is itself of value to the auditor. But the reports themselves will also be useful, particularly for verification work at the year end. For example, a list of overdue sales ledger balances could be produced for the purposes of evaluating the provision for doubtful debts, or a list of slow moving stock could be extracted for the purposes of determining net realisable value.

6. The auditor can himself use *sophisticated techniques* to assist in his audit testing. For example, he may use 'test packs' of artificial data to determine whether the client's program controls are working effectively – compliance testing. Or he may use a computer audit program (note the spelling of program – it is a software program designed for auditing, as opposed to an audit programme

designed for use in a computer audit), either for extracting test data which may otherwise take considerable time to extract by hand, or for the compliance testing of computer controls.

## 20.4 Internal control in a computer-based accounting system

You will already have encountered many of the necessary controls in the context of your computer training, so this area should not be entirely new. But the difficulty I always found, was in remembering them all. So for lectures I developed a chart depicting all the main controls together with their inter-relationship. This chart is reproduced in Fig. 20.1 as an *aide memoire*. And there are also diagrams to remind you of the components of a computer installation, and of the necessary segregation of duties (Figs. 20.2 to 20.4).

U14, entitled 'Internal Control in a computer-based accounting system', is reproduced in Fig. 20.5. Although written many years ago now, the controls contained therein are still very relevant, and constitute a sound basis for our discussion of evaluation technique in the next section. I have commented on certain matters in U14, where I believe further explanation may be useful.

## 20.5 The audit approach to computer-based accounting systems

Reference should be made to Auditing Guidelines 'Internal controls in computer-based accounting systems' for further evidence on how internal controls may be ascertained, evaluated and tested for compliance. Auditing Guideline 'Computer-assisted audit techniques' explains how the auditor may use the computer in obtaining audit evidence. U15 'The audit of computer-based accounting systems' is replaced by these Guidelines, but aspects are still relevant and are reproduced where appropriate in the text that follows.

The audit procedures are a little complex. So to assist your understanding, a decision tree is shown in Fig. 20.6, indicating the various stages which must be completed. A word of warning on the different timing considerations that are involved in a computer audit is given in Fig. 20.7.

### Basic approach

The basic audit approach does not alter when a company converts its accounting records to EDP methods, and can be summarised as follows:
(a) recording the client's accounting systems and controls;
(b) reviewing the potential in the client's systems for errors, and the concealment of defalcations;
(c) compliance testing;
(d) report to management;
(e) substantive testing.

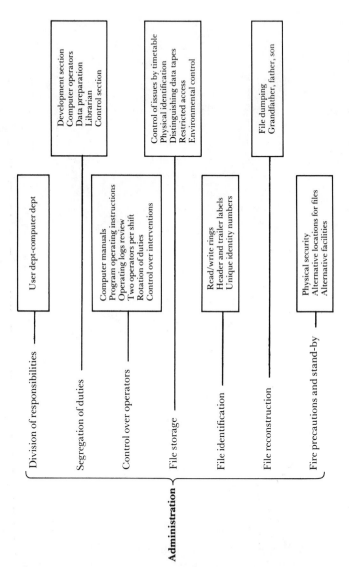

Fig. 20.1 Internal control in a computer-based accounting system

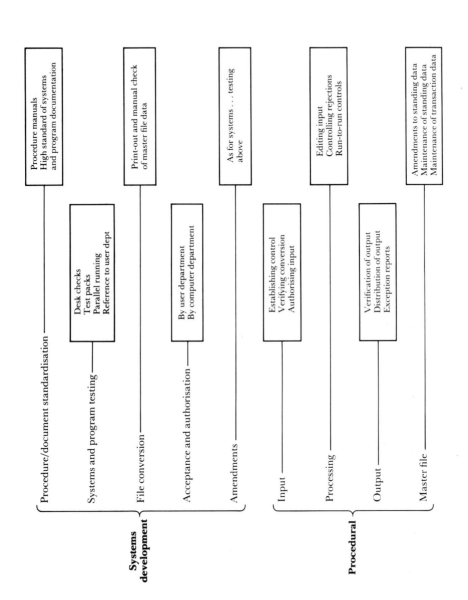

**Systems development**

Procedure/document standardisation —
- Procedure manuals
- High standard of systems and program documentation

Systems and program testing —
- Desk checks
- Test packs
- Parallel running
- Reference to user dept

File conversion —
- Print-out and manual check of master file data

Acceptance and authorisation —
- By user department
- By computer department

Amendments —
- As for systems . . . testing above

**Procedural**

Input —
- Establishing control
- Verifying conversion
- Authorising input

Processing —
- Editing input
- Controlling rejections
- Run-to-run controls

Output —
- Verification of output
- Distribution of output
- Exception reports

Master file —
- Amendments to standing data
- Maintenance of standing data
- Maintenance of transaction data

Fig. 20.2 The workings of a computer

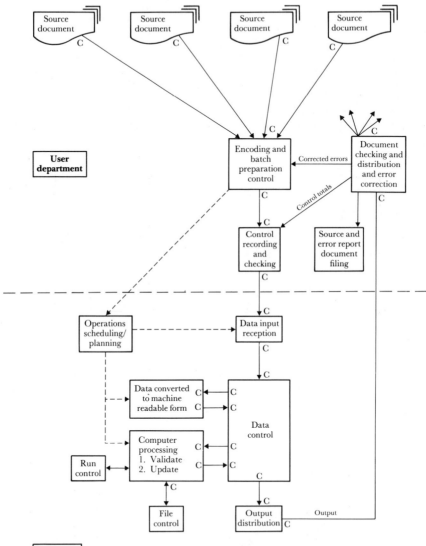

*Data flow in typical batch type computerised data processing system*

Documents arising from transactions in operations
in different sections of user department

C = Control points

*Data flow in typical on-line computerised data processing system*

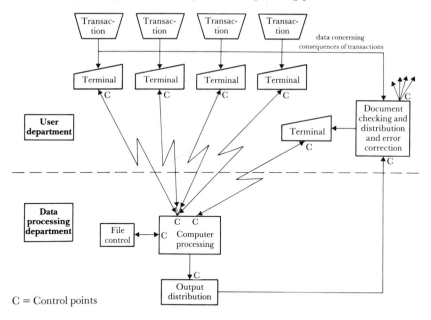

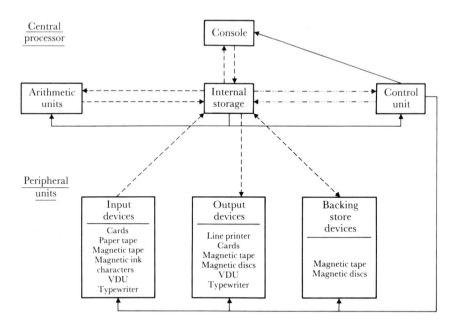

Fig. 20.4  Segregation of duties

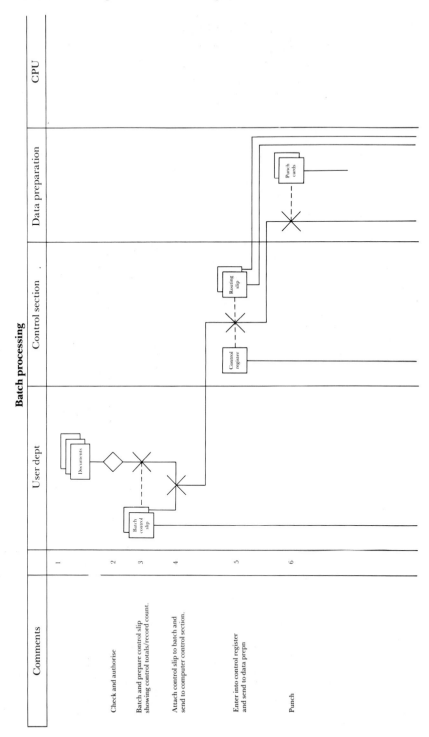

**Batch processing**

| Comments | | User dept | Control section | Data preparation | CPU |
|---|---|---|---|---|---|
| | 1 | Check and authorise | | | |
| Batch and prepare control slip showing control totals/record count. | 2 | | | | |
| Attach control slip to batch and send to computer control section. | 3 | | | | |
| | 4 | | | | |
| Enter into control register and send to data prepn | 5 | | | | |
| Punch | 6 | | | | |

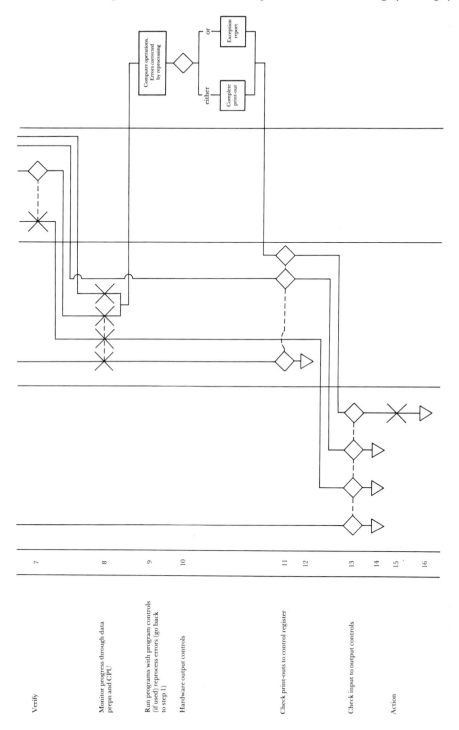

Computer operations. Errors corrected by reprocessing

either

or

Complete print-out

Exception report

7

8    Monitor progress through data prepn and CPU

9    Run programs with program controls (if used) reprocess errors (go back to step 1)

10    Hardware output controls

11

12

13    Check print-outs to control register

14

15

16    Check input to output controls

Verify

Action

Fig. 20.3 Typical organisation structures in a computer department

(a) Minimum

Data processing
manager

Systems analysts
and programmers

Key punch
operators

Machine
operators

(b) Medium/large scale systems

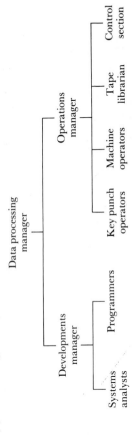

Data processing
manager

Developments
manager

Systems
analysts

Programmers

Operations
manager

Key punch
operators

Machine
operators

Tape
librarian

Control
section

Fig. 20.5 U14. Internal control in a computer-based accounting system (issued
December 1969)

## U14. Internal control in a computer-based accounting system

(Paras. 1 and 2 omitted.)

   3. *Types of internal control in a computer-based system*

   It is usual to distinguish the types of internal control in a computer-based
   system between:
   (a)  administrative controls;
   (b)  systems development controls;
   (c)  procedural controls.

   4. *Administrative controls* are those which are designed to ensure that an
   acceptable standard of discipline and efficiency is maintained over the
   day-to-day running of the computer department. They are usually of more
   importance in computer-based systems than in other accounting systems
   because the system of procedural controls described in paragraph 6 becomes
   increasingly concentrated in the computer department.

   5. *Systems development controls* are those which are designed to ensure a
   satisfactory standard of designing and testing systems and programs, and of
   implementing and documenting them. The complexity of most computer
   systems and the length of time that usually elapses between the original
   outline specification and the final implementation of complex operating
   programs imposes particular importance on systems development controls.
   These controls are necessary to ensure that a computer system operates as
   originally specified and that all the relevant documentation has been
   properly prepared and properly maintained. The same controls should also
   be applied to all changes made to operational systems and programs.

   6. *Procedural controls* are the controls exercised over each separate computer
   application; different techniques will be appropriate for different
   applications. Their purpose is to ensure that the whole of the original data
   relevant to any application is completely and accurately processed from the
   point of origin to the final output, whatever form the latter takes, and that
   the master files used in the application are completely and accurately
   processed, amended and maintained. The procedural controls will either
   be of a clerical nature (commonly known as clerical controls) and exercised
   either in the user departments or in the computer department or will be
   incorporated in, and exercised by, the computer programs (commonly
   known as program controls). Although the distinction between clerical
   controls and program controls is important it should be remembered that,
   generally, both types of procedural control will be present in any
   application.

   7. The main requirements, and the techniques adopted in practice, to establish
   a reliable system of internal control, as regards administrative controls,
   systems development controls and procedural controls are described in the
   following paragraphs.

## Administrative controls

   8. The main requirements and techniques of administrative controls are
   considered below under the following headings:
   (a)  division of responsibilities (paragraphs 9 and 10);

     (b)  control over computer operators (paragraph 11);
     (c)  file control (paragraphs 12 to 16);
     (d)  fire precautions and standby arrangements (paragraph 17).

*Division of responsibilities*

9.  The principal division of responsibilities should be that between the functions of the computer department and the user departments. There are also important divisions of responsibilities within the computer department itself, between:
     (a)  the development section;
     (b)  the operations section, which is usually subdivided between computer operators, ancillary equipment operators and data preparation equipment operators;
     (c)  the librarian;
     (d)  the control section.
    An organisation chart should be prepared and the principal tasks in the department defined and allocated to specified individuals or groups. It is desirable for each section to be staffed by different people who restrict their work to that carried out by their own section. This provides some measure of internal control, as each section checks, either directly or indirectly, the work of the others.

10.  The following safeguards in connection with the proper segregation of duties are desirable, whenever practicable:
     (a)  only the control and data preparation sections should have access to the documents containing the original data to be processed by the computer;
     (b)  computer department staff should not have access to any of the company's clerically maintained financial records;
     (c)  only computer operators should have access to the computer during production runs;
     (d)  only computer operators and the file librarian should have access to files and current programs;
     (e)  only the user department staff and control section should be allowed to amend input data;
     (f)  the staff of the control section and the librarian should not have any other duties within the computer department;
     (g)  computer department staff should not initiate transactions and changes to master files;
     (h)  access to the computer room should be restricted to authorised persons at authorised times.
    The extent to which the above segregation of duties can be achieved in practice will vary with the number of people employed in the computer department. In small installations not all of the jobs described can be carried out by different groups of people at all times, and particular difficulty will often be experienced during shift operations outside normal working hours. In these cases the degree of reliance placed on supervision by responsible officials of the department is increased.

*Control over computer operators*

11.  The computer operators are responsible for operating the equipment in accordance with the operating instructions provided. Their work includes:
     (a)  setting up the equipment for each run (i.e., loading the input devices,

setting up the magnetic backing storage devices and loading the correct stationery into the printer);
(b) running programs on the computer system;
(c) taking the specified action if the computer halts;
(d) maintaining the operating log.
Controls over computer operators include:
  (i)   the use of manuals laying down general standards of operating discipline;
  (ii)  scheduling of work;
  (iii) the provision of detailed operating instructions for each program;
  (iv)  the frequent and independent review of computer usage by reference to time and fault logs prepared by operators, and where there is a console typewriter by reference to operating logs produced thereon;
  (v)   requiring a minimum of two operators per shift;
  (vi)  rotation of operators' duties;
  (vii) programming that all operator intervention appears on the console print-outs where available. Console print-outs should be on pre-numbered paper or alternatively have the intervention numbered consecutively by the computer.
In some cases computer operators carry out checks to verify the completeness and accuracy of processing (e.g. by agreeing control totals on a console print-out). Generally primary reliance on this type of procedural control is not to be recommended, but, in cases where it occurs, control over the computer operators is important in the overall system of control.

*File control*

12. In view of the large number of files held on magnetic backing storage devices in most installations, it is necessary to provide controls to ensure that:
(a) only the correct file can be used;
(b) no file can be used for an unauthorised purpose.
Control employed for this purpose may be considered under the following headings:
(i)  file storage procedures;
(ii) file identification procedures.
In addition it is necessary to have adequate file reconstruction procedures in case files are corrupted.

13. *File storage procedures.* Where the number of files is large, and considerable use is made of them, a member of the department, often designated the librarian, may be appointed on a whole-time basis to control the files and record their use. In small installations or during shift working, it is desirable that a specific member of the department should be made responsible for this work.

14. The duties of the librarian usually include:
(a) controlling the issue and return of files according to scheduled time-tables;
(b) maintaining external file labels;
(c) ensuring that tapes containing information which is no longer of value (generally known as scratch tapes) cannot be confused with data tapes;
(d) allocating identification number to storage devices and maintaining usage records;
(e) ensuring that access to files is restricted to authorised personnel.

Vital files (e.g. programs) should be duplicated and a copy kept in a secure location outside the installation. Copies of files on magnetic tape which are being stored for long periods should be copied at regular intervals to prevent loss of signal strength.

15. *File identification procedures.* The most common procedures include:
   (a) the allocation of a unique identity number to the file. This would be physically recorded on the storage device and checked before use of that device;
   (b) the use, in the case of tape files, of file protection rings (write permit rings) whereby the operator must physically attach the ring before processing involving writing upon the tape (i.e. change the contents of the file) can commence;
   (c) the inclusion of identification data in the file header label (e.g. file name, identity number, retention period). This would be checked by the computer program on set-up with or without operator intervention. It is usual for the results of the check to be printed out on the console. (A header label is software at the commencement of a magnetic tape which identifies the nature of that tape. It is now normal for the computer program to contain an instruction to ensure that tapes match before processing commences – for example, to ensure that a sales ledger transaction tape matches with a sales ledger master file tape, and program.)

16. *File reconstruction procedures.* When no longer required, data held on magnetic file storage devices is overwritten and new data recorded. It is usual for file retention periods to be included in the file identification and library procedures to ensure that files are not overwritten before the due date. Where magnetic tape storage (or direct access devices used in the same way as magnetic tape) is used, it is normal for several generations of master files and the relevant files containing transaction data to be retained. Where direct access devices are used in such a way that new data is written in the same location as that from which the old data was read, it becomes necessary to make other provisions for re-creating files in case of need; these usually involve the use of data copied to another file at a previous date, together with all the transaction data which has subsequently been processed. (The several generations of master file and transaction data are known as 'grandfather', 'father', 'son'. But you should note that with transaction data the generations may only last a few days. Direct access devices (disc storage) will normally be 'dumped' on to other files before processing commences, in order to facilitate reconstruction in the event of loss. The dumping may be on to tape (which is cheaper), as the speed of copying or access will not be relevant in that peripheral machinery can be used.)

## Fire precautions and standby arrangements

17. To safeguard against the dangers of fire or other damage, rules should be established and enforced to provide for the maximum possible physical security within the installation and for the retention of duplicates of important files outside the installation. Standby procedures should be so organised that, in the event of a prolonged breakdown of the equipment, the more essential accounting functions can still be performed. Such procedures may involve either the use of another computer installation or the introduction of manual document preparation. There is the danger that,

if standby procedures have to be employed, normal controls may become inoperative. It is important therefore that standby procedures should incorporate their own methods of control, except where the established controls will continue to apply. The standby arrangements should be reviewed periodically and, if practicable, tested.

18. The main requirements and techniques of systems development controls are considered below under the following headings:
    (a) standard procedures and documentation (paragraphs 19 to 22);
    (b) systems and program testing (paragraph 23);
    (c) file conversion (paragraph 24);
    (d) acceptance and authorisation procedures (paragraph 25);
    (e) systems and program amendments (paragraph 26).

*Standard procedures and documentation*

19. Because of the complexity of most computer systems the procedures for developing, and the documentation supporting, each application should be of a significantly higher standard than for other systems of processing. It is preferable that these requirements are incorporated in a manual for the development section.

20. There are a number of stages in the sequence of planning, recording and testing between the initial idea of a system and the implementation of the computer programs. Initially a feasibility study is carried out and from this review an outline description of the proposed system is prepared. This description forms the framework for subsequent systems development work and provides a basis for agreement between those responsible for developing the system and the management and staff of the user department. This is also an appropriate stage for the auditor to review the general adequacy of the system of internal control and to ensure that sufficient information will be available for him to carry out his audit tests satisfactorily.

21. When the system has been agreed in outline, the second part of the development is the preparation of a detailed description of the computer programs to be written. Procedure manuals for use by the staff of the user department(s) should be prepared at this stage, detailing the clerical procedures to provide input and deal with output. The programs are then written and documented from the instructions included in the detailed specifications. Once the programs have been written, the necessary master files are set up and the programs are tested.

22. Standards should be applied to his work, and the documentation prepared at each stage of development should include:
    (a) as regards systems documentation:
        (i)   a general description of the application to be processed and the system to be employed, together with computer flow charts;
        (ii)  the form(s) of input to be processed, with sample layouts;
        (iii) the form and content of the master files required;
        (iv)  the processing requirements, including error conditions which are to be detected and the data to be rejected or reported upon;
        (v)   the output required and its distribution, with sample layouts;
        (vi)  the overall system of control and the individual controls proposed.
    (b) as regards program documentation:
        (i)   notes on the programming approach adopted;

     (ii)   the current block diagrams cross-referenced as appropriate to the program listings;

    (iii)  descriptions of the control procedures included in the programs;

    (iv)  the processing requirements, including error conditions which are to be detected and the data to be rejected or reported upon;

    (v)   listing of program instructions;

    (vi)  test data and results of testing;

    (vii) amendments made to programs, the reasons why they were made, who authorised them and how they were implemented.

There should be controls to ensure that the documentation is properly prepared and kept up to date for all changes to systems and programs. Where no comprehensive systems description is available, there is an increased risk that the system of internal control may be inadequate and may deteriorate with changes of staff.

*Systems and program testing*

23. Controls are required to ensure that any system is fully tested before it becomes operational. This will normally involve procedures and documentary evidence to ensure that:

    (a)  all individual programs have been exhaustively desk checked and tested with test and 'live' data;

    (b)  the whole system has been tested by pilot running or by running in parallel with the existing system, if practicable. Operational volumes of data should be used;

(In my experience, the period of parallel running is often foreshortened, or omitted altogether, by the client, because of delays in previous development. But this period is vital;

    (a)  to allow the user department staff to familiarise themselves with the new form of documentation, while still having the old available to compare;

    (b)  to iron out the almost inevitable teething problems in the programs.)

    (c)  the user departments are able to provide the input and deal with the output within the specified time cycle of the system under normal working conditions.

*File conversion*

24. Before a computer system becomes operational the master files are set up. Care is required to ensure that:

    (a)  the correct data is set up;

    (b)  the setting up is complete and accurate.

Normally this is achieved by a complete print-out and check of the contents of the files before operational processing begins.

*Acceptance and authorisation procedures*

25. It is important that each major stage of development is reviewed by:

    (a)  a responsible official in the computer department, to ensure that the system is proceeding according to the specified standards; and

    (b)  the user departments concerned, to ensure that the system will provide what the user departments require and specify.

At these reviews further progress is authorised until ultimately the implementation of the new system is approved. It is preferable that the authorisations are obtained in writing and incorporated in the standard documentation.

*Systems and program amendments*

26. Changes to operational systems and programs should be subject to the same controls as the initial development. Many program changes are of a relatively minor nature but they should, nevertheless, be the subject of a formal system of authorisation and control. In all cases it is important for the associated documentation to be kept up to date and for all changes to be tested before being put into use, the type and extent of the test depending on the nature and possible repercussions of the change.

## Procedural controls

*General matters*

27. In considering the requirements and techniques of procedural controls there are certain general matters which should be borne in mind. They concern the structure of control, the types of data to be controlled and work scheduling.

28. *Control structure.* The control structure adopted for each application should take account of the whole sequence of processing from the time when the initial events occur to the time when the management report or other output documents have reached their final destination, and may include work which has to be carried out as a result of the information shown in them (e.g. the clerical investigation of exception conditions).

29. *Types of data to be controlled.* There are often more documents in a computer application than in a conventional accounting system. This is because a document is normally necessary to input any information to a computer. Examples of new types of documents are those for making amendments to standing data. Once the information on documents has been converted into machine readable form as input to the computer, the document loses some of its importance and it is thus common for many of the procedural controls to be applied to the data on the document rather than to the document itself.

30. The data to be processed can be divided into two types:
    (a) standing data to be incorporated in a master file which will affect the accounting for all transactions of a like nature (e.g. selling prices, wage rates or customers' descriptions);
    (b) transaction data which relates to one transaction only (e.g. number of items ordered or number of hours worked in a period).

    Inaccuracies in standing data may have a more far-reaching effect than errors in transaction data and it is therefore usual for higher standards of control to be applied to standing data than to transaction data. The different data fields on input data and file records will also vary in importance. It is usual for higher standards of control to be applied to data fields that contain, or result in, financial or other critical data than for data included merely for reference or identification purposes. (Errors on master file or standing data often have an extensive effect. For example, in the audit of a shipping company, we discovered that the master file data had one too many noughts in the price per ton of fuel – the management were extremely worried by the poor profit per voyage as revealed by the computer! But many of these types of error are easy to spot by virtue of their 'across the board' effect. Fraud may not be so obvious. For example, one programmer employed by a bank changed the master file data in respect of his own overdraft limit, from $200 to $200,000. He was discovered. Very many computer fraudsmen are not.)

31. *Work scheduling.* The planned scheduling of the sequence of work through the computer department is important in ensuring efficient processing. As regards internal control, work scheduling has already been mentioned in relation to control over computer operators (paragraph 11(ii)). It may also be important in procedural controls. The lack of planned scheduling can lead to processing bottlenecks and in extreme cases to breakdowns in procedural controls because of pressure of time.

*Types of procedural controls*

32. It is usual to consider procedural controls under four headings:
   (a) input controls (paragraphs 33 to 39);
   (b) processing controls (paragraphs 40 to 48);
   (c) output controls (paragraphs 49 to 55);
   (d) master file controls (paragraphs 56 to 60).
   While this division facilitates understanding and evaluating a system, it should be remembered that control over data is a continuous process and should be examined as a whole when evaluating any particular aspect of the procedural controls.

*Input controls*

33. The purpose of input controls is to ensure that *all* authorised, and *only* authorised data is presented to the computer for processing only once and that it is correctly converted to machine readable form. Input controls are concerned with the procedures in the user department where the data is originally created, movement of the data to the computer department, where it usually comes under the control of a control section, and its conversion within the data preparation department.

34. The main requirements and techniques of input controls are considered under the following headings:
   (a) establishment of control (paragraphs 35 and 36);
   (b) verification of conversion (paragraphs 37 and 38);
   (c) authorisation of input (paragraph 39).

35. *Establishment of control.* To ensure complete and accurate processing of data it is necessary to establish a control with which the final output can be verified. Whereas completeness of processing can usually be ensured by establishing control over documents, accuracy of processing can normally only be ensured by the establishment of control over the data fields. Depending on the circumstances, it may be appropriate for control to be established in the user department concerned, or clerically in the computer department or by the computer itself. The most common methods by which control is established are:
   (a) by the use of controls from prior procedures (e.g. the totalling of cash received on opening the post would provide a control for the subsequent processing of cash to the sales ledger);
   (b) by clerical sequence checks (e.g. accounting for serially numbered stores issue notes before passing to the computer department);
   (c) by the retention of copies of important documents sent for processing (e.g. amendments to standing data) for subsequent checking with output;
   (d) by establishment, either clerically or by the computer, of batch control

totals. These totals might be document counts, item counts (e.g., the different items on a sales order), sterling totals, quantity totals (e.g. goods despatched or hours worked) or hash totals (e.g. aggregation of stock code numbers);

(e) by program controls (e.g. sequence checks, check digit verification or matching with master file records).

It will be noted that none of the techniques set out in (a) to (e) above necessarily ensures both complete *and* accurate processing. Often a combination of two techniques is employed (e.g. in processing clock cards accuracy might be ensured by a quantity total of hours worked, and completeness by matching with the employees' records on the master file; in processing despatch notes, completeness might be ensured by programmed sequence checking of serially numbered documents, and accuracy by the computer establishing quantity totals).

(*Batching of documents for processing, and controls on batches.* In EDP-based systems, documents are usually batched at some stage in the data flow and processed in batches. Therefore the input controls will usually be based on controlling batches. *Batch Control Slips* (see example A) are usually created in the user department to identify the batch. Control can be established by:

(a) document counts (suitable for batches of mixed documents);
(b) control totals of common fields, either quantitative (e.g. hours worked) or financial (e.g. invoice totals);
(c) hash totals (i.e. numbers not normally added together, such as stock part numbers).

These control totals are usually established manually and checked by the computer in processing, or are printed out for manual verification. *Transmittal and route slips* (see example B) are used for controlling and identification of documents, either singly or batched, on transmission from one location to another. *Batch Registers* (see example C), usually kept by the control section, establish control over the movement of batches. *Cancellation and validation stamps* will be used to indicate the point reached in the data flow, and to safeguard against re-presentation.)

36. It is unusual for control totals to be established over reference data. Normally this type of data is controlled within the computer by check digit verification and by matching with master file records.

37. *Verification of conversion.* The techniques of control vary between installations but usually include:
(a) separation of the duties of punching and verifying;
(b) physical control over the source documents and the input media produced therefrom;
(c) procedures for recording and investigating errors detected at the verification stage and controlling their correction;
(d) control of the progress of punching and verifying.

38. If control is established after the conversion of data into input media (e.g. by control totals established by the computer) the verification of conversion is normally an important part of the control structure as otherwise conversion errors would not normally be revealed.

39. *Authorisation of input.* In many cases the authorisation of input will be part of the conventional manual procedures (e.g. approval of purchase invoices), but it will normally be necessary to lay down formal authorising procedures in the relevant user departments for new documents introduced as a result of transferring an accounting application to a computer (e.g. amendments to

*Example A*              Batch control slip

| Batch no 71 | To DATA CONTROL (EDP) | |
|---|---|---|
| Date 12/1 | From BOUGHT LEDGER | |
| No of document 252 | From 64179 | Numbered To 64431 |
| Control totals | A/C NUMBERS      7149362 | |
| | INVOICE TOTALS    £47, 369 - 61 | |
| Date received 13/1 | Received by   J. SNOOKS | |

*Example B*              Route slips

| 441 | 14/1 | Numbered | | 65 |
|---|---|---|---|---|
| | | 17321 | 17385 | |
| Batch no | Date | From | To | No of docs |
| Dept to | Date fwd | Init | Remarks | |
| ORDER | 14/1 | S.C.H. | | |
| Purchase Control | 15/1 | Q.V. | | |
| Bought Ledger | 16/1 | JN. | 17363 help for query | |
| | | | | |
| | | | | |

*Example C*

Batch control register

| Dept | Batch no | Date in | Control totals (input) | Data prep | | Data proc. | | Control totals (output) | Date out |
|------|----------|---------|------------------------|-----------|------|------------|-----|-------------------------|----------|
| | | | | In | Out | In | Out | | |
| | | | | | | | | | |
| Wages | 42 | 10/1 | 1236 hrs. | 10.a.m. 10/1 | 12.a.m. 10/1 | 3.p.m 10/1 | 3.30.p.m 10/1 | 1144 hrs. 92 hrs. | 11/1 |
| | | | | | | | | | |
| | | | | | | | | | |
| | | | | | | | | | |
| | | | | | | | | | |
| | | | | | | | | | |

standing data). Authorisation procedures do not of themselves ensure that only authorised data will be processed. This will only be the case where the data is authorised after control has been established (e.g. the approval of purchase invoices in pre-listed batches). In cases where control is established after the data has been authorised, it will be necessary, if the data is important, to check that the authorised data has not been changed or suppressed and that unauthorised data has not been introduced before control is established. In certain cases authorisation functions previously carried out clerically may be exercised by program controls in the form of limit and reasonableness checks (e.g. excessive hours worked identified and reported for action).

*Processing controls*

40. The introduction of a computer offers significant improvements in the controls which can be achieved during processing and considerable use is made of this facility in the design of systems of control for computer applications.

41. The main requirements and techniques of processing controls may be considered under the headings:
    (a) editing (paragraphs 42 to 44);
    (b) control over rejections (paragraphs 45 and 46);
    (c) run-to-run controls (paragraphs 47 and 48).

42. *Editing.* One of the most important techniques which is available in the use of computers is 'editing'. This is the term applied to any process by which data is tested by reference to an appropriate standard to determine its validity. Editing of the data is usually carried out during the first computer run,

when data is written to a magnetic backing storage device. The tests carried carried out can include:

(a) check digit verification (e.g. testing that a check digit included in a reference number bears the required relationship to the rest of the number. This protects against most transposition and transcription errors);

(b) reasonableness checks (e.g. ensuring that data lies within predetermined limits – that hours worked are between zero and fifty);

(c) existence checks (e.g. comparing data codes with predetermined lists of codes – that stock codes range from 1,000 to 5,000);

(d) sequence checks (e.g. detecting sequence failures or duplicate records);

(e) format checks (e.g. testing that characters are alphabetic, numeric or blank – that invoice value fields are numeric);

(f) the matching of transactions with master file records.

43. Edit tests can be important in the establishment of control over, and authorisation of, input (e.g. verifying completeness by sequence checks; authorising sales orders by testing for credit-worthiness). Data which fails edit tests will either be rejected from the system, rejected but held on a suspense file (paragraph 46), or accepted for further processing but reported.

44. Tests can also be carried out on data generated by the computer during subsequent processing runs. Limit tests are the most common and test that generated data falls between accepted limits (e.g. the net pay of weekly paid employees is less than £150; a domestic quarterly electricity bill does not exceed £140). Limit checks are often important as they may replace clerical scrutinies and authorising functions.

45. *Control over rejections.* Rejections may occur at various stages in processing and procedures are required to ensure that they are promptly investigated, corrected and reprocessed. In cases where clerical control totals are established prior to processing, control over rejections is normally facilitated by the need to adjust those control totals. Rejections are thus automatically highlighted. If control is not established prior to the processing runs in which rejections can arise, rejections will not automatically be revealed by the disagreement of controls and a higher degree of control over their investigation, correction and reprocessing is appropriate. This should take the form of an independent scrutiny of the rejection records to ensure that they are promptly dealt with. (An example of an *Error Report* is included below, together with an extract from the associated procedures manual. These are intended as illustration only. The particular checks included here have no special significance and are not all explained in detail.)

*Extract from clerical procedures manual*

*Error reports – data vet*

A standard form of error reports has been adopted. Forms 11–29 will always be reported in full and must be checked by the clerical sections concerned to ensure accuracy.

The reason for the report will be shown in code in the fifth column of the error report. These codes are as follows:

0 Parity failure
1 Incorrect range
2 Incorrect radix
3 Incorrect check total

ERROR REPORT

PAYROLL NO.4

ERROR REPORT - DATA VET  POB  PAYROLL 04  PROGRAM JCA0101 RUN80...1  DATE 24/07/80  PAGE 0002

| FORM | PAY | SECT | EMPLY | REPT | ITEM | UPR LMT | LWR LMT | FIELD | BLOCK CONTENTS |
|---|---|---|---|---|---|---|---|---|---|
| 65 / (21)05 40 | 4 | 4824 | 83241 | 1B | | 9 | 1 | 6 | 4824;83241;482400;1;6;7;-;:29 |
| 40 | 4 | 311 | 23487 | 21 | 106 | | | 3 | 106;22.18.0;1072.12,5 |
| 40 | 4. | 4561 | 57205 | 11 | 106 | 166 | | 2 | 106;42.10.8;107;4.19.3 |
| 40 | 4 | 4637 | 78560 | 11 | 96 | | 0 | 1 | 105;580.6.9 |
| 40 | 4 | 4885 | 24148 | 11 | 17 | 4 | 1 | 6 | 7;61;6;2;17;:21;205 |
| 40 | 4 | 7440 | 66409 | 11 | 83 | | | 2 | 83;12;7/168;96;0.0.0 |
| 62 | 4 | 283 | 14000 | B | | | | 1 | 283;02880;750800;1;26.00;14.50 |
| 40 | 4 | 311 | 20515 | 11 | 20 | 11 | 0 | 8 | 7;61;16;2;17;1;20;205 |
| 40 | 4 | 4812 | 27011 | 21 | 48 | | | 10 | 22;43;23;37.00;24;43;31;32;48;ZM647515:49;4812001 |
| 40 | 4 | 4889 | 33762 | 11 | 5 | 9 | 0 | 2 | 5;99;6;1 |
| 62 | 4 | 4564 | 59610 | 10B | | | | 3 | 4564;59610;4564;59610;456402O;37.-75;16.25 |
| 62 | 4 | 4563 | 54240 | 10B | | | | 3 | 4563;54240;:99.00; |
| 62 | 4 | 4563 | 54240 | 10B | | | | 3 | 4563;54240;:58.00;31.00 |
| 62 | 4 | 4894 | 71800 | 1B | | | | 5 | 4894;71800;4894020;; |
| 62 | 4 | 4894 | 96140 | 1B | | | | 5 | 4894;96140;4894020;; |
| 40 | 4 | 4621 | 60928 | 11 | 82 | | | 2 | 82;/7/1968 |
| 43 | 4 | 215 | 37240 | 5B | 149 | | | 7 | 215;37240;149;100.0.0;:0.0.0;+;:;29 |
| 43 | 4 | 215 | 37240 | 5B | 149 | | | 7 | 215;37240;149;100.0.0;:0.0.0;+;:;29 |
| 43 | 4 | 302 | 37400 | 5B | 149 | | | 7 | 302;37400;149;100.0.0;:0.0.0;+;:;29 |
| 43 | 4 | 385 | 54300 | 5B | 149 | | | 7 | 385;54300;149;32.0.0;:0.0.0;+;:;:29 |

    4 Unacceptance form number
    5 Form data incompatible with form no.
    6 Apparent excess of information on form
    7 Miscellaneous check failure
    8 Inadequate information on form
    9 Unacceptable item no.
    10 Incorrect costing code
    11 Control symbol error
    (a) If the whole form is rejected the report type will have a suffix F
    (b) If the block is rejected the report type will have a suffix B
    (c) If the item is rejected the report type will have a suffix I
    e.g. IF = Incorrect range on item specified = whole form rejected.

The remainder of the report will show the payroll, section and employee numbers; the form no.; the item and field number; the upper and lower limits of the item (i.e. the range acceptable to the computer); and the contents of the rejected block.

*Action to be taken on receipt of Error Reports*

*0 – Parity Failure*

This is a machine failure which may be caused by such things as a dirty or broken paper tape. The form or block rejected should be re-submitted.

*1 – Incorrect Range*

By comparison of the block print-out and the upper and lower limits of the item it should be apparent which limit has been exceeded. The cause of this error could be a clerical or punching mistake. The error report should be checked with the original input form and a corrected form should be submitted.

46. In certain systems data which cannot be completely processed is held in backing storage on a suspense file and not rejected (e.g. unidentified cash). Procedures are required to ensure that these items are printed out and promptly investigated and corrected. Correction procedures may be carried out clerically, or the computer may be programmed to transfer items from suspense. In either case evidence of the transfers should be printed out and reviewed. In addition it is important that a periodic review is made of the contents of the suspense file.

47. *Run-to-run controls*. Most computer applications consist of more than one computer run. In order to detect any loss of data occurring during intermediate processing runs it is good practice for the computer to accumulate control totals during each run either for agreement by the computer with totals held on the file, or for clerical agreement with input totals or totals established by the computer and printed out after an earlier run. These are known as run-to-run controls. If the agreement is carried out clerically the totals must be printed out; if carried out by the computer it is good practice to print out details of the agreement which are then usually checked clerically. These print-outs are often called intermediate print-outs of control data.

48. When control over the completeness and accuracy of processing has been established initially by the accumulation of totals other than those of value (e.g. by hash totals, document counts) additional control totals are usually established when sterling values are first generated. These new controls are normally used to verify the completeness and accuracy of subsequent computer runs.

*Output controls*

49. The main requirements and techniques of output controls may be considered under the headings:
    (a) verification of output (paragraphs 50 to 53);
    (b) distribution of output (paragraph 54);
    (c) procedures for acting on exception reports (paragraph 55).
    It is important that the computer should be programmed to write page numbers, descriptive captions and processing dates on all print-outs.

50. *Verification of output.* The verification controls applied to output will be governed largely by the relationship which the output bears to the input and the processing that created it. Output may be considered in these terms under three headings:
    (a) output directly related to input (paragraph 51);
    (b) output indirectly related to input (paragraph 52);
    (c) exception reports (paragraph 53).

51. *Output directly related to input.* This would include:
    (a) output that is identical with input, which usually results from updating or creating a file and takes the form of lists or documents (e.g. lists of master file amendments or purchase invoices, despatch notes and cheques);
    (b) output that is in part identical with input but includes additional information usually involving standing data (e.g. sales invoices produced from despatch notes and prices, payrolls produced from clock cards and rates of pay).
    In these cases it is normal for the output to be verified clerically with the controls established either before or during processing (e.g. by agreeing control totals or checking output individually with retained copies of input documents).

52. *Output indirectly related to input.* This would include output generated by the programs on the basis of:
    (a) current input data (e.g. reports of unmatched and missing items);
    (b) previous or latest input data (e.g. overdue debtor reminder procedures);
    (c) all input for a given period (e.g. personal and nominal ledgers, interest charges and cumulative totals).
    While output of this nature is often verified clerically with the cumulative controls established over the relevant input (e.g. a debtors' control account), more reliance is usually placed on the correct functioning of the computer programs than is normally the case with output directly related to input data.

53. *Exception reports.* These would include reports of items identified by the computer programs from a scrutiny of input data or master files as not satisfying conditions specified in the program (e.g. net pay in excess of a specified amount, or slow moving stock). It is normally practicable to verify exception reports clerically with the controls established over input of master files. Their complete and accurate production almost always depends on the correct functioning of the computer programs.

54. *Distribution of output.* If the user department that verifies the controls also acts on the output it will be apparent to the user department whether it received all that output. If, however, the verification is carried out in the computer department or the output is not verified with the controls established over input or master files (e.g. exception reports) procedures are

required to ensure that the user department responsible receives all output intact. These procedures often take the form of output registers or the sequential numbered exception reports.

55. *Procedures for acting on exception reports.* Exception reports often provide the information on which important control functions are based (e.g. control of overtime). A high degree of control is thus usually required over the investigation of exception reports and the resulting action taken. This will often take the form of an independent review of exception reports to ensure that the exceptional items are promptly investigated and acted upon.

*Master file controls*

56. The main requirements and technique of master file controls may be considered under the headings:
(a) amendments to standing data (paragraph 57);
(b) maintenance of standing data (paragraph 58);
(c) maintenance of transaction data (paragraphs 59 and 60).

57. *Amendments to standing data.* The techniques for control of amendments to standing data are the same as those for transactions and have already been considered in paragraphs 33 to 55. As standing data is normally more important than transaction data it is usual for a higher standard of control to be appropriate.

58. *Maintenance of standing data.* Once standing data has been written onto a master file it is important that there are adequate controls to ensure that the data remains unaltered until an authorised change is made. The most common methods by which this is achieved are:
(a) periodic print-outs of standing data for checking with clerically held information;
(b) the establishment of independent control totals for periodic verification with equivalent totals accumulated on the files;
(c) the establishment and verification of control totals by the computer programs. In these cases it is normal for evidence of the computer reconciliation to be printed out and checked clerically.

59. *Maintenance of transaction data.* The degree of control appropriate to the maintenance of transaction data on master files will vary according to the contents of the file. The maintenance of a sales ledger or stock ledger file is normally of greater importance than a cumulative sales analysis file. In most cases it will be appropriate to maintain control accounts to ensure the correctness of the file on a total basis. The most common methods by which this is done are as outlined in paragraphs 58(b) and (c).

60. It will normally be necessary, in addition to maintaining a total control, to verify independently the correctness of individual balances. The extent of these procedures will depend on the significance of the items and the degree of control which is exercised over the processing of transaction data. In many cases regular print-outs of individual balances will form an automatic part of the processing routine (e.g. debtors, creditors and stock). Conventional controls will often involve the verification of individual balances (e.g. comparison of creditors' balances with statements and comparison of stock balances with physical stock counts). Where individual balances are not regularly verified as part of the routine system, a specific procedure should normally be adopted for their periodic verification.

Fig. 20.7 U15. Extract – timing of audit work

# Timing of audit work

*Timing of initial approach*

The timing of the initial approach by the auditor to a client installing a computer or introducing a new application requires careful consideration. The auditor should develop a sufficiently close working relationship with the client that he is aware of the progress which is planned and is being made. The risk of spending too much time in considering an application in detail in the early stages when substantial changes may still be made to the procedures before they are finalised must be assessed against the considerable expense and inconvenience of modifying the procedures and, in particular, the computer programs if the auditor's examination of the system is left too late. Such modification may be required in order to remedy any weaknesses in the system of internal control or to provide any additional information which may be necessary to enable the auditor to carry out his tests satisfactorily.

The auditor should endeavour to ensure that the client is aware of the requirements and techniques of internal control at an early stage in the installation of a computer. The auditor can at this stage discuss the controls in general terms. Subsequently, when the systems specifications are substantially complete and the controls decided, but before detailed programming is far advanced, he may carry out his review. Any suggestions he may make at this stage can then be considered for incorporation in the system.

In the past it has been the practice at the time of the interim audit to select for examination transactions covering a considerable period of the year, possibly commencing with transactions which arose soon after the date of the previous balance sheet. This approach is likely to become less practicable with computer-based accounting systems due to the reduced availability of data and possibly, where direct access storage devices are used, to the over-writing of data. It may, therefore be necessary for the auditor to confine his tests to recent data. If there is an internal audit department, evidence of a continuous test will be available to the external auditor, otherwise if he considers it necessary to spread his tests over the whole period covered by the audit, it may be necessary to make more frequent visits to his client's office.

The availability of data may be reduced because the client considers that it is not necessary, or practicable, to keep all the print-outs from computers, (e.g. error reports which have been subsequently corrected). The auditor should therefore ascertain from his client the lengths of time for which it is proposed to retain the various kinds of printed output and, where appropriate, make arrangements for these to be kept for audit purposes.

A further difficulty which will affect the timing of detailed tests relates to the manner in which documents are filed. For example if invoices are ultimately filed in supplier order, detailed checking of a batch of invoices and its analysis may not be practicable after a short period of time has elapsed.

Fig. 20.6 Computer audit decision tree

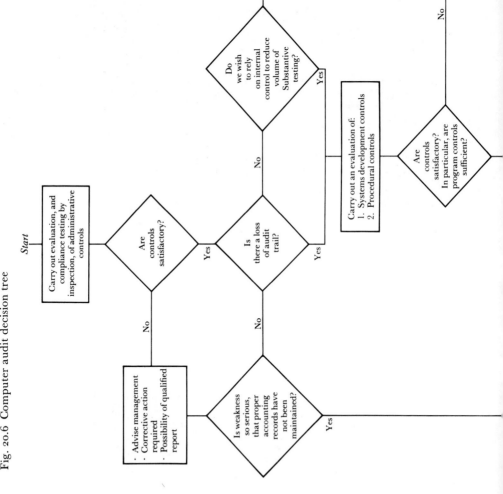

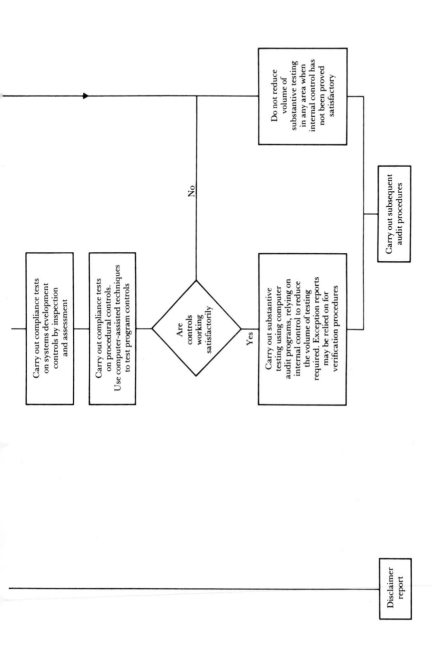

Carry out compliance tests on systems development controls by inspection and assessment

Carry out compliance tests on procedural controls. Use computer-assisted techniques to test program controls

Are controls working satisfactorily

No

Yes

Do not reduce volume of substantive testing in any area when internal control has not been proved satisfactory

Carry out substantive testing using computer audit programs, relying on internal control to reduce the volume of testing required. Exception reports may be relied on for verification procedures

Carry out subsequent audit procedures

Disclaimer report

## 20.6 Recording EDP systems for audit purposes

There must be a clearly defined division of responsibility and segregation of duties within the EDP department. This will probably be best recorded in the form of an organisation chart and detailed descriptions of job functions.

It will be necessary to ascertain and record the system for *each* application. But the first objective in all applications will be to establish the overall basis of control in order to avoid going into unnecessary detail. The sources of information could be:

1. Procedures manual.
2. Job specifications.
3. Computer flow charts.
4. Layout of Master File Records.
5. Operator instructions.
6. Discussions with EDP manager, systems analysts and programmers, and appropriate user department staff.

The following information should be obtained and recorded on file:

1. Organisation chart.
2. Equipment used.
3. For each accounting application:
   (a) brief narrative description;
   (b) computer flow charts;
   (c) specimen input and output documents;
   (d) contents of master files;
   (e) internal controls;
   (f) ICQ/ICE.

## 20.7 Reviewing EDP systems

Where there are comprehensive *manual* procedural controls in an application, the auditor will not necessarily have to examine the computer controls of that application. But procedural controls should be reviewed where the application relies on them to any material degree, or if they are to be relied upon to reduce the volume of substantive testing. It will then also be necessary to review the systems development controls, in order to ensure that the program controls have been correctly designed and implemented.

An ICE for computer applications is shown in Fig. 20.8. The first four questions analyse the overall controls over administration and systems development, and questions 4–8 apply to the procedural controls *in each application*. These 'key control' questions should be read in conjunction with U14.

If the key control questions reveal any material weaknesses, then it will be necessary to look for alternative counter controls, such as independent reconciliations or comparison to manually held records, upon which reliance can then be placed. If there are comprehensive manual controls, the absence of sound computer controls may not be serious. It will just necessitate a greater degree of

Fig. 20.8 ICE for computer applications

## ICE for computer applications

Client _____

Period _____ Prepared by _____ Date _____

| | Tick | | Comments, reference to systems notes etc. |
|---|---|---|---|
| | Yes | No | |

1. Are controls designed to ensure that there is proper segregation of duties within the EDP activity?     _____ _____

   Consider:

   (A) Are EDP personnel debarred from initiating, authorising, or amending data (with the exception of the data control group which may amend data conversion errors)?

   (B) Are the functions of systems and programming separated from operations and are operations controlled by a data control group?

   (C) Are system and programming personnel denied access to live data files and are operating personnel only allowed access to those files when required for authorised processing?

2. Are controls designed to ensure that computerised accounting systems are initially designed and implemented to process data in accordance with management's requirements?     _____ _____

   Consider:

   (A) Is there active participation of management and user departments in the development and design of new systems?

   (B) Is the testing of the system performed or reviewed by persons other than those responsible for the programming to ensure the sufficiency and quality of the tests?

   (C) Is there adequate control over the conversion from the existing to the new system?

3. Are controls designed to ensure that changes to existing programs are only made with proper management authorisation and that after implementing the changes the systems continue to process data in accordance with management's requirements?     _____ _____

   Consider:

   (A) Are there controls to ensure that program amendments are properly authorised and that proper testing procedures are carried out?

   (B) Are there controls to ensure that once a program has been amended only the authorised program is run operationally?

4. Are controls designed to ensure that only
   authorised jobs are processed by the system?          ____   ____
   Consider:
   (A) Does management regularly review reports
       of usage (such as console log, computer
       generated usage reports)?
   (B) Are there always two operators per shift for
       financially vulnerable programs?

5. Are controls designed to ensure that all (and
   only) data intended for processing is completely     ____   ____
   processed?
   Consider if the system is designed so that:
   (A) The loss, omission, or duplication of data
       is detected?
   (B) Output totals are reconciled to input totals
       by a group independent of systems,
       programming, and operations, and by the
       user department?
   (C) Data rejected from processing is
       independently reviewed, and, if appropriate,
       corrected and re-entered into the system?
   (D) All output reports are distributed to the
       designated recipients promptly?

6. Are controls designed to ensure that all (and
   only) data intended for processing is accurately     ____   ____
   processed?
   Consider if the system is designed so that:
   (A) Errors in preparing input documents are
       detected?
   (B) Errors in converting data to computer
       readable form, and, where remote terminals
       are used, errors in data transmission, are
       detected?
   (C) The correct brought forward files are updated
       and programs and equipment perform
       correctly?
   (D) There is control over the physical operation
       of the computer?

7. Are controls designed to ensure that all (and
   only) data intended for processing is authorised?    ____   ____
   Consider if the system is designed so that
   attempts to input data by unauthorised persons
   are detected?

8. Are controls designed to ensure that data which
   changes master files (such as credit limits,
   names, addresses, inventory quantities) or           ____   ____
   financial tables (such as pay rates, selling prices,
   discount and interest rates) is subject to the
   controls outlined in 5, 6 and 7 above?

substantive testing than would otherwise be required. But if manual controls are weak, and if there is poor administration control, then the auditor may be forced to conclude that proper accounting records are not being maintained. In less extreme situations it may still be possible to substantiate the figures by a large quantity of manual testing. But this will not be the case if there is a 'loss of audit trail', arising from the use of exception reporting, incomplete print-outs or computer-generated totals. Such situations can only be met by the use of computer-based techniques. And these can only be used if there are sound computer controls.

## 20.8  Loss of audit trail

A 'loss of audit trail' occurs where it is no longer practical, clerically, to trace through a transaction from its initiation to its final recording. I say 'practical', for it will almost invariably be possible manually to re-create the audit trail by referring back to source documentation. But to resurrect just one or two transactions in this way could take a whole day. And there can be little justification for such time-consuming work. A 'loss of audit trail' may occur in any of the following ways:

1. *Batch processing.* Documents will normally only be retained in batch form, for a short time after processing. So all tests on batch controls and data input controls will have to be performed within a short while of processing. This means in practice that tests must be performed on those batches being processed at the time of the audit attendance; which in turn means that there could be the need for more frequent attendance.

2. *Records will normally only be retained in magnetic form for up to four generations.* So any computer-assisted tests must be performed on current transactions, or the client must be informed of those files which should be retained for testing purposes.

3. *Direct access updating.* Disc stores have the speed advantage of being directly accessible for updating, but this may result in the loss through cancellation of information concerning completed transactions, such as a settled debtor balance. For reconstruction purposes, the client will normally 'dump' such files on to magnetic tape before processing, but if this is not done, then a specific audit request will need to be made. And in any event an audit request will have to be made for the retention of specific files for testing.

4. *Intermediate or final print-outs destroyed* after a given period (because of storage problems).

5. *Print-outs not produced/reliance on exception reports.* It will often not be necessary for the client to have complete print-outs every month; exception reports will

usually be more efficient (consider the example of overdue debtor listings, given earlier).

6. *Computer-generated totals.* The computer may generate a total through one process, and that total may then be used as the input for a subsequent process, there being no intermediate print-out of figures produced. For example, there may be no intermediate print-out of the calculations for the weighted average cost of stock.

Many of these problems can be overcome with advance organisation. For example, special print-outs can be requested, and files can be specially retained. But this alerts the client's staff to those areas to be tested; so strong administration controls are essential for any form of reliance on computer based records.

Special print-outs are, in any event, only a temporary solution, for the client will be reluctant to produce wholesale print-outs specially for the auditor. The line printer is by far the slowest piece of computer equipment, and will take up a large and unnecessary proportion of central processor time. The client can reasonably object to the use of valuable computer time in this way, and it may not even be feasible in terms of his operations schedule. So where there is a lack of hard copy, or where there is a heavy reliance on exception reporting (and hence on program controls), the use of computer-assisted audit techniques (CAATS) (alternatively Special Audit Techniques or SPATS) becomes imperative. They will, in any event, normally be necessary to reduce the quantity of manual substantive testing.

Where there is heavy reliance on program controls, it will be necessary to test that these controls are both sufficient and working satisfactorily in practice. Their sufficiency will be tested by means of examining the systems development controls, and compliance testing can be achieved through the use of 'Test Packs', or computer audit programs.

## 20.9 Compliance testing of program controls

### Test packs

Test Packs consist of test data which will be processed in the same way as actual or live data. The data may either be fictitious as invented by the auditor, or genuine data, selected prior to processing. The essence of a test pack is that data will be chosen to test the workings of each control upon which reliance is to be placed. Data will include both that which falls outside the control parameters (and therefore should be printed out as an error or exception), and that which falls within the parameters (and therefore should be processed normally). For example, assume that stock numbers range from 0 to 3,000, and that any stock movements with a number outside this range should be printed out as an error. So test data with numbers of 2,999 and 3,001 might be chosen. The latter should be printed out as an error, the former should be processed normally. Assume further that all debts over 60 days old should be printed out as exceptions on account of their being overdue. So a debt at 59 days, and one at 61 days might be chosen as the test data. The latter should be printed out as a exception, whereas the former should not appear on the exception report.

The results of the test data can be predetermined, and these anticipated results can then be compared with the error or exception reports produced by the computer. If this compliance testing reveals that the program controls can be relied upon, then it means that the resulting error and exception reports can be regarded as reliable. For if a program control can be proved to work properly, it may be assumed that it will continue to work, unless fradulently interfered with. And the chances of this will have been assessed during the examination of administrative controls.

The auditor will then have to satisfy himself that the appropriate action is taken on all error and exception reports. This he will determine by appropriate compliance testing, such as the review of a sample of error reports, to ensure that all errors have been actioned, and, if necessary, reprocessed. If the results of this compliance testing are satisfactory, the auditor may then be satisfied that the chances of material error existing in the system are small, and he may accordingly reduce the quantity of substantive testing for error, on the basis of reliable internal control.

The exception reports will be an important part of management controls over assets and liabilities, especially in relation to concealed defalcations. And as such, the auditor will want to ensure that they are reliable. But they can also be of considerable audit benefit in substantive testing, particularly at the verification stage. For the exceptions are often exactly those items which the auditor himself would wish to examine. And he would otherwise have to extract such figures by hand. For example, a list of overdue debts would be of value in assessing the provision for doubtful debts.

U15 provides an analysis of the advantages and problems associated with test packs as seen in Fig. 20.9.

Fig. 20.9 U15. Extract – test packs

The advantages of using test packs are:
(a) they provide a positive assurance of the correct functioning of the program controls actually tested;
(b) they can be used on a continuing basis until the programs are changed;
(c) if restricted to testing particular program controls (especially if master files are not required), they are not expensive to develop;
(d) once set up, 'running' costs from year to year are low;
(e) additional tests can be 'grafted' on to basic test packs fairly easily (e.g. a test pack initially set up to test the exercise of credit control over sales orders could be extended to test the production of invoices);
(f) their contents are variable at will.

The difficulties in the use of test packs are:
(a) to ensure that the test data is processed as expected, a more detailed

knowledge is required of the programs than is usual (often including programs not required to be tested);

(b) to test certain program controls may entail either 'passing the data through' previous parts of the system that do not require testing or writing additional programs to by-pass those parts of the processing;

(c) computer time is often difficult to obtain although the difficulty can be minimised by co-operation with the computer department management;

(d) processing halts often occur due to the artificial type and small quantity of data used;

(e) initial set up costs can be high;

(f) amendment may be required for program changes.

The limitations of test packs are:

(a) the difficulty in establishing whether the program tested is the current operational program (*it may have been specially written for the auditors!*);

(b) unless 'live' data is used, they do not test *actual* transactions;

(c) the security risks involved normally make it impracticable to use them against 'live' files.

Test packs are thus usually supplemented by audit tests on actual data and by tests on the organisational controls relating to the security, use and amendments of programs.

It is possible to set up records, solely for audit purposes, on the client's operational master files. Once they have been set up the auditor can process test data against these records at the same time as the client is processing actual data. By this means the need to obtain computer time and to create copy master files for use with test packs is avoided and there is positive assurance that a current operational program is being tested (*alternatively, live transaction data may be selected before processing, and used to achieve the same ends*). Considerable care is required in the use of test packs of this type as it must be assured that the auditors' test data and test records do not affect the company's financial records.

*Computer audit programs*

Because of the difficulties associated with test packs, they are now declining in use, and are being replaced for the compliance testing of program controls by computer audit programs. This has been facilitated by the introduction of computer audit programs which are more sophisticated and flexible in their use than their forbears, which were primarily used for substantive testing. A computer audit program will test program controls by independently reproducing from source data those balances or analyses which are subject to test, and then comparing these with the figures produced by the client's program. In this way, the correct programming and operation of the client's computer can be proved.

## 20.10 Substantive testing using computer audit programs

Much of the data concerning transactions and balances that may need to be examined during the course of substantive testing will be held on magnetic files. In some cases the client's normal procedures will include printing out such files, and these may then suffice for audit purposes. But where print-outs are not obtainable, then computer audit programs can be used to retrieve the relevant data. Even where print-outs can be obtained, it will usually be more effective to use programs, rather than to analyse a client's print-outs manually.

Most of the large firms of auditors have programs especially designed for their audit procedures, and written especially for different makes of computer. Each type of computer will require its own audit program. And as each of these is both expensive to create, and complex to operate, they can often be out of reach of the smaller firm of auditors. However, this problem can be overcome by the association of several firms for training and technical purposes. And most of the computer manufacturers now market standard interrogation packages, which can be used by the auditor to achieve most of the advantages of a specially written audit program.

The use of computer audit programs can have the following advantages:

1. *Independence.* Interrogations can be made independently of the client's systems and programming staff. Normally the client's own computer and operators will be used (though it is essential for the run to be totally under the auditor's control), but if there are any doubts about the independence of the operators then it may be necessary to transfer the run to an independent computer.

2. *Scope of work.* In a manual audit, it is unlikely that the whole population would be tested in detail. However, a computer program can easily encompass an entire file, and hence an entire population. For example, only a proportion of balances would normally be selected for the review of a debtor's ledger kept by an accounting machine. By contrast, a program can cover every debt held on magnetic records – provided that the criteria determining recoverability are specified precisely in advance.

3. *Speed of operation.* The speed of computers enables the performance of tasks which could not, for practical reasons, be carried out manually. For example, an entire payroll could be examined for duplicate payroll or National Health numbers in a matter of minutes.

4. *Use of audit time.* Many time consuming and burdensome procedures can be carried out by the computer, thus freeing the audit staff for those areas where subjective judgement is required. For example, the performance of analytical review procedures and the extraction of information from files can be done more rapidly and probably more accruately by the computer. And this will then allow the audit staff to concentrate their efforts on such tasks as determining the areas for review and test, determining the required parameters and evaluating the results of procedures.

Programs can generally be used for the following procedures:
(a) reading data on magnetically held files;
(b) casting and calculating;
(c) preparing analyses and reports;
(d) selecting items against predetermined criteria;

(e) statistical sampling;
(f) comparing details that are held on two different files.

### Casting

It will almost always be more efficient to use a program for casting a client's file to prove the total value, and for checking other casts and calculations.

### Using statistical sampling

A program can be used to extract statistically based samples from both populations and balances. This will normally be more efficient, and more accurate. And where it is not possible to obtain a print-out, then a program will be the only answer.

### Performing an analytical review

A program can assist in the extraction and calculation of the appropriate figures for the overall review (e.g. on the basis of monthly accounts) and for the detailed review (e.g. on a particular population such as sales). These reviews could of course be carried out manually on the basis of print-outs, albeit less efficiently. But a third type of review, the detailed review of individual items that make up a population, can only be achieved through the use of a suitably designed program. For example, a program could be designed to re-create from source data those critical reports that significantly affect the profit and loss account (for example the provision for stock obsolescence). This would give independent proof that the client's computer had been correctly programmed, and that the program had worked correctly on all the items in the population. Alternatively, the program could be used to create original analyses for examination. For example:
* selecting those sales ledger balances that exceed their authorised credit limits;
* examining all the general ledger items to confirm that they are all of a legitimate type;
* analysing the age rating of any file, particularly debtors;
* confirming that hire purchase interest rates lie within the client's predetermined limits;
* confirming that a payroll contains no duplicate payroll or national health numbers;
* confirming that a payroll contains no duplicate payroll or National Health limit;
* checking a payroll file to ensure that staff and rates of pay agree to those held on an independently produced personnel file.

Such scrutiny of items is in fact a very detailed review. So detailed in fact that it constitutes tests of detail, but on an entire population.

Deloitte, Haskins and Sells have developed two such packages entitled *Auditape* and *CARS 2/3*, which are very flexible in operation and cover a wide range of computers. To achieve their flexibility, they are based on modules, or 'routines', and these routines can be used in varying combinations to suit a particular application. The following are typical functions:

*Edit.* To put the file into the format required for subsequent routines.

*Include/Exclude.* To select records with fields greater or less than specified parameters (for example, to produce a stratified sample).

*Mathematical.* To add, subtract, multiply or divide any records or files (useful, for example, for casting a client's file or producing analyses).

*Match/Merge.* To match or merge records from two separate files (for example, pay rates might be matched from the payroll to independent personnel records).

*Statistical sampling.* To calculate the sample size required, to select the sample and to evaluate the result of the sample once the necessary testing work has been performed.

*Estimation sampling.* To determine the size or value of a population from a small sample. The program will determine the size of sample necessary for a given reliability or confidence. The most common application of estimation sampling is in stock valuation, where it is not possible to count the entire population. Instead a sample may be counted, and this used to estimate the value of the stock as a whole.

*Print-out.* To print out the results of the above procedures.

The programs are so designed that they do not require computer experts to operate them. A short period of training is normally sufficient to familiarise a staff member with the necessary specification forms which are the basis of operating each routine. So in this respect substantive and compliance testing using Computer Audit Programs requires less expertise than compliance tests involving Test Packs.

## *20.11 Remote terminals and real time data processing

Real time data processing involves the input of transaction data at the time the transaction takes place, and/or the reading of stored data in time to influence a transaction. For example, an airline booking terminal may interrogate the airline's reservation file via a VDU, to determine if a seat is available for a potential passenger. If a positive reply comes up on the screen, then the operator can key in a reservation immediately. To take another example, a bank may use a terminal to interrogate its file of customer account balances and credit limits, in order to determine whether a cheque may be cashed.

Terminals are commonly used for the input of cost data, and of sales too. Cash registers are now being marketed in the form of computer terminals, so that detailed records of stock sold can be kept, to provide a perpetual inventory;

and the value of stock sold can be precisely reconciled by the computer, to cash takings. Bar code labels on the individual items of stock can be read by a specially equipped till, to provide both excellent control, and extremely useful management information as to sales per location, and stock on hand.

The use of such sophisticated equipment is spreading rapidly, and used properly it can provide both strong control, and immediate management information, of a sort never before imagined. But on-line, real time systems do bring with them special problems for the auditor:

1. Control over total quantities and values of *input* documentation cannot be achieved in the same way as is possible with batch systems. And there will often be a lack of input documentation at the terminals.
2. It follows that control over *access* to the terminals themselves becomes crucial. And the extent to which terminal users can obtain information from, and input information into, the CPU must be carefully determined at the systems development stage.

### 1. *Control over input*

Not all terminal systems will have real time access to the files for *input* purposes. Sometimes a buffer store will be incorporated, thus enabling input to be validated by program checks, before the live files are accessed. This buffer store could also be dumped before processing, to facilitate reconstruction. A further possibility is that the buffer store could be printed out before processing, to maintain the audit trail, and to facilitate manual checks. Though this latter idea rather clashes with the otherwise sophisticated on-line terminal system.

If a terminal is fully on-line, real time, then files can be instantly up-dated. Such terminals are usually in the form of typewriter keyboards with VDUs (though punched card input can also be used), so it follows that the operator has total control over the input (and edit checks thereon), and can immediately see the results of his work. Furthermore there will often be a total loss of audit trail. In these circumstances, control over the situation of and access to computer terminals must be complete.

### 2. *Control over access*

(a) The situation of the terminals must be carefully considered. It may be appropriate to have a number of read-only terminals (such, for example, as in banks for reading account balances), and no, or very restricted, input access.
(b) Keys may be used to 'unlock' the terminal. These keys may be magnetic or embossed card and can be designed to unlock the computer itself. Alternatively, the computer terminal may be sited in a locked room with alarm and closed circuit TV surveillance.
(c) Passwords may be given to operators, to key into the terminal before the

machine will activate. A further sophistication is for the use of a password numeric code. For example, the code may be a $= 3$, b $= 16$; the computer could give a different formula each time, and the operator would have to give the answer, e.g. $5a - \sqrt{b} = ?-$ the operator would input 11 and the machine would activate. Any other answer and the computer could be programmed to call the security guards!

(d) Even more sophisticated is to use fingerprints to activate the computer – expensive but infallible for preventing unauthorised access.

(e) The CPU could record each occasion on which a terminal was activated, by whom, and the contents of the input. And such data could be regularly examined by the internal auditors. This technique, combined with (d) above, would make for a very strong control indeed. Sophisticated, yes, but then sophisticated techniques necessitate sophisticated control devices.

(f) Authority to operate should be granted by senior officials independent from the computer department, and independent from the intended users.

## 20.12 Service bureaux

Computers are still expensive pieces of machinery to buy and to operate (though this is becoming less so with the new generation of mini-computers). So some clients may decide to use service bureaux, particularly in the following situations:

(a) for economy – cheaper than owning a machine, or if access to a larger computer is required;

(b) an interim measure prior to installing own computer – allowing the gradual build up of computerised applications without incurring expensive overcapacity;

(c) own equipment working to full capacity.

Bureaux are often available from the following sources:

Manufacturers.
Universities.
Banks.
Independent companies.

And the following type of service are normally obtainable:

Time hire.
Application packages, e.g. payroll.
Complete systems.
On-line terminals.

If a client is considering the use of a service bureau, the auditor should consider the following matters, in conjunction with his client:

### 1. *Ownership and stability*

Does the bureau have suitable financial backing to make it a long-term viable proposition, particularly:

(a) Who are the shareholders?

(b) What is its credit rating (Dun & Bradstreet)?
(c) How long has it been in business?
(d) Is it a member of COSBA (Computer Service Bureaux Association)?
(e) Who are its other clients?
(f) Does the bureau already process other commercial applications on a disciplined basis?
(g) What is the type and experience of staff employed?

### 2. *Location*

(a) Is the location of the bureau such as to guarantee performance of processing within the time schedule under all conditions (e.g. bad weather, power failures, strikes, etc.)?
(b) Is the present machine loading of the bureau high? If so are their delivery and turnround proposals reasonable?

### 3. *Back up (stand-by)*

Has the bureau adequate stand-by arrangements to ensure continuity of processing within the client's time schedule, during machine breakdown?

### 4. *Documentation, education and programs, etc.*

(a) Does the bureau provide the user with full systems and program documentation?
(b) Are manuals provided for users, specifying format and purpose of all input and output and suitable processing details (in layman's language) for staff training purposes?
(c) Is all documentation handed over and approved before live processing commences?
(d) Are all proposed system and program changes after commencement of programming agreed in advance with the user?
(e) Who owns copyright of the programs and program documentation?
(f) Who has ownership of data files?

### 5. *Liability*

What is the liability of the bureau for:
(a) Losses due to lateness of processing or inability to process?
(b) Fraud by bureau staff?
(c) Incorrect transmission of data to third parties?
(d) Reconstruction of files due to corruption of magnetic storage?
   If the bureau limits liability under its standard contract, has the user an insurable interest? If the bureau does not limit liability is it adequately insured?

### 6. *Control*

(a) Is the system designed to enable the user to establish significant controls over data processed?

(b) Are these controls adequately evidenced and capable of reconciliation?
(c) In particular, is the treatment of master file amendments and error reports clearly defined?
(d) Are file retention or dumping routines adequate and adhered to?

### 7. Packages

(a) If a standard software package (e.g. an already written payroll package) is offered, para. 6 on control applies with equal emphasis.
(b) In addition, is the package such that the requirements of input and format and contents of output data can be adequately grafted into all existing accounting systems without any loss of control or additional work?

*Audit considerations for computer bureaux*

The same considerations and methods of control apply to the use of service bureaux, as in 'in-house' installations. The principal mode of processing is likely to be the batch method. Controls will be established clerically, but particular attention should be paid to the movement of data outside the client's premises. If data preparation is done at the bureau then it may be necessary to keep copies of raw data sent for processing.

The auditor should particularly ensure that the following matters are considered:

(a) Is there clearly defined liaison between user and bureau, with a senior staff member nominated as liaison officer for each application?
(b) Does the system testing stage involve all related clerical procedures?
(c) Are the responsibilities for, and the checking of file conversion, clearly defined?
(d) Are rejection procedures and responsibilities clearly defined and understood?
(e) Are output procedures clearly defined with particular emphasis on completion of output and receipt of exception reports?
(f) Is there a high degree of control over the maintenance of master files?

The principles and methods of audit tests will be the same as for 'in-house' installations. But there will be some practical difficulties. For example, the auditor will have no legal right to examine the controls in operation at the bureau. Permission for such examination should therefore be arranged at the time the service contract is drawn up. It may well be appropriate to liaise with the bureau's auditors, and/or the auditors of other companies using the bureau. The use of special audit techniques, and the obtaining of special print-outs, may well be logistically more difficult with a service bureau system. So even more attention must be paid to planning in advance, and the auditor should advise the client of the necessity to obtain the relevant permissions prior to the agreement of any contract.

In one respect, of course, the auditor can rely on greater control – a service bureau will be truly independent of the client's user departments.

## 20.13 Bibliography

William C. Mair, Donald R. Wood and Keagle W. Davis. *Computer Control and Audit.* QED Information Sciences Inc. (1978).

Susan Wooldridge, Colin Corder and Claude Johnson. *Security Standards for Data Processing.* Macmillan (1973).

A. Pinkney and B. Jenkins. *An Audit Approach to Computers.* ICAEW (1978).

Donald H. Sanders. *Computers and Management.* McGraw-Hill (1974).

# The legal liability of auditors

## 21.1 Changing standards

There are, in fact, very few decided court cases against auditors, and this makes it somewhat difficult to be precise as to where the auditor's legal liability falls. You may well find this surprising in view of the complaints about auditors' negligence that have been illustrated in previous chapters. But it is less surprising when you realise that the vast majority of actions against auditors are settled behind the scenes, before the cases ever come to court. This, of course, saves what could otherwise be highly expensive court costs. And almost as significant, it saves dragging the name of the professional firm concerned through the courts and through the headlines. Firms are understandably anxious to avoid such bad publicity.

So we have to go back to age old cases of the 1890s to find a general statement about the auditor's duties. In *Re London and General Bank*, Lindley LJ observed:

'Such I take to be the duty of the auditor: he must be honest – i.e. he must not certify what he does not believe to be true, and he must take reasonable care and skill before he believes that what he certifies is true. What is reasonable care in any particular case must depend on the circumstances of that case.'

And in Chapter 1 we saw similar remarks by Lopez LJ in The Kingston Cotton Mill case of about the same date. You will remember that Lopez observed the auditor '. . . is a watchdog, but not a bloodhound'; and that in the absence of suspicious circumstances, the auditor is not obliged to 'sniff out' all fraud and error, provided that he takes reasonable care. Whether such narrow definitions still hold true today, is difficult to say. But there are few positive judgments to extend these general principles. In *Fomento (Sterling Area) Ltd v. Selsdon Pen Co. Ltd* (1958), Lord Denning made the following remarks:

'What is the proper function of an auditor? It is said that he is bound only to verify the sum, the arithmetical conclusion, by reference to the books and all necessary vouching material and oral explanations; . . . I think this is too narrow a view. An auditor is not to be confined to the mechanics of checking vouchers and making arithmetical computations. He is not to be written off as a professional adder-upper and subtractor. His vital task is to take care to see that errors are not made, be they errors of computation, or errors of omission or commission, or downright untruths. To perform this task properly, he must come to it with an enquiring mind – not suspicious of dishonesty, I agree – but suspecting that someone may have made a mistake somewhere and that a check must be made to ensure that there has been none. I would not have thought that *Re Kingston Cotton Mill Co.* . . . relieved an auditor of his responsibility for making a proper check.'

However, it is by no means certain whether the auditor's duties to inquire are as high as Lord Denning suggests. What is clear, is that what constitutes 'reasonable skill and care' is to be judged in the light of *current* professional practice. This was stated by the judge in *Pacific Acceptance v. Forsyth* and was confirmed in *Re Thomas Gerrard* (already discussed in the context of stock). So in a sense, we set the standards by which we are then judged. But it is often difficult for the courts to decide just what are current standards. For each party to a case will invariably provide expert witnesses in support of their definition of current standards. And these definitions are often diametrically opposed. Though the formalised Auditing Standards should help to clarify what is the current position in future cases.

We can be certain that the auditor will be guilty of negligence if:
(a) he fails to detect fraud or error which he should reasonably have detected; and
(b) he fails to comply with generally accepted auditing standards.
Were the court to conclude that current standards were not reasonable, it is possible that it could still find an auditor negligent. However, it is extremely unlikely that the court would usurp the auditing profession's judgement in this way.

We can determine the auditor's liability under a number of specific headings:
1. To clients under contract law.
2. To third parties under the law of tort.
3. Civil and criminal liability under statute law.
And I will now deal with each of these in turn.

## 21.2 Liability to clients under contract law

The auditor is under a duty to report to the shareholders in general meetings, and his contract is with the company as a whole. He has no contract with individual shareholders. Accordingly, individual shareholders whose shares decrease in value as a result of an auditor's failure to detect fraud cannot sue the auditor for negligence in contract law. Such an action must be brought by the company itself . . . or by its liquidator.

For an action by the company to succeed, negligence must be proved, and financial loss must have occurred as a direct result of that negligence. An auditor would probably not be held to be negligent if he failed to detect a fraud which was immaterial to the company's accounts, unless there were suspicious circumstances which he had noticed, or should reasonably have noticed. Even if the fraud was material to the accounts, he may still escape liability if detection could not reasonably have been achieved using normal audit procedures (whatever they may be!). Though this is now a very dubious area of law.

In 1972 the ICAEW issued a statement on professional liability, after consultation with counsel. This statement is still relevant today, so extracts are accordingly reproduced below:

> In a number of cases it appears that . . . claims may have arisen as a result of some misunderstanding as to the degree of responsibility which the accountant was expected to take in giving advice or expressing an opinion. It is therefore important to distinguish between (a) disputes arising from misunderstanding regarding the duties assumed and (b) negligence in carrying out agreed terms.

> The use of engagement letters

> There is a contractual relationship between an accountant and his client. The accountant should therefore ensure that, at the time he agrees to perform certain work for the client, the scope of his responsibilities is made clear, preferably in writing, in that the terms of his contract with his client are properly defined. Wherever possible a letter of engagement should be prepared setting out in detail the actual services to be performed, and the terms of the engagement should be accepted by the client so as to minimise the risk of disputes regarding the duties assumed.

> (Note 1 – remember that the auditor cannot limit the scope of the statutory audit.
> Note 2 – in a 1978 survey of small practitioners by an ICAEW committee, nearly 70% of those members replying still did not use engagement letters at all.)

> Liability to clients

> Section 205 of the Companies Act 1948 makes void any provision in a company's articles, or any contractual arrangement purporting to exempt the auditor from, or to indemnify him against, any liability for negligence, default, breach of duty or breach of trust. Although Section 448 empowers the court, in certain circumstances, to grant relief either wholly or in part from any of such liabilities, it appears that these powers have seldom been exercised and it is prudent to assume that an auditor might not be relieved from liability under Section 205.

> A member desiring to exclude or limit his liability for negligence to his client (other than as auditor of a limited company) should, if possible, ensure that an appropriate reference is made to the exclusion or limitation in the letter of engagement because if an attempt is made to introduce such a provision into an existing relationship or in relation to a transaction for which instructions have already been accepted, difficulty

may be experienced in showing that there is any legal consideration for the client's agreement to submit to the exemption provisions.

Besides reporting as auditors under the Companies Acts 1948 and 1967, accountants are called upon to give opinions and advice, including financial advice, in connection with many other matters, for example, investigations or management consultancy assignments, the preparation or audit of the accounts of sole traders, partnerships and charities, and in the field of taxation. A member undertaking to carry out work of this nature should make clear to his client the extent of the responsibility he agrees to undertake, making particular reference to the information supplied to him as a basis for his work and to those areas (if any) to be excluded from his examination. In particular, if the client requires a 'snap' answer to a complicated problem, a member would be well advised to record in writing (or alternatively to state orally and forthwith to confirm in writing) that the problem is a complicated one, that he has been given a very limited time in which to study it, and that further time is required in order to consider it in depth and that his opinion or advice tendered might well be revised if further time were available to him. Except in the case of a genuine emergency, the client should be warned against acting on the 'snap' advice tendered before the further investigations have been carried out.

*Note that no attempt has been made in this statement to illustrate what would, and what would not, constitute negligence in satutory audit matters.*

## 21.3  Liability to third parties

In the chapter on small companies I made reference to the fact that company and contract law provide no redress for third parties in respect of audit negligence. This is so, but in certain specific circumstances, third parties may be able to obtain damages under the law of tort.

For a long time liability to third parties has existed in respect of physical injury (Donoghue and Stevenson, the famous case of the snail in the ginger beer bottle, is easily remembered). But liability for financial loss is a recent development. As late as 1951, the case of *Candler v. Crane Christmas and Co.* confirmed that there could be no liability for financial loss in the absence of a contractual relationship. In this case, accounts which failed to show a true and fair view were negligently prepared by the defendants (on their own admission). Mr Candler was induced to invest money in the company on the strength of these accounts, and he subsequently lost his investment when the company wound up. He failed in his attempt to sue the auditors by a majority verdict, with Lord Denning dissenting:

'Accountants . . . owe their duty, of course, to their employer or client and also, I think, to any third person to whom they themselves show the accounts, or to whom they know their employer is going to show the accounts so as to induce him to invest money or to take some other action on them. I do not think, however, the duty can be extended still further so as to include strangers of whom they have heard nothing and to whom their employer without their knowledge may choose to show their accounts. Once the accountants have handed the accounts to their employer, they are not, as a rule, responsible for what he does with them without their knowledge or consent.'

But Lord Denning's views were upheld some twelve years later in the famous 1963 case of *Hedley Byrne and Co. Ltd v. Heller and Partners Ltd*. Heller and Partners were sued in respect of losses which resulted from their negligent issuance of a customer reference, in their capacity as merchant bankers. They escaped liability only through a disclaimer clause, and Lord Morris clearly stated:

' . . . If someone possessed of a special skill undertakes quite irrespective of contract, to apply that skill for the assistance of another person who relies upon such a skill, a duty of care will arise.' . . . And then later his Lordship stated the principle even more widely . . . 'If in a sphere in which a person is so placed that others could reasonably rely on his judgement or his skill or upon his ability to make careful enquiry, a person takes it upon himself to give information or advice to, or allows his information or advice to be passed onto another who, as he knows or should know, will place reliance upon it, then a duty of care will arise.'

The Australian case of *Evatt v. Citizens and Mutual Life Assurance Co. Ltd* limits liability to people who are actually in the business of supplying advice or information of the type being relied upon by a plaintiff, or to people who claim to have commensurate skills.

The ICAEW 1972 statement, previously mentioned, contains comments relevant to third party liability:

Examples of occasions when an accountant may run the risk of incurring a liability to third parties under the Hedley Byrne doctrine include the following:

(a) preparing financial statements or reports for a client when it is known or ought reasonably to be expected that they are intended to be shown to and relied upon by a third party (even if the actual identity of the third party is not disclosed at the relevant time to the accountant).

(b) giving references regarding a client's creditworthiness, or an assurance as to his capacity to carry out the terms of contracts (e.g. leases), or giving any other type of reference on behalf of the client.

'Counsel has advised that where an accountant specifically restricts the scope of his report or expresses appropriate reservations in a note attached to and referred to in the financial statements or in his report thereon, this can constitute a disclaimer which will be effective against any action for negligence brought against him by third parties. It may be impossible to foresee whether the person to whom a document may be shown falls within (a) above. The accountant may therefore consider adding to the document a disclaimer on the following lines:

'This report (statement) has been prepared for the private use of X (the client) only. No responsibility to any third party is accepted.' However, such a disclaimer should be introduced only where the circumstances warrant it, as, in the Counsel's view, an indiscriminate use of disclaimers would tend to impair the status of practising accountants by indicating a lack of confidence in the professional work they carry out. It would not, for example, be proper to endorse copies of accounts filed in accordance with Section 127 of the Companies Act 1948 with a disclaimer by the auditor of responsibility to persons other than the shareholders. When giving references or assurances regarding creditworthiness or other matters, the accountant should adopt the normal commercial practice of stating that although the reference or assurance is given in good faith, he accepts no financial liability in respect of it.'

The ICAEW obtained counsel's advice as to the extent of potential liability following the Hedley Byrne decision. It was considered that the following circumstances must apply for liability to result on the basis of the Hedley Byrne decision:

(a) the accountants must have been negligent;
(b) the third party must have suffered a financial loss;
(c) the financial loss must have occurred as a direct result of the accountant's negligence;
(d) the accountant must have known the purpose for which his accounts or report were to be used;
(e) the accountant must have known the specific people or class of people who would be relying on his work, and he must have been aware of their reliance; in other words there must have been a 'special relationship' between the auditor and the third party.

However two recent cases have suggested a break away from the Hedley Byrne 'special relationship principle' – *Jeb Fasteners Ltd v Marks, Bloom and Co.* (1981), and *Twomax Ltd and Goode v Dickson, McFarlane and Robinson* (1982).

### Jeb Fasteners

In 1975, Marks, Bloom and Co. the defending firm of auditors reported on the annual financial statements of B G Fasteners Ltd for the year ended 31 October 1974. Stock had been valued at net realisable value of £23,000 instead of at cost of £11,000 resulting in overstated income and balance sheet figures. The auditors were aware of the company's liquidity problems, and had discussions with Jeb Fasteners, the plaintiffs, at the time of takeover negotiations.

Jeb Fasteners subsequently purchased the company, but the takeover was not a success. Consequently Jeb sued the auditors on the grounds that they were misled into purchasing the company by the misstated financials, and that the auditors had a duty of care to persons whom they could have reasonably foreseen would rely on their audit report. Justice Woolf ruled that such a duty of care did exist, but the auditors escaped liability on the grounds that the alleged negligence was not the cause of the loss. The judge ruled that the primary purpose of the takeover appeared to be the acquisition of the services of the two B G directors, and that a purchase would probably have taken place on the same basis even had the true financial position been known.

Justice Woolf applied a 'reasonable foresight' test, as opposed to the 'special relationship' test of Hedley Byrne. This was based on a judgment by Lord Wilberforce in the 1977 case of *Anns v London Borough of Merton*, in which it was held that:

'First, one has to ask whether, as between the alleged wrongdoer and the person who has suffered damage there is a sufficient relationship of proximity or neighbourhood such that, in the reasonable contemplation of the former, carelessness on his part may be likely to cause damage to the latter, in which case a prima facie duty of care arises.

'Second, if the first question is answered affirmatively, it is necessary to consider whether there are any considerations which ought to negate, or reduce or limit the scope of the duty or the class of person to whom it is owed or the damages to which any breach of it may give rise.'

In Jeb Fasteners, Justice Woolf ruled that the auditors were aware of the liquidity problems of B G and that financial assistance was or would become necessary, and that a takeover was certainly one method which 'was within the contemplation of Mr Marks [the auditor]'. Consequently, the judge decided that the events leading to the takeover of B G were foreseeable, although it was agreed by all parties that at the time of the audit Marks, Bloom and Co. were not aware of reliance by the plaintiffs or even of the fact that a takeover was contemplated.

The Court of Appeal agreed that there was a lack of causal connection between the auditor's negligence and Jeb's loss. It further stated that it was not necessary for it to decide on the extent of liability to confirm in favour of the defendants.

Accordingly, Justice Woolf's ruling has some authority but leaves the extent of third party liability still unconfirmed.

### Twomax Ltd

*Twomax Ltd and Goode v Dickson, McFarlane and Robinson* was a 1982 case decided in Scotland (where the law of negligence is the same as in England). Twomax Ltd acquired a controlling interest in Kintyre Knitwear Ltd of which Dickson, McFarlane and Robinson were the auditors. Twomax and joint plaintiffs Gordon and Goode, stated that they had relied on the audit opinion of Dickson *et al.* in purchasing their respective interest in Kintyre. There were various mistakes in the audited financials, particularly those for 1973, and had they been aware of the true position, the plaintiffs claimed they would not have been interested in the company. The auditors did not attend the stocktake and this contributed towards their being regarded as negligent.

Lord Steward relied on the Jeb case, and decided that although the auditors were not aware of the specific intention of the plaintiffs, they were aware of the fact that Kintyre needed capital. This made the situation forseeable, and the judge accordingly ruled in favour of the plaintiffs.

Although the extent of liability is still by no means certain, it would appear unwise for an auditor or accountant to rely on Hedley Byrne to restrict his liability. It would appear safest to assume that negligently prepared or audited financial statements can result in liability to clients and third parties alike.

A usual argument against the extension of liability to third parties is that company law requires the auditor to report to the existing shareholders, for the purposes of stewardship only. And that the accounts have not necessarily been prepared with others in mind. This latter is not a powerful argument, for it is hard to imagine a situation where accounts which are true and fair to members will be sufficiently misleading to others to provide the basis of a claim for negligence. Financial loss to creditors or other third parties will normally only occur as a result of the auditors' default, if the auditors have made some very significant 'goof'! And auditors' insurers should be well able to cover this risk, which could otherwise unfairly result in individuals bearing the loss.

On the other hand, it can be strongly argued that if company law wants auditors to report to creditors and others, it should clearly say so. And tort should not be used as a backdoor approach for creating such a liability; although on grounds of equity one can question whether the auditor should in fact be held responsible for the financial loss of every potential investor and every creditor who seeks to rely on his report. In the words of Cardozo in the famous American case of the *Ultramares Corporation v. Touche*, . . . it would be wrong for accountants to be exposed 'to a liability in an indeterminate amount for an indeterminate time to an indeterminate class'. The amounts involved could indeed be almost infinite, and the fact of reliance very difficult to prove objectively (herein would lie the auditor's greatest safeguard). Furthermore, it is the directors who should really take primary responsibility for loss through misleading accounts. Yet so often they are 'men of straw' so there is no point in pursuing them; the auditors, with their insurance cover, will prove a much better bet. But should we have to entirely bear this heavy burden, via our insurance premiums, whereas directors can often escape with a suspended jail sentence . . . and their illgotten spoils? Perhaps directors should also carry a mandatory indemnity insurance, as a requirement of holding office.

## 21.4 Liability under statute

Liability under statute can be both *civil* and *criminal*.

### Civil liability

Section 333 of CA 1948 provides that officers of the company (and for these purposes auditors are considered as officers – *Re Kingston Cotton Mill* and *Re London and General Bank*) may be liable for financial damages in respect of the civil offences of 'misfeasance' and 'breach of trust'. This section, which relates only to a winding up, refers to the situation where officers have mis-used their positions of authority for the purposes of personal gain.

*Criminal liability*

Sections 328–332 relate to criminal offences involving officers in a winding-up situation. You will have come across these during your company law studies so no detail is included here. But you should note that the term officer again includes the auditor . . . although of course the CA 1948 specifically states no *officer* of the company shall be appointed as auditor!

Section 438 CA 1948 states that an auditor shall be criminally liable, if he wilfully makes a materially false statement in any report, certificate, financial statement, etc. Wilfully implies fraudulently, and that can be difficult to prove. So cases are seldom brought under this section, because a conviction can be much more easily obtained under the 1968 Theft Act provisions, and the poor auditor could be put in prison for up to seven years under this act, as opposed to only two under Section 438!

Sections 15–19 of the Theft Act 1968 can apply to auditors, who are again treated as officers in this context. These provisions relate to all situations, not just to a winding up.

Sec. 15. 'A person who by any deception dishonestly obtains property belonging to another, with the intention of permanently depriving the other of it, shall on conviction on indictment be liable to imprisonment for a term not exceeding ten years.'

Sec. 16. 'A person who by any deception dishonestly obtains for himself or another any pecuniary advantage shall on conviction on indictment be liable to a term of imprisonment not exceeding five years.'

Sec. 17. 'Where a person dishonestly, with a view to gain for himself or another or with intent to cause loss to another –

(a) destroys, defaces, conceals or falsifies any account or any record or document made or required for any accounting purpose; or

(b) in furnishing information for any purpose, produces or makes use of any account, or any such record or document as aforesaid, which to his knowledge is or may be misleading, false or deceptive in a material particular;

he shall on conviction on indictment, be liable to imprisonment for a term not exceeding seven years'.

Sec. 18. This section extends liability to include officers and shareholders where they consent to, or have connivance in any of the offences in the above sections.

Sec. 19. 'Where an officer of a body corporate . . . with intent to deceive members or creditors . . . publishes or concurs in publishing a written statement or account which to his knowledge is or may be misleading, false or deceptive in a material particular, he shall on conviction on indictment be liable to imprisonment for a term not exceeding seven years.'

412 Legal liability of authors

Few cases have actually been brought against auditors under these sections, for it is seldom that they are actually complicit, or can be proved to be complicit in any fraud. But under the Prevention of Frauds (Investments) Act of 1958 such proof is not necessary.

Section 13 of this Act provides:

'Any person who, by any statement, promise or forecast which he knows to be misleading, false or deceptive, or by any dishonest concealment of material facts, or by the *reckless* making of any statement, promise or forecast which is misleading, false or deceptive, induces or attempts to induce another person to enter into, or offer to enter into, any agreement for . . . acquiring, disposing of, subscribing for, or underwriting securities or lending or depositing money . . ., shall be guilty of an offence and liable to imprisonment for a term not exceeding seven years.' Note that mere recklessness (akin to severe negligence) is sufficient for a criminal prosecution. Fraud is not a prerequisite. So we will have to be careful when we deal with prospectuses in Chapter 22!

# Specialised audit situations and investigations

## 22.1 Introduction

The principles that we have examined during the course of previous chapters will hold good no matter what the audit situation. But when the auditor undertakes certain specialised audits, particular additional considerations will apply. It is not possible here to cover all the specialised audit problems that the auditor may encounter, for each audit undertaken will have its own particular difficulties. Nor indeed is such coverage necessary, for a sound understanding of audit principles will enable the auditor to apply his knowledge to any given situation. But specialised audit situations do necessitate additional specialised knowledge. So the matrix chart (Table 22.1) shows the special rules or legislation governing various specialised businesses, together with the key characteristics which will be encountered during their audit. Sections 22.2 to 22.5 deal in slightly more detail with certain specialised audits which are more commonly encountered by the general practitioner (and are therefore more commonly examined). The remainder of the chapter deals with investigations.

## 22.2 Partnerships and sole traders

Most of this book has concentrated upon the audit of limited companies, for this constitutes the majority of the auditor's work, and hence largely constitutes the basis of examination questions. Limited companies require an audit by law, partnerships and sole traders do not. But they may request a firm of accountants to conduct an audit, as an addition to, or separate from, the function of preparing the accounts. Such an audit could bring advantages as previously cited in sec. 1.3.

As there is no legal requirement for the audit of partnerships and sole traders, there is clearly no legally prescribed basis upon which such work should be undertaken. So the extent and scope of work must be decided by agreement with the client. The client could, for example, specify an audit of wages or cash payments only. On the other hand he could specify a complete audit. But in the latter case it is essential to clarify exactly what is meant by 'complete', and for what purposes the audit is required. And does the client fully appreciate the difference between audit and accountancy work?

Partnerships may require an audit to forestall (or resolve) disputes between partners. Sole traders or partnerships may perhaps request an audit to determine the presence (or extent) of fraud by employees. And both may have an audit forced upon them by the bank, as a condition of granting or continuing a loan. These situations are very different, and none exactly parallels the 'true and fair' audit prescribed by company law. So it follows that the precise nature and scope of the audit must be documented (normally in an engagement letter) before work commences, in order to prevent misunderstandings (and possible law suits) later. And the distinction between audit work and accounts preparation must be clearly made. If a complete audit is specified, with most partnerships and sole traders it will be inherently similar in nature to the audit of a small limited company. For example, there may well be a lack of internal control, and heavy reliance on management representations. In this case, the same reporting principles apply, and it may well be appropriate to use a similar form of wording to that used by the APC in their guideline audit reports for small companies, though obviously reference to company legislation must be omitted. Reference to truth and fairness must only be made, however, if the auditor has had unrestricted access to all the accounting records, and has received all information and explanations that he deems necessary. If the client has in any way restricted the scope of the audit, then the auditor must precisely explain the extent of his work in his report, and no use should be made of the phrase 'true and fair'.

When an accountant has prepared accounts for his client, without audit, then he should clearly state this fact in his report:

'We have prepared the income statement and balance sheet set out on pages
......, without audit, and on the basis of information and explanations
supplied by .......... .'

And it will be advisable to clearly state the word *unaudited* on each page of the accounts.

When auditing the accounts of partnerships and sole traders, the auditor must bear in mind his legal liability to third parties. For example, if a client asks for an audit in response to a bank request, then the auditor may well owe a duty of care to the bank, under the Hedley Byrne rule. So he should take this into account when conducting the audit and making his report.

## 22.3 Building societies

Additional control problems particular to building societies are:
1. The large volume of deposits and withdrawals of small amounts of cash.
2. The granting of loans on mortgage.
3. Control over documents of title.
4. Control over investments and their related income.

The Building Societies Act 1962 recognises these problems and requires the auditor to form an opinion as to the effectiveness of the society's internal control, and of its custody procedures for documents of title. He must also ensure that the value of each property mortgaged is sufficient to cover the loan outstanding. Provision for losses must be calculated on an individual as opposed to cumulative

*Table 22.1*    Specialised Audit Situations

|  | Special Rules or Legal Requirements | Key audit areas |
| --- | --- | --- |
| Clearing banks and merchant banks | Exempted by para. 23, Part III, 2nd Sch. CA 1967, from some of the disclosure provisions of Part I, 2nd Sch., CA 1967. See CA checklist. (Certain Scottish banks no longer have this exemption). Sch. 8 CA 1981 specifies accounting requirements | Internal Control esp. re Computers. Internal audit. Provision for doubtful debts on advances. Manner of describing profit figure and balance sheet items which have included deducted hidden 'inner reserves' (allowed by CA 1967 provided verbal indication given) |
| Finance companies | Institute Statement N23. ED 28 on Leasing | Provision for doubtful debts. Accounting for unearned income. Calculation of turnover. Lease accounting (especially depreciation). Consistency of accounting policies |
| Insurance | Insurance Companies Act 1958. Exempted by para. 24 Part III, 2nd Sch. CA 1967 from some of the disclosure provisions of Part I, 2nd Sch. CA 1967. See CA checklist | Investments. Unearned premiums. Unexpired risks – when a category of business has proved to be unprofitable, provision is made for future losses on risks already accepted. Outstanding claims. Ascertainment of debtors and creditors. Actuarial valuation re life insurance |
| Stock Exchange firms | Rules 79a and 79b of the Rules of the Stock Exchange govern production and audit of accounts | Pledging of securities. Liquidity |
| Friendly societies | Governing Act – 1965 Industrial and Provident Societies Act. Accounts and audit – 1968 Friendly and Industrial and Provident Societies Act (for industrial and provident societies). 1974 Friendly Societies Act (for friendly societies) | See Institute Statement U26 |
| Shipping | Allowed by para. 25 Part III, 2nd Sch. CA 1967 to apply to D of T for exemption from some of the disclosure provisions of Part I, 2nd Sch. CA 1967, provided that D of T satisfied that exemption is in the national interest. See CA checklist | Voyage accounting. Insurance. Provisions for survey and repair. Proof of ownership at Registry of Shipping at ship's port of registration |

| | Special Rules or Legal Requirements | Key audit areas |
|---|---|---|
| Mining and raw material production | Especially: SSAP 9 SSAP 13 | Internal Control esp. re labour and plant. Depreciation and obsolescence of plant. Amortisation provisions re wasting assets, and development expenditure. Valuation of work in progress and finished goods. |
| Hotels and catering | Especially SSAP12 | Internal Control – large number of small value cash transactions. Physical controls against pilferage. Fixed asset registers esp. re fixtures and fittings. Importance of depreciation. Stocks of food, alcohol and tobacco. Overall control to budget and ratio analysis |

basis, as the risks are related to the potential default of individuals. The risk of loss through mortgagor default is not usually high in periods of inflation, for the trend towards increasing property values means that the building society's security automatically increases from the day the loan is granted. But problems can be experienced in periods of recession, or in the slump that often follows a rapid rise in house prices. Loans granted during periods of inflated values may then not be covered by the property values for the time the slump lasts. Mortgagors may then be tempted to pass on their loss to the building society, by defaulting on their payments. In these circumstances, civil action for pursuit of any balance owing after enforced sale of a property will seldom be worthwhile. Accordingly, the auditor of a building society must be especially on his guard in such times of economic slump, and must then be prepared to examine the mortgage portfolio in detail to ensure that the equity cover is sufficient.

Apart from the specific provisions mentioned above, the audit provisions in the Building Societies Act are inherently similar to those in the Companies Acts, in that the auditor must report whether in his opinion: the balance sheet and revenue and appropriation account (instead of profit and loss account) present a true and fair view of the society's affairs at the appropriate date, and of the income and expenditure of the period so ended, and comply with the Building Societies Act 1962.

And he must further report if he is not satisfied that proper accounting records have been maintained, or if he has not had access to such accounting records or to returns from branches, or if he has not received all the information and explanations necessary for the purposes of his audit. The accounting standards apply equally to building societies except in so far as a specific standard gives exemption.

Particular *internal control* matters to which the auditor will have to attend include:

## Cash deposits and withdrawals

Adequate control over deposits and withdrawals hinges upon sound recording procedures and strict supervision. Payments and withdrawals must be supported by vouchers, and these must be reconciled to an individual cashier's till. The reconciliations must be checked by the supervisor with reference to the opening and closing till balances. Deliberate concealment of vouchers by cashiers can be forestalled by supervision, and by ensuring that deposit vouchers and books are initialled by the cashier, so that the originator of any discrepancy could ultimately be traced. It is difficult to forestall misappropriation by cashiers who are not concerned about ultimate detection. The safeguard here is in ensuring that tills are constantly under surveillance so that any attempted concealment of misappropriated cash is likely to be observed. The auditors may consider circularising depositors, to establish the balances on their accounts for compliance and substantive testing purposes.

## Granting of loans

The task of granting loans is a responsible one which should only be assigned to senior personnel. The granting of a loan must be subject to:
(a) evidence of the mortgagor's financial status, and of his ability to cover payments. Character references would normally also be required, to assess the likelihood of default;
(b) report by a building society appointed surveyor to determine the mortgageable value of the property offered as security;
(c) evidence from solicitors that the property title is in order, and that the property is correctly conveyed to the mortgagor. Solicitors would be appointed by the building society for this task, and in practice the payment of the loan would be simultaneous with the conveyancing.

The official granting the loan should not be empowered to proceed without adequate evidence under each of the above heads, and there should be independent checks (by a more senior official, by internal audit, or both) to ensure that such evidence is prima facie in order for each loan granted. If such checks are not performed, the official would be enabled to pledge the society's assets on inadequate or non-existent security. In the event of default by the creditor, or in the case of loans to fictitious individuals then serious loss to the society could result.

## Custody of documents of title

Serious frauds have resulted from inadequate custody of documents of title. The chairman of the Gray's Building Society perpetrated a multi-million pound fraud largely concealed by manipulation of documents of title. It is essential that the auditor should examine a sample of deeds held as security for loans on mortgage, and in this connection it is not satisfactory to merely note that a society seal remains unbroken. The deeds must be carefully examined to ensure that they appear genuine and that the mortgage is properly entered in the name of the society. In the case of new loans entered into by the society, the auditor should select a sample and check for adequate supporting evidence as cited under 'granting of loans' above. And audit work upon such loans should also include an examination of the deeds.

## 22.4 Solicitors' accounts

During the course of his work, a solicitor will receive money from or on behalf of his clients. Solicitors employed by companies, building societies and other entities may also perform work involving the retention of clients' money for a considerable period of time. The handling of, and the accounting for, such money by the solicitor is subject to statutory legislation:

In England and Wales
The Solicitors' Act 1974.
The Solicitors' Accounts Rules 1975.
The Solicitors' Trust Account Rules 1975.
The Solicitors' Accounts (Deposit Interest) Rules 1975.
The Accountant's Report Rules 1975.

### Solicitors' Accounts Rules (SAR)

Statutory regulations require solicitors to maintain books and records in such a manner that clients' money is clearly distinguishable both from office money, and also from trust money. This can either be done using separate accounting records to record clients' money, or by using separate columns in books of account. A ledger account must be kept showing each transaction with a client, and revealing the balances owed to individual clients. Such moneys must be maintained in a separate bank account, identified as a 'client account', and receipts must be banked without delay.

The solicitor is required to reconcile the clients' cash book balances with the clients' account bank statements not less than once in every three month period, and he is also required to keep a copy of the reconciliation statements. No money may be withdrawn from a clients' bank account other than under the signature of either a solicitor who holds a current practising certificate, or an employee of such a solicitor (who is either a solicitor, or a fellow of the Institute of Legal Executives for at least five years and who is confirmed by the Institute as being of good standing).

A decision tree depicting what constitutes 'clients' money' is shown in Fig. 22.1.

*Accountant's Report Rules*

Every solicitor who handles 'clients' money' is required to produce each practice year to the Law Society a report signed by a qualified accountant, confirming that he has complied with the SAR. Such a report is necessary for the renewal of his practising certificate. Each member of an individual practice requires such a report in the event that he handles 'clients' money'. For these purposes, a qualified accountant is a member of the English, Irish or Scottish Institutes of Chartered Accountants, or of the Association of Certified Accountants, provided that he is not an employee of the solicitor and that he is not disqualified by the Law Society.

You should note that there is no requirement for the audit (or even production) of solicitors' accounts, other than those in respect of 'clients' money'.

*Audit work*

1. *All balances in the clients' ledger must normally be checked* with the solicitor's list of balances at two separate dates within the practice year (one of which dates will normally be the year end). In the event that the client has not listed the balances, then they will have to be extracted by the auditor. The list must be compared with the client's cash book balance, as reconciled with bank statements/ certificates.

But in June 1979 the Council of the Law Society agreed to waive the requirements to extract or to check extractions of balances on the clients' ledger accounts under the following circumstances:
(a) that the solicitor uses either a computerised or a mechanised system which automatically produces an extraction of all client ledger balances;
(b) that a satisfactory system of internal control is in operation;
(c) that a test check of the extraction is carried out.
If a reporting accountant relies on this waiver, his report should make this clear by adding the following comment (or similar) to the reverse side of the report: This report has been made in reliance on the waiver rule 4(1)(f) of the Accountant's Report Rules 1975 published by the Law Society on 13 June 1979.

2. *Any debit balances in the clients' ledger must be investigated,* for such balances should not be present. It is possible that they may be covered by credit balances on another account for the same client. But in such cases care must be exercised to ensure that the credit balances held can legally be set off against the debit balances, otherwise the debit balances constitute a breach of the rules. Note that if a solicitor wishes to advance money to or on behalf of a client, he must do so out of an office (firm's) account, or a private account. So no debit balances should appear in the clients' ledger for this cause.

3. *The listing of balances in the clients' ledger should also be checked to ensure that none are in the name of partners in the practice.* A solicitor must not treat himself as a client. Any cheques drawn in favour of partners and debited to clients' accounts should be carefully investigated. If money is properly required for or towards payment of a solicitor's costs it may be drawn from a client account. But only if a

Fig. 22.1 Solicitors' Accounting Rules

**Accounting for clients' and trust money received under the Solicitors' Account Rules 1975 and Solicitors' Trust Account Rules 1975**

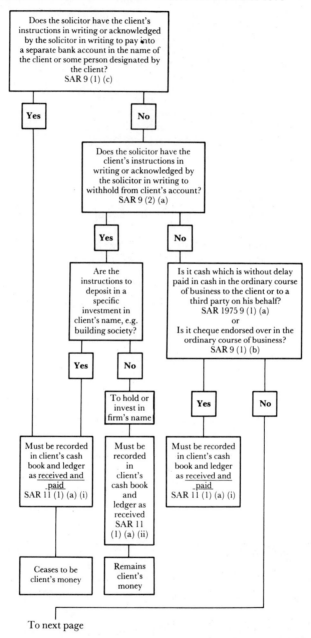

To next page

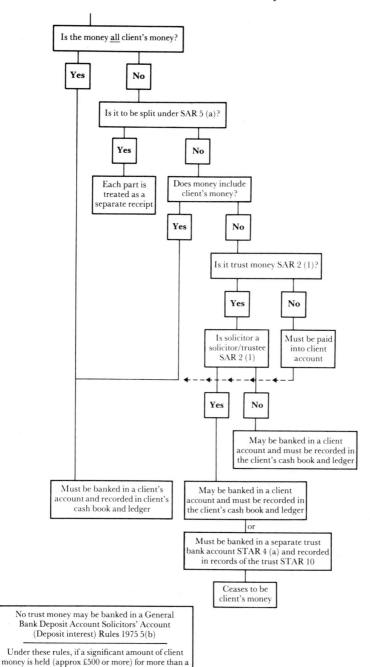

Is the money <u>all</u> client's money?

Yes / No

Is it to be split under SAR 5 (a)?

Yes — Each part is treated as a separate receipt

No — Does money include client's money?

Yes / No

Is it trust money SAR 2 (1)?

Yes — Is solicitor a solicitor/trustee SAR 2 (1)

No — Must be paid into client account

Yes / No

May be banked in a client account and must be recorded in the client's cash book and ledger

Must be banked in a client's account and recorded in client's cash book and ledger

May be banked in a client account and must be recorded in the client's cash book and ledger

or

Must be banked in a separate trust bank account STAR 4 (a) and recorded in records of the trust STAR 10

Ceases to be client's money

No trust money may be banked in a General Bank Deposit Account Solicitors' Account (Deposit interest) Rules 1975 5(b)

Under these rules, if a significant amount of client money is held (approx £500 or more) for more than a short period, interest is due to the client. In these circumstances the solicitor may either deposit the money in a separate bank account, and pass over the interest earned, or pay out of his own money an equivalent amount

N.B. Whenever money ceases to be client's money, it also ceases to fall within the tests under ARR 1975 bill or letter indicating the amount of costs incurred and the fact that money held on the client's behalf is being used in satisfaction of these costs can client money be applied in this way. The auditor should test the dates of such bills or letters with the dates of transfer of funds from client accounts, to ensure that this regulation has not been contravened.

4. *A test examination must be made of suitable documents with a view to ascertaining and confirming that financial transactions involving client money* (including those that gave rise to transfers from one ledger account to another) *are in accordance with SAR 1975.* A test examination must also be made of the entries in the clients' ledger accounts to check that they reflect the transactions in a manner that complies with the rules.

The selection of files should cover at least one client of each partner and each fee earner in the practice. And where a solicitor declines to produce a file or document (for example, on the grounds of privilege) or where a file cannot be found, the accountant's report must be qualified.

5. *A test examination must be made of paid cheques* to ensure that they are signed by an authorised signatory. In this regard an examination of the signature mandate to the bank should also be made.

6. *The office cash book and other accounting records* should be examined to ensure that they do not contain any transactions involving client money, other than permitted transfers.

7. *A check must be made to prove that client bank accounts are maintained at banks permitted by S87(1) Solicitors' Act 1974:*
(a) Bank of England;
(b) Post Office or bank recognised in terms of Banking Act 1979;
(c) Companies recognised as a bank by the Secretary of State in accordance with the Protection of Depositors Act 1963 (Banks so recognised are published quarterly in *Trade and Industry*);
(d) A Trustees Savings Bank.

8. In addition to all these specific requirements of the Accountant's Report Rules, *the normal audit tests* in relation to cash also apply, e.g. casting, posting and reconciling.

### Reporting

A form of the accountant's report is shown in the Schedule to the ARR and a copy of this is reproduced in Fig. 22.2. The report has to be submitted to the Secretary of the Law Society within six months of the end of the practice's financial year and once in every year ending 31 October. A separate report is needed for each partner, including each individual held out to be a partner, covering all addresses from which they practice.

## 22.5 Share transfer audit

A share transfer audit is not part of the statutory auditor's normal responsibilities. Nevertheless, auditors will often be asked to undertake this additional task (for an additional fee of course!), as the risk of loss through errors or fraud in transferring shares can be enormous. For example, an incorrect transfer could result in payment of a dividend to the wrong person, with the resulting necessity of a second, correct, payment. In these circumstances it is unlikely that the original payment would be recovered. Alternatively, the unauthorised transferee could sell the shares, and the correct shareholder would again have to be compensated. Such frauds are not uncommon, and the resulting losses can run into millions of pounds.

As the audit is not a statutory requirement, the directors can decide the extent of the work they wish performed. Accordingly it is very necessary to have the precise scope of the work documented in an engagement letter. The auditor should, however, beware any excessive restrictions on scope, which may restrict him from satisfying himself that proper share transfer procedures have been carried out. For in the event of a fraud subsequently coming to light, the auditor may be in a difficult position, unless he has made it clear that the scope restrictions have prevented him from carrying out a satisfactory audit.

*Internal control*

The auditor must primarily satisfy himself that the internal control procedures in relation to share transfers are satisfactory. In this connection, he should consider the following matters:

1. Is there adequate control over unissued share certificates, and are these only issued on adequate authority?
2. Are transfers made in accordance with the Articles of Association?
3. Is there adequate control over the completion of transfers? Are names, addresses, descriptions and numbers of shares on transfer deeds checked to the register of members, and are transfers checked to ensure that they are properly signed?
4. Are transferors advised of the receipt of transfers in time for them to object to a transfer in the event that it is fraudulent?
5. Is there a check to ensure that the transfer register is kept up to date?
6. Are old certificates relating to transferred shares received, and cancelled after being checked to the register of members?

*Audit tests*

The quantity of audit tests will be dictated as usual by the quality of the internal control. In the event that control is weak, frequent visits may be necessary, as it is important then that the tests should be carried out as soon as possible after transfers are completed. Audit work will largely involve compliance tests to ensure that the above controls have been working satisfactorily in practice throughout the period.

Fig. 22.2 Accountant's Report under SAR

## The form and content of the Accountants Report for England and Wales

*Note:* In the case of a firm with a number of partners, carbon copies of the Report may be delivered provided section 1 below is completed on each Report with the name of the individual solicitor.

(a) BLOCK CAPITALS

(b) *Note*: All addresses at which the Solicitor(s) practice(s) must be covered by an Accountant's Report or Reports. If an address is not so covered, the reason must be stated.

(c) *Note*: The period(s) must comply with Section 34(3) of the Solicitors Act 1974, and the Accountant's Report Rules 1975.

1. Solicitor's Full Name (a) _____

2. Firm(s) Name(s) Address(es) (b) _____
   _____
   _____
   _____
   _____

3. Whether practising alone _____ or in partnership _____

4. Accounting Period(s) (c)
   Beginning _____ Ending _____
   Beginning _____ Ending _____

In compliance with Section 34 of the Solicitors Act 1974, and the Accountant's Report Rules 1975, made thereunder, I have examined to the extent required by Rule 4 of the said Rules the books, accounts and documents produced to me in respect of the above practice(s) of the above-named solicitor.

1. In so far as an opinion can be based on this limited examination I am satisfied that during the above mentioned period(s) he has complied with the provisions of the Solicitors' Accounts Rules 1975, except so far as concerns:

Delete sub-paragraphs not applicable.

   (a) certain trivial breaches due to clerical errors or mistakes in book-keeping all of which were rectified on discovery and none of which, I am satisfied, resulted in any loss to any client;

   (b) the matters set out in the First Section on the back hereof, in respect of which I have not been able to satisfy myself for the reasons therein stated;

   (c) the matters set out in the Second Section on the back hereof, in respect of which it appears to me that the solicitor has not complied with the provisions of the Solicitors' Accounts Rules 1975.

2. The results of the comparisons required under Rule 4(1)(f) of the Accountant's Report Rules 1975, at the dates selected by me were as follows:

Delete (a) or (b) as appropriate.

(i) at _____

    (a) the figures were in agreement.

    (b) there was a difference computed as follows:

Liabilities to clients as shown    £
by clients' ledger accounts

Cash held in client account after allowance for outstanding cheques and lodgments cleared after date

                           £

Delete (a) or (b) as appropriate.

(ii) at _____

    (a) the figures were in agreement.

    (b) there was a difference computed as follows:

Liabilities to clients as shown    £
by clients' ledger accounts

Cash held in client account after allowance for outstanding cheques and lodgements cleared after date

                           £

3. (a) Having retired from active practice as a solicitor the said _____ ceased to hold client's money on _____

   (b) Having ceased to practice under the style of _____ the said _____ ceased to hold client's money on _____

*Particulars of the accountant:*

Full Name _____

Qualifications _____

Firm Name _____

Signature _____ Date_____

First section

To be printed on the reverse of the Report.

Matters in respect of which the accountant has been unable to satisfy himself and the reason for that inability:

Second section

Matters (other than trivial breaches) in respect of which it appears to the accountant that the solicitor has not complied with the provisions of the Solicitors' Accounts Rules 1975:

## *22.6 Investigations

Special investigations undertaken by accountants are many and varied. For example:

(a) reports on prospectuses in connection with the marketing of share capital;
(b) reports on investigations of companies and businesses on behalf of prospective purchasers;
(c) reports on behalf of prospective vendors of companies and businesses;
(d) reports to merchant bankers and others in connection with proposals to provide finance;
(e) reports on profit forecasts and the adequacy of financial resources;
(f) reports on the valuation of businesses and share capital of companies;
(g) reports in connection with the merger of companies;
(h) reports on schemes of reorganisation of share capital;
(i) reports on defalcations;
(j) back duty investigations on behalf of the Inland Revenue;
(k) investigations on behalf of the Department of Trade under Companies Act legislation;
(l) reports on accounting organisation and procedures.

Although the above investigations are very different, they all have one thing in common – the writing of a report. And all the reports will have certain features in common, which we will now examine.

At the outset of an assignment it is necessary to obtain *specific instructions* from the client regarding:

(a) the work to be carried out;
(b) the information expected in the report;
(c) the date by which the report is required.

Where initial instructions are received at a meeting with the client, then a *memorandum* of the matters discussed should be drafted with a copy sent to the client for his agreement. Of course, in the event of a statutory investigation, the scope of the work will be defined by statute. But a letter confirming the undertaking should nonetheless be sent to those responsible for commissioning the investigation.

Once the nature of the work has been established, it will usually then be appropriate to draw up a *questionnaire* detailing the information that will be necessary to carry out the investigation. This information can then be collected by the client prior to the investigating accountant's first visit. The accountant should then prepare a work programme that will enable him to meet the client's reporting date, and to determine how much assistance he will need. Permission should be sought at this stage to confirm factual information with third parties (if appropriate).

After the basic information about the company has been assimilated, and the nature of the investigation problem determined, it may then be appropriate to draw up a *report skeleton* or index. This will then enable the investigating accountant to marshal the necessary information, and to delegate sections to his assisting colleagues. It should also help him to avoid being sidetracked by the welter of detailed information which will inevitably come to light during the course of his investigations.

*The report* itself should be as brief and easy to assimilate as possible; the language in which it is drafted should take into account the financial knowledge of the reader. To preserve the flow, detailed supporting figures should be relegated to appendices, with only primary figures shown in the main report. A scope and a concluding paragraph should always be included in any report:

(a) The scope section should set out:
1. full details of the mandate given by the client,
2. a summary of the purpose of the report, and the extent of the associated investigations,
3. sources of information upon which the report is based.
(b) The concluding paragraph should be short and unambiguous, and should acknowledge assistance received, and express a willingness to have further discussion with the client should he so wish.

## *22.7 Profit forecasts

Many investigations will involve an examination of forecasts of future profits. This of course departs from the auditor's traditional role of expressing an opinion on the truth and fairness of historical accounts. And it should be emphasised immediately that there is no question of profit forecasts being audited. The reporting accountant is only in a position to examine the accounting policies, and calculations used in a forecast. He is not currently expected to comment on the assumptions upon which the forecast is based, for this is the job of the directors (though if it appears to an accountant that an assumption is unrealistic, then he should not allow that assumption to be used).

Profit forecasts are frequently included in prospectuses and are also often sent to shareholders in the context of takeover/merger situations. The 1960s saw many such bid situations, and they also saw some grossly inaccurate profit forecasts. Such forecasts attracted much adverse publicity, and partly as a result of this, the Panel on Takeovers and Mergers was established, assigned with the task of formulating a code for regulating bid situations. The 'City Code on Mergers and Takeovers' was first published in April 1969 and is regularly updated in the light of experience. And this has done much to calm what hitherto were often wildly exaggerated claims. But the assumptions used can still be unrealistic, and it is felt by many that there is room for further strengthening of the requirements for expert examination of forecasts – such examination to include an analysis of the realism of the assumptions upon which the forecasts are based. And a further criticism of the existing arrangements is that the code lacks legal sanctions. The only constraint available to the Panel or the Stock Exchange is the threat to disbar recalcitrants from membership of the relevant body (e.g. the Issuing Houses Association or quotation on the Stock Exchange). By contrast, in America the Securities and Exchange Commission has powerful legal sanctions, and these have proved effective in expediting matters relating to securities regulation.

In November 1978, the CCAB issued statement S23 covering accountants' reports on profit forecasts, and this is now reproduced below.

*S23 Accountants' reports on profit forecasts*

## DEFINITIONS

1. *Profit forecast* is any published estimate of financial results made:
   (a) in advance of completion of financial statements up to publication standard (see paragraph 9 below) for any expired accounting period;
   (b) for a current (or unexpired) accounting period;
   (c) for a future accounting period.
   The definition extends to include other statements which are not expressed in terms of figures, e.g. 'profits would be somewhat higher than last year'. The term profit forecast is used interchangeably with forecast, forecast of profits and profits forecast.

2. *'The Yellow Book'* refers to 'Admission of Securities to Listing', issued by the authority of the Stock Exchange, and dated March 1973, with subsequent revisions to July 1976 which are to be interpreted in accordance with a Notice issued by the council of the Stock Exchange on 6 August 1975.

3. *'The City Code'* refers to 'The City Code on Take-overs and Mergers', issued by the authority of the City Working Party, and dated April 1976.

4. *Practice Notes* are a series of Memoranda of Interpretation and Practice issued as supplements to 'the City Code'. The Stock Exchange regards them as applicable to documents required by the Yellow Book where these contain profit forecasts. (Practice Notes were renumbered in the April 1976 edition of the City Code.)

5. *The regulations* are those contained in 'the Yellow Book' and 'the City Code'; particularly Schedule II, Part A, paragraphs 17 and 32 and Part B, paragraphs 1 and 26, of 'the Yellow Book', and Rules 14, 15 and 16 and Practice Notes 3 and 4 of 'the City Code'. The quotations in this Statement are from these sections of the City Code.

6. *Reporting Accountants* are any practising accountants reporting under the regulations, whether as auditors or otherwise.

7. *Document* is any circular, prospectus or advertisement issued under these regulations.

8. *Assumptions* are the assumptions disclosed in the document relating to both the general economic, commercial, marketing, financial and other conditions under which the company expects to operate, and the assumed position of the Company in relation thereto. (See Practice Note 4.)

9. *Publication standard* is defined in Practice Note 3 paragraph 3 as applying to figures that 'have received the same degree of examination and carry the same degree of authority as normally apply to published but unaudited interim or preliminary final results of the company in question'.

10. *Accounting bases* are the methods developed for applying fundamental accounting concepts to financial transactions and items, for the purpose of financial statements, and in particular (a) for determining the accounting periods in which revenue and costs should be recognised in the profit and loss account and (b) for determining the amounts at which material items should be stated in the balance sheet. (Statement of Standard Accounting Practice No. 2, 'Disclosure of accounting policies', paragraph 15).

11. *Accounting policies* are the specific accounting bases selected and consistently followed by a business enterprise as being, in the opinion of the management, appropriate to its circumstances and best suited to present fairly its results and financial position. (SSAP2, paragraph 16.)

## INTRODUCTION

*Regulations relating to profit forecasts*

12. The only regulations in relation to profit forecasts are contained in the Yellow Book and the City Code. Among other matters, the regulations explain when an accountants' report is required on a profit forecast, the duties placed on the reporting accountants and the responsibility of the directors for the assumptions. The regulations apply when the issuer of a document himself decides to include a profit forecast in that document or is required to do so by the rules of the Takeover Panel.

13. Practice Note 3, paragraph 7, states that:
    'Where practicable when a profit forecast is included in a document

addressed to shareholders there should be included forecasts of turnover, profit before taxation, taxation, profit before extraordinary items, extraordinary items, profit after taxation, and earnings per share before extraordinary items.'

*Requirements for reporting accountants*

14. The regulations require reporting accountants:
    (a) to examine and report on the accounting policies and calculations for the profit forecasts (Rule 16); (Note: The Panel on Take-overs and Mergers have indicated their intention to amend their regulations to include the term 'accounting policies' in place of 'accounting bases');
    (b) to satisfy themselves that the profit forecasts, so far as the accounting policies and calculations are concerned, have been properly compiled on the footing of the assumptions made. (Practice Note 4, paragraph 5.)

15. It is not the reporting accountants' responsibility to report upon the assumptions or to report on the prospects of the company achieving the profit forecast. Nevertheless, Practice Note 4, paragraph 5, states that reporting accountants should not allow an assumption to be published which appears to them to be unrealistic (or one to be omitted which appears to them to be important), without commenting on it in their report (see further paragraphs 24–26 below).

16. It is emphasised that profit forecasts necessarily depend on subjective judgements. They are, to a greater or less extent according to the nature of the business and period the profit forecast covers (see paragraph 19(c) below), subject to numerous and substantial inherent uncertainties. In consequence, profit forecasts are not capable of being substantiated by reporting accountants in the same way as financial statements which present the results of completed accounting periods.

17. It is, therefore, important that reporting accountants should make this clear when they accept instructions to examine the accounting policies and calculations for profit forecasts, and in the wording of their report they should take care to avoid giving any impression that they are in any way confirming, underwriting, guaranteeing or otherwise accepting responsibility for the ultimate accuracy and realisation of forecasts. Moreover, bearing in mind their special

status and authority, reporting accountants should do or say nothing to encourage directors, third parties or the public to place a mistaken degree of reliance on statements as to future profits the achievement of which must always be subject to uncertainty.

## PRACTICE

18. The reporting accountants' work to fulfil the requirements above falls into three main sections:
    (a) preliminary considerations;
    (b) review of profit forecasts;
    (c) the accountants' report.

*Preliminary considerations*

19. Reporting accountants should agree with the directors the following fundamental points before accepting instructions to report:
    (a) the purpose for which the profit forecast has been prepared and the accountants' report is required;
    (b) (i) that the reporting accountants' instructions and responsibilities for reporting are limited to the requirements under the regulations;
        (ii) that the directors assume full responsibility for the profit forecast under review;
        (iii) that the directors will signify their responsibility for formal adoption by the Board;
    (c) that the profit forecast is for:
        (i) an expired accounting period;
        (ii) the current accounting period, or
        (iii) the current and the next following accounting period, provided that a sufficiently significant part of the current period has already elapsed;
    (d) no material restrictions on the scope of the reporting accountants' work (for example, by restricting visits to overseas companies or material factory units) can normally be accepted unless the matter is dealt with in the reporting accountant's report and in the published document;
    (e) that the time within which the accountants' report is required is not so severely restricted that, having regard to the company's circumstances and forecasting experience, and notwithstanding

their best endeavours, it would be plainly impossible for the reporting accountants to obtain sufficient information to enable them properly to exercise their professional judgement.

20. In the case of a profit forecast in a prospectus, the Stock Exchange requires that the issuing house or sponsoring brokers report whether or not they have satisfied themselves that the forecast has been stated by the directors after due and careful enquiry. In the case of a profit forecast in a document connected with an offer the City Code requires that any financial adviser mentioned in the document also report on the forecast. The responsibilities of such persons are distinct from those of the reporting accountants. From the outset, liaison should be established with such other financial advisers to ensure that there is no doubt or misunderstanding on either side as to the respective responsibilities or as to the work which will be carried out by each party to enable it to fulfil its reporting function.

*Review of a profit forecast*

21. In carrying out their review, the main matters to which the reporting accountants will direct their attention are as follows:
    (a) the nature and background of the company's business;
    (b) the accounting policies normally followed by the company;
    (c) the assumptions on which the profit forecast is based;
    (d) the procedures followed by the company in preparing the profit forecast.

22. *The nature and background of the company's business.* The reporting accountants will wish to review the company's recent history, with reference to such matters as the general nature of its activities and its main products, markets, customers, suppliers, divisions, locations, management, labour force and trend of results.

23. *The accounting policies normally followed by the company.* The reporting accountants will wish to establish which accounting policies have been adopted by the company in published financial statements so as to ensure that they are acceptable and have been consistently applied in the preparation of interim accounts and the profit forecast.

24. *The assumptions on which the profit forecast is based.* It is the responsibility of the reporting accountants to determine that the

profit forecast is consistent with and has been properly compiled on the footing of the given assumptions.

25. It has been suggested that Practice Note 4 (referred to in paragraph 15 above) might have changed the reporting accountants' responsibilities for the assumptions. The opinion of Counsel consulted by the Institute of Chartered Accountants in England and Wales is in summary form:

'Practice Note 4 does not change the responsibilities of reporting accountants so far as the choosing, listing or drafting of the assumption is concerned. The Practice Note imposes on reporting accountants no obligation whatever to report on the assumptions. They have no obligation to state that they consider the assumptions to be realistic or to be complete. Their only duty is that if an assumption which is to be published appears to them to be unrealistic or if an assumption is to be omitted which appears to them to be important they must comment upon it in their report. The fact that reporting accountants review the assumptions either as part of their normal practice or on the specific instructions of the company or issuing house, does not extend the duty stated above. This applies whether or not an outside party knows that the reporting accountants have reviewed the assumptions. However, the nature of the instructions accepted by the reporting accountant may involve them in a separate responsibility to the company or issuing house.'

26. Accordingly the reporting accountants have no specific responsibilities for and are not required by the regulations to report on the assumptions. However, in the course of their work on the accounting policies and calculations, they will need to consider the assumptions on which the profit forecast has been based. They should not allow an assumption to be published which appears to them to be unrealistic (or one to be omitted which appears to them to be important) without commenting on it in their report. (Practice Note 4, paragraph 5.) As a result of their work they will be in a position to advise upon the assumptions that should be included in the documents in conformity with the guidance in Practice Note 4, and in particular with the general rules set out in paragraphs 13–15 thereof.

27. *The procedures followed by the company for preparing the profit forecast.* In carrying out their examination of the accounting policies and calculations for the profit forecast, and of the procedures followed by the company for its preparation, the main points which the reporting accountants will wish to consider include the following:
    (a) whether the profit forecast under review is based on forecasts regularly prepared for the purpose of management, or whether

it has been separately and specifically prepared for the immediate purpose;

(b) where profit forecasts are regularly prepared for management purposes, the degree of accuracy and reliability previously achieved, and the frequency and thoroughness with which estimates are revised;

(c) whether the profit forecast under review represents the management's best estimate of results which they reasonably believe can and will be achieved as distinct from targets which the management have set as desirable;

(d) the extent to which profit forecast results for expired periods are supported by reliable interim accounts;

(e) the details of the procedures followed to generate the profit forecast and the extent to which it is built up from detailed profit forecasts of activity and cash flow;

(f) the extent to which profits are derived from activities having a proved and consistent trend and those of a more irregular, volatile or unproved nature;

(g) how the profit forecast takes account of any material extraordinary items and prior year adjustments, their nature, and how they are presented;

(h) whether adequate provision is made for foreseeable losses and contingencies and how the profit forecast takes account of factors which may cause it to be subject to a high degree of risk, or which may invalidate the assumptions (see Practice Note 4);

(i) whether working capital appears adequate for requirements; normally this would require the availability of properly prepared cash-flow forecasts; and where short-term or long-term finance is to be relied on, whether the necessary arrangements have been made and confirmed;

(j) the arithmetical accuracy of the profit forecast and the supporting information and whether forecast balance sheets and sources and applications of funds statements have been prepared – these help to highlight arithmetical inaccuracies and inconsistent assumptions.

*The accountants' report*

28. The accountants' report will be addressed to the directors and will normally include statements dealing with the following matters, so

far as appropriate:

(a) specific identification of the profit forecast and documents to which the report refers;

(b) the fact that the directors are solely responsible for the profit forecast;

(c) the fact that the reporting accountants have examined the accounting policies and calculations used in arriving at the profit forecast;

(d) if, as will frequently be the case, the reporting accountants have not carried out an audit of results for expired periods, a statement to that effect;

(e) whether in the opinion of the reporting accountants the profit forecast, so far as the accounting policies and calculations are concerned has been properly compiled on the footing of the assumptions made by the board of directors, as set out in the document, and is presented on a basis consistent with the accounting policies normally adopted by the company.

29. The report should be qualified if, *inter alia*, the reporting accountants:

(a) have reason for material reservation about the accounting policies or calculations for the profit forecast;

(b) have reason to consider the accounting policies and calculations to be inconsistent with the stated assumptions;

(c) have not obtained all the information they consider necessary (for example the fact that they were unable to review the profit forecasts of material subsidiary or associated companies or because of unduly restrictive time limits).

30. If any of the assumptions which are to be published appear to them to be unrealistic, or if any assumption is to be omitted which appears to them to be important, they should include an appropriate comment in their report.

31. *Specimen report.* An accountants' report might in appropriate circumstances, where there are no grounds for qualifications, read as follows:

To the directors of X Limited

We have reviewed the accounting policies and calculations for the profit forecasts of X Limited (for which the directors are solely responsible) for the

periods .................... set out on pages ............ of this circular.
The forecasts include results shown by unaudited interim accounts for the
period .................... In our opinion the forecasts, so far as the
accounting policies and calculations are concerned, have been properly compiled
on the footing of the assumptions made by the Board set out on page ..........
of this circular and are presented on a basis consistent with the accounting
policies normally adopted by the company.

32. *Letter of consent.* The regulations require that an accountants' report
    contained in a document must be accompanied by a statement that
    the reporting accountants have given in writing, and not withdrawn,
    their consent to its publication.

33. Some of the documents containing profit forecasts are also
    prospectuses for Companies Act purposes, in which case, there is a
    statutory requirement that the consent specifically refers to the
    statement being included, in the form and context in which it is
    included, and that the statement that the consent has been given
    and has not been withdrawn should appear in the prospectus.

34. *Re-issuance of forecast.* In the event of a forecast being re-issued by the
    company, that forecast must contain a statement by the directors
    that the forecast remains valid for the purpose of the offer, and that
    the financial advisers and accountants who reported on the forecasts
    have consented to the extended use of their reports (see Practice
    Note 3, paragraph 5).

35. Before giving their consent to publication or re-publication of their
    report, the reporting accountants should require to see the whole
    text of the document and satisfy themselves that the inclusion of their
    report in the form and context of the document would not be
    inappropriate or misleading.

## *22.8 Prospectuses

As we saw in sec. 1.2, the need for the constraints provided by an audit originally
grew out of the many investment frauds that were perpetrated in the early days
of limited liability companies. The most part of this book has concentrated upon
the statutory audits of the annual accounts of limited companies. But company
law and the Stock Exchange also provide for stringent investigation of documents
presented in support of the public issue of shares or debentures. The legal requirements are incorporated in the Fourth Schedule of the 1948 Companies Act, and
require auditors to report with respect to:
(a) the profits and losses for the company and its subsidiaries (company and

subsidiary profits to be shown separately) for the preceding five years (or for such shorter time as the company has been trading);

(b) the rates of dividend paid on each class of share capital in the five years;

(c) the assets and liabilities at the last date to which the accounts of the company were made up.

These legal requirements are supplemented by the far more demanding *Specifications of the Quotations Department (hereafter Department) of the Stock Exchange*, as incorporated in their 'Yellow Book', the Admission of Securities to Listing. This specifies that the report should deal with:

(a) as regards profits and losses –
  (i) Sales to third parties specifying the method such sales are arrived at, e.g. gross sales less trade discounts, returns and allowances, or other gross income or revenue;
  (ii) Cost of goods sold, being all costs and expenses including those currently specified by the Department to be separately shown, namely:
    (A) Amortisation, depreciation and obsolescence of fixed assets, etc.;
    (B) Financial expenses, e.g. interest and discounts;
  (iii) Other income, e.g. investment income and rents;
  (iv) Share of profits of associated companies;
  (v) Profit before taxation and extraordinary items;
  (vi) Taxation on profits (UK, overseas and share of associated companies) indicating basis;
  (vii) Minority interests;
  (viii) Extraordinary items (less taxation attributable thereto);
  (ix) Profit attributable to shareholders, after taxation and extraordinary items;
  (x) Amount absorbed by preferential dividends;
  (xi) Profit attributable to equity;
  (xii) Amount absorbed by dividends on equity, together with the rate of dividend for each class of shares and details of any waivers of dividends;
  (xiii) Increase in retained profits for the year as shown in the balance sheet; in respect of each of the five completed financial years immediately preceding the issue of the prospectus, or, if incorporated less than five years, in respect of each of the completed financial years since incorporation.

    Other items may require separate disclosure according to the particular circumstances of the company or group;

(b) the balance sheet of the company and of the group at the end of the last accounting period reported upon, together with a summary of the balance sheets of the group (or company if it has no subsidiaries) at the end of each previous accounting period reported upon and at the beginning of the first such period;

(c) the accounting policies followed in dealing with items which are judged material or critical in determining the profits or losses and net assets reported upon; and

(d) any other matters which appear to be relevant for the purposes of the report.

*Further reporting requirements* in the 'Yellow Book' include:
(a) latest financial period reported on to be no more than six months before the date of the prospectus;
(b) accounts should comply with UK and International Accounting Standards, and any significant departures therefrom must be explained in notes;
(c) a report to the effect that profits or losses have been arrived at on defined bases in accordance with accounting standards approved by the accountancy bodies and after making such adjustments as are considered appropriate;
(d) reports containing significant qualifications will not normally be acceptable; in the case of qualified reports appearing in acquisition circulars, the Council of the Stock Exchange may require that the approval of shareholders in general meeting be sought for the relevant acquisition; where a reporting accountant includes any reservation in his report, the extent and materiality of such reservation must be indicated;
(e) an explanation should be included of the trend of profits;
(f) where reliance in the report is placed on the opinion of other experts (valuers or accountants), the names addresses and professional qualifications of such persons should be stated in the report, together with a statement to the effect that they have given and not withdrawn their written consent to the issue of the prospectus including such reference;
(g) where a material proportion of the profits arises overseas or a material proportion of the assets are situated overseas, the document should give a fair indication of the amount and source or situation thereof; the basis of overseas taxation and currency treatment should if material be set out in the report; any restrictions on the repatriation of profits or capital should also be reported;
(h) where plant hire charges on contracts lasting more than a year are material, details should be supplied to the Department who may require disclosure in the prospectus;
(i) a statement signed by the reporting accountants showing the adjustments made by them in arriving at the figures shown in their report must be made available to the public for inspection: adjustment to profits and losses –
*Section A*
This section should begin with the net increase or decrease in the balance at credit or debit on profit and loss account shown by comparison of the balance sheets at the beginning and end of each of the financial periods under review; the net increase or decrease in the balance on profit and loss account for each of the last two years should normally be capable of ascertainment from the accounts which are required to be made available for inspection by the public. There should then be shown and added to or deducted from this amount:
   (a) The items which are required by the Companies Acts 1948 and 1967 ('the Acts') to be stated separately in the profit and loss account, notes being included to disclose any further information required by the Acts

to be disclosed by way of note to the profit and loss account.

(b) Material revenue items which have been dealt with otherwise than through the profit and loss accounts, and other extraordinary items and prior year adjustments shown in compliance with the Accounting Standards approved by the accountancy bodies on the basis that they were in force throughout the period reported upon.

The sum finally arrived at in this section would normally be the profit or loss for the year before taking account of interest and of items which the Acts require in any event to be stated separately.

*Section B*

This section should commence with the final figure of profit or loss shown in Section 'A' and should show in detail the adjustments made thereto in arriving at the profits or losses shown in the accountants' report and giving the reasons therefor.

Adjustment to balance sheets:

If the figures in the final balance sheets of the company, and the group, where applicable, differ from those shown on the corresponding published audited balance sheets, and the relevant adjustments are not set out in the report, a statement should also be submitted showing the adjustments made.

There should be made available for inspection by the public a statement of the detailed balance sheets of the company (or group where applicable) included in the summary in the accountants' report and of any adjustments made thereto.

If the company is a holding company, the statements of adjustments may deal with the consolidated figures of the company and its subsidiaries or with the figures of the separate companies or groups of companies comprising the group. In the latter case, a summary combining the figures so as to arrive at those shown in the accountants' report should be submitted.

*Letter from reporting accountants*

The statement of adjustments must be submitted in draft form at least ten days prior to the date on which it is proposed to publish the prospectus. *In support of the final statement the Department requires a letter from the reporting accountants to the Department confirming that all adjustments which are appropriate for the purposes of the report have been made* to the profits and losses and to the balance sheets (in respect of each year under review) and that no other adjustments have been made.

The reporting accountants' letter to the Department should confirm the following four matters:

(a) Stocks and work in progress

That, save as indicated in their report, they have obtained sufficient information about the stock takings and have examined sufficient records and other evidence to enable them to form the opinion that throughout the period under review stocks and work in progress were properly ascertained and, in arriving at the reported profits and losses, were brought into account on bases and standards in accordance with accepted accounting principles

which were applied consistently.
(b) Depreciation and amortisation
That they have satisfied themselves that the provisions for depreciation and amortisation charged in arriving at the reported profits and losses, considered in conjunction with any qualifications or notes included in their report are in their opinion reasonable having regard, inter alia, to:
   (i)   assets in respect of which it has been or will be the company's practice to make no provisions for depreciation or amortisation (which policy would require to be referred to in their report) and
   (ii)  any revaluation of fixed assets either already incorporated into the company's accounts or to be incorporated therein; where a revaluation is to be incorporated into the accounts, the report should make clear whether the depreciation charged against profits is based on the revalued figures.
(c) Deferred taxation
That the net book value of the fixed assets in respect of which depreciation will have to be provided out of future profits does not exceed by a material amount the corresponding amounts on which capital allowances will be obtained, or how material differences have been taken into account unless apparent from the document. Where no provision for deferred taxation is made on material differences the Department expects the reasons therefore to be explained in the accounting policies note.
(d) Accounting policies
That accounting policies used are in accordance with accounting standards and accepted accounting principles.

*Adjustments to past figures*

Statement N16 of the ICAEW, entitled 'Accountants' reports for prospectuses: adjustments and other matters', was written as long ago as 1953, but much of it is still relevant now. There follows a synopsis of the key issues raised.
   The accountant's report is confined to past results, but because the potential investor is concerned with the future, he will use the past results to assist him in forming his own assessment of future prospects. For this reason it may be necessary for the accountant to adjust the past results so as to portray a more accurate trend of the company's performance.
   *Profits and losses* would be adjusted in the following circumstances:
(a) where material facts having a bearing on reported figures arose subsequent to the issuance of the accounts;
(b) where there have been material sources of revenue or expenses which are expected not to recur (e.g. abnormal or extraordinary items, or debenture interest on a debenture to be redeemed out of the proceeds of the issue);
(c) where there has been a material change in accounting policies during the period of the report.
   *The assets and liabilities* will be stated as at the last balance sheet date, but they

may need to be adjusted in the light of material post-balance sheet events occurring after the date on which the accounts were signed (up until then such events should have been incorporated in the annual accounts), but before the date of the prospectus report. Any significant matters occurring after the balance sheet date which affect asset or liability values after that date should be revealed by way of a note to the accounts. It may be necessary to revalue certain assets, in particular land and buildings, and, indeed, the Department may insist on such revaluation. In these circumstances, a note will have to be made concerning the effect upon related future depreciation charges.

*Acquisitions*

The proceeds of issues are sometimes used for the purpose of acquiring another undertaking. In these circumstances, information as outlined above must also be provided in respect of the undertaking to be acquired. The persons providing such information must be named in the prospectus.

*Reporting accountant's 'consent'*

The CA 1948 in Sec. 40 requires a reporting accountant and other experts (e.g. valuers or engineers or any person whose profession gives authority to a statement made by him) to give written statements to the effect that they consent to the inclusion of their reports or opinions in the prospectus. A statement to the effect that such consent has been given and not withdrawn must be included in the prospectus.

The reporting accountant should beware of any material delay between the issuance of his report and the registration of the prospectus, for events may occur in the meantime that may materially affect his report. So the accountant should monitor the situation to ensure that the prospectus is registered without unreasonable delay. Should such delay occur, then the accountant must consider whether further investigation would appear necessary. And if this is the case, then he must immediately withdrawn his 'consent'.

*Frequency of new issues*

The number of prospectuses appearing has dwindled considerably in recent years, to no more than a handful a year. This is largely the result of recessionary tendencies in the economy, but it also relates to the fact that market issues can be an expensive form of raising capital. Placings, or rights issues, are now more popular in view of their comparative cheapness.

*Stringency of requirements*

The Stock Exchange and legal requirements are onerous with regard to the matters that must be reported in a prospectus. And you will remember from the last chapter that we had to be very careful indeed in fulfilling these requirements, for the 1958 Prevention of Fraud (Investments) Act provides for criminal penalties in regard to mis-statements in prospectus reports on the grounds of mere recklessness – fraud does not have to be proved.

## *22.9 Acquistion of a business or shares

Investigations under this head may relate to:

acquisition of an ongoing sole-tradership;
acquisition of shares in a partnership;
acquisition of a minority or majority of shares in a limited company.

Each specific situation has its own particular considerations, but the main concern in each is to determine the viability of the investment. Investment evaluation relates more to the skills of the financial manager than to those of the auditor. So the auditor must here be careful not to exceed his level of competence. Any acquisition investigation must cover two aspects of the business to be acquired:
1. History and present financial position.
2. An evaluation of future prospects.
The history and present financial position can normally be readily determined by reference to prior year audited accounts and by enquiry. And the figures so derived can then be analysed by the use of ratio analysis, in much the same way as we saw when looking at the principles of analytical review. In particular the profitability trend and liquidity position of the business will need to be thoroughly investigated to ensure that the company is on a sound financial basis. The skills so far required are those necessary for the satisfactory conduct of an audit. But the historic information so derived will be of only limited value in determining the viability of an investment; for this latter must depend on the future performance that the business can expect to achieve.

Future performance implies future forecasts, and forecasts must be based on assumptions. The reliability of such assumptions will normally be in inverse proportion to time – the longer the period of a forecast, the greater the risk. So an investigating accountant may be best advised to merely assemble the information upon which the reliability of an assumption (for instance, in regard to future sales) may be judged. The reader may then make his own evaluation, based on the assembled evidence; although, of course, an investigating accountant should clearly report if he considers an assumption to be unrealistic.

The volume and range of information which may be potentially useful to the purchaser of a business is vast. So to give an indication of the type of matters to be considered, a *check list* of important areas to be investigated is given below:
1. General information
Short history and description of business, names of principal officers and shareholders, number and classes of shares, control.
2. Financial information
(a) compile five-year summary from audited financial statements (more than

five years is usually irrelevant – less than three years is usually inadequate);

(b) project financial statements to as far forward as possible;

(c) establish accounting policies;

(d) banking – full details;

(e) credit reports;

(f) tax assessments;

(g) insurances – policies and premiums;

(h) obtain certified statement re unrecorded liabilities and collectibility of debtors;

(i) stock – investigate stocktaking procedures, costing methods and valuation procedures;

(j) pensions, bonuses, participation, service contracts to be investigated;

(k) macro studies regarding industry – comparative studies; return on investments; assets turnover; calculation of P/E ratio, goodwill;

(l) establish fixed and variable costs; break even point; profit sensitivity to variations in product mix; turnover;

(m) obtain independent valuations of property, plant, equipment, vehicles, etc.

3. Sales and marketing
Establish products, market penetration, projected growth of industry and forecasted future demand; competition and estimated capacity of industry to supply present and future demand. Analyse distribution costs relative to geographic location of plant.

4. Manufacturing
Manufacturing processes – detail plant and equipment and compare with fixed assets register. Obtain technical reports on condition and capability of plant. Check costs of manufacture and any restrictive conditions regarding labour.

5. Purchasing
(a) list principal items of raw materials, products, sub-assemblies, components, etc.;

(b) analyse material content of sales by products;

(c) report on purchasing methods and stock control;

(d) list principal and alternative suppliers and items supplied;

(e) analyse purchases as to number and value of purchase orders; cost of carrying stock and report on general efficiency of purchasing department.

6. Research, planning and development
If any, establish facilities and costs – patents, trademarks – present programme.

7. Commercial, industrial and public relations
(a) list and classify employees; wage agreements; working conditions.

(b) establish labour turnover rate;

(c) analyse system of remuneration, incentive schemes and labour content of sales;

    (d)  analyse administration and overhead content of sales;

    (e)  assess company image and efficiency of present services.

8.  Transport and communication

    (a)  rail, road facilities – tariffs;

    (b)  analyse transport and communication costs as percentage of sales and see if overall savings may result because of the acquisition.

9.  Legal aspects

    (a)  check existing contracts and obligations to third parties (banks, mortgages, leases, etc.);

    (b)  examine Memorandum and Articles;

    (c)  call in legal assistance if complications are apparent;

    (d)  check title deeds, leases, contracts, possible litigation.

The investigating accountant will clearly be expected to reach *a conclusion*, and this should be included in the final section to the report. The conclusion should be short, clear and unambiguous, but it may be unwise to formulate it in terms of 'buy' or 'don't buy'. For in the final analysis this is an entrepreneurial decision, upon which we can only advise as to the relevant facts. The facts we should consider in reaching a conclusion are:

1.  The net asset backing for the investment (if the investment is a risky one, it may be advisable to calculate net assets on a net realisable value basis, and upon a break-up valuation).

2.  The liquidity of the company. Liquidity, and as a consequence perhaps profitability, can be favourably affected by an input of cash from the potential purchaser. Any such necessary input would have to be considered as part of the purchase price when evaluating the return on investment.

3.  The company's past trend of profitability. As discussed in the context of prospectuses, abnormal or non-recurring past profits or expenditure should be adjusted for in determining the profitability trend.

4.  Comparison of profitability to the industry average (allowance should be made for special factors which distinguish the company being investigated).

5.  Projected future profitability. The principles under this head are essentially the same as those dealt with under profit forecasts in sec. 22.7. The accountant will not normally be in a position to evaluate the underlying assumptions, but can present the reader with sufficient information for him to form an opinion.

6.  Return on Investment (ROI). ROI is a complex subject which you will deal with in other courses. Suffice to say here that Accounting Rate of Return, Payback and Discounted Cash Flow techniques can all have their place in analysing an investment decision. In many acquisition situations the assumptions with regard to future profitability and cash flows can give rise to the possibility of wide variation. In these circumstances one should beware giving spurious accuracy to the predictions by the use of over-sophisticated techniques. The calculated return should be compared with the cost of capital, taking into account the risk involved in the investment. The greater the net asset backing, the less the risk.

7. Finally the investigating accountant should consider the potential for improved profitability as a result of greater managerial efficiency.

*Small businesses*

A problem which often besets the accountant who advises small business is the quite natural desire of the owners to minimise their profits for taxation purposes, and yet to show the highest possible profits when it comes to selling the business or seeking a bank loan! Commonly cash takings will be understated, with the amounts involved going directly to the owner. Now, provided the owner is not over-greedy in this regard it may be difficult for an auditor to detect such misstatement. Commonly the only evidence, in the absence of proper internal control, may be a lower than expected gross profit percentage. And understatement is very difficult to prove in these circumstances. Such poor internal control will usually result in a 'subject to' audit report, or in more serious cases where there is a total inability to substantiate cash transactions, then a 'disclaimer' report may be necessary.

An accountant would have to take these matters into consideration when investigating the viability of a small business. In particular he should look back at any qualifications in past accounts on these (or other) matters, and determine any possible effect on the reported profits. A comparison of gross profit percentages over the years under review may also be indicative. An increased percentage for the year immediately prior to the proposed sale may be explained by a desire to show the maximum possible profits.

The desire to show the maximum profits may tempt the owner to distort the accounts by deliberately manipulating key figures. This temptation may not only be confined to small businesses, for directors of larger companies are also often tempted to manipulate the accounts in advance of bid situations. The audit considerations in this regard were examined in sec. 8.7, and the matters that an investigating accountant would need to consider are essentially similar. In particular, profits and asset cover may be manipulated by:

(a) altering judgement valuations, particularly in regard to stock and depreciation;

(b) artificially inflating stock on hand by manipulating stock sheets;

(c) overstating debtors by recording cash received from debtors as an additional sale, or by creating false invoices (this should be easily spotted if an audit is undertaken); alternatively sales/debtors may be overstated by including goods on sale or return;

(d) liabilities may be understated by ignoring them all together (this can be difficult to detect if the control systems are poor);

(e) cut-off may be manipulated by a variety of means such as inclusion of sales subsequent to the year end or exclusion of end of year purchases/liabilities but inclusion of the related stock.

These possibilities have to be borne in mind when evaluating past results, and in this regard a comparison of suitable past ratios can be very informative.

When advising the potential purchaser of a small business, the accountant must bear in mind the involvement of the present owner in the management of the business. Unless the new owner has both the skill and the desire to work full time in the enterprise, it may be necessary to employ an additional manager. Such incremental costs would then have to be taken into account in evaluating the viability of the investment. In any event, the opportunity cost to the potential owner (the amount he could earn in the next best alternative occupation) would have to be taken into consideration in determining the true ROI.

### Small companies

The considerations above apply equally to small limited liability companies. The accountant should add back directors' salaries in determining the profitability of the company, for these will usually be a reflection of the owner's tax position, rather than a proper reward for services rendered. Incremental or opportunity costs should be included in the ROI calculation, as outlined above.

### Partnerships

When acquiring a share in a partnership, certain additional considerations apply:
1.  Details of the partnership agreement:
    What is the basis of sharing profits and losses (is the proposed share equitable in relation to work to be performed)?
    Is a salary to be paid to any working partners?
    What is the basis of capital share on dissolution?
    Are accounts required to be audited?
    Is there an agreed basis for settling partnership disputes?
    What is the possible liability in the event of a partnership failure (remember that partners are jointly and severally liable irrespective of their capital share)?
    In this regard is there adequate professional indemnity insurance cover?
    To what extent can an incoming partner be made liable for debts incurred prior to his admission?
    What are the pension provisions relating to partners who retire – are pensions payable out of future profits of the partnership?
2.  The tax effect caused by the change in the partnership;
3.  The nature of the new partner's workload. Does the profit share constitute an adequate reward for services rendered and provide a reasonable ROI on the capital input, or do the long term prospects outweigh any initial shortfall? In this context it may be appropriate to try and discover the likely reasons for the partnership offer.

### Minority shares in companies

The purchase of a minority share in a proprietary company (where the directors own a majority or controlling number of shares) is potentially dangerous, in that the minority shareholder has little say in the running of the business. Accordingly the directors can manipulate the profits by means of directors' salaries, or by means of suitable accounting policies to ensure that no dividends are payable to minority shareholders. Any profit sharing involvement without management participation is normally best avoided, unless the minority shareholder is associated with the directors either by kinship or long personal association.

### Majority shares in companies

The purchase of a majority of the shares of a proprietary or public company is a straightforward investment decision based on the principles outlined earlier. By holding the majority of shares, the investor has control over both the management and dividend policies; accordingly the primary investment criteria will be the expected future ROI as compared with the investor's opportunity cost of capital.

## *22.10  Bank loans

The advisers of small and large businesses alike will often be asked for assistance in preparing a request for a bank loan. Such a request will undoubtedly stand a far greater chance of success if accompanied by appropriate supporting financial information.

The factors that the bank will normally take into consideration are:

1. The purpose for which the loan is required.
2. The security for the loan (note that security will normally be based on a break-up valuation, for it will only usually be called upon in the event of the company's failure).
3. The funds to be generated by the assets acquired.
4. The ability of the company to pay the interest on the due dates and to repay the loan on expiry.
5. The period of the loan (is a long-term loan required to finance major capital investment, or a short-term overdraft to cover a temporary shortfall in working capital?).
6. The amount of the loan in relation to the assets of the company, and in relation to the investment of the proprietors.
7. The adequacy of the loan in relation to the business requirements of the company (in this regard proprietors are inclined to underestimate the amount of borrowing required by being unduly optimistic; bank managers are not impressed with unrealistic optimism, so a reasonable amount should be built into the request to cover contingencies).
8. The profitability and liquidity of the business as a whole (is it a going concern without the loan, and what are the risks of failure?).
9. The personal status of the business proprietors/directors; in particular, what is the prior business experience of the proprietors, and can they provide

suitable references and/or personal guarantees with appropriate security?

It follows from the above that the advising accountant should prepare, or assist in the preparation of, the following documents for submission to the bank:

(a) a balance sheet clearly depicting the net asset position of the business at the latest possible date (it may be appropriate to obtain professional revaluations of certain assets, particularly land and buildings, in the event that cost is below market value);

(b) income statements for the past three years with appropriate ratios, showing the profitability trend;

(c) a profit forecast covering as much of the duration of the loan as possible (the loan interest should of course be taken into account); obviously the immediately ensuing period can be in the most detail;

(d) a cash budget covering at least the first two years of operation (much more than two years is likely to be too inaccurate to be meaningful); in the early years of a business, cash flow is often much more important than profitability, in that illiquidity is a frequent cause of early failure;

(e) the bank may wish to see figures which demonstrate the range of possible profit, from the most optimistic estimates to the most pessimistic (the forecast will be based on reasonable expectation); and it may also wish to see the most pessimistic estimate of the cash flow position; these estimates should be available at the discussion with the bank, but they will not necessarily be submitted as part of the request and may only be used in the event of a bank enquiry.

## *22.11 Fraud

During the course of Chapter 6 we examined the many ways in which fraud may occur, and in Chapter 8 we discussed how to evaluate the possibility of fraud in specific situations. Should fraud be discovered, the auditor is under a duty to probe that fraud to its full extent, regardless of the materiality of the amount in question.

Fraud can be split into two categories:

1. Misappropriation of stock, cash, fixed assets or investments.
2. Distortion of accounts to show other than a true and fair view:

   (a) by owners for the purpose of raising additional finance or to obtain a better selling price for the business;

   (b) by directors and major shareholders to cause fluctuations in the market price or value of shares; or to justify payment of dividends, or to secure fresh capital;

   (c) by managers to conceal discrepancies, or to obtain more remuneration or commission than should be paid, or to obtain promotion or avoid penalties;

   (d) by other employees to hide discrepancies for which they are responsible.

In all these situations there will be a falsification of records to conceal the true position.

Misappropriation is most likely to be achieved by falsifying expense or revenue records (although temporary concealment of misappropriation may be achieved by overstating assets or understating liabilities). And distortion is most likely to occur through over- or understating assets or liabilities.

The methods to be used by an investigator depend upon the nature of the falsification, but attention should be concentrated upon the motives and likely methods of the people involved.

## Cash frauds

Cash frauds fall into the following groups:
1. Omission or suppression of entries to conceal misappropriation.
2. Manipulated or irregular entries to conceal misappropriation.
3. Outright theft with no concern about discovery.

Investigation into such frauds will involve extensive tests of detail, in particular checking for items omitted from the records or for falsified entries. In designing such tests, consideration should be given to the nature of the defalcation that the suspected party's position in the internal control structure would allow. Matters which may require close examination include:

(a) control over receipt handling and cash recording;
(b) paid cheques, in particular looking for payee names, authorised signatures and supporting vouchers;
(c) signs of alteration to vouchers;
(d) comparison of initial cash records to cash book, to deposit slips (looking for integrity of amounts banked – note that bank copy deposit slips may need to be obtained if the fraud of 'teeming and lading' is suspected), and to the bank statement;
(e) likelihood of 'teeming and lading' as a result of poor segregation of duties between the cashier's department and the sales ledger department;
(f) control over cash sales and travellers' collections;
(g) control over discounts, allowances, credit notes, bad debts written off and journal entries affecting debtor accounts;
(h) if wages are involved – checking of payrolls to personnel records, clock cards, overtime payment authorisation and cash book payments for both net pay and deductions; check control over payout procedures;
(i) the necessity for extensive circularisation of debtors and creditors.

## Stock frauds

It is comparatively easy to determine the extent of a stock fraud in a retail organisation, provided that a physical stocktaking can be held and that the annual accounts at some earlier date can be substantially relied upon. In these circumstances the cost of sales can be determined (assuming purchase records can be relied upon) and this adjusted for known mark-up rates to establish a predicted sales value. If the actual sales value is materially different from the calculated amount, then suppression of cash sales or misappropriation of stock would be indicated. The investigation process will then depend upon the type of defalcation most likely in the context of the prevailing control systems. But in the absence of good internal control with detailed records of stock movements, it may be extremely difficult to pinpoint who is responsible for the fraud. And this is even more the case in a manufacturing organisation with raw materials and work in progress to control as well as finished goods. In such a situation adequate controls must immediately be implemented, and in the process it may be appropriate to instigate a general reshuffle of responsibilities.

In the event that control documentation does exist, extensive tests of detail may reveal the stage of stock loss, and this in turn may reveal the most likely culprits.

### Distortion

The likely motives of persons suspected of distorting accounts can give an investigator a good indication of the probable areas of distortion. For example, directors who are also major shareholders may wish to uplift the profits with a view to paying a higher dividend. They may do so by such means as overstating stock, manipulating cut-off or distorting judgement valuations such as depreciation. So if distortion is suspected, the auditor must:

(a) pay particular attention to asset and liability verification, preferably by direct communication;

(b) conduct extensive cut-off tests;

(c) pay particular attention to any area where there is necessity for judgement valuation.

## *22.12 Inland Revenue investigations

Where taxpayers are suspected of having filed incomplete or inaccurate returns of income, the Inland Revenue authorities may demand an investigation. Known as a 'back duty' investigation, this may be carried out by the Inland Revenue's own staff, or by a local firm of accountants at the request of the Inland Revenue. In either case, the taxpayer may wish to obtain professional advice. So a professional accountant may be called upon to act either for or against the suspected taxpayer.

The number of years under suspicion will be indicated by the Inland Revenue authorities, and the taxpayer will then have to prove that his returns were correct, or to agree an amount for settlement of any understatement. Where the taxpayer maintains adequate accounting records, an investigation may be confined to confirming that the annual returns reflect the income as disclosed by the records. But most 'back duty' cases will arise as a result of the suspicion that adequate records have not been maintained, or that some income has not been disclosed.

So an Inland Revenue investigation will begin by first determining whether adequate accounting records have been maintained. In their absence, an estimate will have to be made of the taxpayer's net assets at the commencement of the investigation period, and of his personal expenditure during the period. It should be possible to determine with reasonable accuracy the net assets at the close of the period, by reference to banks and by observation and enquiry (though balances at Swiss banks can be more difficult to discover!). If the increase between opening and closing net assets is added to the expenditure for the period, then the result must be the (approximate) income for the period. This estimate can then be compared with the declared income, and any understatement established. This can then be used as the basis of a negotiated settlement between the Inland Revenue, and the taxpayer's professional adviser.

The results of an investigation can best be summarised under the following headings:

| | | |
|---|---:|---:|
| Total net wealth of the taxpayer and dependants at the commencement of the investigation period | | £xxx |
| Add | | |
| Income during period under review: | | |
| Income declared for taxation purposes | £xxx | |
| Non-taxable income (e.g. gifts or gambling wins) | xxx | xxx |
| Add | | |
| Inflation-induced increases in asset values | | xxx |
| | | xxx |
| *Less* | | |
| Expenditure for period under review: | | |
| Personal expenditure based on the taxpayer's known standard of living | £xxx | |
| Known capital decreases (e.g. gifts, gambling losses or losses on sale of investments) | xxx | xxx |
| Calculated net wealth as at end of investigation period | | xxx |
| *Less* | | |
| Actual net wealth | | xxx |
| Difference resulting from undisclosed income | | £xxx |

The taxpayer may well wish to show that his closing assets are no higher than opening assets, that his income has mostly come from gambling wins, and that he lives entirely off bread and water! The investigating accountant would have to determine the reasonableness of such claims. The taxpayer would be expected to substantiate such claims by reference to documentary evidence such as:

(a) proof of ownership of existing assets, dating prior to the commencement of the investigation period, or proof of ownership of assets to the equivalent value;

(b) evidence of gambling wins and of any other claimed non-taxable income; such evidence could for example be in the form of remittance advices, betting slips or notification letters;

(c) evidence of standard of living.

The accountant would wish to examine such evidence, and during the course of his investigations he should additionally pay particular attention to:

(a) bank statement credits and deposit slips which may indicate the presence of undisclosed income or assets (e.g. interest on an investment);

(b) large bank statement debits which may reveal the purchase of undisclosed assets, or payments into undisclosed accounts;

(c) the amount of insurance cover, which may indicate the value of assets, or the existence of undisclosed assets;

(d) any documentary evidence in respect of payments and receipts no matter of what amount, as such evidence may be indicative of greater amounts of expenditure/receipt (e.g. a credit card expense for a meal abroad could indicate major undisclosed expenditure on a foreign holiday);

(e) evidence of lifestyle, such as house, type of car/s, club membership, entertainment, number of children, education of children, household amenities, style of dress and holidays.

Any report issued on the basis of such circumstantial information must obviously explain the bases of any estimates and assumptions, and refer to any areas where the limited information available gives rise to doubt as to the reliability of the figures produced.

## *22.13 Companies Acts investigations

Sections 164 to 175 of the CA 1948, and Secs. 35 to 42 of the CA 1967 provide for the inspection of a company's affairs by Department of Trade (hereafter D of T) inspectors.

CA 1948

Sec. 164. The D of T may appoint inspectors on the application of either not less than two hundred members or of members holding not less than one tenth of the issued shares (if the company has no share capital, on application of at least one-fifth of the persons on the register of members); the D of T may require evidence in support of the application, and a deposit against costs.

Sec. 165. The D of T must appoint inspectors if:

(a) the company by special resolution, or

(b) the court by order,

declares that the company's affairs should be investigated. And it may so appoint if it appears to the D of T that there are circumstances suggesting:

(a) that the business is being (Sec. 38 CA 1967 amends this to include 'or has been') carried on with intent to defraud creditors, or in a

       manner oppressive to any part of its members, or for any fraudu-
lent or unlawful purpose; or

(b) that persons concerned with its formation or the management of
its affairs have in connection therewith been guilty of fraud, misfeasance or other misconduct towards it or towards its members; or

(c) that its members have not been given all the information with
respect to its affairs which they might reasonably expect.

Sec. 166.  This section gives inspectors power to investigate the affairs of the
investigated company's holding or subsidiary companies if the consider it relevant to their enquiries.

Sec. 167.  This section provides that all officers and agents of the company (past
and present) shall produce to the inspectors all relevant books or
documents which are in their custody or power, and to give all assistance that they are reasonably able to give. Sec. 40 CA 1967 amends
Sec. 167 to include the requirement for officers and agents to attend
before the inspectors when required so to do.

If an inspector thinks it necessary to examine a person on oath other
than an officer or agent, he may apply to the court which has power to
order such an examination.

Agents include bankers, solicitors and *auditors* of the company, but
Sec. 175 exempts from disclosure privileged communication between
a solicitor and his client (except as respects the name and address of his
client), and information as to the affairs of any of a bank's customers
other than the company, is also exempted.

Any refusals by officers or agents to comply with inspectors' requests
under this section may constitute contempt of court.

Sec. 168.  Inspectors must make interim reports to the D of T if so directed, and
must always make a final report. The D of T must then send a copy of
the report to the company's registered office, and may furnish a copy
on payment of a fee to any member of the company or of any holding
or subsidiary company dealt with in the report and to any creditor
thereof whose interests appear to the D of T to be affected. Where
inspectors are appointed under Sec. 164 above, the D of T must
furnish a copy of the report at the request of the applicants, and where
appointment is made under Sec. 165 a copy must be furnished to the
court.

CA 1967

Sec. 41.  Inspectors appointed under Sec. 164 or Sec. 165 may at any time in the
course of their investigations without the necessity of making an
interim report inform the D of T of matters tending to show that an
offence has been committed. (In these circumstances the D of T would
usually inform the Director of Public Prosecutions.)

Sec. 35.  Section 35 of the CA 1967 provides that if it appears to the D of T
from any report made under Sec. 168 CA 1948 above, or from any
information or document obtained under Part III of the CA 1967

(Inspection of Companies' books and papers) or Sec. 18 or 19 of the Protection of Depositors Act 1963 that it is in the public interest that the company should be wound up, the D of T may present a petition to the court for a winding up (unless it is already being wound up by the court).

Sec. 37. If it appears to the D of T from any of the sources referred to in Sec. 35 above that any civil proceedings ought in the public interest to be brought by any body corporate, they may themselves bring such proceedings in the name and on behalf of the body corporate.

Sec. 170 CA 1948. and Sec. 40 CA 1967. Expenses of investigation are defrayed in the first instance by the D of T, but the following people are liable to repay the D of T:

(a) any person convicted on a prosecution instituted as a result of the investigation;

(b) the applicants for the investigation under Sec. 164 CA 1948, at the D of T's discretion;

(c) any body corporate in whose name proceedings are brought;

(d) any body corporate dealt with by the report unless the investigation was at the D of T's instigation, but again at the D of T's discretion.

Sec. 172 CA 1948 Gives power to the D of T to appoint inspectors to investigate and report on the membership of any company for the purpose of determining the true persons who are or have been financially interested in the success or failure of the company or able to control or materially to influence the policy of the company, where there appears good reason for them so to do. Where application is made to the D of T by equivalent persons to those required by Sec. 164 CA 1948, the D of T must appoint an inspector unless they are satisfied that the request is vexatious. The inspector's appointment must include any matter which the applicant seeks to have included except in so far as the D of T is satisfied that it is unreasonable for the matter to be investigated.

Sec. 32. CA 1967 If it appears to the D of T that there are circumstances suggesting that contraventions may have occurred, in relation to shares in, or debentures of, a company, of Sec. 25 or 27 of CA 1967 (penalisation of dealing by director of a company of options to buy or sell listed shares in, or listed debentures of, the company or associated companies and obligations of a director of a company to notify it of interests of his in shares in, or debentures of, the company or associated companies) or of Sec. 30 (extension of Sec. 25 to spouses and children), they may appoint one or more inspectors to carry out such investigations as are necessary to establish whether or not such contraventions have in fact occurred.

## Part III

CA 1967. This part of the Act gives the D of T wide powers to require virtually any company in the UK to produce books or papers if it believes it has good reason so to do.

The team of inspectors usually consists of one accountant and one Queen's Counsel and they have wide powers of investigation and reporting. Investigations usually take the form of a very extensive audit involving much use of verification, analytical review and tests of detail. The work can often take years, so it is usual for the inspectors to issue interim reports. Many of these reports have been highly critical of directors and auditors (indeed we saw some such comments in sec. 2.9 earlier). And not surprisingly those criticised have hit back at the system which allows for no form of explanation or reply. The CCAB recognised this problem and accordingly issued a memorandum to the D of T in 1978, suggesting a code of practice for company inspectors. The CCAB affirmed the essential role of the inspectors and endorsed their wide-ranging powers. But they recommended that inspectors should recognise that civil and/or criminal proceedings may well arise out of their reports and accordingly should keep their reports free from 'superfluous or flamboyant comment . . . about the personal failings of individuals' in order not to prejudice subsequent proceedings.

# 23
# Contemporary developments

## 23.1 The management audit

There have been many calls recently for a more pluralistic approach to financial reporting, to incorporate (*inter alia*) comments on the efficiency with which the company has conducted its affairs. As directors' comments on the company efficiency are not likely to be entirely objective, this task, it is proposed, will fall to the company's auditors; or to additional auditors appointed especially for the purpose. Proposals for such an audit have been made under various titles such as 'management audit', 'management efficiency audit', 'efficiency audit' or 'operations audit'. And the authors of these proposals often try to draw a subtle distinction between these terms. This is largely semantics, however, and the only practical distinction is whether the audit should be confined to the efficiency of the management team in carrying out the company objectives, or whether it should extend to include the objectives themselves, and hence the effectiveness of the directors. Not surprisingly, most directors concur with the former view!

But a review of the efficiency of the management team would have to be both ongoing and in considerable detail to be meaningful, and it is, therefore, much more suited to an internal audit function. Indeed many companies already have management audit as part of their internal audit procedures. But such audits are for the directors' information. So they are a far cry from an evaluation of the efficiency of the directors themselves, such as is currently being demanded.

There can be little justification for a *mandatory* audit of the efficiency of individual members of the management team. Such an audit may be useful information for the directors. But it is up to them to determine when it is necessary, for the expense of an annual audit could be both prohibitive and unnecessary. On the other hand, an evaluation of the company's objectives, together with its overall success in meeting those objectives, would be of considerable value to shareholders, and could arguably be made a mandatory part of annual reporting.

The precise extent of such an audit is open to debate. The realism of the company's objectives could be examined, and an evaluation could be made of whether these objectives are in the shareholders' interest. And the efficiency of operation could be determined by reference to agreed indicators. These indicators could range from the objective and purely financial, such as liquidity and

456

profit ratios, to highly subjective evaluations of labour relations, the state of research and development, the economic situation of the company's market and potential supply and distribution problems.

Such a move is likely to come by evolution, rather than by revolution in the form of a statutory requirement. For annual reporting is already going some way towards an evaluation of the company's liquidity and financial stability, through the now almost standard 'Going Concern' audit. And comments on efficiency in the auditor's management report will often extend beyond pure internal control (though of course this is not presented to the shareholders). In addition many of the matters indicated in the previous paragraph may well find a place in the directors' report (indeed the Fourth Directive considerably extends disclosure requirements along these lines – see sec. 15.7). And while there is no audit requirement for the complete directors' report, it is now a standard procedure, at least in the larger firms, for the report to be reviewed to ensure that it is in no way misleading.

I would welcome more specific comment by auditors on liquidity and profit performance, which is of very real concern to the shareholders, and third parties alike. Accounting ratios could usefully be compiled and given as an additional statement to the accounts, together with comparative figures, and an analysis of the significance of trends and individual ratios. However, there are many real objections to a more extensive efficiency audit incorporating an evaluation of objectives and ongoing efficiency:

(a) danger of revealing information which could be of value to competitors;
(b) lack of objective indicators of efficiency;
(c) fear of curbing management initiative and willingness to take risk;
(d) necessary greater involvement of auditors in the day-to-day running of the company (to evaluate the basis on which decisions are made), with associated increase in costs and possibly reduction in independence;
(e) lack of personnel to carry out the audit. For an efficiency report to have credibility, it would have to be made by people of equivalent calibre to the directors, and perhaps with a wider range of experience; do such people exist in sufficient numbers?

It is not my intention to extensively debate these points here, merely to illustrate some of the arguments, so that you can determine your own standpoint. But one or two comments are appropriate.

(a) and (b) are valid points which inter-relate. Disclosure of important ratios (e.g. gross margin), such as used by 'Inter Firm Comparison', in conjunction with average figures for the industry would undoubtedly be valuable in assessing the company's performance. But they would also be extremely valuable to competitors. The auditor would have to look less for objective indicators, and more towards making a subjective evaluation of the company's performance in relation to the circumstances in which it operates. Such a move the auditor would be understandably reluctant to make in the current climate of increasing and expensive legal liability.

Whether the greater involvement of the auditors in evaluating management decision making will curb initiative will very much depend on the flexibility and constructiveness with which the auditors approach their task. If they carry out their job in a rigid manner, by reference to predetermined criteria, then the chances are high that management will follow suit and pursue a much more rigid style of management, with potentially disastrous results for profits.

What is certain, is that the increased audit involvement will result in considerably increased costs. Costs which may arguably outweigh any potential benefit derived. An alternative is to have a management audit by request of a specific percentage of shareholders. Such a move may be useful to protect minority interests in the event of dissatisfaction with their directors' performance. But the request, which is tantamount to a vote of no confidence in the directors, is only likely to occur in extreme situations (shareholders normally only take an interest in a crisis), when it may anyway be too late, or when it may be more appropriate to remove the directors completely.

Lack of suitable audit staff is at worst only a temporary problem. For if they are deemed necessary, then they should be trained and financial incentives provided to ensure that suitable people come forward. This problem could be further mitigated by having an audit team incorporating people with different skills as appropriate. But do the benefits to be derived justify the use of highly skilled manpower in this way? I believe that they do not, at least not at the current stage of accounting development.

Management audit is to be encouraged as part of internal audit, aimed at the improvement of a company's operating performance. But before it can be extended to involve the external auditors, there is need for financial reporting itself to have much greater credibility than it currently holds. Standards of audit independence and reporting must be raised, a greater degree of accounting conformity obtained and changes in company law made, particularly with reference to the audit of proprietary limited companies. The issue of to whom the auditor should report – shareholders or the public at large – also needs clarification. Once these difficult matters are resolved, then we are in a stronger position to consider the even more difficult development of management audit. To impose such a change now could be the last straw to a profession already overburdened with change, admittedly much of it overdue.

But in the meantime I do believe that we should extend the existing review of financial stability and make reference to this in the audit report. And an analysis of accounting ratios and trends could usefully become part of reporting requirements.

## 23.2 The social audit

The modern trend towards greater social awareness has now found its way into the once reactionary corridors of the accountancy profession. And this is evidenced by the publication in 1975 of 'The Corporate Report', by the Accounting Standards Steering Committee. This report claimed to take a 'global, economic and pluralistic view of economic organisations'. It certainly recognised that enterprises have responsibilities extending well beyond the maximisation of profit for their shareholders. It acknowledged that enterprises cannot exist but for their host society, and that they have responsibilities to that society, in addition to their obvious (in this enlightened age) responsibilities to creditors, employees and customers. The report concluded that financial reporting should be extended to include these latter sections of the community, but stopped short of advocating full-scale social accounting:

'It is tempting to propose that entities disclose information which will show their impact on, and their endeavours to protect societies, its amenities and environment. In our opinion such a proposal would be impractical at the present time, since the necessary generally agreed measurement techniques are not available.'

Whether their contention about measurement techniques is valid largely depends on what exactly is included in the concept of social accounting. And this is a very hazy area indeed. But we can identify the following potential matters for inclusion:

1. *Employee information.* Training programmes, average wages versus cost of living, absenteeism, employee turnover, accidents, days lost through strikes, social and other amenities provided by the company, etc.

2. *Customer information.* Product range, markets, percentage price rises, customer complaints, details of customer service provision, quality control, advertising details, cost break-down, etc.

3. *Social information.* Details of charitable and other donations, environment protection schemes, noise abatement, energy conservation, etc.

The sky is, proverbially, the limit as regards to the information that could be provided. But much of it becomes nebulous and highly subjective, especially the social information in 3, above. However, aspects of the information in 1 and 2 are capable of objective quantification. For example, the average cost of training per employee could be quantified, a rate of employee turnover could be calculated, and costs incurred in quality control, or complaint rectification could be reported.

The more generalised social information such as environment protection and energy conservation is very difficult to quantify because of the influence of 'externalities' and the lack of a basis of comparison for figures produced. For example, a company may spend enormous sums of money rendering poisonous waste harmless. But it can hardly be praised simply on this score, if the alternative of simply dumping the waste would kill off the surrounding population; though ways can be found to create indicators. For example, a company's success in energy conservation may be measured by the cost of energy per £1,000 value produced. A comparison (in real terms) of the figures in the company over a period of years could be indicative of the company's ability at energy conservation, and these figures could also be compared to an average figure for the industry, thereby giving an indication of the company's performance relative to its competitors. Now critics of social accounting will no doubt argue that such an approach takes a very simplistic view of company operations, in that it completely ignores external factors. While the effect of 'externalities' is undoubtedly significant, the indicators could be amplified by subjective comment, in much the same way as the directors will explain their financial success or failure in the directors' report.

What I do not accept is the attempt by some authors to create a 'social balance sheet', with precise formulae applied to various factors and presented so as to portray a quantitative (and supposedly comparable) picture of the company's social awareness. Such, to me, is an academic irrelevance which has no practical value whatsoever. The keystone of social information provided (indeed of *all* information provided) should be its value to readers. And we should not become weighed down by formulae where a subjective comment would be more valuable.

*Social audit* is the validation of information produced through social accounting; and as such, it is far from merely a concept for academic discussion. In France, a social audit became a legal requirement in 1977 with the following matters specified for disclosure: employment levels, remuneration and fringe benefits, health and safety, training, industrial developments, living conditions of workers, and services provided for employees.

You will note that these mostly relate to matters which are capable of quantification, and do not extend much beyond employee information. In Germany too employee information is generally all that is included in social accounting, which is not anyway mandatory at the moment.

Little has come of 'The Corporate Report', despite the example of France, where the Sudreau Report was published along similar lines, and in the same year. Many reasons have been put forward for this, but it is probably fair to say that the report was before its time in England, where there is a less powerful environmentalist and socialist lobby than in France. And there is a generally held view that 'The Corporate Report' tried to go too far, too quickly, and as a result received little support. Also the latter half of the 1970s was a period of intense and often bitter argument over the issue of inflation accounting, such that other issues of less immediate importance (such as social information) were lost in the debate.

Now that some measure of agreement has been reached on inflation accounting, and impetus has been given by the Fourth Directive for greater disclosure of non-financial information in the Directors' Report, perhaps the time is right to move ahead with some measures of social accountability, at least along the lines of employee and customer information, as previously discussed. Such a move would necessitate a complete overhaul of company law in terms of accountability. But such an overhaul is long overdue, for much of current law bears about the same relationship to the needs of the current business environment, as the abacus does to the computer!

## 23.3 Necessary changes in company law

There seems now to be a relentless stream of company legislation heading towards the statute books, consequent on the EEC directives, and on the antiquated state of the law in the 1970s.

We are now living with five Acts – 1948, 1967, 1976, 1980 and 1981. All with cross-referenced and overlapping requirements. We are now long, long overdue for a consolidating Act to simplify matters . . . just a little. But we can only hope for that.

The 1980 and 1981 Acts go a long way towards modernising our hitherto antiquated company law. But in addition to a consolidating Act, the following matters also require urgent attention, in my opinion:

1. Legislation to recognise the fact that auditors have reporting responsibilities that extend beyond the company itself.
2. Legislation to require the establishment of Audit Committees as discussed in sec. 2.10.
3. Legislation to update auditor independence provisions as discussed in sec. 2.10.
4. Legislation to prevent abuses of limited liability by a small but unscrupulous minority of companies which take advantage of their status by liquidating at an appropriate stage, with their directors/shareholders creaming off creditors' funds in the process. Such companies often liquidate, only to re-appear under another name very shortly afterwards. Very few criminal prosecutions are brought against the directors of such companies, highlighting the weakness of the law in this area. My suggestions are:
   (a) a minimum capital requirement for all companies;
   (b) in the event of small company audits being made non-compulsory, a continuing audit requirement to ensure that the provisions of company law with regard to capital maintenance are being met;
   (c) regardless of any changes in audit and reporting requirements, an effective audit to ensure that the company is solvent, and likely to remain so in the ensuing period;
   (d) directors of proprietary companies which have gone into compulsory liquidation to be prevented from holding office in other companies for a specified period.

## 23.4 Conclusion

The accounting and auditing profession underwent a profound and rapid period of development in the late 1970s, the like of which had not been seen before. Auditing and accounting standards and legal requirements all changed dramatically; in particular formalised auditing standards were introduced, and an inflation accounting standard agreed upon. It is likely, and indeed to be hoped, that the early 1980s will prove to be a period of consolidation and improvement in these new areas. But of one thing we can be certain – the art of auditing will continue to develop, and will now never again suffer from its one time, not entirely unjustified, reputation for being a stagnant area of study. It is up to us all to be part of the evolutionary process.

# Appendices

## Appendix 1

**CHECKLIST FOR THE FINANCIAL STATEMENTS AND THE DIRECTORS' REPORT**

CLIENT.........................................................PREPARED BY .........................DATE ........................
(Accountant-in-charge)

PERIOD ....................................................REVIEWED BY .........................DATE ........................
(Assignment Manager)

### INTRODUCTION

This checklist is designed to enable us to ensure that the financial statements and the directors' report comply with both the accounting and the disclosure requirements of the Companies Acts 1948 to 1981, Statements of Standard Accounting Practice in issue at 31 December 1982 and, where applicable, The Stock Exchange Listing Agreement. Whilst every effort has been made to make the checklist informative, reference must be made to the source documents on any point of doubt or difficulty. Reference should be made also to the company's articles of association for any special requirements regarding the presentation of the financial statements. Additionally, a company may be subject to other legislation that contains accounting and disclosure requirements.

This checklist is not applicable to the financial statements and the directors' report of those banking, insurance and shipping companies, and the group financial statements of those groups that have such a company within them, that continue to be prepared in accordance with Schedule 8A to the Companies Act 1948. The checklist does not cover the special provisions for investment companies that are set out in Part V of Schedule 8 to the Companies Act 1948 and in the Listing Agreement.

To comply with the Companies Acts 1948 to 1981, a company must adopt one of the balance sheet formats and one of the profit and loss account formats that are set out in Schedule 8. Unless there are additional accounting or disclosure requirements, an item that appears in the formats is not specifically referred to in the checklist.

The Listing Agreement requirements apply only to those companies with any class of securities listed on The Stock Exchange. The requirements may be disclosed anywhere in the annual report and financial statements. For convenience, however, they are included in the checklist under the most appropriate heading.

Most of the accounting and disclosure requirements do not apply to immaterial items.

We should consider each step in relation to the company's financial statements and directors' report and, where applicable, in relation to the group financial statements. The answer to each question will be YES, NO or N/A. Where the answer is NO, the matter should be discussed with the Partner or Manager.

The checklist is divided into five parts as follows:

Part I – Format of the financial statements
Part II – Content of the financial statements
Part III – Content of the directors' report
Part IV – Covers loans and other transactions with directors and connected persons
Part V – Covers current cost accounts

Examples of references are as follows:

| | |
|---|---|
| 8 Sch 1(1) | Paragraph 1(1) of Schedule 8 to the Companies Act 1948 (as set out in Schedule 1 to the Companies Act 1981) |
| 8 Sch Note 14 | Note 14 to the required formats for financial statements set out in Schedule 8 |
| 1967 S 8 | Section 8 of the Companies Act 1967 |
| 1948 S 149(2) (1981 S 1(1)) | Section 149(2) of the Companies Act 1948 as amended by Section 1(1) of the Companies Act 1981 |
| SI 1979 No 1618 | Statutory Instrument No 1618 issued in 1979 |
| SSAP 13 para 20 | Paragraph 20 of Statement of Standard Accounting Practice No 13 |
| LA para 10(a) and note 39 | Paragraph 10(a) and note 39 of The Stock Exchange Listing Agreement |

PART I – FORMAT OF THE FINANCIAL STATEMENTS – SCHEDULE 8 COMPANY.

| | Reference | Yes/No N/A Coy Grp. | |
|---|---|---|---|
| The format of the company's financial statements and, where applicable, the group financial statements should comply with the following requirements. | | | |
| 1. Have one of the profit and loss account formats and one of the balance sheet formats set out in Schedule 8 to the Companies Act 1948 been adopted? | 8 Sch 1(1) | ... | ... |
| 2. Are the format for the profit and loss account and the format for the balance sheet the same as those used in the preceding year? | 8 Sch 2(1) | ... | ... |
| If not, does a note disclose both that the directors have adopted a different format and their special reasons for doing this? | 8 Sch 2(2) | ... | ... |
| 3. Are the items in both the profit and loss account and the balance sheet shown in the order and under the headings and sub-headings set out in the chosen format? | 8 Sch 1(1) | ... | ... |
| *Notes:* | | | |
| (a) *Greater detail is permitted.* | 8 Sch 3(1) | | |
| (b) *Additional headings and sub-headings are permitted except that preliminary expenses, expenses of, and commission on, any issue of shares or debentures, and costs of research may not be treated as assets in the balance sheet.* | 8 Sch 3(2) SSAP 13 para 20 | | |
| (c) *Headings and sub-headings are not required where there is no relevant amount in both the current and the preceding year.* | 8 Sch 3(5), 4(3) | | |
| (d) *Items preceded by an Arabic numeral may be combined if immaterial, or if combination results in greater clarity and the breakdown is given in the notes.* | 8 Sch 3(4) | | |
| (e) *The directors must adapt the arrangement and the headings and sub-headings of items preceded by an Arabic numeral where the special nature of the business requires such adaptation.* | 8 Sch 3(3) | | |
| (f) *The letters, Roman numerals and Arabic numerals are not required in published financial statements.* | 8 Sch 1(2) | | |
| 4. Are assets not offset against liabilities and vice versa, and is income not offset against expenditure and vice versa? | 8 Sch 5 | ... | ... |

PART II – CONTENT OF THE FINANCIAL STATEMENTS – SCHEDULE 8 COMPANY.

| | Reference | Yes/No N/A Coy Grp. | |
|---|---|---|---|

The financial statements must comply with the accounting and the disclosure requirements set out below.

**A TRUE AND FAIR VIEW**

1. The overriding requirement is that the profit and loss account must give a true and fair view of the profit or loss for the year and the balance sheet must give a true and fair view of the state of affairs at the end of the year.

   Therefore:

   *Reference:* 1948 S 149(2), (3), 152(2), (3) (1981 S 1(1), 2)

   (a) Where information additional to that which the Companies Acts require is needed for the financial statements to give a true and fair view, has such extra information been given?

   *Reference:* 1948 S 149(3)(a), 152(3) (1981 S 1(1), 2)

   (b) Where the circumstances of the company or the group are such that compliance with a requirement of the Companies Acts would not result in a true and fair view even if additional information were given, has the company or group departed from that requirement?

   *Reference:* 1948 S 149(3)(b), 152(3) (1981 S 1(1), 2)

   If so, are particulars of, the reasons for, and the effect of, the departure given?

   *Reference:* 1948 S 149(4), 152(3) (1981 S 1(1), 2)

**ACCOUNTING PRINCIPLES**

2. Have the amounts to be included in the financial statements been determined in accordance with the following accounting principles:

   *Reference:* 8 Sch 9

   (a) Going concern?

   *Reference:* 8 Sch 10, SSAP 2 para 14

   (b) Consistency?

   *Reference:* 8 Sch 11, SSAP 2 para 14

   (c) Prudence?

   *Reference:* 8 Sch 12, SSAP 2 para 14

   (d) Accruals?

   *Reference:* 8 Sch 13, SSAP 2 para 14

   (e) Separate valuation of assets and liabilities?

   *Reference:* 8 Sch 14

   If not, because the directors consider that there are special reasons for departing from them, are particulars of, their reasons for, and the effect of, the departure given?

   *Reference:* 8 Sch 15, SSAP 2 para 17

**ACCOUNTING POLICIES**

3. Have the significant accounting policies adopted been stated?

   *Reference:* 8 Sch 36, SSAP 2 para 18

   In particular, the policies in respect of:

   (a) Depreciation and diminution in value of assets (including, for each major class of depreciable fixed asset, the depreciation method used)?

   *Reference:* 8 Sch 36, SSAP 12 para 22

   (b) Deferred development expenditure?

   *Reference:* SSAP 13 para 29

   (c) The calculation of cost, net realisable value and attributable profit/foreseeable loss for stock and long-term contract work in progress?

   *Reference:* SSAP 9 para 28

   (d) Deferred taxation?

   *Reference:* SSAP 15 para 37

   (e) The basis of translating amounts denominated in foreign currencies?

   *Reference:* 8 Sch 58(1)

   If the company is listed, is there a statement by the directors as to the reasons for any significant departure from standard accounting practices?

   *Reference:* LA para 10(a) and note 39

| | Reference | Yes/No N/A Coy Grp. | |
|---|---|---|---|

**CORRESPONDING AMOUNTS**

4.  Are corresponding amounts for the immediately preceding year given for all items in the financial statements except where corresponding amounts are specifically not required?

    *Reference:* 8 Sch 4(1), 58(2), (3)    ... ...

5.  Where the corresponding amount is not comparable with the current amount:

    *Reference:* 8 Sch 4(2), 58(2)

  (a) Has the corresponding amount been adjusted?    ... ...

  (b) Have particulars of, and the reasons for, the adjustment been disclosed?    ... ...

**DATE OF APPROVAL**

6.  Is the date on which the financial statements were approved by the board of directors disclosed?

    *Reference:* SSAP 17 para 26    ... ...

**PROFIT AND LOSS ACCOUNT AND RELATED NOTES**

*(Note: If a holding company prepares a consolidated profit and loss account that complies with the requirements of the Companies Acts and shows how much of the consolidated profit or loss for the year is dealt with in the financial statements of the company, it need not prepare a profit and loss account itself (but see step 42).)*

    *Reference:* 1948 S 149(5) (1981 S 1(1))

**Turnover**

    *Reference:* 8 Sch 94

7.  Is the turnover stated exclusive of VAT?

    *Reference:* SSAP 5 para 8    ... ...

**Expenditure**

8.  Do all items of expenditure include any irrecoverable VAT on that expenditure?

    *Reference:* SSAP 5 para 9    ... ...

**Disaggregated Information**

9.  Where two or more classes of business are carried on that, in the opinion of the directors, differ substantially, are the following disclosed:

    *Reference:* 8 Sch 55(1), (3), (4)

  (a) A description of each class?    ... ...

  (b) The amount of turnover attributable to each class?    ... ...

  (c) The amount of the profit or loss before taxation that the directors consider is attributable to each class?    ... ...

10. Where geographically defined markets are supplied that, in the opinion of the directors, differ substantially, is the amount of turnover attributable to each market disclosed?

    *Reference:* 8 Sch 55(2), (3), (4) LA para 10(c) and note 40    ... ...

    If the company is listed and the contribution to profit or loss from a specific market is substantially out of line with the normal ratio of profit to turnover, is the geographical analysis of contribution to trading results disclosed?

    *Reference:* LA para 10(c) and note 40    ... ...

| | Reference | Yes/No N/A Coy Grp. | |
|---|---|---|---|

**11.** Where the directors consider that disclosure of **disaggregated** information would be seriously prejudicial to the interests of the company or group, is there a statement that the information is not disclosed? — 8 Sch 55(5) — ... — ...

*Note:*

*The reason for non-disclosure is not required.*

### Employees

**12.** Is the average number of employees (including directors, and employees working wholly or mainly outside the UK) in the year disclosed both in total and by category of employee? — 8 Sch 56(1), (2), (3) — ... — ...

*Note:*

*When selecting categories, the directors should have regard to the manner in which the company's or group's activities are organised.* — 8 Sch 56(5)

**13.** Where profit and loss account formats 1 or 3 are adopted, is the aggregate of each of the following amounts disclosed in respect of the employees included in 12: — 8 Sch 56(4), 93

   (a)   Wages and salaries paid or payable? — ... — ...

   (b)   Social security costs incurred? — ... — ...

   (c)   Other pension costs incurred? — ... — ...

### Higher-paid Employees' Emoluments

**14.** Is the number of employees (excluding directors, and employees working wholly or mainly outside the UK) whose emoluments fall into each bracket of a scale £30,001-£35,000, £35,001-£40,000, etc. in multiples of £5,000 disclosed? — 1967 S 8 / SI 1979 No 1618 / SI 1982 No 1698 — ... — ...

*Notes:*

   *(a)   Exclude contributions to pension schemes.*

   *(b)   In consolidated financial statements, the provisions apply only to employees of the holding company.* — 8 Sch 63(b)

### Directors' Emoluments

**15.** Are directors' emoluments (divided in each case between amounts receivable in respect of services as director and amounts receivable in respect of other offices) disclosed as follows: — 1948 S 196

   (a)   Aggregate emoluments? — ... — ...

   (b)   Aggregate directors' and past directors' pensions? — ... — ...

   (c)   Aggregate of compensation paid to directors or past directors for loss of office divided between that receivable from the company, its subsidiaries and any other persons? — ... — ...

*Note:*

*In consolidated financial statements, the provisions apply only to directors of the holding company.* — 8 Sch 63(a)

**16.** Are the following disclosed: — 1967 S 6

   (a)   The number of directors whose emoluments fall into each bracket of a scale £0-£5,000, £5,001-£10,000, etc. in multiples of £5,000? — SI 1979 No 1618 / SI 1982 No 1698 — ... — ...

   (b)   The chairman's emoluments, or the emoluments of each person for the period during which he acted as chairman? — ... — ...

   (c)   The emoluments of the highest paid director (or directors, if equal) if in excess of the chairman's emoluments? — ... — ...

| | Reference | Yes/No N/A Coy Grp. | |
|---|---|---|---|

| | | | Reference | | |
|---|---|---|---|---|---|

(d) The number of directors who have waived rights to receive emoluments during the year, and the aggregate amount waived? — **1967 S 7** — ... ...

(e) If the company is listed, particulars of any arrangement under which a director has waived or agreed to waive emoluments from the company or any of its subsidiaries which accrued during the year, or future emoluments? — **LA para 10(m) and note 48** — ... ...

*Notes:*

*(a) The Companies Act requirements do not apply to those companies that are neither holding companies nor subsidiaries and the aggregate directors' emoluments do not exceed £60,000.* — **SI 1982 No 1698**

*(b) Exclude from (a) to (c) directors whose duties were wholly or mainly discharged outside the UK, and contributions to pension schemes.*

*(c) In consolidated financial statements, the provisions apply only to directors of the holding company.* — **8 Sch 63(b)**

## Depreciation

17. Where profit and loss account formats 1 or 3 are adopted:

(a) Are 'cost of sales', 'distribution costs' and 'administrative expenses' stated after deducting provisions for depreciation and diminution in value of related assets? — **8 Sch Note 14** — ... ...

(b) Is the amount of provisions for depreciation and diminution in value of tangible and intangible fixed assets disclosed? — **8 Sch Note 17 SSAP 12 para 22** — ... ...

18. Are the following amounts of additional provisions for diminution in value disclosed:

(a) In respect of temporary diminution in value of fixed asset investments? — **8 Sch 19(1)** — ... ...

(b) In respect of permanent diminution in value of any fixed asset? — **8 Sch 19(2)** — ... ...

(c) Written back because no longer required? — **8 Sch 19(3)** — ... ...

19. Where a fixed asset has been revalued but the depreciation charge included in the profit and loss account either as required by step 17(a) (formats 1 and 3) or under the heading 'depreciation and other amounts written off tangible and intangible assets' (formats 2 and 4) is based on its historical cost, is the difference between that charge and the charge based on the asset's value either shown separately in the profit and loss account or disclosed in the notes? — **8 Sch 32(3)** — ...

## Other Income and Expenditure Items

20. Are the following disclosed:

(a) Income and interest derived from group companies separately from income and interest derived from other sources? — **8 Sch Note 15** — ... ...

(b) The amount of income from listed investments? — **8 Sch 53(4)** — ... ...

(c) Interest and similar charges payable to group companies separately from other interest and similar charges payable? — **8 Sch Note 16** — ... ...

(d) Interest payable on and any similar charges in respect of: — **8 Sch 53(2)**

    (i) Bank loans and overdrafts, and other loans that are repayable:

        — otherwise than by instalments wholly within 5 years of the balance sheet date? — ... ...

        — by instalments wholly within 5 years of the balance sheet date? — ... ...

    (ii) Any other loans? — ... ...

*Note:*

*Not applicable to interest and similar charges payable on loans from other group companies.*

| | | Reference | Yes/No N/A Coy Grp. | |
|---|---|---|---|---|

| | | | Reference | Yes/No N/A | Coy Grp. |
|---|---|---|---|---|---|
| (e) | The amount, where substantial, of the revenue from rents (after deduction of ground rents, rates and other outgoings)? | | 8 Sch 53(5) | ... | ... |
| (f) | Auditors' remuneration including expenses? | | 8 Sch 53(7) | ... | ... |
| (g) | Revenue charges for hire of plant and machinery? | | 8 Sch 53(6) | ... | ... |
| (h) | The amounts set aside for the redemption of: | | 8 Sch 53(3) | | |
| | (i) | Share capital? | | ... | ... |
| | (ii) | Loans? | | ... | ... |
| 21. | Are dividends receivable from UK resident companies stated at the amount of cash received or receivable plus the tax credit? | | SSAP 8 para 25 | ... | ... |

**Profit or Loss Before Taxation**

| | | Reference | Yes/No N/A | Coy Grp. |
|---|---|---|---|---|
| 22. | Is the amount of the profit or loss on ordinary activities before taxation disclosed? | 8 Sch 3(6) | ... | ... |

**Taxation**

| | | | Reference | Yes/No N/A | Coy Grp. |
|---|---|---|---|---|---|
| 23. | If the rate of corporation tax is not known for the whole or part of the year, has the latest known rate been used, and disclosed? | | SSAP 8 para 23 | ... | ... |
| 24. | Are the following elements of the taxation charge separately disclosed: | | 8 Sch 54(1), (3) SSAP 8 para 22 | | |
| | (a) | UK corporation tax, and the amount which it would have been but for the relief from double taxation, and the basis of computation? | | ... | ... |
| | (b) | Transfers to or from the deferred taxation account? | SSAP 15 para 34 | ... | ... |
| | (c) | UK income tax, and the basis of computation? | | ... | ... |
| | (d) | Tax attributable to franked investment income? | | ... | ... |
| | (e) | Irrecoverable ACT? | | ... | ... |
| | (f) | Taxation imposed outside the UK of profits, income and (so far as charged to revenue) capital gains? | | ... | ... |
| | (g) | The amount, if any, of (f) that is unrelieved as a result of the payment or proposed payment of dividends? | | ... | ... |
| | *Note:* | | | | |
| | *Elements (a), (b), (c) and (f) must be stated separately in respect of ordinary activities and extraordinary items.* | | 8 Sch 54(3) SSAP 15 para 36 | | |
| 25. | Has deferred taxation been provided in respect of all short-term timing differences? | | SSAP 15 para 26 | ... | ... |
| 26. | Has deferred taxation been provided in respect of all other originating timing differences except where it can be demonstrated with reasonable probability that the timing differences will not reverse in the future? | | SSAP 15 paras 27 - 31 | ... | ... |
| 27. | Where there is a partial provision for deferred taxation, is the amount provided based on substantiated calculations and assumptions that are explained in the financial statements? | | SSAP 15 para 30 | ... | ... |
| 28. | Is the extent to which the taxation charge for the year has been reduced by timing differences on which deferred taxation has not been provided been disclosed? | | SSAP 15 para 35 | ... | ... |
| 29. | Are any special circumstances that affect the liability in respect of profits, income or capital gains either for the year (for example, stock relief) or for succeeding years (for example, tax losses carried forward) disclosed? | | 8 Sch 54(2) | ... | ... |

| | Reference | Yes/No N/A Coy Grp. | |
|---|---|---|---|

30. Are adjustments to the deferred taxation account that result from a change in the rate of taxation separately disclosed as part of the taxation charge for the year unless the change in rate is associated with a fundamental change in the basis of taxation when the adjustment should be treated as an extraordinary item? — SSAP 15 para 36 ... ...

**Dividends**

31. Is the aggregate amount of any dividends paid and proposed disclosed? — 8 Sch 3(7)(b) ... ...

Do these dividends exclude the related ACT or the attributable tax credit? — SSAP 8 para 24 ... ...

*Notes:*

(a) *A company cannot pay a dividend unless it has profits available for the purpose.* — 1980 S 39(1)

(b) *Profits available for the purpose are:* — 1980 S 39(2), 40(1)

*Accumulated realised profits less accumulated realised losses, less (in the case of a public company) accumulated net unrealised losses.*

*(Such profits and losses may be either revenue or capital in origin.)* — 1980 S 45(4)

(c) *The Companies Act 1980 (as amended by the Companies Act 1981) does not define 'realised' and 'unrealised' but it does give some guidance in specific cases. (See 1980 S 39, 42A, 43A.)*

32. If the company is listed, are particulars of any arrangement under which a shareholder has waived or agreed to waive any dividends (including future dividends) disclosed? — LA para 10(n) and note 49 ... ...

**Reserves**

33. Are any amounts set aside to, or proposed to be set aside to, or withdrawn from, or proposed to be withdrawn from, reserves disclosed? — 8 Sch 3(7)(a) ... ...

**Preceding Year, Exceptional and Extraordinary Items, and Prior-year Adjustments**

34. Are the nature and size of material amounts charged or credited that relate to any preceding year (for example, the normal recurring corrections and adjustments of accounting estimates made in prior years) disclosed? — 8 Sch 57(1) SSAP 6 para 16 ... ...

35. Are items of an abnormal size and incidence that are derived from the ordinary activities of the business included in arriving at the profit for the year before taxation and extraordinary items? — SSAP 6 para 14 8 Sch 57(3) ... ...

Are their nature and size disclosed? — ... ...

36. Do extraordinary items comprise only those items that derive from events or transactions outside the ordinary activities of the business and that are both material and expected not to recur frequently or regularly? — SSAP 6 para 15 8 Sch 57(2) ... ...

Are their nature and size disclosed? — ... ...

37. Do prior-year adjustments comprise only those material adjustments applicable to prior years that arise from changes in accounting policies and from the correction of fundamental errors? — SSAP 6 para 16 ... ...

Are prior year adjustments (less attributable taxation) accounted for by restating prior years with the result that the opening balance of retained profits is adjusted accordingly? — ... ...

Is the effect of the change disclosed where practicable by showing separately in the restatement of the previous year the amount involved? — ... ...

| | Reference | Yes/No N/A Coy Grp. | |
|---|---|---|---|

Is there a statement (immediately following the profit and loss account for the year) of retained profits/reserves that shows any prior-year adjustments? — SSAP 6 para 17 — ... ...

**Earnings Per Share**

*(Notes: 1. SSAP 3 applies only to listed companies.* — SSAP 3 para 13

*2. Appendix 1 to SSAP 3 contains guidelines for the determination of earnings per share.)*

38. Are the earnings per share shown on the face of the profit and loss account on the net basis? — SSAP 3 para 14 — ... ...

Where materially different, are earnings per share shown also on the nil distribution basis? — ... ...

39. Is the basis of calculating earnings per share disclosed? (In particular the amount of the earnings and the number of equity shares used in the calculation.) — SSAP 3 para 15 — ... ...

40. Where a company has at the balance sheet date contracted to issue further shares after the end of the year, or where it has already issued shares that do not rank for dividend until future years, and the effect will be to dilute basic earnings per share by 5 per cent or more, are fully diluted earnings per share also shown on the face of the profit and loss account and is the basis of their calculation disclosed? — SSAP 3 para 16 — ... ...

Is equal prominence given to basic and fully diluted earnings per share? — ... ...

*Notes:*

(a) *A company has 'contracted to issue further shares after the end of the year' where it has issued debentures, loan stock or preference shares that are convertible into equity shares or where it has granted options or issued warrants to subscribe for equity shares.*

(b) *The comparative amount for fully diluted earnings per share is required only if the assumptions on which the amount was based still apply.*

**Consolidated Profit and Loss Account**

41. Is the extent to which the consolidated profit or loss is dealt with in the financial statements of the holding company disclosed? — 1948 S 149(5) (1981 S 1(1)) — N/A ...

42. Where a holding company has taken advantage of the provisions not to prepare its own profit and loss account, is there a statement to that effect in the group financial statements? — 1948 S 149(6) (1981 S 1(1)) — N/A ...

**BALANCE SHEET AND RELATED NOTES**

**Assets — Fixed and Current**

43. Does the purchase price of an asset comprise the actual price paid together with any expenses incidental to its acquisition? — 8 Sch 26(1) SSAP 9 para 18 — ... ...

44. Does the production cost of an asset comprise the purchase price of raw materials and consumables used together with the amount of costs incurred that are directly attributable to the production of that asset? — 8 Sch 26(2) SSAP 9 paras 17, 19, 20 — ... ...

45. Where the production cost of an asset includes a reasonable proportion of costs incurred that are only indirectly attributable to the production of that asset, are these included only to the extent that they relate to the period of production? — 8 Sch 26(3) — ... ...

46. Where the production cost of an asset includes interest on capital borrowed to finance the production of that asset, are the fact that interest is included and the amount of interest included disclosed? — 8 Sch 26(3) — ... ...

| | Reference | Yes/No N/A Coy Grp. | |
|---|---|---|---|
| If the company is listed, is the amount of interest capitalised during the year and an indication of the amount and treatment of any related tax relief disclosed? | LA para 10(g) | ... | ... |
| 47. Where any of the alternative accounting rules have been adopted, are the following disclosed: | 8 Sch 33 | | |
| (a) The items affected and the basis of valuation adopted? | | ... | ... |
| (b) In respect of each balance sheet item affected (except stocks) one of the following: | | | |
| (i) The aggregate cost and aggregate depreciation on an historical cost basis? | | ... | ... |
| (ii) The difference between the aggregate cost and aggregate depreciation as stated and what they would have been on an historical cost basis? | | ... | ... |
| 48. Where any of the alternative accounting rules have been adopted, has the profit or loss on revaluation been transferred to the revaluation reserve? | 8 Sch 34(1), (2) SSAP 6 para 13 | ... | ... |
| *Note:* | | | |
| *The revaluation reserve may be shown under another name.* | 8 Sch 34(3) | | |
| 49. Where the amount repayable on any debt owed by a company is greater than the value of the consideration received and the difference is treated as an asset: | 8 Sch 24 | | |
| (a) Is the difference being written off by reasonable amounts each year so that it will be completely written off before the debt is repaid? | | ... | ... |
| (b) Is the amount of the difference at the year end separately disclosed? | | ... | ... |
| 50. Does the cost of an asset include any irrecoverable VAT on that asset? | SSAP 5 para 9 | ... | ... |
| 51. Where there is no record of the purchase price or production cost of an asset (or such record can be obtained only with unreasonable expense or delay) is the asset included at its earliest known value? | 8 Sch 28 | ... | ... |
| Are particulars given of any case where the earliest known value of an asset is first used? | 8 Sch 51(1) | ... | ... |
| **Assets Included at a Fixed Amount** | | | |
| 52. Are assets that are constantly being replaced included at a fixed quantity and value only under the items 'tangible assets' and 'raw materials and consumables' and only where both their overall value is not material to assessing the state of affairs and their quantity, value and composition are not subject to material variation? | 8 Sch 25 | ... | ... |
| **Fixed Assets — Cost/Valuation** | | | |
| 53. Unless any of the alternative accounting rules are adopted, are fixed assets included at purchase price or production cost less any provisions for depreciation or diminution in value? | 8 Sch 16, 17 | ... | ... |
| 54. Where any of the alternative accounting rules are adopted, have fixed assets been valued on the following bases: | | | |
| (a) Intangible fixed assets (except goodwill) at their current cost? | 8 Sch 31(1) | ... | ... |
| (b) Tangible fixed assets either at a market value as at the date of their last valuation or at their current cost? | 8 Sch 31(2) | ... | ... |
| (c) Fixed asset investments either at a market value as at the date of their last valuation or at a value determined on any basis that the directors consider is appropriate in the circumstances? | 8 Sch 31(3) | | |
| If the latter basis is adopted, are particulars of the method adopted and the reasons for adopting it disclosed? | | ... | ... |

| | Reference | Yes/No N/A Coy Grp. | |
|---|---|---|---|

| | | Reference | | |
|---|---|---|---|---|

55. Where fixed assets (other than listed investments) are included at a valuation, are the following disclosed:

   (a)   The years (so far as they are known to the directors) in which the assets were valued? — 8 Sch 43 — ... ...

   (b)   The respective values? — 8 Sch 43 — ... ...

   (c)   In the case of assets valued during the year: — 8 Sch 43 / SSAP 19 para 12

      (i)   Either the names or the qualifications of the valuers? — ... ...

      (ii)   The bases of valuation used? — ... ...

**Fixed Assets – Depreciation**

56. Where any fixed asset has a limited useful economic life, is the purchase price or production cost or valuation, less the estimated residual value, written off systematically over that life? — 8 Sch 18, 32(1) / SSAP 12 paras 17, 21 / SSAP 13 para 24 — ... ...

   *Note:*

   *Leasehold investment properties should be depreciated at least over the period when the unexpired term of the lease is 20 years or less. Other investment properties should not be depreciated. (Steps 75 – 80 cover investment properties.)* — SSAP 12 para 16 / SSAP 19 para 10

57. If the estimated useful life of an asset is revised, is the unamortised cost/ valuation being charged over the revised remaining useful life? — SSAP 12 para 18 — ... ...

58. In the year in which assets are revalued, is the effect on the depreciation charge disclosed? — SSAP 12 para 21 — ... ...

59. If there is a change from one method of depreciation to another, is the unamortised cost/valuation of the asset being written off on the new basis over the remaining useful life of the asset? — SSAP 12 para 20 — ... ...

   In the year of change, is the effect disclosed? — ... ...

60. If there has been a diminution in the value of any fixed asset and this diminution is expected to be permanent, has additional provision been made? — 8 Sch 19(2) / SSAP 12 para 19 / SSAP 13 para 25 — ... ...

61. Where the reasons for any additional provision against any fixed asset cease to exist to any extent, has the additional provision been written back to that extent? — 8 Sch 19(3) — ... ...

   *Note:*

   *Development costs once written off should not be reinstated even though the uncertainties that led to the write off no longer apply.* — SSAP 13 para 26

62. For each major class of depreciable fixed asset are the useful lives or the depreciation rates used disclosed? — SSAP 12 para 22 — ... ...

**Fixed Assets – Government Grants**

63. Are grants relating to fixed assets credited to revenue over the expected useful·life of the asset by one of the following methods: — SSAP 4 para 9

   (a)   Reducing the cost of the asset by the amount of the grant? — ... ...

   (b)   Treating the grant as a deferred credit and making annual transfers to revenue? — ... ...

   If method (b) is adopted, is the amount of the deferred credit shown separately in the balance sheet (under the heading 'accruals and deferred income')? — ... ...

| | Reference | Yes/No N/A Coy | Grp. |
|---|---|---|---|

**Fixed Assets — Movements**

64. In respect of the cost/valuation of fixed assets under any heading, are the following disclosed: — 8 Sch 42(1), (2) / SSAP 13 para 27

  (a) The aggregate cost/valuation at the beginning of the year? — ... ...

  (b) Any revisions to the amount in respect of a valuation during the year? — ... ...

  (c) Acquisitions during the year? — ... ...

  (d) Disposals during the year? — ... ...

  (e) Any reclassification of assets to or from that heading during the year? — ... ...

  (f) The aggregate cost/valuation at the end of the year? — SSAP 12 para 22 — ... ...

*Note:*

*Comparative amounts are not required.* — 8 Sch 58(3)

65. In respect of provisions for depreciation or diminution in value of fixed assets under any heading, are the following disclosed: — 8 Sch 42(3) / SSAP 13 para 27

  (a) The cumulative provisions at the beginning of the year? — ... ...

  (b) Any such provisions made during the year? — ... ...

  (c) Any adjustments made as a result of disposals of assets during the year? — ... ...

  (d) Any other adjustments made during the year? — ... ...

  (e) The cumulative provisions at the end of the year? — SSAP 12 para 22 — ... ...

*Note:*

*Comparative amounts are not required.* — 8 Sch 58(3)

**Intangible Fixed Assets — Development Costs**

66. Are development costs capitalised only where all of the following conditions apply: — 8 Sch 20(1) / SSAP 13 para 21

  (a) There is a clearly defined project? — ... ...

  (b) The related expenditure is separately identifiable? — ... ...

  (c) The outcome of the project has been assessed with reasonable certainty as to both its technical feasibility and its ultimate commercial viability? — ... ...

  (d) All costs (including future costs to be incurred) are reasonably expected to be more than covered by related future revenues? — ... ...

  (e) Adequate resources exist, or are reasonably expected to be available, to enable the project to be completed, and to provide any consequential increases in working capital? — ... ...

67. Are development costs capitalised only to the extent that their recovery can reasonably be regarded as assured? — SSAP 13 para 22 — ... ...

68. Have the criteria for determining whether development costs may be capitalised been applied consistently? — SSAP 13 para 23 — ... ...

69. In respect of capitalised development costs, are the following disclosed: — 8 Sch 20(2)

  (a) The period over which the costs are being, or are to be, written off? — ... ...

  (b) The reasons for capitalising the costs? — ... ...

  (c) Where appropriate, a statement that the directors have decided not to treat unamortised development costs as a realised loss when calculating distributable profits and the special circumstances that justify their decision? — 1980 S 42A(3) (1981 S 84) — ... ...

| | Reference | Yes/No N/A Coy Grp. | |
|---|---|---|---|

**Intangible Fixed Assets — Concessions, Patents, etc.**

70. Are amounts in respect of concessions, patents, licences, trade marks and similar rights and assets included in the balance sheet only if one of the following applies: — 8 Sch Note 2

   (a) The assets were acquired for valuable consideration and do not represent goodwill? — ... ...

   (b) The assets were created by the company? — ... ...

**Intangible Fixed Assets — Goodwill**

71. Is goodwill capitalised only to the extent that it was acquired for valuable consideration? — 8 Sch Note 3 — ... ...

72. In respect of capitalised goodwill, are the following disclosed: — 8 Sch 21

   (a) The period that the directors have chosen for writing off the goodwill? — ... ...

   (b) The reasons why the directors chose that period? — ... ...

   *Note:*

   *Goodwill arising on consolidation does not have to be written off.* — 8 Sch 66

**Tangible Fixed Assets**

73. Is the cost of fixed assets acquired or constructed to provide facilities for research and development activities over a number of years capitalised and written off over the useful life of those assets? — SSAP 13 para 19 — ... ...

**Tangible Fixed Assets — Land and Buildings**

74. Is the division of the net book amount of land and buildings between freehold, long leases (50 or more years to run) and short leases disclosed? — 8 Sch 44, 82 — ... ...

**Tangible Fixed Assets — Investment Properties**

*(Note: SSAP 19 does not apply to investment properties owned by charities.)* — SSAP 19 para 9

75. Are investment properties (as defined in SSAP 19 paras 7, 8) included in the balance sheet at their open market value? — SSAP 19 para 11 — ... ...

76. Are changes in the value of investment properties disclosed as a movement on an investment revaluation reserve? — SSAP 19 para 13 — ... ...

   *Note:*

   *Not applicable to the long-term business of insurance companies where changes in value are dealt with in the relevant fund account.* — SSAP 19 para 14

77. If a deficit on revaluation exceeds the balance on the investment revaluation reserve, has the excess been charged in the profit and loss account? — SSAP 19 para 13 — ... ...

78. If the persons making the revaluation are employees or officers of the company or group that owns the property, is this fact disclosed? — SSAP 19 para 12 — ... ...

79. Are both the carrying value of investment properties and the investment revaluation reserve displayed prominently? — SSAP 19 para 15 — ... ...

80. Are particulars of, the reasons for, and the effect of, the departure from the specific requirement to provide depreciation on any fixed asset that has a limited useful economic life given? — SSAP 19 para 17 1948 S 149(4), 152(3) (1981 S 1(1), 2) — ... ...

|  | Reference | Yes/No N/A Coy Grp. | |
|--|-----------|---------------------|--|

**Investments — Fixed Asset and Current Asset**

81. In respect of listed investments under any heading, are the following disclosed:  —  8 Sch 45

   (a) The amount that has been granted a listing on a recognised stock exchange?  ... ...

   (b) The amount of other listed investments?  ... ...

   (c) The total amount of all listed investments?  ... ...

   (d) The aggregate market value (unless the investments are included in the balance sheet at market value)?  ... ...

   (e) Both the market value and the stock exchange value of any investments where the market value is higher?  ... ...

82. If the company is holding any of its own shares, is the nominal value of those shares disclosed?  —  8 Sch Note 4  ... ...

**Significant Shareholdings (excluding subsidiaries)**

83. For shareholdings in a company at the balance sheet date where  —  1967 S 4(1), (1A), (2) (1981 S 3(1))

   (i) the investing company's holding in any class of the equity share capital of that company exceeds one-tenth of the nominal value of the allotted shares of that class, or

   (ii) the investing company's holding in the share capital of that company exceeds one-tenth of the nominal value of the allotted share capital of that company, or

   (iii) the aggregate amount of the share holdings exceeds one-tenth of the total assets as stated in the investing company's balance sheet,

are the following disclosed:

   (a) The name of the company?  ... ...

   (b) Its country of incorporation, if outside Great Britain?  ... ...

   (c) Its country of registration (England or Scotland) if different from the investing company?  ... ...

   (d) The identity of, and the proportion of, the nominal value of the allotted shares of each class held?  ... ...

   (e) A statement, where appropriate, that the information given deals only with the companies within (i) and (ii) whose results principally affect the profit or loss or amount of assets of the investing company?  —  1967 S 4(4), (5) (1981 S 3(2)(b))  ... ...

*Notes:*

   *(a) Comparative amounts are not required.*  —  8 Sch 58(3)

   *(b) In consolidated financial statements, the provisions apply only to investments by the holding company.*  —  8 Sch 63(b)

   *(c) A company need not disclose particulars in respect of bodies corporate incorporated, or carrying on business, outside the UK if it would be harmful to the business of the company or the other body corporate and the Department of Trade agrees to the non-disclosure.*  —  1967 S 4(3)

84. For shareholdings in a company at the balance sheet date where the investing company's holding exceeds one-fifth of the allotted share capital of that company, are the following disclosed:  —  1981 S 4(2), (3)

   (a) The aggregate amount of the capital and reserves of that company as at the end of its financial year ending with, or last before, the financial year of the investing company?  ... ...

   (b) The profit or loss of that company for its financial year ending with, or last before, the financial year of the investing company?  ... ...

| | Reference | Yes/No N/A Coy Grp. | |
|---|---|---|---|

*Notes:*

*(a)   Not required if the investment is included in, or in a note to, the investing company's accounts by way of the equity method of valuation.* — 1981 S 4(5)

*(b)   In consolidated financial statements, the provisions apply only to investments by the holding company.* — 8 Sch 63(d)

85. If the company is listed and the group has an interest of 20% or more in the equity capital of another company, are the following disclosed in respect of each such interest:   —   LA para 10(e) and notes 42, 43

| | | | | |
|---|---|---|---|---|
| (a) | The principal country of operation? | | ... | ... |
| (b) | Particulars of its issued share and loan capital? | | ... | ... |
| (c) | The total amount of its reserves (unless the investment is dealt with as an associated company)? | | ... | ... |
| (d) | The percentage of each class of loan capital attributable to the interest (direct or indirect)? | | ... | ... |
| (e) | A statement, where appropriate, that the information given deals only with those companies whose results principally affect the profit or loss or amount of assets of the investing group? | | ... | ... |

**Associated Companies**

86. If there are investments in associated companies (as defined in paragraphs 13 - 16 of SSAP 1), has Part 5 been completed?   —   ... ...

**Investments in Subsidiaries**

87. For each subsidiary at the balance sheet date, are the following disclosed:   —   1967 S 3(1), (2) SSAP 14 para 33

| | | Reference | | |
|---|---|---|---|---|
| (a) | The name of the subsidiary? | | ... | ... |
| (b) | Its country of incorporation, if outside Great Britain? | | ... | ... |
| (c) | Its country of registration (England or Scotland) if different from the holding company? | | ... | ... |
| (d) | The identities and proportions of the nominal values of the allotted shares of each class held by: | | | |
| | (i)   The company and its nominees? | | ... | ... |
| | (ii)  Subsidiaries and their nominees? | | ... | ... |
| (e) | If the company is listed, the name of the principal country in which each subsidiary operates? | LA para 10(d) and note 41 | ... | ... |
| (f) | A statement, where appropriate, that the information in (a) to (e) is given only for those companies whose results principally affect the profit or loss or the amount of the assets of the group? | 1967 S 3(4), (5) | ... | ... |
| (g) | The aggregate amount of the capital and reserves of the subsidiary as at the end of its financial year ending with, or last before, the financial year of the holding company? | 1981 S 4(1), (3) | ... | ... |
| (h) | The profit or loss of the subsidiary for its financial year ending with, or last before, the financial year of the holding company? | | ... | ... |
| (i) | For each principal subsidiary, an indication of the nature of its business? | SSAP 14 para 33 | ... | ... |

*Notes:*

*(a)   Comparative amounts are not required for the information in (a) to (f).* — 8 Sch 58(3)

*(b)   A company need not disclose the information required by (a) to (d) in respect of subsidiaries incorporated, or carrying on business, outside the UK if it would be harmful to the business of the company or subsidiary and the Department of Trade agrees to the non-disclosure.* — 1967 S 3(3)

| | | Reference | Yes/No N/A Coy Grp. | |
|---|---|---|---|---|
| (c) | The information in (g) and (h) is not required if one of the following applies: | 1981 S 4(4) | | |
| | (i) The holding company is exempt from preparing group accounts because it is the wholly-owned subsidiary of another company incorporated in Great Britain. | | | |
| | (ii) The accounts of the subsidiary are included in the group accounts. | | | |
| | (iii) The investment of the company in the shares of the subsidiary is included in, or in a note to, the company's financial statements by way of the equity method of valuation. | | | |
| (d) | In consolidated financial statements, the provisions in (g) and (h) apply only to investments by the holding company. | 8 Sch 63(d) | | |

**Group Companies**

| | | | | |
|---|---|---|---|---|
| 88. | Are the aggregate amounts of each of the following disclosed: | 8 Sch 59 | | |
| | (a) Amounts owed to or by, and any interests in, any holding company or fellow subsidiary? | | ... | ... |
| | (b) Amounts owed to or by, and any interests in, any subsidiary? | | ... | ... |
| | Note: | | | |
| | In consolidated financial statements, the provisions apply only to subsidiaries not consolidated. | 8 Sch 67 | | |

**Group Accounts**

| | | | | |
|---|---|---|---|---|
| 89. | If the company has subsidiaries, have the relevant sections of Part 6 been completed? | | ... | ... |

**Current Assets**

| | | | | |
|---|---|---|---|---|
| 90. | Unless any of the alternative accounting rules are adopted, is each current asset included at the lower of purchase price or production cost and net realisable value? | 8 Sch 16, 22, 23(1) SSAP 9 para 26 | ... | ... |
| | Does production cost exclude distribution costs? | 8 Sch 26(4) | ... | ... |
| 91. | Where the reasons for a provision to reduce purchase price or production cost to net realisable value cease to exist to any extent, has the provision been written back to that extent? | 8 Sch 23(2) | ... | ... |
| 92. | Where any of the alternative accounting rules are adopted, have current assets been valued on the following bases: | | | |
| | (a) Current asset investments at their current cost? | 8 Sch 31(4) | ... | ... |
| | (b) Stocks at their current cost? | 8 Sch 31(5) | ... | ... |

**Stocks and Fungible Assets**

| | | | | |
|---|---|---|---|---|
| 93. | Is the purchase price or production cost of stocks and fungible assets determined using FIFO, LIFO, weighted average price or any other similar method? | 8 Sch 27(1), (2) | ... | ... |
| | Is the method chosen one which appears to the directors to be appropriate in the circumstances of the company? | | ... | ... |
| | Note: | | | |
| | Fungible assets are assets that are substantially indistinguishable one from another (for example, identical shares in a particular company). | 8 Sch 27(6) | | |
| 94. | Where the purchase price or production cost of stocks and fungible assets is determined using one of the methods referred to in step 93 and it is materially different from the replacement cost (or, if more appropriate, the most recent actual purchase price or production cost) of those stocks or fungible assets, is the amount of the difference disclosed for each category? | 8 Sch 27(3), (4), (5) | ... | ... |

**Long-term Contract Work in Progress**

| | | | |
|---|---|---|---|
| 95. Is long-term contract work in progress stated at cost plus attributable profit less any foreseeable losses and progress payments received and receivable? | SSAP 9 para 27 | ... | ... |
| If anticipated losses on a contract exceed costs incurred to date less progress payments received and receivable, is the excess shown separately as a provision? | | ... | ... |
| If progress payments on a contract exceed costs incurred to date plus attributable profit, is the excess included in payments received on account under the heading 'creditors'? | 8 Sch Note 8 | ... | ... |
| 96. If long-term contract work in progress includes attributable profit, are particulars of, the reasons for, and the effect of, the departure from the statutory valuation rules for current assets given? | 1948 S 149(4), 152(3) (1981 S 1(1), 2) | ... | ... |
| 97. In respect of long-term contracts, are the following disclosed: | SSAP 9 para 30 | | |
|     (a) The amount of work in progress at cost plus attributable profit, less foreseeable losses? | | ... | ... |
|     (b) The progress payments received and receivable on account of contracts in progress? | | ... | ... |

**Debtors**

| | | | |
|---|---|---|---|
| 98. For each item included under debtors, is the amount falling due after more than one year separately disclosed? | 8 Sch Note 5 | ... | ... |

**Loans for Acquisition of Own Shares**

| | | | |
|---|---|---|---|
| 99. Is the aggregate amount of any outstanding loans in respect of financial assistance for acquisition of own shares and authorised by 1981 S 42(6)(b) or (c) or S 43 disclosed? | 8 Sch 51(2) | ... | ... |

**Loans and Other Transactions with Directors**

| | | | |
|---|---|---|---|
| 100. Has Part 4 been completed? | | ... | ... |

**Loans and Other Transactions with Officers**

| | | | |
|---|---|---|---|
| 101. In respect of transactions, arrangements and agreements made by the company, and in the case of a holding company by its subsidiary, for persons who were, at any time during the year, officers, but not directors, of the company, do the notes contain the following particulars: | 1980 S 56(1), (2), (4A) (1981 3 Sch 52(b)) | | |
|     (a) The aggregate amounts outstanding at the end of the year of: | | | |
|         (i) Loans (including guarantees, securities, arrangements and agreements relating to loans)? | | ... | ... |
|         (ii) Quasi-loans (including guarantees, securities, arrangements and agreements relating to quasi-loans)? | | ... | ... |
|         (iii) Credit transactions (including guarantees, securities, arrangements and agreements relating to credit transactions)? | | ... | ... |
|     (b) The number of officers that each of the aggregate amounts in (a) cover? | | ... | ... |
| *Notes:* | | | |
|     *(a) Where the aggregate amount outstanding at the end of the year under transactions, arrangements and agreements made for the officer does not exceed £2,500, the amount may be excluded from the aggregate amounts disclosed under (a).* | 1980 S 56(2A) (1981 3 Sch 52(a)) | | |
|     *(b) Comparative amounts are not required.* | 8 Sch 58(3) | | |
|     *(c) In consolidated financial statements, the provisions apply only to officers of the holding company.* | 8 Sch 63(c) | | |

| | Reference | Yes/No N/A Coy | Grp. |
|---|---|---|---|

**Creditors and Other Liabilities**

| | | Reference | Yes/No N/A Coy | Grp. |
|---|---|---|---|---|
| 102. | Is there separate disclosure of the amount of convertible debenture loans? | 8 Sch Note 7 | ... | ... |
| 103. | In respect of debentures issued during the year, are the following disclosed: | 8 Sch 41(1) | | |
| | (a) The reason for making the issue? | | ... | ... |
| | (b) The classes of debentures issued? | | ... | ... |
| | (c) For each class: | | | |
| |    (i) The amount issued? | | ... | ... |
| |    (ii) The consideration received by the company? | | ... | ... |
| 104. | Are particulars disclosed of any redeemed debentures that the company has power to reissue? | 8 Sch 41(2) | ... | ... |
| 105. | In respect of any of the company's debentures held by a nominee of, or trustee for, the company, are the following disclosed: | 8 Sch 41(3) | | |
| | (a) The nominal amount of the debentures? | | ... | ... |
| | (b) The book value of the holding? | | ... | ... |
| 106. | Are the number, description and amount of the company's debentures held beneficially by subsidiaries or their nominees disclosed? | 8 Sch 60 | ... | ... |
| | *Note:* | | | |
| | *In consolidated financial statements, the provisions apply only to subsidiaries not consolidated.* | 8 Sch 67 | | |
| 107. | If balance sheet format 2 is used, is the amount falling due within one year and after more than one year shown separately for each item included under creditors and in aggregate for all items? | 8 Sch Note 13 | ... | ... |
| 108. | In respect of each item included under creditors falling due after more than one year, are the following disclosed: | 8 Sch 48(1) | | |
| | (a) The aggregate amount of debts that are payable or repayable otherwise than by instalments more than five years after the balance sheet date? | | ... | ... |
| | (b) The aggregate amount of debts that are payable or repayable by instalments any of which fall due more than five years after the balance sheet date? | | ... | ... |
| | (c) The aggregate amount of the instalments in (b) that fall due more than five years after the balance sheet date? | | ... | ... |
| 109. | In relation to each debt within 108, is one of the following disclosed: | 8 Sch 48(2), (3) | | |
| | (a) The terms of payment or repayment and the rate of interest payable? | | ... | ... |
| | (b) If the above statement would be excessively long, a general indication of terms of payment or repayment and the rates of interest payable? | | ... | ... |
| 110. | If the company is listed, is there a statement detailing the aggregate amounts repayable | LA para 10(f) | | |
| |    (i) in one year or less, or on demand, | | | |
| |    (ii) between one and two years, | | | |
| |    (iii) between two and five years, | | | |
| |    (iv) in five years or more, | | | |
| | in respect of: | | | |
| | (a) Bank loans and overdrafts? | | ... | ... |
| | (b) Other borrowings? | | ... | ... |

| | Reference | Yes/No N/A Coy Grp. | |
|---|---|---|---|

111. In respect of each item shown under creditors, are the following disclosed: — **8 Sch 48(4)**

   (a) The aggregate amount in respect of which any security has been given? — … …

   (b) An indication of the nature of the securities given? — … …

112. Is the amount for creditors in respect of taxation and social security shown separately from the amount for 'other creditors'? — **8 Sch Note 9** — … …

113. Is the aggregate amount that is recommended for distribution by way of dividend disclosed? — **8 Sch 51(3)** — … …

   Do proposed dividends and dividends declared but not yet payable exclude the related ACT? — **SSAP 8 para 26** — … …

   Is the ACT on proposed dividends (whether recoverable or irrecoverable) included as a current tax liability? — … …

   If the ACT on proposed dividends is regarded as recoverable, has it been deducted from the deferred taxation account, or, in the absence of such an account, shown under 'prepayments and accrued income'? — **SSAP 8 para 27** — … …

114. For arrears of fixed cumulative dividends, are the following disclosed: — **8 Sch 49**

   (a) The amount of the arrears? — … …

   (b) The period for which the dividend on each class of shares is in arrears? — … …

### Provisions for Liabilities and Charges

115. In respect of provisions under any heading or sub-heading where there has been a transfer to the provision, or from the provision otherwise than for the purpose for which the provision was established, are the following disclosed: — **8 Sch 46**

   (a) The amount of the provision at the beginning of the year? — … …

   (b) The amount and the source of transfers to the provision? — … …

   (c) The amount and the application of transfers from the provision? — … …

   (d) The amount of the provision at the end of the year? — … …

   *Note:*

   *Comparative amounts are not required.* — **8 Sch 58(3)**

116. Are particulars disclosed of each material provision included under the heading 'other provisions'? — **8 Sch 46(3)** — … …

117. Is the amount of any provision for taxation other than deferred taxation disclosed? — **8 Sch 47** — … …

### Provisions for Liabilities and Charges — Deferred Taxation

118. Is there disclosure of the potential amount of deferred tax for all timing differences? — **SSAP 15 paras 33, 37** — … …

   Does this distinguish between the various principal categories of deferred tax and show for each category the amount that has been provided? — … …

119. Are debit balances on the deferred taxation account carried forward only if there is reasonable certainty of their recovery in future years? — **SSAP 15 para 32** — … …

120. Where the financial statements disclose the value of an asset by way of note and that value differs from the book value of the asset, does the note also disclose the tax implications that would result if the asset was sold at that value? — **SSAP 15 para 39** — … …

### Guarantees and Other Financial Commitments (excluding contingencies)

121. Are particulars (including amount secured, where practicable) of any charge on the assets to secure the liabilities of any other person disclosed? — **8 Sch 50(1)** — … …

| | Reference | Yes/No N/A Coy Grp. | |
|---|---|---|---|
| 122. Are the following amounts of capital expenditure disclosed: | 8 Sch 50(3) | | |
|   (a)  Contracted but not provided for? | | ... | ... |
|   (b)  Authorised but not contracted for? | | ... | ... |
| 123. Are particulars of the following pension commitments disclosed: | 8 Sch 50(4) | | |
|   (a)  Those included under any provision in the balance sheet? | | ... | ... |
|   (b)  Those for which no provision has been made? | | ... | ... |
|   (c)  Those in (a) and (b) in respect of pensions payable to past directors? | | ... | ... |
| 124. Are particulars disclosed of any other financial commitments that have not been provided for and that are relevant to the assessment of the state of affairs? | 8 Sch 50(5) | ... | ... |
| 125. Is there separate disclosure of commitments in 121 to 124 that are undertaken on behalf of or for the benefit of: | 8 Sch 50(6) | | |
|   (a)  Any holding company or fellow subsidiary? | | ... | ... |
|   (b)  Any subsidiary? | | ... | ... |

**Contingencies**

| | Reference | Yes/No N/A Coy Grp. | |
|---|---|---|---|
| 126. Have material contingent losses been accrued where it is probable that a future event will confirm a loss that can be estimated with reasonable accuracy at the date on which the financial statements are approved by the board of directors? | SSAP 18 para 15 | ... | ... |
| 127. Except where the possibility of loss is remote, have material contingent losses not accrued been disclosed? | SSAP 18 para 16 | ... | ... |
| 128. Have material contingent gains been disclosed only where it is probable that the gain will be realised? | SSAP 18 para 17 | ... | ... |
| 129. In respect of each contingency (or group of similar transactions) that require disclosure, are the following disclosed: | SSAP 18 paras 18, 21 8 Sch 50(2) | | |
|   (a)  The nature of the contingency? | | ... | ... |
|   (b)  The uncertainties that are expected to affect the ultimate outcome? | | ... | ... |
|   (c)  A prudent estimate of the financial effect (made at the date on which the financial statements are approved by the board of directors), or a statement that it is not practicable to make such an estimate? | | ... | ... |
| In addition, in respect of any contingent liability not provided for, are the following disclosed: | 8 Sch 50(2) | | |
|   (a)  Its legal nature? | | ... | ... |
|   (b)  Whether any valuable security has been provided and if so, what? | | ... | ... |
| 130. If an estimate of the financial effect of a contingency is disclosed, does this take into account the probable outcome of any related counter-claim or claim by or against a third party such that only the potential financial effect is disclosed? | SSAP 18 paras 6, 19 | ... | ... |
| 131. In the case of a contingent loss, has the potential effect that is disclosed been reduced by: | SSAP 18 para 19 | | |
|   (a)  Any amounts accrued? | | ... | ... |
|   (b)  Any amounts where the possibility of loss is remote? | | ... | ... |
| 132. Has the estimate of the financial effect been disclosed before taking account of taxation, and have the taxation implications of the contingency crystallising been explained where this is necessary for a proper understanding of the financial position? | SSAP 18 para 20 | ... | ... |

| | Reference | Yes/No N/A Coy Grp. | |
|---|---|---|---|
| 133. Is there separate disclosure of contingent liabilities that are undertaken on behalf of or for the benefit of: | 8 Sch 50(6) | | |
|   (a)  Any holding company or fellow subsidiary? | | ... | ... |
|   (b)  Any subsidiary? | | ... | ... |
| **Share Capital** | | | |
| 134. Is the authorised share capital disclosed? | 8 Sch 38(1)(a) | ... | ... |
| 135. Where more than one class of shares has been allotted, are the number and the aggregate nominal value of each class of share allotted disclosed? | 8 Sch 38(1)(b) | ... | ... |
| 136. Are the amount of allotted share capital and the amount of called up share capital that has been paid separately disclosed? | 8 Sch Note 12 | ... | ... |
| 137. In respect of allotted redeemable shares, are the following disclosed: | 8 Sch 38(2) | | |
|   (a)  The earliest and the latest dates on which the company has power to redeem them? | | ... | ... |
|   (b)  Whether they must be redeemed in any event or at the option of the company? | | ... | ... |
|   (c)  The premium, if any, payable on redemption? | | ... | ... |
| 138. Where a class of preference shares (or participating or preferred ordinary shares) was issued before 6 April 1973 and indicates a fixed rate of dividend, is the new effective rate of dividend that is paid to shareholders also incorporated in the description of the shares? | SSAP 8 para 28 | ... | ... |
| 139. In respect of shares allotted during the year, are the following disclosed: | 8 Sch 39 | | |
|   (a)  The reason for making the allotment? | | ... | ... |
|   (b)  The classes of shares allotted? | | ... | ... |
|   (c)  For each class: | | | |
|     (i)  The number allotted? | | ... | ... |
|     (ii)  The aggregate nominal value? | | ... | ... |
|     (iii)  The consideration received by the company? | | ... | ... |
| 140. In respect of any option to subscribe for shares and for any other right to require the allotment of shares to any person, are the following disclosed: | 8 Sch 40 | | |
|   (a)  The number, description and amount of shares involved? | | ... | ... |
|   (b)  The period during which the option or right is exercisable? | | ... | ... |
|   (c)  The price to be paid for the shares? | | ... | ... |
| 141. Are the number, description and amount of the company's shares held beneficially by subsidiaries or their nominees disclosed? | 8 Sch 60 | ... | ... |
| *Note:* | | | |
| *In consolidated financial statements, the provisions apply only to subsidiaries not consolidated.* | 8 Sch 67 | | |
| 142. Are the name of the company's ultimate holding company and its country of incorporation disclosed? | 1967 S 5(1) | ... | ... |
| **Reserves** | | | |
| 143. In respect of reserves under any heading or sub-heading where there has been a transfer to or from the reserve, are the following disclosed: | 8 Sch 46 | | |
|   (a)  The amount of the reserve at the beginning of the year? | | ... | ... |
|   (b)  The amount and the source of transfers to the reserve? | | ... | ... |

| | Reference | Yes/No N/A Coy | Grp. |
|---|---|---|---|

(c)  The amount and the application of transfers from the reserve?  | | ... | ... |

(d)  The amount of the reserve at the end of the year?  | | ... | ... |

*Note:*

*Comparative amounts are not required.*  — 8 Sch 58(3)

144. Is the treatment for taxation purposes of amounts credited or debited to the revaluation reserve disclosed? — 8 Sch 34(5) ... ...

Are any amounts transferred to or from the deferred taxation account shown separately as part of such movements? — SSAP 15 para 38 ... ...

145. Has the revaluation reserve been reduced to the extent that amounts standing to the credit of the reserve are in the opinion of the directors no longer necessary for the purpose of the accounting policies adopted? — 8 Sch 34(4) ... ...

Has an amount been transferred from the revaluation reserve to the profit and loss account only where one of the following applies:

(a)  It was previously charged to the profit and loss account? ... ...

(b)  It represents realised profit? ... ...

**Merger Relief**

146. If during the year the company entered into an arrangement to which 1981 S 37 applied, are the following disclosed: — 8 Sch 74A(1) (SI 1982 No 1092)

(a)  The name of the company acquired? ... ...

(b)  The number, the nominal value and the class of shares allotted for the acquisition? ... ...

(c)  The number, the nominal value and the class of shares the acquired company issued or transferred to the company, or cancelled, as part of the arrangement? ... ...

(d)  Particulars of the accounting treatment that the company adopted in respect of the issue, transfer or cancellation referred to in (c)? ... ...

(e)  Where the company prepares group accounts, particulars of the extent to which, and the manner in which, the group profit or loss for the year is affected by any profit or loss of the acquired company (and any of its subsidiaries) that arose before the allotment? N/A ...

147. If during the year, or during either of the two immediately preceding years, the company entered into an arrangement to which 1981 S 37 applied, is there disclosure of any amounts in (a) to (c) below that are included in its consolidated profit and loss account, or where consolidated financial statements are not prepared, in its own profit and loss account: — 8 Sch 74A(2), (3) (SI 1982 No 1092)

(a)  The net amount of any profit or loss that the company (or any of its subsidiaries) realised on the disposal of shares in the acquired company? ... ...

(b)  The net amount of any profit or loss that the company (or any of its subsidiaries) realised on the disposal of any assets that were fixed assets of the acquired company (or any of its subsidiaries) at the date of the acquisition and that were subsequently transferred to the company (or any of its subsidiaries)? ... ...

(c)  Any net profit or loss (or part thereof) that the company (or any of its subsidiaries) realised on the disposal of shares in a company (X) other than the acquired company where the amount was attributable to the fact that at the time of the disposal the assets of X (or any of its subsidiaries) included one or both of the following:

(i)  Shares in the acquired company? ... ...

(ii)  Assets that had been fixed assets of the acquired company (or any of its subsidiaries) at the date of the acquisition but which had been subsequently transferred to X? ... ...

| | Reference | Yes/No N/A Coy Grp. | |
|---|---|---|---|

148. Where any amount is disclosed under step 147, is there an explanation of the transaction that gave rise to the amount?

*Reference:* 8 Sch 74A(2), (3) (SI 1982 No 1092) ... ...

**Post Balance Sheet Events**

*(Note: Financial statements should be prepared on the basis of conditions existing at the balance sheet date.)*

*Reference:* SSAP 17 para 21

149. Do amounts included in the financial statements take account of a material post balance sheet event where:

*Reference:* SSAP 17 para 22

(a) It is an adjusting event? ... ...

(b) It indicates that the application of the going concern concept to the whole or a material part of the company is inappropriate? ... ...

150. Has a material post balance sheet event been disclosed where:

*Reference:* SSAP 17 para 23

(a) It is a non-adjusting event of such materiality that its non-disclosure would affect the ability of the users of the financial statements to reach a proper understanding of the financial position? ... ...

(b) It is 'window dressing'? ... ...

151. In respect of each material post balance sheet event that requires disclosure, are the following disclosed:

*Reference:* SSAP 17 para 24

(a) The nature of the event? ... ...

(b) An estimate of the financial effect, or a statement that it is not practicable to make such an estimate? ... ...

152. Has the estimate of the financial effect been disclosed before taking account of taxation, and have the taxation implications been explained where this is necessary for a proper understanding of the financial position?

*Reference:* SSAP 17 para 25 ... ...

**STATEMENT OF SOURCE AND APPLICATION OF FUNDS**

153. Where an entity has turnover or gross income of £25,000 or more per annum, do the financial statements include a statement of source and application of funds?

*Reference:* SSAP 10 paras 9,10 ... ...

*Note:*

Where group accounts are prepared, the statement should reflect the operations of the group.

*Reference:* SSAP 10 para 12

154. Does the statement show the profit or loss for the year together with the adjustments required for items that did not use (or provide) funds in the year?

*Reference:* SSAP 10 para 11 ... ...

Are the following other sources and applications of funds also shown where material:

(a) Dividends paid? ... ...

(b) Acquisitions and disposals of fixed assets? ... ...

(c) Funds raised by increasing, or expended in repaying or redeeming, medium or long-term loans or the issued capital of the company? ... ...

(d) The increase or decrease in working capital sub-divided into its components, and movements in net liquid funds? ... ...

*Notes:*

(a) There should be a minimum of 'netting off'. The figures should generally be identifiable in the profit and loss account, in the balance sheet and in the related notes. If adjustments to those figures are necessary, details should be given to enable the related figures to be located.

*Reference:* SSAP 10 para 4

(b) The effects of acquiring, or disposing of, a subsidiary should be reflected. (See the examples in the Appendix to SSAP 10.)

| | Reference | Yes/No N/A Coy Grp. | |
|---|---|---|---|

**CURRENT COST ACCOUNTS**

155. If the entity falls within the scope of SSAP 16 (as set out in paragraph 46), has Part 7 been completed?

*Note:*

*A holding company that produces current cost group accounts need not produce current cost accounts for itself as a single company where historical cost accounts are the main accounts.* — SSAP 16 para 60

156. If the historical cost accounts are the main accounts, are the supplementary current cost accounts prominently displayed? — SSAP 16 para 48

157. If the current cost accounts are the main or only accounts, do they comply with the requirements of the Companies Acts 1948 to 1981? — SSAP 16 para 48

**DISCLOSURE IN THE EVENT OF NON-COMPLIANCE WITH A SSAP**

If there is a departure from a SSAP, and if its effect is material, is such departure referred to in:

(a) The financial statements (or, in the absence of a reference in the financial statements, in our audit report)?

(b) Our audit report, in all cases where we do not concur with the departure?

**THE AUDITORS' STATUTORY DUTIES**

Where the details required by steps 14,15,16, 101 and Part 4 are not disclosed in the financial statements, have we included in our audit report, so far as we are reasonably able to do so, a statement giving the required particulars? — 1948 S 196(8) 1967 S 6(4), 7(3), 8(4) 1980 S 59

If we have qualified our opinion on the financial statements and if the company proposes to pay a dividend, have we made an additional statement to the members of the company as to whether the subject matter of the qualification is material in determining the legality of the proposed dividend? — 1980 S 43(3)(c)

PART III – CONTENT OF THE DIRECTORS' REPORT – SCHEDULE 8 COMPANY.

| | | Reference | Yes/No N/A |
|---|---|---|---|
| | Does the directors' report contain the following information: | | |
| 1. | A description of the principal activities of the company (and its subsidiaries) during the year and of any significant changes in those activities? | 1967 S 16(1) | ... |
| 2. | A fair review of the development of the business of the company (and its subsidiaries) during the year and of their position at the end of the year? | 1948 S 157(1) (1981 S 13(1)) | ... |
| 3. | An indication of likely future developments in the business of the company (and its subsidiaries)? | 1967 S 16(1)(f)(ii) (1981 S 13(3)) | ... |
| 4. | Particulars of any important events affecting the company (or its subsidiaries) that have occurred since the end of the year? | 1967 S 16(1)(f)(i) (1981 S 13(3)) | ... |
| 5. | An indication of any activities of the company (and its subsidiaries) in the field of research and development? | 1967 S 16(1)(f)(iii) (1981 S 13(3)) | ... |
| 6. | The amount, if any, the directors propose to transfer to reserves? | 1948 S 157(1) | ... |
| 7. | The amount, if any, the directors recommend should be paid by way of dividend? | 1948 S 157(1) | ... |
| 8. | If the company is listed, an explanation of any material difference between the trading results for the year and any published forecast made by the company? | LA para 10(b) | ... |
| 9. | Particulars of any significant changes in the fixed assets of the company (and its subsidiaries) during the year? | 1967 S 16(1)(a) | ... |
| 10. | The difference (as precisely as practicable) at the year end between the market value and the balance sheet value of land if, in the opinion of the directors, the difference is of such significance that it should be drawn to the attention of the members and the debenture holders? | 1967 S 16(1)(a) | ... |
| | *Note:* | | |
| | *Under Section 3 of the Interpretation Act 1889, 'land' means 'land and buildings'.* | | |
| 11. | The amount of money given to UK charities and the amount given for political purposes (if together they exceed £200)? | 1967 S 19 SI 1980 No 1055 | ... |
| | In the case of any individual amount exceeding £200 for political purposes, the name of the recipient or political party concerned and the amount given? | | ... |
| | *Note:* | | |
| | *Not applicable to directors' reports of wholly-owned subsidiaries of companies incorporated in Great Britain.* | | |
| 12. | A statement of the company's policy during the year in respect of: | SI 1980 No 1160 | |
| | (a) Applications for employment from disabled persons? | | ... |
| | (b) Employees that become disabled? | | ... |
| | (c) Training, career development and promotion of disabled persons? | | ... |
| | *Notes:* | | |
| | *(a) Not applicable to employees who work wholly or mainly outside the UK.* | | |
| | *(b) Not applicable to directors' reports of companies that employ on average 250 or fewer persons in the UK.* | | |
| 13. | If the company is listed, a statement of whether or not, so far as the directors are aware, the company is a close company for taxation purposes and whether there has been any change in that respect since the end of the year? | LA para 10(j) and note 46 | ... |

| | | Reference | Yes/No N/A |
|---|---|---|---|

14. In respect of purchases by the company of its own shares during the year: — **1967 S 16A (1981 S 14)**

   (a) The number and nominal value of shares purchased? — ...

   (b) The percentage of called-up capital purchased? — ...

   (c) The aggregate consideration paid? — ...

   (d) The reasons for the purchase? — ...

15. In respect of acquisitions (other than purchases) by the company of its own shares: — **1967 S 16A (1981 S 14)**

   (a) The number and nominal value of shares acquired or charged during the year, and the percentage of called-up capital? — ...

   (b) The maximum number and nominal value of shares acquired or charged at any time that were held during the year, and the percentage of called-up capital? — ...

   (c) The number and nominal value of shares acquired or charged at any time that were disposed of or cancelled during the year, and the percentage of called-up capital? — ...

   (d) The consideration received in respect of disposals during the year where the shares were originally acquired for money or money's worth? — ...

   (e) The amount of any charge? — ...

*Note:*

*Acquisitions (other than purchases) by the company of its own shares comprise:*

   *(i) Shares acquired by forfeiture, by surrender in lieu of forfeiture or by way of gift.*

   *(ii) In the case of a public company, shares any person acquires with the financial assistance of the company and the company has a beneficial interest in those shares.*

   *(iii) In the case of a public company, shares that a nominee of the company acquires from a third party without the company providing any financial assistance and the company has a beneficial interest in those shares.*

   *(iv) In the case of a public company, shares over which the company takes a lien or a charge (express or implied) for any amount payable in respect of those shares.*

   *(v) Shares on which the company held a charge immediately before applying to re-register or register as a public company under the Companies Act 1980.*

   *(vi) In the case of an old public company, shares on which the company held a charge immediately before the end of the re-registration period if it had not by then applied to re-register as a public company.*

16. The names of persons who were directors of the company at any time during the year? — **1967 S 16(1)** — ...

17. If the company is listed, the unexpired period of any service contract of each director proposed for re-election at the annual general meeting? — **LA para 11(d)** — ...

18. The interests of each person who was a director at the end of the year in shares and debentures of both the company and any other company in the group at both the beginning of the year (or date of appointment, if later) and the end of the year? — **1967 S 16(1)(e), S 27, S 28 (1981 3 Sch 29), S 31 LA para 10(h) and note 44** — ...

*Notes:*

   *(a) Details to be according to the register kept by the company.* — **1967 S 16(1)(e)**

| | Reference | Yes/No N/A |
|---|---|---|
| (b) The main exemptions are: | | |
| (i) Directors' nominee shareholdings in wholly-owned subsidiaries. | 1967 S 27(13) | |
| (ii) Interests of directors of wholly-owned subsidiaries of companies incorporated in Great Britain who are also directors of the holding company. | SI 1968 No 1533 | |
| (iii) Interests of directors of wholly-owned subsidiaries of companies incorporated outside Great Britain in companies incorporated outside Great Britain. | SI 1968 No 1533 | |
| (c) Other exemptions are set out in SI 1967 No 1594 and SI 1968 No 865. | | |
| (d) Directors' interests may be given in the notes to the financial statements. | 1967 S 16(4A) (1981 S 13(4)) | |
| (e) If the company is listed, interests in shares in the company and its subsidiaries should distinguish between beneficial and non-beneficial interests and particulars should be given of the extent of any duplication that occurs. | | |
| 19. If the company is listed, any change in directors' interests between the end of the year and a date not more than one month prior to the date of the notice of meeting, or the fact that there have been no changes? | LA para 10(h) and note 44 | ... |
| 20. If the company is listed, particulars of, and the amount of, an interest of any person (other than a director) in 5% or more of the nominal value of any class of voting capital at a date not more than one month prior to the date of the notice of meeting, or the fact that there are no such interests? | LA para 10(i) and note 45 | ... |
| Note: | | |
| Details to be according to the register kept by the company under 1981 S 73. | | |
| 21. A statement that describes the action that the company has taken during the year to introduce, maintain or develop arrangements aimed at: | 1967 S 16(1)(h) (Employment Act 1982 S 1(2)) | |
| (a) Providing employees systematically with information on matters of concern to them as employees? | | ... |
| (b) Consulting employees or their representatives on a regular basis so that the views of employees can be taken into account in making decisions that are likely to affect their interests? | | ... |
| (c) Encouraging the involvement of employees in the company's performance through an employees' share scheme or by some other means? | | ... |
| (d) Achieving a common awareness on the part of all employees of the financial and economic factors that affect the performance of the company? | | ... |
| Notes: | | |
| (a) The provisions apply only to directors' reports for periods commencing on or after 1 January 1983. | | |
| (b) Not applicable to employees who work wholly or mainly outside the UK. | 1967 S 16(8) (Employment Act 1982 S 1(4)) | |
| (c) Not applicable to directors' reports of companies that employ on average 250 or fewer persons in the UK. | 1967 S 16(1A) (Employment Act 1982 S 1(3)) | |

## THE AUDITORS' STATUTORY DUTY

| | Reference | Yes/No N/A |
|---|---|---|
| Is the information in the directors' report consistent with the financial statements? | 1967 S 23A (1981 S 15) | ... |
| If not, is that fact stated in our audit report? | | ... |

## PART IV – LOANS AND OTHER TRANSACTIONS WITH DIRECTORS AND CONNECTED PERSONS

*Note: Special provisions apply to recognised banks and to money-lending companies.*

| | Reference | Yes/No N/A |
|---|---|---|
| If the company is listed and no contract of significance in which a director of the company is or was (for Stock Exchange purposes) materially interested subsisted during or at the end of the year, is there a statement of that fact? | LA para 10(l) | ... |
| If loans or other transactions with directors and connected persons have been entered into, or subsisted, during the course of the year, the notes to the financial statements must contain the disclosures set out below. | | |
| In respect of: | | |
| (i) Any transaction or arrangement of a kind described in 1980 S 49 entered into by the company, and in the case of a holding company by a subsidiary of the company, for a person who at any time during the year was a director of the company, or of its holding company or was connected with such a director. | 1980 S 54(1)(a), (2)(a) (1981 3 Sch 51(a)) | |
| (ii) An agreement by the company, and in the case of a holding company by a subsidiary of the company, to enter into such a transaction or arrangement. | 1980 S 54(1)(b), (2)(b) (1981 3 Sch 51(a)) | |
| (iii) Any other transaction or arrangement with the company, and in the case of a holding company with a subsidiary of the company, in which a person, who at any time during the year was a director of the company or of its holding company, had directly or indirectly, a material interest. (A director is also treated as being interested in a transaction or arrangement between a company and any of his connected persons.) | 1980 S 54(1)(c), (2)(c) (1981 3 Sch 51(a)) LA para 10(l) 1980 S 54(4)(a) | |
| Do the notes contain the following particulars: | 1980 S 54(1), (2), (2A) (1981 3 Sch 51(b)) | |
| (a) The principal terms of the transaction, arrangement or agreement? | 1980 S 55(1) | ... |
| (b) A statement that the transaction, arrangement or agreement was made during the year, or that it subsisted during the year? | 1980 S 55(1)(a) | ... |
| (c) The name of the person for whom the transaction, arrangement or agreement was made and where that person is connected with a director, the name of the director? | 1980 S 55(1)(b) | ... |
| (d) If the transaction or arrangement is one in which the director has a material interest, the name of the director and the nature of that interest? | 1980 S 55(1)(c) | ... |
| (e) In respect of a loan, or an agreement for a loan, or an arrangement within 1980 S 49(3) or (4) relating to a loan: | | |
| (i) The amount of the liability for both the principal and the interest outstanding at both the beginning and the end of the year? | 1980 S 55(1)(d)(i) | ... |
| (ii) The maximum amount of the liability during the year? | 1980 S 55(1)(d)(ii) | ... |
| (iii) The amount of interest which, having fallen due, has not been paid? | 1980 S 55(1)(d)(iii) | ... |
| (iv) The amount of any provision that the company has made against the failure of the borrower to repay the whole, or any part, of the principal or the interest? | 1980 S 55(1)(d)(iv) | ... |
| (f) In respect of a guarantee, or security, or an arrangement within 1980 S 49(3) relating to a guarantee or security: | | |
| (i) The amount for which the company (or its subsidiary) was liable under the guarantee, or in respect of the security, both at the beginning and at the end of the year? | 1980 S 55(1)(e)(i) | ... |
| (ii) The maximum amount for which the company (or its subsidiary) may become liable? | 1980 S 55(1)(e)(ii) | ... |
| (iii) Any amount paid, and any liability incurred, by the company (or its subsidiary) in fulfilling the guarantee or discharging the security? | 1980 S 55(1)(e)(iii) | ... |
| (g) In the case of any other transaction, arrangement or agreement, the value of the transaction or arrangement, or the value of any transaction or arrangement to which the agreement relates? | 1980 S 55(1)(f), 65(4) | ... |

| | | Reference | Yes/No N/A |
|---|---|---|---|

*Notes:*

*(a)*    *The transactions or arrangements of the kind described in 1980 S 49 include:*

    *(i)*    *A loan.*

    *(ii)*    *A quasi-loan.*

    *(iii)*    *A credit transaction.*

    *(iv)*    *A guarantee or security in connection with a loan, quasi-loan or credit transaction.*

    *(v)*    *An assignment of any rights, obligations or liabilities to the company under a transaction which, if it had been entered into by the company, would have fallen within (i), (ii), (iii) or (iv) above.*

    *(vi)*    *An arrangement by the company for another person to enter into such a transaction.*

*(b)*    *The disclosure requirements do not apply to the following transactions, arrangements or agreements:*

    *(i)*    *A transaction, arrangement or agreement between one company and another company in which a director of the first or of its subsidiary or holding company is interested only by virtue of his being a director of the other.*      1980 S 54(6)(a)

    *(ii)*    *A contract of service between a company and one of its directors or a director of its holding company or between a director of a company and any of that company's subsidiaries.*      1980 S 54(6)(b) (1981 3 Sch 51(c))

    *(iii)*    *A transaction, arrangement or agreement which was not entered into during the year in question and which did not subsist at any time during that year.*      1980 S 54(6)(c) (1981 3 Sch 51(d))

    *(iv)*    *A transaction, arrangement or agreement which was made before 22 December 1980 and which does not subsist on or after that day.*      1980 S 54(6)(d)

    *(v)*    *Any credit transaction, guarantee, security, or agreement or arrangement falling within 1980 S 49(3) or (4) that is made in connection with a credit transaction, where the amount outstanding of the value as defined in 1980 S 65(4) does not exceed £5,000 for any one director and his connected persons during the year.*      1980 S 58(1), (2)

    *(vi)*    *A transaction or arrangement (covered by 1980 S 54(1)(c) and (2)(c)) between a company and a director of the company or of its holding company or a person connected with such a director in which the director has an interest and the majority of the directors (other than the director) of the company which is preparing the financial statements in question are of the opinion that the interest is not material.*      1980 S 54(4)(b)

    *(vii)*    *A transaction or arrangement (covered by 1980 S 54(1)(c) and (2)(c)) in which a director has a material interest if (a) the value as defined in 1980 S 65(4) of any such transaction made in that year, and (b) the value as defined in 1980 S 65(4) of any such transaction previously made less the amount by which the liabilities of the person for whom the transaction was made have been reduced, at no time during the year exceeded £1,000 or, if more, the lower of £5,000 and 1% of the value of the net assets of the company preparing the financial statements as at the end of the year.*      1980 S 58(3) (1981 3 Sch 53)

*(c)*    *Comparative amounts are not required.*      8 Sch 58(3)

*(d)*    *In consolidated financial statements the above provisions apply only to directors of the holding company and its holding company.*      8 Sch 63(c)

PART V – CURRENT COST ACCOUNTS.

| | SSAP16 Para. | Yes/No N/A |
|---|---|---|

If an entity falls within the scope of SSAP 16 (as set out in paragraph 46), the financial statements should include current cost accounts that comply with the accounting and the disclosure requirements set out below. — 47

**Current Cost Profit and Loss Account**

1. Does the current cost profit and loss account show the following (although not necessarily in the order below): — 55

(a) The current cost operating profit or loss? — ...

(b) The interest/income that relates to the net borrowing on which the gearing adjustment has been based? — ...

(c) The gearing adjustment? — ...

(d) The taxation charge? — ...

(e) The extraordinary items? — ...

(f) The current cost profit or loss (after tax) attributable to shareholders? — ...

2. Is there a reconciliation between the current cost operating profit or loss and the historical cost profit or loss before interest and taxation? — 56 ...

Does this reconciliation give the amounts of the following:

(a) The depreciation adjustment? — ...

(b) The cost of sales adjustment? — ...

(c) The monetary working capital adjustment and, where appropriate, interest that relates to monetary working capital? — ...

(d) Other material adjustments made to profits calculated on the historical cost basis when determining current cost operating profit? — ...

*Note:*

*The adjustments for cost of sales and monetary working capital may be combined.*

3. If the company is listed, are current cost earnings per share disclosed and are these based on the current cost profit attributable to equity shareholders before extraordinary items? — 59 ...

4. Is the depreciation adjustment calculated as the difference between the proportion of the value to the business of the fixed assets consumed in the year and the depreciation calculated on the historical cost basis? — 49 ...

5. Is the cost of sales adjustment calculated as the difference between the value to the business and the historical cost of stock consumed in the year? — 49 ...

6. Is the monetary working capital adjustment calculated as the amount of additional (or reduced) finance needed for monetary working capital as a result of changes in the input prices of goods and services the business has used and financed? — 49, 11 ...

7. Where a proportion of net operating assets is financed by net borrowing, has a gearing adjustment been made? — 50 ...

Has this gearing adjustment been calculated by expressing net borrowing as a proportion of the net operating assets using average figures for the year from current cost balance sheets and applying this proportion to the total of the charges or credits made to allow for the impact of price changes on the net operating assets of the business? — ...

8. Has the current cost profit and loss account been charged with amounts, if any, to reduce the assets from net current replacement cost to recoverable amount? — 54 ...

| | | SSAP16 Para. | Yes/No N/A |
|---|---|---|---|
| 9. | Is the treatment within the current cost profit and loss account of gains and losses on asset disposals, extraordinary and exceptional items, prior year items, group consolidation adjustments, minority interests and the translation of foreign currencies, where practicable, consistent with the definitions of current cost operating profit and current cost profit attributable to shareholders? | 52 | ... |
| | If this is impracticable, is the treatment adopted disclosed? | | ... |
| | *Note:* | | |
| | *The treatment of income from associated companies is covered in steps 26 to 28 of Part 5.* | | |

**Current Cost Balance Sheet**

| | | | |
|---|---|---|---|
| | *(Note: The current cost balance sheet should include only those assets that are reflected in the historical cost balance sheet.)* | 29 | |
| 10. | If the current cost balance sheet is in a summarised form, do the financial statements include the full historical cost balance sheet? | 57 | ... |
| 11. | Are the following included in the current cost balance sheet at their value to the business: | 53 | |
| | (a) Land and buildings? | | ... |
| | (b) Plant and machinery? | | ... |
| | (c) Stocks on which a cost of sales adjustment has been made? | | ... |
| 12. | Are investments (except those treated either as associated companies or as current assets) included in the current cost balance sheet at the directors' valuation? | 53 | ... |
| | Where the directors' valuation of a listed investment is materially different from the mid-market value, have both the basis of valuation and the reasons for the difference been stated? | | ... |
| | *Note:* | | |
| | *The treatment of investments in associated companies is covered in steps 26 and 29 of Part 5.* | | |
| 13. | Have intangible assets (excluding goodwill) been included at the best estimate of their value to the business? | 53 | ... |
| 14. | Has the premium or discount that arises on consolidation been included on the basis set out in SSAP 14? | 53 | ... |
| | Has goodwill that arose on consolidation before the introduction of SSAP 14 been reduced to the extent that it represents those revaluation surpluses that relate to the assets that were held at the date of the acquisition? | | ... |
| 15. | Are the following included in the current cost balance sheet at the same amount as in the historical cost balance sheet: | 53 | |
| | (a) Current assets (except stocks on which a cost of sales adjustment has been made)? | | ... |
| | (b) All liabilities? | | ... |
| 16. | Do reserves in the current cost balance sheet include the following: | 54 | |
| | (a) Revaluation surpluses or deficits? | | ... |
| | (b) Adjustments made to allow for the impact of price changes in arriving at the current cost profit attributable to shareholders? | | ... |

| | SSAP16 Para. | Yes/No N/A |
|---|---|---|

**Notes to the Current Cost Accounts**

17.  Do the notes to the current cost accounts include the following:  **57, 58**

    (a)  Disclosure of both the main elements and the totals of net operating assets and net borrowing?  ...

    (b)  Summaries of the fixed asset accounts?  ...

    (c)  Movements on the reserves?  ...

    (d)  A description of the bases and the methods that were adopted to prepare the current cost accounts, in particular:

        (i)  The value to the business of fixed assets?  ...

        (ii)  The depreciation adjustment?  ...

        (iii)  The value to the business of stocks?  ...

        (iv)  The cost of sales adjustment?  ...

        (v)  The monetary working capital adjustment?  ...

        (vi)  The gearing adjustment?  ...

        (vii)  Other material adjustments to the historical cost figures?  ...

        (viii)  The basis of translating foreign currencies and dealing with translation differences that arise?  ...

        (ix)  The corresponding amounts?  ...

**Other SSAPs**

18.  Except where a conflict exists because of the conceptual difference between the historical cost accounting system and the current cost accounting system, do the current cost accounts comply with other SSAPs?  **62**  ...

# Appendix 2
## How to pass auditing examinations

My experience in marking auditing examinations suggests that failure to answer all the questions and poor expression are every bit as frequent causes of failure as lack of knowledge. Lack of knowledge necessitates more learning, but the two other problems may not be so easily (!) solved. They are essentially inter-related, and while not exclusive to auditing, they are perhaps more apparent in this subject. So the following ideas may help you to give your best performance 'on the day'.

Remember that you gain most marks by citing the main concepts in response to a question. You gain little by going into immense detail. So it follows that you can score relatively the most marks in the first few minutes of your answer attempts – provided that you know the main concepts. And if you do not, then the examiner will not be impressed by a profusion of irrelevant detail. Indeed he may become annoyed, and this may cloud his view as to the rest of your paper. Examiners are only human (nearly!), remember.

To ensure that you have the opportunity of scoring on all the questions, you must answer all of them! Even if you can produce four perfect answers, five adequate ones will normally score better. And perfect auditing answers are very rare. So it is essential to divide your time up equally between the questions, leaving a bit over for reading and review time. Be ruthless about the cut-off time. For if you creep over on your first few answers, you risk having too little time for even the main concepts in your final answer.

Auditing answers require planning and a structure. Without this, expression will invariably be poor. And the introduction of unnecessary detail often makes matters worse. So concentrate on quality rather than quantity. And quality must apply to both your written English, which should be in a professional style (it is after all a professional examination), and to your handwriting. Examiners try to decipher the indecipherable (usually), but the temptation to put a large cross through illegible work is very strong at the end of a long marking session.

Answer the question is an obvious point, which applies to any examination. But it is amazing how many candidates do not. So you must read the question carefully – perhaps once quickly through the complete paper to gather the main topics from each question, and then again in more detail to ensure that you have a proper understanding before you commence your answers. Then give your answers in the form that is required. For example, if a letter is asked for, give your answer in letter format. You will lose marks for an essay.

Examiners regretfully do not always supply perfect questions, so if you find one that is ambiguous, choose another one if possible; but if not possible then state your assumptions and proceed logically from there. Even if the examiner disagrees with your assumptions, he should award marks for a logical, practical exposure. But he may not, just as he may not award marks if you are highly critical (of his opinions) in a question involving a controversial issue. So I would avoid such questions also, but if you cannot avoid them, ensure that you put both sides to the debate, and do not state your opinions in too forceful a manner. Where you are expressing your own opinion (to which you are perfectly entitled), ensure that this is distinguished in your answer from where you cite the opinions of others, or rely on recognised publications.

The auditing syllabus is large. And becomes larger with each new Auditing Standard and Accounting Statement. Questions are now being written much more imaginatively than in the past, and often test several aspects of the syllabus in just one question. So you need to be familiar with all of the matters discussed in this book. But you can be scientific about your approach to learning. An analysis of past papers will reveal certain aspects of the syllabus which examiners (rightly) concentrate upon (for example, stock, debtors and computers). While it is highly dangerous to 'question spot' to the extent that your preparation for the examination involves only five topics, it is common sense to pay particular attention to those topics that are frequently examined.

Good luck!

# Index